Quantitative Analysis for Business

Quantitative Analysis for Business

Andrew Vazsonyi

St. Mary's University

Herbert F. Spirer

The University of Connecticut

Prentice-Hall, Inc., Englewood Cliffs, New Jersey 07632

Library of Congress Cataloging in Publication Data

Vazsonyi, Andrew.
  Quantitative analysis for business.

  Bibliography: p. 706
  Includes index.
  1. Management science. 2. Industrial management--
Mathematical models. I. Spirer, Herbert F. II. Title.
HD30.25.V39 1984   658   83-23093
ISBN 0-13-746578-5

Editorial/production supervision and text design: Linda C. Mason
Text openings and Cover design: Judith A. Matz
Manufacturing buyer: Ed O'Dougherty

Printed in the United States of America

10 9 8 7 6 5 4 3 2 1

ISBN 0-13-746578-5

Prentice-Hall International, Inc., *London*
Prentice-Hall of Australia Pty. Limited, *Sydney*
Editora Prentice-Hall do Brasil, Ltda., *Rio de Janeiro*
Prentice-Hall Canada Inc., *Toronto*
Prentice-Hall of India Private Limited, *New Delhi*
Prentice-Hall of Japan, Inc., *Tokyo*
Prentice-Hall of Southeast Asia Pte. Ltd., *Singapore*
Whitehall Books Limited, *Wellington, New Zealand*

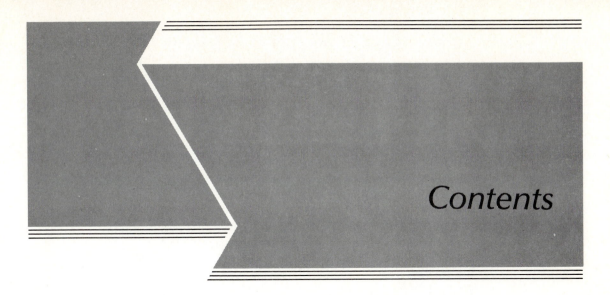

Contents

6 *Solving Decision Analysis Problems*   206

7 *Individual Preferences and Multiple Objectives Under Uncertainty*   232

12 *The Transportation Problem and Applications*   422

13 *Mathematical Programming: A Survey*   450

14 *Goal Programming and Multiobjectives*   492

15 *Markov Processes*   516

16 *Waiting Lines: Queuing Theory* 553

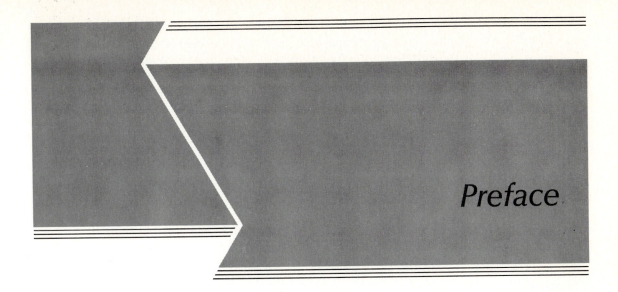

Preface

This three-part educational package—Text, Study Guide and Instructor's Manual—provides an introduction to the basics of quantitative methods of managerial decision making for students with limited mathematical skills. The package presents recent developments in the theory and practice of quantitative methods, using accepted pedagogical principles. It has been fully tested in classroom use for several years.

WHY A NEW TEXT

During the last five years there has been a dramatic increase in successful applications of quantitative methods of management, Operations Research, Management Science and Decision Support Systems. These applications provide new insights in *what* and *how* to teach students so they can become successful practitioners of quantitative methods of managerial decision making.

These applications imply what is important, what is not, and establish priorities in teaching. For example, we now know that a fundamental understanding of optimization, including decision analysis, concepts of multiple objectives, personal preference and goal programming are important. Mathematical models are essential, but tedious hand calculation and detailed knowledge of algorithms are no longer necessary.

The student needs to learn at an early stage that computers are important as both information processors and "number crunchers." The student also needs to know that quantitative methods support decision makers but do not replace judgment. This viewpoint, recently so successfully stressed by Decision Support Systems, is incorporated into the text.

Using this three-part educational package, instructors can integrate these recent advances in theory and practice into classroom instruction and give students a text which combines theory and the best of current practice. Thus this package provides the means to motivate students with limited knowledge of mathematics and management.

TEACHING OBJECTIVES

The principal objective of the text is to provide step-by-step *procedures* with which the student masters the use of the various tools of quantitative methods. This primary objective is supported by the following secondary objectives:

- Provide a vocabulary of quantitative methods
- Clarify the central issues of decision making and resource allocation
- Clarify the relationship between quantitative methods, computers and information systems
- Familiarize the student with the scope of quantitative methods and include applications, both for the private and public sectors of our society

A managerial situation is first described in plain English and concrete terms. The human element and need for judgment is stressed. Then, an intuitive mathematical discussion is given. Lastly, formal techniques and mathematical discussions are introduced, followed at this point with solutions.

Throughout mathematical notation is kept to a minimum, yet retaining the rigorous logic of the approach. Whenever there is need for a new type of mathematical argument, reference is made to the Appendix: Review of Basic Mathematics.

While the text stresses advantages and benefits derived from quantitative methods, it also fully discusses potential traps and disadvantages.

Seventeen "Socratic dialogs" appear at critical points in the text to provide provocative material for substantive discussions.

The histories of 18 recent successful applications provide the instructor with further material for discussion and shows the practical application of the material discussed in the chapter.

A large number of exercises (over 725 for the book) are given in each chapter. They are designed to lead the student back to the text, thereby demonstrating that every topic in the text is necessary.

In addition to exercises, essay-type discussion questions are provided, which also lead back to the text, including the dialogs and case histories. These essay questions reinforce the student's understanding of the underlying philosophy of quantitative methods.

DISTINCTIVE FEATURES

- Risk Analysis, an important technique of Decision Support Systems, is introduced in Chapter 5 and further discussed in Chapter 17.

- Individual preferences and multiple objectives under uncertainty are discussed in Chapter 7.
- An entire Chapter (14) is devoted to Goal Programming and multiple objectives.
- The importance of computers is stressed throughout the text but no prior knowledge of computers is required.
- Multi-channel waiting-line problems can be solved with little calculation by use of a special table.
- The Khintchine-Pollaczek formula is included to solve single-channel waiting-line formulas for any service-time distribution.

PEDAGOGICAL FEATURES

- The text is written in easy-to-read plain English
- The presentation is designed to alleviate any possible anxiety on the part of students as to mathematics.
- Socratic dialogs are included to explain some key issues in the text, and provide a basis for stimulating class discussions.
- Key Words and Concepts, both technical and managerial, are printed in boldface when they first appear and are fully defined textually.

THE STUDY GUIDE

This optional learning aid reenforces the learning process and provides means for students to check their progress. The *Study Guide* starts with an Introduction to show How to Build a Mathematical Model. The material follows the text chapter by chapter and contains for each chapter:

- Vocabulary review
- Study hints
- True/False and multiple choice questions
- An illustration of the method of how to Build a Mathematical Model
- New exercises with solutions

THE INSTRUCTOR'S MANUAL

Solutions to the Exercises are presented in the *Instructor's Manual*.

ACKNOWLEDGMENTS

It gives us great pleasure to acknowledge our profound, indebtedness to Laura T. Vazsonyi without whose invaluable editorial support the quality of this textbook would not have been possible. We also acknowledge our gratitude for technical assistance to Dr. M. S. Dueker and Vinayuk Kudva, and for editorial assistance to Louise Spirer.

1

Why Quantitative Methods? A Few Introductory Applications

1.1. WHAT THIS TEXTBOOK IS ABOUT

Managerial Decision Making

Our objective in this textbook is to teach ways to make better managerial and executive decisions. Look around you in today's world where many people work on large and complex problems. You will find a great need to manage the world better and many opportunities for people who can manage well, who can contribute to effective **management**, and/or who can support managers so that our quality of life will be improved.

Management is a large field of endeavor, and managers carry out many tasks. Libraries are full of books about management; schools and colleges are dedicated to teaching management. Although this textbook is about management, it is about a certain aspect of management. In this textbook you will learn about the art and science of **managerial decision making.** You will learn about examining **alternatives** and about the process of selecting an alternative that meets your **goals.**

Many, perhaps most, of our decisions are simple and require no particular effort or study. However, in this textbook you will learn about decision making in complex and difficult situations where there are many possible alternative actions. It is not a simple matter to determine which action or choice leads to the desired goal, and thus the need for **quantitative** techniques arises.

> This textbook is about quantitative techniques of managerial decision making under complex and difficult situations.

Resource Allocation

All of us continuously make decisions, but in this textbook we focus on a particular class of important decisions. Typically, managers are faced with the need to examine resources available to them (such as labor, material, capital energy, etc.) and to choose alternatives which will convert these resources into goods and services that enhance the quality of life. There is a growing recognition that the resources of this planet are limited. Hence, if resources are allocated in the wrong way, our goals cannot be achieved, and our quality of life suffers. So in this textbook we take a very broad view of managerial decision making.

> Managerial decision making allocates limited resources to meet specified goals.

There are many ways to make decisions, but in this textbook we focus on one approach to decision making. Decisions can be, and often are, made on the basis of experience, custom, habit, or "seat-of-the-pants" intuition. Or decisions may be made as an automatic reflex reaction to conditions by hunch or even by chance. This kind of decision making, so common and necessary, is qualitative and nonscientific. In this textbook we concentrate on decision making under complex and uncertain situations where this **qualitative** kind of decision making is inadequate and there is need for a better, scientific approach.

Do not be misled by the words quantitative or scientific. We explicitly recognize the human element, that goals are personal; one person wants one thing and another quite a different thing. Even the same person aspires to many goals, some contradictory to others. Quantitative techniques can and must include consideration of the human element.

Neither should you be misled by the many symbols, diagrams, graphs, and mathematical equations. They are the necessary features of quantitative techniques, but this is not a textbook on mathematics, and you need not become a mathematician to master quantitative techniques of management.

Before we delve deeper into our subject, we must stress that managers cannot make good decisions unless they have information and knowledge about the problem at hand, the organization they work in, and the environment they live in. Thus, quantitative analysis in management relies heavily on **information systems** and specifically on computer-based systems. You need not become an expert on the computer but must realize that providing information is the bread and butter of quantitative analysis.

Before we continue our discussion of the subject, we present a brief historical background.

During World War II some serious military problems developed, first in Great Britain and in the United States, and an appeal was made to scientists to provide help. So, with great success, the **scientific method** was applied to problems of antisubmarine warfare, the development of early warning radar systems, bombing raids, etc.

Scientists were so successful in World War II that after the completion of the war, the same scientists organized to provide help to management, both in the private and public sectors of our lives. It was also recognized that the scientific method had been applied prior to World War II to managerial decision making, although only occasionally and in a scattered manner. So starting in the late 1940s, and at an ever-accelerating rate, the scientific method has been applied to managerial decision problems with ever-increasing scope and great success. A number of professional organizations, such as the Operations Research Society of America (ORSA), the Institute of Management Sciences (TIMS), and the American Institute of Decision Sciences (AIDS), were formed, and the process of applying scientific techniques to managerial decision making became a profession. A number of journals were started, a great many meetings were held, and the techniques developed spread from Great Britain and the United States to other nations. As the field developed, universities and colleges recognized the importance of these techniques, and courses and curricula were organized to teach these techniques to an ever-growing number of students. In matching the names of the various organizations and other key characteristics, these techniques today go under the names of **operations research**, **management science**, **decision analysis**, and **quantitative analysis** and techniques. Today these techniques penetrate all areas of management, finance, marketing, and production. There are numerous applications in both the private and public sectors of our society.

To complete this brief history of quantitative analysis, here are a few words about information systems and computers. During World War II, under the pressure of difficult scientific problems, the electronic digital computer was developed. Also, due to the complexity of business operations, more and more elaborate accounting and information systems were developed. In the 1960s it was recognized that computers are not only high-speed calculators but machines to deal with information, and thus the concept of the modern computer-based management information system (MIS) was born. The main thrust of the MIS is to replace manual, clerical processes with more efficient computerized systems. Thus the main payoff comes from the improvement in efficiency and reduction in costs. Also, many tasks that before the advent of the computer were impractical or impossible to perform could be dealt with by standard operating procedures.

In addition to replacing clerical tasks, computers supported quantitative techniques of management and resulted in improved managerial decision making. The use of computers in decision making has been greatly accelerated during the last few years, and the concept of the decision support system (DSS) has emerged. Advocates of the DSS stress that the computer is a most important decision-making tool, that decision makers must play an integral part in the decision-making process, and that the computer must remain under the direct control of managers. Computers, models, and managerial judgment are all required in effective managerial decision making.

In this textbook our goal is to provide you with knowledge of quantitative decision making, and we are not too concerned with the particular name attached to the technique we are describing. Consequently, we mention the specific name of a particular technique only when it is to your benefit to make the distinction.

Now let us discuss some successful applications of quantitative methods of decision making.

Successful Applications of Quantitative Methods

There have been thousands of successful applications of quantitative methods in all fields of management both in the private and public sectors of life, and therefore it is impossible to provide even a list of them. But to give you insight into the scope of quantitative methods of business, we provide here a selected list of the most successful recent applications.

Our method of selection is as follows. Each year the College on the Practice of Management Science of the Institute of Management Sciences sponsors the Annual International Management Science Achievement Award Competition. The purpose is to focus the attention of the management community and the public on the great value of the practice of management science and operations research. Since 1972 an annual competition has been held to recognize and honor outstanding examples of successful, high-impact management science practice. Each year the prize itself is awarded to the client or host organization for the winning project in that year's competition. At the same time cash awards are made to the management science practitioners who developed and implemented the winning works.

First we provide the list of the winner and runners-up in the 1981 prize competition*:

1. From Freight Flow and Cost Patterns to Greater Profitability and Better Service for a Motor Carrier.
2. Reducing Uncollectible Revenue from Residential Telephone Customers.
3. Simulation Modeling Improves Operations, Planning and Productivity of Fast Food Restaurants.

---

* *Interfaces*, Vol. 11, No. 6, Dec. 1981, pp. 4–100.

4. Matching Supplies to Save Lives: Linear Programming the Production of Heart Valves.
5. Scientific Management of Inventory of Hand-Held Calculator.
6. Keeping Ahead of a $2 Billion Canal.
7. Using a Dialysis Need-Projection Model for Health Planning in Massachusetts.

Here are the winner and runners-up for the 1980 competition*:

1. Coordinating Decisions for Increased Profits.
2. Naval Ship Production: A Claim Settled and a Framework Built.
3. Improving Strength Forecast: Support for Army Manpower Management.
4. Boxcars, Linear Programming and the Sleeping Kitten.
5. Implementing Effective Risk Analysis at Getty Oil Co.
6. Evaluating a New Market: A Forecasting System for Nonimpact Computer Printers.

Here are the winner and runners-up for the 1979 competition†:

7. A Long Island Blood Distribution System as a Prototype for Regional Blood Management.
8. An Integrated Production, Distribution and Inventory Planning System.
9. Optimum Bond Calling and Refunding.
10. Management Science Application in the Planning and Design of a Water Supply System for a Nuclear Power Plant.
11. Queuing Theory Applied to Machine Manning.

Here are the winner and runners-up for the 1978 competition‡:

12. A Planning System for Facilities and Resources in Distribution Networks.
13. Applying Capital Marketing Theory to Investing.
14. Helicopter Fleet Mix.
15. Development of a Comprehensive Land-Use Plan by Means of a Multiple Objective Mathematical Programming Model.
16. Fuel Management and Allocation Model.

Now we are ready to start the study of our discipline in earnest. There are many ways to begin, but the best way is to start with an application. So now we proceed to a hypothetical case study, the Loud and Clear Playback Corporation.

---

* *Interfaces*, Vol. 10, No. 6, Dec. 1980, pp. 1–87.
† *Interfaces*, Vol. 9, No. 5, Nov. 1979, pp. 1–63.
‡ *Interfaces*, Vol. 9, No. 2, Part 2, Feb. 1979, pp. 1–86.

The Business Situation

The Loud and Clear Playback Corporation (L&C) is in the business of manufacturing and distributing electronics equipment: radios, stereos, tape recorders, speakers, etc. The corporation decided to market a new two-way citizen's band (CB) radio. The question is, What should be the price of the new two-way CB radio? This is the decision problem to which we address ourselves.

The Pricing Problem

As a consequence of market research and comparison with other products management agrees that the product could be priced anywhere between $60 and $100 and still compete effectively in the marketplace. Thus the problem to decide what the price should be reduces the choice to between $60 and $100. We further simplify our analysis: We reduce the choice to the prices of $60, $70, $85, and $100. Consideration of the full range of prices is postponed for a later analysis.

Thus the decision-making process reduces to the selection of one of these four prices. So what should be the price of the two-way CB radio? What is the *best* price?

All problems must have alternative solutions, and the answer to the problem is the best (or at least an acceptable) alternative.

To come to a logical answer regarding the best price for the CB radio, we must determine the consequences for each of the alternatives. If the product is priced low, more units will be sold than if it is priced high. **Market research** predicts that the quantities sold at prices of $60, $70, $85, and $100 would be 2600, 2200, 1600, and 1000 units, respectively. For the time being we make the assumption that market research can predict exactly the demand corresponding to each price, an assumption surprisingly valid for the analysis of many practical situations.

Using this information, Sally Marks, Vice President of Sales and Marketing, determines the **revenue** associated with each of the four prices. For example, if

$$PRICE = \$100$$

then the quantity of units sold is

$$QUANTITY = 1000$$

and the revenue is

$$REVENUE = QUANTITY \times PRICE = 1000 \times \$100 = \$100,000$$

However, the objective of the corporation is to maximize profits and not sales. Thus the criterion to be used for the selection of the best price is maximization of the profit, given by

$$\text{PROFIT} = \text{REVENUE} - \text{COST}$$

So Sally Marks needs to know the cost associated with producing the CB radio and consults John Shepard, Vice President of Production and Manufacturing.

John Shepard prepares production estimates for the various possibilities. For example, he estimates that to manufacture the

$$\text{QUANTITY} = 1000$$

units corresponding to

$$\text{PRICE} = \$100$$

requires a cost of

$$\text{COST} = \$85,000$$

meaning that the **unit cost of production** is

$$\frac{\text{COST}}{\text{QUANTITY}} = \frac{\$85,000}{100} = \$85$$

Thus the profit on each unit would be $100 − $85 = $15, and the total profit on the 1000 units would be

$$\text{PROFIT} = 1000 \times \$15 = \$15,000$$

On the other hand, if

$$\text{QUANTITY} = 1600$$

for

$$\text{PRICE} = \$85$$

we have

$$\text{COST} = \$106,000$$

and the unit cost of production is

$$\frac{\text{COST}}{\text{QUANTITY}} = \frac{\$106,000}{1600} = \$66.25$$

This results in a profit on each unit of $85.00 − $66.25 = $18.75 and a total profit of

$$\text{PROFIT} = 1600 \times \$18.75 = \$30,000$$

To find the best price, we show in Figure 1.1 all the necessary values. For each of the four alternatives, in the line headed by P (price), the alternate prices are given; in the row headed by Q (quantity), the

	ALTERNATIVES			
	1	2	3	4
P	$60	$70	$85	$100
Q	2,600	2,200	1,600	1,000
C	$141,000	$127,000	$106,000	$85,000
R	$156,000	$154,000	$136,000	$100,000
Z	$15,000	$27,000	$30,000	$15,000

FIGURE 1.1 Determining the selling price of the CB radio for the L&C Corporation. There are four alternatives to the price P: $60, $70, $85, and $100. The second and third rows show predicted quantity Q of sales and cost C. The revenue R and profit Z can be easily computed and the price with the largest profit Z chosen.

corresponding quantities sold; and in the row headed by C (cost), the corresponding costs are shown. The next row, headed by R, shows the revenue. The revenue is computed by multiplying the price by the quantity*:

$$REVENUE = QUANTITY \times PRICE$$

We abbreviate this English language statement by using mathematics:

$$R = Q \times P$$

In the last row, the profit Z, corresponding to each of the four alternatives, is shown:

$$PROFIT = REVENUE - COST$$

or, in mathematical language,

$$Z = R - C$$

Note that Z is the **gross profit**: Taxes and many other costs must be subtracted in a real-life situation to get the **net profit**. To simplify, let us assume that L&C management uses this **criterion** to make the *decision*: Maximize Z, the gross profit. We can now rank the four alternatives in order of decreasing gross profit (Figure 1.2). The *optimum solution* **maximizes** the **payoff**, in this case the gross profit. This optimal solution is obtained for a price of $P = $85 when the payoff (the profit) is $Z = $30,000. The second best choice is the price of $P = $70 with a gross profit of $Z = $27,000. The prices of $P = $60 and $P = $100 both give a gross profit of $Z = $15,000.

---

* The notation for multiplication is inconsistent and confusing. Some authors write 2.5×3.1; others write $(2.5)(3.1)$. You may write $A \times B$ or $A \cdot B$, but in an algebra text you find mostly just AB. You may write $2.5 \times C$ or $2.5C$. We shall use the simplest notation that is not confusing.

| ALTERNATIVE | | GROSS PROFIT, |
Number	Selling Price, P	Z
3	$85	$30,000
2	$70	$27,000
1 & 4	$60, $100	$15,000

FIGURE 1.2 The four ranked alternatives of the selling price of the CB radio for the L&C Corp. The best selling price is $85, the second best is $70, and the third best, $60 and $100, form a tie.

Solution Procedure

To solve this kind of problem, you must answer five crucial questions:

> 1. What are the alternatives?
> 2. What are the consequences and payoffs for each alternative?
> 3. What is the criterion for choosing an alternative?
> 4. How do the alternatives compare in terms of the criterion?
> 5. Which alternative is the optimal solution in terms of the criterion?

In our case the answers are as follows:

1. The prices $60, $70, $85, and $100.
2. Profits of $15,000, $27,000, $30,000, and $15,000.
3. Profit.
4. $85 is best, $70 is next best, and $60 and $100 tie for worst.
5. $85.

Finally we list the assumptions under which this solution is the optimum:

1. Only the prices $60, $70, $85, and $100 are possible.
2. The corresponding sales and costs are known exactly.
3. The criterion is to maximize the average profit.

   If any of these assumptions do not hold, the answer found may not be best, and the analysis would have to be modified to incorporate the correct assumptions.

1.3 THE SCIENTIFIC APPROACH TO UNCERTAINTY

One of our assumptions was that market research can make a perfect **forecast**. For example, in the analysis of Section 1.2 it was assumed that if the CB radio is priced at $60, exactly 2600 units will be sold. Of course we know in reality that this is only an estimate of future sales. No one knows the future, and there is always **uncertainty** involved in prediction. What can be done to make the analysis more realistic by including uncertainty?

In everyday life we continuously make qualitative assessments of uncertainty. We guess a solution, or we just assume that the same thing will happen in the future as happened in the past, etc. The scientific method gives us an objective basis for dealing with uncertainty.

> The scientific method deals with uncertainty by the application of **probability theory** and **statistics**.

This is the approach we follow in this textbook. So we proceed to study the pricing problem under uncertainty but first clarify when and how probability theory and statistics should be used.

There are many managerial situations where reliable estimates of values can be made for the variables involved and acceptable answers can be obtained under the assumption that the future can be accurately predicted. When such conditions prevail, we say that we are dealing with a **deterministic** problem and talk about getting a solution under the deterministic assumption or conditions of **certainty**. Thus, we can say that we have so far resolved the pricing problem only under the deterministic assumption. As we said before, the deterministic analysis often stands on its own and can provide sufficient clarification of the situation so that a decision can be made and action can be taken. Also, even when the situation is uncertain and requires probabilistic analysis, it may still be a good first step to attack the problem by first assuming deterministic conditions and then to proceed to a probabilistic analysis. This is precisely how we are dealing with the L&C pricing problem. We completed the deterministic analysis in Section 1.2 and now proceed to the consideration of uncertainty.

Pricing Under Uncertainty

Sally Marks cannot know in advance precisely how many units will be sold. To simplify, let us continue with the price alternatives $60, $70, $85, and $100. Let us first examine the alternative when the product is priced at the highest amount, namely $100.

We question market research analysts as to sales corresponding to this price. To simplify matters, we ask that they restrict their estimates to only *two* sales levels. The analysts think this is reasonable and state that either 900 or 1100 units would be sold and feel that the chances of selling either quantity are the same. In the upper part of Figure 1.3 we show the costs (as given by L&C's manufacturing department) associated with producing either quantity and the revenues and profits obtained. You can see that if the product is priced at $100 there is a 50–50 chance for a profit of $8500 or $21,500. What next?

If you know some probability theory, you know that *equal chances* means that the probability is 1/2 of selling 900 units and 1/2 of selling

	Possibilities for selling price P = $100	
	1	2
	Equal chances	
Q	900	1,100
C	$81,500	$ 88,500
R	$90,000	$110,000
Z	$ 8,500	$ 21,500

Roulette wheel

Wheel of fortune

Lottery bag

FIGURE 1.3
What to do when sales are uncertain. Market research analysts estimate that 900 or 1100 CB radios will be sold with equal *odds* or *chances* if the price is $100. The lower part of the diagram presents the problem as a gamble with a roulette wheel or a lottery bag. Owing to the equal odds, the average value of the two profits ($8500 + 21,500)/2 = $15,000 is suggested for the value of the profit to be considered.

1100 units. However, Sally Marks does not want to use formal probability theory and wants to solve the problem in her own way.

It happens that Ms. Marks is an expert on gambling. Not that she is so foolish as to gamble away her money! Her rich uncle owns a share of the Platinum Nugget Casino in Las Vegas, and Ms. Marks has spent quite a few weekends there observing **roulette wheels**, wheels of fortune, blackjack, and other systems of gambling. She has observed that half of an ordinary roulette wheel is black and half red (she ignores the zero), so she reasons to herself as follows: "If red comes up, our profit is $8500; if black, $21,500. So let's take the average: ($8500 + $21,500)/2 = $30,000/2 = $15,000." In the lower part of Figure 1.1 we show pictorially her way of reasoning. In addition to showing a roulette wheel (with black and red numbers), we show a balanced true wheel of fortune, where precisely one-half of the wheel indicates a profit of $8500 and the other half a profit of $21,500. If you spin the wheel many times, Ms. Marks claims, roughly half the time you will win $8500 and the other half $21,500.

On the right-hand side of Figure 1.3 we present the same uncertain situation with the aid of a bag such as used in **lotteries**. In the bag we have two chips: one with $8500 and the other with $21,500 written on it. The uncertainty involved in our problem can be represented by drawing chips from this lottery. The average profit will, of course, again be $15,000.

Let us turn now to the situation where the product is priced at $85.

Figure 1.4 shows the prediction of sales by market research: namely, quantities of 1200, 1600, and 1800. Again they feel that the chances for selling each of these quantities are the same, which we know means that each of the probabilities is 1/3. So again we compute the costs, revenues, and profits, and we accept as a criterion for our decision the average of the three profits: $8000, $30,000, and $40,000. So we

Possibilities for selling price P = $85		
1	2	3
Equal odds or chances		
1,200	1,600	1,800
$94,000	$106,000	$113,000
$102,000	$136,000	$153,000
$8,000	$30,000	$40,000

(Rows labelled Q, C, R, Z)

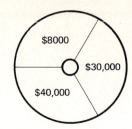

FIGURE 1.4
Resolution of uncertainty when the price is $85 is a little more complicated. Possible sales are in quantities of 1200, 1600, and 1800, and the odds or chances are equal for all three alternative profits. (Observe that on the roulette wheel the profits, not the quantities, are marked.) The average profit is $26,000.

agree that if the product is priced at $85 we should expect a profit of $26,000.

Let us proceed now to the case in which the product is priced at $70 (Figure 1.5). Now we have a new kind of problem. Once again market research says that there are two possibilities. The product will sell 2000 or 2400 units. But they think the chances are better that 2400 units will be sold. How much better? They say the *chances are 2 to 1 in favor of selling 2400 units*. What kind of roulette wheel should we use now? Divide the roulette wheel into *three* equal sectors. Write $20,000 in one sector and $34,000 profit in each of the other two sectors. If the wheel is spun, the chances will be 2 to 1 that the ball will stop on $34,000.

Using probability theory, we would say that the probability of selling 2000 units is 1/3 and of selling 2400 units is 2/3. What should the criterion for the decision be? We can take the average of $20,000, $34,000, and $34,000. So we add as follows: $20,000 + $34,000 + $34,000 = $88,000. Then we divide by 3 to get the average, $29,333. Thus we agree that if the product is priced at $70 we should use the expected profit of $29,333.

Consider, finally, the most complex case, when the product is priced at $60. As shown in Figure 1.6, the market research analysts tell us that there are four possibilities: namely, that the quantities will be 2200, 2400, 2600, and 2900. The corresponding profits are $5000, $10,000, $15,000, and $22,500.

Here is the heart of the problem. Using probability theory, we could say that the probabilities for selling 2200, 2400, 2600, and 2900 units are 1/6, 1/6, 1/3, and 1/3, respectively.

Using our earlier approach, we can determine the decision criteri-

Possibilities for selling price $70	
1	2
Odds or chances	
1 to 2	
2,000	2,400
$120,000	$134,000
$140,000	$168,000
$ 20,000	$ 34,000

(Rows labelled Q, C, R, Z)

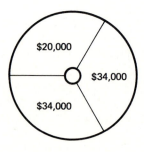

FIGURE 1.5
The problem of pricing at $70 is more difficult. The two possibilities are selling at levels of 2000 and 2400 units, but the odds or chances are 2 to 1 in favor of selling 2400 units. The right-hand side shows that the uncertainty is resolved by using a roulette wheel with three equal sectors with the profits $20,000, $34,000, and again $34,000. The average profit is $29,333.

on by dividing our roulette wheel into six equal sectors. We mark the sectors as follows: one with $5000, one with $10,000, two with $15,000, and two with $22,500. To get the average profit, we must add the profits $5000, $10,000, $15,000, $15,000, $22,500, and $22,500 and divide the sum by 6. We get a total of $90,000 and an average profit of $15,000.

Do you like bags better than roulette wheels? Drop six chips into your bag with the numbers $5000, $10,000, $15,000, $15,000, $22,500, and $22,500 on them. If you draw many times, on the average you will get $15,000.

Confused? The reason is that we have not yet presented a theory for decision making under uncertainty. You will have to wait until we develop the knowledge required for such a theory. However, a diagram will be helpful.

Tree Diagrams to Represent Decision Making

An important pictorial **modeling** technique to help in decision making is the use of the **decision tree** illustrated in Figure 1.7. We show by the *square box* on the left, the **decision fork** at the *root* of the tree, that we have a decision to make. We must choose one of the four branches emanating from the square box representing the prices $60, $70, $85, and $100. Each decision branch leads to a *circle*, a **chance fork** representing a roulette wheel. When we reach a chance fork, we do not make decisions; chance takes over. The roulette wheel is spun, and we proceed along the branch specified by the spot at which the ball stops. We show individual profits and average computed profits at the **tips** of the tree. Now you can see that the optimum solution to the pricing problem is the price of $70, taking our criterion to be maximizing average profit.

Thus we have a two-step procedure to deal with uncertainty.

> 1. Convert the managerial situation into a problem described by a **thought experiment**.
> 2. Find the best solution to the problem by using probability theory.

Possibilities for selling price $60			
1	2	3	4
Chances			
1 to 1	1 to 2	2 to 2	

	1	to	1	to	2	to	2
Q	2,200		2,400		2,600		2,900
C	$127,000		$134,000		$141,000		$151,500
R	$132,000		$144,000		$156,000		$174,000
Z	$ 5,000		$ 10,000		$ 15,000		$ 22,500

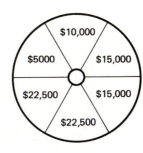

FIGURE 1.6
Pricing the CB radio at $60 is the hardest to deal with. There are four possibilities. The first two have equal chances; the second two also have equal chances, but the second two have odds twice as high as the first two. The roulette wheel to be used has six equal sectors. The average profit is $15,000.

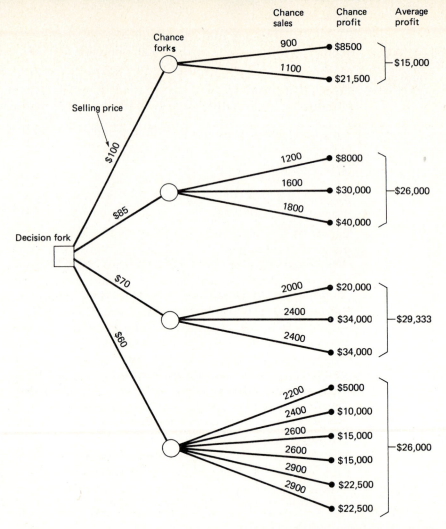

FIGURE 1.7 Tree diagram summarizes pricing the CB radio at four different price levels. The square box represents a decision fork, and the circles represent roulette wheels at chance forks. The price of $70 yields the highest average profit of $29,333.

Gamble Ventures and Thought Experiments

Note how Ms. Marks finds a way to deal with problems of uncertainty. First she converts the business problem into a gambling problem, and then she imagines that a gambling experiment is performed. Of course she has no need to actually perform the experiments. Physicists call such imaginary experiments *gedanken* (German for "thought") experiments, and in our textbook we often borrow the physicist's term and speak of thought experiments.

Note also that Ms. Marks does not use formal probability theory.

For more complex situations, probability theory becomes indispensable, and therefore in Chapters 2 and 3 we shall review probability theory.

This then concludes our preliminary discussion of the Loud and Clear Playback Corp., and we are ready to go deeper into our subject by introducing quantitative analysis with the aid of mathematical models.

1.4. AN EXAMPLE OF A MATHEMATICAL MODEL

Why Mathematical Models?

The word *model* has many meanings. Models have long been used for various purposes. Engineers test model airplanes in wind tunnels. Architects use scale models of buildings and cities. We use maps which are models of a land, a territory, etc. We might even say that all our discussions are verbal models of the real world. However, to deal with managerial decision making, verbal models are often inadequate, so verbal information needs to be replaced by **symbolic representation** of thought, that is, by symbolic information. This is also necessary when a computer is used, since a computer program is a particular symbolic representation of a management situation and its resolution.

Now we show how symbolic and in particular mathematical representation can be considered an extension of common sense, how words can replace mathematical equations, and how mathematics can aid in clarifying confused situations. We argue that you need not become a mathematician. All that is required is to learn the basic techniques of manipulating mathematical symbols.

To summarize, **mathematical models** are used because verbal descriptions and information are inadequate in dealing with complex and uncertain decision situations. Specifically, they are inadequate in

1. *Describing* the economic characteristics associated with managerial decision making
2. *Predicting* the probable consequences of decisions
3. *Articulating* criteria required to evaluate the relative merits of alternate decisions

To illustrate our point, we present here a mathematical model for the Loud and Clear Playback Corp.

Mathematical Model for the Loud and Clear Playback Corp.

We have already solved the pricing problem for the CB radio when the only price alternatives were $60, $70, $85, and $100. Now we want to extend our analysis to include any pricing alternative between and including $60 and $100, although we shall conduct our analysis under the assumption that there are no uncertainties involved.

To solve this problem under this more general condition, we need

mathematical formulas, expressions, and **relationships** for the problem. First we inquire of the Vice President of Production and Manufacturing how the cost of production depends on the quantity produced. Without going into detail of how Shepard obtains his answer, we simply report here that he says the following formula is to be used*:

COST OF PRODUCTION = 35 × QUANTITY PRODUCED + 50000

We now introduce mathematical notation for the variables of the problem,

$$C = \text{COST OF PRODUCTION}$$

$$Q = \text{QUANTITY PRODUCED}$$

and write the mathematical formulas

$$C = 35Q + 50000$$

(Note that we omitted the multiplication sign between the 35 and Q.)

We also need a relationship between Q, the quantity sold, and the price of the CB radio. The Vice President of Sales and Marketing tells us that we can use the following relationship:

QUANTITY SOLD = 5000 − 40 × PRICE

So we designate the price by P and write

$$Q = 5000 - 40P$$

We should, however, qualify these relationships by saying that they hold only when P, the price, is between and including \$60 and \$100. In other words, P must be (1) greater than (or equal to) \$60 and (2) less than (or equal to) \$100. We write this in mathematics as

$$P \geqslant 60 \qquad \text{or} \qquad 60 \leqslant P$$

and

$$P \leqslant 100 \qquad \text{or} \qquad 100 \geqslant P$$

or in abbreviated form,

$$60 \leqslant P \leqslant 100$$

There are corresponding restrictions for Q. Namely, if $P = 60$,

$$Q = 5000 - 40P = 5000 - 40 \times 60 = 2600$$

and if $P = 100$,

$$Q = 5000 - 40 \times 100 = 1000$$

Thus Q must be between and including 2600 and 1000 or

$$1000 \leqslant Q \leqslant 2600$$

---

* To avoid confusion, mathematical formulas often omit commas and write 50000 instead of 50,000 and so on.

To help visualize these relationships, we show them in graphical form in Figures 1.8 and 1.9.

Note that both relationships in Figures 1.6 and 1.7 are represented by a straight line. Such relationships are called **linear**. Note from the cost-quantity relationships that if an additional unit is produced, the cost *increases* by $35. The quantity-cost relationship tells us that if the price is increased by $1, then sales will *decrease* by 40 units.

To complete our model, we need R, the revenue, which equals price times quantity,

$$\text{REVENUE} = \text{PRICE} \times \text{QUANTITY}$$

$$R = PQ$$

and the profit Z, which is the difference between the revenue and the cost,

$$\text{PROFIT} = \text{REVENUE} - \text{COST}$$

$$Z = R - C$$

Now we have the mathematical model of our problem, as shown in Figure 1.10. The model implies the following calculation procedure:

Step 1. Compute the quantity for given price from

$$Q = 5000 - 40P$$

Step 2. Calculate cost from

$$C = 50000 + 35Q$$

Step 3. Calculate revenue from

$$R = PQ$$

Step 4. Calculate profit from

$$Z = R - C$$

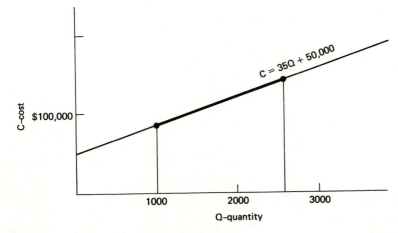

FIGURE 1.8
Graphical representation of the cost-quantity relationship for the CB radio.

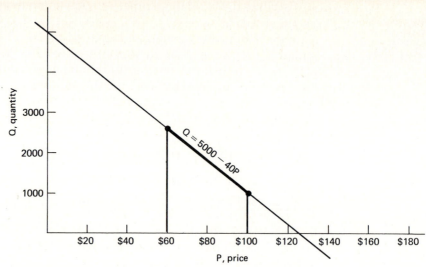

FIGURE 1.9 Graphical representation of the quantity-price relationship for the CB radio.

The Profit Function

Our problem is to determine the optimum price, that is, the one which maximizes profit. We shall accomplish this task by developing a single *formula* which relates Z, the profit, to P, the price. First we develop a formula for C, then for R, and finally for Z.

Therefore we take the cost-quantity relationship and eliminate Q, the quantity, with the aid of the price-quantity relationship. We get the formula

$$C = 50000 + 35Q = 50000 + 35(5000 - 40P) = 225000 - 1400P$$

Now we can determine the formula for revenue by eliminating Q, the quantity, with the aid of the quantity-price relationship:

$$R = PQ = P(5000 - 40P) = 5000P - 40P^2$$

Now we have formulas for C and R and can derive the formula for the profit:

$$Z = R - C = (5000P - 40P^2) - (225000 - 1400P)$$

$$Z = -40P^2 + 6400P - 225000$$

$$\boxed{\begin{aligned} &Q = 5000 - 40P, \; 60 \leqslant P \leqslant 100 \\ &C = 50000 + 35Q, \; 1000 \leqslant Q \leqslant 2600 \\ &R = PQ \\ &Z = R - C \end{aligned}}$$

FIGURE 1.10 The mathematical model of the pricing situation.

Note that this is a **quadratic function** of P because P appears raised to the second power. We show the function graphically in Figure 1.11 and you can see that the optimum price which yields the highest profit is somewhere in the neighborhood of $80.

The Concept of Algorithm

Before we continue our analysis, we stress that the preceding formula for the profit Z indicates a computational procedure to calculate Z from a given P. The procedure is as follows:

> *Step 1.* Calculate the square of P.
> *Step 2.* Multiply the result of step 1 by 40.
> *Step 3.* Change the sign of the result of step 2.
> *Step 4.* Designate by A the result of step 3.
> *Step 5.* Multiply P by 6400.
> *Step 6.* Designate the result of step 5 by B.
> *Step 7.* Add A and B.
> *Step 8.* Subtract 225,000 from the result of step 7.
> *Step 9.* Designate the result of step 8 by Z.

Such a precise step-by-step rule to calculate an answer is called an **algorithm.** As we proceed, you will study algorithms to solve more complex problems. You will also learn that computers are most superior tools for carrying out algorithms, and, in fact, before a computer can do useful work, it must be given an algorithm to follow.

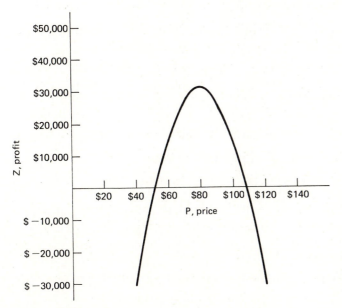

FIGURE 1.11
Graphical representation of the profit as a function of price.

Finding the Optimum Price

So far we determined the approximate optimum value of P by inspecting Figure 1.11. Now we need an **optimization technique** to compute accurately the optimum value of P.

In Appendix A, Section 7.5, we give the formula for determining the maximum of a quadratic function. The general form of the equation is

$$y = ax^2 + bx + c$$

where a, b, and c are given constants. The optimum occurs at

$$x = -\frac{b}{2a}$$

which implies the following three-step algorithm:

> *Step 1*. Divide b by a.
> *Step 2*. Divide by 2.
> *Step 3*. Reverse the sign.

In the problem at hand we have

$$x = P$$

$$a = -40$$

$$b = 6400$$

$$c = -225000$$

Consequently, the optimum value of the price is

$$P^* = -\frac{6400}{2x(-40)} = \$80$$

where the asterisk reminds us that we are dealing with optimum values. We can also compute the optimum value of all our other variables:

$$Q^* = 5000 - 40 \times 80 = 1800$$

$$C^* = 50000 + 35 \times 1800 = \$113,000$$

$$R^* = 80 \times 1800 = \$144,000$$

$$Z^* = \$144,000 - \$113,000 = \$31,000$$

It is worth comparing these answers with the best solution obtained in Figure 1.1. There the best solution was the price of $85, which resulted in a profit of $30,000. Now that we allow any price, we can realize $1000 more profit.

Note that without mathematical analysis we could not have obtained this result.

> The primary advantage of a mathematical model is in clarifying the situation, providing information, and supporting the manager so the best decision can be made.

Note also that the mathematical analysis provides the best solution to the mathematical model. However, the mathematical model at best is an approximate description of the situation.

> An optimum solution means the best solution to a model, nothing more or less.

This then completes our first illustration of what a mathematical model is and what it does. Now we are ready to discuss the most essential feature of the quantitative approach—the scientific method.

1.5 THE SCIENTIFIC METHOD

The word **science** comes from the Latin *scientia* meaning "knowledge" or "to know." *Science covers the broad field of human knowledge concerned with facts held together by rules or principles.* These facts and principles are discovered by the scientific method, an orderly technique of solving problems. Any subject which can be studied using the scientific method and other special rules of thought may be called a science.

When we speak about applying the scientific method to managerial situations, we mean there is a considerable store of accumulated knowledge which can be applied to a specific situation faced by a manager. Thus science includes the systematic approach to solving a problem using accumulated knowledge.

> The scientific method implies the application of a well-developed body of knowledge in a systematic and well-structured sequence of five phases.

The Five Phases of the Scientific Method

1. Stating a problem or question
2. Forming a **hypothesis** based on a theory
3. Experimentation, that is, gathering data bearing on the hypothesis
4. Interpretation of the data and drawing conclusions
5. Revising the theory for deriving further hypotheses for testing

Putting the hypothesis in a form that can be tested is the foundation of the **empirical** verification of science. In addition, all the sciences try to express their hypotheses, theories, and conclusions in quantitative form. Now we shall apply the scientific method to managerial decision making.

1. *Exploration.* When a manager faces a new and complex situation, usually there is confusion, "fuzziness," about what really is the problem. The scientific method specifies that the situation must be explored, observations must be made, and data and facts and information must be gathered and analyzed and verified. Experimentation and trial solutions are often required to clarify the situation. The exploratory phase is more art than science and is often described as the qualitative, explorative analysis of the situation.

2. *Model building.* The first phase of a quantitative study results in formulation of the problem and a clarification of the situation. After the problem is clearly formulated, a logical model of the situation must be built, usually a mathematical model. One of the central themes of this textbook is how to build such logical, mathematical models needed to resolve managerial problems. Building the mathematical model often leads to writing computer programs and the use of computers.

3. *Model interpretation.* After the model has been built and used, it becomes possible to determine on the basis of the model how goals can be achieved. However, to aid the decision maker, the model must be interpreted in plain English. Thus, in this third phase the situation is clarified for the decision maker, and the implications of decisions are precisely stated. Again, this phase of the work is more art than science.

4. *Decision making.* The manager starts originally with a confused and poorly defined situation. Through the three phases—exploration, model building, and model interpretation—the situation is clarified, and it becomes apparent which alternative is to be chosen, and a decision is made.

5. *Implementation.* After the decision is made, it must be put into effect. The decision must be executed. In fact, this last phase of the project must be kept in mind during the first four phases, and careful plans must be made to assure acceptance by management. During the implementation phase final support by management is obtained, and the benefits to be gained from the study are carefully explained to all personnel involved. Detailed procedures to put the solution into operation are developed, and all operating personnel are fully educated and trained to put the results of the project into actual fulfillment. (Often the implementation phase culminates in the delivery of a computer-based information system, which then serves as the primary vehicle for taking advantage of the results of the quantitative analysis.)

This brief outline of the scientific method and its application to managerial decision making serves only as a background. You will fully understand what is involved only as you progress in the study of this textbook, and we shall make references as we proceed to specifics of the application of the scientific method.

Finally, let us say that this textbook is based on a faith in science and its well-established success in its application to problems of management. But we most emphatically do not claim that science can save us and solve all our problems. Science alone cannot specify our overall objectives and desired quality of life.

Now we proceed to provide some recent case studies where Operations Research or Management Science, OR/MS has been successfully applied to managerial decision making.

1.6. INTERACTIVE FINANCIAL PLANNING: THE DECISION SUPPORT SYSTEM APPROACH

In the pricing model developed for the Loud and Clear Playback Corporation we considered only a single product, a single time period, and a bare minimum of relationships leading to the profit. In practical situations financial planning may involve many products, factories, warehouses, and so on and several years of operations. Such models may cover any or all facets of the operation of a corporation and may involve hundreds or even thousands of equations. Therefore, such models are invariably computer based.

Financial planning models are perhaps the most successful and popular applications of quantitative methods. Thousands of corporations are either using, developing, or planning to use such models. Financial planning models are used in every type of organization, both in the private and public sectors of our economy, and by executives and managers at all levels. They are used daily, weekly, monthly, and whenever necessary to make decisions.

As in the Loud and Clear corporate pricing model, financial planning models consist of a system of equations derived from accounting relationships, statistical forecasting, and other relationships of quantitative analysis. Financial planning models support planning and decision making, for example, in

1. Capital decisions (to borrow money, issue stock or bonds, etc.)
2. Capital investments (to build a new warehouse, production facility, etc.)
3. Marketing decisions (for pricing strategy, advertising, promotional budgets, distribution of goods, etc.)
4. Merger of corporations, acquisition analysis, and so on

Financial planning models provide past, present, and projected information important to decision making and are based on *interactive* computer facilities. This means that the decision maker can actually sit down in front of a computer equipped with a TV-like screen and obtain information directly from the computer. The manager can input data, query the computer, and rapidly obtain answers to questions; he or she can have man-machine dialogs.

There are so many financial planning models in use that it is impractical to select a representative one. Therefore in what follows we describe a disguised case, the La Brea Oil Company, but stress that all the material is based on work performed in actual corporations.

The La Brea Oil Company

This major corporation is a fully integrated enterprise, has 30 or so subsidiaries employing about 30,000 people, and has revenues of about $2 billion and assets of about $2.5 billion. Top executives of the corporation were dissatisfied with their planning and control system and their ability to react with timely analysis to impending changes. They had only limited capability for evaluating alternate possible actions in spite of the mass of pertinent data available. Management desired to take a firmer and longer look into the future, develop many alternate plans quickly, and in general improve the decision-making capability.

At this point the management decided to install a decision support system (DSS) and explored the possibility of purchasing a commercial computer package of programs, a *decision support system generator*. Such a computer package would have made it easier and less costly to develop and install the DSS. However, due to the fact that the corporation had both an excellent operations research group and management information systems division, management decided to develop the model and programs in-house. This had the advantage that the model could be better tailored to the needs of La Brea and also resulted in very efficient computer programs.

On completion of the project the model had 1500 input variables, 500 environmental variables, 1000 decision variables, and about 5200 output variables. The model was capable of providing in a matter of minutes outputs of 61 various reports consisting of 132 pages and enabled decision makers to conduct man-computer dialogs.

Components of the La Brea Model

The central feature of the La Brea model is the capability to provide outputs fashioned after the annual reports of the company. In addition, many of the outputs of the model simulate the traditional financial reports of the company, so decision makers have little difficulty interpreting the outputs. To create these outputs, company processes and accounting practices were translated into mathematical equations, and then these equations were programmed for the computer. Corporate and departmental revenues and expenses were examined, component by component, and related to physical activities of the corporation. Mathematical equations for each account and subaccount were established for the four principal submodels making up the total model: (1) production model related to finding and extracting oil, (2) transportation model describing the use of tankers and pipelines, (3) manufacturing or refining model, and (4) marketing model dealing with the gasoline stations of the company.

The principal quantitative technique for the establishment of the equations was statistics (see Chapters 2–4). For example, direct selling expense was statistically related to the number of service stations operated by the company and the volume of sale of gasoline. The equation has the form

$$\text{selling expense} = a_1 + a_2 \times (\text{number of service stations})$$

$$+ a_3 \times (\text{gasoline sales})$$

$$+ \text{marketing depreciation expense}$$

$$+ \text{advertising expense}$$

where a_1, a_2, and a_3 are coefficients derived by regression analysis (see Chapter 4).

As a further example we point out that refining expense was related to such variables as operating labor, pension cost, plant throughput, gasoline volume, refinery and equipment volume, refinery and equipment value, and the length of time of operation.

The model generates a projection based on such input variables as (1) product prices and volumes, (2) raw material costs, (3) economic conditions, (4) investments, (5) subsidiary company income, and (6) discretionary expense items. The general economic conditions predicated include (1) import restrictions, (2) rates for U.S. taxes and mineral depletion allowance, and (3) allowable levels of crude oil production as set by state regulatory agencies. Proposed investments for the various marketing and production areas are either specified beforehand or are determined by the model.

Advantages of Decision Support Systems

Perhaps the greatest benefit to the decision makers of La Brea is the freedom to experiment with ideas via man-computer dialogs. They can explore alternatives in allocating resources and testing the many assumptions they hold about the enterprise. Also important is the capability to predict the impact of trial decisions on such financial factors as net income, cash flow, and profit. Executives ask *what* happens *if* any of the inputs change, and the decision support system provides answers for decision making. Because the system can be operated for various segments of the company, these advantages are available not only to corporate executives but also to executives of the operating divisions, lower-level managers, and even to operations personnel.

The model also provides capability to keep budgeted plans accurate, up to date, and in line with current results. Also, income projections can be revised in terms of various conditions and alternative strategies. Answers can either be displayed on computer terminals or printed on paper by computer-driven printers.

Decision support systems may encompass all the operations of a corporation and can provide a common medium of communication for top management, middle management, and operating personnel. While organizational problems often arise due to faulty assumptions, lack of information, misunderstanding, and so on, the preciseness of models promotes a clear understanding of goals and responsibilities. Thus the impact of models is not only on financial improvements but also in promoting cooperation, goal clarification, and motivation. The behavioral importance of decision support systems cannot be overemphasized.

1.7 A DIALOG

For 24 centuries the Socratic method of teaching by question and answer has been practiced. To reinforce and expand the material of this textbook, we present dialogs at the ends of chapters between instructor and student, fashioned after Plato's *Republic*.

Q. *What evidence is there that the quantitative approach pays off?*

A. We cannot offer scientific proof but can offer testimony as in court trials to prove beyond reasonable doubt that the quantitative approach is useful. Consider, for example, financial planning models. They have been used for years in practically all large corporations of the United States. These models are being revised and expanded, and management keeps spending money to maintain these systems. This then is evidence that managers are satisfied. There are many successful cases, and you will learn about a few of them later in this textbook.

Q. *Do quantitative techniques save money?*

A. Often the success of a system is measured by the satisfaction of the manager. However, there are many other applications where dollar savings have been verified by accepted auditing standards. There are also many situations where the system leads to **value added**, such as an increase in sales or profits.

Q. *Can quantitative techniques deal with any kind of situation?*

A. Not so! There are many problems which are so ill-defined and ill-structured that they are yet unsolvable by quantitative analysis. Suppose, for instance, you want to determine whether you should stay single or get married. Such a situation is so full of intangibles, immeasurables of the quality of life, that it would be difficult, nay impossible, to conceive a rational mathematical analysis to resolve the problem.

Q. *Are quantitative techniques used only in business?*

A. Not at all! The quantitative approach has been used in many aspects of the public sector. Just to mention a few examples: pollution control, control of water resources, running of hospitals, menu planning for institutions, pension reform of veterans, traffic control, urban development, crime abatement, etc., etc.

Q. *Do I need to become a mathematician to perform a quantitative analysis?*

A. No. Mathematics is an important but not the most important facet of quantitative analysis. You can see in the corporate model that no advanced mathematics is required. The mathematical review in Appendix A is adequate to cover the mathematical prerequisites for quantitative analysis. Some of the most successful practitioners of quantitative analysis have only a limited mastery of mathematics. Often there is a need for advanced techniques, but then many practitioners rely on the advice of experts and consultants.

Q. *Must I use a computer?*

A. Almost always. Most people believe that computers compute only numbers. Not so! Computers are machines to process information. In fact, they *compute* not only numbers but also information. The primary purpose of quantitative techniques is to provide information to managers, and without computers it may be impractical to do so.

Q. *Do I need to become a computer expert?*

A. Computers are extremely useful and are being used in practically all cases where quantitative techniques are used. But today there are many software packages available which can be used without being a computer expert. There are also English-language-oriented programming techniques, so a nonexpert can use the computer. Then again, if in difficulty, you may consult an expert to help solve your problem.

Q. *What are the most important traits of successful analysts?*

A. They must have a mastery of how to apply quantitative techniques. This means they must know the elements of the various techniques available and how to apply them. But more important, they must have an understanding of management and managers. Successful analysts must have a good grasp of the various functional areas of management: finance, production, marketing, accounting, etc. Successful analysts must have good conceptual abilities to think rationally and in a logical manner. They must be creative, original, practical, and oriented toward problem solving. They must have behavioral skills to master interpersonal relationships; they need to be good communicators and to possess a degree of self-awareness. They must be highly motivated and understand not only the technical but social and psychological aspects of our society.

Q. *Do quantitative techniques always provide the optimum?*

A. Not so! Think again about the decision support system we discussed. We stressed that managers operate the model with what-if types of questions, and the computer provides projected sales, profits, profit-and-loss statements, etc. The manager experiments with various alternatives and by judgment selects an acceptable solution. In such situations no optimization techniques are used, and we speak of *satisficing*.* In fact DSS advocates stress that in practice decision makers mostly satisfice.

Optimization provides additional information to the manager, but you must clearly understand in what sense the optimum holds. Consider, for example, the model in Figure 1.10. The best solution is valid only *if* (1) profit is the sole criterion for decision, (2) the formulas for cost and price are correct, (3) only a single time period is considered, etc.

Q. *Suppose some of these assumptions do not hold?*

A. Then you must expand the model to include more of the realities of the situation. But you cannot go on indefinitely making the model more complicated. Judgment must be used when to stop. So there is room for common sense even in the most sophisticated model. Decision making is never completely automated because in the final analysis assumptions are accepted on the basis of intuition.

So you can see that some situations admit optimization, while in others optimization is not possible or even required. You must make a distinction between the model and the optimization technique. The model, that is, the collection of relations and formulas, is an indispensable instrument to examine, describe, and clarify complex situations. Optimization is a powerful tool which provides additional and better information to the decision maker.

Q. *Your models do not completely represent reality. Many aspects are missing. How can they be useful?*

A. Models do not aim to portray reality perfectly. Models are tools of analysis to aid decision makers.

Q. *It is clear that a deterministic model is a system of equations, but it is not so clear about models of uncertainty.*

A. For the time being you can consider the thought experiment as a model—converting the problem into a gambling problem and imagining that the gambling experiment is performed. As we develop probability theory, you will be able to firm up your views of models, including uncertainty.

SUMMARY

1. Quantitative analysis provides information for managers and executives so they can make better decisions.
2. Resource allocation is a central issue to management.
3. Quantitative techniques of management had their roots in the use of scientific techniques in solving military problems in World War II.
4. Decision making means choosing one alternative.

* The word was coined by the Nobel laureate economist Herbert A. Simon.

5. Pricing products is one of the important problems in managerial decision making.

6. To analyze a management decision problem quantitatively, you must
   a. Determine the alternatives
   b. Establish the consequences for each alternative
   c. Define the criterion to be used
   d. Evaluate the alternatives in terms of the criterion
   e. Choose an acceptable or perhaps optimal alternative in terms of the criterion

7. Two types of management decision problem are considered in this textbook: when conditions are (a) certain or deterministic and (b) uncertain or probabilistic.

8. Theories of probability and statistics provide the scientific bases for decision making under uncertainty.

9. Tree diagrams provide a convenient, graphical way to analyze management decision problems quantitatively.

10. Decision-making problems under uncertainty will often be studied (modeled) with the aid of thought experiments, that is, gamble ventures utilizing chance devices.

11. Mathematics is a most effective and convenient language to clarify and support managerial decision making and provides a bridge to the use of computers.

12. The use of mathematical models is central to quantitative approaches to managerial decision making.

13. The five phases of quantitative analysis of decision making are
    a. Exploration
    b. Model building and operation
    c. Model interpretation
    d. Decision making
    e. Implementation

14. The competent analyst must be clearly aware of the limitations of the scientific method.

15. Interactive financial planning systems employ the computer and a system of equations derived from accounting, statistical, forecasting, and other relationships connecting the variables of a corporation.

16. The computer and mathematics are necessary instruments for management decision making, and the design of information systems can only enhance, not replace, human judgment.

SECTION EXERCISES

1. **What This Textbook is About**
   1.1 Give examples from your own experience of each of the following:
      a. A manager (job title, position, or function)
      b. Decisions made by this manager
      c. A person who supports this manager in decision making

1.2 Give an example of a "confusing and uncertain situation" where there are many alternatives to be considered and it is not a simple matter to determine which alternative leads to the desired goal. *Hint*: Many personal and/or everyday situations are of this type.

1.3 Identify and list the scarce resources in each of the following situations where resources are converted to goods or services.
  a. Manufacture of wooden furniture
  b. Utility supplying private homes with electricity
  c. Airline
  d. Manufacture of aluminum cans
  e. Research and development department of a microcomputer company

1.4 Resources do not have to be limited on a global scale (as, for example, in the case of fossil fuels). Any decision maker may get into a situation where the supply of some resource is limited for *this* decision maker at *this* time. Give an example of such a situation; your example can be from your own experience. *Hint*: Be sure you know the definition of *resource*.

1.5 Give an example of an information system that provides information used in decision making. Note that information systems need not be computer based, as mentioned in the text, and that you see a great deal of information system support of decision making in your daily life.

1.6 Several professional societies concerned with scientific decision making are mentioned in Section 1.1. Pick one of them, look up a copy of its journal, and summarize the kinds of situations in which decision making is discussed in articles in the journal.

1.7 The following is a list of journal articles on applications of scientific decision making. Pick one of them, read it, and report on the benefits obtained. (What are the benefits in terms of better service, lower cost, greater revenue, better control, etc., as they fit in the case you choose?)
  a. L. C. Edie, "Traffic Delays at Toll Booths," Journal of the Operations Research Society of America, (*JORSA*), Vol. 2, May 1954, pp 107–138.
  b. G. Brigham, "On a Congestion Problem in an Aircraft Factory," *JORSA*, Vol. 3, No. 4, Nov. 1955, pp 412–428.
  c. Levinson, "Experiences in Commercial Operations Research," *JORSA*, Vol. 1, No. 4, Aug. 1953, pp 220–239.

1.8 To get an idea of the breadth of applications of quantitative methods, complete the following table. The first three entries have been done for you. Note that you may not have sufficient information for all applications to complete their entry.

NO.	TYPE OF PROBLEM SOLVED	TYPE OF USER
1.	Decision making	Tire company
2.	Settling a claim	Naval shipbuilding
3.	Forecasting strength	U.S. Army (military)
4.		
5.		
⋮		

2. *Loud and Clear Playback Corporation*

2.1 Figure 1.1 summarizes the pricing situation for the sale of CB radios under the conditions given in Section 1.2. Assume that the cost of producing the radios has been changed by the use of new microprocessors; the unit cost for producing a radio is $65 at any volume of production.

a. Make a new version of Figure 1.1 in which you revise the total costs (*C*) in accordance with this new condition.
b. Make a new version of Figure 1.2.
c. What is the optimal alternative?
d. What is the optimal selling price?
e. What is the gross profit at the optimal selling price?
f. What is the next best selling price?
g. What is the gross profit at the next best selling price?

2.2 The Loud and Clear Playback Corporation wishes to consider a new type of CB product which can be sold at the prices shown in Figure 1.1 plus $65, $75, $80, $85, $90, and $95. For this new product, the unit costs are the same as those in Figure 1.1, but the quantity sold is determined from the following relationship: $Q = 5000 - 40 \times P$.
a. Revise Figure 1.1 to fit these new conditions.
b. Complete the analysis, and make a new version of Figure 1.2.
c. What is the optimal alternative?
d. What is the optimal selling price?
e. What is the gross profit at the optimal selling price?
f. What is the next best selling price?
g. What is the gross profit at the next best selling price?

2.3 Big Byte Stores is a personal computer store selling at a discount. They are trying to decide at what price to market the 173MBI chip; prices under consideration are $19.95, $24.95, $29.95, and $32.50. Price tests show that they can expect to sell 3000 units at the lowest price and the following quantities for each successively higher price: 2500, 2000, and 1000. For quantities of 3000, 2500, 2000, and 1000, the manufacturer has quoted unit prices to Big Byte of $22, $24, $27, and $30.
a. What is the optimal selling price?
b. What is the gross profit at the optimal selling price?
c. What is the next best price, and what is the gross profit at that price?
d. The manufacturer has idle time in his plant and has asked Big Byte to set a price for the chips from him at which they will be willing to buy 3000. At what price from the manufacturer will the gross profit at a volume of 3000 be equal to the optimal gross profit determined in part b?
e. The manufacturer wants to go out of the business of producing the 173MBI chip and has offered Big Byte the entire inventory of chips at a price of $16 per unit. What is the minimum price at which all 10,000 chips in the inventory must be sold to yield the same gross profit as that determined in part b to be optimal?

2.4 Pop Rikka, a musical star, is thinking of marketing his most popular song. A marketing consultant has told him that he can sell 1 million at $3, 800,000 at $4, and 600,000 at $6. The costs of producing the record at the three successively lower quantities have been estimated at (per record) $2.60, $3.00, and $3.80.
a. What is the optimal selling price?
b. What is the gross profit at that price?

2.5 The Engels Toy Company is making a decision on a TV advertising campaign. Three different campaign efforts have been proposed; the dollars to be expended in each are $1 million, $1.5 million, and $2 million. The sales that can be generated by each of these campaign efforts are estimated to be $16 million, $21 million, and $24 million, respectively. A profit analysis by Engels shows that the gross profit not counting the advertising campaign costs is $2,400,000, $3,150,000 and $3,600,000, respectively.
a. What is the optimal expenditure for the TV advertising campaign?
b. What is the profit (taking advertising costs into account) at the optimal expenditure?

c. Suppose that the sales in millions of dollars generated by the advertising campaign (S) can be related to advertising expenditure in millions of dollars (A) by the formula

$$S = 20 \times A - 4 \times A^2$$

Assuming that advertising expenditure can be changed only in increments of $100,000, what is the optimal expenditure for the TV advertising campaign?

d. Under the conditions of part c, what is the profit (taking advertising costs into account) at the optimal expenditure?

3. *The Scientific Approach to Uncertainty*

3.1 This exercise refers to the situation for Loud and Clear Playback Corporation pricing when the market response is uncertain, as illustrated by Figures 1.3–1.6. New information from the Marketing Department indicates that, while the profits remain unchanged, the chances of selling different quantities should be revised as follows:

SELLING PRICE, P	NEW CHANCES	REFERENCE FIGURE FOR DATA
$100	Odds are 2 to 1 in favor of selling 1100 instead of 900	1.3
$85	Odds are 1 to 1 to 2 for selling 1200, 1600, and 1800	1.4
$70	Odds are equal for selling 2000 or 2400	1.5
$60	Odds are equal for selling 2200, 2400, 2600, and 2900	1.6

a. Create new versions of Figures 1.3–1.6, and compute the average profit to be obtained for each of the four selling prices.

b. What is the optimal selling price now?

c. What is the average profit at the optimal selling price?

d. Show this new situation in a decision tree similar to Figure 1.7.

3.2 The Marketing Department of the Loud and Clear Playback Corp. reports that all estimates of sales should be increased by 10%. Thus in Figure 1.3, 1100 should be increased to 1210 and 900 to 990; similar increases in Q will hold for all cases, Figures 1.3–1.6 (but costs remain the same).

a. Change all values of Q accordingly, and create the revised versions of Figures 1.3–1.6.

b. Find the optimal selling price.

c. What is the average profit at the optimal selling price?

3.3 Marcel Joseph is the finance commissioner for the city of Cummerbund, which has been criticized by a local newspaper for its tax collection methods. The newspaper claims that $1 million in taxes are uncollected because of poor record keeping. The Executive Committee of Cummerbund met, and the best opinion of the committee was that there is a 50–50 chance that the newspaper is right. While recognizing that the final decision may be based on purely political concerns, the mayor wants to have an "unemotional" analysis of the situation so that he can balance the purely analytical results against the political costs and benefits when he meets with the City Council. One approach that could be taken is to do nothing. Another is to hire an outside firm for $330,000 to carry out a detailed audit; this firm is known for its skill and is certain to discover uncollected taxes if there are any. However, if there are uncollected taxes of $1 million, then this firm will charge an additional $270,000 to collect them. Another alternative is to hire a firm specializing in municipal affairs; they will charge only $230,000 for the investigation and offer a guarantee to find any missing taxes. However, they want $530,000 to collect the outstanding taxes.

a. From the purely analytical standpoint (using the methods of this chapter), which alternative is best?

b. What is the average return for this alternative?

c. The Executive Committee reevaluates the estimate that the chances of a variance existing are 50–50; they now feel that they are 3 to 1. Under these conditions, what is the best alternative?

d. What is the average return to the city for the best alternative in part c above?

e. Marcel Joseph discussed the situation with the second firm, arguing that a fee of $530,000 to collect any outstanding taxes that might be found is excessive. A new fee was negotiated on this basis: $300,000 for the investigation and $380,000 to collect the taxes if found to be owing. What is the best alternative if the chances of the existence of unpaid taxes are 50–50?

f. What is the best alternative under the revised conditions of part e if the chances of unpaid taxes existing are 3 to 1?

g. What are the average returns to the city in both cases e and f?

3.4 Refer to the problem of pricing under uncertainty illustrated in the decision tree of Figure 1.7. Assume that the probabilities have been revised as follows:

| | SELLING PRICE | | | |
	$60	$70	$85	$100
Sales	2200	2000	1200	900
Probability	.1	.4	.3	.4
Sales	2400	2400	1600	1100
Probability	.1	.6	.3	.6
Sales	2600		1800	
Probability	.2		.4	
Sales	2900			
Probability	.6			

Find the optimal price.

3.5 The Happy Valley Authority is sending a team to a remote area to search for new sources of natural gas. The team will travel in a vehicle with a special transmission for rapid movement through sand in adverse conditions. Experience with these vehicles shows that the number of spare transmissions that might be needed for a year's service (the planned time for the upcoming trip) is none, one, two, or three. They must decide how many spares to ship with the vehicle on this trip. The probability of needing 0, 1, 2, or 3 spares is .1, .5, .3, or .1, respectively. The cost of each spare shipped with the team is $2000. For each spare that is needed but not available in the vehicle, a special helicopter flight must be made at a cost per flight of $10,000. What is the optimal number of spares to ship, and what is the expected cost for the optimal alternative?

4. An Example of a Mathematical Model

4.1 Which of the following expressions describes a linear relationship:
  a. $Q = 10,000 - 2 \times P$
  b. $Y = X - X^2$
  c. The cost is found by adding the fixed cost of $10,000 to the product that results by multiplying the number produced by $45.
  d. The price of the product is inversely proportional to the amount demanded.

4.2 Sally Marks has determined that the quantity-price relationship for a new product is $Q = 10,000 - 20 \times P$.
  a. Plot this relationship on a graph similar to Figure 1.9.
  b. Sally finds that this relationship holds only for prices from $50 to $125. Modify the graph of part a to show this.
  c. Express the determination of Q as a function of P algorithmically, taking into account the conditions of part b.

4.3 The model for revenue is $R = P \times Q$. For a price of $P = \$50$, draw a graph of total revenue vs. quantity for all values of Q from 0 to 100. Express the determination of R as a function of Q algorithmically. *Hint*: Be sure to account for the constraints on values of Q.

4.4 The model for profit is $Z = R - C$. Assume that $R = \$75$ and that cost can vary from $10 to $100. Draw the graph of the relationship. Express the determination of Z algorithmically. Be sure to account for constraints on values of the variables.

4.5 The cost relationship for a dictating machine relating total cost (C_2) and quantity (Q_2) is $C_2 = 50 \times Q_2 + 140,000$; the relationship between quantity sold (Q_2) and price (P_2) is $Q_2 = 6000 - 30 \times P_2$. Assume that these models hold only in the range of prices from $100 to $150.
  a. Express the total revenue (R_2) as a function of the variables Q_2 and P_2.
  b. Express the profit (Z_2) as a function of the variables R_2 and C_2.
  c. Substitute the relationships among cost, price, and quantity into the formulas of parts a and b, and obtain a formula relating profit (Z_2) to the price (P_2).
  d. Using the formula obtained in part c, find the optimal value of the price.
  e. What is the profit at the optimal value of price?
  f. What is the total cost of production at the optimal quantity?
  g. What is the quantity corresponding to the optimal price?
  h. What is the revenue at the optimal price?
  i. Algorithmically, express the determination of profit as a function of price.

4.6 The State University has agreed to open a branch in a community remote from the main campus. However, the state government has been reducing the education budget, so the branch is required to pay its own way; it must support itself from tuition charges. To carry out the educational mission on such a basis, the branch has undertaken many novel forms of education, including self-study using courses purchased only as students need them, payment of instructors by the number of students, etc. The consequence of these approaches has been to make the cost of instruction (C) nearly linear with the number of students (S), the relationship being $C = 30,000 + 50 \times S$. Like most other products, the educational services of the school are subject to a decreasing demand with increasing price (here tuition is denoted by T), the relationship being known from other branches to be $S = 1500 - 7.5 \times T$, where T is the tuition cost per student and ranges from $10 to $200 (a constraint imposed by public law).
  a. Express the total cost as a function of the tuition per student.

b. Express the total revenue as a function of the tuition per student.

c. Express the total profit as a function of the tuition per student.

d. Find the tuition fee for the maximum profit.

e. What is the profit for the optimal tuition fee?

f. What is the number of students for the optimal fee?

g. At a hearing on establishing the new branch, the governor says that it is not the purpose of the university's branches to make a profit but to serve the maximum number of residents at a reasonable tuition charge. On the other hand, they do not want to have to put tax-derived funds into supporting the operation, nor is the university willing to provide funds. What is the tuition fee at which the branch makes neither a profit nor a loss?

h. Under the conditions of part g, what is the number of students when the branch is making neither a profit nor a loss?

i. Algorithmically, express the determination of profit as a function of tuition fee.

5. *The Scientific Method*

5.1 State three examples of inventions or discoveries. Discuss whether the scientific method was used in making these inventions or discoveries. Note that your examples should be similar to the sewing machine, smallpox vaccine, radio, transistor, etc.

5.2 Give three examples of creative human activities such as writing a poem, composing a symphony, proving a theorem in geometry, etc. Discuss whether or not the scientific method has been or can be applied to such activities.

5.3 Why can you not start making a model of a management situation without doing exploration?

5.4 Why is the model alone, without interpretation, not sufficient?

5.5 Why is it that the scientific approach—by itself—cannot tell you what career to choose?

5.6 The benefits of science have been accompanied by costs. For example, the use of medical science to increase lifetimes of inhabitants of countries with subsistence economies has led to food shortages. Give three examples of costs resulting from benefits of applications of the scientific method.

5.7 Why can science without morality lead to societal difficulties? Discuss briefly.

6. *Interactive Financial Planning: The Decision Support System Approach*

6.1 Why is it likely that a practical planning model will have hundreds or thousands of equations and possibly be computer based?

6.2 How might a planning model be used to support decision making in the following areas:

a. Making a capital decision to borrow money, issue stocks or bonds, etc.

b. Making capital investment decisions such as building a new warehouse, production facility, etc.

c. Making marketing decisions such as pricing, strategy, advertising, promotion, etc.

6.3 When determining coefficients for models using regression analysis (as exemplified by the equation for selling expense), the statistical analysis may come up with negative or positive coefficients. It is helpful to have a feel for the *sign* of the coefficient based on judgment against which to compare the analytical result. What do you think are the likely signs of the coefficients for operating labor, pension cost, plant throughput, gasoline volume, refinery and equipment value, and length of time of operation when obtaining a model for refining expense as mentioned in Section 1.6?

7. *Quantitative Methods: A Dialog**

7.1 From your own knowledge, is there one piece of evidence you can offer of a specific case in which you can show there was a savings as the consequence of the use of a quantitative model? If so, explain it.

7.2 Can you give an example from your own economic activities where a quantitative model cannot be conceived to resolve the issue?

7.3 Can you give an example other than those in Section 1.7 where the quantitative approach is used in a nonbusiness situation?

7.4 It is one thing to determine the optimal solution of a mathematical formula: You have seen ways of doing that (for example, where you pick the highest point of a quadratic curve). Why is it impossible in most business situations to know if you have made the decision which gives the optimal solution?

CHAPTER EXERCISES AND DISCUSSION QUESTIONS

C1. *Dealing with two products.* Assume that the Loud and Clear Playback Corp. has to make a pricing decision for a dictating machine as well as the CB radio.

a. Figure 1.12 shows the situation in tabular form for the dictating machine (this is a chart for the dictating machine which is similar to Figure 1.1 for the CB radio). Complete the chart by determining the missing entries for revenue and profit. Note that we use the subscript 2 for the dictating machine.

	ALTERNATIVES			
	1	2	3	4
P_2	$100	$120	140	$150
Q_2	3,000	2,400	1,800	1,500
C_2	$290,000	$260,000	$230,000	$215,000
R_2				
Z_2				

FIGURE 1.12 Determining the selling price of the dictating machine for L&C.

b. Consider the problem of marketing the dictating machine as a separate and independent activity from the marketing of the CB radio. Assuming that the sole criterion for making the decision is to maximize the gross profit, what is the optimal selling price, and what is the gross profit at optimum?

c. If both products are marketed at the same time and are independent,

---

* Exercises for dialogs are expressed as questions in the Socratic format. Students are to provide answers, the role between the student and the teacher being reversed here.

what is the gross profit if both are marketed at the optimal selling price?

d. L&C does not have the skilled workers to produce 1600 CB radios and 2400 dictating machines. Such a shortage is called a *constraint*. Each unit of CB radio production requires 2 hours of skilled labor, each unit of dictating machine production requires 3 hours, and the corporation has only 10,000 hours of such skilled labor available. Figure 1.13 shows all possible pricing alternatives for the CB radio and the dictating machine, and the number of hours to produce each under that alternative. The table shows the total manufacturing hours required. A dark line separates the shaded *feasible* region from the *infeasible region* (because total hours exceed 10,000). Fill in the missing entries in Figure 1.13.

e. Figure 1.14 shows a similar table except that it is for *gross profit* instead of hours. The entries in the body of the table are total gross profit, and the same convention for showing feasible and infeasible regions holds. Complete the missing entries in the table.

f. Based on your completed version of Figure 1.14, make a table ranking the feasible solutions by gross profit obtained. Your table should have columns for price of CB radio, price of dictating machine, and gross profit. What is the selling price of both machines, and what is the gross profit realized at optimum? Compare to the gross profit for independence given as your answer to part c.

C2 Your completed Figure 1.12 shows the pricing situation for selling dictating machines. New manufacturing equipment leads to a *unit cost* for each dictating machine of $100, a constant with respect to quantity. This means a revision of the total costs is in order, possibly giving new optimal values.

a. Make a new version of the table of Figure 1.12 for the new costs.

b. What is the optimal selling price, and what is the gross profit at optimum?

c. What is the next best selling price, and what is the gross profit at that price?

C3 Refer to Figure 1.12. Add columns for prices of $105, $110, $115, $125, $130, $135, and $145. The relationship for quantity sold is to be determined from $Q = 6000 - 30 \times P$.

a. What is the optimal selling price, and what is the gross profit at optimum?

b. What is the next best selling price, and what is the gross profit at that price?

C4 Refer to Figures 1.13 and 1.14, which summarize the situation when the Loud and Clear Playback Corporation is producing both the dictating machine and CB radio. Rework the table to include prices for the CB radio of $65, $75, $80, $90, and $95 and prices for the dictating machine of $105,

				Alternatives for CB radio			
				1	2	3	4
				$P_1 = 60$	$P_1 = 70$	$P_1 = 85$	$P_1 = 100$
			Labor hours	$H_1 = 5200$	$H_1 =$	$H_1 = 3200$	$H_1 =$
Alternatives for dictating machine	1	$P_2 = \$100$	$H_2 = 9000$	14,200	13,400	12,200	11,000
	2	$P_2 = \$120$	$H_2 =$			10,400	
	3	$P_2 = \$140$	$H_2 = 5400$	10,600	9,800		7,400
	4	$P_2 = \$150$	$H_2 =$	9,700		7,700	

FIGURE 1.13
Table showing skilled labor requirements for the dependent sales situation. Note the use of the subscript 1 for the CB radio and 2 for the dictating machine.

Alternatives for dictating machine		Selling price	Profit	Alternatives for CB radio			
				1	2	3	4
				$P_1 = \$60$	$P_1 = \$70$	$P_1 = \$85$	$P_1 = \$100$
		Selling price	Profit	$15,000	$	$30,000	$
	1	$P_2 = \$100$	$10,000	$25,000	$37,000	$40,000	$15,000
	2	$P_2 = \$120$	$			$58,000	
	3	$P_2 = \$140$	$22,000	$37,000	$49,000		$37,000
	4	$P_2 = \$150$	$	$25,000		$40,000	

FIGURE 1.14
Table showing profits for the dependent sales situation.

$110, $115, $125, $130, $135, and $145. The quantity-price relationship for the CB radio is $Q_1 = 5000 - 40 \times P_1$; for the dictating machine, $Q_2 \times 6000 - 30 \times P_2$.

   a. What is the optimal selling price for the CB radio?
   b. What is the optimal selling price for the dictating machine?
   c. What is the value of gross profit when selling both products at their optimal selling prices?
   d. What are the next best selling prices for both products?
   e. What is the gross profit when both products are sold at the next best price?
   f. Assume that the constraint on the availability of skilled labor has changed; only 8899 hours of skilled labor are available. What are the optimal selling prices for the two products?
   g. Under the constraint of only 8899 hours of skilled labor, what is the value of gross profit when the two products are sold at their optimal prices?
   h. Under the constraint of only 8899 hours of labor, what is the gross profit when the products are selling at the next best prices?

C5. Engels Toy Company is considering its magazine advertising campaign. There are two media available to advertise in; each of these generates sales in accordance with the formula $S = 20 \times A - 4 \times A^2$, where S is sales generated in millions of dollars and A is the amount spent in millions of dollars advertising in that medium. Assume that advertising expenditures can be changed only in increments of $100,000 and that there is a total of $2 million to be allocated between the two media.
   a. Make a table of alternatives (similar to Figures 1.13 and 1.14).
   b. Indicate the infeasible alternatives as in Figures 1.13 and 1.14.
   c. What is the optimal combination of advertising expenditures?
   d. What is the profit for the optimal combination of advertising expenditures?
   e. Engels has access to additional funds; the total funds can be between $2 million and $4 million in increments of $500,000. What is the optimal combination of advertising expenditures?
   f. Under the conditions of part e, what is the profit for the optimal combination of advertising expenditures?

C6. In the real world, we may choose not to operate at the optimal values. Give the longest possible list of reasons for this which you can imagine or give from your experience. You should have at least five items in your list.

C7. What are the human factors which you believe operate to make decision makers shy away from using quantitative models?

C8. What are the nonhuman but practical factors which you believe reduce the efficacy of quantitative models?

C9. How many quantitative models could exist in a given decision-making situation? How many models should a manager making decisions examine?

1.	Sales	$15,000
2.	Cost of goods = $6,000 + 30% of sales	$10,500
3.	Gross profit	$4,500
4.	Operating expenses	$900
5.	Net operating profit	$3,600
6.	Other revenue	$500
7.	Gross income before taxes	$4,100
8.	Taxes = 48% of Gross income	$1,968
9.	Net income after tax	$2,132
10.	Prior retained income	$808
11.	Retained income before dividend	$2,940
12.	Dividend paid	$1,000
13.	Retained income	$1,940
14.	Net income/sales	14.21%

FIGURE 1.15 Financial information for preparing a 5-year forecast for the Pioneer Construction Corporation.

C10. Give an example of how you could use a quantitative model to help in some decision-making situation in your personal life.

C11. Figure 1.15 gives a financial statement for the current year, year 1 of the Pioneer Construction Corporation. The problem is to prepare a 5-year forecast for each of the line items. The following information is provided for preparation of the forecast:
1. Sales are assumed to increase each year by 10%.
2. The cost of goods is computed from the formula

$$\text{cost of goods} \times \$6000 + 30\% \text{ of sales}$$

3. Gross profit = sales − cost of goods.
4. Operating expenses start at 6% of sales and decrease by .5% each year, that is, to 5.5, 5.0, 4.5, and 4.0% by the end of the fifth year.
5. Net operating profit = gross profit − operating expenses.
6. Other revenue is $500 each year.
7. Gross income before taxes = net operating profit + other revenue.
8. Taxes = 48% of gross income.
9. Net income after taxes = gross income before taxes − taxes.
10. Prior retained income = retained income from last year (line 13).
11. Retained income before dividends = net income after tax + prior retained income.
12. The dividend paid is $1000 each year.
13. Retained income = retained income before dividend − dividend paid.
14. Net income/sales is line 9 divided by line 1, in %.

C12. The management of the Pioneer Construction Corporation (Discussion Exercise 11) wants a new 5-year forecast under the following three new assumptions:
   a. Sales increase at 20% each year.
   b. Other revenue increases 10% each year.
   c. The dividend paid is $2000 each year.
Prepare the forecast.

2

Review of Basic Concepts of Probability Theory

In Chapter 1 we showed that the scientific approach to decision making under uncertainty relies on probability theory. Now we develop the foundation of probability theory required in the quantitative analysis of business decisions.

The foundation of probability theory was laid by two French mathematicians: Pierre de Fermat (1601–1665) and Blaise Pascal (1643–1662). Sometimes science responds to the frivolous side of life. Fermat and Pascal worked out their theories in response to the decision problems of a gambler friend, Chevalier de Méré (1610–1685).

Antoine Gombault de Méré posed the following problem: In throwing a pair of dice, how many tosses are needed to have at least an even chance of getting two sixes?

Gamblers knew from experience that the answer was 25, but there was no scientific calculation to prove this number. Pascal showed that the probability of getting two sixes in 24 throws is 0.491, while it is 0.505 in 25 throws. Thus the first step in probability theory was made. More than 100 years later Pierre Simon de Laplace (1749–1820) established the foundations of probability theory in his classic essay "Concerning Probability." So it became possible to spell out rigorously the laws of chance and to reduce uncertainty to calculations.

As stated in Chapter 1, we deal with a decision problem under uncertainty by first stating the situation in terms of thought experiments where random devices are used to describe chance. Thus the use of random devices is a part of developing thought experiments, and so the approach of the classics, presenting probability theory via random devices, is most appropriate for our textbook. Our objective in developing the theory is to derive rules and procedures to calculate probabilities associated with performing **experiments** with random devices.

Typical Random Devices and Experiments

Figure 2.1 shows some of the random devices used in our studies. The experiment of tossing a coin has the two possible **outcomes**: (1) heads, (2) tails. A roulette wheel has the list of outcomes for the numbers 0 to 36 inclusive. A wheel of fortune may be divided into four uneven sectors: The possible outcomes are sectors 1, 2, 3, and 4. A bag may contain 6 numbered marbles: 2 red, 1 black, and 3 gray. The possible outcomes are the numbers 1 to 6. Instead of marbles we may have chips with inscriptions or different objects. Figure 2.2 shows a chessboard to be used as a dart board. The possible outcomes are the 64 squares of the board.

Suppose now we toss a penny twice in sequence or two pennies simultaneously. We call such experiments composite, in contrast to our earlier simple experiments. Further examples of composite experiments are the following: (1) spin a roulette wheel three times in sequence; (2) draw chips from a bag but put the chip back into the bag after each draw; (3) draw chips from a bag without putting any back.

In this textbook, unless specifically stated otherwise, we deal with discrete, noncontinuous experiments where the number of outcomes can be explicitly listed by a finite number of possibilities.

Events

Suppose two coins are tossed and we are interested in the outcomes when the results *match*: namely when we toss (1) heads and heads or (2) tails and tails. We refer to these two outcomes as the matching event. An outcome itself is a **simple event**. When two or more outcomes are involved, we refer to them as **compound events**.

For example, tossing a die with the result of getting an even number of dots implies the outcomes of 2 or 4 or 6, which is a compound event; tossing two dice so the sum is 5 implies a compound event. In Figure 2.2 throwing the dart at a black square implies a compound event.

Coin   Roulette wheel   Wheel of fortune   Bag of marbles

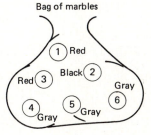

FIGURE 2.1
Four typical random devices.

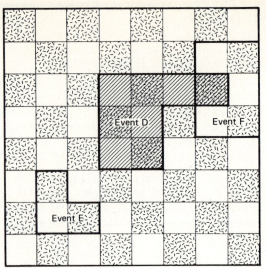

FIGURE 2.2
Chessboard to be used as a dart board.

Calculating Probability

Our main interest is to state theoretical rules and procedures to calculate probabilities of complex and compound events. Consider the random experiment of drawing marbles from the bag shown in Figure 2.1. Note that it is equally likely that we draw balls 1, 2, 3, 4, 5, or 6. Designate by *A* the *event* that we draw a red marble. Note in Figure 2.1 that outcomes 1 and 2 result in occurrence of event *A*. What is the probability of event *A*? Here is the procedure to find the answer:

> *Step 1.* Count the total number of equally likely outcomes (six in Figure 2.1).
>
> *Step 2.* Count the number of outcomes resulting in the occurrence of event *A* (two in Figure 2.1).
>
> *Step 3.* Divide the results of step 1 by the results of step 2: probability of event *A* occurring
>
> $$= \frac{\text{number of outcomes resulting in occurrence of event } A}{\text{total number of outcomes}}$$

Now we introduce a precise and brief mathematical notation for probabilities. We abbreviate*:

$$P[\text{of event } A \text{ happening}] = P[A]$$

$$A = \text{drawing a red marble}$$

$$P[\text{drawing a red marble}] = P[A] = \tfrac{2}{6} = \tfrac{1}{3}$$

Denote by *B* the event that a black marble is drawn and by *C* the

---

* For emphasis we use brackets and not parentheses.

event that a gray marble is drawn. Then by using the preceding notation,

$$P[B] = \tfrac{1}{6}$$

$$P[C] = \tfrac{3}{6} = \tfrac{1}{2}$$

Consider a second random experiment of throwing a dart at a dart board. Imagine that the dart board is made of a rectangular-shaped piece of material. To determine the probability of event D (Figure 2.2), that is, the probability the dart lands in area D, imagine that the shape represented by event D is cut out of the piece of material. Then the procedure for calculating the probability of the dart landing in area D is given by

$$P[D] = \text{probability of event } D = \frac{\text{weight of shape } D}{\text{total weight of rectangle}}$$

$$= \frac{\text{area of shape } D}{\text{total area of rectangle}}$$

In Figure 2.2 you find by counting squares and recognizing that the weight of each square is the same that

$$P[D] = \tfrac{8}{64} = \tfrac{1}{8}$$

$$P[E] = \tfrac{3}{64}$$

$$P[F] = \tfrac{6}{64} = \tfrac{3}{32}$$

Basic Rules of Probability Theory

Reflect for a moment about our procedure of calculating the probability of the occurrence of event A by (1) counting the total number of outcomes, (2) counting the outcomes resulting in event A, and (3) dividing the first count into the second. Neither of the counts can be negative, and so the ratio cannot be negative. Neither can the ratio be greater than 1:

> No negative probabilities exist.
> No probability is greater than 1.

We can state these rules mathematically:

> *Rule 1.* $P[A] \geq 0$.
> *Rule 2.* $P[A] \leq 1$.

If there is no outcome resulting in event A, then A is impossible; if all outcomes result in A, then A is certain:

> *Rule 3.* $P[A] = 0$ implies that A is impossible.
> *Rule 4.* $P[A] = 1$ implies that A is certain (sure).

If your calculation violates the preceding rules, you can be certain you have made an error.

Mutually Exclusive and Collectively Exhaustive Events

When you toss a coin, you may observe heads or tails; the two simple events are **mutually exclusive**. On a roulette wheel the events red, black, and zero are also mutually exclusive. But the events of tossing a die with a face value of (1) less than five or (2) more than three are not mutually exclusive, because the outcome of tossing the number four is common to both events.

In Figure 2.2 events D and E are mutually exclusive because a dart cannot land in both areas D and E. Events D and F are not mutually exclusive.

A list of events is **collectively exhaustive** if all possible events are represented in the list. For example, heads or tails, black or white on the chessboard, and red, black, and zero on the roulette wheel are collectively exhaustive events.

Suppose we wish to calculate the probability of an event A which consists of the occurrence of either B or C, where B and C are mutually exhaustive. The addition law for mutually exclusive events provides a three-step procedure for such a calculation:

Step 1. Calculate $P[B]$.
Step 2. Calculate $P[C]$.
Step 3. If B and C are mutually exclusive, then

$$P[A] = P[B \text{ or } C] = P[B] + P[C]$$

For example, on a roulette wheel there are 18 red numbers, 18 black numbers, and the zero. For a balanced roulette wheel,

$P[$ball stopping on any given number between 0 and 36 inclusive$]$
$$= \tfrac{1}{37}$$

The outcome of the numbers is mutually exclusive, and if we assume that the odd numbers are red,* we can apply the addition law:

$P[$ball stopping on red$] = P[\text{RED}]$

$\qquad = P[$ball on 1$] + P[$ball on 3$] + \cdots + P[$ball on 35$]$

$\qquad = \tfrac{1}{37} + \tfrac{1}{37} + \tfrac{1}{37} + \cdots (18 \text{ times})$

$\qquad = P[\text{RED}] = \tfrac{18}{37}$

---

* This is an unusual way of using colors on a roulette wheel, but we do it for simplicity of exposition.

Also,

$$P[\text{BLACK}] = \tfrac{18}{37}$$

$$P[\text{ZERO}] = \tfrac{1}{37}$$

The events RED and BLACK are mutually exclusive, and so by the addition law,

$$P[\text{RED or BLACK}] = P[\text{RED}] + P[\text{BLACK}] = \tfrac{18}{37} + \tfrac{18}{37} = \tfrac{36}{37}$$

Also, RED and ZERO are mutually exclusive, and so

$$P[\text{RED or ZERO}] = P[\text{RED}] + P[\text{ZERO}] = \tfrac{18}{37} + \tfrac{1}{37} = \tfrac{19}{37}$$

In Figure 2.2 events D and E are mutually exclusive:

$$P[D] = \tfrac{8}{64} \quad \text{and} \quad P[E] = \tfrac{3}{64}$$

Therefore,

$$P[D \text{ or } E] = \tfrac{8}{64} + \tfrac{3}{64} = \tfrac{11}{64}$$

The addition law holds for any number of events.

For example, if events X, Y, and Z are mutually exclusive, then

$$P[X] + P[Y] + P[Z] = P[X \text{ or } Y \text{ or } Z]$$

If the set of events is *also* collectively exhaustive, the sum must be 1, because one of the events must occur. For example, assume that for a crooked coin the probability of tossing heads is 1/3 and of tossing tails is 2/3:

$$P[\text{HEADS}] = \tfrac{1}{3}, \quad P[\text{TAILS}] = \tfrac{2}{3}$$

Then

$$P[\text{HEADS or TAILS}] = P[\text{HEADS}] + P[\text{TAILS}] = \tfrac{1}{3} + \tfrac{2}{3} = 1$$

For a roulette wheel the probability that it stops on red, black, or zero is

$$P[\text{RED or BLACK or ZERO}] = P[\text{RED}] + P[\text{BLACK}] + P[\text{ZERO}]$$

$$= \tfrac{18}{37} + \tfrac{18}{37} + \tfrac{1}{37} = 1$$

This law also holds for any number of events. For example, if P, Q, R, and S are mutually exclusive and collectively exhaustive, then

$$P[P \text{ or } Q \text{ or } R \text{ or } S] = P[P] + P[Q] + P[R] + P[S] = 1$$

If a set of events is mutually exclusive and collectively exhaustive, then the sum of probabilities must be equal to 1.

If you get answers violating the preceding law, you can be certain of an error in your calculations.

Mutually Nonexclusive Events

You know how to calculate the probability of an event which is composed of mutually exclusive events. Now we extend our theory to cover nonexclusive events.

As an example, consider first events D and F in Figure 2.2 which events are not mutually exclusive; namely, the square in the third row, seventh column is common to both D and F. Thus the probability of the dart landing in areas D or F, that is

$$P[D \text{ or } F] \text{ does not equal } P[D] + P[F]$$

In fact, there are eight squares in D and six in F, but there is a common square X. So there are only $8 + 6 - 1 = 13$ squares in total. So

$$P[D \text{ or } E] = \tfrac{8}{64} + \tfrac{6}{64} - \tfrac{1}{64} = \tfrac{13}{64}$$

and

$$P[D] + P[E] = \tfrac{8}{64} + \tfrac{6}{64} = \tfrac{14}{64}$$

and the two probability values 13/64 and 14/64 are not the same. Note then that the procedure of the addition laws consists of the following four steps:

> *Step 1.* Calculate $P[D]$.
> *Step 2.* Calculate $P[E]$.
> *Step 3.* Calculate $P[D \text{ and } E]$.
> *Step 4.* Whether D and E are mutually exclusive or not,
> $$P[D] + P[E] = P[D \text{ or } E] - P[D \text{ and } E]$$

Namely, if D and E are mutually exclusive, then $P[D \text{ and } E] = 0$. When they are not mutually exclusive, $P[D \text{ and } E]$ removes the common elements from D and E and gives the correct probability value.

Now we turn our attention to another interpretation of probability often used in the everyday world as well as in management.

The Frequency Interpretation of Probability

Past records of births in the United States show that twins occur once in 83 births. The obstetrician will tell you that the probability of twins is 1/83. The sales manager of a supermarket may examine the past sales history of cans of sardines and observe that out of 120 days it occurred 30 times that over 100 cans were sold. He may say that the probability of selling more than 100 cans of sardines in a single day is 30/120 = .25. We are describing here the **relative frequency** approach to probability.

Suppose now you toss an unbiased coin that is fair 1000 times. The statistician will say you have taken a **sample** of 1000. The process of gathering data from several performances of a chance experiment is called **sampling**. You know from everyday experience that in the sample about half of the tosses will be heads and half tails, because the probability of tossing heads (or tails) is .5. In other words, the relative frequency of heads (or tails) is approximately given by the probability. You also know that the larger the sample, the closer you get to the probability of .5. Thus according to the relative frequency approach to probability,

> Probability is approximately equal to the relative frequency of occurrence in a large sample.

As a further example, suppose you build a roulette wheel with 83 numbers and mark 82 as "singles" and 1 as "twins." If you spin this wheel, you are representing the chance occurrence of twin births. Or again build a roulette wheel with 100 numbers and mark 75 as "100 or less than 100 cans" and 25 as "more than 100 cans." If you spin this wheel, you are representing the chance occurrence of sales of cans of sardines in the supermarket.

> A random experiment can represent the chance occurrence of events associated with the relative frequency approach to probability.

The Judgmental Interpretation of Probability

Now suppose a manager considers introducing an entirely new product and says the probabiity of success is .5. He can introduce the product only once and so cannot mean that if he introduced it 1000 times it would be successful about 500 times. In no way can he prepare a sample of the chance experiment of introducing the product. But he can and does mean that the probability of success is the same as tossing heads or tails with a coin. This probabilty is called a **judgmental** approach to probability, because in the judgment of the manager tossing coins models his problem. Thus

> A random experiment can represent the chance occurrence of events associated with both the relative frequency and the judgmental approach to probability.

This supports our approach of using thought experiments when dealing with decision making under uncertainty.

2.2 APPLICATION OF PROBABILITY THEORY: PART I

The Used Car Lot Problem

There are 15 cars on a small used car lot: five two-door sedans, six four-door sedans, and four convertibles. Of the five two-door sedans there are two green, two black, and one white. Of the six four-door sedans, there are three green, one black, and two white. Of the four convertibles, one is green, one white, and two black.

For promotional purposes one of the cars is raffled off. What is the probability that the car is a two-door, a four-door, a convertible, green, black, white, etc.?

Solution

In Figure 2.3 the problem is stated as a thought experiment using the random device of a specially designed dart board. There are 15 rectangles representing the cars and the events of the dart landing in any of the 15 rectangles for a mutually exclusive and exhaustive list of events. Thus, the probability of the dart landing in any of the rectangles is the same and equals 1/15. Therefore the probability that a two-door car is raffled off is

$$P[\text{2-door}] = \tfrac{5}{15} = \tfrac{1}{3}$$

Similarly,

$$P[\text{4-door}] = \tfrac{6}{15}$$

$$P[\text{convertible}] = \tfrac{4}{15}$$

$$P[\text{white}] = \tfrac{4}{15}$$

$$P[\text{black}] = \tfrac{5}{15}$$

$$P[\text{green}] = \tfrac{6}{15}$$

White and black are mutually exclusive and so

$$P[\text{white or black}] = P[\text{white}] + P[\text{black}] = \tfrac{4}{15} + \tfrac{5}{15} = \tfrac{9}{15}$$

White, black, and green are mutually exclusive and exhaustive and so

$$P[\text{white or black or green}] = P[\text{white}] + P[\text{black}] + P[\text{green}]$$
$$= \tfrac{4}{15} + \tfrac{5}{15} + \tfrac{6}{15} = \tfrac{15}{15} = 1$$

White and nonwhite are mutually exclusive and collectively exhaustive and so

$$P[\text{white}] + P[\text{nonwhite}] = 1$$

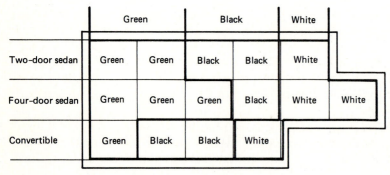

FIGURE 2.3
Used car lot problem converted to throwing darts at a dart board.

or

$$P[\text{nonwhite}] = 1 - P[\text{white}] = 1 - \tfrac{4}{15} = \tfrac{11}{15}$$

which of course means

$$P[\text{black or green}] = \tfrac{11}{15}$$

Further examples of the probabilities are

$$P[\text{2-door or convertible}] = \frac{5 + 4}{15} = \frac{9}{15} = \frac{3}{5}$$

$$P[\text{2-door or green}] = \frac{5 + 3 + 1}{15} = \frac{9}{15} = \frac{3}{5}$$

$$P[\text{convertible and black}] = \frac{2}{15}$$

The events convertible and black are not mutually exclusive. Therefore it would be wrong to say

$$P[\text{convertible or black}] = P[\text{convertible}] + P[\text{black}]$$

The correct formula is obtained by using the multiplication law of probability:

$$P[\text{convertible or black}] = P[\text{convertible}] + P[\text{black}]$$
$$- P[\text{convertible and black}]$$
$$= \tfrac{4}{15} + \tfrac{5}{15} - \tfrac{2}{15} = \tfrac{7}{15}$$

You can verify the probability by observing

$$P[\text{convertible or black}] = P[\text{2-door sedan and black}]$$
$$+ P[\text{4-door and black}] + P[\text{convertible}]$$
$$= \tfrac{2}{15} + \tfrac{1}{15} + \tfrac{4}{15} = \tfrac{7}{15}$$

2.3 BASIC PROPERTIES OF PROBABILITIES

Decision makers are often concerned about the occurrence of events which are somehow related or connected with other events. For example, in many businesses when this month's sales are high, there is a good probability that sales will be high next month also. If sales are high in the north, the probability is they will be high in the south. On the other hand, if customers overspend this month, perhaps they will underspend next month.

Next we extend our theory of probability to deal with such situations and develop suitable concepts and procedures to calculate such probabilities.

Joint and Marginal Probabilities

To illustrate the theory we present a special dart board (Figure 2.4). First
we divide the board into LEFT and RIGHT areas by the broken line
ABCD [Figure 2.4(a)]. Then we extend the horizontal line *BC* and
divide the board into UP and DOWN areas [Figure 2.4(b)]. The resulting
board now has four areas: (1) UP and LEFT, (2) UP and RIGHT, (3)
DOWN and LEFT, and (4) DOWN and RIGHT [Figure 2.4(c)].

Figure 2.4(d) shows the dimensions of the board: Height = 21
inches, width = 20 inches. The figure also shows the dimensions of the
subdivisions and the respective areas. The total area is 20 × 21 = 420
square inches.

Managerial Interpretation

Before we continue the discussion, we interject a possible business
interpretation of this experiment:

UP means sales are HIGH in the north
DOWN means sales are LOW in the north

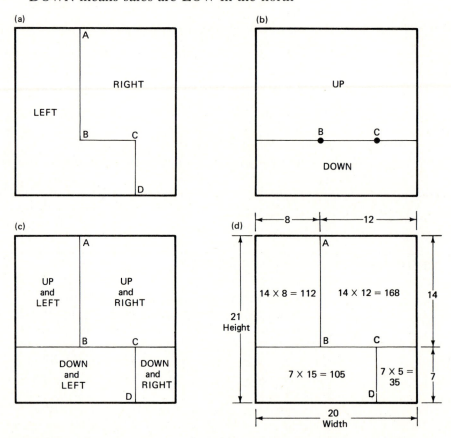

FIGURE 2.4 Special dart board to illustrate joint and marginal probabilities.

RIGHT means sales are HIGH in the south

LEFT means sales are LOW in the south

Now you can translate all that follows into terms of this business problem.

Back to the Dart Board

What is the joint probability that the dart lands both UP and LEFT? We apply the rule from Section 2.1 that the ratio of respective areas gives the probability. The area of the UP and LEFT rectangle [Figure 2.4(d)] is 14 × 8 = 112 square inches. The total area is 420 square inches, and so the probability that the dart lands both UP and LEFT is

$$P[\text{UP and LEFT}] = \frac{112}{420} = \frac{4 \times 28}{15 \times 28} = \frac{4}{15}$$

You can now calculate the other three joint probabilities:

$$P[\text{UP and RIGHT}] = \frac{168}{420} = \frac{2 \times 84}{5 \times 24} = \frac{2}{5}$$

$$P[\text{DOWN and LEFT}] = \frac{105}{420} = \frac{105}{4 \times 105} = \frac{1}{4}$$

$$P[\text{DOWN and RIGHT}] = \frac{35}{420} = \frac{35}{12 \times 35} = \frac{1}{12}$$

What is the probability of UP? This can happen in two mutually exclusive ways: [UP and LEFT] or [UP and RIGHT]. We know from the summation rule that the probabilities of these two events are to be added:

$$P[\text{UP}] = \tfrac{112}{420} + \tfrac{168}{420} = \tfrac{280}{420} = \tfrac{2}{3}$$

By similar agreement,

$$P[\text{DOWN}] = \tfrac{105}{420} + \tfrac{35}{420} = \tfrac{140}{420} = \tfrac{1}{3}$$

$$P[\text{LEFT}] \;= P[\text{UP and LEFT}] + P[\text{DOWN and LEFT}]$$

$$= \tfrac{112}{420} + \tfrac{105}{420} = \tfrac{217}{420} = \tfrac{31}{60}$$

$$P[\text{RIGHT}] = \tfrac{168}{420} + \tfrac{35}{420} = \tfrac{203}{420} = \tfrac{29}{60}$$

In Figure 2.5 we show these probabilities in tabular form. Due to the appearance of the table, $P[\text{UP}]$, $P[\text{DOWN}]$, $P[\text{LEFT}]$, and $P[\text{RIGHT}]$ are called marginal probabilities.

Note in Figure 2.5 that the sum of the probabilities in each row adds up to the marginal probabilities:

$$P[\text{UP and LEFT}] + P[\text{UP and RIGHT}] = \tfrac{4}{15} + \tfrac{2}{3} = \tfrac{2}{3}$$

	LEFT	RIGHT	
UP	$\frac{4}{15}$	$\frac{2}{5}$	$\frac{2}{3}$
DOWN	$\frac{1}{4}$	$\frac{1}{12}$	$\frac{1}{3}$
	$\frac{31}{60}$	$\frac{29}{60}$	

FIGURE 2.5
Joint probabilities are inside the heavy frame; the marginal probabilities are outside.

and
$$P[\text{DOWN and LEFT}] + P[\text{DOWN and RIGHT}] = \tfrac{1}{4} + \tfrac{1}{12} = \tfrac{1}{3}$$

The same holds for the column sums:
$$P[\text{UP and LEFT}] + P[\text{DOWN and LEFT}] = \tfrac{4}{15} + \tfrac{1}{4} = \tfrac{31}{60}$$

$$P[\text{UP and RIGHT}] + P[\text{DOWN and RIGHT}] = \tfrac{2}{5} + \tfrac{1}{12} = \tfrac{29}{60}$$

Conditional Probabilities

Suppose you are blindfolded and are told the dart landed on UP. What is the probability it landed on LEFT? To put it differently, what is the **conditional** probability that the dart landed on left?

$$P[\text{ landing } \text{LEFT }_{\text{if it has landed }} \text{UP}]$$

The mathematical symbolism for this statement is

$$P[\text{LEFT} \mid \text{UP}]$$

Also, the landing of the dart LEFT is said to be *conditioned* by the occurrence of the event of the dart landing UP first.

You *know* the dart is UP. So you are dealing with the dart board experiment shown in Figure 2.6 where only the *reduced* dart board, the upper part of the original board, is shown. Using the area rule, we obtain

$$P[\text{LEFT} \mid \text{UP}] = \frac{\text{area of UP and LEFT rectangles}}{\text{area of UP rectangle}}$$

So

$$P[\text{LEFT} \mid \text{UP}] = \frac{112}{112 + 168} = \frac{112}{280} = \frac{2}{5}$$

You can derive the same answer by working with probabilities:

$$P[\text{LEFT} \mid \text{UP}] = \frac{P[\text{UP and LEFT}]}{P[\text{UP}]}$$

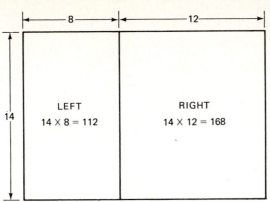

FIGURE 2.6
Reduced UP dart board. The total area is $14 \times 20 = 280$.

We already determined

$$P[\text{UP and LEFT}] = \tfrac{4}{15}$$

and

$$P[\text{UP}] = \tfrac{2}{3}$$

and so

$$P[\text{LEFT} \mid \text{UP}] = \frac{4/15}{2/3} = \frac{2}{5}$$

Similarly,

$$P[\text{RIGHT} \mid \text{UP}] = \frac{P[\text{UP and RIGHT}]}{P[\text{UP}]} = \frac{2/5}{2/3} = \frac{3}{5}$$

$$P[\text{LEFT} \mid \text{DOWN}] = \frac{P[\text{DOWN and LEFT}]}{P[\text{DOWN}]} = \frac{1/4}{1/3} = \frac{3}{4}$$

$$P[\text{RIGHT} \mid \text{DOWN}] = \frac{P[\text{DOWN and RIGHT}]}{P[\text{DOWN}]} = \frac{1/12}{1/3} = \frac{1}{4}$$

Figure 2.7 summarizes the joint, marginal, and conditional probabilities.

Marginal probabilities are also called **unconditional** probabilities to contrast with conditional probabilities, because marginal probabilities have no conditions put on them.

We can now state the law of unconditional probability. Namely, replace LEFT by A and UP by B. Then the basic formula we have used becomes

---

Law of conditional probability: For events A and B,

$$P[A \mid B] = \frac{P[A \text{ and } B]}{P[B]}$$

		LEFT					RIGHT			
Up	$P[UP]$	×	$P[LEFT \mid UP]$	=	$P[UP$ and $LEFT]$	$P[UP]$	×	$P[RIGHT \mid UP]$	=	$P[UP$ and $RIGHT]$	$P[UP]$
	2/3	×	2/5	=	4/15	2/3	×	3/5	=	2/15	2/3
Down	$P[DOWN]$	×	$P[LEFT \mid DOWN]$	=	$P[DOWN$ and $LEFT]$	$P[DOWN]$	×	$P[RIGHT \mid DOWN]$	=	$P[DOWN$ and $RIGHT]$	$P[DOWN]$
	1/3	×	3/4	=	1/4	1/3	×	1/4	=	1/12	1/3
					31/60					29/60	

FIGURE 2.7 Joint, marginal, and conditional probabilities for the dart board experiment shown in Figure 2.4.

This formula is often useful in the form of the

> *Law of multiplication:* For events A and B,
>
> $$P[A \text{ and } B] = P[A \mid B] \times P[B]$$

Probability Tree Models

The same situation may be described by a different thought experiment. To illustrate, we replace the simple random experiment shown by the dart board in Figure 2.4 with a **probability tree** model using roulette wheels in a composite experiment.

Returning to the dart board model, observe that

$$P[\text{UP}] = \tfrac{2}{3} \qquad P[\text{DOWN}] = \tfrac{1}{3}$$

In Figure 2.8, at the *foot* of the tree is roulette wheel 1 such that the UP sector is twice the size of the DOWN sector. Thus the probabilities of the ball stopping in UP or DOWN are the same as of the dart landing UP or DOWN on the dart board. Suppose we spin the wheel and the outcome is UP. We move along the upper branch and reach wheel 2. This wheel has sectors in the proportion of 3 and 2, marked RIGHT and LEFT. Thus if we reach wheel 2, the probabilities of the ball stopping LEFT or RIGHT are

$$P[\text{LEFT}] = \tfrac{2}{5} \qquad P[\text{RIGHT}] = \tfrac{3}{5}$$

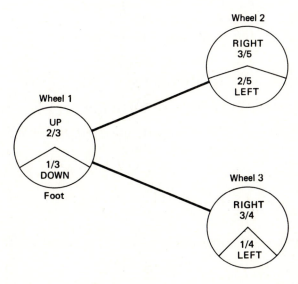

FIGURE 2.8
Probability tree model using roulette wheels.

but these probabilities are conditioned by having UP as the outcome of wheel 1. So the more complete statement is that the probability of the ball stopping in RIGHT if the ball first stops in UP is

$$P[\text{RIGHT} \mid \text{UP}] = \tfrac{3}{5}$$

But these are precisely the conditional probabilities associated with the dart board experiment in Figure 2.4.

What if the outcome on wheel 1 is DOWN? We reach wheel 3 for which

$$P[\text{LEFT} \mid \text{DOWN}] = \tfrac{3}{4} \qquad P[\text{RIGHT} \mid \text{DOWN}] = \tfrac{1}{4}$$

These values again correspond to the conditional probabilities of the experiment in Figure 2.4.

> The two random experiments are equivalent when the outcomes and probabilities are the same.

Probability trees are used extensively when dealing with uncertainty, and the traditional tree diagram is simplified by not showing the roulette wheels. Thus in Figure 2.9 only the tree is shown, and the wheels are represented by the *forks* of the tree. Along the branches emanating from the foot of the tree the *unconditional* probabilities are listed. From then on along each branch the conditional probabilities are listed.

Now we compute the joint probabilities and list them at the tips of the tree. By the multiplication law,

$$P[\text{UP and LEFT}] = P[\text{UP}] \times P[\text{LEFT} \mid \text{UP}] = \tfrac{2}{3} \times \tfrac{2}{5} = \tfrac{4}{15}$$

and we list this joint probability at tip 1. Note the rule that to get the joint probability we must draw a path from the foot of the tree to the tip and multiply the probabilities.

Similarly, the other joint probabilities are

$$P[\text{UP and RIGHT}] = \tfrac{2}{3} \times \tfrac{3}{5} = \tfrac{2}{5}$$

$$P[\text{DOWN and LEFT}] = \tfrac{1}{3} \times \tfrac{3}{4} = \tfrac{1}{4}$$

$$P[\text{DOWN and RIGHT}] = \tfrac{1}{3} \times \tfrac{1}{4} = \tfrac{1}{12}$$

Now we can get the marginal, unconditional probabilities by the addition rules, as shown in Figure 2.9.

$$P[\text{LEFT}] = P[\text{UP}]P[\text{LEFT} \mid \text{UP}] + P[\text{DOWN}]P[\text{LEFT} \mid \text{DOWN}]$$
$$= \tfrac{2}{3} \times \tfrac{2}{5} + \tfrac{1}{3} \times \tfrac{3}{4} = \tfrac{4}{5} + \tfrac{1}{4} = \tfrac{31}{60}$$

Also,

$$P[\text{RIGHT}] = P[\text{UP}]P[\text{RIGHT} \mid \text{UP}] + P[\text{DOWN}]P[\text{RIGHT} \mid \text{DOWN}]$$
$$= \tfrac{2}{3} \times \tfrac{3}{5} + \tfrac{1}{3} \times \tfrac{1}{4} = \tfrac{1}{12} = \tfrac{29}{60}$$

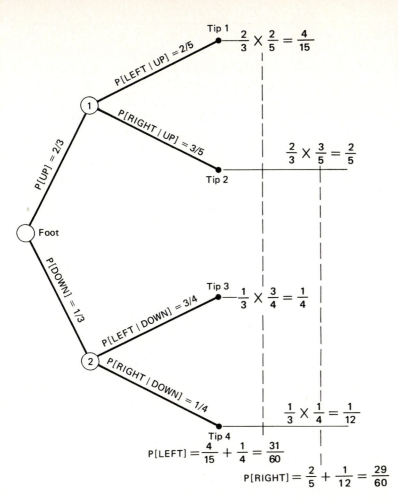

FIGURE 2.9
Probability tree model of the random experiment shown in Figure 2.8.

Each branch of the tree not leading to a tip terminates in a fork. The branches emanating from each fork represent a set of mutually exclusive and collective events, and therefore the following rule holds:

> The probabilities associated with the set of branches emanating from a fork of a tree must add to 1.

If your results violate this rule, you can be certain you made a mistake somewhere.

We can now summarize the procedure to carry out calculations with a probability tree model:

> *Step 1.* Multiply the probabilities along each *path* of the tree, and list the results at the *tips* of the tree.
>
> *Step 2.* Obtain the marginal probabilities by adding the respective values at the *tips* of the tree.

Suppose a major oil corporation is drilling for oil in Mexico, Canada, and Venezuela. The striking of oil in any place depends on chance, of course, but the three strikes have nothing to do with each other; they are independent of each other. Management wants to know the probability of striking oil in at least one of the places. How does one put into numbers the belief that the three strikes are independent?

On the other hand, the management of a department store believes that the sale of luxury items goes up in times of prosperity. Economists predict prosperity for next year. How does one put into numbers the belief that the sale of luxury items is dependent on prosperity?

Probability theory provides precise rules to determine whether events are statistically **independent** or **dependent**. As before, we present our theory via random experiments.

Statistical Independence

If you pick a coin and toss it 1000 times, you expect to get about 500 HEADS and 500 TAILS because you expect the coin to be fair, that is, unbiased. But crooked gamblers know how to alter a coin, and then the coin may be biased to fall on one side rather than the other. Assume that for a very crooked coin

$$P[\text{HEADS}] = \tfrac{2}{3} \qquad P[\text{TAILS}] = \tfrac{1}{3}$$

Consider now the experiment of tossing the crooked coin twice in succession.

The probability tree model of tossing twice is shown in Figure 2.10. First we toss at the foot of the tree. We can reach either fork 1 or 2, depending on whether we toss HEADS or TAILS. In either case we toss the same coin again. We multiply the probabilities along the branches and list the marginal probabilities at the tips. We note, for example, that

$$P[\text{HEADS and TAILS}] = \tfrac{2}{3} \times \tfrac{1}{3} = \tfrac{2}{9}$$

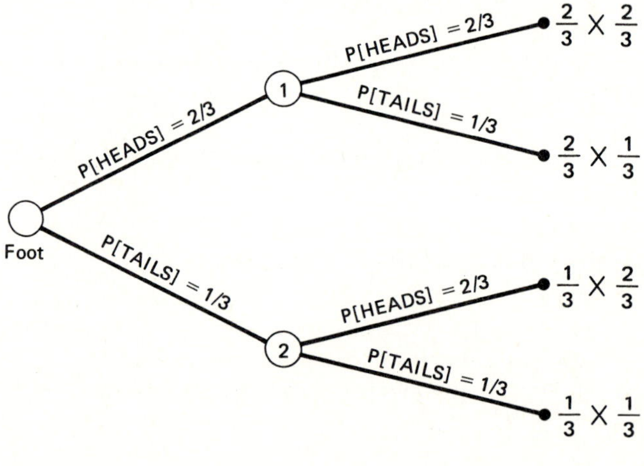

FIGURE 2.10
Probability tree model for tossing two pennies.

Note that

$$P[\text{HEADS and HEADS}] = P[\text{HEADS}] \times P[\text{HEADS}]$$

Generalization of this observation leads to the following three-step procedure to calculate the probability of the joint occurrence of events A and B under the condition of statistical independence:

> *Step 1.* Determine $P[A]$.
> *Step 2.* Determine $P[B]$.
> *Step 3.* $P[A \text{ and } B] = P[A] \times P[B]$.

Statistical Dependence

The concept of statistical dependence can be illustrated with the dart board experiment in Figure 2.4. The probabilities of the dart landing UP and LEFT are given by

$$P[\text{UP}] = \tfrac{2}{3} \qquad P[\text{LEFT}] = \tfrac{31}{60}$$

But

$$P[\text{UP and LEFT}] = \tfrac{4}{15}$$

which does not equal

$$P[\text{UP}] \times P[\text{LEFT}] = \tfrac{2}{3} \times \tfrac{31}{60} = \tfrac{31}{90}$$

The fact is that UP and LEFT are statistically dependent.

> Two events are statistically independent if the probability of joint occurrence equals the product of the individual probabilities.

> Two events are statistically dependent if the probability of joint occurrence does not equal the product of the individual probabilities.

The concept can be easily generalized for three, four, or a number of events. Events A and B are statistically independent if

$$P[A \text{ and } B] = P[A] \times P[B]$$

Events A, B, and C are statistically independent if

$$P[A \text{ and } B \text{ and } C] = P[A] \times P[B] \times P[C]$$

and so on.

Understanding Statistical Dependence and Independence

We can now provide further insight into the meaning of dependence and independence. Suppose you are blindfolded when the dart board experiment is performed and are told the dart landed on UP. Your knowledge as to the event of LEFT is given by the conditional probability

$$P[\text{LEFT} \mid \text{UP}] = \tfrac{2}{5}$$

as shown in the tree in Figure 2.8. But if you are told the dart landed on DOWN, you have

$$P[\text{LEFT} \mid \text{DOWN}] = \tfrac{3}{4}$$

The event UP influences the event LEFT; they are statistically dependent.

But now consider tossing a penny twice, as shown in Figure 2.10. If you are told that the first toss was HEADS, this in no way helps you to form an opinion about the second toss. The second HEADS is independent of the first HEADS. So

$$P[\text{second toss being HEADS} \mid \text{first toss being HEADS}] = \tfrac{2}{3}$$

$$= P[\text{toss being HEADS}]$$

Thus when A and B are statistically independent,

$$P[A \mid B] = P[A]$$

$$P[B \mid A] = P[B]$$

meaning that the conditional probabilities equal the unconditional probabilities. This is the reason that in the tree in Figure 2.10 the branches emanating from forks 1 and 2 are marked by *unconditional* probabilities, which in the case of statistical independence equal the conditional probabilities. This then leads to the following important procedure for probability tree models:

If a branch starts in event A and terminates in event B and A and B are statistically independent, then along the branch the unconditional probability of B is to be listed, because

$$P[B] = P[B \mid A]$$

2.5 APPLICATIONS OF PROBABILITY THEORY: PART II

A Department Store Problem

In a certain department store 30% of the shoppers have credit cards and 70% do not. Forty percent of the shoppers holding a credit card make a purchase; 30% of the shoppers with no credit cards make a purchase. What percent of the shoppers made a purchase?

Solution

We interpret the percents as probabilities and use the dart board model in Figure 2.11.

$$P[\text{HAVING CARD}] = .3$$

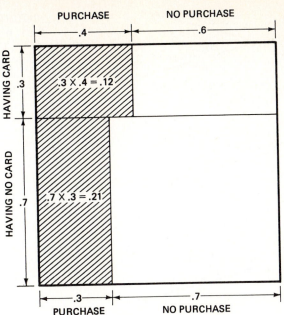

FIGURE 2.11
Department store problem converted to throwing darts at a dart board.

$$P[\text{HAVING NO CARD}] = .7$$

$$P[\text{PURCHASE} \mid \text{HAVING CARD}] = .4$$

$$P[\text{PURCHASE} \mid \text{HAVING NO CARD}] = .3$$

We compute the areas of each of the rectangles. The combined shaded areas give the desired probability:

$$P[\text{PURCHASE}] = .12 + .21 = .33$$

Balancing a Stock Portfolio

RJ is an investor who is concerned about recession and decides to invest in airline and bus stocks, believing that in the case of prosperity airline stocks go up and bus stocks go down but that in the case of recession the opposite occurs. RJ believes that there is a 50-50 chance for recession. RJ also believes that in the case of prosperity, airline stocks will go up with a probability of .85 and bus stocks down with a probability of .8; in the case of recession, airline stocks will go down with a probability of .7 and bus stocks up with a probability of .9. What is the probability that both stocks go up? Both go down?

Solution

We use the probability tree in Figure 2.12, multiply the probabilities along each pertinent path of the tree, and add the respective values at the tips:

$$P[\text{BOTH STOCKS GO UP}] = .085 + .135 = .220$$

$$P[\text{BOTH STOCKS GO DOWN}] = .06 + .035 = .095$$

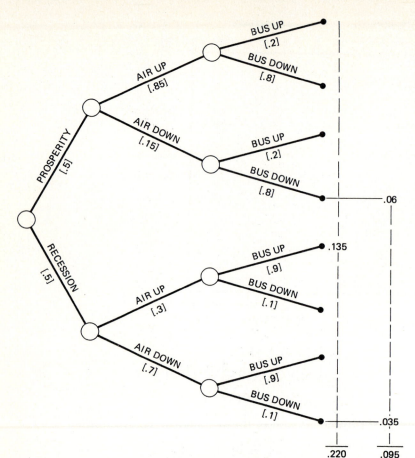

FIGURE 2.12
Tree representation of the stock portfolio balancing problem.

A Problem in Auditing

A certain firm has an internal auditor, Smith, but also hires an outside auditor, Jones. Yearly audits are performed separately, and the probability that an auditor finds a deficiency is .7. The events of auditors finding deficiencies are statistically independent. However, the auditors themselves may be in error, and the firm wants to determine whether the accounting system is truly deficient, requiring an overhaul. The probability of true deficiency, that is, the probability for a need to overhaul, depends of course on what the auditors find. From past experience the firm knows the conditional probabilities for the need to overhaul. Namely, the conditional probability for the need to overhaul the accounting system is as follows: (1) if both auditors find a deficiency, .85; (2) if only one auditor finds a deficiency, .6; and (3) if neither auditor finds a deficiency, .2. What is the unconditional probability that the accounting system needs overhauling?

Solution

We use the probability tree shown in Figure 2.13, multiply the probabilities along each pertinent path of the tree, and add the values at the respective tips:

$$P[\text{need for overhaul}] = .4165 + .1260 + .1260 + .0180 = .6865$$

The Used Car Lot Problem

Return to this problem stated in section 2.2. Determine the following probabilities of raffling off cars:

$$P[\text{SEDAN}], \qquad P[\text{SEDAN and GREEN}], \qquad P[\text{GREEN}]$$

Are the events SEDAN and GREEN statistically independent?

Solution

We can get the answers by direct count from Figure 2.3:

$$P[\text{SEDAN}] = \tfrac{11}{15}$$

$$P[\text{SEDAN and GREEN}] = \tfrac{5}{15} = \tfrac{1}{3}$$

$$P[\text{GREEN}] = \tfrac{6}{15} = \tfrac{2}{3}$$

$$P[\text{SEDAN}] \times P[\text{GREEN}] = \tfrac{11}{15} \times \tfrac{2}{3} = \tfrac{22}{45}$$

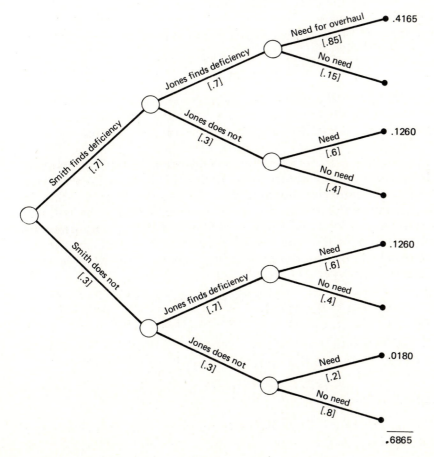

FIGURE 2.13
Tree representation of the problem in auditing.

which does not equal 1/3. Thus the two events are statistically dependent.

2.6 REVISION OF PROBABILITIES AND BAYES' THEOREM

When we contemplate future events, our estimate of the probability that the events will occur may change as time goes by and new information is received. For example, a manufacturer of stereo records may think that the record sale of a popular singer will be high and plans to manufacture many of the records. But if he receives information from retailers that the records do not sell well, the manufacturer may cancel some of the production.

In fact, decision makers are continuously seeking new information, expend a great deal of money, and use computers to obtain new information to update their views of the future. Therefore, as you progress in this textbook, you will learn more and more how information and computers enter the world of the decision maker.

We already touched on this subject when discussing conditional probability, and now we go further and show how probability theory provides a precise method to incorporate new information into the decision-making process.

Review now the dart board experiment shown in Figure 2.4. We have

$$P[\text{UP}] = \tfrac{2}{3}$$

As before you are blindfolded when the dart is thrown and do not know where the dart has landed. You are given the information that the dart landed in the RIGHT area. What is the probability that the dart landed in the UP area?

The original probability $P[\text{UP}] = \tfrac{2}{3}$ is the **prior** probability, and you must *revise* this prior probability in the light of the information received and calculate the **posterior** probability.

Now examine Figure 2.4. You *know* that the dart is in the RIGHT area, but you do not know whether it is UP or DOWN. So your problem can be represented by the reduced RIGHT part of the board as shown in Figure 2.14. Thus the posterior probability is given by dividing the area for UP and RIGHT by the entire RIGHT area, or

$$P[\text{UP} \mid \text{RIGHT}] = \frac{P[\text{UP and RIGHT}]}{P[\text{RIGHT}]}$$

(This also follows from the law of conditional probability.) We already computed that the area of the upper rectangle is

$$P[\text{UP and RIGHT}] = \tfrac{2}{5}$$

and the total area is

$$P[\text{RIGHT}] = \tfrac{29}{60}$$

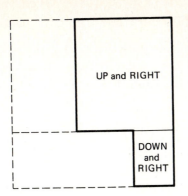

FIGURE 2.14
If you know that the dart *is* in the RIGHT area of Figure 2.4, then your problem is equivalent to throwing darts at the dart board shown here.

Thus the posterior probability is

$$P[\text{UP} \mid \text{RIGHT}] = \tfrac{2}{5} / \tfrac{29}{60}$$
$$= \tfrac{2}{5} \times \tfrac{60}{29} = \tfrac{24}{29}$$

Note also that

$$P[\text{RIGHT and UP}] = P[\text{RIGHT} \mid \text{UP}] \times P[\text{UP}]$$

$$P[\text{RIGHT}]$$
$$= P[\text{RIGHT} \mid \text{UP}] \times P[\text{UP}] + P[\text{RIGHT} \mid \text{DOWN}] \times P[\text{DOWN}]$$

and so

$$P[\text{UP} \mid \text{RIGHT}]$$

$$= \frac{P[\text{RIGHT} \mid \text{UP}] \times P[\text{UP}]}{P[\text{RIGHT} \mid \text{UP}] \times P[\text{UP}] + P[\text{RIGHT} \mid \text{DOWN}] \times P[\text{DOWN}]}$$

Applying this formula to Figure 2.4, for the right-hand side of the equation we get

$$\frac{\tfrac{3}{5} \times \tfrac{2}{3}}{\tfrac{3}{5} \times \tfrac{2}{3} + \tfrac{1}{4} \times \tfrac{1}{3}} = \frac{24}{29}$$

which agrees with our earlier calculation. The formulas discussed here, giving the posterior probabilities in terms of the prior and conditional probabilities, are called Bayes' formulas after the Reverend Thomas Bayes (1702–1761), a British pioneer of probability theory. The most important of these formulas is often referred to as Bayes' theorem. All you need do to get Bayes' theorem is to replace UP by A and RIGHT by D:

Bayes' theorem: For events A and B,

$$P[A \mid B] = \frac{P[B \mid A] \times P[A]}{P[B]}$$

Probability Tree Approach

As an alternative approach we can use the probability tree in Figure 2.9. We *know* that the dart landed on RIGHT and therefore need consider only the lower branches emanating from forks 1 and 2. Thus,

$$P[\text{UP}] \times P[\text{RIGHT} \mid \text{UP}] = \tfrac{2}{3} \times \tfrac{3}{5} = \tfrac{2}{5}$$

$$P[\text{DOWN}] \times P[\text{RIGHT} \mid \text{DOWN}] = \tfrac{1}{3} \times \tfrac{1}{4} = \tfrac{1}{12}$$

$$P[\text{RIGHT}] = \tfrac{2}{5} + \tfrac{1}{12} = \tfrac{29}{60}$$

and so

$$P[\text{UP} \mid \text{RIGHT}] = \frac{\tfrac{2}{5}}{\tfrac{29}{60}} = \frac{24}{29}$$

which agrees with our previous answer.

Thus the probability tree approach for determining the posterior probability of an event A consists of the following five steps:

> *Step 1.* Draw the probability tree.
> *Step 2.* Mark the probabilities along the branches.
> *Step 3.* Multiply the probabilities along each path, and list the joint probabilities at the tips.
> *Step 4.* Encircle the probabilities related to event A.
> *Step 5.* Add the encircled probabilities. This is the posterior probability of A.

The Process of Updating Probabilities

Figure 2.15 summarizes the four-step procedure to update probabilities:

> *Step 1.* Start with the given prior probabilities.
> *Step 2.* Obtain new information.
> *Step 3.* Update the probabilities by Bayes' theorem.
> *Step 4.* Use the posterior probabilities in your problem.

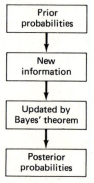

FIGURE 2.15
Bayes' procedure for updating probabilities.

As time goes by the decision maker may repeat the whole cycle. Posterior probabilities now become prior probabilities, new information is received, new posterior probabilities are calculated, and so on.

2.7 APPLICATION OF BAYES' THEOREM

The Department Store Problem

Return to this problem as stated in Section 2.5. What is the probability that a purchaser has a credit card?

Solution

We need

$$P[\text{HAVING CARD} \mid \text{PURCHASE}]$$

We use the dart board model in Figure 2.11. We *know* that the dart landed in the shaded area, and so the shaded area is our new reduced dart board. We have

$$P[\text{HAVING CARD and PURCHASE}] = .3 \times .4 = .12$$

$$P[\text{HAVING NO CARD and PURCHASE}] = .7 \times .3 = .21$$

Only purchasers in the upper shaded rectangle have cards:

$$P[\text{HAVING CARD} \mid \text{PURCHASE}] = \frac{.12}{.12 + .21} = \frac{.12}{.33} = .364$$

A Problem with Imperfect Information

You are in a casino in Monte Carlo, Monaco and are offered the gamble of drawing a marble blindfolded from a bag. There are 20 red and 40 blue marbles. You have a friend who whispers in your ear the color of the marble. Unfortunately, he is partially color-blind and so not reliable. The fact is that if the marble is red, he will whisper "rouge" with a probability of 3/4 and "bleu" with a probability of 1/4. If the marble is blue, he will whisper "bleu" with a probability of 3/5 and "rouge" with a probability of 2/5. You draw a marble, and your friend whispers "rouge." What is the probability that the marble is red?*

Note: This type of problem will lead in Chapter 5 to the discussion of information systems with imperfect information and the monetary value of an information system.

Solution

We decide to use a dart board model, and so our first task is to construct the dart corresponding to the given probabilities. We know

---

* We use English to describe the color of the marbles and French to describe the information received about the color of the marbles.

that

$$P[\text{RED}] = \frac{20}{20 + 40} = \frac{1}{3}$$

and

$$P[\text{BLUE}] = \frac{40}{20 + 40} = \frac{2}{3}$$

so in the rectangle in Figure 2.16 we draw the horizontal line *AB* which divides the rectangle into proportions 1/3 to 2/3.

The upper part is RED, and we draw the vertical line *CD* so the proportions are 1/4 to 3/4 to correspond to the conditional probabilities:

$$P[\text{BLEU} \mid \text{RED}] = \tfrac{1}{4} \qquad P[\text{ROUGE} \mid \text{RED}] = \tfrac{3}{4}$$

Finally we divide the lower BLUE rectangle by the line *EF* into proportions 3/5 to 2/5 to match the conditional probabilities:

$$P[\text{BLEU} \mid \text{BLUE}] = \tfrac{3}{5} \qquad P[\text{ROUGE} \mid \text{BLUE}] = \tfrac{2}{5}$$

Now we know that the dart landed in the shaded area. We have

$$P[\text{RED and ROUGE}] = \tfrac{1}{3} \times \tfrac{3}{4} = \tfrac{1}{4}$$

$$P[\text{BLUE and ROUGE}] = \tfrac{2}{3} \times \tfrac{2}{5} = \tfrac{4}{15}$$

and so

$$P[\text{RED} \mid \text{ROUGE}] = \frac{\tfrac{1}{4}}{\tfrac{1}{4} + \tfrac{4}{15}} = \frac{15}{31}$$

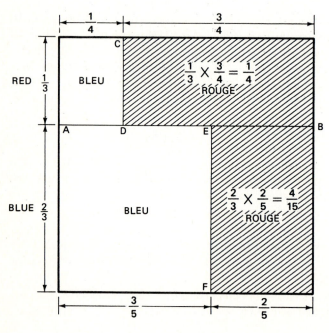

FIGURE 2.16
Converting the problem with imperfect information to throwing darts at a dart board.

Before probability theory was discovered, there were great scientific controversies about calculating probabilities. Even today those who do not know probability theory can easily fall into traps, compute erroneous probabilities, and make wrong decisions. Here are some common traps.

Trap 1. Confusing "or" with "and"

For example, consider tossing a single fair die,

$$P[\text{FACE VALUE} = 1] = \tfrac{1}{6}$$

$$P[\text{FACE VALUE} = 6] = \tfrac{1}{6}$$

and therefore concluding erroneously that

$$P[(\text{FACE VALUE} = 1) \text{ or } (\text{FACE VALUE} = 6)] = \tfrac{1}{6} \times \tfrac{1}{6} = \tfrac{1}{36}$$

The connective *or* requires the addition law, not the multiplication law.
Or by knowing that

$$P[\text{FACE VALUE greater than } 1] = \tfrac{5}{6}$$

and

$$P[\text{FACE VALUE less than } 5] = \tfrac{4}{6}$$

it is wrong to conclude that

$$P[\text{FACE VALUE is between 1 and 5}] = \tfrac{5}{6} + \tfrac{4}{6} = \tfrac{9}{6} = \tfrac{3}{2}$$

Trap 2. Using the rule of addition for events which are not mutually exclusive

For example, if

$$P[\text{STOCK of GENERAL ELECTRIC goes up}] = .7$$

and

$$P[\text{STOCK of IBM goes up}] = .3$$

it is erroneous to assume that one of these events is certain to occur.

Trap 3. Assuming that statistically independent events are dependent

For instance, a gambler may argue that after red comes up in sequence five times on the roulette wheel, it is better to bet on black or that one should bet on *heads* because a "lucky" person already bet on heads.

Trap 4. Misunderstanding the meaning of mutually exclusive and collectively exhaustive events

For example, assume that a car lot manager has a total of two cars and that he can sell on the next Saturday (1) no car, (2) one car, or (3) two cars, all with equal probability. Then

$$P[\text{SELL NO CAR}] = \tfrac{1}{3}$$

but

$$P[\text{SELL ALL CARS}] \neq \tfrac{2}{3}$$

because selling *no* car and selling *all* cars are not collectively exhaustive. But

$$P[\text{SELL SOME CARS}] = \tfrac{2}{3}$$

because selling no car and selling some cars are mutually exclusive and collectively exhaustive events.

Trap 5. Confusing mutually exclusive with statistically independent

For example, when tossing a penny, the outcome is HEADS or TAILS, and the outcomes are mutually exclusive. But tossing a penny twice can lead to HEADS and HEADS, though these outcomes are statistically independent.

Trap 6. Confusing statistical dependence with physical dependence

A bag contains four chips with the inscriptions UP/RIGHT, UP/LEFT, DOWN/RIGHT, and DOWN/LEFT. The events UP and RIGHT are physically connected; they are written on the same chip. But

$$P[\text{UP}] = \tfrac{1}{2} \qquad P[\text{RIGHT}] = \tfrac{1}{2}$$

and

$$P[\text{UP and RIGHT}] = \tfrac{1}{4}$$

so the events UP and RIGHT are statistically independent. But if you remove one of the chips, they become dependent.

Trap 7. Using the wrong thought experiment or model

This is the most dangerous of all traps because all your calculations may be correct and yet you have the wrong answer to the real problem.

The following example from the classics is attributed to Pierre de Fermat, the mathematician cited at the beginning of this chapter. Cast in modern context, it runs as follows.

Management believes it is equally likely there will or will not be prosperity. If there is prosperity, it is believed equally likely that sales will be high or low. If there is no prosperity, it is twice as likely that sales will be low.

Represent high sales by red balls and low sales by black balls. In the case of prosperity, there is one red and one black ball. If there is no prosperity, there is one red and two black balls. Thus there are two red and three black balls, a total of five balls. What is the probability of high sales (red balls)?

An analyst proposes the following thought experiment. Place all the balls into a bag, and pull a ball at random. Then

$$P[\text{HIGH SALES}] = P[\text{RED BALL}] = \tfrac{2}{5}$$

and so the probability of high sales (red balls) is 2/5.

This reasoning is erroneous because it ignores the piece of information that management believes it is equally likely that prosperity will or will not occur. The correct thought experiment is modeled by the probability tree of Figure 2.17. At the foot of the tree there are two branches corresponding to whether or not there is prosperity. At fork 1 there are two branches corresponding to high and low sales with the conditioned probabilities of 1/2 and 1/2. At fork 2 again there are two branches, but now the conditional probabilities are 1/3 and 2/3, corresponding to high and low sales.

We mark the joint probability at tip 1:

$$P[\text{HIGH} \mid \text{PROSPERITY}] = P[\text{PROSPERITY}] \times P[\text{HIGH} \mid \text{PROSPERITY}]$$

$$= \tfrac{1}{2} \times \tfrac{1}{2} = \tfrac{1}{4}$$

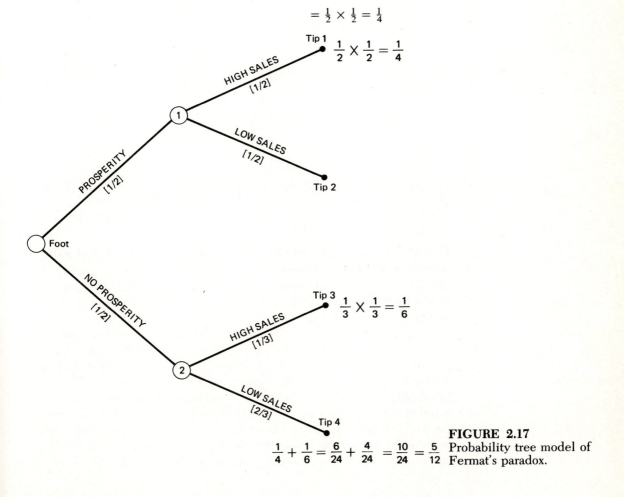

FIGURE 2.17 Probability tree model of Fermat's paradox.

At tip 3 we mark

$$P[\text{HIGH} \mid \text{NO PROSPERITY}] = P[\text{NO PROSPERITY}] \times P[\text{HIGH} \mid \text{NO}$$
$$\text{PROSPERITY}]$$
$$= \tfrac{1}{2} \times \tfrac{1}{3} = \tfrac{1}{6}$$

Thus

$$P[\text{HIGH}] = \frac{1}{4} + \frac{1}{6} = \frac{6+4}{24} = \frac{10}{24} = \frac{5}{12}$$

Following the tree model, the correct thought experiment is the following: Make up two bags, one for prosperity and one for no prosperity. Put one red and one black ball into the prosperity bag and one red and two black balls into the no prosperity bag. Now consider the following *composite* random experiment:

> *Step 1.* Draw one of the bags at random.
> *Step 2.* Draw a ball from the chosen bag.
> *Step 3.* $P[\text{RED}] = P[\text{HIGH}]$.

The verification of the validity of this thought experiment is left as an exercise.

2.9 A DIALOG

Q. *What does a random device have to do with management?*

A. Quantitative approaches to management rely on models, and when decision making is under uncertainty, mathematical models use probability theory. Random devices and thought experiments are easily understandable forms of probabilistic models. It helps you to divide the work into two steps: first identify the thought experiment using random devices, that is, the model, and, second, analyze the model.

Q. *What is the difference between a thought experiment and using random devices?*

A. Let me give you a classical example. Aristotle taught that heavy, that is, large bodies, fall faster than small or light bodies. Everyone believed this until Galileo Galilei, the great Italian astronomer, mathematician, and physicist of the seventeenth century, proved by a thought experiment that Aristotle was wrong. Galileo argued as follows: Take a large body and a small body. According to Aristotle, the large body falls faster than the small one. Now tie the two bodies together into a single combined body and repeat the experiment with the new body. This new body will fall slower than the large body and faster than the small body because the large body will speed up the small one, and the small will slow down the large body. Therefore, the speed of the combined body would be at an intermediate speed between that of the large body and the speed of the small one. But here is the rub: The combined body is even larger than the large body because it contains not only the large body but the small one. Thus, according to Aristotle, the combined body should fall even faster than the large body. But this is clearly a contradiction, and the resolution of the paradox is that all three bodies will fall at the same speed. Note therefore that Galileo used a thought experiment to disprove Aristotle, but he did not use random devices.

Q. *So the concept of a thought experiment is broader than experiments with random devices?*

A. Yes indeed!

Q. *I see now what you mean, so let me go to another subject. Why didn't you say anything about decision making?*

A. Decision making involves calculating probabilities and payoff. So far we have discussed only probabilities. You must be patient until we get further into the theory.

Q. *Do I always have to use random devices and thought experiments?*

A. Not at all. What you need is probability theory. Thought experiments and random devices are only props to keep you thinking straight. When you get more experience, you will work directly with probability theory. However, if in doubt, or if you are not clear on how probability theory applies, thought experiments come in very handy.

Q. *You use probability trees and formulas. Which one is the right model?*

A. It depends on the problem and individual preference. Some people are geometrically inclined, and use probability trees; others use only formulas. The scientific method implies that *no holds are barred*, and you proceed in the manner most suitable to your individual thinking style. Also when you explain models to managers, you must consider their style.

Q. *How can I be sure I am using the right thought experiment or model?*

A. You can never be absolutely sure, but with practice you increase your batting average. For guidance, read again the five steps of the scientific method in Chapter 1. Still, model building remains more of an art than a science. When dealing with uncertainty, you also need statistical theory to analyze the data, identify the model, and estimate the probabilities and other parameters involved.

Q. *Do managers really use probability theory?*

A. We all use probability in an intuitive manner. But in many cases probability theory puts intuition on a firm basis, and so the use of probability theory is increasing. In some fields probability theory has been used for many years, such as in quality control, sampling, opinion polls, auditing, inventory control, etc. Looking into the future, that is, forecasting, is a field where probability theory is used more and more. In other fields, such as finance and marketing, the use of probability theory is expanding.

Q. *Can you think of a trap I must avoid?*

A. Perhaps the worst trap is to assume that managers are familiar with probability theory and will act when you present a rational probabilistic analysis. You must never ignore behavioral aspects and the managerial style of the decision maker.

SUMMARY

1. Decision making under uncertainty is based on probability theory.
2. Probability theory was originally developed to solve gambling problems.
3. Typical random devices used in this book are (1) balanced or fair coin, (2) biased or bent coin, (3) roulette wheel, (4) wheel of fortune, (5) bag of marbles (balls) or chips, and (6) dart board.
4. If the outcomes of an experiment are equally likely, then the probability of event A is

$$P[A] = \frac{\text{number of outcomes resulting in occurrence } A}{\text{total number of outcomes}}$$

5. According to the basic laws of probability,

$$0 \leqslant P[A] \leqslant 1$$

$$P[A] = 0 \text{ implies that } A \text{ is impossible}$$

$$P[A] = 1 \text{ implies that } A \text{ is certain (sure)}$$

6. If events $A, B, C, \ldots$ are mutually exclusive, then

$$P[A] + P[B] + P[C] + \cdots = P[A \text{ or } B \text{ or } C \text{ or } \ldots]$$

7. If events $A, B, C, \ldots$ are also collectively exhaustive, then

$$P[A] + P[B] + P[C] + \cdots = P[A \text{ or } B \text{ or } C \text{ or } \ldots] = 1$$

8. According to the multiplication law for any event of A and B,

$$P[A \text{ or } B] = P[A] + P[B] - P[A \text{ and } B]$$

9. While there are two distinct interpretations of probability, the frequency and the judgmental, the calculating procedures are the same.

10. You need to distinguish between joint, marginal (unconditional), and conditional probabilities where

$$P[A \text{ and } B] = P[B] \times P[A \mid B]$$

11. According to the law of conditional probability,

$$P[A \mid B] = \frac{P[A \text{ and } B]}{P[B]}$$

12. Probability tree models are useful procedures for calculating probabilities.

13. The basic concepts in probability tree models are the foot, the fork, the branch, the tip, and the paths of the probability tree.

14. If events A and B are statistically independent, then

$$P[A \mid B] = P[A]$$
$$P[B \mid A] = P[B]$$

and

$$P[A \text{ and } B] = P[A] \times P[B]$$

15. If events A and B are statistically dependent, then

$$P[A \text{ and } B] \text{ does not equal } P[A] \times P[B]$$

16. When information is received, prior probability is to be revised by Bayes' theorem to obtain posterior probability:

$$P[A \mid B] = \frac{P[B \mid A] \times P[A]}{P[B]}$$

SECTION EXERCISES

1. *Foundations of Probability Theory*

1.1 Figure 2.1 shows four typical random devices. Give three more examples of typical random devices.

1.2 Tossing a die with six sides numbered by spots from 1 to 6 is a frequently used illustration of a random device.

   a. Show how a wheel of fortune (draw it, too) can be made to give the same results as tossing a die randomly.

   b. Show how a dart board can be made to give the same results as tossing a die randomly; draw your dart board.

   c. Show how a roulette wheel can be used to give the same results as randomly tossing a die; illustrate your wheel.

   d. Why can you not use a coin to give the same results in a random experiment in one toss?

   e. If you do not let the person who wants to know the outcome of the random experiment see the experiment that you are using (you only report the result of each spin, toss, or dart throw), is there any way he or she can find out from the results the nature of your experiment? Explain.

1.3 If a coin is bent and when tossed 10,000 times yields 6000 heads, what would you estimate the probability of getting a head to be?

1.4 A composite experiment can be converted into a simple one. For example, tossing two unbiased coins is equivalent to a wheel of fortune with four equal sectors.

a. Show that the preceding statement is valid.

b. Run an experiment to verify this. In the case of the coin tossing, follow the following format:

		Cumulative proportion of time result			
Toss no.	*Result* (TT, HH, TH, HT)	is: *HH*	*TT*	*TH*	*HT*

Note the following: (1) You must identify the coins; otherwise HT is the same as TH. Use a spot of color or different coins. (2) The cumulative proportion must be calculated for each result (HH, TT, TH, HT) after each toss. It is the proportion of times out of all the tosses in which that result occurred. For the wheel of fortune, make one with a spinner (a paper clip can be used for a spinning pointer), and label sectors TT, HH, TH, and HT. Or you can make a circle on a piece of paper and spin a pencil (carefully). Use the same format for results. Do at least 25 spins or tosses.

1.5 The three-step formula given in Section 2.1 is for the probability of event *A* happening knowing the total number of outcomes and the number of outcomes resulting in the occurrence of event *A*. Using this formula, determine the probability of

a. Drawing a black card on a single cut of a standard poker deck

b. Drawing a queen on a single cut of a standard poker deck

c. Drawing a heart on a single cut of a standard poker deck

d. Drawing the queen of hearts on a single cut of a standard poker deck

1.6 The first formula given in Section 2.1 is for the probability of an event *A* happening knowing the total number of outcomes and the number of outcomes resulting in the occurrence of event *A*. Using that formula, determine the probability of

a. Getting a 1 or 2 when rolling a single six-sided die

b. Getting two 1s ("snake eyes") on one toss of two six-sided dice

c. Getting two numbers of the same value on one toss of two six-sided dice

d. Getting a sum of seven for the values showing when tossing two six-sided dice

1.7 The first formula given in Section 2.1 is for the probability of an event *A* happening knowing the total number of outcomes and the number of outcomes resulting in the occurrence of event *A*. Using that formula, determine the probability of

a. Winning a lottery in which 5 million tickets have been sold where 500 winners are drawn from a drum containing all the ticket stubs

b. Being the interviewee chosen in a market research study which randomly picks 500 persons to interview from a city directory of 3.5 million names

c. Losing a raffle in which two ticket purchasers are chosen from 1728 ticket stubs

1.8 Which rule (1, 2, 3, or 4) of probability given in Section 2.1 is violated in the following cases:

a. "The price freeze on beef ended at midnight Sunday. But on the first day of the thaw, many industry officials said they had no idea what would happen next. 'I'd say there's a 50–50 chance of prices going up, 50–50 they'll go down, and 50–50 they'll stay the same,' said a spokesman for Grand Union" (from *Newsday* as quoted in *The New Yorker*).

b. "I'm 130% certain you will be satisfied."

1.9 The second formula given in Section 2.1 is for relating the probability of an event D to the relative weight of an area. Use this formula to determine the probability of
   a. A dart landing on the red squares of a checkerboard
   b. A dart landing on the squares along one edge (side) of a checkerboard
   c. A dart landing on a red square or along one edge of a checkerboard
   d. A dart landing on any of the squares along the diagonal of a checkerboard

1.10 The second formula given in Section 2.1 is for relating the probability of an event D to the relative weight of an area. Use this formula to determine the probability of
   a. Winning your bet on 1 of the 20 numbers on a wheel of chance at a fair
   b. Obtaining a 1 or a 2 on a game spinner divided into 10 sectors of equal size where the sectors are labeled 1, 2, 3, . . . , 9, 10

1.11 Can an event whose probability is .000000001 ever happen? Substantiate your answer with a random experiment.

1.12 If someone reports a probability that is 1.1, what interpretation should you give to the statement?

1.13 Give three examples of collectively exhaustive sets of events.

1.14 Give three examples of mutually exclusive events.

1.15 Use the appropriate form of the addition law to find the probability of
   a. Getting a 3 or a 5 on a roll of a six-sided die
   b. Drawing a face card or a heart from a deck of standard poker cards on one cut
   c. Getting a 1 on either of two six-sided dice on one throw
   d. In Figure 2.2, getting a dart into either area D or E.

1.16 The addition formula for computing probabilities where the events are nonmutually exclusive is given in Section 2.1. Use that formula to find the probabilities requested below for the situation where there are two machines producing parts (I, II) and two outcomes (GOOD, BAD) and the probabilities are as follows:

$$P(\text{I}) = .8 \qquad P(\text{II}) = .2$$
$$P(\text{GOOD}) = .6 \qquad P(\text{BAD}) = .4$$
$$P(\text{GOOD and from machine I}) = .52$$
$$P(\text{GOOD and from machine II}) = .08$$
$$P(\text{BAD and from machine I}) = .28$$
$$P(\text{BAD and from machine II}) = .12$$

   a. The probability that a part chosen at random is from machine I or II
   b. The probability that a part chosen at random is GOOD *or* from machine I
   c. The probability that a part chosen at random is BAD *or* from machine II

1.17 Nickles, a mail order firm, sent out 100,000 catalogs in a test mailing. They received 5000 orders from the test mailing catalogs. Use the relative frequency approach to probability to determine what probability they should assign to the event that an order will result from a catalog they have just mailed into the same demographic sector. Describe a random experiment that will have the same probability.

1.18 M. Endel has an experimental farm developing new pea varieties. An experiment on peas results in 315 smooth yellow peas, 101 wrinkled yellow peas, 108 smooth green peas, and 32 wrinkled green peas. What is the probability of occurrence of each kind of pea?

1.19 P. Limpton, softball star, has been at bat 480 times and struck out 320 times; all other times at bat, she got a hit. What is the probability she gets a hit when up at bat?

1.20 An industry official says that there is a probability of .9 that a major airline will fail in the next year. What kind of probability is this? How do you interpret this?

1.21 Robert Schlaifer in *Probability and Statistics for Business Decisions* (McGraw-Hill, New York, 1959, p. 17) discusses judgmental probabilities as being assigned by a "reasonable person" in accordance with the following rule:

If a person assessing the probability of a given event under a given set of conditions feels absolutely sure that the event would occur with relative frequency *p* in a great number of trials made under the same conditions, he will assign probability *p* to the event.

Relate this to the discussion of judgmental probability in the text, and give an example of the application of this rule.

2. Application of Probability Theory. Part 1

2.1 Refer to the used car lot problem of Section 2.2, conceptualized as a dart-throwing problem in Figure 2.3. What is the probability that the car drawn will be
  a. Black?
  b. Black or convertible?
  c. Black or four-door?
  d. White or black?
  e. A white convertible?
  f. Black or two-door?

3. Basic Properties of Probabilities

3.1 Refer to Figure 2.4. As shown, there are 112 units of area in the category LEFT and UP. Move the dividing line to the right so that there are now 126 units of area in the category LEFT and UP.
  a. Make a table similar to Figure 2.5 summarizing the new joint and marginal probabilities.
  b. Find all the conditional probabilities for this revised situation.

3.2 The following is a table of joint and marginal probabilities which is incomplete:

	A	A'	
B	1/4	?	3/8
B'	?	?	5/8
	3/4	?	

  a. Complete the entries in the table.
  b. Find all conditional probabilities for this table.

3.3 The following is a table of joint and marginal probabilities which is incomplete:

	LEFT	RIGHT	
Up	1/4	?	3/4
Down	?	1/3	?
	?	?	?

  a. Complete the entries in the table.
  b. Represent this table as a dart board, similar to Figure 2.4.

c. Find all conditional probabilities for this table.

3.4 Express all the probabilities—both in the tables and computed by you—of Exercises 3.2 and 3.3 in formulas using the $P[\ ]$ notation.

3.5 Refer to the tree of Figure 2.9. Suppose that the marginal probability of UP were changed from 2/3 to $P[\text{UP}] = 1/3$.
   a. Revise the tree of Figure 2.9 to account for this change.
   b. Find the new values for $P[\text{LEFT}]$ and $P[\text{RIGHT}]$.
   c. Show that all the probabilities for each set of branches emanating from a fork add to 1. What practical use can be made of this fact?

3.6 A bank has discovered that the probability that a customer will close a new account in the first year is 1/20. Also, a survey of records shows that if the customer closes the account in the first year, there is a 1/5 chance that he or she is still a resident of the area which the bank serves. If the customer does not close the account in the first year, there is a 9/10 chance that he or she is still a resident of the area served by the bank.
   a. Draw a probability tree (similar to Figure 2.9) for this situation.
   b. Find all probabilities for this situation: the probabilities that the customer is still a resident and not a resident.
   c. Show that all the probabilities for each set of branches emanating from a fork add to 1.

3.7 The Environmental Protection Bureau of a community has found that the probability that any factory in their town will be a violator of pollution regulations in a given month is 1/100. Their records also show that if a factory is a violator, there is a 18/20 chance that it has been in operation more than 2 years. If the factory is not a violator, the chances are 4 to 1 that it has not been in operation for more than 2 years.
   a. Construct a probability tree (similar to Figure 2.9) for this situation.
   b. Show all the probabilities for this situation: the probabilities that the factory is older than 2 years and 2 years or less old.
   c. Show that all the probabilities for the set of branches emanating from each fork add to 1.

3.8 Describe in words the process of drawing a probability tree.

4. *Independent versus Dependent Events*

4.1 Make the tables (similar to Figure 2.5) and the probability trees for the following situations in which statistical independence holds between the two events or variables:
   a. Tossing two coins where the events of interest are heads or tails on the first coin and heads or tails on the second coin.
   b. Tossing two dice where the events of interest are getting 2 or less on the first die and 4 or more on the second die.
   c. Being first in line or not first in line for a movie and being male or female. Assume that the line is always exactly 20 persons long and that the probability of being female in this community is .55.
   d. A professor chooses five homework papers by lot out of each class of 30 students; these papers are graded. Assume that one-third of the students in the classes wear contact lenses or glasses.

4.2 The following is a series of tables showing counts of events or probabilities. For each, show whether or not the two events are statistically independent.

a.		A	A'	
	B	.03	.75	.78
	B'	.03	.19	.22
		.06	.94	1.00

b.

	YES	NO	
Male	25	75	100
Female	25	75	100
	50	150	200

c.

	LIKES	DISLIKES	
Over 50	.068	.272	.34
50 or less	.132	.528	.66
	.2	.8	1.00

5. *Applications of Probability Theory. Part II.*

5.1 Refer to the used car lot problem of Section 2.2, discussed in Section 2.5 as the used car lot problem.

    a Determine the following probabilities:

      i.   *P*[convertible or 4-door]

      ii. *P*[convertible or 4-door and black]

      iii. *P*[black]

    b. Are the events convertible or four-door and black statistically independent?

5.2 In a bank, 20% of the depositors hold mortgages and 80% do not. In a particular period, 70% of the depositors with a mortgage make a withdrawal; 40% of the depositors with no mortgage make a withdrawal. What percent of the depositors make a withdrawal? (*Hint:* Use a model as shown in Figure 2.12.)

5.3 Jimmie Crater is an investor who is concerned about a recession coming and decides to invest in cashew bars and peanuts, believing that in times of prosperity cashew bars rise in value and peanuts go down. In times of adversity, he reasons that the extra value in peanuts makes them more attractive and that they will go up, while the processed cashew bars will fall because they give lower food value. He believes that there is a 70–30 chance of a recession. He also believes that in the case of prosperity, the chance that cashew bars will rise in value is .9 and that peanuts will decline is .7. In the case of a recession, he believes that peanuts will go up with a probability of .9 and that cashew bars will go down with a probability of .65.

    a What is the probability that both types of nutty investments will go up?

    b. What is the probability that both types of nutty investments will go down?

(*Hint:* Use a probability tree of the type shown in Figure 2.12.)

5.4 A certain firm has an internal auditor named Miller and hires an outside auditing firm named Friedman and Volcker. The internal auditor and the outside firm perform audits separately; the probability that an auditor—internal or external—will find a deficiency is .8. The events—internal or external auditor finds a deficiency—are independent as it has been many years since the two groups of auditors have spoken to each other. If both auditors find a deficiency, then the probability that the accounting system must be revised is .7. If only one auditor finds a deficiency, the probability of a need for revision is estimated to be .6. If neither finds a deficiency, the probability of a call for revision is believed to be .1. What is the probability that the accounting system will be revised? (*Hint:* Use a probability tree similar to Figure 2.13.)

6. *Revision of Probabilities and Bayes' Theorem*

6.1 Suppose you are blindfolded when a dart is thrown at the dart board of Figure 2.4. You are told that the dart has landed in the LEFT area.
    a. Find the posterior probability that the dart has landed in the DOWN area using the step-by-step logical reasoning of Section 5 which precedes the introduction of the formula for Bayes' Theorem.
    b. Verify your result in a), above, by using the formula for Bayes' Theorem.
    c. Find the posterior probability that the dart has landed in the UP area using the formula for Bayes' Theorem.

6.2 Refer to the Department Store Problem of Section 4, which is contained in Section 5. Recent changes in store policy have caused a shift in the probabilities. Now 60% of the shoppers carry credit cards and 40% do not. Twenty percent of the shoppers with no credit card make a purchase.
    a. What percent of the shoppers make a purchase?
    b. What is the probability that a purchaser has a credit card?

6.3 The Fort Apache Police Department has accumulated records on the bookings of suspects and behavior of witnesses. In some cases, the suspects have been caught "red-handed," and all that is lacking is a movie of the suspect committing the crime. However, in Fort Apache, airtight eyewitness confirmation in court is required. The Fort Apache Police find that 72% of their arrests are of red-handed suspects and 28% of suspects where the police officer's evidence is not of the red-handed variety. Records show that if the suspect is of the red-handed type, the probability that eyewitness testimony will lead to conviction is .86. If the suspect is of the other type, the probability that eyewitness testimony will lead to conviction is .17. Assume that there is always an eyewitness.
    a. Knowing that a suspect was convicted, what is the probability that the suspect was of the red-handed type?
    b. Knowing that a suspect was not convicted, what is the probability that the suspect was not caught red-handed?
    c. What is the probability of conviction?

7. *Applications of Bayes' Theorem*

7.1 This exercise refers to the problem with imperfect information, introduced in Section 2.7. You have become discontented with the color-blind friend and have brought in another friend to help you. The game still involves drawing a marble blindfolded from a bag with 20 red and 40 blue marbles. Unfortunately, your friend does not remember his French well. If the marble is red, he can be expected to whisper "rouge" with a probability of .9 and "bleu" with a probability of .1. If the marble is blue, he will whisper "bleu" with a probability of .8 and "rouge" with a probability of .2.
    a. What is the probability that the marble is red if he whispers "rouge" to you?
    b. What is the probability that the marble is blue if he whispers "bleu" to you?
    c. Which friend do you prefer, the color-blind one or the poor linguist? Why?
    d. What is the probability that your friend will whisper "rouge?"

7.2 The problem of imperfect information discussed in Section 2.7 and illustrated in Figure 2.16 can be modeled and solved using a probability tree. Do so. Which method do you prefer and why?

8. *Traps in Using Probability Theory*

8.1 Trap 1 shows two erroneous conclusions. Calculate the correct probabilities for each of these two cases which are defined as follows:
   a. $P[(\text{FACE VALUE} = 1) \text{ or } (\text{FACE VALUE} = 6)]$
   b. $P[1 < \text{FACE VALUE} < 6]$

8.2 Trap 3 occurs when it is assumed that independent events are dependent; the example given is from the game of roulette where a gambler incorrectly assumes dependence, a common failing of amateur gamblers. However, independence holds only under certain conditions. What are the conditions that must hold in a roulette situation for independence of outcomes? [*Hint:* Explore first the *mechanical* conditions. Then consider the human influences (legal and/or illegal) that might be brought to bear.]

8.3 Trap 6 discusses the confusion of statistical and physical independence and gives a particular example. Model that example with a tree.

8.4 Trap 7 is about using the wrong thought experiment. Model the example given with four chips.

8.5 Trap 7 discusses the use of the wrong model for a situation involving probability. How will you avoid this type of error? (*Hint:* There are behavioral, organizational, and scientific ways of reducing the chance of using the wrong model. One simple approach is to have someone check your work. More formal approaches exist; in engineering, formal design reviews are used. Can you think of other ways or extensions of these ways? Can this type of trap be totally eliminated?

9. *A Dialog*

9.1 Is it possible to use quantitative approaches to management in conditions of uncertainty without using models of random devices for thought experiments?

9.2 Which do you prefer, probability trees or formulas? Why?

9.3 Which do you think would be better to use in explaining a decision to the board of directors of a large company, probability trees or formulas? Why?

9.4 In managerial decision making you may never be able to verify if your thought experiment or model was correct. However, in scientific work, it is often possible. *How* is it possible?

CHAPTER EXERCISES AND DISCUSSION QUESTIONS

C1. Probability trees are not limited to two-stage situations (two coins, two dimensions, two random experiments in sequence). Use trees to model the following:
   a. Tossing a coin three times in succession
   b. Tossing three differently colored dice simultaneously
   c. Throwing three differently colored darts at the dart board in Figure 2.4

C2. It is helpful to be able to express the formula for probabilities in colloquial English. Do so for the following:
   a. The formula for finding the probability of events where the total number of outcomes are all equally likely

b. The basic laws of probability
c. The addition formula for mutually exclusive events
d. The additional formula for mutually and collectively exclusive events
e. The multiplication law
f. The laws of conditional probability
g. The rules for statistically dependent and independent events
h. Bayes' theorem

3 Review of Random Variables and Probability Distributions

In Chapter 2 we reviewed the basic concepts of probability. Now we introduce some new concepts, extend the theory, and provide a bridge to decision making under uncertainty by introducing payoffs into our framework. Again we introduce theory by discussing random devices.

3.1 RANDOM VARIABLES

Consider the chance experiment in part (a) of Figure 3.1. The values of the payoffs are $5, $15, $20, and $30, and the respective probabilities are 1/6, 1/6, 2/6 = 1/3, 2/6 = 1/3, as shown in tabular form in part (b) of Figure 3.1. Part (c) of Figure 3.1 shows graphically the **probability distribution function (PDF)** associated with the random experiment. This probability function has four values: $5, $15, $20, and $30, indicated on the horizontal axis. The corresponding probabilities are 1/6, 1/6, 2/6 = 1/3, 2/6 = 1/3, as indicated on the vertical axis. When we are dealing only with a finite number of (discrete) values, the probability distribution function is called a **probability mass function (PMF)**. Thus the PMF provides the probabilities associated with each outcome of a random experiment and summarizes all the data pertinent to it.

Note that the concept of the probability distribution function is more general than the concept of the probability mass function, as a probability mass function is always a probability density function but the converse is not true. The concept of the PMF applies only when there are a finite number of (discrete) values.

The outcomes described by the PMF are mutually exclusive and collectively exhaustive. Therefore,

> The sum of the probabilities in the probability mass function must add to 1.

Now we show an alternate, useful method to summarize data

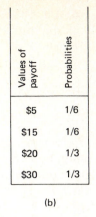

Values of payoff	Probabilities
$5	1/6
$15	1/6
$20	1/3
$30	1/3

(a)

(b)

FIGURE 3.1
(a) Random experiment; (b) the tabular representation of data; (c) the associated probability mass function (PMF); (d) the cumulative distribution function (CDF). (Calculations in the text show that $\mu = \$20$, Var $= 75$, and $\sigma = \$8.660$.)

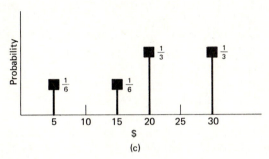

(c)

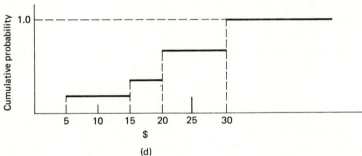

(d)

associated with a random experiment. Note that the probability of the value of the payoff being less than $5 in Figure 3.1 is zero, or

$$P[\text{PAYOFF less than } \$5] = 0$$

We write this in mathematical notation as

$$P[\text{PAYOFF} < \$5] = 0$$

Similarly,

$$P[\text{PAYOFF} < \$15] = \tfrac{1}{6}$$

$$P[\text{PAYOFF} < \$20] = \tfrac{1}{6} + \tfrac{1}{6} = \tfrac{1}{3}$$

$$P[\text{PAYOFF} < \$30] = \tfrac{1}{6} + \tfrac{1}{6} + \tfrac{1}{3} = \tfrac{2}{3}$$

$$P[\text{PAYOFF} < \$50] = 1$$

The values 0, 1/6, 1/3, 2/3, and 1 define the **cumulative distribution function (CDF)** of the random experiment. Further examples of the values of the CDF are

$$P[\text{PAYOFF} < \$14.99] = \tfrac{1}{6}$$

$$P[\text{PAYOFF} < \$15.01] = \tfrac{1}{3}$$

$$P[\text{PAYOFF} < \$100] \quad = 1$$

We now want to augment the concept of a random experiment with numerical outcomes by the precise mathematical concept of a **random variable**. Such a random experiment can be characterized by a probability distribution function, and therefore a random variable is defined by a probability distribution function. A discrete random variable is defined by its probability mass function. The outcomes of the experiments are the numerical **values** of the random variable.

Do not confuse the values of the random variables with the probabilities. In Figure 3.1 the *probabilities* are 1/6, 1/6, 1/3, and 1/3; the *values* of the random variable are $5, $15, $20, and $30.

The Expected Value of a Random Variable

Suppose the payoffs from the sales for some goods can be characterized by the PMF in Figure 3.1. For a manager it is not enough to know the probabilities and the corresponding values. For example, suppose he wants to estimate the payoff from 600 trials. Inspecting part (a) of Figure 3.1, we can directly calculate this payoff. Namely, we expect the ball to stop about 100 times in each sector of the wheel. Thus the payoffs will be about

$$100 \text{ times } \$5 = \$\ \ 500$$

$$100 \text{ times } \$15 = \$1{,}500$$

$$100 \text{ times } \$20 = \$2{,}000$$

$$100 \text{ times } \$20 = \$2{,}000$$

$$100 \text{ times } \$30 = \$3{,}000$$

$$100 \text{ times } \$30 = \$3{,}000$$

$$\overline{\qquad\qquad}$$

$$\$12{,}000$$

This means that the expected or mean payoff per trial is $12,000/600 = $20. We now need a general procedure to solve problems of this nature.

We define the **expected value** (or **mean**) of random variables in the following way.

Designate by* x_1, x_2, x_3, ..., x_n the n respective values of the random variable and by p_1, p_2, p_3, ..., p_n the respective probabilities.

---

* A review of subscripted notation is given in Appendix A, Section 10.

> The expected value of a random variable is
> $$\mu = p_1 x_1 + p_2 x_2 + p_3 x_3 + \cdots + p_n x_n$$

(Here μ is the greek letter mu.)

If all the probabilities are the same, we must have

$$p = \frac{1}{n}$$

and the expected value (or mean) is given by

$$\mu = \frac{x_1 + x_2 + \cdots + x_n}{n}$$

Figure 3.2 illustrates how to calculate the expected value of the random variable shown in Figure 3.1. Note that our result of $20 agrees with our previous result.

Our formula for calculating the expected value can be stated as a two-step procedure.

> *Step 1.* Calculate the product of each probability times the value.
> *Step 2.* Add all the products.

Formal Notation

We designated the values of our random variable by the lowercase letters $x_1, x_2, \ldots$ It is customary to designate the random variable itself by the corresponding capital letter, that is, X in our case. You can think of X as the name of a random device such as a roulette wheel; the xs stand for the numbers on the wheel, the values of the random variable. The customary notation for the expected value is $E(X)$, where E is an abbreviation of Expected. In this formal notation,

> $$\mu = E(X) = p_1 x_1 + p_2 x_2 + \cdots + p_n x_n$$

	x	p	px
1	$5	1/6	5/6
2	$15	1/6	15/6
3	$20	1/3	20/3 = 40/6
4	$30	1/3	30/3 = 60/6

$$\downarrow$$

Expected value = μ = (5 + 15 + 40 + 60)/6
= 120/6 = $20

FIGURE 3.2 Calculating the expected value of the random variable shown in Figure 3.1.

Note then that the mathematical formula $E(X)$ is an abbreviated form of the English statement of how to calculate the expected value of a random variable with values x_1, x_2, . . . and respective probabilities p_1, p_2, ...

The Variance and Standard Deviation

While the mean of a random variable provides important information about a chance experiment, it provides no information as to the variability of the outcomes in the experiment. To a corporation it makes a great deal of difference whether profits will be (1) $900,000 or $1 million with equal chance or (2) a loss of $1,100,000, or a gain of $3 million with equal chance, in spite of the fact that the expected value is the same for both.

expected value for first venture   = .5 × 900,000 + .5 × 1,000,000

= $950,000

expected value for second venture = −.5 × 1,100,000 + .5 × 3,000,000

= $950,000

In probability theory some indication of the degree of variability is given by two important quantities, the **variance** and the **standard deviation**.

> The variance is the expected value of the square of the difference between the values of the random variable and the mean.

Figure 3.3 shows how to calculate the variance for the random variable shown in Figure 3.1.

The procedure for calculating the variance is as follows:

> *Step 1.* Calculate the mean of the random variable.
> *Step 2.* Subtract the mean from each value of the random variable.
> *Step 3.* Calculate the square of each term in step 2.
> *Step 4.* Multiply each probability by the corresponding term in step 3.
> *Step 5.* Add all the terms in step 4.

The procedure can be briefly stated by the formulas

> $$\text{Var} = p_1(x_1 - \mu)^2 + p_2(x_2 - \mu)^2 + \cdots + p_n(x_n - \mu)^2$$
>
> or
>
> $$\text{Var} = E[(X - \mu)^2]$$

Note that mathematics serves as a concise language for describing the procedure required.

	x	p	$x - \mu =$ $x - 20$	$(x - \mu)^2$	$p(x - \mu)^2$
1	$5	1/6	−15	225	$\dfrac{225}{6}$
2	$15	1/6	−5	25	$\dfrac{25}{6}$
3	$20	1/3	0	0	0
4	$30	1/3	+10	100	$\dfrac{200}{6}$

$$\downarrow$$

$$\text{Var} = (225 + 25 + 0 + 200)/6 = 75$$

FIGURE 3.3 Calculating the variance of the random variable in Figure 3.1.

The standard deviation, a direct measure of variability, is the square root of the variance:

$$\sigma = \sqrt{\text{Var}}$$

where σ (sigma) is a Greek letter. For the random variable in Figure 3.1,

$$\sigma = \sqrt{75} = \$8.660$$

When all the probabilities are the same, the formula for the variance simplifies to

$$\text{Var} = E[(X - \mu)^2] = \frac{(x_1 - \mu)^2 + (x_2 - \mu)^2 + \cdots + (x_n - \mu)^2}{n}$$

Note that the standard deviation is measured in the same units as the random variable itself. For example, if the random variable is in dollars, hours, feet, etc., the standard deviation will be, respectively, in dollars, hours, feet, etc. This is *not* so for the variance, and therefore the standard deviation is a preferred measure of variability.

How to Add Random Variables

In Chapter 1 we developed a mathematical model for the pricing situation of the Loud and Clear Playback Corporation (Figure 1.10). We also described a decision support system for the La Brea Oil Company. Both models were deterministic, and now we start to pave the way for a probabilistic analysis.

Consider as an example the quantity-cost relationship:

$$Q = 5000 - 40P$$

in Figure 1.10. Suppose both the coefficients 5000 and 40 are uncertain and must be represented by random variables. How do we calculate the new random variable, the quantity Q? We need procedures to combine random variables.

In this section we show only how to add and subtract random

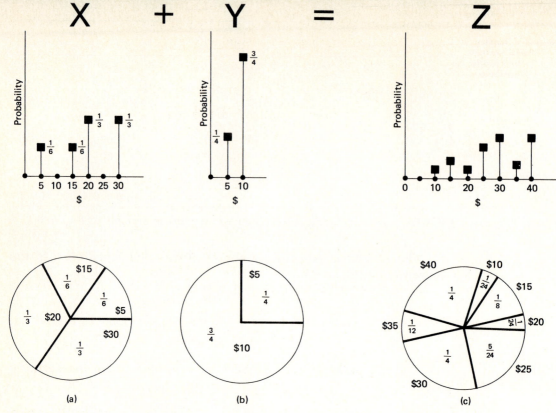

FIGURE 3.4 Adding two random variables means combining two wheels of fortune.

variables and how to multiply a random variable by a constant and postpone to later chapters the calculations required for more complex models. First we pose the question of how to add two random variables X and Y.

To answer the question, we fall back on an example using wheels of fortune. Suppose a corporation is selling goods in the north and the south. Sales in the north are given by the random variable X defined in part (a) of Figure 3.4 and in the south by the random variable Y defined in part (b) of Figure 3.4. Combined sales will be a new random variable Z, and our problem is to determine the PMF of Z. The values of Z will be all the possible combinations of (1) $5, $15, $20, and $30 and (2) $5 and $10. Thus there will be seven values of Z: $10, $15, $20, $25, $30, $35, and $40. The probability tree in Figure 3.5 shows how to calculate the corresponding probabilities. The event $x_1 = \$10$ can occur only a single way (tip 1 of the tree), and so

$$p_1 = \tfrac{1}{6} \times \tfrac{1}{4} = \tfrac{1}{24}$$

The event $x_2 = \$15$ can occur only a single way (tip 2), and so

$$p_2 = \tfrac{1}{6} \times \tfrac{3}{4} = \tfrac{3}{24} = \tfrac{1}{8}$$

Similarly, for $x_3 = \$20$, $p_3 = 1/24$.

However, the event $x_4 = \$25$ can occur two ways (tips 4 and 5). These events are mutually exclusive, and so

$$p_4 = \tfrac{1}{6} \times \tfrac{3}{4} + \tfrac{1}{3} \times \tfrac{1}{4} = \tfrac{3}{24} + \tfrac{1}{12} = \tfrac{5}{24}$$

The other probabilities can be determined directly:

$$x_5 = \$30 \qquad p_5 = \tfrac{1}{3} \times \tfrac{3}{4} = \tfrac{3}{12} = \tfrac{1}{4} \qquad \text{(tip 6)}$$

$$x_6 = \$35 \qquad p_6 = \tfrac{1}{3} \times \tfrac{1}{4} = \tfrac{1}{12} \qquad \text{(tip 7)}$$

$$x_7 = \$40 \qquad p_7 = \tfrac{1}{3} \times \tfrac{3}{4} = \tfrac{1}{4} \qquad \text{(tip 8)}$$

We verify that the sum of the probabilities is indeed 1:

$$\frac{1}{24} + \frac{1}{8} + \frac{1}{24} + \frac{5}{24} + \frac{1}{4} + \frac{1}{12} + \frac{1}{4} = \frac{1 + 3 + 1 + 5 + 6 + 2 + 6}{24} = 1$$

In part (c) of Figure 3.4 we show the PMF of the new random variable Z and the corresponding wheel of fortune.

Note that the PMF of Z is obtained by *combining* in a specific

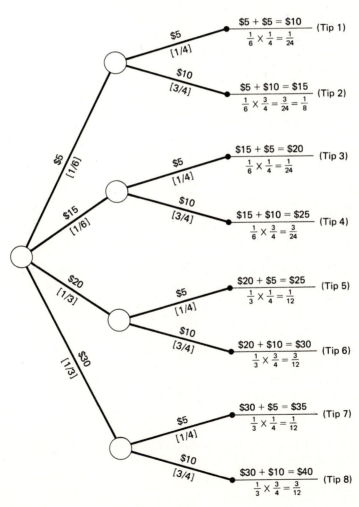

FIGURE 3.5
Probability model of adding two random variables.

manner the PMF of X and Y as shown in Figure 3.4. We can also say that the roulette wheel of X is combined with that of Y to obtain the combined wheel of Z.

Note also that Z may be represented by the composite experiment of spinning two wheels and adding the numerical outcomes or by the simple experiment of spinning the wheel corresponding to Z.

> The same random variable may be represented by simple or composite random experiments.

Often all you want is the expected value and the variance of the sum of random variables. The probability theory provides a shortcut method of calculation. We present this theory without mathematical proofs.

The Expected Value and Variance of the Sum of Random Variables

Let X, Y, ... be given random variables. The sum of these random variables is a new random variable. *The expected value of the sum of random variables equals the sum of the expected values of the individual variables:*

$$E(X + Y + \cdots) = E(X) + E(Y) + \cdots$$

If C is a constant, then

$$E(C + X) = C + E(X)$$

and when a random variable is multiplied by a factor,

$$E(FX) = FE(X)$$

The formula for variances is

$$\text{Var}(X + Y + \cdots) = \text{Var}(X) + \text{Var}(Y) + \cdots$$

provided X, Y, ... are generated by random experiments that are statistically independent. Further formulas for the variances are

$$\text{Var}(C + X) = \text{Var}(X)$$

$$\text{Var}(FX) = F^2 \, \text{Var}(X)$$

The formulas for standard deviations are

$$\sigma(C + X) = \sigma(X)$$

$$\sigma(FX) = F\sigma(X)$$

Each of the preceding formulas represents procedures for carrying out calculations. Development of the corresponding English language statements is left as an exercise.

Example 1

In a certain harbor accurate records of ships being unloaded were kept for 100 days:

> 1 ship unloaded: 50 times
> 2 ships unloaded: 50 times

What is the expected value of ships unloaded per day?

Solution

$$P[\text{1 ship unloaded}] = 50/100 = .5$$

$$P[\text{2 ships unloaded}] = 50/100 = .5$$

The expected value is

$$\mu = .5 \times 1 + .5 \times 2 = .5 + 1.0 = 1.5 \text{ ships/day}$$

Note that it is impossible to unload 1.5 ships.

The expected value may not be a possible outcome.

Example 2

A salesman kept record of his net quarterly earnings for the last 10 years:

> Bad earnings: loss of $5000, 4 times
> So-so earnings: gain of $6000, 12 times
> Good earnings: gain of $10,000, 20 times
> Excellent earnings: gain of $27,000, 4 times

Determine the expected value, variance, and standard deviation of quarterly earnings.

Solution

$$P[\text{bad earnings}] = \tfrac{4}{40} = .1$$

$$P[\text{so-so earnings}] = \tfrac{12}{40} = .3$$

$$P[\text{good earnings}] = \tfrac{20}{40} = .5$$

$$P[\text{excellent earnings}] = \tfrac{4}{40} = .1$$

The expected value is

$$\mu = -5000 \times .1 + 6000 \times .3 + 10,000 \times .5 + 27,000 \times .1 = \$9000$$

The variance is

$$\text{Var} = [(-5 - 9)^2 \times .1 + (6 - 9)^2 \times .3 + (10 - 1)^2 \times .5 + (27 - 9)^2 \times .1]$$
$$\times 1000^2 = 95,200,000$$

The standard deviation is

$$\sigma = \sqrt{\text{Var}} = \sqrt{95,200,000} = \$9757.05$$

Example 3

A building contractor constructs buildings in the north and the south. Sales can be represented by two statistically independent generated random variables X and Y. X can be represented by the random experiment in Figure 3.1 and Y by Figure 3.6a where all dollar values represent millions of dollars. Combined sales can be represented by the sum of the random variables X and Y. Determine the expected value, the standard deviation, and the PMF of combined sales.

Solution

From Figure 3.1,

$$\mu(X) = E(X) = \$20$$

$$\text{Var}(X) = 75$$

$$\sigma(X) = \$8.660$$

With the aid of Figure 3.6a,

$$\mu(Y) = E(Y) = 0 \times \tfrac{1}{3} + 5 \times \tfrac{2}{3} = \tfrac{10}{3} = \$3.3333$$
$$\text{Var}(Y) = \tfrac{1}{3}(0 - \tfrac{10}{3})^2 + \tfrac{2}{3}(5 - \tfrac{10}{3})^2 = 5.5556$$
$$\sigma(Y) = \sqrt{5.5556} = \$2.3570$$

Thus for combined sales,

$$\mu = E(X + Y) = \$20 + \$3.3333 = \$23.3333$$
$$\text{Var}(X + Y) = 75 + 5.5556 = 80.5556$$
$$\sigma = \sqrt{80.5556} = \$8.9753$$

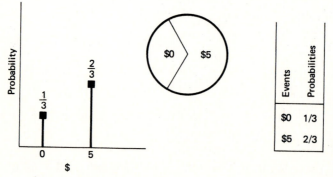

FIGURE 3.6a
Random experiment representation of sales for the building contractor in the south.

The PMF can be determined with the probability tree shown in Figure 3.6b. At the tip of the tree we list the sum of the dollars and the products of the probabilities.

Figure 3.6c graphically shows the PMF and the CDF.

Example 4

Consider the random variable of Figure 3.1 and add \$5 to each of the dollar values. Determine the expected value, variance, and standard deviation of this new random variable.

Solution

We must add the constant

$$C = \$5$$

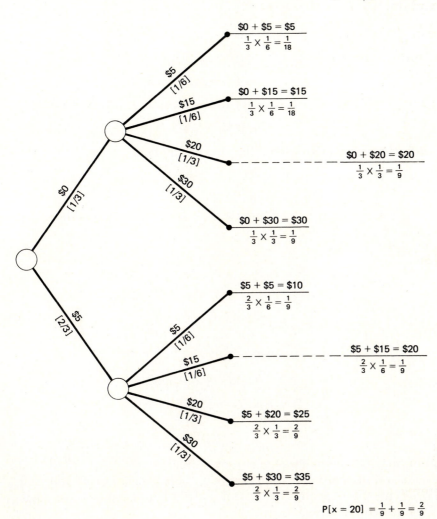

FIGURE 3.6b
Probability tree representation of combined sales for the building contractor.

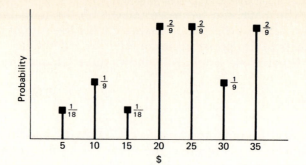

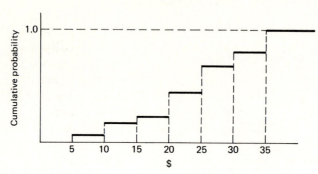

FIGURE 3.6c
Probability mass function (PMF) and cumulative probability function (CPF) of combined sales for the building contractor.

to a random variable, which has an expected value of $20. Thus,

$$E = \$20 + \$5 = \$25$$

The variance and standard deviation remain unchanged.

Example 5

This example is similar to Example 2 except all dollar values are multiplied by 2.

Solution

The constant factor is

$$F = 2$$

and so

$$E = 2 \times \$20 = \$40$$

$$\text{Var} = 2^2 \times 58.3333 = 233.3333$$

$$\sigma = 2 \times 7.6376 = 15.2753$$

Example 6

A central hospital serves three geographic areas. The expected number of patients and standard deviations are 500, 1000, 2000 and 100, 150, and 210. What are the expected value and standard deviation of the combined number of patients?

Solution

Assuming statistical independence, we obtain

$$E = 500 + 1000 + 2000 = 3500$$

$$\text{Var} = 100^2 + 150^2 + 210^2 = 76,600$$

$$\sigma = \sqrt{76,600} = 276.77$$

3.3 THE UNIFORM PROBABILITY DISTRIBUTION

In many practical problems one can assume that any value of a random variable is just as likely to occur as any other value. For instance, the sales manager may believe that it is equally likely that sales are anywhere between $5 million and $10 million. Or in a bank it may be assumed that customers are equally likely to arrive any time between 10:00 a.m. and 11:00 a.m. In these situations we are dealing with random variables with continuous **uniform distribution**.

Contrast such random variables with the ones considered in Section 3.2. There the values were discrete and finite in number; now the values are continuous and infinite in number.

To develop the theory of such continuous random variables, consider first a wheel of fortune such that the pointer may stop at any point with the same probability. We mark the edge of the wheel with the fractions between 0 and 1 [Figure 3.7(a)]. The corresponding random variable X is equally likely to assume any value between 0 and 1 and is said to be *uniformly* distributed between 0 and 1. The **probability density function** of X is [Figure 3.7(b)]

$$1 \qquad \text{when } 0 \le x \le 1$$

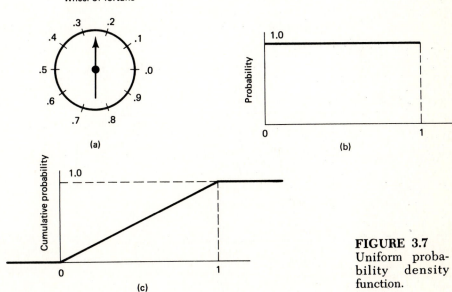

FIGURE 3.7
Uniform probability density function.

and

$$0 \quad \text{otherwise}$$

The cumulative distribution function (CDF) of X is [Figure 3.7(c)]

$$0 \quad \text{for } x < 0$$

$$x \quad \text{for } 0 \leq x \leq 1$$

$$1 \quad \text{for } x \geq 1$$

Meaning of Probability Density Function

We now show how to interpret the uniform probability density functions just introduced. For example, let us ask the question, What is the probability of the event that the needle of the wheel of fortune stops on or between 0 and .1? In other words, what is the probability that the value x of the random variable is between 0 and .1 inclusive. We now introduce abbreviated mathematical notation. The event of x being between 0 and .15 inclusive is written as

$$0 \leq x \leq .15$$

and the corresponding probability as

$$P[0 \leq x \leq .15]$$

To get this probability, consider part (b) of Figure 3.7 as a dart board (shown in Figure 3.8). The total area of the dart board is $1.0 \times 1.0 = 1.0$. The area of the crosshatched rectangle $ABCD$ is $.15 \times 1.0 = .15$. Thus, using the area rule from Chapter 2, we obtain

$$P[0 \leq x \leq .15] = \frac{\text{area of } ABCD}{\text{total area}} = \frac{.15}{1.0} = .15$$

Replace .15 by a general algebraic symbol u where, of course, $u \leq 1$:

$$P[0 \leq x \leq u]$$

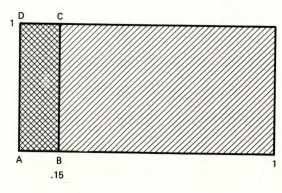

FIGURE 3.8
Dart board model of uniform probability density function.

The quadrangle *ABCD* has a base length of *u* and height of 1, and so

$$P[0 \le x \le u] = u \qquad \text{provided } 0 \le u \le 1$$

By similar argument,

$$P[v \le x \le 1] = 1 - v \qquad \text{provided } 0 \le v \le 1$$

because now the base of the quadrangle has the length of $1 - v$.
Finally,

$$P[u \le x \le v] = v - u$$

provided

$$0 \le u \le 1$$
$$0 \le v \le 1$$

and

$$u \le v$$

What is the probability that *x* is *exactly* .15? Because any value between (and including) 0 and 1 is possible, this probability is zero. Therefore, the symbols $P[u \le x \le v]$, $P[u < x \le v]$, $P[u \le x < v]$, and $P[u < x < v]$ all designate the same value. Note that this is so for the sole reason that we are discussing continuous random variables. For discrete variables you must be careful, because it may make a difference which inequality sign you use.
Note finally that

$$P[0 \le x \le u] = 1 \qquad \text{provided } u \ge 1$$

and that

$$P[x < u] = 0 \qquad \text{provided } u \le 0$$

because the first event is certain, and the second is impossible.

The General Uniform Distribution Function

We now replace 0 by *a* and 1 by *b*, where $b > a$, and consider a continuous random variable *X* such that it is equally likely that *X* assumes any value between *a* and *b* [Figures 3.9 (a) and (b)]. Then *X* is *uniformly* distributed between *a* and *b*. The *probability density* function of *X* is

$$\frac{1}{b - a} \qquad \text{when } a \le x < b$$

and

$$0 \qquad \text{otherwise}$$

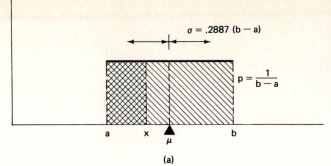

FIGURE 3.9
Uniform probability
density function
and cumulative dis-
tribution function.

(a)

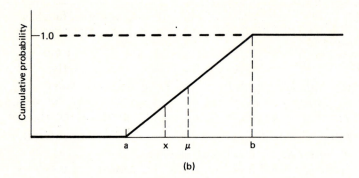

(b)

The *cumulative distribution function* of X is

$$0 \quad \text{for } x < a$$

$$\frac{x - a}{b - a} \quad \text{for } a \le x < b$$

$$1 \quad \text{for } x \ge b$$

as shown in Figure 3.9(b).

The expected value or mean of X can be shown to equal

$$\mu = \frac{a + b}{2}$$

The **range** s is

$$s = b - a$$

The variance can be shown to equal

$$\text{Var} = \frac{(b - a)^2}{12}$$

The standard deviation is

$$\sigma = \sqrt{\text{Var}} = \frac{b - a}{\sqrt{12}} = .2887(b - a) = .2887s$$

The area under the probability density function [the area of the entire quadrangle in Figure 3.9 (a)] equals

$$\text{area} = \text{base} \times \text{height} = (b - a)p$$

but

$$p = \frac{1}{b - a}$$

and therefore we conclude that the area under the uniform probability distribution function equals 1. In fact, this statement holds for *any* probability distribution function.

> The area under any probability distribution function equals 1.

The explanation is that the random variable must assume *some* value and the events are mutually exclusive and collectively exhaustive, so the sum or area must equal 1, representing certainty.

We now derive further probability values for the uniform distribution. The probability that $x < \mu$ is given by the shaded area in Figure 3.10(a):

$$P[x < u] = \frac{u - a}{b - a} \qquad \text{provided } a \leq u \leq b$$

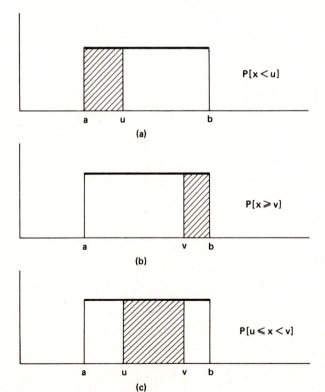

FIGURE 3.10
The shaded area shows various probabilities associated with the uniform probability density function.

The shaded area in part (b) shows

$$P[x \geq v] = \frac{v - a}{b - a}$$

The shaded area in part (c) shows

$$P[u \leq x < v] = \frac{v - u}{b - a}$$

Height Versus Range

The *shape* of probability functions is of great importance to the decision maker. A narrow function means little variability and relatively small uncertainty in the values of the random variable, while a broad function implies a great deal of uncertainty.

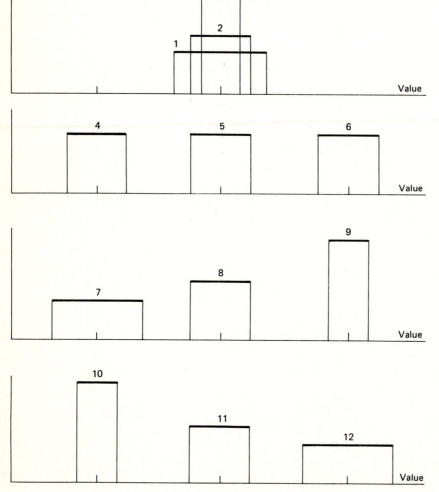

FIGURE 3.11
Comparing 12 uniform probability density functions in terms of the mean, the height, and the range.

For the uniform probability distribution function the area of the rectangle always equals 1, and so the HEIGHT and RANGE of the rectangle are related by

$$\text{HEIGHT} \times \text{RANGE} = 1$$

or

$$\text{HEIGHT} = \frac{1}{\text{RANGE}}$$

meaning that HEIGHT and RANGE are inversely proportional. Thus a high height value implies a narrow range and a low height value a wide range. Figure 3.11 compares 12 uniform distributions. Distributions 1, 2, and 3 have the same mean, increasing height, and decreasing range. Distributions 4, 5, and 6 have increasing mean and the same height and range. Distributions 7, 8, and 9 have increasing mean and increasing height but decreasing range. Distributions 10, 11, and 12 have increasing mean, decreasing height, and increasing range.

An Application

The number of people x crossing a toll bridge daily is uniformly distributed between 10,000 and 30,000 people. Calculate (1) the mean; (2) the range; (3) the variance; (4) the standard deviation; (5) $P_1 = P[x \leq 16,000]$, the probability that less than (or equal to) 16,000 people cross; (6) $p_2 = P[x > 20,000]$, the probability that more than 20,000 people cross; and (7) $p_3 = P[12,000 \leq x \leq 27,000]$, the probability that between 12,000 and 27,000 (inclusive) people cross.

Solution

See Figure 3.12.

$$a = 10,000 \qquad b = 30,000$$

$$\mu = \frac{10,000 + 30,000}{2} = 20,000$$

$$s = 30,000 - 10,000 = 20,000$$

$$\text{Var} = \frac{(30,000 - 10,000)^2}{12} = \frac{20,000^2}{12} = 33,333,333$$

$$\sigma = \frac{20,000}{\sqrt{12}} = 5773.50$$

$$p_1 = \frac{16,000 - 10,000}{20,000} = .3$$

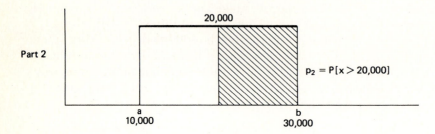

Part 1

$p_1 = P[x \leqslant 10,000]$

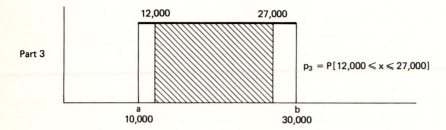

Part 2

$p_2 = P[x > 20,000]$

Part 3

$p_3 = P[12,000 \leqslant x \leqslant 27,000]$

(shaded area in Figure 3.12, part 1),

$$p_2 = \frac{30,000 - 20,000}{20,000} = .5$$

(shaded area in Figure 3.12, part 2), and

$$p_3 = \frac{27,000 - 12,000}{20,000} = .75$$

(shaded area in Figure 3.12, part 3).

3.4 THE DISCRETE UNIFORM PROBABILITY MASS FUNCTION

Consider again the problem of people crossing a bridge. Can this problem really be modeled by a continuous random variable? We cannot have 15,000.35 people crossing the bridge. Of course intuition tells us that we can round off to 15,000 people. But what about a problem where it is equally likely to have 100 to 200 or 50 to 100 people crossing? In this section we present formulas for the expected value, variance, and standard deviation of the discrete uniform random variable. First we present an example.

Example 7: The New Car Dealer Problem

A dealer in new cars sells 0, 1, 2, . . ., 15 cars, respectively, each week. Sales are uniformly distributed from 0 to 15 cars. What is the probability that sales are less than 5 cars or less than or equal to 5 cars? What is the expected value, variance, and standard deviation of sales?

To solve such problems first we need to introduce mathematical notation for the random variable. Designate the following:

n: the number of values
b: the first value
d: the difference between the successive values

In our example

$$n = 16$$

$$a = 0$$

$$d = 1$$

With this notation we can now proceed to the formulas needed.

Formulas

Consider the discrete random variable which assumes n values, starting at a, terminating in b, and always increasing by d, and with the uniform probability of $p = 1/n$. (Figure 3.13)

The difference between the largest and smallest value, the range, is s:

$$s = (n - 1)d = b - a$$

It can be shown that the expected value or mean is

$$\mu = \frac{a + b}{2} = a + \frac{s}{2}$$

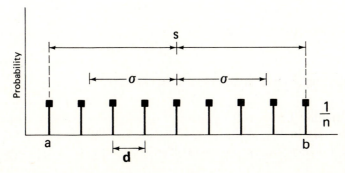

FIGURE 3.13
Uniform probability mass function.

where b is the largest value

$$b = a + (n - 1)d$$

The variance is

$$\text{Var} = \frac{1}{3}\left(\frac{s}{2}\right)^2 \frac{n+1}{n-1} = \frac{1}{12} s^2 \frac{n+1}{n-1}$$

and the standard deviation is

$$\sigma = \sqrt{\text{Var}} = \frac{s}{\sqrt{12}} \sqrt{\frac{n+1}{n-1}} = .2887s \sqrt{\frac{n+1}{n-1}}$$

Comparing these formulas with the uniform continuous distribution, we conclude that the mean and the range are the same but that the variance and standard deviation contain the factors

$$\frac{n+1}{n-1} \quad \text{and} \quad \sqrt{\frac{n+1}{n-1}}$$

When these factors are close to 1, the formulas for the continuous variable give a close approximation.

Solving the New Car Dealer Problem

We have the following solution.

Solution

$$a = 0, \quad d = 1, \quad n = 16, \quad b = 15$$

so

$$P[\text{SALES} < 5] = \tfrac{5}{16} = .3125$$

$$P[\text{SALES} \leq 5] = \tfrac{6}{16} = .3750$$

$$b = b - a = 15 - 0 = 15$$

$$\mu = \frac{a+b}{2} = \frac{0+15}{2} = 7.5$$

$$\text{Var} = \frac{1}{12} s^2 \frac{n+1}{n-1} = \frac{1}{12} \times (15)^2 \times \frac{17}{15} = 21.25$$

$$\sigma = \sqrt{\text{VAR}} = \sqrt{21.25} = 4.61 \text{ cars}$$

Example 8: The Bridge Problem Again

We have

$$a = 10{,}000, \quad d = 1, \quad n = 20{,}001$$

$$b = a + (n-1)d = 10{,}000 + 20{,}000 \times 1 = 30{,}000$$

$$s = b - a = 30,000 - 10,000 = 20,000$$

$$\mu = \frac{10,000 + 30,000}{2} = 20,000$$

All are in agreement with the continuous case. To calculate the variance and standard deviation, we evaluate the factor

$$\frac{n + 1}{n - 1} = \frac{20,002}{20,000} = 1.0001$$

This is so close to 1 that the results given by the continuous random variable can be considered accurate for any practical purpose.

3.5 THE NORMAL DISTRIBUTION

The uniform probability distribution is rectangle-shaped [Figure 3.9 (a)]; the often used **normal distribution** is *bell*-shaped [Figure 3.14 (a)]. It is characterized by the mean μ and the standard deviation σ. Figure 3.15 (which is to be compared with Figure 3.11) shows 12 different normal distributions. The area under each distribution equals 1, so high probability values imply slender bells and small standard deviations and low probability values wide bells and large standard deviations. Distributions 1, 2, and 3 have the same mean but increasing height and

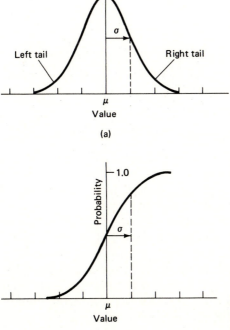

(a)

(b)

FIGURE 3.14
The normal probability density function and cumulative probability distribution function.

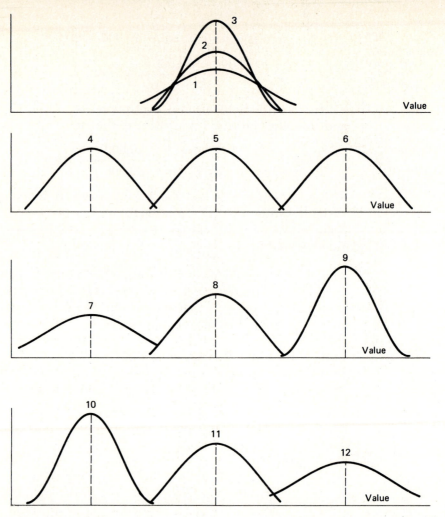

FIGURE 3.15 Comparing 12 normal probability distributions in terms of the mean and standard deviation.

decreasing standard deviation; distributions 4, 5, and 6 have the same height and standard deviation but increasing mean; distributions 7, 8, and 9 have increasing mean and height and decreasing standard deviation; distributions 10, 11, and 12 have increasing mean and standard deviation and decreasing height.

Figure 3.16 compares the uniform and normal distributions with the same mean and standard deviation. As you can see, the two cumulative distributions are not totally unlike, and in fact under some conditions the uniform instead of the normal distribution may be used.

In many practical managerial problems the uniform distribution is actually used, thereby simplifying the computations involved. This practice is particularly common when many random variables are involved and computer-based solutions are used. However practical this

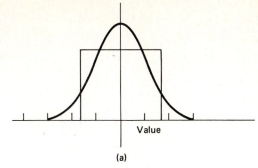

FIGURE 3.16
Comparing the uniform and normal distributions having the same
mean and standard deviation.

Value

(a)

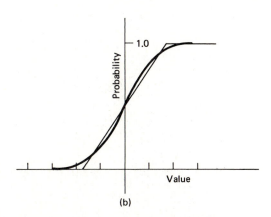

Probability

1.0

Value

(b)

approach, the answers may be suspect, and only using the correct distributions (normal or otherwise) can assure valid answers.

Note, however, that the normal distribution always provides both positive and negative values because the range is from minus to plus infinity. If a manager encounters a negative number of goods sold, even with a small probability, he or she may doubt the validity of the approach. The uniform distribution avoids this difficulty because the range can be set as desired.

The Standard Normal Probability Distribution

While problems with uniform distribution can be solved by formulas, problems with normal distribution require Table 1 of Appendix B. This table provides the areas under the standard normal probability distribution, that is, the normal distribution having a 0 mean and a standard deviation equal to 1 (Figure 3.17). A random experiment will help you understand this table.

Figure 3.18 shows a peculiar, bell-shaped dart board. Note that the shape is precisely the standard normal distribution shown in Figure 3.17. Suppose you are blindfolded and throw a dart against the board at random, keeping in mind that you want to hit the board. If you miss, the throw does not count, and you throw again. Suppose you hit. What is the probability that you hit the crosshatched area of the board left of the line

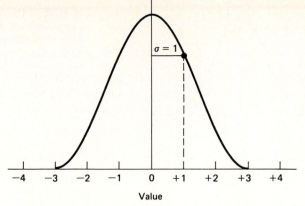

FIGURE 3.17
Standard normal proba-
bility distribution. The
mean equals zero; the
standard deviation equals
1.

AB? Line AB goes through the point $x = 1.53$. Formally speaking, we want to calculate

$$P[x < 1.53]$$

where x is a random variable with the standard normal distribution.

To calculate the probability, we use the area rule described in Section 2.1:

$$P[x < 1.53] = \frac{\text{area under curve left of line } AB}{\text{total area under curve}}$$

But the total area under the curve of any probability distribution is 1, and so

$$P[x < 1.53] = \text{area under the curve left of line } AB$$

This is precisely what is tabulated in Table 1 of Appendix B, and so you can find the answer in Table 1. Here is the procedure.

Enter Table 1, the leftmost column. Run down to the value 1.5.

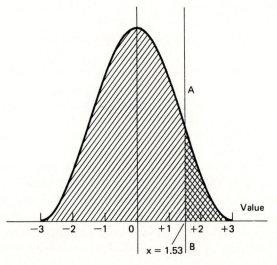

FIGURE 3.18
Dart board model of normal
distribution.

Now move to the right to the column headed by 3. This is the probability you are looking for:

$$P[x < 1.53] = .9370$$

You should become somewhat familiar with the probabilities in the table. Suppose the line AB is moved to the left, to -2. You do not have much chance of hitting the board left of AB. You find

$$P[x < -2.0] = .0228$$

Suppose the line moves to the right to 2.5. You are quite certain you will hit left of the line. Indeed,

$$P[x < 2.5] = .9938$$

Now suppose you want $P[x \leq 1.53]$. You will recall from our previous discussion of continuous distribution that it makes no difference whether we use the symbol $\leq$ or $<$. Thus,

$$P[x \leq 1.53] = P[x < 1.53] = .9938$$

So far we have used Table 1 for the standard normal distribution. Now we show by example how the table is to be used for any normal distribution.

Example

The number of people x crossing a toll bridge daily is normally distributed with a mean of $\mu = 20,000$ and a standard deviation of $\sigma = 5000$. Determine the following probabilities:

$$p_1 = P[x < 27,000]$$
$$p_2 = P[x < 20,000]$$
$$p_3 = P[x < 12,000]$$
$$p_4 = P[x \geq 27,000]$$
$$p_5 = P[x \geq 20,000]$$
$$p_6 = P[x \geq 12,000]$$
$$p_7 = P[12 \leq x < 27,000]$$

Procedure to Solve Problem

Step 1. Compute

$$z = \frac{x - \mu}{\sigma}$$

which gives the value of the random variable measured in standard deviations from the mean.

Step 2. Look up the values corresponding to the limiting x in Table 1 of Appendix B.

Probability $p_1 = P[x < 27,000]$:

$$x = 27,000$$

$$z = \frac{27,000 - 20,000}{5000} = \frac{7000}{5000} = 1.4$$

Table 1 gives .9192. So $p_1 = .9192$ (shaded area in Figure 3.19, part 1).

Probability $p_2 = P[x < 20,000]$:

$$x = 20,000$$

$$z = \frac{20,000 - 20,000}{5000} = 0$$

Table 1 gives .5000. So $p_2 = .5000$ (shaded area in Figure 3.19, part 2).

Probability $p_3 = P[x < 12,000]$:

$$z = \frac{12,000 - 20,000}{5000} = \frac{-2000}{5000} = -.4$$

Table 1 gives .3446. So $p_3 = .3446$ (shaded area in Figure 3.19, part 3).

Probability $p_4 = P[x \geq 27,000]$: This is the unshaded area in part 1

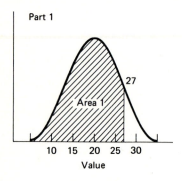

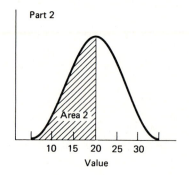

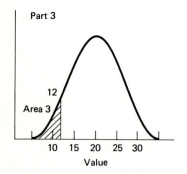

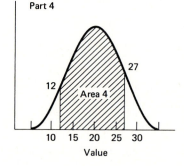

FIGURE 3.19
Various probabilities associated with the problem of crossing a toll bridge.

Figure 3.19. The total area is 1, and so

$$\text{unshaded area} = 1 - \text{shaded area}$$

$$p_4 = 1 - p_1 = 1 - .9192 = .0808$$

Probability $p_5 = P[x \geq 20{,}000]$: This is the unshaded area in Figure 3.19, part 2:

$$P_5 = 1 - .5000 = .5000$$

Probability $p_6 = P[x \geq 12{,}000]$: This is the unshaded area in Figure 3.19, part 3:

$$P_6 = 1 - .3446 = .6554$$

Probability $p_7 = P[12{,}000 \leq x < 27{,}000]$: This is the shaded area in Figure 3.19, part 4:

$$\text{shaded area 4} = \text{shaded area 1} - \text{shaded area 3}$$

and so

$$p_7 = p_1 - p_3 = .9192 - .3446 = .5746$$

Sum of Normally Distributed Random Variables

We have already explained how to add random variables and the rules of computing the expected value, variance, and standard deviation of the sum. Now we state an important theorem:

> The sum of normally distributed random variables is itself normally distributed.

The mean of the sum equals the sum of the means, and if the variables are independent, then the variance equals the sum of the variances.

This theorem is of great importance because it allows us to determine immediately the distribution of the sum. Several exercises will illustrate its usefulness.

3.6 THE BINOMIAL DISTRIBUTION

Toss a fair or biased coin a fixed number of times. Such a sequence of experiments is called a **Bernoulli trial** process. Namely,

1. Each trial (toss) has only two possible outcomes: heads or tails, yes or no, success or failure.
2. The probability of heads or tails, yes or no, success or failure never changes.
3. The trials are statistically independent.

Example

A biased coin has a probability of .6 of landing on heads (or success) and .4 of landing on tails (or failure). Toss the coin five times. What is the probability of tossing exactly three heads (or successes)?

Solution

Figure 3.20 shows the corresponding probability tree. There are 32 tips, and we are interested in tips 4, 6, 7, 10, 11, 13, 18, 19, 21, and 25, a total of 10 tips. To obtain the tip probabilities, we multiply the probabilities leading to each tip. There are three successes and two failures, so the tip probabilities are

$$.6 \times .6 \times .6 \times .4 \times .4 = .03456$$

There are 10 paths, with three successes and two failures (Figure 3.20), and so the probability of three successes and two failures is

$$10 \times .03456 = .3456$$

Formula Approach

Introduce the following notation:

p: probability of success
$q = 1 - p$: probability of failure
r: number of successes specified
n: number of trials

The procedure for calculating the required probability can be stated by the formula

$$\boxed{\text{probability of } r \text{ successes in } n \text{ trials} = \frac{n!}{r!(n-r)!} p^r q^{n-r}}$$

Here the symbol ! designates the factorial and means

$$0! = 1$$
$$1! = 1$$
$$2! = 2 \times 1 = 2$$
$$3! = 3 \times 2 \times 1 = 6$$
$$4! = 4 \times 3 \times 2 \times 1 = 24$$
$$5! = 5 \times 4 \times 3 \times 2 \times 1 = 120$$

and so on.

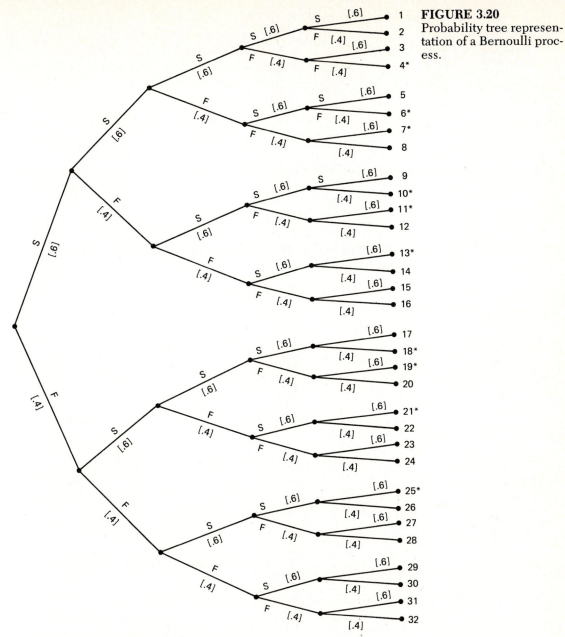

FIGURE 3.20
Probability tree representation of a Bernoulli process.

Example

In our coin-tossing problem,

$$p = .6$$

$$q = 1 - .6 = .4$$

$$r = 3$$

$$n = 5$$

115

so the desired probability is

$$\frac{5!}{3!2!} \times .6^3 \times .4^2 = \frac{5 \times 4 \times 3 \times 2 \times 1}{(3 \times 2 \times 1) \times (2 \times 1)} \times .6^3 \times .4^2$$

$$= \frac{120}{6 \times 2} \times .6^3 \times .4^2 = .3456$$

The Binomial Probability Distribution

Consider again the random experiment of tossing a coin five times. *The number of successes is a discrete random variable.* Designate by p_0, p_1, p_2, p_3, p_4, and p_5 the probability of 0, 1, 2, 3, 4, and 5 successes, respectively. This PMF is called the binomial probability distribution. For our coin-tossing example,

$$p_0 = \frac{5!}{0!5!} \times .6^0 \times .4^5 = .01024$$

$$p_1 = \frac{5!}{1!4!} \times .6 \times .4^4 = .07680$$

$$p_2 = \frac{5!}{2!3!} \times .6^2 \times .4^3 = .23040$$

$$p_3 = \frac{5!}{3!2!} \times .6^3 \times .4^2 = .34560$$

$$p_4 = \frac{5!}{4!1!} \times .6^4 \times .4 = .25920$$

$$p_5 = \frac{5!}{5!0!} \times .6^5 \times .4^0 = .07776$$

Figure 3.21 shows the PMF.

Note that for each number of trials n there is a different discrete random variable, PMF, and binomial probability distribution.

The Cumulative Binomial Distribution

What is the probability that in our coin experiment the number of successes is more than or equal to 3? Clearly,

$$P[S \geq 3] = p_3 + p_4 + p_5 = .34560 + .25920 + .07776 = .68256$$

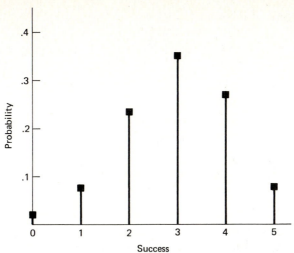

FIGURE 3.21
Probability mass function
(PMF) of a binomial proba-
bility distribution.

Table Lookup Approach

You can save a great deal of computational work by using Table 2 of Appendix B, which provides values for the cumulative probability distribution.

Example 1

Suppose

$$n = 10$$

$$r = 4$$

$$p = .3$$

What is the probability of having four or less than four successes?

Solution

The leftmost column of Table 2 of Appendix B shows n. The first grouping is for $n = 5$ and the second for $n = 10$. This is the one we need.

The next column to the right shows the value of r. We need $r = 4$. In this row we move to the right until we reach the column headed by $p = .30$. Here we find the desired probability, .84973.

Example 2

What is the probability in Example 1 of having five or more successes?

Solution

The two events are mutually exclusive, and so the desired probability is

$$1 - .84973 = .15027$$

Example 3

What is the probability in Example 1 of having exactly five or six successes?

Solution

probability[five or six successes] = probability[six or less than six successes] − probability[four or less than four successes] = $p_6 - p_4$

From Table 2 we get

$$p_6 = .98941$$

We already have

$$p_4 = .84973$$

and so the desired probability is

$$.98941 - .84973 = .13968$$

Example 4

Consider again our coin-tossing experiment. Here the probability of success is .6, and Table 2 gives values only for $p \le .50$. However, you can use the table by recognizing that the probability of having *three or more successes* is the same as having *two or fewer failures*. So we need values from Table 2 for

$$n = 5$$
$$r = 2$$
$$p = .4$$
$$q = .6$$

We find the value .68256 in agreement with our previous result.

The Contractor's Problem

A swimming pool contractor bids on 15 pools, each at $10,000. The probability of a contract award is .3, and winning contracts is statistically independent. Determine the following success probabilities:

$$p_1 = P[S \le 5]$$
$$p_2 = P[S > 5]$$
$$p_3 = P[S \le 6]$$
$$p_4 = P[S = 6]$$

Solution

Using Table 2, we obtain

$$p_1 = .72162$$

Clearly,

$$p_1 + p_2 = 1$$

so

$$p_2 = 1 - p_1 = 1 - .72162 = .27838$$

From Table 2,

$$p_3 = .86886$$

Clearly,

$$P[S = 6] = P[S \leq 6] - P[S \leq 5] = p_3 - p_1$$
$$= .86886 - .72162 = .14724$$

Expected Value, Variance, and Standard Deviation of Successes

It can be shown that

$$\mu = np$$
$$\text{Var} = npq$$
$$\sigma = \sqrt{npq}$$

Example

A contractor bids on 100 jobs, each worth $10,000. The process of capturing contracts is a Bernoulli process with $p = .3$. What are the expected number of successes and standard deviation of successes and the expected sales and the standard deviation of sales?

Solution

The givens are

$$n = 100, \quad p = .3, \quad q = .7$$

so the expected number of successes is

$$\mu = np = 100 \times .3 = 30$$

and the standard deviation of successes is

$$\sigma = \sqrt{npq} = \sqrt{100 \times .3 \times .7} = \sqrt{21} = 4.5826$$

Sales are also a random variable, and this second random variable is obtained from the first one (the number of successes) by multiplying by a factor of 10,000, as each success is worth $10,000. In Section 3.1 we stated the theorem that if a random variable is multiplied by a factor F, then both the expected value and standard deviation are to be multiplied by the same factor F. Thus in our problem the factor $F = 10,000$, and the expected value of sales is given by

$$10,000\mu = 10,000 \times 30 = \$300,000$$

and standard deviation of sales is

$$10,000\sigma = 10,000 \times 4.5826 = \$45,826$$

Binomial Versus Normal Distribution

We state the following theorem:

> For large n the binomial distribution can be approximated by a normal distribution with
>
> $$\mu = np$$
>
> and
>
> $$\sigma = \sqrt{npq}$$

How large should n be? In computer-based analysis often $n = 13$ is considered large enough, provided p is close enough to 1/2. Figure 3.22 compares the binomial distribution $n = 13$, $p = q = \frac{1}{2}$ with the normal distribution when

$$\mu = np = 13 \times \tfrac{1}{2} = 6.5$$

$$\sigma = \sqrt{npq} = 13 \times \tfrac{1}{2} \times \tfrac{1}{2} = 1.8028$$

More specifics about the closeness of this approximation are given in the exercises.

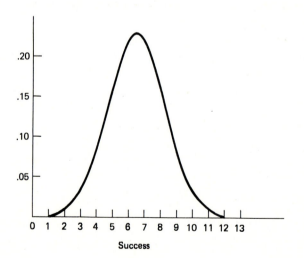

FIGURE 3.22
Comparing the binomial distribution with $n = 13$ with the normal distribution.

Q. *I am still not clear as to what a random variable is.*

A. I don't blame you. It took me years to master the concept. You know what a probability mass function (PMF) is. You can forget about the expression *random variable* and think simply in terms of the PMF. Just as a criminal is characterized by a thumb print, a discrete random variable is characterized by the PMF. When you consider the discrete random variable X, you can think of X as the name of a wheel of fortune like the one in Figure 3.1. As I said before, the values $x_1, x_2, \ldots$ are the numbers written on the wheel.

Q. *Is the random variable a basic concept?*

A. Indeed it is. The concept of the *variable* is a most basic concept of mathematics. When there is no uncertainty, we have deterministic variables; otherwise we have random variables. In each mathematical model there are variables and of course constants. We speak of controllable, uncontrollable, decision variables, and so on.

Q. *What are some other basic concepts?*

A. There are two more. *Functions* are procedures for relating variables to each other. For example, we ask how profit depends on price. What is the profit function? *Algorithms* we discussed in Chapter 1. These are step-by-step procedures for obtaining answers. If you get the concepts (1) variable, (2) function, and (3) algorithm straight, you are in good shape.

Q. *You said the expected value may not necessarily occur as an outcome. Why is it called "expected?"*

A. The word comes from the frequency interpretation of probability. The long-run average value from repeated experiments will be close to the *expected* value.

Q. *What about the concept of a continuous random variable and the probability density function?*

A. Think about a dart board experiment as in Figures 3.8, 3.10, 3.12, 3.18, and 3.19. The bottom of the board is straight, the top is the probability density function, and the area of the board is 1.

Q. *Are there other important probability distributions not covered here?*

A. Yes, there are many of them: the triangular, Poisson, beta, gamma, and hypergeometric distributions, just to mention a few.

Q. *Why didn't you say more about techniques of data collection and analysis?*

A. They are proper subjects for statistics. The science of collecting, summarizing, sampling, estimating, and hypothesis testing are all covered in courses in statistics. Here we cover only the interface between statistics and quantitative approaches to management.

Q. *You showed how to add the random variables* X *and* Y. *How about multiplying?*

A. Yes, you can multiply, divide, and combine random variables in many ways. We shall treat the subject in Chapter 5. But if you use models of probability trees, you will see that the problem is not really difficult.

Q. *How do I know which probability distribution to use?*

A. You need data and statistical analysis to fit the best probability distribution. For theoretical reasons the normal distribution is often preferred, though for computational purposes the uniform distribution is often used because of its convenience. However, in many real-life situations past data are analyzed, and an empirical probability distribution is constructed, which is then used in the analysis.

Q. *When you add two uniform distributions, do you get a new uniform distribution?*

A. No! This holds only for normal distribution. However, if you add many identical, including uniform distributions, it can be shown that you get approximately a normal distribution.

Q. *Can you think of any traps I should be particularly careful to avoid?*

A. People often assume that all distributions are normal or at least symmetrical. Another common trap is to disregard variability (standard deviation) and work only with expected values. This may lead to wrong answers. In fact, often when making decisions under uncertainty, it is not even enough to consider both the expected value and the standard deviation. You need the entire distribution, as you will see later.

Q. *One last question. All this business of looking up numbers in tables and using formulas bores me. Is there a shortcut?*

A. Yes, many organizations provide computer-based tables and formulas. All you need do is call the table or formula and enter the numbers. The computer presents the answers.

SUMMARY

1. A random variable is defined via the probability distribution function.

2. A discrete random variable is defined via the probability mass function (PMF).

3. The expected or mean value of the discrete random variable X is

$$\mu = E(X) = p_1 x_1 + p_2 x_2 + \cdots p_n x_n$$

4. The variance is

$$\text{Var} = E[(X - \mu)^2]$$

$$= p_1(x_1 - \mu)^2 + p_2(x_2 - \mu)^2 + \cdots + p_n(x_n - \mu)^2$$

5. The standard deviation is

$$\sigma = \sqrt{\text{Var}}$$

6. If X, Y, and so on are random variables, then

$$E(X + Y + \cdots) = E(X) + E(Y) + \cdots$$

7. If X is a random variable and C and F are constants, then

$$E(C + X) = C + E(X)$$

and

$$E(FX) = FE(X)$$

Also

$$\text{Var}(C + X) = C + \text{Var}(X)$$

and

$$\text{Var}(FX) = F^2 \, \text{Var}(X)$$

Furthermore,

$$\sigma(C + X) = \sigma(X)$$

$$\sigma(FX) = F\sigma(X)$$

8. If X, Y, and so on are independent random variables, then

$$\text{Var}(X + Y + \cdots) = \text{Var}(X) + \text{Var}(Y) + \cdots$$

9. For a uniformly distributed continuous random variable, the probability of assuming any of the possible values between the given limits is constant.

10. For the uniformly distributed continuous random variables,

$$\mu = \frac{a + b}{2}$$

$$\text{Var} = \frac{(b - a)^2}{12}$$

$$\sigma = \frac{b - a}{\sqrt{12}}$$

$$P[u \le x < v] = \frac{v - u}{b - a}, \qquad a \le u < v \le b$$

where a and b are the lower and upper limits of the random variable.

11. For the uniformly distributed discrete random variable,

$$s = b - a$$

$$\mu = \frac{a + b}{2} = a + \frac{s}{2}$$

$$\text{Var} = \frac{1}{12} s^2 \frac{n + 1}{n - 1}$$

$$\sigma = \frac{s}{\sqrt{12}} \sqrt{\frac{n + 1}{n - 1}}$$

where b is the largest and a the smallest of n values, and s is the range.

12. The normal distribution characterized by the mean μ and standard deviation σ is one of the most commonly used probability functions.

13. In practical applications of the normal distribution one uses tables (Table 1 in Appendix B) or the computer.

14. The sum of normally distributed variables is normal.

15. The probability of r successes in n trials equals

$$\frac{n!}{r!(n - r)!} p^r q^{n-r}$$

where p and q are the probabilities of success and failure, respectively.

16. The probability mass function (PMF) of 0, 1, 2, 3, and so on successes of n trials is called the binomial probability distribution.

17. The expected value, variance, and standard deviation of the binomial probability distribution are

$$\mu = np$$

$$\text{Var} = npq$$

$$\sigma = \sqrt{npq}$$

18. In practical application of the binomial distribution one uses tables (Table 2 in Appendix B) or the computer.

19. For a large n the binomial distribution can be approximated by a normal distribution with

$$\mu = np$$

$$\sigma = \sqrt{npq}$$

SECTION EXERCISES

1.   *Random Variables*

1.1   Refer to Figure 3.1. Assume that the chance experiment described in Figure 3.1(a) and the related text of 3.1 is changed so that the values and probabilities are as follows:

Values of payoff	Probabilities
$20	1/3
$50	1/6
$80	1/6
$100	1/3

   a. What is the random variable?
   b. What are the outcomes of the chance experiments? [List as in Figure 3.1(b).]
   c. Describe the probability mass function in symbols as in the text.
   d. Draw the probability distribution function for this experiment using Figure 3.1(c) as a guide.
   e. Describe the cumulative mass function in symbols as in the text.
   f. Draw the cumulative distribution function using Figure 3.1(d) as a guide.

1.2   Refer to Figure 3.1. Assume that the probabilities have changed as described in the following probability distribution function:

$$P[\$5] = \tfrac{1}{2} \qquad P[\$15] = \tfrac{3}{8} \qquad P[\$20] = \tfrac{1}{8} \qquad P[\$30] = 0$$

   a. What is the random variable?
   b. What are the outcomes of this experiment? [List as in Figure 3.1(b).]
   c. Describe the experiment with a drawing similar to Figure 3.1(a).
   d. Draw the probability mass function for this experiment using Figure 3.1(c) as a guide.
   e. Describe the cumulative distribution function using Figure 3.1(d) as a guide.

1.3   During the vacation season, the Hondius Park Environmental Control Board issues licenses to anglers who wish to fish for the rare spetzelfish in the park. The director of the board models occurrences each day as a chance experiment since he never knows exactly how many people will apply for licenses. Records show that they never have 0, 1, or 2 people apply or more than 7. Examination of the records indicates that the same number of days are recorded for 3, 4, 5, 6, and 7 people.
   a. Based on this information, what outcomes of the experiment can be used to model this process?
   b. What is the probability mass function for this experiment (show both numerically and graphically)?
   c. What is the cumulative distribution function for this experiment (show both numerically and graphically)?

1.4   Definitions of four random variables are given in I through IV:
   I. The random variable of Exercise 1.1.
   II. The random variable of Exercise 1.2.
   III. The random variable, the number of people applying for licenses, of Exercise 1.3.

IV. The probability mass function for the number of cars per minute arriving at a toll booth on the Pestabuda Bridge is

$$P[0] = .606 \qquad P[2] = .076$$
$$P[1] = .303 \qquad P[3] = .013$$
$$P[4] = .002$$

For these random variables,
a. Compute the mean as done in Figure 3.2
b. Make a probability tree similar to Figure 3.5.
c. Use the probability tree found in part b to obtain the expected value. Show your computation.
d. Compute the variance.
e. Compute the standard deviation.

1.5 What does the variance tell us about a probability mass function?
1.6 Verify the following values for standard deviation:
a. $P[1] = .5$, $P[0] = .5$; $\sigma = .5$.
b. $P[0] = .779$, $P[1] = .195$, $P[2] = .024$, $P[3] = .002$; $\sigma = .5$.

1.7 Find the variance and standard deviation for the random variable defined in
a. Exercise 1.1.   c. Exercise 1.3.
b. Exercise 1.2.   d. Part IV of Exercise 1.4.

2. *Applications of Random Variables*
2.1 Refer to Example 1 in text Section 3.2. The number of times one ship was unloaded was 40 times, and the number of times two ships were unloaded was 80. What is the expected value of ships unloaded per day?
2.2 Refer to Example 2 in text Section 3.2. The salesperson's record for the most recent years was

Bad earnings: 3 times
So-so earnings: 8 times
Good earnings: 5 times
Excellent earnings: 0 times

Determine the expected value, variance, and standard deviation of quarterly earnings.
2.3 Refer to Example 4 in text Section 3.2. Add an additional $10 to all the dollar values of this example. Compute the new values of expected value, variance, and standard deviation.
2.4 Refer to Example 5 in text Section 3.2. Multiply the values obtained there by .6. Compute the new values of expected value, variance, and standard deviation.
2.5 Refer to Example 6 in text Section 3.2. Assume that the expected number of patients and standard deviation are 1200, 1600, and 3200 and 300, 900, and 1000. What is the expected value and standard deviation of the combined number of patients?
2.6 Refer to Example 3 in text Section 3.2 concerning a corporation which sells goods in both the north and the south. Assume that the random variable Y is defined by the PMF

$$P[\$5] = \tfrac{2}{3} \qquad P[\$10] = \tfrac{1}{3}$$

Assuming that all other conditions remain the same, find the PMF for Z,

the total sales in both the south and the north:
  a. Make a table for this situation similar to Figure 3.6a.
  b. Draw a probability tree like Figure 3.6b.
  c. Summarize the PMF of Z in a table similar to Figure 3.6c.
  d. Find the expected values of X, Y, and Z by direct computation.
  e. Find the variances and standard deviations of X, Y, and Z by direct computation.
  f. What conclusions can you draw about the expected value of Z with respect to X and Y?
  g. What conclusions can you draw about the variance of Z with respect to X and Y?

2.7 Verify your results in Exercise 2.6 using the rules for the expected value and variance of the sum of random variables given in text Section 3.2.

2.8 If someone offered to gamble with you on the toss of a coin with (1) heads, you pay them $10 and (2) tails, they pay you $5, you would not play. Interpret your reason for not playing in terms of expected value. What is the expected value of a fair game?

2.10 An insurance company will insure your life for $3 on a particular trip, meaning that they will pay $20,000 to your beneficiary if you do not survive the trip because of an airline accident.
  a. What is the *maximum* probability they have assigned to a fatal airline accident to you on this trip?
  b. Why is this the maximum value, and what are the additional factors that may be involved?

3. **The Uniform Probability Distribution**

3.1 Refer to the discussion of the principles of the general uniform distribution in text Section 3.3. Assume that $a = 0$, and give formulas for
  a. The probability density function
  b. The cumulative distribution function
  c. The expected value
  d. The width (or range)
  e. The variance
  f. The standard deviation
  g. The probability that $x \leq u$

3.2 Refer to the application in the text concerning the number of people crossing a toll bridge daily. Assume that the number of people crossing is uniformly distributed between 2300 and 9800. Calculate the mean, range, variance, and standard deviation.

4. **The Discrete Uniform Probability Mass Function**

4.1 Refer to Example 7 in text Section 3.4, the new car dealer problem. Assume that the dealer sells 1, 2, . . . , 8 cars each week, sales being uniformly distributed between 1 and 8. What is the probability that sales are
  a. Less than 5 cars?
  b. Less than or equal to 5 cars?

4.2 Refer to Exercise 4.1. What is the expected value, variance, and standard deviation of sales?

4.3 Refer to Exercise 3.2. Follow the text analysis of Example 8 in text Section 3.4 for the values given in Exercise 3.2, finding the mean, variance, and standard deviation. What conclusions do you draw?

4.4 To select a simple random sample of homeowners to estimate the mean percentage of mortgage payments, the Municipal Reserve Board of Dingchester Township has numbered all 1000 homeowners from 1 to 1000. Tags bearing these numbers have been thrown into a large barrel mounted on a barbeque spit; the barrel is rotated to thoroughly mix the tags. To determine a homeowner to be included in the sample, a tag is chosen at random from the barrel.

    a. What kind of uniform distribution is thereby created (discrete or continuous)?

    b. What is the probability that any one homeowner will be included in the sample?

    c. What is the range of the distribution?

    d. What is the mean of the distribution?

    e. What is the standard deviation of the distribution?

    f. What is the probability that homeowners who have numbers of 586 or higher will be chosen in the sample?

5. The Normal Distribution

5.1 Maintenance payments for condominiums in Miasma Beach are normally distributed with a mean of $\mu = \$290$ and $\sigma = \$40$. Determine the following probabilities:

    a. $P[\text{maintenance payments} < \$230]$

    b. $P[\text{maintenance payments} < \$210]$

    c. $P[\text{maintenance payments} \geq \$410]$

    d. $P[\text{maintenance payments} \geq \$250]$

5.2 The pay X of municipal employees in Miasma Beach is normally distributed with a mean of $\$340$ and a standard deviation of $\$25$. Find the following probabilities:

    a. $P[X < \$350]$

    b. $P[\$315 \leq X < \$390]$

    c. $P[X \geq \$150]$

5.3 The city inspector of weights is about to inspect the output of a candy factory. The factory produces boxes of candy that have an advertised net weight of 500 grams. The factory's record shows a standard deviation of 20 grams and that the distribution of weights is normally distributed.

    a. If the inspector will reject any packages that have a net weight below 470 grams, what proportion of the packages that he inspects can he expect to reject?

    b. The manager of the factory decides that he does not want to have the inspector reject more than .01 of the packages inspected. To what level should the mean of the process be set?

6. The Binomial Distribution

6.1 Consider the example of the biased coin which starts Section 3.6. Assume that the coin has a probability of .7 of coming up heads. Toss the coin four times.

    a. What is the probability of exactly three heads?

    b. Draw the corresponding probability tree, referring to Figure 3.20.

    c. Solve by using the formula approach.

    d. Obtain the complete PMF for this situation.

    e. Is this PMF a binomial probability distribution?

    f. Draw the PMF, referring to Figure 3.21.

    g. What is the probability that the number of successes is more than or equal to 3?

    h. Verify your answers using the table lookup approach.

6.2 Consider Example 1 in Section 3.6. Let $n = 8$, $r = 3$, and $p = .2$.

    a. What is the probability of having four or fewer successes?

    b. What is the probability of having five or more successes?

    c. What is the probability of having exactly five or six successes?

6.3 Refer to Example 4 in Section 3.6. If the probability of success is .8 and $n = 5$, what is the probability of two successes?

6.4 Refer to the contractor's problem in Section 3.6. Assume that the contractor bids on 20 pools, each valued at $15,000. The probability of a contract award is .4, and winning contracts is statistically independent. Determine the following success probabilities:

  a. $P[S \leq 5]$
  b. $P[S > 5]$
  c. $P[S \leq 6]$
  d. $P[S = 6]$

6.5 What are the expected value, variance, and standard deviation for

  a. Exercise 6.1?
  b. Exercise 6.2?
  c. Exercise 6.3?
  d. Exercise 6.4?

6.6 An artful Dodger has a batting average of .4; this represents his historical record which may be interpreted as the probability that he will get a hit each time at bat. If he goes to bat five times, what are the probabilities for the following possible outcomes:

  a. No hits
  b. One hit
  c. At least three hits
  d. Fewer than four hits

6.7 A new cure for a disease has cured 60% of the patients suffering from the disease. Twelve patients are now being treated with the cure. What is the probability that

  a. All the patients will be cured?
  b. None of the patients will be cured?
  c. At least 1 patient will be cured?
  d. Exactly 2 patients will be cured?
  e. More than 3 patients will be cured?
  f. Eight or fewer patients will be cured?
  g. Ten or more patients will be cured?

6.8 The production line at a factory has been producing 10% defective units of a new product. Quality control takes samples of five units at regular intervals.

  a. What is the expected value of the number of defective units per sample of five?
  b. What is the standard deviation of the number of defective units per sample of five?
  c. What is the probability of no defective units in a sample?

6.9 A biased coin has a probability of .7 of coming up heads. If the coin is tossed four times, what is the probability of

  a. Getting four heads?
  b. Getting two heads?
  c. Getting three heads?

  (Use the formula approach.)

6.10 For the coin of Exercise 6.9, draw a probability tree similar to Figure 3.20. If you have done Exercise 6.9, verify your formula results.

6.11 For the coin of Exercise 6.9,

  a. Draw the PMF, making a graph similar to Figure 3.21.
  b. Determine the cumulative distribution function, and make a graphic representation similar to Figure 3.1(d).

6.12 If you have done either Exercise 6.9 or 6.10, verify the results by table lookup.

6.13 Refer to the contractor's problem discussed in Section 3.6. Assume that the probability of contract award is estimated to be .45 and that the contractor is bidding on 10 pools, each at $10,000. The probability of winning contracts is statistically independent.

a. Determine the following probabilities:
    i. $P[S \leq 5]$
    ii. $P[S > 5]$
    iii. $P[S \leq 6]$
    iv. $P[S = 6]$

b. What is the expected value of sales?

c. What is the standard deviation of sales?

d. Compare the results of parts a, b, and c which duplicate the results found in the text of Section 3.6 for different probabilities of success and number of trials; discuss. (For example, which situation would you prefer to invest in?)

6.14 The normal distribution is often used to find binomial probabilities using the approximation theorem given in Section 3.6. In the text the statement is made that $n = 13$ is "often" considered large enough. To make this statement more precise and to determine the nature of the approximation, complete the following table:

$n = 13, p = .4$ CUMULATIVE PROBABILITIES

x	EXACT BINOMIAL	NORMAL APPROXIMATION
0		
2		
4		
6		
8		
10		

6.15 Repeat Exercise 6.14 for $n = 13$ and $p = .2$.

6.16 Repeat Exercise 6.14 for $n = 6$ and $p = .5$.

6.17 Repeat Exercise 6.14 for $n = 6$ and $p = .2$.

7. *A Dialog*

7.1 Give another example of a random variable different from the one given in the first question in Section 3.7. Take an example from games of chance.

7.2 In what way is the telephone directory a probability mass function?

7.3 The definition of expected value given in the fourth question and answer pair is circular. Explain why, and give a definition you like better, thinking in terms of a gambler. (*Note:* A circular definition is one which uses the word being defined.)

7.4 Find a book which discusses one of the other probability distributions mentioned in the sixth question and answer pair of Section 3.7, and describe it. Draw a PDF, and tell how and where it might be used.

CHAPTER EXERCISES AND DISCUSSION QUESTIONS

C1. T. H. Rani sells carpets in Carrizozo. He obtained an MBA from Yale and now models each day's activities as a chance experiment. Records he keeps show that it is reasonable for him to assume that the probability mass function for the business is as follows:

X, TOTAL DAILY REVENUE ($000)	PROBABILITY, P[X]
0	.17
1	.36
2	.31
3	.13
4	.02
5	.01

a. What is the expected daily revenue from this business activity?
b. What is the variance of the daily revenue from this business activity?
c. If Rani has three identical stores in similar cities, what is the total expected daily revenue from all three?
d. For part c, what is the variance of the total daily revenue?

C2 Refer to Exercise C1, the one-store case. The success of the rug business in Carrizozo has led the town council to put a *progressive* tax on revenues of rug stores. A progressive tax is one which raises the rate of taxation as the amount of revenue increases. The schedule of the new tax is as follows:

STORE'S DAILY REVENUE ($000)	AMOUNT OF TAX ($000)
0	0
1	0
2	.3
3	.8
4	1.5
5	2.5

a. What is the expected value of the owner's net revenue with this tax in effect?
b. What is the variance of the owner's net revenue with this tax in effect?
c. Looking at this situation from the standpoint of the town government, what is the expected daily revenue from this tax?
d. Following up on part c, what is the variance of the town's daily revenue?
e. A businessman enlisted the support of a local representative and was able to get the progressive tax dropped, and a flat 10% tax was imposed. The tax is 10% of the daily revenues, whatever they may be. Use the appropriate formula from the text, and find the expected value of the net daily revenue under this new tax.
f. Refer to part e. What is the variance of the net daily revenue under this new tax?
g. T. H. Rani's enthusiasm for the new, nonprogressive 10% tax on all revenues was lessened when he found that he now had to keep more comprehensive records costing $50 per day. What is the expected value of the net revenue taking into account the flat 10% tax and the added costs?
h. What is the variance of the net revenue under the conditions of part g?

C3. The Offshore Revenue Service (ORS) of Lower Vaynig has five revenue agents collecting taxes from the mussel farmers; experience shows that the five agents—as a consequence of their territories and respective diligence—have expected returns to the ORS of $75,000, $80,000, $30,000, $25,000, and $100,000 a year each. The standard deviation of all agents, surprisingly enough, is the same: $5000.

    a. What is the expected combined return from all five agents?

    b. What is the standard deviation of the combined return from all five agents?

    c. The governing council of Lower Vaynig is meeting to estimate the total revenue from the agents of the ORS for the coming year. As pointed out by their consultant, they must take into account that the expected values and standard deviations given are in 1976 dollars and that for the next year it is expected that the rise above 1976 will be 180%, due to inflation. Compute the expected combined revenue for the next year in current dollars.

C4. Some manufacturing processes involve a final step after which the manufactured items are inspected to see if any are beyond tolerance limits. Those which are outside tolerance limits are thrown away. The result is a uniform distribution of the characteristic of interest in the remaining items. For example, low-cost resistors for electrical circuits are sold according to their tolerance. A factory has produced a lot of 1000-ohm resistors to a ±10% tolerance; all resistors outside those limits are discarded. The result is a uniform distribution in the range 1000 ohms ± 10%.

    a. What is the mean of this distribution?

    b. What is the range of this distribution in ohms?

    c. What is the variance of this distribution?

    d. What is the standard deviation of this distribution?

    e. An engineer wishes to build a circuit that will not work if the resistor he picks is outside the limits of ±5% of the nominal value of 1000 ohms. What is the probability that a resistor picked at random lies within that range?

    f. After the resistors are purchased by a manufacturing organization, they discover that they cannot use any resistor with values above 1075 ohms. What proportion of the resistors they have purchased can they expect to have to discard?

4

Art and Science of Forecasting

When you pick up a popular business journal or magazine and examine the contents, you find that much of the material is historical and descriptive. But much is concerned with forecasting or predicting the future. For the manager and decision maker the most important thing is to look ahead, because all decisions are made with the intent of impacting on the future. So managers study the business outlook, the Washington outlook, predictions of recession or prosperity, inflation, competitors, and so on. Today business people rely heavily on forecasts based on quantitative technique, economic theory, and econometric models.

Man was always much occupied with predicting the future. Joseph deciphered the Pharoah's dream about the seven fat-fleshed kine (cows) and seven lean-fleshed kine and was rewarded by being made governor over the land. The Oracle of Delphi swayed the decisions of Roman emperors and soothsayers; fortune tellers and astrologers have been much in vogue for thousands of years. Even today practically every newspaper carries daily astrological forecasts. So there is nothing new about forecasting; what is new is that today scientific methods are available to make better forecasts with greater degrees of confidence and credibility.

Bear in mind that every manager is looking to the future and so must intuitively forecast and predict. A sales forecast is fundamental to the success of any business enterprise, but often the words sales budget or sales goal are used, although these words may really mean something different. The trend today is to make forecasting more formal and more explicit and to establish specific and well-articulated procedures for forecasting. More and more often a corporate policy states who is to make the forecast, who controls and approves it, and how the forecast is to be used. The question, then, is not *whether* to forecast or not but *how* to forecast and how *explicit* should the forecasting procedure be.

Quantitative analysis of business problems aims to provide decision makers with information, so they can better conduct their business. But information about the past and present is not enough, as they need information about the future, which requires explicit and formal techniques of forecasting.

Forecasting is fundamental to quantitative approaches to management.

In this chapter we review the most commonly used quantitative techniques of forecasting in business.

4.1 HOW BUSINESS FORECASTS

Quantitative analysis provides information for decision makers and must blend in with judgmental aspects of decision making. Therefore, before we present quantitative forecasting techniques, we must say a few words on how forecasting fits into the business world.

Why Forecasting?

Suppose you are introducing a new product and want to plan product development. It would make no sense to introduce the product unless you are convinced that there is a market for the product and you have some estimate as to the quantity in which the product will sell. You want to know something before you go ahead about the success or failure of similar products and how much money you should allocate to research and development efforts. You also want to know how the product will fit into the market 5 or 10 years from now and the type of actions you would expect from competitors.

After the product is developed and you are faced with the issue of introducing the product into the market, you will ask many questions. What will the marketing plan be? Which markets should you enter and in what quantity? How much manufacturing capacity will be required? As demand grows, how should capacity be expanded?

After the product is introduced, there will, you hope, be a rapid growth in sales. What will this growth be? How long will the rapid growth rate prevail? At what level and at what time will sales level off? When will there be a need to redesign or phase out the product?

Every one of these questions can be answered only if forecasts and predictions for the future are made.

Factors Influencing a Sales Forecast

You need to distinguish between two classes of factors: the **uncontrollables,** which cannot be influenced by managers, and the **controllables,** which are subject to decision making. First we review five examples of uncontrollable factors.

1. Past sales volume

2. Economic indicators for the world and for the United States, the gross national product, related industries, personal income, employment, prices, industrial production, interest rates, etc.

3. The logical and mathematical relationship connecting sales and other factors with general economic indicators

4. Past competition

5. Broad trends of growth and decrease and long-range economic variability, such as business cycles

While decision makers cannot control these factors, forecasts are required so appropriate decisions can be made on the controllable factors. Six examples of controllable factors, that is, decision variables, are

1. Product selection

2. Pricing policies

3. Advertising and promotional budget

4. Size and quality of production and sales force

5. Production capacity

6. Inventory levels

Note that controllable factors are subject to decisions; so we also call them **decision variables.**

What to Forecast

Before a forecasting system can be developed, one must examine what and how business decisions will be made and by whom. That is, the business requirement for the forecast must be established. Is there need for a short- or long-range forecast? How many periods should the forecast include? Should it be yearly, quarterly, monthly? What variables should be forecast?

There is also a need to know what the output of the forecasting system should be. Is it adequate to predict expected values of sales? Should high (maximum) value and low (minimum) value also be forecast?

Is it necessary to provide alternative estimates in addition to single estimates? Or should it be stated that the forecast value of sales is so and so and that the probability is 90% that sales will be within certain upper and lower bounds. Should the standard deviation of the probability mass function of sales be forecast? Or is it necessary to go into more detail and forecast the entire probability mass function (PMF)?

Before going into further details, we should discuss various forecasting approaches.

Forecasting Approaches

It is useful to classify forecasting approaches into two classes: **judgmental** and **statistical**.

Judgmental Approach to Forecasting

You must realize that there is always judgment involved in a forecasting system. The question is to what degree judgment enters into the system. Quantitative analysis serves to sharpen and make more reliable forecasts and thereby support decision makers.

It is common business practice to have those responsible for sales participate in preparing the forecast. Thus, often individual salespersons and district sales managers provide input to the system. Previous sales volumes are examined, extraordinary events are pinpointed, and discussions about prospective sales are held. Also the market research group usually plays a major role in the preparation of sales forecasts. Finally, tentative sales forecasts are presented to high-level executives, and by judgment a consensus on the final sales forecasts is reached.

Judgmental forecasting is a basic step in looking into the future, and the additional benefits from the process of developing these forecasts are (1) articulating the participants' thinking, (2) broadening and firming up opinion, (3) creating a consensus, and (4) reaching a workable plan based on the forecast.

Judgmental forecasting is particularly suited to long-range forecasting (many years) where regularities of the past are not too significant. On the other hand, statistical forecasting is most applicable to short-range time spans (months).

Statistical Approach to Forecasting

Our main concern in this chapter is to present quantitative techniques of forecasting based on the statistical analysis of past data. The basic objective is to examine and analyze past data and establish patterns in the data which will then be applied to the future.

Statistical techniques attempt to extrapolate the past into the future and to exploit our fundamental belief that regularities underlying the past will also prevail in the future or at least in the near future. Such extrapolation of past into future, such bootstrapping of historical data, must be applied with caution, as it does not include the occurrence of extraordinary events. Thus, before formal statistical methods can be applied, there is always a need for exploratory, judgmental analysis of data.

Such analysis includes the examination of columns of data grouped in various ways and alternate graphical representations of data. Data which do not seem to fit into patterns are identified and examined. The occurrence of extraordinary events is pinpointed, and their impact on the data is assessed. Thus before a formal statistical approach is applied, past historical data are examined, interpreted, and if necessary adjusted.

As an example, consider the data shown in Figure 4.1 where value (such as sales, profits, labor hours, etc.) is plotted versus time. The human eye immediately notices the sharp peak represented by what statisticians call an **outlier** data item. So the analyst proceeds to examine the data to find a **causal** explanation. It may be that for some extraordi-

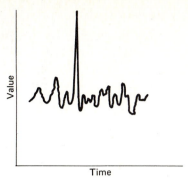

Value

Time

FIGURE 4.1
Sharp peak in the data requires causal explanation.

nary reason sales were high, and it is not to be expected that these high sales will recur in the future. Or again, it is possible that a mistake was made when the data were collected, transmitted, or recorded. Thus exploratory analysis would identify this data item, and the analyst would replace it with a value which would have occurred without the extraordinary event.

> The first rule of forecasting: Look at the data.

Advantages of Statistical Forecasting

Judgmental forecasts are subjective, difficult to explain, and therefore ill-suited to reaching consensus. When statistical forecasts are used, there is a clear and explicit separation of judgment and science. The mathematical aspects are unambiguous, and the calculations are reproducible and can be carried out by the computer. The forecast values can be compared with actuals, and as time goes on the values of the parameters can be modified to suit new data. Statistical forecasts can be integrated with other quantitative models of decision making and can be performed on computer systems.

Mathematical Models in Forecasting

You need to make a distinction between **independent** and **dependent variables** in forecasting. Independent variables are forecast by judgment and/or statistical methods; dependent variables are computed by the equations of the model.

As a simple example, assume that both sales and expenses are forecast as independent variables. The difference between the two, the profit, is obtained by simple subtraction; it is a dependent variable, and no judgment or statistics is involved.

Another example is the Loud and Clear Playback Corporation discussed in Chapter 1. Once the cost-quantity and quantity-price relationships (Figures 1.8 and 1.9) are forecast, the rest follows from the model (Figure 1.10).

The real-life approach to combining forecasts and models is related to the approach discussed in Chapter 1 where the technique of financial planning models is described. There sales, wage rates, taxes, inflation, etc., are forecast by judgment and/or statistical techniques and economic models. Then the model, that is, a system of equations, is developed for the dependent variables, such as selling expense, profit, return on investment, etc.

Note then that judgmental, statistical, and modeling techniques are used jointly when making executive decisions. However, in this chapter we focus on statistical techniques of forecasting, both from the theoretical and practical points of view.

4.2 STATISTICAL FORECASTING

Statistical theory allows us to examine historical data and infer the nature and characteristic of the underlying process generating the data. Thus **statistical inference** leads to conclusions as to the processes governing the events under scrutiny. Statistics is used in all sciences and provides a greater degree of confidence in reaching conclusions and allows the calculation of the probabilities involved in the underlying processes. Statistics helps us in sharpening our ability to find patterns in data. Before proceeding to formal statistical analysis, we discuss how statistics does this.

Patterns of Data

Look at Figure 4.2(a). It appears that there is a random set of values around the solid line. Thus the judgmental forecast for the future is the line shown. Statistics help sharpen judgment and to determine the position of the line by calculating the *mean*.

Figure 4.2(b) shows random variations around a straight-line **trend**. Statistical analysis allows fitting the best straight line to the data. Then the procedure for forecasting is provided by the formula for the straight line.

Figure 4.2(c) illustrates **seasonal variations** in the sales of a product. For example, the sale of beer is higher during the hot summer than during the cold winter. Statistics allows the determination of **seasonal indices** which, for instance, would indicate that sales in December are 80% but in July 150% of average sales.

Figure 4.2(d) illustrates fluctuations around a **growth curve** apparently leading to a saturation level. The data may be sales for a maturing product for which sales are still growing but at a diminishing rate.

Figure 4.2(e) shows random variations around the growth curve of a product for which the sales are still accelerating.

Figure 4.2(f) shows random variations with a **drift**. There seems to be no average or no particular trend in the data.

Figure 4.2(g) shows **cyclic variations** related to long-time variations such as the business cycle. Variability here involves time spans of 2, 3, or more years.

Statistical forecasting allows the examination of data and the inference of patterns shown in data. In most practical situations the main

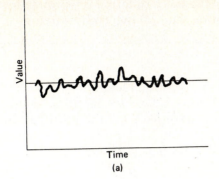

(a)

FIGURE 4.2
Patterns of data.

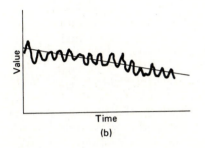

(b)

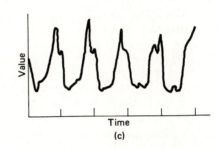

(c)

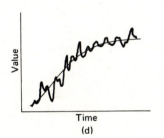

(d)

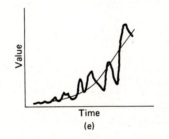

(e)

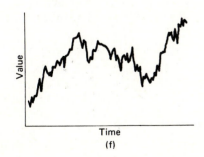

(f)

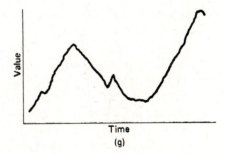

(g)

problem is to identify the three different types of patterns: (1) the trend, (2) the seasonal variation, and (3) the cyclic variation.

4.3 MOVING AVERAGES

We begin the study of forecasting techniques by describing the **moving average** procedure. Figure 4.3 shows monthly sales (in thousands of dollars) for 3 years for Wearever, Inc., a subsidiary of the Aluminum Corporation of America.* Column 2 in Figure 4.4 shows the approximate data in tabular form for the first year. Our problem is to forecast next month's sales.

Before we describe the moving average procedure, consider the naive approach of assuming that

> next month's sales forecast = this month's (actual) sales.

For example, January (actual) sales are $2.0 (line 1, column 2 of Figure 4.4), so the forecast F for the next month, February, is $2.0 (line 2, column 3). Forecast for March is February (actual sales or $1.4). This forecast is shown in column 3 of Figure 4.4.

The weakness of this procedure is that no attention is given to earlier sales; only the last month's sales count, and they may have been influenced by unusual conditions. The procedure of moving averages remedies this weakness. We illustrate this procedure by examples.

Average of Last Two Values

Consider the forecast to be made on March 1 for sales in March. Last month's sales, that is, sales in February, were $1.4. Two months ago, that

---

* A brief review of regression analysis is given in Section 4.8.

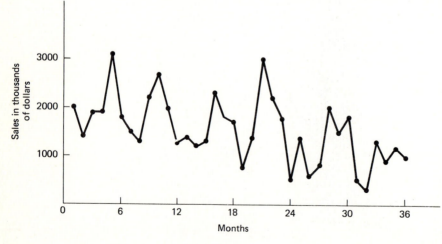

FIGURE 4.3
Monthly sales for 3 years for Wearever, Inc.

(1) MONTH	(2) ACTUAL SALES	(3) SALES LAST MONTH	(4) AVERAGE OF LAST 2 MONTHS	(5) WEIGHTED AVERAGE OF LAST 2 MONTHS	(6) AVERAGE OF LAST 3 MONTHS	(7) WEIGHTED AVERAGE OF LAST 3 MONTHS
1. Jan.	2.0	—	—	—	—	—
2. Feb.	1.4	2.0	—	—	—	—
3. March	1.9	1.4	$(1.4 + 2.0)/2 = 1.70$	$(3 \times 1.4 + 2 \times 2.0)/5 = 1.64$	—	—
4. April	1.9	1.9	$(1.9 + 1.4)/2 = 1.65$	$(3 \times 1.9 + 2 \times 1.4)/5 = 1.70$	$(1.9 + 1.4 + 2.0)/3 = 1.77$	$(7 \times 1.9 + 2 \times 1.4 + 1 \times 2.0)/10 = 1.81$
5. May	3.1	1.9	$(1.9 + 1.9)/2 = 1.90$	$(3 \times 1.9 + 2 \times 1.9)/5 = 1.90$	$(1.9 + 1.9 + 1.4)/3 = 1.73$	$(7 \times 1.9 + 2 \times 1.9 + 1 \times 1.4)/10 = 1.85$
6. June	1.8	3.1	$(3.1 + 1.9)/2 = 2.50$	$(3 \times 3.1 + 2 \times 1.9)/5 = 2.62$	$(3.1 + 1.9 + 1.9)/3 = 2.30$	$(7 \times 3.1 + 2 \times 1.9 + 1 \times 1.9)/10 = 2.74$
7. July	1.5	1.8	$(1.8 + 3.1)/2 = 2.45$	$(3 \times 1.8 + 2 \times 3.1)/5 = 2.32$	$(1.8 + 3.1 + 1.9)/3 = 2.27$	$(7 \times 1.8 + 2 \times 3.1 + 1 \times 1.9)/10 = 2.07$
8. Aug.	1.3	1.5	$(1.5 + 1.8)/2 = 1.65$	$(3 \times 1.5 + 2 \times 1.8)/5 = 1.62$	$(1.5 + 1.8 + 3.1)/3 = 2.13$	$(7 \times 1.5 + 2 \times 1.8 + 1 \times 3.1)/10 = 1.72$
9. Sept.	2.2	1.3	$(1.3 + 1.5)/2 = 1.40$	$(3 \times 1.3 + 2 \times 1.5)/5 = 1.38$	$(1.3 + 1.5 + 1.8)/3 = 1.53$	$(7 \times 1.3 + 2 \times 1.5 + 1 \times 1.8)/10 = 1.39$
10. Oct.	2.7	2.2	$(2.2 + 1.3)/2 = 1.75$	$(3 \times 2.2 + 2 \times 1.3)/5 = 1.84$	$(2.2 + 1.3 + 1.5)/3 = 1.67$	$(7 \times 2.2 + 2 \times 1.3 + 1 \times 1.5)/10 = 1.39$
11. Nov.	2.0	2.7	$(2.7 + 2.2)/2 = 2.45$	$(3 \times 2.7 + 2 \times 2.2)/5 = 2.50$	$(2.7 + 2.2 + 1.3)/3 = 2.07$	$(7 \times 2.7 + 2 \times 2.2 + 1 \times 1.3)/10 = 2.46$
12. Dec.	1.3	2.0	$(2.0 + 2.7)/2 = 2.35$	$(3 \times 2.0 + 2 \times 2.7)/5 = 2.28$	$(2.0 + 2.7 + 2.2)/3 = 2.30$	$(7 \times 2.0 + 2 \times 2.7 + 1 \times 2.2)/10 = 2.16$

FIGURE 4.4 Forecasting in moving averages for Wearever, Inc. (only the first year is shown).

is, January, sales were \$2.0. The forecast is calculated by taking the average of the last 2 months' sales:

$$F = \text{forecast for March} = \tfrac{1}{2} \times (\text{actual sales in February})$$
$$+ \tfrac{1}{2} \times (\text{actual sales in January})$$

Now we introduce mathematical abbreviations:

S_1 = actual sales last month   (ONE month ago)

S_2 = actual sales TWO months ago

And so

$$F = \frac{S_1 + S_2}{2}$$

But

$$S_1 = 1.4, \qquad S_2 = 2.0$$

and so the March forecast is

$$F = \frac{1.4 + 2.0}{2} = \$1.70$$

On April 1 the forecast for April is made:

S_1 = actual sales ONE month ago (March) = \$1.9

S_2 = actual sales TWO months ago (February) = \$1.4

Thus the April forecast is

$$F = \frac{S_1 + S_2}{2} = \frac{1.9 + 1.4}{2} = \$1.65$$

Note that the same formula and procedure hold for all the forecasts. The forecast is shown in column 4 of Figure 4.4.

Weighted Average of Last Two Values

The formula

$$F = S_1$$

neglects S_2, and the formula

$$F = \frac{S_1 + S_2}{2}$$

gives equal weight to S_1 and S_2. Forecasters may learn by experience that better forecasts can be obtained by weighting S_1 and S_2 with different weights. Suppose, for example, that the forecaster finds that last month's sales S_1 are more important than sales 2 months ago, S_2. So the formula

$$F = \frac{3S_1 + 2S_2}{3 + 2} = \frac{3S_1 + 2S_2}{5}$$

where the weights are in the proportion 3 to 2, is tried. For example, the March forecast is now

$$F = \frac{3 \times 1.4 + 2 \times 2.0}{5} = \$1.64$$

These values are tabulated in column 5 of Figure 4.4. Thus the analyst tries various weights and selects the ones that give the most suitable forecast.

Average of Last Three Values

Assume that a forecast is to be made on April 1 for April. Experience has shown that in many situations the forecast for any month can be obtained by taking the average actual sales for the past 3 months. The moving average formula for the forecast is

$$F = \frac{S_1 + S_2 + S_3}{3}$$

where S_1 is *last* month's actual sales, S_2 is actual sales 2 months prior, and S_3 is actual sales 3 months prior.

Now

$$S_1 = \$1.9, \qquad S_2 = \$1.4, \qquad S_3 = \$2.0$$

and the April forecast is

$$F = \frac{1.9 + 1.4 + 2.0}{3} = \$1.77$$

This forecast is shown in column 6 of Figure 4.4.

Weighted Average of Last Three Values

The forecaster may find that recent sales values are more important than the values for last month and 2 months ago. Thus the formula

$$F = \frac{7S_1 + 2S_2 + 1S_3}{10}$$

may be used where the weights are in the proportions 7 to 2 to 1. This forecast is shown in column 7 of Figure 4.4.

Figure 4.5 gives a comparison between actual and forecasted sales.

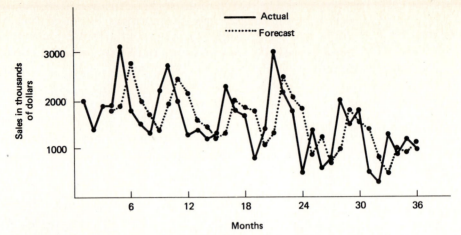

Sales in thousands of dollars

— Actual

········ Forecast

Months

FIGURE 4.5 Comparing forecast with actuals for Wearever, Inc. The forecast is computed by taking the weighted average of the last 3 months of actual sales as shown in column 7, Figure 4.4.

Again the analyst experiments with various weights and selects the most suitable ones.

Critique of Moving Average Method

The general forecasting formula is

$$F = \frac{W_1S_1 + W_2S_2 + \cdots + W_nS_n}{W_1 + W_2 + \cdots + W_n}$$

where the weights (the Ws), must be nonnegative (positive or zero) numbers. Note that each forecast requires n past actual values.

One problem with the technique is that there is no generally accepted theory for determining the number of periods n and the weights to be used and so little advice can be given to the analyst choosing values. Therefore we now present another popular statistical forecasting technique.

4.4 EXPONENTIAL SMOOTHING

The procedure of exponential smoothing combines last month's actual sales and last month's *forecast* by taking a weighted average of the two. We illustrate the procedure again with the data from Wearever, Inc. in Figure 4.4. Assume that January 1 a judgmental beginning forecast of $3.00 for January is made (first number in column 5, Figure 4.6). Actual sales are $2.0 in January. Thus, on February 1 a forecast is made by calculating the weighted average of the actual sales of $2.0 in January and the forecast of $3.00. Suppose the weights of 7 and 3 or .7 and .3 are used. The forecast for February is

.7 × (actual sales in January) + .3 × (forecast for January)

	MONTH	(1) ACTUAL SALES	(2) SALES LAST MONTH	(3) PREVIOUS FORECAST	(4)	(5) α × COL. 3 + (1 − α)COL. 4
1.	Jan.	2.0	—	—		Beginning forecast = 3.00
2.	Feb.	1.4	2.0	3.00		.7 × 2.0 + .3 × 3.00 = 2.30
3.	March	1.9	1.4	2.30		.7 × 1.4 + .3 × 2.30 = 1.67
4.	April	1.9	1.9	1.67		.7 × 1.9 + .3 × 1.67 = 1.83
5.	May	3.1	1.9	1.83		.7 × 1.9 + .3 × 1.83 = 1.88
6.	June	1.8	3.1	1.88		.7 × 3.1 + .3 × 1.88 = 2.73
7.	July	1.5	1.8	2.73		.7 × 1.8 + .3 × 2.73 = 2.08
8.	Aug.	1.3	1.5	2.08		.7 × 1.5 + .3 × 2.08 = 1.67
9.	Sept.	2.2	1.3	1.67		.7 × 1.3 + .3 × 1.67 = 1.41
10.	Oct.	2.7	2.2	1.41		.7 × 2.2 + .3 × 1.41 = 1.96
11.	Nov.	2.0	2.7	1.96		.7 × 2.7 + .3 × 1.46 = 2.48
12.	Dec.	1.3	2.0	2.48		.7 × 2.0 + .3 × 2.48 = 2.14

FIGURE 4.6 Forecast obtained by exponential smoothing for Wearever, Inc. (only the first year is shown).

or

$$.7 \times 2.0 + .3 \times 3.0 = \$2.30$$

(See the third row in column 5, Figure 4.6.) The March forecast is

$$.7 \times (\text{actual sales in February}) + 3 \times (\text{forecast for February})$$

or

$$.7 \times 1.4 + .3 \times 2.30 = \$1.67$$

It is customary to designate the weight on the actual sales by the Greek letter α (alpha). The procedure for exponential smoothing is

forecast = α(actual sales last month)

$+ (1 - \alpha)$(forecast for last month's sales)

where α must be between 0 and 1. In our example we arbitrarily chose

$$\alpha = .7, \qquad 1 - \alpha = .3$$

Figure 4.6 shows the forecast for the first year, and Figure 4.7 compares actual sales with the forecast.

Figure 4.8 compares the six different forecasts for 36 months for Wearever, Inc. (The forecasts were prepared on a computer.)

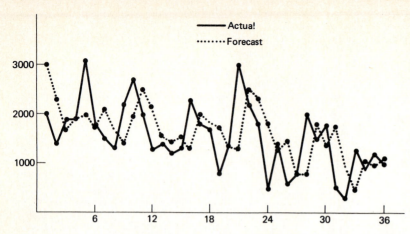

Critique of Exponential Smoothing

The problem with this technique is the selection of α. How much weight should be given to actual sales and to the forecast? One practical approach is to plot the data and the forecasts for various values of alpha, "look" at the data, and choose the value of alpha by judgment. A value close to 1 will give a forecast responding quickly to changes in sales because a relatively large weight is given to the last value of sales. A low alpha gives a slow response.

A more quantitative procedure is the following:

1. Calculate the deviations between actuals and forecasts.
2. Calculate the squares of the deviations.
3. Take the average of the deviations.
4. Repeat the first three steps for various values of alpha and select the alpha with the lowest value of the average.

In actual practice this procedure is often combined with experience and judgment in the selection of alpha.

Note, however, that the same critique applies to choosing weights for the moving average method and in fact to selecting the technique of forecasting itself. Thus the preceding four steps apply to any forecasting system except that in step 4 the value of alpha is to be replaced by other parameters of the forecasting system. One advantage of exponential smoothing is that only one number is to be chosen. In the moving average technique, two, three, four, or more numbers must be selected—a more difficult task.

4.5 TREND PROJECTION BY REGRESSION ANALYSIS

In many situations there is a prevailing direction or *trend* for growth or decline. By fitting a straight trend line with the use of **linear regression analysis**,* a forecast for the future can be made.

---

*Adapted from P. E. Winters, "Forecasting Sales by Exponentially Weighted Moving Averages," *Management Science*, Vol. 6, No. 3, April 1960, pp. 324–342.

(1) MONTH	(2) ACTUAL SALES	(3) SALES LAST MONTH	(4) AVERAGE OF LAST 2 MONTHS	(5) WEIGHTED AVERAGE OF LAST 2 MONTHS	(6) AVERAGE OF LAST 3 MONTHS	(7) WEIGHTED AVERAGE OF LAST 3 MONTHS	(8) EXPONENTIAL SMOOTHING WITH $\alpha = .7$
1	2.00	—	—	—	—	—	3.00
2	1.40	2.00	—	—	—	—	2.30
3	1.90	1.40	1.70	1.64	—	—	1.67
4	1.90	1.90	1.65	1.70	1.77	1.81	1.83
5	3.10	1.90	1.90	1.90	1.73	1.85	1.88
6	1.80	3.10	2.50	2.62	2.30	2.74	2.73
7	1.50	1.80	2.45	2.32	2.27	2.07	2.08
8	1.30	1.50	1.65	1.62	2.13	1.72	1.67
9	2.20	1.30	1.40	1.38	1.53	1.39	1.41
10	2.70	2.20	1.75	1.84	1.67	1.95	1.96
11	2.00	2.70	2.45	2.50	2.07	2.46	2.48
12	1.30	2.00	2.35	2.28	2.30	2.16	2.14
13	1.40	1.30	1.65	1.58	2.00	1.58	1.55
14	1.20	1.40	1.35	1.36	1.57	1.44	1.45
15	1.30	1.20	1.30	1.28	1.30	1.25	1.27
16	2.30	1.30	1.25	1.26	1.30	1.29	1.29
17	1.80	2.30	1.80	1.90	1.60	1.99	2.00
18	1.70	1.80	2.05	2.00	1.80	1.85	1.86
19	.80	1.70	1.75	1.74	1.93	1.78	1.75
20	1.40	.80	1.25	1.16	1.43	1.08	1.08
21	3.00	1.40	1.10	1.16	1.30	1.31	1.31
22	2.20	3.00	2.20	2.36	1.73	2.46	2.49
23	1.60	2.20	2.60	2.52	2.20	2.28	2.29
24	.50	1.60	1.90	1.84	2.27	1.86	1.81
25	1.40	.50	1.05	.94	1.43	.89	.89
26	.60	1.40	.95	1.04	1.17	1.24	1.25
27	.80	.60	1.00	.92	.83	.75	.79
28	2.20	.80	.70	.72	.93	.82	.80
29	1.50	2.20	1.50	1.64	1.20	1.76	1.78
30	1.80	1.50	1.85	1.78	1.50	1.57	1.58
31	.50	1.80	1.65	1.68	1.83	1.78	1.74
32	.30	.50	1.15	1.02	1.27	.86	.87
33	1.30	.30	.40	.38	.87	.49	.47
34	.90	1.30	.80	.90	.70	1.02	1.05
35	1.20	.90	1.10	1.06	.83	.92	.95
36	1.00	1.20	1.05	1.08	1.13	1.15	1.12

FIGURE 4.8 Comparing six forecasts for Wearever, Inc. Columns 2–7 correspond to averaging (see Figure 4.4) and column 8 to exponential smoothing (see Figures 4.6 and 4.7).

Example

In a certain suburb in the southwest there has been growth in the number of students attending college. The growth is shown graphically (Figure 4.9) and numerically (columns 1, 2, and 3, Figure 4.10). What is the prediction for 1982 and 1983?

Notation and Formulas

We introduce the following notation for the data points and number of students in thousands:

$$X_1 = 1, \quad X_2 = 2, \quad X_3 = 3, \quad X_4 = 4, \quad X_5 = 5, \quad X_6 = 6$$
$$Y_1 = 15, \quad Y_2 = 17, \quad Y_3 = 18, \quad Y_4 = 20, \quad Y_5 = 20.5, \quad Y_6 = 21$$

Then

$$\Sigma X = X_1 + X_2 + X_3 + X_4 + X_5 + X_6$$
$$\Sigma Y = Y_1 + Y_2 + Y_3 + Y_4 + Y_5 + Y_6$$
$$\Sigma XY = X_1Y_1 + X_2Y_2 + X_3Y_3 + X_4Y_4 + X_5Y_5 + X_6Y_6$$
$$\Sigma X^2 = X_1^2 + X_2^2 + X_3^2 + X_4^2 + X_5^2 + X_6^2$$

Notation for the Means

$$\overline{X} = \frac{X_1 + X_2 + X_3 + X_4 + X_5 + X_6}{6}$$

$$\overline{Y} = \frac{Y_1 + Y_2 + Y_3 + Y_4 + Y_5 + Y_6}{6}$$

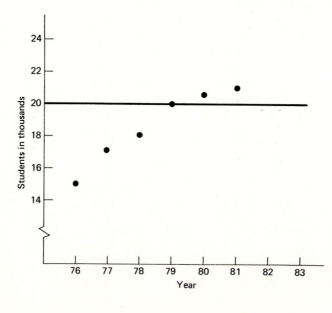

FIGURE 4.9
Scatter diagram to show the growth in the number of students attending college.

(1) YEAR	(2) DATA POINT (X)	(3) STUDENTS IN THOUSANDS (Y)	(4) (X)(Y)	(5) X²
1976	1	15	15	1
1977	2	17	34	4
1978	3	18	54	9
1979	4	20	80	16
1980	5	20.5	102.5	25
1981	6	21	126	36
$\Sigma X = 21$ $\overline{X}(\Sigma X)/n$ $= 21/6$ $= 3.5$		$\Sigma Y = 111.5$ $\overline{Y} = (\Sigma X)/n$ $= 115.5/6$ $= 18.5833$	$\Sigma XY = 411.5$	$\Sigma X^2 = 91$

FIGURE 4.10 Linear regression analysis of the growth in number of students attending college. The number of data points is $n = 6$.

The **slope** of the best fitting straight line is given by the formula (see Section 4.8)

$$b = \frac{(\Sigma XY) - n(\overline{X})(\overline{Y})}{(\Sigma X^2) - n(\overline{X})^2}$$

where n is the number of data points ($n = 6$ in our example). The **intercept** is given by the formula

$$a = (\overline{Y}) - b(\overline{X})$$

Do not confuse

$$(\overline{X})^2 = \left(\frac{X_1 + X_2 + X_3 + X_4 + X_5 + X_6}{6}\right)^2$$

with

$$\Sigma X^2 = X_1^2 + X_2^2 + X_3^2 + X_4^2 + X_5^2 + X_6^2$$

The Best Fitting Straight Line

We determine the best fitting straight line by a procedure consisting of nine steps:

Step 1. $\Sigma X = 21$ (column 2, Figure 4.10)

Step 2. $\Sigma Y = 111.5$ (column 3, Figure 4.10)

Step 3. $\Sigma XY = 411.5$ (column 4, Figure 4.10)

Step 4. $\Sigma X^2 = 91$ (column 5, Figure 4.10)

Step 5. $\overline{X} = \dfrac{\Sigma X}{n} = \dfrac{\Sigma X}{6} = \dfrac{21}{6} = 3.5$ (column 2, at the bottom of Figure 4.10)

Step 6. $\overline{Y} = \dfrac{\Sigma Y}{n} = \dfrac{\Sigma Y}{6} = 18.5833$ (column 3, at the bottom of Figure 4.10)

Step 7. $b = \dfrac{411.5 - 6 \times 3.5 \times 18.5833}{91 - 6 \times 3.5^2} = \dfrac{411.5 - 390.25}{91 - 73.5}$

$= \dfrac{21.25}{17.5} = 1.2143$

Step 8. $a = 18.5833 - 1.2143 \times 3.5 = 14.3200$

Step 9. The best fitting straight line is (Figure 4.11)

$$Y_c = 14.3200 + 1.2143X$$

The Forecast

For 1982 we have $X = 7$, and so

$Y_c = 14.3200 + 1.21 \times 7 = 22.79$ thousand students

For 1983, $X = 8$, and so

$Y_c = 14.3200 + 1.21 \times 8 = 24.00$ thousand students

(See the two crosses in Figure 4.11)

Adapting the Trend to New Data

Suppose in the preceding example that actual attendance for 1982 turns out to be 21,000 students. What should the new forecast be for 1983?

One approach is to take the new data and perform a regression analysis on the seven values. However, one may object that the 1975 enrollment should not influence the 1983 forecast and that therefore only the last six values should be used—or perhaps the last five. This leads to the concept of self-adapting regression analysis.

Forecast by regression analysis, using the last n data points.

Experience, experimentation, and calculation of error helps in determining the best value of n.

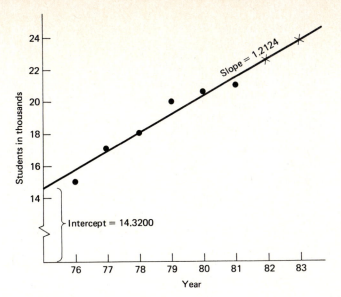

FIGURE 4.11
Best fitting straight
line for scatter dia-
gram of the number
of students attend-
ing college (Figure
4.9).

4.6 FORECASTING AT AMERICAN CAN COMPANY: A CASE STUDY*

Practically every corporation uses more or less sophisticated forecasting techniques, and the purpose of this discussion is to present how the Packaging Division of American Can Company developed and implemented a simple short-range forecasting model. The emphasis is not on the technical aspects of the model but on the successful approach used by the OR/MS group of American Can Company.

Background

American Can Company, having sales of over $3 billion and over 45,000 employees is the major manufacturer of containers, packaging products, metal cans, collapsible tubes, etc. But American Can is more than just a can company. Consumer products and distributions are about 34% of its domestic packaging business.

The Packaging Division of the American Can Company is the major operating division of the corporation, accounting for about 60% of company sales. The division consists of four specialized marketing departments: food, beverage, meat and special products, and general packaging. Each department has a profit center headed by a general manager with ultimate responsibility for sales and profits.

In the early part of 1976 Mr. B. F. Larson, Director, Material and Production Planning, was given the responsibility of improving the

* Carl Kallina, "Development and Implementation of a Simple Short Range Forecasting Model—A Case Study," *Interfaces*, Vol. 8, No. 3, May 1978, pp. 32–40.

monthly sales forecasting system. According to B. F. Larson, the fore-casting system had numerous shortcomings:

First, there wasn't any accumulation of historical data which either the sales or marketing groups could turn to for a record. Second, there wasn't any assistance given in the area of statistical trend projections. In essence, all that we had was a best guess feel, based on whatever notes had been kept, and what the customers thought they would need for the coming months.

The projections had the inherent bias of being too high and completely misinterpreted recurring situations such as an announced price increase. Forecast errors ranged between -21 and $+25\%$.

B. F. Larson solicited the help of Carl Kallina, Business System Manager of American Can Company, to improve the forecasting system. Within a short time period and at a low budget the OR/MS group developed and implemented a successful forecasting system. However, to understand how this was possible, it is necessary to digress a little and describe the history of forecasting at American Can.

History of Model Development: Two Failures

It is a well-established custom in describing quantitative methods of management to deal exclusively with successes. We depart now from this custom because you can learn a great deal from studying failures. The fact is that six years prior to Larson's request a complex forecasting system was developed at American Can Company. However, it failed to reach acceptance. The analysts who developed the system left American Can, and the forecasting effort was abandoned.

In late 1974 the OR/MS group was approached by a senior manager for a monthly forecasting system to deal with a small number of highly aggregated products with extensive sales histories. The OR/MS group accepted the assignment on a modest budget with the condition that a practical forecasting system would be developed which would be understandable to operating managers.

The OR/MS group considered the problem as fairly traditional and was convinced that a simple forecasting technique in a short period of time could be developed. However, recalling the failure of the 1970 effort, an investigation was started to find out why the earlier effort had failed. A series of discussions was held with operating managers, and it was found that the 1970 model was mistrusted not only because of the forecast errors themselves but also because the analysts were unable to explain either the model or the cause of these errors. Managers had no feeling for the logic of the model and how the model computed the forecast. Managers knew that a small number of customers accounted for the bulk of sales but noticed that the model failed to take this into account. Historical data were unadjusted to past extraordinary activities of key customers, and upcoming extraordinary events were also ignored. In our terminology no exploratory analysis of the data was made, and the computerized forecasting system blindly accepted historical data and produced useless forecasts.

Recognizing the significance of the findings, the OR/MS group set out to develop a simple and explainable forecasting model. A series of available forecasting models and computer programs was examined, and a fairly traditional forecasting model, using extrapolation of trends and adjustments by seasonal indices, was developed. Fine tuning of the parameters was reached by extensive trial and error analysis. The resulting forecasting equations were simple and easy to explain to operating personnel.

During a trial period, comparisons with the existing judgmental forecasts were made. Oddly enough, during the trial period there was a dramatic drop in sales, and the forecasting system performed poorly. However, the sponsor had a good understanding of the system and realized that failures were due to the unusual pattern of sales, and so the sponsor "forgave" the errors of the system. Thus the sponsor was ready to install the system. However, at this point in time an unfortunate incident occurred. The sponsor was assigned to a new position, and the project was suddenly abandoned—a second failure for quantitative methods.

However, the OR/MS group continued on its own to further develop the forecasting system, and so when in 1976 B. F. Larson asked Carl Kallina to develop a forecasting system, the stage was set for a successful application.

The OR/MS group quickly realized that the forecasting system they developed earlier was suitable for solving Larson's problem, and so, in a relatively short time period and with a low budget, a successful forecasting system was developed and implemented. Thus the two earlier failures were changed to a final success.

Conclusion

B. F. Larson attested that the earlier forecast variability of -21 to $+25\%$ in the judgmental forecasting system was reduced to -5 to $+8.8\%$ and stated that the system was highly successful.

Carl Kallina attributed the success of the project not to sophisticated mathematical techniques or a highly innovative technical approach but rather to the simplicity of the model. The equations could be explained to operating managers, and they trusted and used the model because they felt it to be valid.

As a final remark, note that the success of the project is measured simply by managerial satisfaction. The system performs well because it is better than the judgmental forecasting system previously used. Management satisfaction did not come from sophisticated statistical analysis or cost benefit analysis but simply from the fact that the new system performed better than the old one.

4.7 A DIALOG

Q. *You cannot foretell the future, so what is the point of all this?*

A. We are not trying to predict the future. We want to be prepared for various contingencies and need answers to what-if types of questions to make good decisions. Forecasting provides a scientific technique of analysis of alternative futures to support decision making. Regularities of the past tend to carry into the future. Statistical regularity makes businesses such as insurance and gambling casinos possible. In many other businesses regularities of the past are not that important but are more useful than looking at tea leaves or gazing into a crystal ball. Better forecasts lead to better planning, better projections, and better business performance.

Q. *Is forecasting fundamental to all quantitative analysis? How about deterministic analysis?*

A. When you are very certain about the future, you don't call it a forecast. When you make a deposit in the bank, you know you will get a fixed percent return. But with costs you may think you know what costs will be, when in fact you are actually making assumptions. The value of parameters in deterministic analysis is often nothing more than expected values in which people have great confidence. When you go to work in the morning, you are in fact forecasting that the car will start and you will get there on time. Of course in reality you occasionally have trouble and are late.

Q. *There is too much judgment, trial and error in the whole thing. Is this science?*

A. Executives often complain that forecasts put too much reliance on past statistical data; the future is different from the past, and more judgment should be used. On the other hand, there are often complaints that the past is neglected and decisions are based solely on speculation. There are two sides to every coin. Looking into the future is a combination of art and science, and it is a subjective matter to decide how much of science and how much of judgment.

Q. *Why didn't you use probabilities when forecasting?*

A. I did! The underlying theory, not presented here, is based on probability theory. Moreover, recall our dialog in Chapter 3, which discusses the practical aspects of determining probability distributions. The fact is that analyzing past data, deriving a probability distribution, is really a forecast of the future, though typically the approach is not called forecasting. In real-life situations the combination of (1) determining probability distributions and (2) statistical forecasting—as described in this chapter—is rarely utilized.

Q. *You mentioned seasonal variations, cyclic variations, and other types of variability. Why did you not cover these in the text?*

A. There is a considerable body of knowledge on forecasting, and here we present only the most popular approaches. In a more advanced text, for example, you can learn about the *decomposition* approach, which separates these different types of variability.

Q. *Why does exponential smoothing ignore all except data from the last period?*

A. The simplicity of exponential smoothing is deceiving. You are

using the last actual value and the last forecast. But the last forecast used the actual value from two periods prior and the forecast from two periods prior, etc. Exponential smoothing in reality uses all the past data but with the aid of ever-decreasing weights. The fact is that exponential smoothing can be considered as a moving average process.

Q. *Why do you keep reemphasizing exploratory analysis?*

A. Let me give you an illustration. A certain group was given historical data and asked to prepare a forecasting equation. The group tried a whole slew of computer programs, using more and more sophisticated forecasting techniques to match the data. After many trials, a very complex system was finally developed and the forecast made and given to the user. The user found the forecast to be ridiculous. Then a more practical analyst examined the data, plotted the points on graph paper, and discovered that in one data point the decimal point was misplaced. This of course completely disrupted the computer program and led to impossible answers. The moral: *Look at the data.*

Q. *When does statistical forecasting really apply?*

A. When regularities of the past carry into the future. Technical writers talk about a process homogeneous in time and also about statistical equilibrium. For a precise definition, you have to consult advanced texts which cover the theory of stochastic processes.

Q. *What do you mean when you say that budgets and forecasts are often confused?*

A. A budget is a quantitative expression of a plan of action and an aid to communication, coordination, and implementation. A forecast is an important input to a budget, but it is not a plan of action. Neither is a sales forecast a sales goal. A sales goal is a target for performance toward which a group takes aim. Sales goals may be set high to get salespersons enthused or may be set lower to show realistic goals. On the other hand, sales potential often means the upper limit for sales under optimal conditions. So realistic sales goals may be set under sales potential not to discourage salespersons but above the forecast of actual sales. All this may sound confusing, but remember that basically we are dealing with information which is to be provided to managers to support decision making.

Q. *Is there a most important trap to avoid?*

A. Do not assume that just because you have a sophisticated system of equations, management will accept your recommendations. Bear in mind that a forecasting system is an information system to support managerial decision making. Trends, numbers, and computer printouts contain no information for executives unless they have a gut feeling for how the information was developed, why the information is pertinent to their situation, why the information is valid, and when and where judgment is required to improve performance.

Regression analysis is a statistical technique which fits a line to a given set of data. It provides a formula which relates the dependent variable (sales, for example) to one or more independent variables (price and number of salespersons, for example).

Least squares analysis fits a line to a given set of data so that the sum of the squares of the errors (residuals) between the estimated points on the line and the given data is minimized. We discuss here only fitting a straight line by least squares analysis to a given set of data.

Linear Regression Analysis

In Figure 4.12(a) we show a scatter diagram of given pairs of data X and Y. Our problem is to fit a best straight line to the data by least squares analysis. The formula we seek is

$$Y_c = a + bX$$

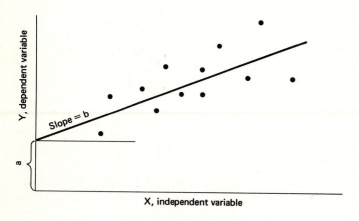

(a)

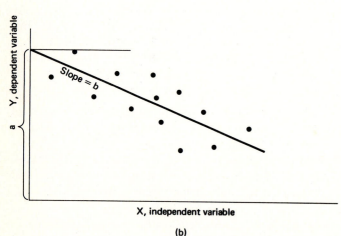

(b)

FIGURE 4.12
Scatter diagrams to illustrate linear regression analysis.

where Y_c is the computed value of the dependent variable and a and b are the unknowns. Bear in mind that a is the *intercept* in the Y axis and b is the *slope* of the straight line. Our problem is to calculate the values of a and b. Note that in Figure 4.12(a) the slope b is positive and that in Figure 4.12(b) the slope b is negative.*

Least Squares Analysis

Suppose we have four data points: (1) x_1, y_1, (2) x_2, y_2, (3) x_3, y_3, and (4) x_4, y_4 and we seek the best fitting line:

$$Y_c = a + bX$$

The four errors (residuals) provided by the equation will be

$$e_1 = y_1 - (a + bx_1)$$

$$e_2 = y_2 - (a + bx_2)$$

$$e_3 = y_3 - (a + bx_3)$$

$$e_4 = y_4 - (a + bx_4)$$

How should we choose a and b? We want the errors to be small. At first blush you may think that a good thing to do is to minimize the sum of the errors:

$$e_1 + e_2 + e_3 + e_4$$

But this is clearly a bad criterion because plus and minus errors will cancel each other. A better approach is to *minimize the sum of the squares of the errors*, because both plus and minus errors yield positive squares.

> The least squares error principle chooses the straight line for which the sum of the squares of the errors is minimum.

For our four point example we should minimize

$$\text{sum} = e_1^2 + e_2^2 + e_3^2 + e_4^2 = [y_1 - (a + bx_1)]^2 + [y_2 - (a + bx_2)]^2$$
$$+ [y_3 - (a + bx_3)]^2 + [y_4 - (a + bx_4)]^2$$

Without proof we now state how to calculate a and b. First we introduce the following notation:

X: independent variable
Y: dependent variable
ΣX: sum of the independent variables
ΣY: sum of the dependent variables
$\overline{X}$: mean of independent variable

---

* The mathematics of straight lines is reviewed in Appendix A, Section 3.

$\overline{Y}$: mean of dependent variable

n: number of data points

ΣXY: sum of the respective products of the independent and dependent variables

ΣX^2: sum of the squares of the independent variable

where Σ is a capital Greek *sigma* standing for *summation*. Note that

$$\overline{X} = \frac{\Sigma X}{n}$$

$$\overline{Y} = \frac{\Sigma X}{n}$$

The slope b can be calculated from

$$b = \frac{(\Sigma XY) - n(\overline{X})(\overline{Y})}{(\Sigma X^2) - n(\overline{X})^2}$$

The intercept a can be calculated from

$$a = \overline{Y} - b(\overline{X})$$

Do not confuse ΣX^2 (sum of the squares) with $\overline{X}^2$ (square of the mean).

Many electronic calculators are capable of calculating a and b automatically, so all you have to do is to enter the values of X and Y. Also most computers provide programs to perform the calculations.

An Example: Quantity-Price Relationship for the Loud and Clear Playback Corporation

In Chapter 1 we used the relationship

$$Q = 5000 - 40P$$

where P is price and Q is quantity sold. Now we make a more accurate calculation by using better data and linear regression analysis.

Figure 4.13 shows the scatter diagram of five data items obtained by market research. The diagram shows pairs of X, the price, and Y, the quantity sold. In Figure 4.14 we show X in column 2 and Y in column 3. In column 4 we compute XY and in column 5, X^2. At the bottom of the table we list X, $\overline{X}$, Y, $\overline{Y}$, XY, and X^2. From our formulas

$$b = \frac{686,000 - 5 \times 80 \times 1800}{33,000 - 5 \times 80^2} = \frac{686,000 - 450,000}{33,000 - 32,000} = -34$$

$$a = 1800 - (-34) \times 80 = 1800 + 2720 = 4520$$

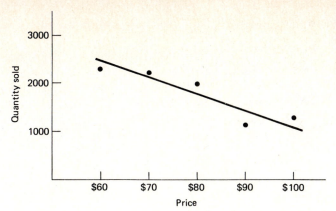

FIGURE 4.13
Scatter diagram for quantity-price rela-tionship.

Thus sales are to be computed from

$$Y_c = 4520 - 34X$$

(See the solid line in Figure 4.13.) Column 5 in Figure 4.14 shows the computed values.

Multiple Regression Analysis

Suppose in the preceding example it is found that the number of salespersons employed by Loud and Clear influences the quantity sold. In such a situation there is need for a formula to relate the dependent

(1)	(2)	(3)	(4)	(5)	(6)
DATA POINT	PRICE (X)	SALES IN THOUSANDS OF DOLLARS (Y)	(X)(Y)	X^2	Y_c
1	$60	2400	144,000	3,600	2480
2	70	2200	154,000	4,900	2140
3	80	2000	160,000	6,400	1800
4	90	1200	108,000	8,100	1460
5	100	1200	120,000	10,000	1120

$$\Sigma X = 400 \qquad \Sigma Y = 9000 \qquad \Sigma XY = 686,000 \qquad \Sigma X^2 = 33,000$$
$$\overline{X} = \Sigma X/n \qquad \overline{Y} = \Sigma Y/n$$
$$= 400/5 \qquad = 9000/5$$
$$= 80 \qquad = 1800$$

FIGURE 4.14 Linear regression analysis for quantity-price relationship.

variable of quantity sold to *two* independent variables: price and number of salespersons.

The statistical technique of relating one dependent variable to two or more dependent variables is called multiple regression analysis. If you know how to apply simple regression analysis, you should have no difficulty in applying multiple regression analysis. This is particularly true because multiple regression analysis is usually done on the computer. All you need do is input the data, and the computer automatically provides the answers.

SUMMARY

1. Today most corporations use a quantitative approach to forecasting because it leads to better performance than the purely judgmental approach.

2. Forecasting involves three considerations: (a) judgment, (b) statistical theory, and (c) mathematical models.

3. The most important prerequisite to good forecasting is careful judgmental examination of data and the separation of extraordinary and repetitive statistical occurrences.

4. Forecasting provides information on uncontrollable factors; decision making focuses on the choice of controllable factors, the decision variables.

5. Statistical forecasting uncovers underlying patterns in data and by extrapolation forecasts the future in a probabilistic sense.

6. A practical forecast usually has three components: (a) trend, (b) seasonal variation, and (c) cyclic or long-term variation.

7. The practice of forecasting heavily depends on the computer.

8. The moving average forecast is based on using the weighted past *n* values of a variable:

$$\text{forecast} = \frac{w_1 x_1 + w_2 x_2 + \cdots + w_n x_n}{w_1 + w_2 + \cdots + w_n}$$

9. The formula for forecasting by exponential smoothing is

$$\text{forecast} = \alpha(\text{value last month})$$
$$+ (1 - \alpha)(\text{previous forecast of current value})$$

10. The trend in a variable can be forecast by fitting a straight line, using linear regression analysis between time and the respective values of the variable.

11. The equation for the best fitting straight line by least squares analysis is

$$Y_c = a + bX$$

where

$$b = \frac{(\Sigma\ XY) - N(\overline{X})(\overline{Y})}{(\Sigma\ X^2) - n(\overline{X})^2}$$

and

$$a = \overline{Y} - b\overline{X}$$

12. Whether a forecasting system is adopted by management depends a great deal on the ability of the analyst to present the proposed system.

13. Without reliable data it is impossible to make a valid statistical forecast.

14. Least squares analysis fits a line to a given set of data by minimizing the sum of the squares of the errors (residuals).

15. Multiple regression analysis develops a relationship between a dependent variable and two or more independent variables.

SECTION EXERCISES

1. *How Business Forecasts*

1.1 Forecasts of future events are often reported in newspapers and magazines. An example of such an area is *housing starts* which are forecast. Can you report two other such areas in which forecasts have recently been discussed in the newspapers and magazines that you read?

1.2 Assume that you are the manager of a factory producing one model of automobile tire. To determine production schedules, you wish to forecast the demand for your tires in the future. The following is a list of factors which influence your demand forecast:
    1. The selling price you set for the tire
    2. Demand in the past
    3. Number of distribution outlets
    4. Advertising and promotion budget
    5. Forecasts of automobile production
    6. Results of a consumer intent-to-purchase survey
    7. Seasonal variation in tire demand
    8. Availability of white-wall models
        a. Which of these factors are controllable?
        b. Which of these factors are uncontrollable?
Hint: See the definition of controllable and uncontrollable factors in Section 4.1.

1.3 The Local Paper Company has tree farms of fast-growing trees which take 10 years to be ready to harvest and convert to paper. The company wants to forecast the plantings necessary today to meet future demand for their special papers. Is this a need for a long-range or short-range forecast?

1.4 The Swinger's Bank wants to offer a special savings certificate that will pay an interest rate which they can pay for the next 6 months. The bank wants to forecast the interest rates so that they can offer an attractive interest rate which will not cost them unnecessarily. Is this a need for a long-range or short-range forecast?

1.5 The following is a list of forecasts:
   1. Market research performed a statistical analysis on the sales of the competition during the past 10 years.
   2. The president of the company says that, in his opinion, the housing market will revive in 1990.
   3. Five economists were brought together as a panel for a whole day to forecast the trend of the Gross National Product.
   4. Census Bureau data on the Minneapolis metropolitan region was analyzed with a computer program to forecast unemployment for the next decade.
   5. The chief of the forecasting section asked his barber what he thought would happen to used car sales next year.

   For each of these forecasts, indicate whether it is a judgmental or statistical forecast.
   Hint: See the discussion of judgmental and statistical forecasts—Section 4.1.

1.6 The text states "Statistical techniques ... extrapolate the *past into the future* ...." What is the danger in "extrapolating the past into the future?"

1.7 Refer to Figure 4.1. The text in Section 4.1 suggests two possible reasons for the peak in the data shown in Figure 4.1: some special extraordinary reason for high sales or an error in the data.
   a. Give an example of some "special extraordinary reason" for a peak in sales.
   b. Give an example of the kind of error that might be made to lead to such a peak in sales.

   Hint: Simple, obvious answers are the best.

1.8 A plot is made of measurements of a standard voltage source; this is a special cell which holds its voltage constant for long periods of time. When the readings are plotted, they form a bell-shaped curve with the exception of one reading at approximately 10 times the voltage of the standard.
   a. What do you call such a value?
   b. What is the causal explanation which you think applies here?

1.9 Refer to Exercise 1.8. If the standard voltage source were rated at 1.08 volts and the unusual reading was 11.1 volts, what value would you use to replace it?

1.10 Why is it an advantage that statistical forecasts can be prepared on computer systems?

2. *Statistical Forecasting*

2.1 The following is a list of situations which might arise in statistical forecasting:
   1. Sales data for a product are decreasing steadily.
   2. Sales data for a product are decreasing at a decreasing rate.
   3. The pattern of demand for a product is to have high seasonal demand at Christmas and Easter.
   4. The pattern of demand for a product is to have high seasonal demand at Christmas and Easter and demand has been slowly increasing from year to year.
   5. Oil price pattern from 1970 to the present.
      a. Make up a table of data which you think might apply to these cases. You are not obligated to be accurate.
      b. Make a graph for each case similar to those shown in Figure 4.2.

2.2 Why is it that forecasting can involve "large masses of data?"

3. *Moving Averages*

3.1 The method called "assuming that tomorrow = today" in Section 4.3 is called by two other names: the *naive method* and *persistence forecasting*.

a. Explain why this method might be called the naive method.
b. Explain why this method might be called persistence forecasting.
c. This method has been used to forecast weather, daily retail store sales, cafeteria demand for certain food items, and payroll cash needs. Why might this be a good method in some cases for these variables?

3.2 Refer to the Wearever data of Figure 4.4 for actual sales data by month.
  a. Obtain the forecast defined by assuming that tomorrow = today.
  b. Plot the forecast.
  c. Complete the *average of last two values* moving average forecast for the monthly data.
  d. Plot the forecast you made in part c.
  e. With the results of parts a–d in hand, compare the two forecasting methods.

Hint: You have the actual values available so that you can compare how each of these forecasts compared to what actually happened in this case.

3.3 The following are sales data for a hypothetical corporation:

YEAR	SALES
1974	106.5
1975	94.82
1976	98.28
1977	120.45
1978	122.09
1979	103.79
1980	116.19
1981	133.36
1982	152.88
1983	141.88

Forecast sales for 1977–1983 using these data by the following methods:
  a. Assuming that tomorrow = today.
  b. Average of last two values.
  c. Weighted average of last two values.
  d. Average of last three values.
  e. Weighted average of last three values.
  f. With the results of parts a–e in hand, compare the five forecasting methods.

Hint: You have the actual values available so that you can compare how each of these forecasts compared to what actually happened in this case.

3.4 The following is shipments (number of cases shipped) data for a hypothetical corporation:

YEAR	SHIPMENTS
1974	7302
1975	3545
1976	3520
1977	2477
1978	3509
1979	4134
1980	3389
1981	4820
1982	7205
1983	6805

Forecast shipments for 1977–1983 using these data by the following methods:
  a. Assuming that tomorrow = today.
  b. Average of last two values.
  c. Weighted average of last two values.
  d. Average of last three values.
  e. Weighted average of last three values.
  f. With the results of parts a–e in hand, compare the five forecasting methods.

Hint: You have the actual values available so that you can compare how each of these forecasts compared to what actually happened in this case.

3.5 The following is data on payroll costs for a hypothetical corporation:

YEAR	PAYROLL, $(000)
1974	8,181
1975	7,414
1976	7,249
1977	8,121
1978	10,067
1979	12,646
1980	16,397
1981	14,479
1982	14,969
1983	13,600

Forecast sales for 1977–1983 using these data by the following methods:
  a. Assuming that tomorrow = today.
  b. Average of last two values.
  c. Weighted average of last two values.
  d. Average of last three values.
  e. Weighted average of last three values.
  f. With the results of parts a–e in hand, compare the five forecasting methods.

YEAR	MONTH	DISTANCE, KM (000)
1981	Jan.	13,171
	Feb.	11,977
	March	13,651
	April	15,871
	May	16,495
	June	19,762
	July	18,723
	Aug.	18,627
	Sept.	19,979
	Oct.	15,506
	Nov.	13,023
	Dec.	14,932
1982	Jan.	13,409
	Feb.	12,710
	March	16,080
	April	16,216
	May	17,379
	June	20,837

Hint: You have the actual values available so that you can compare how each of these forecasts compared to what actually happened in this case.

3.6 The following are data on the distances flown by the Freddie Ponder Airlines for an 18-month period (by month):
Forecast sales for April 1981–June 1982 using these data by the following methods:
   a. Assuming that tomorrow = today.
   b. Average of last two values.
   c. Weighted average of last two values.
   d. Average of last three values.
   e. Weighted average of last three values.
   f. With the results of parts a–e in hand, compare the five forecasting methods.
Hint: You have the actual values available so that you can compare how each of these forecasts compared to what actually happened in this case.

4. Exponential Smoothing

4.1 For what value of the weight alpha is the exponential smoothing method the same as the assume that tomorrow = today method?

4.2 Refer to the Wearever data of Figure 4.4 for actual sales data by month. Using the data for the first 12 months, carry out an exponential smoothing forecast for alpha of .1, .4, .8:
   a. Make a table showing your exponential smoothing forecasts.
   b. Make a plot of your forecasts.
   c. Which value of alpha do you judge to be the "best"?

4.3 Refer to the sales data of Exercise 3.3. Carry out an exponential smoothing forecast for these data using alpha of .1, .4, and .8:
   a. Make a table showing your exponential smoothing forecasts.
   b. Make a plot of your forecasts.
   c. Which value of alpha do you judge to be the "best?"

4.4 Refer to the shipments data of Exercise 3.4. Carry out an exponential smoothing forecast for these data using alpha of .2, .5, and .8:
   a. Make a table showing your exponential smoothing forecasts.
   b. Make a plot of your forecasts.
   c. Which value of alpha do you judge to be the "best?"

4.5 Refer to the payroll cost data of Exercise 3.5. Carry out an exponential smoothing forecast for these data using alpha of .1, .5, and .7:
   a. Make a table showing your exponential smoothing forecasts.
   b. Make a plot of your forecasts.
   c. Which value of alpha do you judge to be the "best?"

4.6 Refer to the distances flown data of Exercise 3.6. Carry out an exponential smoothing forecast for these data using alpha of .3, .5, and .7:
   a. Make a table showing your exponential smoothing forecasts.
   b. Make a plot of your forecasts.
   c. Which value of alpha do you judge to be the "best?"

5. Trend Projection by Regression Analysis

5.1 Refer to the sales data of Exercise 3.3.
   a. Using all the data given, perform a trend analysis by linear regression (determine the linear regression line).
   b. Use your linear regression to forecast the values for the next four periods.
   c. Draw a plot showing the data and the regression line of your forecast.

5.2 Refer to the shipments data of Exercise 3.4.
   a. Using all the data given, perform a trend analysis by linear regression (determine the linear regression line).

b. Use your linear regression to forecast the values for the next four periods.

c. The actual data for the next four periods were 6882, 8242, 8181, and 7414. Draw a plot showing the actual data and your forecast.

5.3 Refer to the payroll data of Exercise 3.5.

a. Using all the data given, perform a trend analysis by linear regression (determine the linear regression line).

b. Use your linear regression to forecast the values for the next four periods.

c. The actual data for the next four periods were 15,203, 14,986, 12,122, and 11,090. Draw a plot showing the actual data and your forecast.

5.4 Refer to the distances data of Exercise 3.6.

a. Using all the data given, perform a trend analysis by linear regression (determine the linear regression line).

b. Use your linear regression to forecast the values for the next four periods.

c. The actual data for the next four periods were 19,665, 19,704, 21,369, and 16,679. Draw a plot showing the actual data and your forecast.

6. *Forecasting at American Can Company: A Case Study*

6.1 Can *statistical* forecasting deal with "recurring situations such as an announced price increase?"

6.2 How would *you* go about making sure that a forecasting system was "understandable to operating managers?"

6.3 Why was it important that the model developed be "explainable?"

6.4 How could management come to the conclusion that "the new system performed better than the old one" without "sophisticated statistical measures and cost benefit analysis?"

6.5 Refer to Exercise 6.4. *Should* management use "sophisticated statistical measures and cost benefit analysis" in judging forecasting models?

7. *A Dialog*

7.1 Why is it an advantage to have a "scientific technique of analysis of alternative futures?"

7.2 Why do you think that people do not want to "look at the data?"

7.3 Make a list of the reasons that management might not accept the recommendations based on a "sophisticated set of equations." Use all your knowledge of mathematical models, people, and the business world. If you do not have first-hand experience in business, ask someone who does to get some ideas. Be imaginative, and don't hesitate to ask.

8. *Appendix: Review of Regression Analysis*

8.1 Find the regression equation for the following data:

MONTHLY SALES, Y	MONTHLY EXPENDITURES, X
3.2	.0
7.9	1.0
1.8	.0
12.6	2.0
12.1	2.0
.8	.0
5.8	2.0
10.6	2.0
16.0	3.0
4.9	1.0

8.2 Find the regression equation for the following data:

QUANTITY PURCHASED, X (TONS)	COST PER TON, Y ($)
125	4.80
100	5.50
125	4.50
140	4.50
150	4.30
150	4.60
110	5.60
110	5.60
100	5.40
105	5.80
150	4.30

8.3 Find the regression equation for the following data:

YEARS OF SERVICE, X	REPAIR COST, Y ($)
2	15.50
1	11.10
11	62.60
6	35.40
5	24.90
7	28.10
3	23.20
10	42.00
1	10.00
4	20.00
8	47.50

8.4 Find the regression equation for the following data:

LENGTH OF STALKS, X (CM)	PRICE OF BUNCH, Y (CENTS)
16	87
14	69
18	93
14	64
16	82
16	86
18	96
18	98

CHAPTER EXERCISES AND DISCUSSION QUESTIONS

C.1 Why would an organization want to make the making of a forecast a matter of organizational policy?

C.2 What is the characteristic of long-term trends that makes it relatively easy to forecast the near future?

C.3 As accuracy of the forecast declines, how does the cost of forecasting vary? Draw a plot of the relationship of cost of forecasting vs. accuracy (declining to the right on the x axis).

C.4 As the accuracy of the forecast declines, how does the cost of inaccuracy vary? On the same axis as you used in C.3, draw the plot for the cost due to inaccuracy vs. declining forecast accuracy.

C.5 Combine the curves in C3 and C4 to give a total cost curve. What guidance do you get from it?

C.6 What are the ways you can "look at the data?" That is, what kinds of plots can you make? Use your imagination, and look in other texts more directly oriented to forecasting. You can start by listing scatter plots (mentioned in the text), and take it from there.

C.7 In what situations (what kind of behavior of the variable to be forecasted) do you feel exponential smoothing has the greatest applicability?

C.8 How would *you* obtain a regression forecast if you had a set of data? Would you solve the equations in the text? Think of the computational aids you might have access to.

C.9 If your answer to C.8 would be to use some computer-calculator to do the computations, how would you try to be sure that they have been done right?

5

Decision Analysis

In Chapter 1 we discussed the two main classes of decision problems: deterministic or certain and probabilistic or uncertain. In Chapters 2 and 3 we reviewed probability theory to deal with uncertainty. In Chapter 4 we showed the scientific approach to dealing with uncertain and uncontrollable factors of the future. Now we proceed to study in depth decision making under uncertainty where the problem is the choice of controllable factors or decision variables. Our discussion will include the decision support system (DSS) approach which stresses the use of computers in making decisions.

Before developing our material, we must realize that a manager operates in a world of uncertainty. To begin with, no one can predict with certainty what will happen. Furthermore, neither the present nor past world is completely known to the manager. In fact, it is not practical to obtain the infinite variety of data needed to describe the world. **Decision analysis** is the quantitative and rational approach to decision making under uncertainty. Decision analysis provides the decision maker with the tools and information to deal with uncertainty and is concerned with two aspects of decision making: *what* information to obtain and *how* to make the best decision.

The fundamental approach of decision analysis is to express uncertainty in terms of probability theory. Thus the first step in applying decision analysis is to convert the problem into a thought experiment and to describe the problem with the aid of a probability model. The model establishes the mathematical relationship among the various deterministic and random variables of the problem. Then information is obtained to specify probabilistic inputs to the model, and the probabilistic outputs are computed. Finally, an action is chosen by selecting the one which provides the most desirable probabilistic payoff.

We develop this approach to decision making via illustrative examples. There is a large variety of applications to choose from, and here we select a few typical situations which illustrate both theory and practice.

5.1 THEORY AND PRACTICE OF DECISION MAKING: SELLING STRAWBERRIES

Managers are often faced with the problem of manufacturing and distributing perishable products which cannot be kept in storage for extended time periods. Illustrations that come easily to mind are fish, fruit, vegetables, milk, airline seats, albums of popular songs, etc.

To be specific, consider Mr. S. T. Berry who recently acquired from a friend a roadside fruitstand selling strawberries. The selling price of a basket of strawberries is $1.50, and the cost to Berry is $1.20. These values are assumed to be *certain*, but the demand for strawberries is *uncertain*; it is a random variable. Let us assume that the demand can be modeled by a thought experiment using a roulette wheel, shown in Figure 5.1(a). The decision problem with which Berry is faced is to determine how many baskets of strawberries to buy each morning.

Berry's friend has a policy or decision rule: to buy 14 baskets of strawberries each morning. Berry is not sure that this is the best or even a good decision rule and wants to consider other decision rules and evaluate and compare them. As a first step he evaluates the rule of buying 14 baskets.

Berry evaluates a decision rule in terms of profit. Note that demand, sales, and profit are all random variables. Berry wants to maximize profit, but how can he do this if profit is a random variable? He decides to calculate the average or expected *value* of the profit and use it as the evaluator of the decision rule. So now Berry needs to express the uncertainty of the problem in terms of probabilities.

Let us assume that Berry accepts the thought experiment in Figure 5.1(a). Berry may have reached his conviction by examining records of past sales of strawberries, by believing us, by guessing, or by other means. Berry agrees that the demand will be 13, 14, 15, or 16 baskets of strawberries and that the respective probabilities are .1, .3, .4, and .2, as shown in Figure 5.1(b). *This is the random variable specifying the demand.* A graphical representation of the demand and probabilities is given by the probability mass function (PMF) in Figure 5.1(c).

The next step is to determine the random variable of sales, that is, the number of baskets sold. The probability is .1 that the demand is 13, so the probability is .1 that sales are 13 baskets. In column 3 of Figure 5.2 we show sales. Note that sales are never more than 14 baskets because Berry buys 14 baskets.

Revenue is obtained by multiplying sales by the selling price of $1.50. The values of this random variable are shown in column 4 of Figure 5.2. Column 5 shows the (constant) cost of buying 14 baskets or $14 \times 1.20 = \$16.80$. Column 6 shows the values of the payoffs or profits of the random variable specifying the payoffs-profits.

The final step is to calculate the expected payoff. You will recall the

(a)

Probability of demand	Demand for baskets of strawberries
.1	13
.3	14
.4	15
.2	16
1.0	

(b)

(c)

two-step procedure for calculating the expected value of a random variable:

Step 1. Multiply each probability by each value of the random variable (shown in column 7, Figure 5.2).

Step 2. Add all the products (shown on the bottom line of Figure 5.2 as $4.05, the expected daily profit).

Note that this result holds because (1) Berry accepts the decision rule, and (2) Berry accepts the PMF of Figure 5.1 for the demand. We call this expected daily profit the **expected monetary value** or **EMV**.

This answer is obtained under the assumption that Berry will continue to buy 14 baskets each morning. However, there is no reason to believe that this policy of buying 14 baskets is the best policy. How many should Berry buy?

(1)	(2)	(3)	(4)	(5)	(6) PAYOFF- PROFIT: (4) − (5)	(7)
PROBABILITY OF DEMAND	DEMAND	SALES	REVENUE	COST		PRODUCT OF (1) and (6)
.1	13	13	$19.50	$16.80	$2.70	$ .27
.3	14	14	21.00	16.80	4.20	1.26
.4	15	14	21.00	16.80	4.20	1.68
.2	16	14	21.00	16.80	4.20	.84
1.0						

Expected daily profit, EMV = $4.05

FIGURE 5.2 Expected daily profit for strawberry problem if Berry uses the decision rule of buying 14 baskets each morning.

Decision Criteria

Berry may never want to lose a sale; thus he buys 16 baskets each morning. Or he may never want to throw away strawberries and buys only 13 baskets each morning. Neither of these two decision rules relates directly to the long-range profitability of the business venture. We present now the following rule as the criterion for decision making:

> The best act is one which maximizes the expected payoff.

This rule is called Bayes' decision rule after the English clergyman and mathematician Thomas Bayes (not to be confused with Bayes' theorem in Section 2.6).

Theory of Decision Making

We can now formulate the mathematical theory of decision making. As an example, assume that the decision maker is to choose an act from three acts, a_1, a_2, and a_3 and that for each **act** there are five outcomes: x_1, x_2, x_3, x_4, and x_5. (Of course we may have any number of acts and any number of outcomes.)

For each outcome-act pair there is a payoff. Designate by V_{11} the value of the payoff for outcome x_1 and act a_1, by V_{12} the payoff for outcome x_1 and act a_2, and so on, a total of $5 \times 3 = 15$ for our example.* The payoff matrix (table) is as follows:

OUT- COMES	ACTS		
	a_1	a_2	a_3
x_1	V_{11}	V_{12}	V_{13}
x_2	V_{21}	V_{22}	V_{23}
x_3	V_{31}	V_{32}	V_{33}
x_4	V_{41}	V_{42}	V_{43}
x_5	V_{51}	V_{52}	V_{53}

* In Appendix A1, Section 10, there is a review of doubly subscripted notation and matrices.

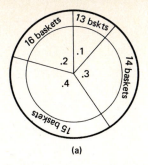

(a)

Probability of demand	Demand for baskets of strawberries
.1	13
.3	14
.4	15
.2	16

1.0

(b)

(c)

two-step procedure for calculating the expected value of a random variable:

Step 1. Multiply each probability by each value of the random variable (shown in column 7, Figure 5.2).
Step 2. Add all the products (shown on the bottom line of Figure 5.2 as $4.05, the expected daily profit).

Note that this result holds because (1) Berry accepts the decision rule, and (2) Berry accepts the PMF of Figure 5.1 for the demand. We call this expected daily profit the **expected monetary value** or **EMV**.

This answer is obtained under the assumption that Berry will continue to buy 14 baskets each morning. However, there is no reason to believe that this policy of buying 14 baskets is the best policy. How many should Berry buy?

(1)	(2)	(3)	(4)	(5)	(6)	(7)
PROBABILITY OF DEMAND	DEMAND	SALES	REVENUE	COST	PAYOFF- PROFIT: (4) – (5)	PRODUCT OF (1) and (6)
.1	13	13	$19.50	$16.80	$2.70	$ .27
.3	14	14	21.00	16.80	4.20	1.26
.4	15	14	21.00	16.80	4.20	1.68
.2	16	14	21.00	16.80	4.20	.84
1.0						

Expected daily profit, EMV = $4.05

FIGURE 5.2 Expected daily profit for strawberry problem if Berry uses the decision rule of buying 14 baskets each morning.

Decision Criteria

Berry may never want to lose a sale; thus he buys 16 baskets each morning. Or he may never want to throw away strawberries and buys only 13 baskets each morning. Neither of these two decision rules relates directly to the long-range profitability of the business venture. We present now the following rule as the criterion for decision making:

> The best act is one which maximizes the expected payoff.

This rule is called Bayes' decision rule after the English clergyman and mathematician Thomas Bayes (not to be confused with Bayes' theorem in Section 2.6).

Theory of Decision Making

We can now formulate the mathematical theory of decision making. As an example, assume that the decision maker is to choose an act from three acts, a_1, a_2, and a_3 and that for each **act** there are five outcomes: x_1, x_2, x_3, x_4, and x_5. (Of course we may have any number of acts and any number of outcomes.)

For each outcome-act pair there is a payoff. Designate by V_{11} the value of the payoff for outcome x_1 and act a_1, by V_{12} the payoff for outcome x_1 and act a_2, and so on, a total of $5 \times 3 = 15$ for our example.* The payoff matrix (table) is as follows:

OUT-COMES	ACTS		
	a_1	a_2	a_3
x_1	V_{11}	V_{12}	V_{13}
x_2	V_{21}	V_{22}	V_{23}
x_3	V_{31}	V_{32}	V_{33}
x_4	V_{41}	V_{42}	V_{43}
x_5	V_{51}	V_{52}	V_{53}

* In Appendix A1, Section 10, there is a review of doubly subscripted notation and matrices.

Similarly, for each outcome-act pair there is a conditional probability. Designate by p_{11} the conditional probability of x_1 occurring provided act a_1 is taken, by p_{21} the conditional probability of x_2 occurring provided act a_1 is taken, and so on. The probability matrix (table) is as follows:

OUT-COMES	ACTS		
	a_1	a_2	a_3
x_1	p_{11}	p_{12}	p_{13}
x_2	p_{21}	p_{22}	p_{23}
x_3	p_{31}	p_{32}	p_{33}
x_4	p_{41}	p_{42}	p_{43}
x_5	p_{51}	p_{52}	p_{53}

Note that for each act (or column in the table) there are five probabilities and five payoffs.

> For each act the payoffs are given by a random variable.

For example, for act a_1 the outcome probabilities are p_{11}, p_{21}, p_{31}, p_{41}, and p_{51}, and the values are V_{11}, V_{21}, V_{31}, V_{41}, and V_{51}.

For each act there is a random variable specifying the payoffs, and so for each act there is an expected value of the payoff. For example, the expected payoff for act a_1 is

$$z_1 = p_{11}V_{11} + p_{21}V_{21} + p_{31}V_{31} + p_{41}V_{41} + p_{51}V_{51}$$

and for a_2 is

$$z_2 = p_{12}V_{12} + p_{22}V_{22} + p_{32}V_{32} + p_{42}V_{42} + p_{52}V_{52}$$

and so on. For each act a the expected payoff is the corresponding z.

> The decision maker's problem is to choose an act a such that for act a the corresponding expected payoff z becomes a maximum. The decision rule is a procedure to find act a.

We can express our theory in terms of a thought experiment. Suppose for each act a we have a wheel of fortune marked with the respective dollar values. *Choosing an act means choosing a wheel of fortune.* Each wheel represents a random variable. So we can write the expected value of the random variable on the wheel. *The problem is to choose the wheel of fortune with the highest expected value of payoffs.*

For many practical problems the outcome probabilities are the same for all the acts. Then

$$p_{11} = p_{21} = p_{31} = p_{41} = p_{51}$$

and so on for all the other columns. Then all the wheels of fortune are the same, except that the dollar values marked are different. This, then, simplifies the calculations required. The rest of this chapter applies the theory to practical decision problems.

Solving the Strawberry Problem

To solve this decision problem, first we develop the payoff table. As shown in Figure 5.3, at the top we list the various acts, which in this case are to order 13, 14, 15, or 16 baskets. Each row of the payoff table corresponds to one of the outcomes, namely, to the possibility that the demand is 13, 14, 15, or 16 baskets. Each number in the table is the dollar payoff. For example, for act a_3 15 baskets are ordered. If the outcome is x_2, the demand is 14. The payoff-profit is

$$\text{revenue from 14 baskets sold} = 14 \times \$1.50 = \$21.00$$

$$\text{cost of buying 15 baskets} = 15 \times \$1.20 = \$18.00$$

$$\text{Profit} = \$21.00 - \$18.00 = \$3.00$$

A graphical model by a decision tree (Figure 5.4) is useful for explaining the meaning of the payoff table. At the foot of the tree the square box designates a decision fork. Here a decision is to be made on which act to choose, that is, how many baskets to buy. Each act leads to a chance fork (a wheel of fortune) shown by small circles. Each chance fork leads to the four outcomes of having a demand of 13, 14, 15, or 16 baskets. The respective probabilities are independent of the acts and are listed under the branches, and the values of the payoff table are listed at the tips of the tree.

With the aid of the payoff table (Figure 5.3) or with the decision tree in Figure 5.4, we can compute the expected payoff for each act, as shown in Figure 5.5. In Figure 5.6 we write these values in the circles corresponding to the chance forks. Note that the best act is to buy 14 baskets of strawberries, because this act yields the highest expected daily profit of $4.05.

There are two important points to make. If the demand is less than 14 baskets, there will be a waste of spoiled strawberries.

> Planned waste may be profitable.

OUTCOME-DEMAND	DEMAND FOR BASKETS	PROBABILITIES	ACTS, NUMBER OF BASKETS PURCHASED EACH MORNING			
			a_1 13	a_2 14	a_3 15	a_4 16
x_1	13	.1	3.90	2.70	1.50	.30
x_2	14	.3	3.90	4.20	3.00	1.80
x_3	15	.4	3.90	4.20	4.50	3.30
x_4	16	.2	3.90	4.20	4.50	4.80

FIGURE 5.3 Payoff table (profit in dollars) for the strawberry problem.

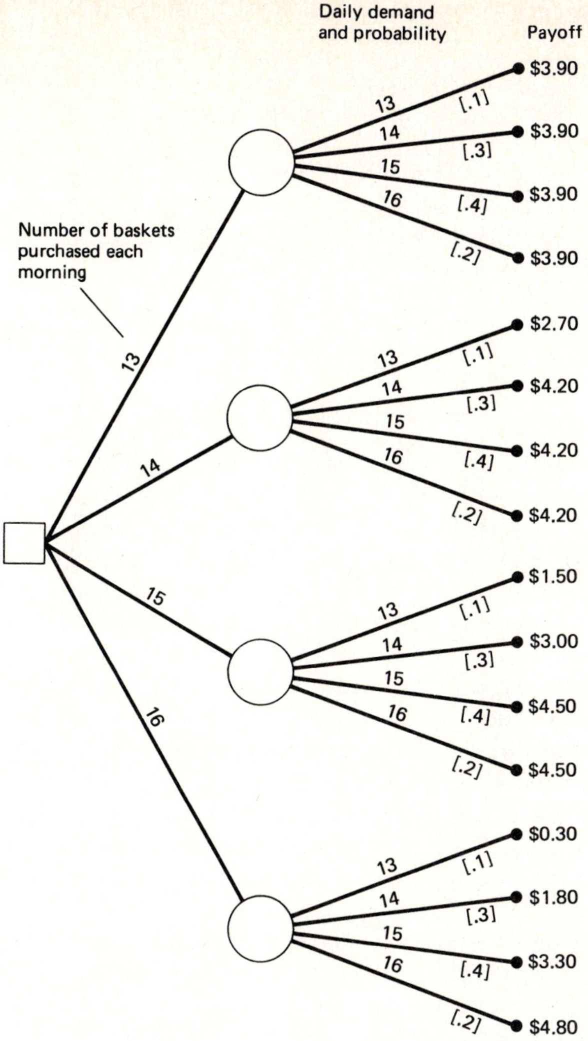

Number of baskets
purchased each
morning

Daily demand
and probability   Payoff

FIGURE 5.4
Decision tree for the
strawberry problem.

Second, if the demand is over 14 baskets, there will be a loss of sales or shortage.

Planned loss of sales may be profitable.

The Four-Step Procedure for Solving Decision Problems

Step 1. List potential actions, outcomes, and payoffs.
Step 2. Assign probabilities to outcomes.
Step 3. Compute the expected payoff for each act.
Step 4. Choose the act with the maximum expected payoff.

ACTS, NUMBER OF BASKETS PURCHASED EACH MORNING

Demand	Probability	BUY 13 BASKETS			BUY 14 BASKETS			BUY 15 BASKETS			BUY 16 BASKETS		
		Sales	Payoff	Probability × payoff	Sales	Payoff	Probability × payoff	Sales	Payoff	Probability × payoff	Sales	Payoff	Probability × payoff
13	.1	13	3.90	.39	13	2.70	.27	13	1.50	.15	13	.30	.03
14	.3	13	3.90	1.17	14	4.20	1.26	14	3.00	.90	14	1.80	.54
15	.4	13	3.90	1.56	14	4.20	1.68	15	4.50	1.80	15	3.30	1.32
16	.2	13	3.90	.78	14	4.20	.84	15	4.50	.90	16	4.80	.96
Expected daily profit				$3.90			$4.05			$3.75			$2.85

FIGURE 5.5 Strawberry problem when all four possible acts are considered. The best act is to order 14 baskets of strawberries.

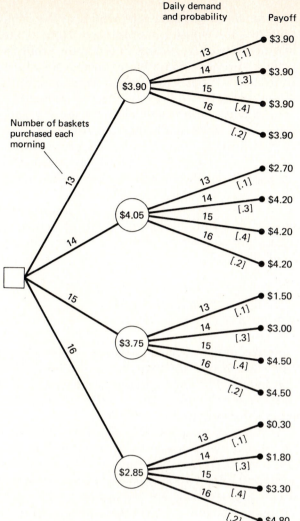

Daily demand
and probability

Payoff

FIGURE 5.6
Solving the strawberry
problem with a decision
tree.

Other Decision Criteria

So far we have accepted the principle of selecting the best decision by
maximizing the expected payoff. However, several other principles have
also been proposed.

For example, one may argue that a pessimist will ignore probabilities and consider only the worst possible case. For instance, in the
strawberry problem, Figure 5.3, he may argue that if he chooses act a_3,
that is, if he purchases 15 baskets of strawberries in the morning, his
profit could be only $1.50. So this decision maker examines the worst
outcome for each decision, that is, he looks at the smallest number in
each column in Figure 5.3. These numbers are as follows: $3.90, $2.70,
$1.50, and $.30. The maximum of these worst cases occurs for the first act
a_1, which assures a profit of $3.90. This pessimistic decision maker uses

the so-called *maximin* decision rule, which, as the name implies, selects the maximum of the worst possible case. Here it means ordering 13 baskets of strawberries, resulting in a certain profit of $3.90. Compare this with the criterion of using the expected payoff which results in an expected profit of $4.05 if 14 baskets of strawberries are purchased.

An alternate argument is to take the point of view of the incorrigible optimist. He examines the payoff table in Figure 5.3 and observes that if he purchases 16 baskets of strawberries, he could possibly reap a profit of $4.80. The probability of this occurring is only .2, but the optimist ignores this and proceeds to order 16 baskets of strawberries. He is hoping for a profit of $4.80, which is of course more than the $4.05 obtained by maximizing the expected profit.

There are also other suggestions for decision criteria, but none of them have obtained wide acceptance in the practical managerial world. Therefore, in this textbook we shall ignore these alternate approaches to decision making.

The Mind as an Informal Synthesizer: The DSS Approach

You must realize, of course, that the theory of decision making requiring complete payoff and probability matrices can only approximate real-life decision problems. The better the approximation, the better the solution, though there will always be room for judgment. However, it often occurs that it is difficult, impractical, or in fact impossible to develop the required matrices in a sufficiently complete manner so that decision theory can be explicitly used. It is said that the problem cannot be sufficiently *structured* or that the decision maker's problem is an *unstructured* problem. Advocates of decision support systems stress that such unstructured problems are the proper area for DSS.

The problem may be unstructured, yet a lot of relevant information can be stored in the computer, and so the decision maker can conduct dialogs to obtain information required to make a decision. The decision maker may specify certain sets of possible acts and examine the outcomes indicated by the computer. The computer response may not be just a payoff but may be a whole set of factors, such as profits for the present and for future years, cash flows, cost, and other factors occurring in traditional financial reports. The decision maker then by judgment conducts the dialog, examines uncertainties, and informally makes a choice by selecting an acceptable alternative. In such systems there may not be explicit statements as to all the possible acts, outcomes, probabilities, etc., and it is up to the judgment of the decision maker to make the choice. The analysts or designers of such systems provide mathematical models, data, and dialog systems to support the decision maker in the choice. For this reason some people refer to decision support systems as *mind* support systems.

Consider Harold Trojinski, comptroller of the Loud and Clear Playback Corporation, who reviews the inventory records of tape recorders and finds that according to those records there is a total of 4500 units stored in the various warehouses of the corporation. Trojinski knows from past experience there is often some discrepancy in the records, or, as accountants often say, there is (an **accounting**) **variance**—a difference between the count in the records and the actual inventory. Why? Human errors enter into record keeping, such as the failure to record a sale of goods, a return of goods, or an incoming shipment. Defective items are scrapped, some items deteriorate in storage, and others are misplaced. Or, in some cases, there may be theft.

To simplify the situation, we assume that Trojinski has a lot of experience with Loud and Clear and knows with certainty that there is a variance. He also knows that if this variance is not found, the corporation will suffer a certain loss of $30,000. The corporation wants an **audit** to determine the exact number of tape recorders in inventory and wants to pinpoint the cause of the variance. To conduct an audit, which is a form of investigation, costs money. There may be alternate ways to conduct the audit, each involving a different cost.

> Whether or not to investigate is a decision problem in itself.

Let us now model the alternatives available to Trojinski with the aid of the tree diagram in Figure 5.7.

Alternative 1 is to do nothing. This will cost the corporation a certain $30,000.

Alternative 2 is to conduct an **internal audit**, which means using L&C's own staff. However, the accountants are already quite busy and would have to work overtime on Saturdays, which makes the audit costly. It is estimated that the cost of conducting the investigation is $35,000. Clearly, alternative 1, doing nothing, is $5000 less costly than alternative 2, and so the proposition of conducting an internal audit is immediately discarded. In addition, Trojinski is considering three proposals for **external audits**.

Alternative 3 is offered by an external auditor. It guarantees to find and correct the variance for $25,000. This is $5000 better than the do-nothing alternative 2 and so is the best of the three alternatives considered so far. But there are two other alternatives to be considered.

The external audit of alternative 4 costs only $18,000. This is $7000 less than alternative 3. But here is the catch: This investigation involves a partial audit, and the auditor estimates that there is a probability of 1/5 of missing the variance or a probability of 4/5 of finding it. Thus there still is the possibility that after the $18,000 is paid to the external auditor,

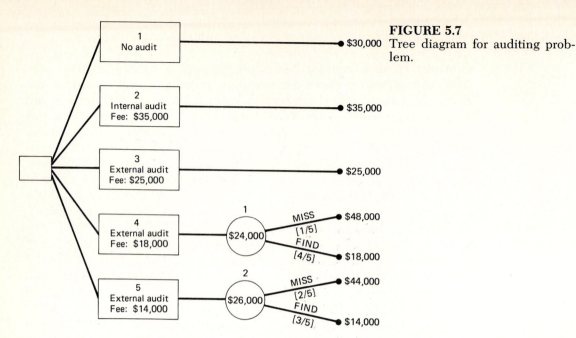

FIGURE 5.7
Tree diagram for auditing problem.

the variance will not be found, and the corporation will suffer the additional loss of $30,000.

Note that if the variance is missed, the loss is

$$\$30,000 + \$18.000 = \$48,000$$

and if the variance is found, the loss is $18,000, as shown in the respective tips of the decision tree in Figure 5.7. Thus the expected loss for alternative 4 is

$$\tfrac{1}{5} \times \$48,000 + \tfrac{4}{5} \times \$18,000 = \$24,000$$

as shown in chance fork 1.

Finally, consider alternative 5 when the fee is $14,000 and the probability of missing the variance is 2/5. Now the expected loss is

$$\tfrac{2}{5}\,(\$30,000 + \$14,000) + \tfrac{3}{5} \times \$14,000 = \$26,000$$

as shown in chance fork 2.

To apply Bayes' decision rule, we must *minimize* the expected loss. Thus the optimal act is alternative 4, that is, to pay $18,000 and permit a 1/5 probability of missing the variance.

5.3 PERFECT INFORMATION AND MONETARY VALUE OF INFORMATION

Here we point out that in the Loud and Clear audit problem it made good sense to pay for information, that is, to purchase the audit. Information is in fact a resource somewhat like material, capital, labor, and so on and can be assigned a dollar value. So now we return to the strawberry problem to discuss a second feature of decision theory, namely finding the *monetary value of information*. First, assume that Berry, the seller of strawberries, can at no cost get the advice of a *clairvoyant*, who can foresee the future. Sales of strawberries are uncertain, but such a person can provide a perfect schedule of sales for Berry, who then can order the exact amount to meet the demand for strawberries. There will be no lost sales because Berry always acts in the best way. What is the **expected value** of such **perfect information, EVPI,** to Berry?

The clairvoyant foresees the future, and so there are no lost sales; expected sales are equal to expected demand. In Figure 5.8 we determine that expected demand is 14.7 baskets.* Berry makes 30 cents on each sale, so his expected profit, or the expected monetary value with perfect information, is

$$\text{EMVPI} = 14.7 \times \$3 = \$4.41$$

We refer to the expected monetary value (EMV) without the information system (the no-information case) as $(\text{EMV})_0$ when it is necessary to state explicitly that we refer to the no-information case.

We stress that EMVPI is computed under the assumption that perfect information can be obtained free. In a practical case, when there is a fee, EMVPI is only the gross EMVPI, and the net EMV is $\text{EMVPI} - F$, where F is the fee.

The expected value of perfect information (EVPI) is the difference between what Berry can expect to earn with (free) perfect information and what he can earn without perfect information:

$$\text{EVPI} = \text{EMVPI} - (\text{EMV})_0 = \$4.41 - \$4.05 = \$.36$$

Note again that if there is a fee F to buy the information system, EVPI provides only a gross value.

What gain accrues to the decision maker if he buys the information system? The value of this gain is given by the expected net gain, or

$$\text{ENG} = (\text{EMVPI} - F) - (\text{EMV})_0$$

or

$$\text{ENG} = \text{EVPI} - F$$

---

* Note that actual demand never equals expected demand.

DEMAND	PROBABILITY OF DEMAND	PRODUCT
13	.1	1.3
14	.3	4.2
15	.4	6.0
16	.2	3.2

Expected daily demand = 14.7 Baskets

FIGURE 5.8 Expected daily demand for strawberry problem.

Suppose Berry can purchase the perfect information for $.20. We have

$$\text{ENG} = \text{EVPI} - F = \$.36 - \$.20 = \$.16$$

indicating that Berry should buy the information system. However, if F is $.50, then

$$\text{ENG} = \text{EVPI} - F = \$.36 - \$.50 = -\$.14$$

and Berry should not buy the information system because the fee F is greater than EVPI, the expected value of perfect information.

Using our theory, we get the following procedure for calculating the monetary value of perfect information.

Step 1. Calculate the expected monetary value of the venture with perfect information, EMVPI.

Step 2. Calculate the expected monetary value of the venture without perfect information, $(\text{EMV})_0$.

Step 3. Calculate the expected net gain:

$$\text{ENG} = \text{EMVPI} - (\text{EMV})_0 - F$$

Step 4. If ENG is positive, buy the perfect information.

Insofar as Berry's problem is concerned, we can summarize our calculations for the four situations considered. The value of the venture is as follows:

1. Without perfect information: $(\text{EMV})_0 = \$4.05$.
2. With free perfect information: EMVPI = $4.41.
3. With perfect information at a cost of $.20: $\$4.41 - \$.20 = \$4.21$.
4. With perfect information at a cost of $.50: $4.05. (Berry refuses to buy the perfect information at $.50.)

Note that perfect information removes uncertainty from the problem for Berry. The clairvoyant provides a schedule of future sales, so Berry will never be faced with an unexpected demand. (Imperfect information, which does not remove uncertainty, will be discussed in Chapter 6.)

5.4 BREAK-EVEN ANALYSIS UNDER UNCERTAINTY

The Presto Corporation is faced with the problem of increasing labor costs and considering the introduction of an automatic machine to replace manual labor. For purposes of analysis, it is assumed that the machine will wear out in 1 year, that the fixed cost of obtaining the machine is $8400, and that for each hour of manual labor saved there is a cost avoidance or cost benefit of $4.00. Thus,

$$\text{COST BENEFIT} = 4 \times \text{HOURS} - 8400$$

Figure 5.9 shows the traditional break-even analysis in a graphical form. For example, if there is a replacement of 3000 hours of labor, there is a cost benefit of

$$3000 \times \$4.00 - \$8400 = \$3600$$

If only 2000 hours are replaced,

$$2000 \times \$4.00 - \$8400 = -\$400$$

which means a loss of \$400.

The **break-even point**, where the benefit is zero, is at

$$\frac{8400}{4.00} = 2100 \text{ hours}$$

If Presto knew how many labor hours would be replaced, the benefit (or loss) could be determined and a decision made whether to purchase the automatic machine. However, management is uncertain about the number of labor hours that will be replaced. Should they purchase the machine?

Solving the Problem with Decision Analysis

First we convert the uncertainties of the problem to probabilities, which can be done by agreeing on a thought experiment representation of the problem.

After reviewing the various product lines of the corporation and much soul searching, management agrees that there is a 50–50 chance that the machine will save either 2550 hours or 1950 hours. *The number of hours saved is a random variable: the values are 2550 and 1950 hours, and the probabilities are 1/2 and 1/2.* The expected number of hours saved is 1/2 × 2550 + 1/2 × 1950 = 2250 hours. The chance device in the thought experiment may be a coin or a wheel of fortune with two equal

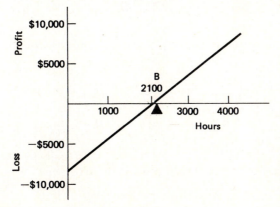

FIGURE 5.9
Break-even analysis for Presto Corporation.

sectors [Figure 5.10(a)]. Referring to the higher figure (2550) as success and to the lower figure (1950) as failure, we can say that if the ball stops at success on the wheel of fortune, Presto would have done better to bet on the venture; otherwise, Presto should have passed the bet. Success means a gross benefit of 4 × $2550 = $10,200, and failure means 4 × $1950 = $7800. The net benefit, the payoff, after the fixed cost of $8400 is subtracted, is a gain of $1800 or a loss of $600. Now we can prepare the decision tree and the payoff table for the venture [Figures 5.10(b) and (c)], which shows the payoff (net benefit) for each pair of outcomes and acts.

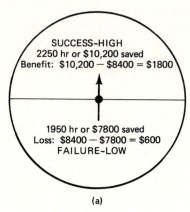

SUCCESS–HIGH
2250 hr or $10,200 saved
Benefit: $10,200 − $8400 = $1800

1950 hr or $7800 saved
Loss: $8400 − $7800 = $600
FAILURE–LOW

(a)

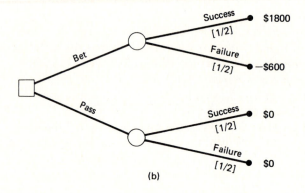

(b)

		Acts	
		Buy–bet	Not buy–pass
Outcomes	Success–high	$1800	0
	Failure–low	− $600	0

(c)

FIGURE 5.10
Thought experiment, decision tree, and payoff table for break-even analysis under uncertainty.

Now we can apply decision theory to our problem. The expected payoff or expected net gain is the sum of two terms:

$$\text{for success:} \quad \tfrac{1}{2} \times 1800 = \$900$$

$$\text{for failure:} \quad \tfrac{1}{2} \times 600 \quad = -\$300$$

The decision for Presto, then, is to acquire the labor-saving machine, because if the machine is purchased, there is an expected gain of $900 − $300 = $600.

Expected Value of Perfect Information

Suppose that a more detailed analysis of the manufacturing situation can predict precisely whether 1950 or 2550 hours will be saved. How much should Presto be willing to pay for this information? That is, what is the expected value of perfect information?

First determine the expected monetary value of the venture with perfect information. Presto would know in advance where the ball stops on the wheel of fortune; that is, Presto could *wait and see* until the ball stops. Consequently, Presto would bet only after the ball stops on success. The probability of the ball stopping either on success or failure is 1/2. The gain is $1800 when the ball stops on success and zero when it stops on failure, because Presto would not bet after it knows that the outcome is failure. Therefore, the expected monetary value of the venture with perfect information is

$$\text{EMVPI} = \tfrac{1}{2} \times \$1800 + \tfrac{1}{2} \times \$0 = \$900$$

Note then that perfect information increases the expected monetary value of the venture from $600 to $900. Consequently, the expected value of perfect information is

$$\text{EVPI} = \$900 - \$600 = \$300$$

Thus if the cost of perfect information is over (or equal to) $300, Presto should not bother to obtain the information but just acquire the machine. If the cost is less than $300, the perfect information should be obtained and the machine acquired only if the high saving of $2250 is predicted. If, for example, the cost is $50, then the net expected value is

$$\$900 - \$50 = \$850$$

which is $250 better than the expected value without perfect information. To summarize,

---

If the cost of perfect information is greater than (or equal to) the expected value of perfect information (EVPI), the information should not be purchased.

So far in our problems the demand for goods or the labor-saving potential of a machine has been uncertain. In real life managers have many similar types of uncertainty to face. Now we want to examine a problem where timeliness in completing a product is uncertain but is of major importance.

The Bop & Rock Studio, Inc. records and markets 8-track cartridges of popular music. The duration of popularity of such cartridges is short, and it is of paramount interest for the corporation to be ready to "meet the market," that is, to produce the cartridges fast before popularity wanes.

The difficulty in making a logical analysis of such a problem lies in the fact that the concept of meeting the market is vague and ill-defined. Only translating the problem into mathematical terms can lead to a satisfactory solution.

The critical factor in the problem is the time span or speed of production. This factor is obtained by taking the elapsed time between placing the order, the start date, and the delivery date, the completion date. Assume that a study is made of how profits depend on the time span of producing the cartridge. The scatter diagram in Figure 5.11 shows that a fast production schedule leads to a good profit but that a slow production schedule leads to a loss. Assume that Bop & Rock makes a linear regression analysis and finds the profit formula of

$$P = \$4300 - \$70S$$

where S is the span in days and P the profit in thousands of dollars.

Can Bop & Rock meet the market? Management is uncertain about the time span it takes to produce the cartridge but has the following information.

Production of the cartridge involves three activities: A_1, A_2, and A_3. Activities A_1 and A_2 can both be started immediately. But A_3 cannot be started before both A_1 and A_2 are completed (Figure 5.12). For example,

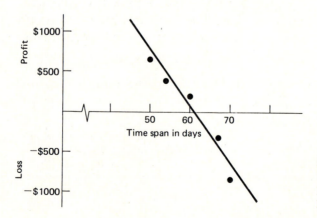

FIGURE 5.11
Scatter diagram relating profits to time span of production.

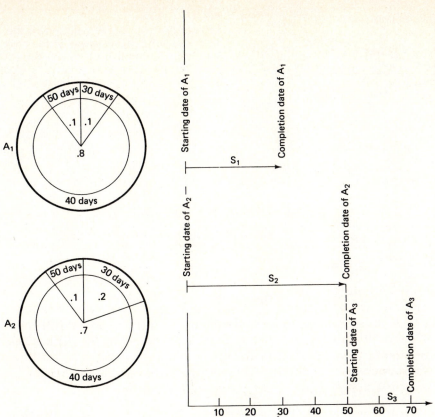

FIGURE 5.12
Thought experiment for the scheduling problem of the Bop & Rock Studio. The starting date of A_3 equals the larger of the completion dates of A_1 and A_2.

if A_1 takes 30 days, A_2 takes 50 days, and A_3 takes 20 days, the whole project takes 70 days.

Management knows that S_3, the span of A_3, is exactly 20 days but is uncertain about the spans of S_1 and S_2; S_1 *and* S_2 *are random variables.* Management agrees on the thought experiment (Figure 5.12) to generate the time spans of A_1 and A_2 with the wheels. For example, the probability that S_1 is 40 days is .8, and the probability that S_2 is 40 days is .7. It is also believed that the two activities are statistically independent. To solve the problem, we construct the probability tree in Figure 5.13 and list at the tips the starting date of A_3 which equals the larger of the durations of A_1 and A_2.

There is only one way to complete A_1 and A_2 in 30 days, and so this probability is $.1 \times .2 = .02$, as shown in the diagram. The diagram also shows that there are three ways to complete A_1 and A_2 in 40 days, and so this probability is

$$.1 \times .7 + .8 \times .2 + .8 \times .7 = .79$$

There are five ways to complete A_1 and A_2 in 50 days, and so this probability is

$$.1 \times .1 + .8 \times .1 + .1 \times .1 + .1 \times .7 + .1 \times .2 = .19$$

187

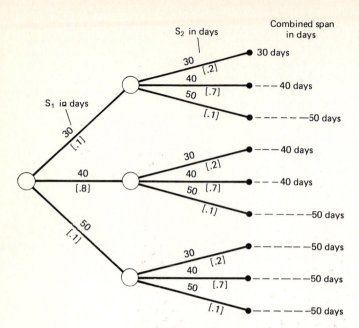

Activity A_3 takes 20 days, so we find that the completion probabilities for 50, 60, and 70 days are .02, .79, and .19, respectively. *This defines the completion time as a random variable.*

Now we can compute the expected value of completion time:

$$.02 \times 50 + .79 \times 60 + .19 \times 70 = 61.7 \text{ days}$$

What is the expected value of the profit? *Profit is a random variable.* You can calculate the profit associated with each time span, shown at the tips of the tree, multiply by the respective probability, and obtain the expected profit by addition. We leave this calculation as an exercise. A simpler approach is to apply our linear profit formula directly to 61.7 days, the expected value of completion. For the expected profit we get

$$4300 - 70 \times 61.7 = -\$19.00$$

which you can verify when working the exercise.

So the decision for Bop & Rock is not to market the 8-track cartridge. What is the EVPI, the expected value of perfect information?

Note that there are three posible time spans: 50, 60, and 70 days, corresponding to profits of $800, $100, and $-$600. So we conclude that (under this wait-and-see condition) the manager should bet only if the combined time span is 50 or 60 days and pass when it is 70 days. Using this decision rule, we can compute the expected monetary value of the venture with perfect information:

$$(\text{EMV})_1 = .02 \times 800 + .79 \times 100 = \$95.00$$

But without perfect information the expected monetary value of the venture is zero because Bop & Rock will not market the product. Therefore,

$$\text{EVPI} = (\text{EMV})_1 - (\text{EMV})_0 = \$95.00 - \$0 = \$95.00$$

If perfect information is offered for less than $95.00, Bop & Rock should buy it; otherwise it should not. If the information is bought and the combined span is 50 or 60 days, Bop & Rock should market the cartridge. If it is 70 days, it should not.

5.6 A DECISION SUPPORT SYSTEM APPROACH: RISK ANALYSIS

In Section 1.6 we described interactive financial planning using a decision support system (DSS) approach. To all appearances we used a deterministic analysis because there were no probabilities involved. However, in reality the DSS approach does assume uncertainty, because by *what-if* types of dialogs the manager can consider uncertainty and determine how solutions are influenced by uncertainty. For example, in an initial analysis an inflation factor of 10% may be assumed, but then by *what-if* types of questions the manager can examine what happens if inflation is 8 or 12%. Or the executive may inquire what happens if the assumed 6% growth rate of sales drops to 5.4% and the projected price of the product drops from $50 to $45. A DSS will produce the output variables to such *what-if* types of questions. Thus, with the aid of sensitivity analysis the manager can develop a judgment about uncertainty. Risk analysis augments deterministic analysis and sensitivity analysis by considering probabilities explicitly. Specifically, it is assumed that the uncertain variables of the problem are random variables and that the decision maker can develop probability distributions characterizing these random variables.

We have already touched on the approach to be used in Section 3.1 when we showed how to add random variables. Now we go further and show how to combine the random variables occurring in a mathematical model.

The thought experiment associated with this approach is shown in Figure 5.14. Each of the random variables of the problem can be represented by a roulette wheel, and the model specifies computations to be performed on the outcomes of the chance devices. On the basis of these computations, invariably performed by computers, the probability mass function of the derived random variables are determined, including the probability mass function of the profit or payoff. Finally the decision maker chooses an alternative.

The specific computer-based computational technique for carrying out risk analysis will be discussed in Chapter 17.

We can thus say that there are three levels of sophistication in carrying out such analysis.

The Three Levels of Analysis

Level 1. Deterministic Analysis

No uncertainty is considered. You can take the view that only the expected values of the input variables are used and that outputs are calculated by a deterministic model. Our first discussion of the Loud and Clear Playback Corp. in Chapter 1 was at this level.

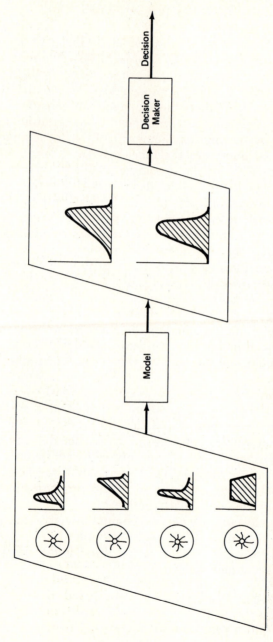

FIGURE 5.14 Thought experiment associated with risk analysis.

Level 2. Sensitivity Analysis

A more or less systematic review of a panorama of solutions by considering various possible combinations of inputs. Our discussion of the La Brea Oil Company in Chapter 1 was at this level.

Level 3. Risk Analysis

If the uncertainty in an input variable cannot be dealt with adequately by sensitivity analysis, the input variable is considered as a random variable. First the probability distribution of such input variables is determined, and then the output random variables are calculated. Our second discussion of the Loud and Clear Playback Corp. in Chapter 1 was at this level.

Managerial judgment enters into risk analysis in two ways: (1) The probability distribution of input variables is influenced by managerial judgment; (2) the selection of the preferred alternative is not taken by maximizing the expected profit but by examining the various probability distributions of output variables and applying judgment as to which alternative provides the most desirable solution to the problem.

Advantages of Risk Analysis

Risk analysis offers a scientific approach to resolving issues of uncertainty without imposing specific decision rules on the manager when making decisions. Thus risk analysis offers a logical approach to uncertainty, but the final decision still remains with managers.

It is to be stressed that different managers have a different perception of uncertainty, and so natural conflicts arise when making decisions. Risk analysis (1) imposes a rigorous discipline on managers who must state their probability estimates precisely and (2) promotes the establishment of a consensus of opinion. When a decision is made using risk analysis, there is a feeling between managers that all facts and judgments have been considered and incorporated into the making of the decision. Thus risk analysis provides information important from the organizational and behavioral points of view.

5.7 EFFECTIVENESS OF THE OCCUPATIONAL SAFETY AND HEALTH ACT OF THE U.S. CONGRESS: A CASE STUDY

In passing the Occupational Safety and Health Act, the U.S. Congress declared that its purpose was to "assure so far as possible every working man and woman in the nation safe and healthful working conditions." In establishing the law, Congress recognized that many firms would voluntarily obey the law but that some would comply only if forced to do so. Thus Congress decreed that those companies which operate in a "reckless" manner should be dealt with firmly and effectively.

Messrs. Gleason and Barnum undertook to study this act of Congress and applied quantitative techniques to determine whether "reckless" companies would be deterred from unsafe and unhealthful conditions by the penalty of the law.

Messrs. Gleason and Barnum* assumed that firms dedicated to providing maximum profit to stockholders would consider two alternatives: (1) put money into "healthful" ways, that is, correct working conditions, or (2) invest the money otherwise. Thus the question is, What is more profitable, providing safe and healthful working conditions or investing in business?

For each of these two alternatives there are five possible government acts:

1. No inspection occurs.
2. No violation is cited.
3. A nonserious violation is cited.
4. A serious violation is cited.
5. A willful violation is cited.

The penalties for each of these violations are known to firms and will not be listed here. However, to do a quantitative analysis, there is need also to determine the probability for the occurrence of each of these possibilities. It took a great deal of analysis of data for Messrs. Gleason and Barnum to determine these probabilities.

It was found that enforcement officers exercise substantial discretion in classifying violations as serious or nonserious. This often results in the same type of violation being classified differently depending on the inspector involved. Due to the lack of uniformity in classification of violations, it was found that it is impossible to determine with certainty that a certain type of violation would be classified as nonserious, serious, or willful. Furthermore, it is extremely difficult to prove willfulness, and few violations are classified as such. Thus there is a good possibility that an employer will not be convicted of a willful violation even if one exists, unless it is a blatantly obvious case.

After much study of the data and applying common sense and judgment, Messrs. Gleason and Barnum established the following probabilities:

No inspection; .9
Inspection, no citation: .0259
Nonserious citation: .0730
Serious citation: .0009
Willful citation: .0002

By using these probabilities and known penalties, the expected cost of nonconformance with the law was established. This expected penalty was then compared with the expected return if the same amount

---

*J. M. Gleason and D. T. Barnum, "Effectiveness of OSHA Penalties: Myth or Reality?," *Interfaces*, Vol. 7, No. 1, Part 1, 1977 pp. 1–13.

of money is invested in ventures. For purposes of analysis, a range of rate of return on investment from 8 to 20% was assumed.

The analysis indicated that the probabilities and penalties were so low that they were of little value in preventing violations of the act. Those employers who obey the law do so regardless of the penalty. Employers at whom the penalties are aimed, those who will correct violations only if it is economically profitable for them to do so, are not being affected. Thus the law antagonizes employers who obey the law but has little impact on those who obey the law only if it is profitable.

5.8 UNCERTAINTY, PROBABILITY, AND INFORMATION: A DIALOG

Q. *Why is the demand for strawberries uncontrollable? Can't Berry advertise?*

A. We assumed that Berry cannot change the demand. You are proposing a more advanced problem which can be well dealt with by decision analysis.

Q. *What is the rationale for Bayes' rule?*

A. Think of the frequency interpretation of probability. When you maximize expected value, you maximize the long-run average gain.

Q. *But in real life does the decision maker decide the same issue many times?*

A. There are examples of repeated decisions where the frequency interpretation applies. But most of the time we deal with *one-shot* decisions, and here you must fall back on the judgmental interpretation. We said many times that judgment and science must be mixed.

Q. *How does perfect information eliminate uncertainty? This makes no sense to me because even if Berry knows in advance the demand for strawberries, he sells different quantities each day.*

A. You are confusing variability with uncertainty. Variability means that a quantity may assume any one of a set of values. No information system can eliminate or even change variability. You must accept variability as a fact of life. On the other hand, uncertainty implies lack of information. Suppose that in a holdup several shots are fired, and a wounded man is taken to the hospital. There will be some bullets in the body but uncertainty as to actually how many bullets. An X-ray machine can provide perfect information and indicate exactly how many bullets are in the wounded man. But an X-ray machine has no influence on the aiming or firing of bullets or on the variability in the number of bullets in victims.

Getting back to games of chance, suppose you are playing blackjack in Las Vegas. There is a deck of cards face down on the gambling table. There is nothing uncertain about the way the deck is laid out on the table, as the deck will not be shuffled after the game starts. However, you do not know the sequence of the cards, so the uncertainty is in your mind. If you had a device to read the faces of the cards to provide perfect information, there would be no uncertainty. Perfect information provides Berry with a schedule of the demand for strawberries.

Or consider a custom tailor who only makes suits to order. He will wait and see until the orders come in, so there is no uncertainty or surprise in his problem.

Q. *I find it easier to understand this wait-and-see concept than perfect information. How about hindsight? I would have done so-and-so had I only known in advance. Are all these concepts the same?*

A. Yes, you are thinking correctly. The goal is to assure the manager that he is making the best decision in the light of information available at that time.

Q. *Why bother with perfect information? There is no practical way to get it.*

A. Perfect information provides an insight to uncertainty. Its value gives an upper limit to the value of any kind of information.

Q. *Does decision analysis predict the future?*

A. No one can do that. In Chapter 4 you learned how forecasting supports decision making. Decision analysis puts all data together and provides a quantitative approach to decision making under uncertainty.

Q. *When do you use decision analysis?*

A. As Professor Ronald Howard of Stanford University, a pioneer in the field, puts it, if you do not know what to do, then you do decision analysis.

Q. *Can decision analysis guarantee success?*

A. No! You must distinguish between good and bad decisions and good and bad luck. For example, the man who leaves his tenth-floor office by jumping out the window instead of walking down the stairs does not have bad luck. He made a bad decision. The player of blackjack who wants to win by collecting 21 points and takes another card when he already has 20 is making a bad decision but may win by drawing an ace. The firm that maximizes profit by maintaining dangerous working conditions may be making an "economically sound" decision. If it is caught and penalized, it has "bad luck." Let me tell you a story.

My friend, George, falls suddenly ill and calls the doctor. The doctor says that it is quite possible poor George has had a heart attack. If so, he should be rushed to the hospital emergency ward to save his life. George believes in quantitative analysis. He finds out from the doctor that the probability is ½ that he actually has had a heart attack and that if he stays home the probability of dying is .8. If he goes to the hospital, the conditional probability of dying drops to .1. He decides to go to the hospital and calls an ambulance. The driver turns on the siren and so fails to hear an oncoming fire engine. The two cars collide, and poor George dies in the accident. He made a good decision but had bad luck.

Q. *In the break-even analysis problem, first you assumed that only the demand is uncertain and then that the fixed cost is uncertain. Is this realistic?*

A. You have a point. In real life you would assume that the variable cost and other variables are uncertain.

Q. *What is subjective probability?*

A. The word probability has many shades of meaning. One of the important meanings relates to the frequency of outcomes displayed in chance devices. When you toss an unbiased coin, there is a certain regularity between heads and tails, and when you say the probability is one-half to get heads or tails, you are interpreting probability in the sense of the regularity of heads or tails appearing.

Another meaning of probability, often referred to as subjective probability, refers to judgment and opinion on the occurrence of events. When you say that you think that the probability is .3 that in the next election a Democrat will be elected President, you are expressing your view or belief on the election. When a corporation bids on a new contract and executives feel that the probability is .8 for capturing the contract, they are expressing an opinion on what is going to happen. People often express opinions on events that have never occurred previously or have occurred only a few times.

Let me tell you a story to illustrate what I mean when I say that judgmental probability is not attached to real physical things but resides in your mind.

The Elevators of the Empire State Building

Suppose you are sightseeing in New York City and decide to go to the top of the Empire State Building. You get up early because you want to do many other things than stand in line for elevators going to the tower. The tower is not yet open, but you know how many people each elevator can handle and figure that you will be going on elevator 5. There is one thing, however, that bothers you. The night before, in one of the friendly bars, a nondescript customer told you there is trouble with the elevators in the Empire State Building: not that they fall down, or anything like that, but that they have a bad habit of getting stuck. When that happens, the unfortunate passengers spend hours under most uncomfortable conditions before getting out of the elevator. So it crosses your mind that maybe you should not be going up, since you might get stuck. The operators waiting to serve you seem to be unmindful of any difficulty and are going about their business in their usual self-assured manner. How would you judge the probability of elevator 5 getting stuck?

I wouldn't worry. After all, the fellow in the bar probably didn't know what he was talking about, and I don't believe in rumors. I would think that it is practically certain that elevator 5 would reach the top.

Good thinking! So there you stand in line, the tower opens, and the first elevator starts up. Behold! It gets stuck! What do you think now?

Well, once in a long while elevators do get stuck, so I wouldn't really be too worried.

Okay! Now you watch elevator 2, and it also gets stuck and so do elevators 3 and 4. What now?

I would be sure that something is wrong and that elevator 5 will also get stuck.

Very good! But let me ask if there has been any change in elevator 5. Ten minutes earlier you had great confidence in elevator 5; now your confidence is gone. Is this due to a change in the mechanical equipment or anything else in elevator 5?

No, I don't think so. I don't think there was any change in the mechanics of elevator 5. I changed my mind because if four elevators already got stuck, there must be something wrong.

You see, then, that in the outside world nothing has changed about things you can see and touch but in your mind the probability of failure of the elevator has been drastically revised. This is what I mean by saying that probability is in your mind; it is subjective and is not attached in any sense to elevator 5.

Q. *Why did the elevators get stuck?*

A. An investigation revealed that the night before the elevator brakes were greased and by mistake the wrong grease was used. The nondescript customer in the bar guessed correctly what was coming.

Q. *You made your point in this story. But then how do you deal with subjective probability?*

A. Our approach of using thought experiments clearly separates judgmental and frequency probabilities. When dealing with decision making under uncertainty, we model the situation by chance devices. Data must be gathered and opinions must be expressed to arrive at the conclusion that the thought experiment describes the situation in accordance with the best knowledge of the decision makers. Once the thought experiment is agreed upon, the calculations are performed strictly on an objective basis, and there is no further room for judgment. Of course, after the calculations have been performed and the decision is made as to which of the alternatives to choose, there will be judgment applied to the outcomes of the thought experiment. Thus judgment comes into accepting the thought experiment and in making the decision.

Q. *All this sounds too individual and personal.*

A. Yes, but this is a scientific way to incorporate the human element into the analysis. This is a good example of how science can incorporate behavioral aspects into its framework.

SUMMARY

1. Decision analysis is the basic quantitative technique of aiding managers in making decisions under uncertainty.

2. Whether or not to buy information is an important decision problem.

3. Probabilities, acts, outcomes, payoffs, and/or the decision tree are the important elements of decision analysis.

4. The most common criterion for choosing the best act is Bayes' rule, which maximizes expected payoff (or minimizes the expected loss or cost).

5. The decision maker's problem is to choose the act a_i for which

$$z_i = p_{1i}V_{1i} + p_{2i}V_{2i} + \cdots + p_{ni}V_{ni}$$

becomes a maximum. Here the ps are the probabilities and the Vs are the payoffs.

6. The solution to the decision problem is the decision rule which states how to find i.

7. The decision to investigate is itself an important managerial decision.

8. A managerial accounting system provides information to decision makers, and the selection of an accounting system is an important decision problem.

9. Perfect information removes uncertainty from the problem. Depending on the conditions of the problem, perfect information may or may not have a monetary value.

10. EVPI, the expected value of perfect information, is given by the difference between the expected monetary value EMV of the venture with and without information:

$$\text{EVPI} = (\text{EMV})_1 - (\text{EMV})_0$$

11. EVPI is a gross value as it assumes that the information is free.

12. If F, the fee for buying information, is greater than (or equal to) EVPI, the expected value of perfect information, it is not worthwhile to buy the information.

13. The expected net gain from buying information is given by

$$\text{ENG} = (\text{EMV})_1 - (\text{EMV})_0 - F = \text{EVPI} - F$$

The decision maker should not buy information unless ENG is positive.

14. Deterministic break-even analysis is a fundamental managerial technique of analysis, and decision analysis extends its usefulness by incorporating the uncertainties of the situation.

15. Risk analysis extends the scope of decision support systems by providing computer-based probabilistic information to managers under conditions of uncertainty.

16. Risk analysis is often used as a sequel to (1) deterministic analysis and (2) *what-if* types of sensitivity analysis.

17. Subjective probability is a quantitative expression of a person's state of mind.

18. When people receive information, they update their subjective probabilities.

SECTION EXERCISES

1. **Theory and Practice of Decision Making: Selling Strawberries**

1.1 A year later, S. T. Berry finds that his probability of demand distribution (see Figure 5.1) is as follows:

PROBABILITY OF DEMAND	DEMAND FOR BASKETS
.3	13
.4	14
.2	15
.1	16

a. Draw the wheel of fortune for this situation as in Figure 5.1(a).
b. Make the PMF as in Figure 5.1c.
c. Find the expected daily profit, under the decision rule of buying 14 baskets each morning, making a table as shown in Figure 5.2.
d. Find the expected daily profit, under the decision rule of buying 13 baskets each morning, making a table as shown in Figure 5.2.

1.2 Going into the business of selling bushels of boysenberries, S. T. Berry finds that the probability of demand distribution (similar to Figure 5.1) is as follows:

PROBABILITY OF DEMAND	DEMAND FOR BUSHELS
.2	1
.4	2
.1	3
.3	4

The selling price of a bushel is $10.00 and the cost to Berry is $6.00. Berry's initial rule for purchasing bushels is to purchase three.

a. Make a wheel of fortune for this case, similar to Figure 5.1(a).
b. Make a PMF similar to Figure 5.1(c).
c. Find the expected daily profit, under the decision rule of buying three baskets each morning, making a table as shown in Figure 5.2.
d. Find the expected daily profit, under the decision rule of buying four baskets each morning, making a table as shown in Figure 5.2.

1.3 Refer to Exercise 1.1. S. T. Berry wants to decide the optimal act to take in this circumstance.
a. Make a payoff table for this situation similar to Figure 5.3.
b. Make a decision tree for this situation similar to Figure 5.4.
c. Make a table for showing the optimal act similar to Figure 5.5.
d. Choose the optimal act.
e. Solve this situation using a decision tree similar to Figure 5.6.

1.4 Refer to Exercise 1.2. S. T. Berry wants to decide the optimal act to take in this circumstance.
a. Make a payoff table for this situation similar to Figure 5.3.
b. Make a decision tree for this situation similar to Figure 5.4.
c. Make a table for showing the optimal act similar to Figure 5.5.
d. Choose the optimal act.
e. Solve this situation using a decision tree similar to Figure 5.6.

2. *Problems in Accounting*

2.1 Refer to the Harold Trojinski auditing problem of Section 5.2 and the tree diagram of Figure 5.7. How would your decision be changed if the cost of the alternative 3—the guaranteed audit—were reduced to $22,000?

2.2 Refer to the Harold Trojinski auditing problem of Section 5.2. If alternative 5 were deemed to have a 1/5 chance of missing the variance, how would Trojinski's decision be changed?

2.3 Refer to the Harold Trojinski auditing problem of Section 5.2. Suppose that the offeror of the guaranteed audit of alternative 3 offered to lower the price to $20,000 but would quote only a probability of finding the variance (if it exists) of 9/10. What would your decision be?

3. *Perfect Information and Monetary Value of Information*

3.1 Refer to Exercise 1.1. Assuming that the fee for perfect information is $.50.
a. Calculate the expected monetary value of the venture with perfect information EMVPI.
b. Calculate the expected monetary value of the venture without perfect information $(EMV)_0$.
c. Calculate the expected net gain $ENG = EMVPI - (EMV)_0 - F$.
d. Find the optimal decision for the purchase of the information.

3.2 Refer to Exercise 1.1. Assuming that the fee for perfect information is $.20,
a. Calculate the expected monetary value of the venture with perfect information EMVPI.
b. Calculate the expected monetary value of the venture without perfect information $(EMV)_0$.
c. Calculate the expected net gain $ENG = EMVPI - (EMV)_0 - F$.
d. Find the optimal decision for the purchase of the information.

3.3 Refer to Exercise 1.2. Assuming that the fee for perfect information is $1.00,
a. Calculate the expected monetary value of the venture with perfect information EMVPI.
b. Calculate the expected monetary value of the venture without perfect information $(EMV)_0$.
c. Calculate the expected net gain $ENG = EMVPI - (EMV)_0 - F$.
d. Find the optimal decision for the purchase of the information.

3.4 Refer to Exercise 1.2. Assuming that the fee for perfect information is $10.00,

    a. Calculate the expected monetary value of the venture with perfect information EMVPI.

    b. Calculate the expected monetary value of the venture without perfect information $(EMV)_0$.

    c. Calculate the expected net gain $ENG = EMVPI - (EMV)_0 - F$.

    d. Find the optimal decision for the purchase of the information.

4. *Breakeven Analysis Under Uncertainty*

4.1 Consider the Presto Corporation example of Section 5.4. Assume that the fixed cost of obtaining the machine is $10,000 and that for each hour of manual labor saved there is a cost benefit of $10.00.

    a. What is the cost benefit if there is a replacement of 3000 hours of manual labor?

    b. What is the cost benefit if there is a replacement of 2000 hours of manual labor?

    c. What is the break-even point?

    d. Draw a break-even chart similar to Figure 5.9.

Assume the probability of saving either 2550 or 1950 hours is .7 and .3, respectively.

    e. Draw a wheel of fortune for this case similar to Figure 5.10(a).

    f. Draw the decision tree for this case similar to Figure 5.10(b).

    g. Draw the decision table for this case similar to Figure 5.10(c).

    h. Make the decision.

    i. Find the expected monetary value of the venture with perfect information (EMVPI).

    j. Find the expected value of perfect information (EVPI).

    k. At and below what cost would you purchase perfect information?

4.2 Consider the Presto Corporation example of Section 5.4. Assume that the fixed cost of obtaining the machine is $10,000 and that for each hour of manual labor saved there is a cost benefit of $5.00.

    a. What is the cost benefit if there is a replacement of 3000 hours of manual labor?

    b. What is the cost benefit if there is a replacement of 2000 hours of manual labor?

    c. What is the break-even point?

    d. Draw a break-even chart similar to Figure 5.9.

Assume the probability of saving either 2550 or 1950 hours is .6 and .4, respectively.

    e. Draw a wheel of fortune for this case similar to Figure 5.10(a).

    f. Draw the decision tree for this case similar to Figure 5.10(b).

    g. Draw the decision matrix for this case similar to Figure 5.10(c).

    h. Find the optimal decision.

    i. Find the expected monetary value of the venture with perfect information (EMVPI).

    j. Find the expected value of perfect information (EVPI).

    k. At and below what cost would you purchase perfect information?

4.3 Consider the Presto Corporation example of Section 5.4. Assume that the fixed cost of obtaining the machine is $5000 and that for each hour of manual labor saved there is a cost benefit of $7.00.

    a. What is the cost benefit if there is a replacement of 3000 hours of manual labor?

    b. What is the cost benefit if there is a replacement of 2000 hours of manual labor?

    c. What is the break-even point?

    d. Draw a break-even chart similar to Figure 5.9.

Assume the probability of saving either 2550 or 1950 hours is .3 and .7, respectively.

  e. Draw a wheel of fortune for this case similar to Figure 5.10(a).
  f. Draw the decision tree for this case similar to Figure 5.10(b).
  g. Draw the decision matrix for this case similar to Figure 5.10(c).
  h. Make the decision.
  i. Find the expected monetary value of the venture with perfect information (EMVPI).
  j. Find the expected value of perfect information (EVPI).
  k. At and below what cost would you purchase perfect information?

4.4 Consider the Presto Corporation example of Section 5.4. Assume that the fixed cost of obtaining the machine is $24,500 and that for each hour of manual labor saved there is a cost benefit of $12.00.

  a. What is the cost benefit if there is a replacement of 3000 hours of manual labor?
  b. What is the cost benefit if there is a replacement of 2000 hours of manual labor?
  c. What is the break-even point?
  d. Draw a break-even chart similar to Figure 5.9.

Assume the probability of saving either 2550 or 1950 hours is .2 and .8, respectively.

  e. Draw a wheel of fortune for this case similar to Figure 5.10(a).
  f. Draw the decision tree for this case similar to Figure 5.10(b).
  g. Draw the decision matrix for this case similar to Figure 5.10(c).
  h. Make the decision.
  i. Find the expected monetary value of the venture with perfect information (EMVPI).
  j. Find the expected value of perfect information (EVPI).
  k. At and below what cost would you purchase perfect information?

5. *When Time is Uncertain*

5.1 The management of Bop & Rock has revised the probabilities assigned in the scheduling problem discussed in Section 5.5:

ACTIVITY A_1		ACTIVITY A_2	
S_1	$P[S_1]$	S_2	$P[S_2]$
30	.2	30	.2
40	.2	40	.1
50	.6	50	.7

  a. Make a thought experiment diagram similar to Figure 5.12.
  b. Make a new probability tree similar to Figure 5.13.
  c. Find the expected value of the completion time.
  d. Determine the profits associated with each terminal leaf of the probability tree.
  e. Find the EMVPI.
  f. What is the EVPI?

5.2 The management of Bop & Rock has revised the probabilities assigned in the scheduling problem discussed in this section:

ACTIVITY A_1		ACTIVITY A_2	
S_1	$P[S_1]$	S_2	$P[S_2]$
20	.3	35	.2
40	.2	45	.2
60	.5	50	.6

a. Make a thought experiment diagram similar to Figure 5.12.
b. Make a new probability tree similar to Figure 5.13.
c. Find the expected value of the completion time.
d. Determine the profits associated with each terminal leaf of the probability tree.
e. Find the EMVPI.

6. A Decision Support System Approach: Risk Analysis

6.1 Give an example of a sensitivity analysis you have carried out in regard to some personal decision.

6.2 Computer program packages for carrying out risk analysis (such as PAUS from Bonner & Moore Associates, New York, and PASA1 used in the General Electric Company) have high costs: $10,000 to $20,000 for purchase or equivalent value. Why would it be worth the cost to a company?

6.3 If you read the preceding Exercises for this chapter, you will see that they involve setting different values for variables and then carrying through the analysis. Discuss how working a set of such exercises (called *scenarios* in the text) is in fact carrying out a sensitivity analysis.

7. Effectiveness of Occupational Safety and Health Act of U. S. Congress: A Successful Application

7.1 Draw a probability tree for the case discussed in Section 5.7.

7.2 If governmental policy is to reduce the power of regulatory agencies such as OSHA, how would the probabilities and/or branches of the tree be changed?

8. Uncertainty, Probability and Information: A Dialog

8.1 There are a number of variables (demand, probability, prices, costs, etc.) in the S. T. Berry situation. Which ones can be changed by advertising and in what way?

8.2 Give an example of the difference between variability and uncertainty which is different from the one given in Section 5.8.

8.3 There are many ways in which the examples given in Section 5.8 do not correspond to the real world; one of them is mentioned in the question concerning the break-even analysis problem. Make a list of all such instances you can find. Do they all matter? (That is, can we get guidance for our decision making even though gross simplifications have been made?) Put the items you list in order of increasing importance to the decision-making process.

CHAPTER EXERCISES AND DISCUSSION QUESTIONS

C.1. S. T. Berry, whose strawberry stand is discussed in Section 5.1, has received bad news. A competitor sells strawberries of the same quality for $1.35 per basket. Berry is sure that he can keep the demand schedule of Figure 5.1(b) unchanged if he lowers his selling price to $1.30 per basket.
   a. Of the six illustrations of this situation, Figures 5.1 through 5.6, which will be affected as a result of the price change?
   b. Revise the illustrations specified by you in part a to account for the new selling price.
   c. Choose the best act under these new conditions. How many baskets should Berry order?

d. Compare the optimal expected daily profit at the new price of $1.30 to the optimal value for the old price.

e. C. Herry, a friend of Berry who is not skilled in quantitative methods, suggested on intuitive grounds that Berry should not drop the price even if sales were lower. "You will make it up on the increased profit," said Herry. To prove or disprove this contention quantitatively, Berry and Herry estimated that if Berry held his price to $1.50 per basket while the competitor sold at $1.35 per basket Berry's demand schedule would be as follows:

DEMAND FOR BASKETS OF STRAWBERRIES	PROBABILITY OF DEMAND
11	.2
12	.4
13	.3
14	.1

Under these conditions, what is the optimal act?

f. Should Berry sell at $1.50 or $1.30 under the competitive conditions described in part e? Why?

g. For parts a–d, where Berry sells at the competitive price of $1.30, what is the expected monetary value of the venture with perfect information (EMVPI)? What is the expected value of perfect information (EVPI)?

h. For parts e and f, where Berry sells at the price of $1.50 in the competitive situation, what is the EMVPI? What is the EVPI?

i. Compare the values of EMVPI and EVPI obtained in parts g and h with the values for the noncompetitive situation of Section 5.1. Explain the differences.

C.2 Z. A. Barr runs a gourmet food shop, selling the high-priced Cuchinaro Food Processor at $250. Experience has shown that the weekly demand schedule for this item is as follows:

DEMAND FOR FOOD PROCESSORS	PROBABILITY OF DEMAND
0	.082
1	.205
2	.214
3	.184
4	.134
5	.097
6	.058
7	.026

Due to a disagreement with the wholesaler, he can obtain processors only on a weekly basis. He must order a fixed quantity a week in advance, and any unsold units must be returned at the end of the week. The cost of the units is $150, and a $50 charge is assessed by the wholesaler for any unit that is returned. While Barr searches for an alternate source, he wants to analyze the current situation for the best strategy.

a. List the order quantities that you regard as reasonable alternative actions for Barr.

b. For each of the order quantities in part a, make a table similar to Figure 5.2 for the expected weekly revenue and profit.

c. Make a payoff table similar to Figure 5.3 for Barr.

d. Make a table similar to Figure 5.5; what is the optimal act?

e. What are the EMVPI and the EVPI for this situation?

C.3 Presto Corporation is considering the use of automatic machinery in a production operation. The situation is essentially similar to that of the text with the following values holding:

Fixed cost of automatic machinery: $15,000
Savings for each hour of labor saved: $10
Possible values of labor saving: 1200 or 2000 hours
Probability: $P(1200) = .3$

    a. Make a break-even chart (similar to Figure 5.9).
    b. What is the EMV?
    c. What is the optimal decision?
    d. Make a wheel of fortune for this case as shown in Figure 5.10(a).
    e. Make a decision tree for this case as shown in Figure 5.10(b).
    f. Make a payoff table as shown in Figure 5.10(c).
    g. Find the EMVPI and the EVPI.

C.4 The management of the S. H. Petzel Company is considering an advertising campaign for their line of home grinders for paprika. The campaign could be helpful (increasing sales without increasing competition) or hurtful (increasing competition and decreasing their sales). In the absence of any campaign, they now sell 50,000 grinders per year and are breaking even. If the campaign is helpful, they expect to sell 100,000 grinders with a total profit of $200,000. If the campaign is not helpful, they expect sales to drop to 25,000 grinders for a loss of $100,000. Management estimates that the probability of a helpful campaign is 3/4.

    a. Make a break-even chart (similar to Figure 5.9).
    b. What is the EMV?
    c. What is the optimal decision?
    d. Make a wheel of fortune for this case as shown in Figure 5.10(a).
    e. Make a decision tree as shown in Figure 5.10(b).
    f. Make a payoff table as shown in Figure 5.10(c).
    g. Find the EMVPI and the EVPI.

C.5 The Hungarian space agency is sending an unmanned spacecraft to the planet Buda. The sooner the spacecraft can be launched, the lower will be the costs; an early flight means less fuel and greater payload. The profit relationship is $P = 10,000 - 50D$, where D is the time from the start of the project until launch. The spacecraft can be launched as soon as both activities A and B are completed, but B cannot start until A is finished. The time duration for activity B is known with certainty to be 50 days. However, activity A involves new technology and is uncertain. For this reason the space agency has given out two contracts for activity A to different contractors. Whichever one completes A first determines the duration time of activity A. The management of the agency estimates the probabilities of completion at different times for the two contractors as follows:

CONTRACTOR 1		CONTRACTOR 2	
Time to finish A (days)	Prob.	Time to finish A (days)	Prob.
25	.1	25	.3
50	.4	50	.2
75	.4	75	.2
100	.1	100	.3

The two contractors work independently of each other.

a. Illustrate this situation with a thought experiment similar to that shown in Figure 5.14.
b. Make a probability tree representation similar to that shown in Figure 5.13.
c. Determine the expected profit.
d. What is the EMVPI?
e. What is the EVPI?

Solving Decision Analysis Problems

In Chapter 5 we laid the groundwork for decision analysis and showed several applications. Now we want to further apply the concepts and techniques of decision analysis.

So far most of the problems we solved have involved relatively few alternatives. Now we present procedures to solve problems with a very large number or even an infinite number of possibilities.

6.1 DECISION ANALYSIS BY ENUMERATING STRATEGIES

Combined Marketing and Production Problem

The Ham-Gear Instruments Corporation is considering the marketing of a new product. The combined marketing and production problem is modeled by the alternatives and chance events illustrated in the decision tree in Figure 6.1. Note that decision forks are represented by squares and chance forks by circles. The very first act or decision (A) at the foot of the tree, 1, specifies that Ham-Gear must decide whether to market the product or not. At the second decision point, 2, a decision (B) must be made whether to produce the intrument manually or automatically. If sufficient demand develops for the instrument, the capital investment required to tool up and produce automatically is worthwhile. Otherwise, manual production is better. Forks 3 and 9 are chance forks showing events leading to whether or not a competitor will enter the market to make a competitive instrument. We shall not show a detailed analysis for manual production, but let us follow the two branches emanating from chance fork 3. At fork 4 (C) or 5 (D) a marketing decision must be made about the product.

For example, it might be decided to go into mass production, price the product low, package it with no frills, and advertise in newspapers. Or a distinctive design may be selected, and it may be decided to price the product high and advertise in trade journals. Or a compromise

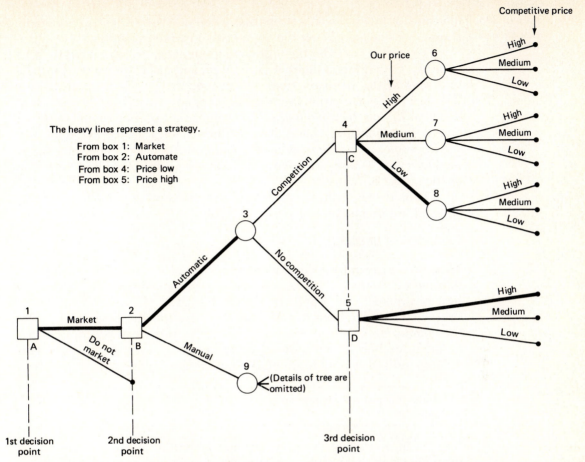

FIGURE 6.1 Decision tree representation of the marketing problem of the Ham-Gear Instruments Corporation. The square boxes are decision forks and the circles are chance forks.

between these two may be decided upon. To simplify our discussion, we shall say that there are three possibilities: Price the product (1) high, (2) medium, or (3) low. Let us pause a moment to examine the information available to Ham-Gear for decision making.

The decision tree is drawn in an **informational chronology** to model the time sequence of (1) information received by the decision maker and (2) decision made. Observe that at the time when decisions *A* and *B* are made, it is not yet known whether the competitor will enter or not. On the other hand, when decisions *C* and *D* are made, Ham-Gear knows whether the competitor will enter or not. We analyze and evaluate possible pricing and marketing strategies at decision forks 4 and 5 and at chance forks 6, 7, and 8. Due to the fact that the competition knows the pricing and marketing strategy of Ham-Gear, it will respond with its own marketing strategy. To simplify, we mark on the decision tree (chance forks 6, 7, and 8) how the competitor responds to our high, medium, or low pricing level. The competitor is assumed to respond with high, medium, or low price. We stress that when decisions *C* and *D* are made, Ham-Gear does not know the competitive marketing action.

To clarify, consider the following thought experiment. Start to drive your car, beginning at the foot of the tree, and make your way along the branches of the decision tree. At decision *A* you are in control. You decide whether to market the instrument or not. You are also in control at decision *B*. You decide whether to automate or not. But when you reach chance fork 3 or 9, you lose control of the wheel. Imagine that a random device such as a roulette wheel is spun and that a chance decision is made for you. You regain control at decisions *C* and *D* but lose control at chance forks 6, 7, and 8.

Thus the outcomes at the tip of the tree and the payoffs are partly determined by choice and partly by chance.

Concept of Strategy

What do we mean by a solution to a problem of this sort? Due to the fact that the decisions are made in sequence, you must define a **strategy** of how to proceed under any conditions. For example, here is a possible strategy: (1) Market the instrument; (2) use automatic production; (3) if the competitor enters, price the product low; if the competitor does not enter, price it high, as shown by the heavy lines in Figure 6.1. This strategy tells you what to do under any circumstance.

> A strategy is a decision rule specifying what to do in any and all foreseeable situations.

As an everyday example of what a strategy means, consider the problem of driving to school in the morning. Suppose you decide before you start that your strategy is to follow Main Street and if the line of cars waiting for the traffic light at the intersection of Main and Broad Streets is short, you continue on Main Street, but if there is a long line, you turn right on Broad Street. If you continue on Main Street and the line at Franklin Street is short, you continue on Main; otherwise you take a right on Franklin. On the other hand, if you made the right-hand turn on Broad Street, when you reach North Street, you continue on Broad if the line is short but make a left on North if the line is long. Etc.

Returning to Figure 6.1, observe that once you decide on a strategy there will be only one branch coming out from each decision box, because the strategy tells you what to do. If we call a tree having only chance forks a **probability tree**, then

> Each strategy turns the decision tree into a probability tree.

Note also that once you decide on a strategy you still do not know the profit with certainty. Uncertainty still remains. In fact,

> Each strategy makes the profit into a random variable.

How many strategies does Ham-Gear have if (1) it enters the market and (2) considers only automatic production? In Figure 6.2 we show the probability trees associated with the nine possible strategies. For example, strategy 1 assumes that the product is priced high irrespective of whether the competitor enters or not. (The heavy lines show the acts to be taken; light lines, representing forbidden acts, are blocked by the double slashes.) Strategy 2 assumes that the product is (1) priced medium if the competitor enters and (2) priced low if the competitor does not enter. We have already mentioned strategy 3. And so on.

To clarify, observe the following. In strategies 1, 5, and 9 Ham-Gear does not care whether the competitor enters or not. It prices the product high, medium, or low. In strategies 3 and 6, if the competitor enters, Ham-Gear prices the product low. You might consider the strategies as a top management policy which tells the marketing department what acts to undertake under any circumstances.

There will be nine other strategies for manual production, and finally there is the obvious strategy of not entering the market. We have, then, a total of 19 strategies to consider. How can we evaluate a strategy? We have seen that each strategy turns the decision tree into a probability tree and makes the profit a random variable. Each probability tree generates a PMF (probability mass function) of payoff, and therefore the best strategy is found by choosing the most desirable PMF.

How to Choose the Best Strategy

So far in all our work we have accepted Bayes' rule of finding the optimum solution by maximizing the expected payoff. As long as we

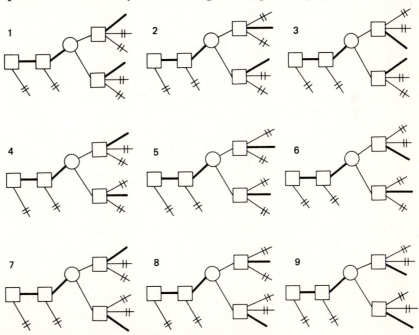

FIGURE 6.2 Nine possible strategies for Ham-Gear, provided it (1) enters the market and (2) uses automatic production.

continue with this rule, we can simply say that

> There is an expected payoff associated with each probability tree, and the best strategy is the one which provides the highest expected payoff.

However, in Chapter 7 we shall show that in many practical situations this rule is not applicable and shall develop a broader theory of optimization. Our presentation of evaluating strategies in terms of the PMF will be directly applicable to the broader theory. For this reason in this chapter we stress that first the PMF of the payoff must be calculated and then the expected value.

Evaluation of a Strategy

Of course we need a great deal of information to evaluate the PMF associated with strategies. To begin with, we need production costs for various possibilities for both automatic and manual production. We also need the demand, that is, the number of instruments sold. Then we can calculate the profits for each case. Finally we need the probabilities of possible competitive action.

We omit details here on how this information is obtained and report only the results.

In Figure 6.3, part (a), we show that if the competitor does not enter, the gross profits (excluding marketing costs) are $150,000, $200,000, and $250,000 depending on whether the product is priced high, medium, or low, respectively.

In part (b) of Figure 6.3 we show gross profit when the competitor does enter and how the gross profit depends on the competitive price.

(a)

OUR PRICE	COMPETITOR DOES NOT ENTER
High	$150
Medium	200
Low	250

(b)

	COMPETITOR DOES ENTER		
OUR PRICE	High Competitive Price	Medium Competitive Price	Low Competitive Price
High	$100	$ 90	$ 80
Medium	150	120	100
Low	180	100	90

FIGURE 6.3 Profits of Ham-Gear Instruments Corp. (in thousands of dollars) associated with various pricing combinations, not including fixed marketing expense.

For example, if our price is high and the competitor does not enter, our gross profits were $150,000 from part (a). But if he enters at a high price, our gross profits will drop to $100,000. If he enters at a medium price, our gross profits drop to $90,000, and if at a low price, to $80,000, etc.

So far we have excluded marketing costs because later we want to make a sensitivity analysis on this cost. For the time being we assume that a marketing cost of $135,000 must be deducted from the gross profits listed in Figure 6.3.

Now we need probabilities with regard to competitive action. Assume that the probability of the competitor entering or not entering the market is 1/2. We also need the conditional probabilities of how the competitor will price the product. This is shown by the numbers in Figure 6.4. For example, if our price is high, the conditional probability that the competitor too will price his product high is .4, that his price will be medium is .5, and that it will be low is .1. Etc.

Figure 6.5 shows the decision tree for strategy 8, where if the competitor enters the market, we price our product medium, and if he does not enter, we price it low. (The double slashes again block the forbidden acts of strategy 8. The probability values for the branches emanating from fork 7 were obtained from the second row of Figure 6.4.)

In Figure 6.6 we show evaluation of the probability tree associated with strategy 8. To calculate the expected payoff, we multiply the probabilities along each path of the tree and the payoff at the tips:

$$.5 \times \quad .1 \times 150 = \quad 7.5$$
$$.5 \times \quad .6 \times 120 = \quad 36.0$$
$$.5 \times \quad .3 \times 100 = \quad 15.0$$
$$.5 \times 1.0 \times 250 = \underline{125.0}$$
$$183.5$$

Thus the expected value is $183,500 at fork 3. There is, however, the $135,000 marketing expense represented in Figure 6.5 as a *toll* to pass the gate for marketing the product. So the net expected profit is $48,500 at the foot of the tree.

To better understand what is involved in strategy 8, we show in Figure 6.7 the PMF associated with this strategy. The PMF gives complete information on payoffs and probabilities.

OUR PRICE	High Competitive Price	Medium Competitive Price	Low Competitive Price
High	.4	.5	.1
Medium	.1	.6	.3
Low	.1	.2	.7

FIGURE 6.4 Conditional probability of how the competitor will price the product.

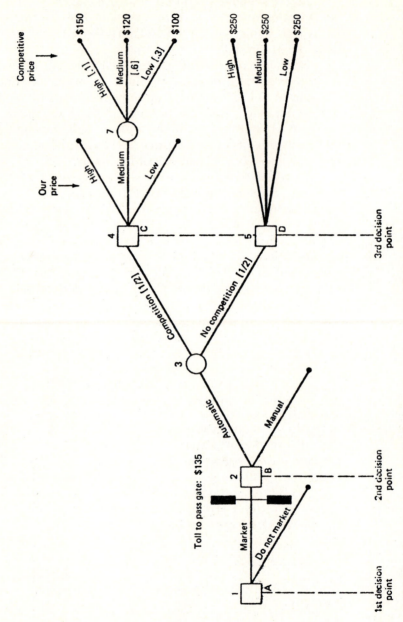

FIGURE 6.5 Decision diagram for strategy 8: If the competitor enters the market, we price our product medium; if he does not enter, we price it low.

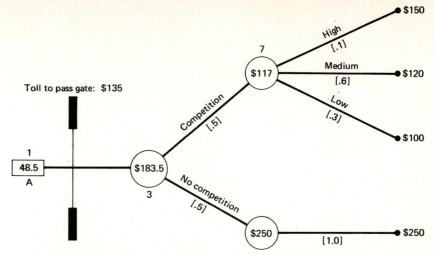

FIGURE 6.6 Evaluation of probability tree associated with strategy 8.

Finding the Best Strategy

Using the expected profit as a decision criterion, we see that it is worthwhile indeed to market the product, but we still do not know whether strategy 8 is the best. We have 17 other strategies to evaluate. (The strategy of not entering the market has already been eliminated.) In Figure 6.8 we show the nine strategies for automatic production and on the bottom line the expected profit for each. Details of the calculations are omitted and are left as an exercise. Note that the optimum strategy is 8 with the expected profit of $48,500, which profit of course agrees with our earlier result.

Finally we report, without including calculations, that the optimum expected payoff with manual production is only $150,000. *Thus automatic production with strategy 8 is the optimum solution to the*

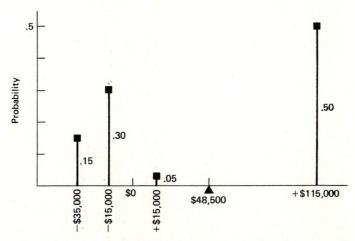

FIGURE 6.7 Net PMF of dollars associated with strategy 8.

STRATEGIES FOR AUTOMATIC PRODUCTION

	1	2	3	4	5	6	7	8	9
Competitor does enter	High	Medium	Low	High	Medium	Low	High	Medium	Low
Competitor does not enter	High	High	High	Medium	Medium	Medium	Low	Low	Low
Expected profit (thousands of dollars)	−13.5	−1.5	−9.5	11.5	23.5	15.5	40.5	48.5	40.5

FIGURE 6.8 Nine strategies available to Ham-Gear Instruments Corp. for automatic production.

problem. Apparently there is high enough demand for the instruments to warrant the capital outlay for automatic equipment.

Incidentally, observe in Figure 6.3, part (a), that if the competitor does not enter, the optimum act is to price the product low. Thus strategies 1–6 need not be evaluated, as they specify high or medium prices. Only strategies 8 and 9 are serious contenders. Often such commonsense observations can cut drastically the number of strategies to be searched.

The procedure used here examines all possible strategies and is called **normal analysis**. But in real-life situations there may be myriad strategies, and it would be impractical to evaluate each of them. We need some shortcut procedure to deal with large problems. Before proceeding with this alternate approach, let us summarize how to evaluate a strategy with the normal analysis.

The Six Steps of the Normal Analysis

1. Draw the decision tree.
2. Mark all probabilities and payoffs.
3. List all possible strategies.
4. For each strategy, determine the associated probability tree.
5. Calculate the PMF for each probability tree.
6. Choose the strategy with the "best" PMF. If you are using Bayes' criterion, the best strategy is the one which provides the highest expected payoff.

6.2 TREE PRUNING BY BACKWARD INDUCTION

To illustrate the procedure called **extensive analysis**, we redraw Figure 6.1 in Figure 6.9 and add the computations involved in the technique of **backward induction** or **dynamic rollback**. We start at the tips of the branches and move toward the foot of the tree, **pruning the tree** through two kinds of operation: **averaging out** and **folding back**.

Consider first chance fork 6. The expected profit for this chance fork is

$$.4 \times 100 + .5 \times 90 + .1 \times 80 = 40 + 45 + 8 = 93$$

or $93,000. So let us write number 93 (thousand) in the circle. Similarly, write in the circle for chance forks 7 and 8 the expected values of 117 and 101 (thousand). Observe that we can *forget about all the information to the right of these three chance forks* because when we want to make a decision at decision fork 4, all we need consider are the three values of $93,000, $117,000, and $101,000. *We have averaged out chance forks 6, 7, and 8 and pruned our tree.*

What is the decision problem at decision fork 4? We must choose

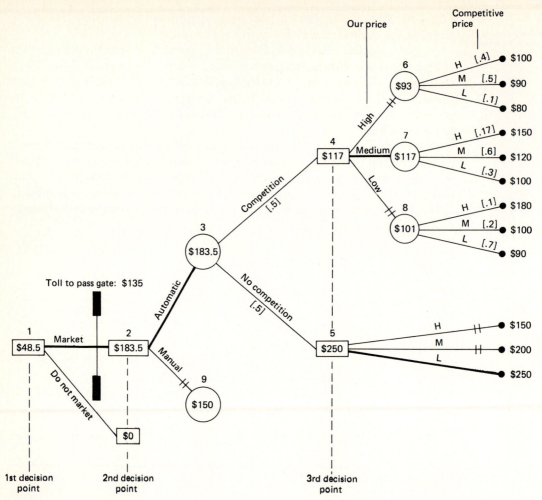

FIGURE 6.9 New version of Figure 6.1 to illustrate the technique of backward induction and dynamic rollback.

between the three values of $93,000, $117,000, and $101,000, and the obvious choice is the largest one, $117,000, which corresponds to pricing the instrument at a medium level. So we prune the *high* and *low* branches by double slashes, mark the *medium* branch by a heavy line, and put the number 117 (thousand) into decision fork 4. *We have folded back chance forks 6, 7, and 8.* What is the problem at decision fork 5? We must choose between the three deterministic payoffs of $150,000, $200,000, and $250,000. Of course we already said that by looking at the numbers in Figure 6.3, part (a), you know that if the competitor does not enter, we should price our product low. So we prune *high* and *medium* by double slashes, mark the *low* branch heavy, write the best profit of 250 (thousand) in decision box 5, and we have *folded back the decision to be made at fork* 5.

Inspect chance fork 3. We can average out by writing the expected value

$$.5 \times 117 + .5 \times 250 = 58.5 + 125.0 = 183.5$$

or 183.5 (thousand) in the circle.

Let us assume that a corresponding analysis was made for manual production and that chance fork 9 was averaged out to be $150,000.

What is the decision at fork 2? It is clearly better to automate than go into manual production, so we prune manual production by double slashes and write into fork 2 the number 183.5 (thousand). *We have folded back forks 3 and 9.* To get the net expected profit we must subtract next the cost of marketing, $135,000, and finally write the net amount of 48.5, representing $48,500, at the foot of the tree. The decision? Go ahead and market the product. The strategy? Follow the unblocked heavy branches emanating from decision boxes 1, 2 and 4. This of course agrees with the result we obtained with the normal analysis.

What is the advantage of the backward induction of dynamic rollback technique when compared with the normal analysis of evaluating each strategy? As we said at the end of the preceding section, in real life situations the normal analysis may require an impractical amount of calculation. With our new approach we do much less work. If in this problem we had five pricing levels, we would have 25 strategies for automatic, 25 for manual, and finally the strategy of not entering the market, a total of 51. As the problem gets more complicated, the number of possible strategies increases greatly.

The Four Steps of the Extensive Analysis

> *Step 1.* Draw the decision tree.
> *Step 2.* Mark all probabilities and payoffs.
> *Step 3.* Starting with the tips, prune the tree by
>   a. Averaging out
>   b. Folding back
> *Step 4.* Choose the strategy with the highest expected payoff.

What-If the Situation Changes

Suppose a new estimate of the marketing cost is made and the new cost turns out to be $160,000. What is the best strategy now? All we need do is to change the *toll* in Figure 6.9 from $135,000 to $160,000. The strategy stays the same, but the expected net profit is only $183,000 − $160,000 = $23,000.

What if the marketing cost is $200,000? This is more than the $183,500 at decision fork 2, and so the best strategy is not to market the product.

Suppose now that the marketing cost is still $135,000 but that we definitely know the competitor will enter the market. Decision box 4

(Figure 6.9) shows the value $117,000, which is $18,000 less than the $135,000 required to market the product. Thus, if we definitely know that the competitor will enter, there is no point in marketing the instrument.

Now suppose you must decide to price the product *before* knowing if the competitor will enter the market. This problem is modeled by the decision tree in Figure 6.10. Now you must decide whether to price the product high, medium, or low at decision fork 3 (Figure 6.10). If you carry out the computations by backward induction, you will find that the net expected value of the venture is only $40,500, which is $8000 less than the value we obtained previously.

Consider the situation when we allow the competitor to price his product and *wait and see* what his pricing strategy will be. This problem is modeled in Figure 6.11. Observe in the upper right corner that if he prices it at a medium or low level, we should respond with a medium level. (You can also conclude that this is the best thing to do directly

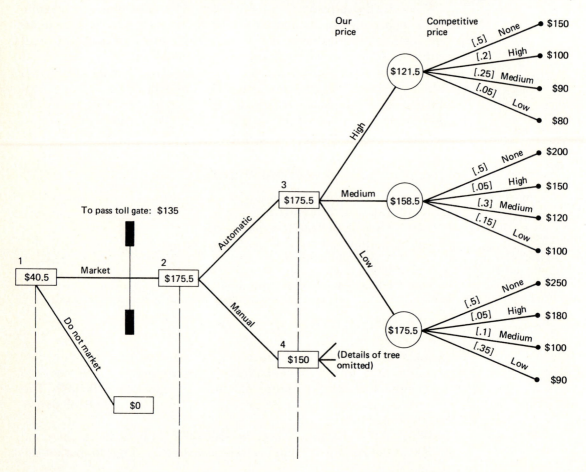

FIGURE 6.10 Decision tree representation of the problem if we must decide on pricing the product *before* knowing the competitor will enter the market.

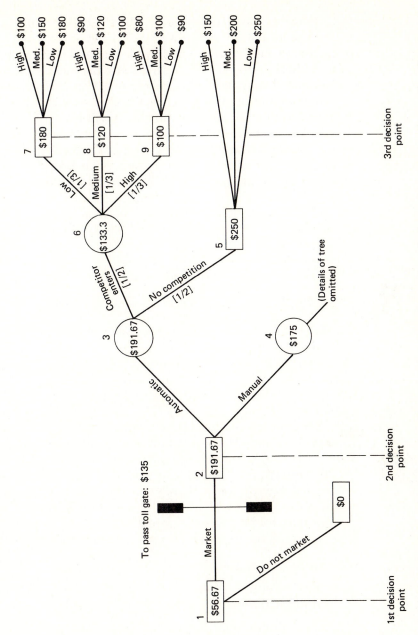

FIGURE 6.11 Decision tree representation of the problem provided we price our product only *after* we know the competitor's price.

219

from Figure 6.3.) Before we can average out, we need to know which probabilities to assign to the various pricing levels set by the competitor. Assume that each of the probabilities is $\frac{1}{3}$. Now we can average out fork 6 and find the expected value of $133,333. We can average out again forks 5 and 6 and find the value of $191,670. A similar calculation for manual production (not shown) yields the value of $175,000. Thus we prune the manual route by double slashes and write in box 2 the number 191.67 (thousand). We must still deduct the marketing cost of $135,000, which leaves us with a net expected profit of $56,670. Observe that with this kind of information we have a higher expected profit.

Consider again the situation shown in Figure 6.11, but assume that you know the competitor will enter the market. Now we have only a value of $133,333 at chance fork 3, and so at decision fork 2 it is better to decide on manual production. Now we have $175 (thousand) at fork 2 and a net expected profit of $175,000 − $135,000 = $40,000. Note that

> When the problem is altered, the model must be altered too, and the computations performed must be repeated more or less anew.

6.3 DECISION ANALYSIS IN THE PUBLIC SECTOR: CASE STUDIES

Fire Protection for the Santa Monica Mountains*

The Santa Monica Mountains, northwest of Los Angeles, face one of the most serious wildfire threats of any area in the world. Weather, vegetation, and the large population in the area combine to make large fires an inevitable phenomenon. Driven by hot, dry winds, Santa Anas, the fires can quickly reach a size and intensity that are virtually impossible to control.

Because of the 100,000 residents and 30,000 homes threatened, fires in the Santa Monica Mountains are of great concern. The Wright Fire of 1970 swept a distance of 8 miles to the Pacific Ocean in 6 hours, and the Bel Air Fire of 1971 destroyed nearly 500 homes.

A number of proposals have been made to improve fire protection in the Santa Monica Mountains to avoid the destruction of millions of dollars worth of property and threat to life. This case study describes the decision analysis approach aimed at selecting the best alternative.

The Three Alternatives

After examination of the various proposals to limit fire destruction, the following three alternatives were analyzed:

1. Limit the number of fires reaching significant size by establishing better programs for prevention and initial fire fighting.
2. Establish large strips of land on which inflammable material is

---

* This case study is based on an article by D. W. North, F. L. Offensend, and C. N. Smart, "Planning Wildfire Protection for the Santa Monica Mountains, an Economic Analysis of Alternatives," *Fire Journal*, Vol. 69, Jan. 1975, pp. 355–363.

reduced to (a) permit access to fire suppression crews, (b) increase the effectiveness of fire suppression, and (c) provide greater safety to crews.

3. Reduce damage by making homes and structures more fire resistant.

Elements of Cost and Loss

The following nine classes of cost and loss were considered:

1. Losses in property value of insured homes
2. Losses in property value of uninsured homes
3. Insurance cost
4. Partial destruction loss and loss of other improvements
5. Watershed damage
6. Loss of life
7. Disruption of public services and damage to aesthetics, wildlife, and recreation
8. Brushfire fighting cost
9. Program implementation cost

After each of these costs and/or losses were developed, a cost benefit analysis for each of the three alternatives was made. The analysis showed that the most promising approach is to reduce damage by making homes and structures more fire resistant. So this analysis was carried out in greater detail and cost and expected losses determined, assuming fire-resistant roofs and different levels of brush clearance around each home. Brush clearances of (1) 0–30, (2) 30–60, (3) 60–100, and (4) over 100 feet were assumed.

Conclusions

The analysis, supported by sensitivity studies, showed that the most effective means for protecting the homes in the Santa Monica Mountains from wildfire is for all houses to have fire-resistant roofs and 100 feet of brush clearance. The analysis showed that the number of structural losses would be reduced by a factor of almost 10.

Note that the most effective means of protection does not try to prevent all fires, which is essentially impossible, but balances the cost of fire protection measures against expected losses.

The Decision to Seed Hurricanes*

The average yearly property damage in the United States from hurricanes is $440 million. Hurricane Betsy in 1965 and Hurricane Camille in 1969 each caused property damage of approximately $1.5 billion. Any

---

* This case study is based on an article by R. A. Howard, J. E. Matheson, and D. W. North, "The Decision to Seed Hurricanes," *Science*, Vol. 176, June 16, 1972, pp. 1191–1202.

means of reducing the destructive force of hurricanes therefore has great economic and societal implications.

The possibility of reducing the force of hurricanes by seeding with silver iodide was suggested by R. H. Simpson in 1961, and experiments indicated that seeding could indeed reduce the intensity of hurricanes.

In 1970 Stanford Research Institute began a study for the Environmental Science Service Administration of U.S. with the objective of resolving the decision problems related to hurricane modifications. Typical questions to be answered were as follows:

1. How does one decide whether to seed a hurricane?
2. What is the expected value of expanding research in this field?
3. What is the value of making additional field experiments?

The decision to seed a hurricane is typically a decision to be made under uncertainty. The decision must be made about 12 hours before the hurricane is predicted to strike. Due to uncertainty in hurricane wind changes, there is no way to predict with certainty where and with what intensity the hurricane will strike. Furthermore, the property damage the hurricane may cause is uncertain. Therefore, to apply decision analysis, probability distributions for the variables needed to be established.

Results of decision analysis showed that the cost of seeding was less than the expected property damage. However, it was found that thinking solely in terms of property damage cannot resolve the issue, because if a hurricane is seeded and an unusual level of damage occurs, there could be a public outcry against the government, which might lead to substantial government liability. Thus the issue of the cost of government liability arose.

Government Liability Cost

The analysis showed there is a probability of .36 that a seeded hurricane might increase in intensity, and, in fact, there is a .18 probability that the intensity will increase more than 10%. This situation is inevitable because of the variability in the intensity of hurricanes. Such situations may then lead to suits against the government, and a legal study showed that the laws of the United States provide the government with only partial and unpredictable protection against such lawsuits. Thus analysts were unable to determine the government liability cost involved in seeding hurricanes; one of the recommendations made was that better legal bases for government seeding activities were needed before hurricane seeding could be considered other than as an extraordinary emergency action.

Recognizing that government liability costs were largely unknown, the study determined *how high these liability costs must be to reverse the decision to seed.* Calculations using decision analysis showed that for a hurricane with potential damage of $100 million there would have to be an expected government liability cost of $22 million to reverse the decision to seed. For $1 billion hurricane damage, the government liability cost would have to be $200 million.

Conclusions

Due to uncertainty in government liability cost, the recommendation was made that seeding be permitted only on an emergency basis. However, recommendations were also made that it is worthwhile to (1) make further seeding experiments and (2) initiate a detailed decision analysis to find the decision rule for whether or not to seed.

The final recommendation to the National Oceanic and Atmospheric Administration stressed that the decision to seed hurricanes cannot be resolved on strictly scientific grounds and that appropriate legal and political institutions must be designated to make hurricane seeding decisions.

6.4 A DIALOG

Q. *I do not understand how strategy 8 can be the best for the Ham-Gear Instruments Corporation. This strategy specifies that if the competitor enters the market, the product should be priced medium, and that if he does not, the product should be priced low. It seems to me that the strategy should be just the opposite.*

A. Did you check the numbers?

Q. *Yes, I did, but I couldn't find anything wrong.*

A. Sometimes these things are hard to figure out, and the answers may be counterintuitive. Remember, though, that when we said pricing the product low, we really meant the marketing strategy associated with a low price. For example, it is possible that the competitor's strength is in the mass market, and therefore if the competitor enters, Ham-Gear should price the product medium and not try to compete in the mass market. However, if the competitor does not enter, then perhaps the best approach is to go for the mass market and price the product low.

Q. *This seems to make sense. Now I have another question. You said little about information. Why?*

A. In this chapter we described the two procedures to solve decision problems represented by decision trees. If you must make a decision on whether to acquire information or not, you need to add more forks and branches to the tree but use one of the procedures presented to solve the problem.

Q. *It sounds easy.*

A. The procedure is the same, but actual application may get complex. We shall take this subject up in Chapter 8.

SUMMARY

1. The concept of strategy is fundamental to decision analysis.
2. A strategy is a sequential decision rule which specifies what to do under any and all conditions.

3. Each strategy turns the decision tree into a probability tree.

4. Each strategy makes the profit into a random variable.

5. The best strategy is selected by maximizing the expected payoff.

6. For problems with few alternatives the best strategy can be found by normal analysis which enumerates and evaluates all strategies.

7. The six steps of normal analysis are as follows:
   a. Draw the decision tree.
   b. Mark all probabilities and payoffs.
   c. List all possible strategies.
   d. For each strategy, determine the induced probability tree.
   e. Determine and evaluate each induced PMF.
   f. Choose the strategy which induces the best PMF.

8. For problems with many alternatives, extensive analysis, that is, tree pruning by backward induction—averaging out and folding back—is needed.

9. The four steps of extensive analysis are as follows:
   a. Draw the decision tree.
   b. Mark all probabilities and payoffs.
   c. Starting with the tips, prune the tree by
      (1) averaging out
      (2) folding back
   d. Choose the strategy with the highest payoff.

10. Extensive analysis is an important example of a procedure which is required only if the number of alternatives is numerous.

SECTION EXERCISES

1. **Decision Analysis by Enumerating Strategies**

1.1 This exercise refers to the Ham-Gear Instrument Corporation problem discussed in this section.
   a. Refer to Figure 6.1. Complete the tree for the branches following chance fork 9.
   b. Refer to Figure 6.2. Make a similar illustration for Ham-Gear provided (1) it enters the market and (2) uses manual production.
   c. Make a complete study of the strategies for manual production using normal analysis and giving the PMF for each strategy. "Common-sense" evaluations must be clearly explained. Refer to the six steps of the normal analysis which appear at the end of Section 6.1.

   Note: To do this exercise, you will need the following table. The table of probabilities in Figure 6.4 still holds.

Profits Associated with Various Pricing Combinations, Not Including the Fixed Marketing Expense (in thousands of dollars): manual production.

OUR PRICE	COMPETITOR DOES NOT ENTER	COMPETITOR ENTERS		
		High Price	Medium Price	Low Price
High	$190	$130	$100	$80
Medium	120	120	90	60
Low	50	100	70	50

1.2 Ham-Gear Corporation is considering automation of their line for producing antennas of one type. When a competitor enters the market, the quantity of the product which can be sold is determined by this model: $Q = 4000 - 40 \times P + 10 \times P'$, where P is the Ham-Gear price and P' is the competitor's price. When a competitor does not enter, the quantity sold is $Q = 5100 - 40 \times P$. The production cost using automatic equipment is $C_1 = 50,000 + 35 \times Q$; the production cost using current manual methods is $C_2 = 7500 + 50 \times Q$. A study of the competition indicates that their only competitor is likely to price only at $110, $105, $100, or $95. The joint probabilities for pricing in the competitive situation are estimated to be those shown in the following table:

Pricing Probabilities

HAM-GEAR'S PRICE	COMPETITOR'S PRICE			
	$110	$105	$100	$95
$105	.1	.4	.3	.2
100	.1	.2	.5	.2
95	0	.2	.2	.6

Profit is defined as the difference between total revenue and total costs; the company will make its decision based on the criterion of maximizing the expected profit.

a. Perform a complete analysis to determine an optimal strategy using *normal analysis*; assume that the probability of competition is .5.

b. Would your decision be changed if the probability of competition were 1.0? If yes, how? If no, why not?

1.3 The town of Roccoco Baton is in the hurricane zone. Over the years, the town has been able to classify the outcomes of hurricanes as BAD, MODERATE, and INSIGNIFICANT. The losses incurred for these outcomes may be considered to be $10, $5, and $0 million, respectively. When the town takes precautions, the probability that a hurricane's outcomes will fall into one of the three outcome categories is as follows:

OUTCOME OF HURRICANE	PROBABILITY
BAD	.6
MODERATE	.3
INSIGNIFICANT	.1

The cost of taking precautions is $.5 million. When the town does not take precautions, the probabilities are as follows:

OUTCOME OF HURRICANE	PROBABILITY
BAD	.8
MODERATE	.1
INSIGNIFICANT	.1

A new early warning system for hurricanes is available for local forecasting at an annual cost of $3 million. With this system, the town can put its precautionary measures into effect sooner, and the following probabilities hold:

OUTCOME OF HURRICANE	PROBABILITY	
	Without Precautions	With Precautions
BAD	.3	.2
MODERATE	.4	.3
INSIGNIFICANT	.3	.5

With this new system the cost of precautions is still $.5 million. Climatic conditions at Roccoco Baton are such that there is only one hurricane or no hurricane in any given year.

    a. Assume that the probability of a hurricane in a year is .5; draw the decision tree.

    b. Use normal analysis to determine the optimal strategy under the conditions of part a.

    c. Assume that the probability of a hurricane in a year is .8; draw the decision tree.

2   *Tree Pruning by Backward Induction*

2.1   Refer to the Ham-Gear Instrument Corporation problem discussed in Sections 6.1 and 6.2. Carry out the complete extensive analysis for the section of the tree following chance fork 9, the manual operation. Show all steps in the pruning and folding back. Refer to the four steps of the extensive analysis which appear in Section 6.2.

2.2   Refer to Exercise 1.2. Perform a complete analysis to determine the optimal strategy using *extensive analysis*; assume that the probability of competition is .8. Would your decision change if it is certain that the competitor enters. If yes, how? If not, why not?

2.3   Refer to Exercise 1.3.

    a. Under the condition of part b of Exercise 1.3, use extensive analysis to determine the optimal strategy.

    b. Assume that the probability of a hurricane occurring in any year is q. Determine the range of q for which the first decision would be to accept and use the new hurricane warning system.

    c. How much would the cost of precautions have to be before you would decide not to take precautions, expressing your answer as a function of q?

3.   *Decision Analysis in the Public Sector: Successful Applications*

3.1   In Section 6.3, three alternatives for limiting fire destruction are proposed.

    a. Can you think of any other alternatives which could be proposed? (Try to list at least two.)

    b. On what grounds do you believe that the investigators were able to reduce *their* longer list to only three?

    c. Do you think that the two or more alternatives you offer in part a should have been considered in a decision analysis?

3.2   Add at least one more item to the list of nine classes of cost and loss which were considered by the investigators.

3.3   Draw a decision tree for the Santa Monica Mountain fire protection example in Section 6.3. Of course, you do not have sufficient information to complete such a table; do the best you can to outline what it would look like, leaving blanks for information which you think should have been shown if you cannot estimate it.

3.4 Draw a decision tree for the hurricane seeding example. Of course, you do not have sufficient information to complete such a table; what further information would you want to collect?

4. *A Dialog*

4.1 Would you make a decision, in your own life, using decision analysis? If yes, why? If no, why not? If yes, give several examples.

CHAPTER EXERCISES AND DISCUSSION EXERCISES

C.1 The Space Agency is sending a spacecraft and crew to a nearby asteroid for a year to explore for commercial potential. The crew travels in a special space desert vehicle which has a unique ventilating system. Experience with this ventilating system has shown that the number of spare units that might be needed during a year's service is 0, 1, 2, or 3. The agency's director must decide whether to ship 0, 1, 2, or 3 spares with the vehicle. Past records of trips of a similar type show that the probabilities of requiring 0, 1, 2, or 3 spares are .1, .5, .3, and .1, respectively. Each spare shipped with the expedition costs $20,000. If a spare is needed but none is available on the trip, one must be shuttled to the expedition at a cost of $100,000. What is the optimal strategy?

C.2 The rapid growth in the personal computer installations following IBM's introduction of a personal computer in late 1981 caused a strong demand for microprocessor chips at a time when the high cost of money limited the development of new capacity. Pico Microprocessor Corporation is fortunate in having the capacity to produce large quantities of competitively priced "jelly beans" (commodity-type PROM chips).

Alan Sabret, the president of Pico, was contemplating a significant bid opportunity from Microx, a major OEM (original equipment manufacturer) when Edna Samantha, director of industrial relations, reported that the union had just given an ultimatum, breaking off the current wage negotiations. Despite a company-wide bonus given only 6 months ago to offset cost of living increases, the union demands a 12% across-the-board wage increase.

"And suppose they don't get it?" asked Sabret.

"Then they strike at midnight tonight. They have a strike vote in hand which overwhelmingly favors a strike. The union negotiators can do what they want, and they seem to know that we are particularly vulnerable to a shutdown with the increase in bidding activity," replied Samantha. "Their demand will lead to a cost increase from $7.60 to $8.15 per chip for the PROM chip which is now most of our business."

"*And* the subject of our upcoming bids. Look, you and I both know that we can take this strike if we have to in order to hold the wage scale. These aren't skilled workers. What do you figure it will cost us to hold firm and outsit them?"

"About $600,000. But will you be able to bid to Microx if the employees are out on strike?"

"No, unfortunately. And they are looking for 10 million PROM chips! The contract is to be let within the next 30 days, and we certainly won't be able to bid if we let them walk out. On the other hand, if we give in to this wage demand, we still can't be sure of getting the contract unless we are the lowest cost bidder," said Sabret.

"What do you know about the competitive bidding situation?" asked Samantha.

"Marketing has a pretty good feel for contract conversion chances. Here's what they think we can do."

UNIT PRICE	CONVERSION PROBABILITY
$8.30	30%
8.24	50
8.20	60
8.14	80

At this point, Ken Matty, director of marketing, came into the room and said, "Good news! Microx is going to come out with a second buy later in the year for PROM chips. But because they are concerned with capacity limitations of both ourselves and the second sources, they will *only* give us this contract if we don't get the first. It's a good contract, too. They want this PROM to fly in the NASA black hole shoot, so if we can get up the environmental test equipment, we have a good chance."

"But Ken," said Sabret, "we don't have a test facility like that on hand."

"Yes, but we have a fighting chance to get it. First of all, there is a staged requirement, so we don't necessarily have to go all the way. Of course, we do have to show that we can get the financial backing. Here's what you can do for different levels of test equipment investment."

EQUIPMENT INVESTMENT	CONVERSION PROBABILITY
$2,000,000	20%
2,400,000	40
2,600,000	50
2,900,000	60

Sabret asked for time to look into this and called for a rush effort to evaluate this opportunity. By early afternoon, it was clear that Pico could anticipate a net profit for this venture of $6 million at a unit PROM cost of $8.15 and $8 million at a unit cost of $7.60. The financial analysts did point out that these figures do not include the capital investment in special test equipment which must be written off over the life of the contract.

    a. Make the decision tree for this situation.

    b. Carry out the analysis by the easiest method (normal or extensive), and recommend a strategy for the management to follow.

C.3 Parker Company sued Denner Industries for allegedly infringing on its recently issued manufacturing patent for certain chemical powders.* Denner held that its manufacturing process was a straightforward application of published research, involving no new, patentable concepts. Both sides needed specially skilled attorneys and technical experts because of the nature of the manufacturing process. The legal issue is whether Denner's process infringes Parker's patent and if so, what damage would be awarded to Parker. If Parker wins the case, the court sets a royalty percentage of Denner's sales of the powders. Royalties on prior sales are

---

    * This exercise is based on an article by Samuel E. Bodily, "When Should You Go to Court?" *Harvard Business Review*, May–June 1981, pp. 103–113, 1981 by the President and Fellows of Harvard College.

due at the time of the announcement of the award, and royalties on later sales are due from the time of sale until the 17-year patent expired.

It was clear from the start that the royalty awarded, if any, would be between 1 and 10%. Denner had current sales of $20 million per year and publicly announced they would continue making and selling at that rate in any event. However, privately, Denner's officers decided that if 5% or more of royalty is going to Parker, they would reserve the option of switching to a more costly, patent-free process.

The president of Denner Industries, Shirley Dominguez, decided to use decision analysis on the case. Her first step was to determine the financial consequences of each alternative. To simplify the initial analysis, she assumed that the alternatives facing her were to fight the suit or to offer a settlement.

Exhibit I shows the financial consequences of following a path through the tree. The present value figures reflect the 20% discount rate.

Dominguez also needed to know probabilities. They will lose to Parker if the court holds first that the process is patentable and then if the court rules that Denner's process infringes. Dominguez had the legal department estimate the probability of the court ruling that the process infringes given that the process is deemed patentable. Data were examined, but in the final analysis, it was a judgmental decision that the chance of Denner being ruled to be infringing was 60%.

Based on a study of prior cases of a similar nature and the historical record of the judge most likely to hear the case, a committee formed for this purpose concluded on the probabilities shown in Exhibit II. Now Dominguez's remaining problem was what action to take. Your assignment is as follows:

a. Draw the decision tree for this situation.
b. Determine the best strategy of Dominguez to follow. Note that you will have to choose some discrete values for settlement values, using Exhibit II as your guide.

Exhibit I

Parker v. Denner

Memo to S. Dominguez from Financial Analyst

To: S. Dominguez

From: Stu Ross

Subject: Financial Analysis re Parker v. Denner

If we do not settle, the legal department informs me that the projected legal costs are $420,000. In the event of a settlement, we will incur no legal costs.

In the event we go to an alternative production process, the present value of extra costs is $2,700,000. The estimated present values of royalties given three levels of royalty awards are as follows:

ROYALTY	PRESENT VALUE OF ROYALTIES $(000)
1%	$100
5	1800
10	4200

Exhibit II

Parker v. Denner

Probabilities of Royalty Settlements

CHANCE (%)	THAT ROYALTY SETTLEMENT WILL BE	LESS THAN (%)
95		9
75		6
50		4
25		2
5		1

C.4 The Utel Corporation manufactures the TRASH-81, a personal pocket-size computer. They expect to sell 200,000 of the small machines at a profit of $10 per unit. Monkey Ward, a large retailer, has offered Utel a proposal that they produce a private-label version (to be sold by Monkey Ward and called the CHIMP-A/N/Z). Monkey Ward will guarantee a purchase of 400,000 units at a price that will give Utel a $2 profit per unit. Some of the sales of the CHIMP-A/N/Z would reduce sales of Utel's version of the TRASH-81. If they turn down Monkey Ward's offer, there is a good chance that one of their competitors may choose to take it. If a competitor does supply Monkey Ward, then Utel can either do nothing, increase their promotional expenses by $500,000 per year, or cut the price to reduce their profit to $7 per unit as a competitive action. Of course, if they cut their price, the competition may do so also. The question facing Utel's management was what strategy to follow.

    J. W. Apple, head of the quantitative analysis section, made the following presentation to the executive committee: "If you agree to private-label the TRASH-81 for Monkey Ward, we estimate that the probability of losing 30% of your TRASH-81 sales is .7; the probability of losing 50% is .2; the probability of losing 70% is .1. On the other hand, if you do not make a deal with them, we think that the probability of a competitor doing so (in particular, the successful Banana Corporation with its SKIN-III) is .5.

    "If the competitor buys the deal and we do nothing, then we could experience losses of unit sales as follows:

LOSS (%)	PROBABILITY OF LOSS
15	.6
30	.3
50	.1

    "But if the competitor buys the deal and we spend $500,000 for sales promotion, we have the following probability distribution:

LOSS (%)	PROBABILITY OF LOSS
0	.4
5	.3
10	.3

"On the other hand, if we do not do either of the preceding but cut prices, we have the following probability distribution for losses:

LOSS (%)	PROBABILITY OF LOSS
0	.5
5	.4
10	.1

"But then there is a .8 probability that the competition will also cut prices, resulting in the following."

LOSS (%)	PROBABILITY OF LOSS
0	.1
5	.3
10	.6

   a. Draw the decision tree for this situation.
   b. What strategy would you recommend to Utel management?

C.5 Longlife Assurance, Limited, has categorized potential customers for life insurance according to whether or not they have received a call from a salesperson and the time since their last purchase of insurance:

CUSTOMER TYPE	YEARS SINCE LAST PURCHASE	SALES CALL LAST YEAR
I	2	No
II	3	Yes
III	3	No
IV	≥ 4	Yes
V	≥ 4	No

The gross profit on a sale is $3000, and it costs $50 per prospect to have a sales call made to customers in class I, $100 to customers in classes II and III, and $200 to customers in classes IV and V.
A study of available records shows that the probability of sales can be described by the following table:

CUSTOMER TYPE	NO CALL	CALL
I	.30	.35
II	.28	.33
III	.24	.30
IV	.10	.15
V	.05	.10

   a. Draw the decision trees for these situations.
   b. What strategy for sales calls and types of customers would you recommend to the management of Longlife?

7

Individual Preferences and Multiple Objectives Under Uncertainty

In Chapters 5 and 6 we developed the important technique of decision analysis to aid managers in making decisions under uncertainty. We assumed that the rule of maximizing expected payoff provides an adequate criterion for decision making in practice. Now we show that under many conditions this rule needs to be modified, because people greatly differ in their individual preferences and often do not choose ventures maximizing expected payoff. Furthermore, in many decision problems there are nonmonetary and often conflicting objectives to be considered.

For example, a corporation may want to simultaneously (1) maximize profit, (2) maximize return on investment, (3) maximize customer satisfaction, (4) have a sales volume of at least $10 million, (5) have at least a 30% market share, (6) provide stable employment, (7) keep capital expenditure below $500,000, (8) minimize total cost, etc. The corporation may want to achieve these goals for this and the next year. It may want (1) at least a 10% increase in sales next year, (2) to reduce total cost at least by 5%, etc.

In the public sector a city may want to (1) provide the best health care, (2) minimize traffic accidents, (3) maximize the flow of traffic, (4) minimize air pollution, (5) provide fast ambulance service, (6) reduce the crime rate by 10% in a year, (7) reduce city noise by 20% in 2 years, (8) minimize adverse health effects and improve the quality of life for senior citizens, and (9) minimize taxes.

In this chapter we describe resolution of such problems by **preference-utility theory** which provides tailor-made criteria for individual decision making and choice in both private industry and the societal environment for both single and **multiobjectives**.

We begin our study by a critical examination of the expected payoff criterion.

Compare the three ventures illustrated in Figure 7.1. Each has a different random variable as the payoff. In Figure 7.1(a) we have a PMF where there are probabilities of 1/2 to get nothing and 1/2 to get $100,000. Figure 7.1(b) illustrates a PMF where the probabilities are still 1/2 and 1/2 but the gains are $45,000 and $55,000. Finally, Figure 7.1(c) shows a venture obtaining $50,000 with certainty. Suppose tickets are sold for the opportunity of playing the ventures. What would the tickets be worth?

The expected value is $50,000 for each venture, and so if we accept the expected value as a measure, we must accept all three ventures as equally attractive. However, most people would not consider the three opportunities equivalent.

> Different people may act differently under identical conditions.

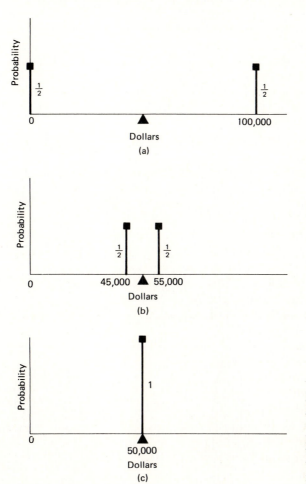

FIGURE 7.1
All three ventures have the same expected value, but part (a) is a high-risk venture, part (b) is a low-risk venture, and part (c) has no risk or uncertainty at all.

How much would *you* be willing to pay for venture (a)? Most of us would not be willing to pay the $50,000 for a 50–50 chance of winning $100,000 or nothing. Few of us have that kind of cash available to play a game. I may be willing to pay $5000 and another person $10,000, and you may not be able to raise more than $1000. But a wealthy person who is involved in various risky investments may be willing to pay $40,000 or perhaps even $60,000 for the possibility of winning $100,000.

The situation for winning $45,000 or $55,000 [Figure 6.1(b)] is quite different; it is worth at least $45,000. You may be able to get together with some others, or may even be willing and able to raise a loan of $45,000 to get your money back or to gain an additional $55,000 − $45,000 = $10,000. If you happen to have $45,000 lying around, you would certainly consider this a good venture.

Of course you would have an even easier time raising say $45,000 to play venture (c), which is absolutely certain to provide you with $50,000.

Expected value alone cannot serve as a common measure for all people.

How about combining expected value and standard deviation? The PMF of Figure 7.1(a) has a larger standard deviation than Figure 7.1(b),

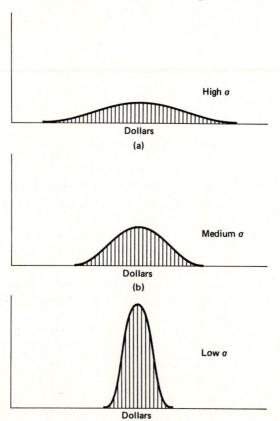

FIGURE 7.2
The three mass functions have the same expected value, but part (a) has a low σ and represents a low-risk venture; part (b) represents a medium risk, and part (c) with a high σ represents a high-risk venture.

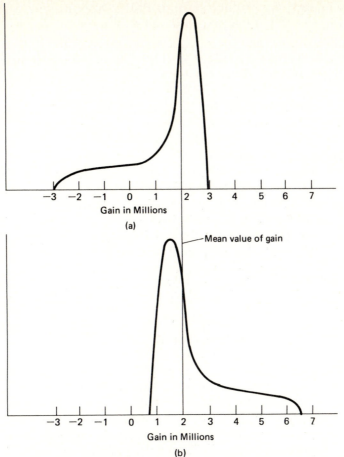

FIGURE 7.3
The two ven-
tures have the
same expected
value and stan-
dard deviation.
(The distribu-
tions are the mir-
ror images of
each other.)

which has a larger standard deviation than Figure 7.1(c). Similarly, in Figure 7.2, as you go from part (a) to part (b) and then to part (c), the standard deviation decreases, which means less risk. *However, now we show that expected value and standard deviation combined can still be misleading.*

In Figure 7.3 we show two PMFs with identical expected values and standard deviations. (The PMFs are the mirror images of each other.) However, in Figure 7.3(a) there is a possibility of a loss of $2 million, while in Figure 7.3(b) no loss can be incurred. Thus these two risks are quite different. For example, a corporation wants to be very certain not to be exposed to large losses leading to bankruptcy. So uncertainty as to large losses is viewed with extreme alarm. On the other hand, when building a skyscraper, the uncertainty of being early may be of no significance. But uncertainty as to being late may be of the greatest importance. In many practical situations the *decision maker needs to know the PMF before a decision can be made.*

In Section 5.6, when discussing risk analysis, we introduced the point of view of decision support systems and left it to the manager to compare and evaluate various PMFs. Now we go beyond this approach and develop an approach based on theory.

> Preference-utility theory provides procedures for comparing and evaluating the PMFs of different ventures.

7.2 UTILITY FUNCTIONS AND PREFERENCES

We must recognize that the consequences of our actions may not necessarily be monetary rewards and also that individual preferences toward money widely differ. Our actions and choices are governed by individual subjective preferences as to our perception of how our needs, desires, and hopes are satisfied. Person A may prefer a concert ticket to a football ticket, while person B may prefer the football ticket. Person C may prefer job security to advancement, while person D may think that a large salary is the most important thing. Utility theory first converts preferences, monetary rewards, and risks into personal **utiles,** * and then all calculations are performed in utiles instead of dollars.

How Utiles Measure Preferences

You might think of utiles as a foreign currency different from dollars. The decision maker first converts all benefits into utiles and then performs the calculations and makes the decision by comparing utiles.

Or you might think in terms of a point system where the points are called utiles. As an illustration, you may rate jobs offered you on a scale of 0 to 100 points. You choose the job with the highest points or utiles.

An Example

Consider, for example, John Robbins' perception of preferences as to dollar gains. Suppose the conversion from dollars to utiles can be performed by the **utility function** (curve) shown in Figure 7.4. (We stress that different individuals will have different utility functions.) For example, a gain of $100,000 is converted into about 85 utiles. We shall describe later in Section 7.5 how by appropriate interviews this utility function for John Robbins can be determined. To carry out calculations, we need an accurate formula to describe the utility function. Without going into mathematical details, we just report here the result, that if D is the dollar gain in thousands of dollars, then U, the utiles for John

---

* There is no uniformly accepted terminology for the units of measure of individual preferences. To simplify our discussion, we accept the term *utiles* used by some investigators.

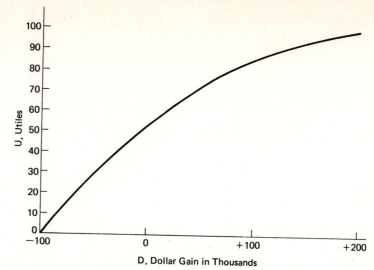

FIGURE 7.4 Dollars can be converted into utiles by using the individual utility function (curve) of John Robbins:

$$U(D) = 190 \times \left(\frac{D + 100}{300}\right) - 90 \times \left(\frac{D + 100}{300}\right)^2$$

Robbins, can be computed with the aid of the utility **function**[*]

$$U(D) = 190 \times \left(\frac{D + 100}{300}\right) - 90 \times \left(\frac{D + 100}{300}\right)^2$$

where D is in thousands of dollars. Note in Figure 7.4 (or from the formula) that a loss of \$100,000 ($D = -\$100,000$) corresponds to zero utile and a gain of \$200,000 to 100 utiles. We assume that John Robbins is not faced with ventures involving a loss larger than \$100,000 or a gain greater than \$200,000.

Suppose John Robbins is offered the venture in Figure 7.5(a). What would this venture be worth to him in utiles? We need to apply the following two-step procedure:

Step 1. Convert the dollars of the PMF into utiles
Step 2. Calculate the expected utiles

We can obtain from the formula the utiles corresponding to the dollar returns of \$0 and \$100,000 by setting $D = 0$ and $D = 100,000$, respectively,

$$U(0) = 190 \times \left(\frac{0 + 100}{300}\right) - 90 \times \left(\frac{0 + 100}{300}\right)^2 = 53.33 \text{ utiles}$$

---

[*] Functional notation is reviewed in Appendix A.

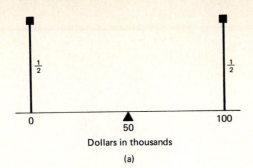

FIGURE 7.5
When applying utility theory the PMF of dollars is converted into the PMF of utiles.

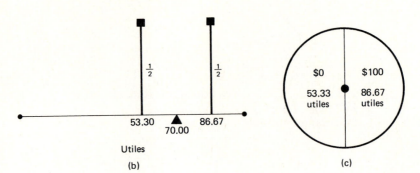

(a)

(b)

(c)

$$U(100) = 190 \times \left(\frac{100 + 100}{300}\right) - 90 \times \left(\frac{100 + 100}{300}\right)^2 = 86.67 \text{ utiles}$$

and so the expected utility value is

$$\tfrac{1}{2} U(0) + \tfrac{1}{2} U(100) = \frac{53.33}{2} + \frac{86.67}{2} = 70.00 \text{ utiles}$$

Thus this venture is worth 70.00 utiles to John Robbins. In Figure 7.5(b) we show the PMF in utiles. Figure 7.5(c) shows the random device to generate either dollars or utiles.

What is the expected utility of the venture shown in Figure 7.1(c)? We get

$$U(50) = 190 \times \tfrac{1}{2} - 90 \times (\tfrac{1}{2})^2 = 72.50 \text{ utiles}$$

meaning that this venture is worth 72.50 utiles to John Robbins. Therefore, Robbins concludes that the *certainty of getting $50,000 is to be preferred to the 50–50 chance of getting nothing or $100,000.*

7.3 CERTAINTY MONETARY EQUIVALENT (CME)

How many dollars should John Robbins be willing to pay for the 50–50 chance of getting nothing or $100,000 [Figure 7.5(a)], that is, for 70 utiles? Designate this number of dollars by x. You can see in Figure 7.4 that 70 utiles corresponds to about $42,000. A more accurate value of x can be obtained by solving the equation

$$190\left(\frac{x + 100}{300}\right) - 90\left(\frac{x + 100}{300}\right)^2 = 70$$

or

$$90y^2 - 190y + 70 = 0$$

where

$$y = \frac{x + 100}{300}$$

This is a quadratic equation for y which we can solve with the formula*

$$\text{unknown } y = \frac{-b \pm \sqrt{b^2 - 4ac}}{2a}$$

where

$$a = 90$$
$$b = -190$$
$$c = 70$$

Thus,

$$y = \frac{-(-190) \pm \sqrt{(-190)^2 - 4 \times 90 \times 70}}{2 \times 90} = \begin{cases} .4755 \\ 1.6356 \end{cases}$$

Now we calculate the corresponding values of x by solving

$$y = \frac{x + 100}{300}$$

We get

$$x = 300y - 100$$

and so $y = .4755$ corresponds to $x = 42.661$, and $y = 1.6356$ corresponds to $x = 390.68$. The first solution leads to \$42,661 and the second to \$390,680. We discard the latter, as it does not apply, and conclude that John Robbins is indifferent to the venture with 70 utiles or its certainty monetary equivalent (CME) of \$42,661.

> The utility of a venture can be measured either by utiles or by the certainty monetary equivalent (CME). The best venture has the highest expected utility or the highest certainty monetary equivalent (CME).

---

* See Appendix A.

To further clarify the use of preference-utility theory, we present now an application from the field of capital investments.

7.4 PROTECTION AGAINST UNCERTAINTY: HEDGING

As the saying goes, "Do not put all your eggs in one basket; diversify." Why? You might drop the basket and break all your eggs. Presumably if you carry your eggs in two baskets, you will be safer. Similarly, a prudent investor can go even further and *hedge*, that is, invest simultaneously in ventures which react oppositely to economic changes. For example, an investor may buy stocks in the leisure industry, betting on prosperity in the economy, and also in companies selling bread or water, because even in times of depression people must buy bread and water.

To illustrate, consider the portfolio of Eleanor Chauncy of Houston, Texas, who has $4 million in cash and also owns an amusement park. Income from the park is a random variable, and the PMF is shown in Figure 7.6(a). The expected value of this investment is .5 × 0 + .5 × 4 = $2 million, but the risks involved are quite high because the probabilities of getting nothing or $4 million are both equal to 1/2. The combined expected value of the portfolio is $4 million + $2 million = $6 million, as shown in the upper part of Figure 7.7 by strategy 1.

Eleanor Chauncy is concerned about the high risk of the investment and is considering a cash offer of $1,700,000 for the amusement park. Ms. Chauncy has $4 million in cash, so the sale of the amusement park will make her portfolio a cash amount of $5,700,000. Thus, after the sale the expected value drops to a certain $5,700,000 (strategy 2 in Figure 7.7). However, Ms. Chauncy feels that keeping her assets all in cash is less risky than the alternate portfolio of owning an amusement

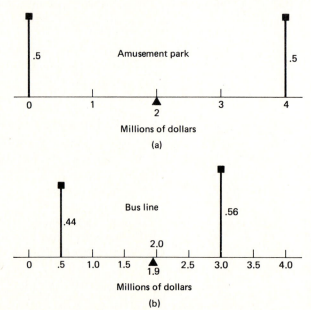

FIGURE 7.6
Part (a) shows the PMF of the income from the amusement park and part (b) the PMF of the income from the bus line.

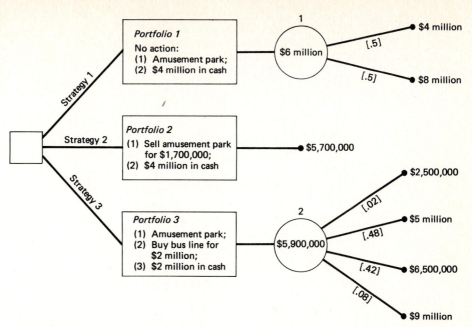

FIGURE 7.7 Decision tree description of Ms. Chauncy's portfolio problems.

park and holding $4 million in cash. Should Ms. Chauncy sell the amusement park?

It so happens that as a third alternative she is offered a local bus line for $2 million. The PMF of this venture is shown in Figure 7.6(b). When considering the purchase of the bus line as a separate investment, it looks like this purchase makes no sense. The investment is $2 million, and the expected value is only .44 × .5 + .56 × 3.0 = $1,900,000 with the possibility that the income will be only $500,000. Why should she consider this venture at all?

Her reasoning is as follows. The return on these investments depends on the state of the economy. She feels that in the case of prosperity, it is more likely that the amusement park will have a high value and the bus line will have a low value. On the other hand, in the case of recession, the amusement park will be more likely to have a low value and the bus line more likely to have a high value. The two investments are not independent. She feels that a portfolio having both the amusement park and the bus line provides an opportunity for hedging. However, to make a decision on a quantitative basis, we need probabilities and Ms. Chauncy's utility function.

Portfolio Analysis by Expected Payoff Functions

Ms. Chauncy accepts the following thought experiment to describe the problem. Consider a bag with 100 chips, each chip describing the outcome of the investments. For example, Figure 7.8 illustrates a *prosperity* chip. It says that the value of the amusement park will go up

Amusement park will go up to $4 million.
Bus line will go down to $500,000.
(prosperity)

FIGURE 7.8 Sample "prosperity" chip
for Ms. Chauncy's thought
experiment.

to $4 million and that that of the bus line will go down to $500,000. In Figure 7.9 we show the eight types of chips placed in the bag. For example, in the second line we show that there will be 40 chips of the type shown in Figure 7.8. Thus there is a 40% chance or a probability of .4 for drawing the chip shown in Figure 7.8.

To make a comparison with the original portfolio, we need to calculate the PMF of the new portfolios. However, first we ignore the cash and calculate the PMF of the portfolio consisting of the amusement park and bus line. Our procedure is summarized in the four cells of Figure 7.10. Observe that the expected dollar value of this venture is

$$.02 \times 500,000 + .48 \times 3,000,000 + .42 \times 4,500,000$$
$$+ .08 \times 7,000,000 = \$3,900,000$$

Now it is simple to get the PMF and expected value of the venture of $2 million and the amusement park and bus line. All we need do is add the $2 million to all the values. In Figure 7.11(a), we show the PMF for the original investment of the amusement park plus $4 million. In Figure 7.11(b) we show the PMF for the new combined portfolio. Observe that the expected value is $5,900,000, which is $100,000 less than the expected value for the original portfolio.

Let us return now to Figure 7.7 to summarize the problem and the three strategies.

LINE NUMBER	NUMBER OF CHIPS	TOTAL	STATE OF ECONOMY	VALUE OF INVESTMENT Amusement Park	Busline
1	5		Prosperity	$4,000,000	$3,000,000
2	40		Prosperity	$4,000,000	$500,000
3	4		Prosperity	$0	$3,000,000
4	1		Prosperity	$0	$500,000
		50			
5	3		Recession	$4,000,000	$3,000,000
6	2		Recession	$4,000,000	$500,000
7	44		Recession	$0	$3,000,000
8	1		Recession	$0	$500,000
		50			
Grand total		100			

FIGURE 7.9 Eight types of chips will be put into the bag for the thought experiment dealing with Ms. Chauncy's problem.

		AMUSEMENT PARK	
		Down	**Up**
BUS LINE	**Down**	*Use lines 4 & 8 (Figure 7.9)* Probability = (1 + 1)/100 = .02 Outcome = $0 + $500,000 = $500,000	*Use lines 3 & 7 (Figure 7.9)* Probability = (4 + 44)/100 = .48 Outcome = $0 + $3,000,000 = $3,000,000
	Up	*Use lines 2 & 6 (Figure 7.9)* Probability = (40 + 2)/100 = .42 Outcome = $4,000,000 + $500,000 = $4,500,000	*Use lines 1 & 5 (Figure 7.9)* Probability = (5 + 3)/100 = .08 Outcome = $4,000,000 + $3,000,000 = $7,000,000

FIGURE 7.10 Calculation of the PMF for the portfolio consisting of the amusement park and bus line.

Strategy 1. Take no action. Keep the amusement park and $4 million in cash. The expected value is $6 million.

Strategy 2. Sell the amusement park for $1,700,000. Together with the $4 million, this result is $5,700,000 in cash.

Strategy 3. Buy the bus line for $2 million. The combined investments in the amusement park and bus line plus $2 million in cash yield an expected value of $5,900,000.

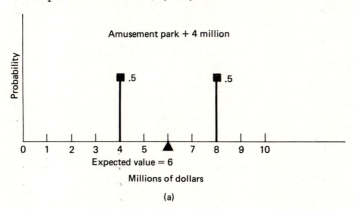

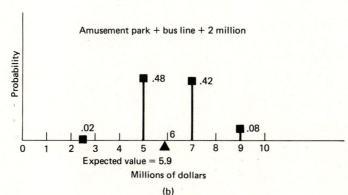

FIGURE 7.11 PMF of two alternate portfolios for Ms. Chauncy.

Thus if the expected payoff criterion is used, strategy 1 appears to be best. However, the correct answer to the problem can be obtained only if Ms. Chauncy's utility curve is used.

Applying Preference Theory

Suppose after lengthy discussion and probing, we determine that Ms. Chauncy's utiles are to be computed from

$$U = 170 \times \left(\frac{D}{10}\right) - 70 \times \left(\frac{D}{10}\right)^2$$

where D is in millions of dollars. (Note that Ms. Chauncy's utility function is quite different from John Robbins' utility function in Figure 7.4.) Ms. Chauncy's utility function is shown in Figure 7.12. Let us proceed to compute the expected utiles. The utility of portfolio 2 with the cash value of $5,700,000 presents no problem, as it is given by

$$U(5.7) = 170 \times .57 - 70 \times .57^2 = 74.16 \text{ utiles}$$

as shown in Figure 7.13.

However, calculating the utility of portfolio 1 presents a problem because the payoff is a random variable. We need a three-step procedure.

Step 1. Convert each payoff into utiles.
Step 2. Multiply each probability by the respective utile.
Step 3. Add the products to obtain the expected value of utility.

To compute the utility of portfolio 1 (amusement park plus cash), we need the utility of the two payoffs of $4 million and $8 million:

$$U(4.0) = 170 \times .4 - 70 \times .4^2 = 56.80 \text{ utiles}$$

$$U(8.0) = 170 \times .8 - 70 \times .8^2 = 91.20 \text{ utiles}$$

From this we can compute the expected utility of portfolio 1:

$$\tfrac{1}{2}U(4.0) + \tfrac{1}{2}U(8.0) = \tfrac{1}{2} \times 56.80 + \tfrac{1}{2} \times 91.20 = 74.00 \text{ utiles}$$

(chance fork 1 in Figure 7.13). Note that the all-cash portfolio 2 (74.16 utiles) is better for Ms. Chauncy than the original portfolio 1 (74.0 utiles) of the amusement park plus cash.

Now compute the expected utility of the combined investment, portfolio 3. To do this, we compute from the formula the utility value for the payoffs of $2.5 million, $5 million, $6.5 million, and $9 million:

$$U(2.5) = 38.13$$

$$U(5.0) = 67.50$$

$$U(6.5) = 80.92$$

$$U(9.0) = 96.30$$

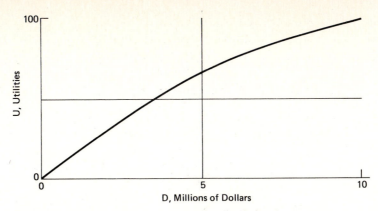

FIGURE 7.12 Utility curve for Ms. Chauncy:

$$U(D) = 170 \times \left(\frac{D}{10}\right) - 70 \times \left(\frac{D}{10}\right)^2$$

Now we can compute the expected utility as

$$.02 \times U(2.5) + .48 \times U(5.0) + .42 \times U(6.5) + .08 \times U(9.0) = 74.85 \text{ utiles}$$

(chance fork 2 in Figure 7.13). Thus it is concluded that for Ms. Chauncy the best portfolio is the combined investment of portfolio 3 because this provides the highest expected utility, notwithstanding the fact that strategy 1 yields the highest expected payoff.

Certainty Monetary Equivalents

For the original portfolio 1 of the amusement park plus cash we need to solve

$$170\frac{x}{10} - 70\left(\frac{x}{10}\right)^2 = 74$$

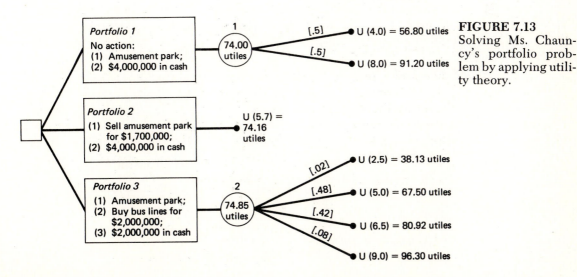

FIGURE 7.13
Solving Ms. Chauncy's portfolio problem by applying utility theory.

or

$$70\left(\frac{x}{10}\right)^2 - 170\left(\frac{x}{10}\right) + 74 = 0$$

Solving the quadratic, we get*

$$\frac{x}{10} = \frac{170 - \sqrt{170^2 - 4 \times 70 \times 74}}{2 \times 70} = .5682617$$

and

$$x = 5.682617$$

Thus the certainty monetary equivalent of the original investment is \$5,682,617, which is indeed less than the all-cash possibility of \$5,700,000.

For the combined investment, portfolio 3, we need to solve

$$170\frac{x}{10} - 70\left(\frac{x}{10}\right)^2 = 74.85$$

or

$$70\left(\frac{x}{10}\right)^2 - 170\left(\frac{x}{10}\right) + 74.85 = 0$$

So

$$\frac{x}{10} = \frac{170 - \sqrt{170^2 - 4 \times 70 \times 74.85}}{2 \times 70} = .5777293$$

and

$$x = 5.777293$$

Thus the certainty monetary equivalent of the combined investment portfolio 3 is \$5,777,293, which is indeed higher than the equivalents of the other two portfolios.

Summary of Procedure

Step 1. Convert the PMF of dollars into the PMF of utiles.
Step 2. For each strategy, compute the expected utility measured in utiles or/ and the certainty monetary equivalent.
Step 3. Choose the alternative with the highest expected utility and/or highest certainty monetary equivalent.

---

* As before, the second root of 1.860397 does not apply.

Now we provide a brief description of how individual utilities can be assessed when a decision maker is faced with a single objective. As an example, we show how the utility curve of John Robbins (Figure 7.4) can be determined.

First we establish that John Robbins is interested in gains of less than $200,000 and losses not to exceed $100,000. This sets the horizontal scale in Figure 7.4 from −$100,000 to $200,000. Then we decide that we will establish utilities on a scale of 0 to 100, and so the −$100,000 corresponds to 0 utile and the +$200,000 to 100 utiles.

Our next task is to establish the number of utiles John Robbins assigns to a zero dollar gain, that is, to the venture of doing nothing. To accomplish this task, we establish **standard gamble ventures**, meaning ventures which either lead to a gain of $200,000 or to a loss of $100,000, that is, to utiles of 100 or 0. We ask John Robbins whether he would prefer doing nothing or obtaining a .9 probability of gaining $200,000 and a .1 probability of losing $100,000. That is, would he prefer zero dollars or the expected utility value of $.9 \times 100 + .1 \times 0 = 90$ utiles? Suppose he says he prefers this gamble venture to doing nothing. So we conclude that the utility to be assigned to a zero dollar gain must be less than 90 utiles.

Now we ask Robbins whether he prefers a .1 probability of gaining $200,000 and a .9 probability of losing $100,000 to doing nothing. Robbins replies that he prefers doing nothing. The expected utility of the venture is $.1 \times 100 + .9 \times 0 = 10$ utiles, and we conclude that the utility to be assigned to 0 dollars must be more than $.1 \times 100 = 10$ utiles. Now we know that the utiles to be assigned to a zero dollar gain must be between 10 and 90 utiles.

Next we ask Robbins whether he prefers a .7 probability of gaining $200,000 and a .3 probability of losing $100,000 to doing nothing. Robbins prefers this gamble venture to doing nothing, and so we conclude that zero dollar gain should be assigned a value which is less than $.7 \times 100 + .3 \times 0 = 70$ utiles. Now we know that the utiles in question are more than 10 but less than 70.

We proceed with a series of questions until we bracket the utiles in question with sufficient accuracy. Suppose we find that the value of 54 utiles approximately corresponds to a zero dollar gain. Then we have a single point established on the utility curve of John Robbins (Figure 7.4).

Next we repeat the sequence of questions, using a dollar gain of $100,000. After a sufficient number of questions and answers, we establish that approximately 80 utiles correspond to $100,000. So we have a second point on the curve. Then we repeat the entire sequence for a loss of $50,000 and obtain a third point on the utility curve. We proceed with this method of analysis until we obtain a sufficient number of points on the curve, and then we fit by some suitable statistical technique a best fitting curve to the points established. This, then, is the utility curve of John Robbins.

It is to be stressed that this type of investigation must be performed for each individual, so the different utility curves of different people can be established.

In this description we determined utilities for a single objective: dollar gain. A similar approach can be carried out for a nonmonetary objective.

The approach can also be extended to multiobjective problems, and in Chapter 14 when discussing goal programming, we return to this subject.

Finally it must be mentioned that the time-consuming question-and-answer procedures have been computerized, and so it may be possible for a decision maker to hold a dialog with a computer terminal and thus ferret out the utility function by an automated process.*

7.6 PROCEDURE TO FIND THE OPTIMUM DECISION

Now we can summarize the three basic steps for finding the optimum solution to a decision-making problem.

Step 1. Derive subjective probabilities.
Step 2. Assess the preferences, and derive the utility function.
Step 3. Find the strategy for which the expected utility is maximized.

Subjective probability has been treated in earlier chapters and the preference and utility function approach in this chapter. Now we can state the principle of applying the utility-preference theory.

Once the utility function is determined, the problem becomes a standard maximization problem, and all available techniques become candidates for solving the problem.

You should recall that the technique to be used will depend on whether we have a small or large number of alternatives. When the number of alternatives is small, we compute the expected utility for each strategy and select the best. When working with decision trees, this implies the *normal* form of analysis (see Section 6.1), used for Ms. Chauncy's portfolio problem (Figure 7.13).

---

*A. M. Geoffrian, J. S. Dyer, and A. Feinberg, "An Interactive Approach for Multicriterion Optimization with an Application to the Operation of an Academic Department," *Management Science*, Vol. 19, No. 4, 1972, pp. 357–368.

The Eight Steps of the Normal Analysis

Step 1. Draw the decision tree.
Step 2. Mark all probabilities along the branches and dollar payoffs at the tips of the tree. (If there are gates and fees as in Figure 6.3, they must be absorbed in the payoffs at the tips.)
Step 3. List all possible strategies.
Step 4. For each strategy, determine the associated probability tree.
Step 5. Convert each payoff into utiles.
Step 6. For each probability tree, calculate the PMF of the utiles.
Step 7. Calculate the expected utility for each probability tree.
Step 8. Choose the strategy with the highest expected utility.

As an alternative you can work with the certainty monetary equivalent (CME). Then steps 7 and 8 are replaced by

Alternate Step 7. Calculate the CME for each probability tree.
Alternate Step 8. Choose the strategy with the highest CME.

When the Number of Possibilities Is Large

When the number of possibilities is large, we may need a computer, and if decision trees are used, the *extensive* form of analysis must replace the *normal* form of analysis (see Section 6.2).

When the number of alternatives is myriad or infinite, mathematical algorithms are required to find the optimum. Typically, techniques of linear programming and mathematical programming, discussed in Chapters 10–14, lead to the solution of such problems. A particularly important technique for multiple objectives, goal programming, will be covered in Chapter 14.

7.7 SUCCESSFUL APPLICATIONS

Air Pollution Control

Congressmen, mayors, city councilors, and other public officials are making major decisions on what measures should be taken to control air pollution. Should a new electric power generation station be established in the city? Should the current station be expanded? Should there be stringent limits established on the sulfur content of fuel? What standards should be established for carbon monoxide, hydrocarbons, and nitrogen oxides emitted by motor vehicles?

While there is agreement that we want clean air, it is recognized that improving conditions leads to higher utility costs, manufacturing costs, automobile costs, etc. Thus the impact of preventive measures must be considered not only in terms of improved living standards but also of cost.

The principal stumbling block in applying quantitative analysis to situations of this nature is that the goals to be established are ill-defined and not explicitly stated. In the broadest sense, officials are concerned with improving the well-being of their constituents. But such a general statement is inadequate for decision makers trying to deal or even think effectively about their problems. The situation is so complex and has so many facets that it becomes difficult, nay impossible, to deal with the problem even in a qualitative sense. Thus the objective of making a quantitative analysis is not only to obtain precise quantitative answers but also to provide a qualitative insight into the situation. One of the purposes of quantitative analysis is to force decision makers to think harder about their problem than they are ordinarily accustomed and to provide decision makers with readily defensible assessments of the situation.

In this brief overview of a quantitative study of air pollution, we concentrate on the work of Howard N. Ellis, who was the principal investigator for making an air pollution control study for New York City.* Ellis started—as is always the case in quantitative analysis—by building a general model for evaluating air pollution control programs. The model includes *inputs* (demand for electric power, weather, air pollution control technology, air pollution programs and legislation), the *pollution problem* (air pollution emissions, air pollution concentrations), *outputs* (adverse effects on residents, adverse effects on the city's economy), and *control* (proposed air pollution control legislation and programs). However, the difficulty in finding a quantitative model lies in the vague definition of the output. After serious thought and through an evolutionary process, Howard Ellis divided the overall objectives of the air pollution system into five subobjectives:

1. Decrease the adverse health effects on residents
2. Decrease the adverse economic effects on residents
3. Decrease the adverse effects on the residents' psychological well-being
4. Decrease the net cost to the city government
5. Achieve as desirable a political "solution" as possible

After identifying these subobjectives, Ellis decided that the alternatives are to be evaluated in terms of the following seven variables:

1. Per capita increase in the number of days of remaining lifetime
2. Per capita decrease in the number of days of bed disability per year
3. Per capita annual net cost to low-income residents
4. Per capita annual net costs to other residents

---

* R. L. Keeney and H. Raiffa, *Decisions with Multiple Objectives: Preferences and Value Tradeoffs*, Wiley, New York, 1976, pp. 355–365.

249

*Individual
Preferences and
Multiple Objectives
Under Uncertainty*

5. Daily sulfur dioxide concentrations in parts per million
6. Total annual net cost to city government
7. Subjective index of political desirability

After establishing these seven variables as appropriate in evaluating air pollution control legislation, Ellis proceeded to evaluate in specific terms the sulfur decision problem of New York City. Namely, the city council was considering whether *the legal limit on the sulfur content of fuels burned in the city should be lowered.*

Now that Ellis had formulated the air pollution problems in a quantitative manner, he was able to proceed and apply decision analysis to the problem. He determined the explicit impact of the proposed legislation and developed a detailed program for air pollution control. He presented his recommendations to the New York City Environmental Protection Administration and also to the New York City Council in its legislative dealings on the proposed new air pollution control code. The code was approved by the city council, and Ellis continued to consult with the city after his work was completed.

Location of an Airport*

What should Secretary Bracamontes, head of the Ministry of Public Works, recommend to President Echeverria of Mexico regarding the development of future airport facilities in Mexico City? Should Mexico modernize its present facilities at Texcoco or build a new airport at Zumpango, north of the city? The decision is not a static one (Texcoco or Zumpango now!) but instead a dynamic one that considers phased developments over a number of years. There are many uncertainties, including the possibility of technological breakthroughs (e.g., noise suppressants, new construction methods for building runways on shallow lakes or marshlands, and increased maneuverability of commercial aircraft), the possibility of changes in demand for international travel, the possibility of future safety requirements being imposed by international carriers, and the like. But even if Secretary Bracamontes had a reliable clairvoyant, his problem of making a choice is still complex. He must balance such objectives as how to

Minimize the *costs* to the federal government
Raise the *capacity* of airport facilities
Improve the *safety* of the system
Reduce *noise* levels
Reduce *access time* to users
Minimize *displacement* of people for expansion

---

* R. de Neufville, and R. L. Keeney, "Use of Decision Analysis in Airport Development for Mexico City," in *Analysis of Public Systems*, A. W. Drake, R. L. Keeney, and P. M. Morse, eds., M.I.T. Press, Cambridge, Mass, 1972.

Improve *regional developments* (roads, for instance)

Achieve *political* aims

These objectives are too vague to be operational, but decision analysis, based on utility theory, transformed the objectives to quantitative form and assisted Secretary Bracamontes in reaching a rational recommendation for President Echeverria.

Treatment of Heroin Addiction

Heroin addiction has reached alarming proportions in New York City and something must be done about it. But what? The problem has been studied and restudied, yet experts differ widely in their proposed strategies. The reason is partly because the problem is so complex that experts honestly disagree about the implications of any specific treatment. Technically they differ on what a reasonable model of the situation should include and on what rate of flow of addicts from one category to another should be acceptable. Therefore, their probabilistic predictions of the future vary. However, if these experts had crystal balls and their disagreements about uncertainties disappeared, the controversy would still continue. It would focus only on preferences instead of on both preferences and uncertainties. The mayor of New York City would like to:

> Reduce the size of the addict pool (this is more complicated than it sounds, since there are different types of addicts and trade-offs must be made among the sizes of the categories)
>
> Reduce costs to the city and its residents
>
> Reduce crimes against property and persons
>
> Improve the "quality of life" (whatever that may mean) of addicts and reduce their mortality
>
> Improve the quality of life of nonaddicts, make New York City a more pleasant place to live, and reverse the disastrous trends of in-and-out migration of families and businesses
>
> Curb organized crime
>
> Live up to the high ideals of civil rights and civil liberties
>
> Decrease the alienation of youth
>
> Get elected to higher political office

By using decision analysis and utility theory,* it became possible for the mayor to combine uncertainties and preferences, thus developing a more reliable approach to decision-making.

---

* M. H. Moore, *Policy Towards Heroin Use in New York City*, doctoral dissertation, Harvard University, Cambridge, Mass., 1973.

Doctor William Schwartz,* Chief of Medicine at Tufts Medical School, makes the rounds of the wards with his students and insists on sharing his thought processes with them: "Well, this patient I think has either disease A, or B, or C. I think the respective probabilities are .2, .3, .5. Now I can prescribe treatments X, Y, or Z. After the treatment starts I'll know more about what ails the patient, but I'll still not be certain. I'll have to revise my probabilities before continuing treatment. But of course I also must consider the side effects, discomfort, and cost to the patient, too."

Not all physicians can state their thought processes with such clarity. However, all doctors must constantly combine probabilities with preferences. Some preferences are not easy to make. Not only is cost to the patient a consideration but also costs to insurance companies, fees to doctors, and utilization of scarce resourses (doctors, nurses, surgical facilities, and hospital beds, for example). Doctor Schwartz must be concerned about pain, suffering, anxiety, the time of the patient's incapacitation, and the possibility of death. Then, societal factors are involved in the problem such as contagious effects, information gained from one patient that can be useful in the treatment of other patients, and development of resistant bacterial strains. These societal considerations often create a conflict for the doctor: what's right for his patient may not be right for society. But all these matters must be considered, and decisions must be made.

The physician begins by constructing a *generalized* decision tree to describe possible actions and their potential consequences. At this stage he tries to avoid subjective judgments as to the particular patient considered. Then he starts to prune the tree, using judgment to eliminate or consolidate branches which represent unlikely alternatives or outcomes which can be ignored without significantly influencing the decisions. Thus a *particularized* decision tree is constructed, and the final decision is reached by applying both qualitative and quantitative analysis to this decision tree.

Thus with the aid of decision analysis and utility theory it became possible to include the subjective elements of the problem into the decision-making process. While there was no claim that an "objectively correct solution" was obtained, the systematic and quantitative nature of the approach raised confidence that the "right" solution was obtained.

Establishing Corporate Preferences

According to a simplistic view, the purpose of business is to make profit. But in reality corporations issue all sorts of policy statements about their goals and objectives. The corporation has responsibilities to the stock-

---

* W. B. Schwartz, G. A. Gorry, J. P. Kassirer, and A. Essig, "Decision Analysis and Clinical Judgment," *The American Journal of Medicine*, Vol. 55, 1973, pp. 459–472.

holders, the employees, the public, the government, etc. However, from the viewpoint of operating a corporation, such general statements of goals and objectives are of little use.

Since early 1972, Woodward Clyde, a holding firm for several professional service consulting firms, has used utility theory to establish corporate preferences.*

All the shareholders of Woodward Clyde are senior professionals on the staff or at one of the affiliates. Thus, the overall objective of Woodward Clyde was stated as follows: "The combined efforts of Woodward Clyde Consultants and its Affiliates are directed toward the creation and maintenance of an environment in which the employees can realize their personal, professional and financial goals." To apply utility theory, this general statement of goals was converted to a detailed set of objectives such as financial growth, increase of shareholders' investment, compensation plan, scope of services offered, etc. Then these objectives were converted to numerical assessable attributes such as retained earnings, growth in retirement plan, base compensation, incentive compensation, etc.

Using 10 significant factors, a utility function for the corporation was developed. This corporate utility function was not used for making specific decisions or for attempting to maximize utility for the corporation but to run the business. Benefits obtained by utility theory can be summarized in the following way: (1) aid communication among the decision makers, (2) support managers in grappling with fundamental issues of the firm, (3) determine and examine differences of opinion in a quantitative fashion, (4) aid in generating creative alternatives in solving corporate problems, and (5) identify areas where the corporation is deficient in meeting objectives.

In 1974 Woodward Clyde Consultants reorganized its operations to better serve its clients. In evaluating the desirability of the organizational changes, many members of the board of directors used the information developed by utility theory.

7.8 HOW PRACTICAL IS UTILITY THEORY? A DIALOG

Q. *How often is utility theory used?*

A. The word *used* has several meanings, and so I have several answers. First, utility theory provides an understanding of how people behave and how they make their choices. As an example, consider barter or trade. Why do farmers exchange their produce for other goods? Both the farmer and the buyer make a "good deal." Utility theory provides the explanation, because surplus grain is not of much use to the farmer, but machinery is. To the manufactur-

---

* R. L. Keeney, "Examining Corporate Policy Using Multiattribute Utility Analysis," *Sloan Management Review*, Vol. 17, 1975, pp. 63–76.

er of farm equipment the machinery has no direct utility, so the manufacturer trades the equipment for money.

Consider why people buy insurance. Insurance originated when merchants became concerned over considerable investment in ships, the loss of which could mean bankruptcy to the owner. So some people went into the business of taking the risk of ships sinking and formed insurance companies. The shipowner is willing to share the cost of running the insurance company and providing a profit, because the shipowner cannot take the risk of losing the ship. The insurance company insures many shipowners and so can take the risk.

The same holds for those who buy life insurance, fire insurance, theft insurance, etc. We cannot take these risks and so are willing to share the cost of running and providing a profit to insurance companies.

Q. *What other uses of utility theory can you give?*

A. The modern theory of social and economic choice and finance is based on utility theory. The current theory of capital investments is based on economic theory, which in turn uses utility theory. New marketing theory dealing with the choice of consumers again uses utility theory.

Q. *Can you give a specific list of areas where utility theory has supported managerial decision making?*

A. Budget allocation problem of a school district

Fire department operations

Computer systems selection

Siting and licensing of nuclear power facilities

Safety of landing aircraft

Strategic and operational policy concerning frozen blood

Sewage sludge disposal in the metropolitan Boston area

Selecting a job or a profession

Transport of hazardous substances

Treatment for cleft lip and cleft palate

Development of water quality indices

Examining foreign policy

Forest pest management

Also I want to stress that specific applications of utility theory are still growing in number. Bear in mind that the purpose of quantitative analysis is to provide better information for decision making. Utility theory provides consistent information and consensus of objectives for decision makers. It provides a systematic examination of objectives, trade-offs, and risks. It makes people think hard and carefully and provides a method to augment intelligence and common sense.

Q. *Can you name a field where utility theory has been most successful?*

A. In the article "An Annotated Bibliography of Decision Analytic Applications to Health Care,"* 110 applications are cited. The applications span 15 years and are reported in widely dispersed journals, half of which are aimed at medical audiences.

Q. *When we discussed corporate models in Chapter 1, you said the output of the model is "fashioned after the annual report of the company." Instead of all these data, why don't they simply use a single utility measure?*

A. Well, we have not gotten that far yet, although the Woodward Clyde case should convince you that we are moving in that direction.

Q. *Now that I have you on the defensive, tell me why in risk analysis, discussed in Chapter 5, executives don't use utility theory?*

A. You have a knack for pointing out the direction in which applications should move.

Q. *What evidence is there that utility theory can accurately represent human preferences?*

A. There has been research to answer this question, and the answer is mostly affirmative. The growth of applications is not limited by lack of agreement between theory and reality.†

Q. *Does it not take an inordinate amount of time and effort to ferret out the utility function of an executive?*

A. Yes, it is time-consuming. To help, as mentioned earlier, research is being conducted to design computer programs, so by man-machine dialogs the process can be accelerated.‡

Q. *Suppose you find the optimum solution but there is another solution unknown to the decision maker for which the utility is only slightly lower? How would he know this?*

A. The utility function is only an approximate measure of preference. For this reason in practice the most attractive alternatives are ranked and presented for consideration.

Q. *I must admit you have convinced me that individual judgment can indeed be incorporated into quantitative methods. Will you present more evidence?*

---

* J. P. Krischer, *Operations Research*, Vol. 28, No. 1, Jan.–Feb. 1980, pp. 97–113.

† See G. W. Fischer, "Utility Models for Multiple Objective Decisions: Do They Accurately Represent Human Preferences?" *Decision Sciences*, Vol. 10, No. 3, July 1979, pp. 451–479.

‡ A. M. Geoffrian, J. S. Dyer and A. Feinberg, "An Interactive Approach for Multicriterion Optimization with an Application to the Operation of an Academic Department," *Management Science*, Vol. 19, No. 4, 1971, pp. 357–368.

A. Yes, goal programming in Chapter 13 will give you more food for thought.

SUMMARY

1. Utility-preference theory recognizes that individual preferences are subjective and differ in both monetary and nonmonetary rewards.
2. Utility-preference theory allows a systematic and scientific assessment of individual preferences even when several and conflicting objectives must be considered.
3. Individual preferences can be assessed in terms of utiles by carefully conducted question-and-answer sessions.
4. The key to applying utility theory is the replacement of rewards and objectives by utiles.
5. The best strategy for each individual is chosen by the principle of maximizing expected utility and/or maximizing the certainty monetary equivalent.
6. Solving a problem with utility theory involves three steps: (a) assessing probabilities, (b) deriving the utility function, and (c) maximizing expected utility.
7. The actual step-by-step computations, that is, the algorithm, for finding the decision which minimizes the expected utility depend on the number of alternatives to be considered.

SECTION EXERCISES

1. *What is wrong with the Expected Payoff Criterion?*
1.1 How much would you—taking into account your personal financial situation—be willing to pay for each of the ventures in Figures 7.1(a), (b), and (c)?
1.2 Consider the venture in Figure 7.1(b).Do you think that you could get someone to lend you the money to play this venture? If the answer is yes, why? If the answer is no, why?
1.3 Consider the ventures in Figures 7.1(a) and (b). Design a way in which these two ventures could be set up in the real world. (*Hint:* Don't overlook the obvious, elementary kind of gambling situation.)
1.4 With the spurt in U.S. oil drilling activities, a consultant is asked to decide on whether to drill on a candidate's drilling site. There is a 50–50 chance of oil at the site. Should they drill and strike oil, his profit would be $300,000. But if the well turns up dry, his net loss would be $100,000.

a. Should the consultant advise for or against drilling?

b. A seismologist is available to help the consultant arrive at the decision. What is the largest amount the consultant should consider paying for such seismic information?

2. *Utility Functions and Preferences*

2.1 Using Figure 7.4 or the formula from which it is derived given in Section 7.2, find the following:

a. The utiles John Robbins would assign to a certain gain of $50,000.

b. The utilities John Robbins would assign to the opportunity to gain an additional $50,000 over the original $50,000 (for a total of $100,000). Compare the value of the additional $50,000 after the initial $50,000, as seen by John Robbins in utiles.

c. What is the dollar gain corresponding to 40 utiles? 80 utiles?

2.2 Using John Robbins' utility function given in Section 7.2,

a. Find the expected utility to John of the venture in Figure 7.1(a).

b. Find the expected utility to John of the venture in Figure 7.1(b).

c. Find the expected utility to John of the venture in Figure 7.1(c).

2.3 An individual is faced with three gambles, each costing $15 to play. The first has outcomes of $10 and $20 with probabilities of .9 and .1; the second has outcomes of $10 and $24 with probabilities of .6 and .4; the third has outcomes of $10 and $20 each with a probability of .5. For each of the utility functions described below, determine whether the individual would accept, reject, or be indifferent to the gamble:

a. $U(D) = 3D + 5$.

b. $U(D) = D + 10$.

c. $U(D) = \log_e(D + 10)$.

2.4 The utility function for money may be used as a basis for describing risk attributes of a person. A *risk seeker* is one who will pay a premium for the privilege of participating in a gamble, a *risk-neutral* individual assigns the face value of money as its true worth, and a *risk-averse* individual takes only favorable gambles. Classify each of the utility functions in Exercise 2.3 as to its risk preference if they fall into any of the preceding categories. If not, state so.

3. *Certainty Monetary Equivalent (CME)*

3.1 Refer to the example discussed in Section 7.3 concerning John Robbins.

a. How many dollars should John Robbins be willing to pay for this venture: a 40% chance of losing $50,000 and a 60% chance of winning $200,000.

b. What is the indifference relationship, utiles vs. CME?

3.2 Refer to the example discussed in Section 7.3 concerning John Robbins.

a. How many dollars should John Robbins be willing to pay for this venture: a 20% chance of losing $100,000 and an 80% chance of winning $200,000.

b. What is the point at which John Robbins is indifferent to the venture in utiles and CME? (*Hint:* See the discussion at the end of Section 7.3 concerning John Robbins.)

3.3 John Robbins, with the utility function as given in Exercise 3.2, has two choices:

a. A 30% chance of losing $60,000 and a 70% chance of winning $120,000

b. A 40% chance of losing $50,000 and a 60% chance of winning $75,000

Assuming John Robbins is indifferent toward risk, which choice would he prefer? (*Hint:* Choose the choice with the higher CME.)

4. Protection Against Uncertainty

4.1 In Figure 7.6, the PMF derived in Section 7.4 for Ms. Chauncy's portfolio is presented. Prepare a probability tree representation of the PMF obtained.

4.2 In Section 7.4, Ms. Chauncy's utility function is determined and utiles computed. Suppose that she senses a change in her attitude toward risk and obtains a new utility function:

$$U(D) = 100(1 - e^{-D})$$

Where *e* is the base of the natural logarithms.
  a. Compute the expected utility for portfolio 1.
  b. Compute the expected utility for portfolio 2.
  c. Compute the expected utility for portfolio 3.
  d. Find the CME for each of the three portfolios. (*Note:* You will have to solve for *D* as a function of *U*.)
  e. Which portfolio is now the best? How does this compare to the decision made in Section 7.4?

4.3 Refer to Figure 7.9 and the hedging situation in Section 7.4. A review of the figures has led Ms. Chauncy to revise the section of Figure 7.9 called *value of investment*. That section of the table in Figure 7.9 is to be replaced by the following:

Value of Investment

Amusement Park	Bus Line
$3,000,000	$1,000,000
3,500,000	750,000
100,000	4,000,000
100,000	2,000,000
3,000,000	1,000,000
3,500,000	750,000
100,000	4,000,000
100,000	2,000,000

As a consequence of these new values, portfolio 3 must be completely reevaluated.
  a. Make a probability tree to determine the PMF for portfolio 3 as revised.
  b. Make a graph of the PMF for the revised portfolio 3.
  c. Using the utility for Ms. Chauncy determined in Section 7.3, find the expected utility for portfolio 3.
  d. Compute the EMV of portfolio 3 as revised.
  e. Compute the CME of portfolio 3 as revised.
  f. What is the optimal portfolio?
  g. Assume that Ms. Chauncy wants to evaluate the revised situation using the utility function of Exercise 4.2. Find the expected utility.
  h. Refer to part g. Compute the CME.
  i. Refer to parts g and h. Has the optimal decision been altered by application of this new utility function?

4.4 Ms. Chauncy has a hunch that the probabilities given in the analysis of section 7.4 (as represented by the experiment in Figure 7.9) are incorrect.

Her estimates would lead to changing the column *number of chips* to the following:

LINE NUMBER	NUMBER OF CHIPS
1	5
2	37
3	4
4	4
5	3
6	2
7	41
8	4
Grand total	100

As a consequence of these new values, portfolio 3 must be completely reevaluated.

a. Make a probability tree to determine the PMF for portfolio 3 as revised.

b. Make a graph of the PMF for the revised portfolio 3.

c. Using the utility function for Ms. Chauncy determined in Section 7.3, find the expected utility for portfolio 3.

d. Compute the EMV of portfolio 3 as revised.

e. Compute the CME of portfolio 3 as revised.

f. Which is the optimal portfolio?

g. Assume that Ms. Chauncy wants to evaluate the revised situation using the utility function of Exercise 4.2. Find the expected utility.

h. Refer to part g. Compute the CME.

i. Refer to parts g and h. Has the optimal decision been altered by use of this new utility function?

4.5 In Exercise 4.3, new values of return are given for portfolio 3. In Exercise 4.4, new values for probability are given. Using the values of return from Exercise 4.3, and the probabilities of Exercise 4.4, create new versions of Figures 7.9 and 7.10.

a. Make a probability tree to determine the PMF for portfolio 3 as revised.

b. Make a graph of the PMF for the revised portfolio 3.

c. Using the utility function for Ms. Chauncy determined in Section 7.3, find the expected utility for the revised portfolio 3.

d. Compute the EMV.

e. Compute the CME.

f. Which is the optimal portfolio?

g. Assume that Ms. Chauncy wants to evaluate the revised situation using the utility function of Exercise 4.2. Find the expected utility.

h. Refer to part g. Compute the CME.

i. Refer to parts g and h. Has the optimal decision been altered by this new utility function?

4.6 A contractor must determine whether to buy or rent equipment required to do a job up for bid. Because of lead-time requirements in getting the equipment, he must decide before knowing whether the contract is won or not. If he buys, a contract would result in $120,000 profit, net of equipment resale returns, but should he lose the job, the equipment will have to be sold at a $40,000 loss. By renting, his profit from the contract, if he wins it, will be only $50,000, but there will be no loss of money if the job is not won. The contractor's utility function is $U(D) = D + 40,000$.

    a. Calculate the expected utility payoff for each act.

    b. Which act provides the maximum expected utility?

5. Assessment of Individual Utilities

5.1   a. Insurance companies have established that historically 2 out of every 1000 of a particular type of home burn down each year. Assume that there are only two relevant events, fire and no fire, and also assume that the homeowner in the insurance example values the dollar changes in his assets according to the following utility function:

$$U(F) = F + 90,000 - 300$$

where F expresses the change in cash position associated with each outcome. The acts are to buy or not buy an annual policy with a $150 premium charge. Should there be a fire, we assume his home and all contents (valued at $90,000) will be completely destroyed. From the homeowner's point of view, is buying or not buying fire insurance the optimal choice? (*Hint:* Find the utility of buying and not buying insurance. Then decide.)

    b. Suppose the price of a policy is raised to $450. Does the decision to buy or not buy insurance change, other things remaining equal?

    c. At what premium level will the homeowner be indifferent between buying or not buying insurance?

5.2 Plot the points obtained for Mr. Robbins' utility curve on a plot, and draw the curve.

5.3 Assume that we set the lower limit of the utility scale at 0 utile and the upper limit at 100. Find the utility curve (plot utiles vs. dollars) for the following situation: The chief financial analyst says that she is indifferent to a certain profit of $50,000 and a gamble venture with an 80% probability of earning $150,000 and a 20% chance of no return. On further questioning, she says that she is also indifferent to a gamble venture with a certain profit of $20,000 and a 30% chance of winning $150,000 and a 40% chance of no return. The upper dollar limit for this utility function is $150,000 and the lower limit, $0.

5.4 Assume that we set the lower limit of the utility scale at 0 utile and the upper limit at 100. Find the utility curve (plot utiles vs. dollars) for the following situation: The head of operations research is indifferent to a gamble venture with a 70% chance of returning $100,000 and a 30% chance of no return and a certain return of $60,000. He is also indifferent to a 20% chance of returning $100,000 and an 80% chance of no return and a certain return of $10,000. The upper dollar limit for this utility function is $100,000, and the lower limit is $0.

    a. Draw the utility curve for this person.

    b. What is the utility associated with a certain $15,000 for this operations researcher?

5.5 While there is a prevalence of insurance coverage for thefts, fire, etc., there is a paucity of protection against natural disasters, such as earthquakes, tornados, or floods. Explain why.

6. Procedure to Find the Optimum Decision

(Since this section is only a formal summary of methods which have been developed in the preceding sections and chapters, no exercises are given for it.)

7. *Successful Applications*

7.1 In this section, a list of five subobjectives for an air pollution control system is given. Can you add any subobjectives to this list?

7.2 In this section, a list of seven variables for an air pollution control system is given. Can you add any variables to this list which you think might be relevant?

7.3 In this section, a list of seven variables for an air pollution control system is given. Are there any variables in this list which you think might be irrelevant? Use and give your own opinion.

7.4 In this section, the example of a location of an airport is given. Some of the objectives set by Secretary Bracamontes are readily quantified. Which are they?

7.5 In this section the example of a location of an airport is given. Some of the objectives set by Secretary Bracamontes are *not* readily quantified. Which are they?

7.6 In this section, the example of heroin addiction policy in New York is given. Some of the objectives are quantifiable, but this does not mean that the effect of a policy on this subject can be verified in the data. What are the problems in quantification and measurement of subsequent effect for the objectives "improve the quality of life of nonaddicts" and "curb organized crime?"

7.7 In this section, there is a discussion of decision making in the field of medicine. When a physician who is systematic in decision making considers such issues, do you think that he or she conceives of the problems in quantitative terms? In terms of utiles as an explicit measure? Why or why not?

7.8 In this section, there is a discussion of how Woodward Clyde sets utility functions. Why is it that such an approach seems (is?) so much more relevant and applicable in a business situation than in matters of public policy and medicine?

8. *How Practical is Utility Theory? A Dialog*

8.1 In Section 7.8, it is stated that modern theories of capital investment and social, economic choice and finance are based on utility theory. What will this mean to you in your working career in business?

8.2 How do you think utility theory might be used to get a consensus among decision makers in a large corporation who are trying to decide on how to apportion capital for new investments in plants and facilities? (*Hint:* Think of the value of having a quantified formula for the group, representing an agreed-upon attitude to risk.)

8.3 If a corporation were to have all middle managers work with the computer to develop their own utility functions, what general shape do you think they would have? Why? (*Hint:* Do you think they are risk seekers, risk neutral, or risk averse (these terms are defined in Exercise 2.4 of this chapter)? What general shape of curve results in each case?

8.4 What do you think the shape of the utility function for entrepreneurs is? Why? (*Hint:* Do you think they are risk seekers, risk neutral, or risk averse (these terms are defined in Exercise 2.4 of this chapter)? What general shape of curve results in each case?

CHAPTER EXERCISES AND DISCUSSION QUESTIONS

C.1 The following is a venture offered to the investor with the utility function $U(D) = 200 \times (D + 50)/200 - 100 \times (D + 50)/200^2$ (D is in thousands of dollars):

AMOUNT OF RETURN	PROBABILITY
−$40,000	.25
10,000	.25
50,000	.50

a. Show the PMF for this venture.
b. Find the EMV of this venture, and indicate it on your graph of the PMF.
c. Find the utiles corresponding to each return, and plot them.
d. Find the expected utility of this venture, and indicate it on your graph of the PMF of the utility.
e. Find the CME for this expected utility.
f. How do the EMV and CME compare?

C.2 A wary investor has been found to have a utility function defined as follows (where D is in thousands of dollars):

$$U(D) = 53 + D, \qquad D \leq 0$$

$$U(D) = 53 + .2D, \qquad D \geq 0$$

This investor has been offered the choice of one of the three ventures shown in Figure 7.1.
a. Make a graph of this utility function.
b. What is the expected utility for each venture?
c. Based on the three values for expected utility, which venture should the investor choose?
d. What is the certain monetary equivalent of this venture?
e. What is the CME of each of the other ventures?

C.3 The following are three ventures offered at the same time:

VENTURE	AMOUNT OF RETURN	PROBABILITY
I	$10,000	5/8
	50,000	3/8
II	$10,000	.4
	32,500	.4
	40,000	.2
III	$20,000	.5
	30,000	.5

a. What is the expected value of each venture?
b. What is the standard deviation of each venture?
c. If the criterion is to maximize expected value, which venture would you choose?

d. If the criterion is to minimize standard deviation, which venture would you choose?

e. If $25,000 is required to "play" one of these three ventures, which would you choose if you have no assets but could borrow the $25,000 from the Vigorish National Bank at 5% per week? Which would you choose to play if you have just won $1 million in the Caledonian sweepstakes?

f. Assume that the utility function $U(D) = 190 \times (D + 100)/300 - 90 \times [(D + 100)/300]^2$ holds (D is thousands of dollars). Find the expected utility for each of the three preceding ventures. Which venture has the highest expected utility?

g. The venture originator has offered it for $25,000. To determine whether this is a fair offer, find the CME for the expected utility of the venture with the highest expected utility.

h. Find the CME of the two other ventures. With the result from part g, what do you conclude about the "fairness" of these ventures?

C.4 The Kahn Cave Corporation manages tourist cave attractions. They have been offered land containing some unusual caves at a cash price of $60 million; they will draw the funds from their stock of gold held in one of their caves. If a new interstate highway is routed near the caves, they estimate earnings will be such that they can sell the property within a year for $140 million. If the highway is not so routed, they would have to sell the land for $5 million on a distress basis. They have estimated that the probability of favorable location of the highway is .4.

a. Assume that it is reasonable to estimate the utility function of the corporation in two parts:

$$U(D) = .9D \quad \text{for } D \le 0$$

$$U(D) = D^2/100 \text{ for } D \ge 0$$

where D is measured in millions of dollars. What is the expected utility of this venture?

b. Refer to part a. What is the EMV of this venture?

c. Refer to part a. What is the CME of this venture for Kahn Cave?

d. The Kahn Vex Corporation holds a majority interest in Kahn Cave Corporation and reviews all their major decisions involving over $10 million. Kahn Vex is noted for its financial conservatism, and their utility function can be estimated in two parts:

$$U(D) = .9D \quad \text{for } D \le 0$$

$$U(D) = 10D \quad \text{for } D \ge 0$$

where D is measured in millions of dollars. What is the expected utility to them of this venture? How might their decision differ from the Kahn Cave decision?

e. The controller of Kahn Cave discovered gross errors in computation. Along with his resignation, he submitted the following revised figures:

Cost of land including fees that were overlooked: $95 million

Resale value of land: $5 million

Sales value of land if project successful, including mineral rights: $215 million

Find the EMV and the expected utilities for both Kahn Cave and Kahn Vex, and tell how the decision is affected.

C.7 Draw your own utility curve for values of money from −$250,000 to $1 million.

C.8 One view is that insurance started because of merchants being concerned over the safety of their large investments in ships at a time when piracy, storms, mutinies, and inadequacies of ship construction and navigation made shipping a highly uncertain business. Draw the utility functions you would expect the following to have:

    a. The shipowner
    b. The insurer

With these in hand, you now can show where the shipowner's loss fails on the insurer's utility function. Do so.

C.9 The Hunyadi family has had medical insurance for 25 years. During that time they have paid over $10,000 in premiums and collected only $3000 in benefits. Why do they continue to pay premiums?

C.10 It has been found that the president of a company is indifferent to an investment giving a certain $50,000 return and another gamble venture which has a 60% chance of a $200,000 return with a 40% chance of a loss of $10,000. The president's utility function is roughly the following:

$	UTILES
−6,000	−10
0	0
30,000	50
120,000	100
180,000	150

A new investment is up for consideration; it involves the possible gain of $90,000 or no gain whatsoever. Unfortunately, the management committee has been unable to agree on a chance of success for this investment. What probability of success would make the president indifferent to the venture of a certain gain of $50,000?

8 Information Systems Analysis

We all live in an uncertain environment and seek knowledge and information to learn more about our world so we can have a better chance to achieve our goals. Managers spend a great deal of their time inquiring about the state and future of their business, the government, and the environment in which they must operate. We spend billions of dollars both in the private and public sectors of our economy with the objective of conducting our business better and supporting decision making. In the past such information was generated manually by clerks, bookkeepers, and accountants. But today the delivery of information comes from many sources, mainly from computers.

The scientific approach to information systems analysis is based on quantitative analysis and the use of models. In this chapter we present the fundamental concepts and models used in information systems analysis.

8.1 INFORMATION ANALYSIS AND DECISION ANALYSIS

Our basic approach is to apply the theory of decision analysis to the problem of acquiring an information system. In Chapter 5 we developed and applied the theory to perfect information; now we extend the theory to imperfect information and more complex situations.

Assume that the manager is offered an information system at a fee or cost of F dollars (Figure 8.1). The venture without the information system (the no-information case) based on *prior probabilities** has an **expected monetary value of $(EMV)_0$**. The venture with the information system, based on *posterior probabilities*, has an **expected monetary value of $(EMV)_1$**. This is a gross EMV because the fee F must be

---

* You need to review the concepts of prior and posterior probabilities in Chapter 2.

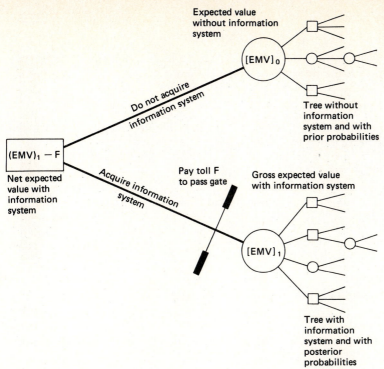

Expected value
without information
system

$[EMV]_0$

Tree without
information
system and with
prior probabilities

$(EMV)_1 - F$

Net expected
value with
information
system

Do not acquire
information system

Acquire information
system

Pay toll F
to pass gate

Gross expected value
with information system

$[EMV]_1$

Tree with
information
system and with
posterior
probabilities

FIGURE 8.1
Decision tree model for the problem of acquiring an information system.

subtracted to get the *net expected monetary value*:

$$(EMV)_1 - F$$

The decision maker will acquire the information system and choose the lower branch of the tree in Figure 8.1 only if the net expected value with the information system is higher than the value without the information system:

$$(EMV)_1 - F > (EMV)_0$$

The difference between the two expected values is the **expected net gain:**

$$ENG = (EMV)_1 - F - (EMV)_0$$

The decision maker should buy the information system if the expected net gain is greater than 0:

$$ENG > 0$$

The **expected value of an information system (EVXI)** can be calculated as the difference between the expected monetary value of the venture (1) with the information system $(EMV)_1$ and (2) without the information system $(EMV)_0$. Thus,

$$EVXI = (EMV)_1 - (EMV)_0$$

and

$$ENG = EVXI - F$$

> If the information system is free,
> $$ENG = EVXI$$

If the information system is perfect, EVXI is called EVPI, the expected value of perfect information.

The Four Phases of Decision Analysis

In Section 5.6, when discussing risk analysis, we stated three levels of sophistication:

1. Deterministic analysis
2. Sensitivity analysis
3. Risk analysis

Now we add a fourth level*:

4. Information analysis

In this chapter we concentrate on this fourth and most sophisticated analysis.

> Information analysis guides the decision maker whether to buy an information system or not.

8.2 EXAMPLES OF INFORMATION ANALYSIS

The Oil Drilling Problem

A wildcatter is a person who drills oil wells in the hope of finding oil. Ms. Carla Castellana of Guadalajara has an option to drill 130 kilometers west of Guadalajara in the village of Ixtlan del Rio. Castellana is uncertain about the geology of the area and tries to determine whether she should drill or not. Her decision problem is described by the decision tree in Figure 8.2.

From past experience on similar sites, she knows the prior probability of whether the site is WET, meaning that there is oil:

$$P[WET] = .25$$

Consequently,

$$P[DRY] = .75$$

---

* This approach is based on the research of Ronald A. Howard. See, for example, "The Foundations of Decision Analysis," *IEEE Transactions on Systems Science and Cybernetics*, Vol. SSC-4, No. 3, Sept. 1968, pp. 1–9.

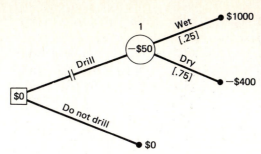

FIGURE 8.2
Decision tree representation of the problem of the wildcatter of Ixtlan when no information is available.

where DRY means there is no oil (see the branches emanating from chance fork 1). Castellana also knows that if the site is WET there is a profit of $1000.* If the site is DRY, there is a $400 loss. By averaging out, at chance fork 1 we get

$$.25 \times \$1000 - .75 \times \$400 = -\$50$$

Therefore Castellana decides not to drill, and the expected value of the venture without information $(EMV)_0$ equals zero.

Perfect Information

It so happens Don Genaro, a clairvoyant, offers his services to Castellana for $320. The clairvoyant can predict with absolute certainty whether the site is WET or DRY. Therefore Castellana drills only if the site is WET, and so the expected monetary value of the venture, with information but before paying the fee (gross EMV), is

$$(EMV)_1 = .25 \times \$1000 + .75 \times \$0 = \$250$$

To get the expected net gain ENG, we must deduct the fee and $(EMV)_0$:

$$ENG = (EMV)_1 - F - (EMV)_0 = \$250 - \$320 - \$0 = -\$70$$

This is a negative value, so Castellana decides not to purchase the perfect information from Don Genaro and not to drill. But now a second clairvoyant, Don Juan, offers perfect information for $200. So the expected net gain is

$$ENG = (EMV)_1 - F - (EMV)_0 = \$250 - \$200 - \$0 = \$50$$

So Castellana decides to purchase the perfect information. If Don Juan says MOJADO,[†] Castellana will drill. If Don Juan says SECO, she will not.

What is the EVPI, *the expected value of perfect information?* We get

$$EVPI = (EMV)_1 - (EMV)_0 = \$250 - \$0 = \$250$$

---

* The $ sign stands for gold pesos now. All numerical values have been altered to protect Ms. Castellana.

† *Mojado* and *seco* are, respectively, wet and dry in Spanish.

We shall make a systematic study of various drilling sites and information systems and summarize the results in Figure 8.3. Line 1 under Ixtlan shows that with no information Castellana will not drill and lines 2 and 3 that she will not purchase perfect information from Don Genaro but will from Don Juan. For the time being, ignore lines 4, 5, and 6 and the Tequila site, which will be discussed later.

Imperfect Information

To be more realistic, consider seismic sounding which provides information on the underlying geological structure of the soil. Note that seismic sounding provides only imperfect information, as the instruments and technique used are not infallible. Consider the seismic sounding firm Imperfecto Inc., which is willing to provide seismic tests to Castellana for $58. Should she purchase this information? To make a decision, Castellana needs information about the reliability of the seismic soundings. Suppose from past records of Imperfecto Inc. she finds that the probability is .8 that a correct prediction will be made if the site is WET. This is a conditional probability meaning that if the site is WET the probability is .8 that the recommendation will be Mojado and .2 that it will be SECO:

$$P[\text{MOJADO} \mid \text{WET}] = .8 \qquad P[\text{SECO} \mid \text{WET}] = .2$$

This is the reliability when the site is WET. Castellana also knows the reliability of the prediction when the site is DRY*:

$$P[\text{MOJADO} \mid \text{DRY}] = .3 \qquad P[\text{SECO} \mid \text{DRY}] = .7$$

To apply decision theory to the problem, a decision tree in the spirit of Figure 8.1 must be constructed.

Assume that Ms. Castellana is trying to decide in January whether she should buy the information (decision fork 1, Figure 8.4). If she does not buy information, she reaches the upper part of the decision tree which is similar to Figure 8.1. If she decides to buy the information, she must pass the gate and pay the fee for the information to reach chance fork 3. Suppose Imperfecto Inc. reports MOJADO by February, and thus Ms. Castellana reaches decision fork 4. She must decide whether or not to drill. If she drills, she reaches chance fork 5, and the site may be WET or DRY.

On the other hand, if Imperfecto reports SECO at chance fork 3, Ms. Castellana finds herself at decision fork 6, and again she may drill (chance fork 7) or not. If she does drill, then chance fork 7 may lead to WET or DRY.

To complete the analysis, we need to assign the payoffs of $1000

---

* Bear in mind: DRY means no oil, SECO means that Imperfecto thinks there is no oil, WET means there is oil, and MOJADO means that Imperfecto thinks there is oil. English words refer to the states of the oil fields and Spanish to the information received about them.

| | F | IXTLAN SITE | | | | TEQUILA SITE | | | |
---	FEE	Buy Info?	Drill?	ENG	EVXI	Buy Info?	Drill?	ENG	EVXI
1. No information	—	—	No	—	—	—	Yes	—	—
2. Sole source Don Genaro	$320	No	No	-$70	$250	No	Yes	-$40	$280
3. Sole source Don Juan	$200	Yes	If MOJADO	$50	$250	Yes	If MOJADO	$80	$280
4. Sole source Imperfecto, Inc.	$58	Yes	If MOJADO	$52	$110	Yes	If MOJADO	$78	$136
5. Sole source Defectuoso, Inc.	$150	No	No	-$40	$110	No	Yes	-$14	$136
6. Either Don Juan or Imperfecto Inc.	—	From Imperfecto for $58	If MOJADO	$52	$110	From Don Juan for $200	If MOJADO	$80	$280

FIGURE 8.3 Results of the analysis of the problem of the wildcatter of Ixtlan. EVXI stands for the expected value of either perfect or imperfect information: ENG = EVXI − F.

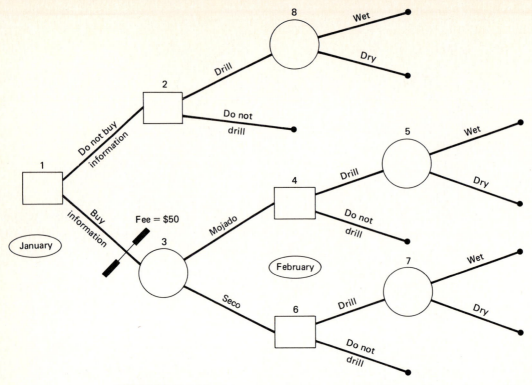

FIGURE 8.4 Decision tree representation on the problem of the wildcatter of Ixtlan when information is obtainable.

and −$400 to the tips of the tree, include the $58 fee for buying information, and determine the probabilities for the branches emanating from the chance forks (Figure 8.5).

Prior and Posterior Probabilities

The prior probabilities of WET and DRY for the branches emanating from chance fork 8 (on the top of figure) are

$$P[\text{WET}] = .25 \qquad P[\text{DRY}] = .75$$

Imperfecto Inc. offers information for $58 with the reliability of

$$P[\text{MOJADO} \mid \text{WET}] = .8 \qquad P[\text{SECO} \mid \text{WET}] = .2$$

$$P[\text{MOJADO} \mid \text{DRY}] = .3 \qquad P[\text{SECO} \mid \text{DRY}] = .7$$

First we calculate the unconditional probabilities:

$$P[\text{MOJADO}] = P[\text{MOJADO} \mid \text{WET}] \times P[\text{WET}] + P[\text{MOJADO} \mid \text{DRY}] \times P[\text{DRY}]$$

$$= .8 \times .25 + .3 \times .75 = .425$$

and

$$P[\text{SECO}] = 1 - P[\text{MOJADO}] = 1 - .425 = .575$$

Then we compute the posterior probabilities from Bayes' theorem:

$$P[A \mid B] = \frac{P[B \mid A] \times P[A]}{P[B]}$$

If A is WET and B is MOJADO, then

$$P[\text{WET} \mid \text{MOJADO}] = \frac{P[\text{MOJADO} \mid \text{WET}] \times P[\text{WET}]}{P[\text{MOJADO}]}$$

$$= \frac{.8 \times .25}{.425} = .4706$$

and

$$P[\text{DRY} \mid \text{MOJADO}] = 1 - .4706 = .5294$$

If A is WET and B is SECO, then

$$P[\text{WET} \mid \text{SECO}] = \frac{P[\text{SECO} \mid \text{WET}] \times P[\text{WET}]}{P[\text{SECO}]} = \frac{.2 \times .25}{.575} = .0870$$

and

$$P[\text{DRY} \mid \text{SECO}] = 1 - .0870 = .9130$$

In Figure 8.6 we redraw the decision tree, mark the probabilities,

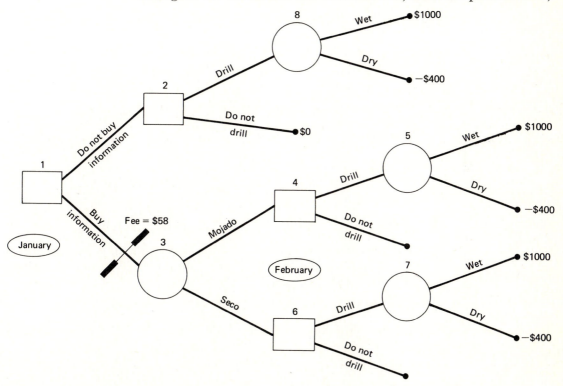

FIGURE 8.5 Probabilities and conditional payoffs for wildcatter's problem of Ixtlan.

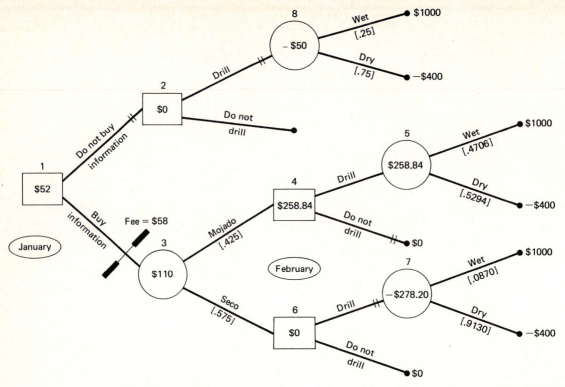

FIGURE 8.6 Extensive analysis of the problem of the wildcatter of Ixtlan.

and apply extensive analysis and backward induction. At chance fork 8, averaging out gives

$$.25 \times \$1000 - .75 \times \$400 = -\$50$$

At decision fork 2, folding back gives $0. At chance fork 5, averaging out gives

$$.4706 \times \$1000 - .5294 \times \$400 = \$258.84$$

At chance fork 7,

$$.0870 \times \$1000 + .9130 \times (-\$400) = -\$278.20$$

We fold back to decision fork 4 and find that *drill* gives $258.84. At decision fork 6, we get $0; it is better not to drill. Now we can average out at chance fork 3 and get

$$(EMV)_1 = .425 \times \$258.84 + .575 \times \$0 = \$110.01$$

Finally, we fold back to decision fork 1 and arrive at the expected net gain of

$$ENG = (EMV)_1 - F - (EMV)_0 = \$110 - \$58 - \$0 = \$52$$

(See line 4, Figure 8.3, Ixtlan site.)

The best strategy is to buy the imperfect information and drill only when Imperfecto Inc. reports MOJADO.

The expected value of the imperfect information is

$$\text{EVXI} = (\text{EMV})_1 - (\text{EMV})_0 = \$110 - \$0 = \$110$$

(See line 4, Figure 8.3, Ixtlan site.)

Analysis by Actual Chronology

The decision trees in Figures 8.4, 8.5 and 8.6 are drawn in **informational chronology**, meaning that the forks appear in the same sequence as the information is received by the decision maker. An alternate approach, using **actual chronology**, is shown in the lower part of Figure 8.7. The site is either WET or DRY, and the information in each case is either MOJADO or SECO.

The upper part of Figure 8.7 shows a corresponding thought

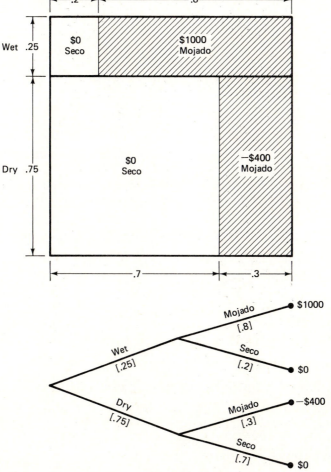

FIGURE 8.7
Thought experiment and probability tree in actual chronology for the problem of the wildcatter of Ixtlan.

experiment. You are blindfolded and throw a dart. The area above the heavy line, representing WET, has an area of .25 and the one below, DRY, an area of .75. When you throw a dart blindfolded (and hit the board), the probability of the dart landing in the WET area is .25 and correspondingly in the DRY area is .75.

But you have a Spanish-speaking assistant with poor vision, who is not quite reliable. He observes where the dart lands and whispers his observation in your ear for a fee of $58. If the dart lands on WET, he whispers with a probability of .8 MOJADO and with a probability of .2 SECO. On the other hand, if the dart lands in the DRY area, he whispers with a probability of .7 SECO and with a probability of .3 MOJADO.

This thought experiment corresponds precisely to the problem of Castellana when she purchases imperfect information from Imperfecto Inc. So now we repeat the computation of the expected net gain if she buys the imperfect information.

Castellana will bet only if the dart lands in the shaded areas marked MOJADO in Figure 8.7. If the dart lands in the upper part, her expected gain is

$$.25 \times .2 \times 0 + .25 \times .8 \times \$1000 = \$200$$

and if in the lower part,

$$.75 \times .7 \times 0 - .75 \times .3 \times \$400 = -\$90$$

Thus, the gross EMV is

$$(EMV)_1 = \$200 - \$90 = \$110$$

which agrees, of course, with our previous calculation using informational chronology.

In what follows we shall always use the technique of actual chronology to simplify the calculations in our examples. However, exercises will also be provided for informational chronology, because in practice both approaches are used.

The Value of Imperfect Information

Suppose Imperfecto Inc. goes bankrupt before performing the seismic sounding and Defectuoso Inc. offers precisely the same service for a fee of $150. Should Castellana buy the information from Defectuoso?

We still have

$$(EMV)_1 = \$110$$

But now the fee is $150, and

$$ENG = (EMV)_1 - F - (EMV)_0 = \$110 - \$150 - \$0 = -\$40$$

So the decision is not to buy the information (line 5, Figure 8.3, Ixtlan site). You will recall that the decision was not to drill without information (line 1, Figure 8.3, Ixtlan site), and so the decision for not drilling is not changed by the offer of Defectuoso Inc.

Suppose that Castellana has a choice to buy perfect information for $200 from Don Juan or imperfect information from Imperfecto Inc. for $58. Which is better? Observe in Figure 8.3, Ixtlan site, that the ENG for Don Juan is $50 but for Imperfecto is $52. Thus, the imperfect information is a better buy than the perfect information (line 6, Figure 8.3, Ixtlan site).

> Buy imperfect information if the price is right.

8.3 THE WILDCATTER OF TEQUILA

While Ms. Castellana is driving back from Ixtlan to Guadalajara, she stops halfway in Tequila and purchases an option to drill for oil. It is her judgment that this is a better site because the probability of the site being WET is .3:

$$P[\text{WET}] = .3 \qquad P[\text{DRY}] = .7$$

The gain is still $1000 if the site is WET, and the loss is $400 if it is DRY. To analyze the problem, we use the approach of actual chronology. Figure 8.8 shows the thought experiment and the probability tree. The expected monetary value is

$$(\text{EMV})_0 = .3 \times \$1000 - .7 \times \$400 = \$300 - \$280 = \$20$$

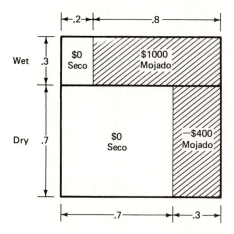

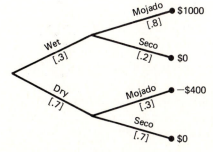

FIGURE 8.8
Thought experiment and probability tree representation of the problem of the wildcatter from Tequila.

Thus Castellana decides to drill (line 1, Figure 8.3, Tequila site).

Now Don Genaro offers perfect information for $320. This gives Ms. Castellana a gross EMV of

$$(EMV)_1 = .7 \times \$0 + .3 \times \$1000 = \$300$$

The EVPI, the expected value of perfect information, is

$$EVPI = (EMV)_1 - (EMV)_0 = \$300 - \$20 = \$280$$

The expected net gain is

$$ENG = (EMV)_1 - F - (EMV)_0 = EVPI - F = \$280 - \$320 = -\$40$$

The decision is not to buy the perfect information but to proceed to drill (line 2, Figure 8.3, Tequila site).

Don Juan still offers perfect information for $200. Now the expected net gain is

$$ENG = EVPI - F = \$280 - \$200 = \$80$$

So Castellana decides to purchase perfect information from Don Juan and drill if MOJADO is indicated (line 3, Figure 8.3, Tequila site).

Defectuoso Inc. still offers imperfect information for $150. The realiability of the service is the same whether they drill in Tequila or Ixtlan, and so

$$P[MOJADO \mid WET] = .8 \qquad P[SECO \mid WET] = .2$$

$$P[MOJADO \mid DRY] = .3 \qquad P[SECO \mid DRY] = .7$$

The gross EMV is

$$(EMV)_1 = .3 \times .2 \times \$0 + .3 \times .8 \times \$1000 - .7 \times .7 \times \$0 - .7 \times .3 \times \$400$$

$$= \$0 + \$240 - \$0 - \$84 = \$156$$

The expected value of imperfect information is

$$EVXI = (EMV)_1 - (EMV)_0 = \$156 - \$20 = \$136$$

The expected net gain is

$$ENG = EVXI - F = \$136 - \$150 = -\$14$$

So Castellana does not buy the imperfect information and proceeds to drill (line 5, Figure 8.3, Tequila site).

But now Imperfecto Inc. is back in the act and offers the same service for $58. Now

$$ENG = EVXI - F = \$136 - \$58 = \$78$$

Thus the decision is to buy the imperfect information from Imperfecto and to drill only if Imperfecto indicates MOJADO (line 4, Figure 8.3, Tequila site).

Note that the value of imperfect information for the Ixtlan site is $110 and for the Tequila site, $136. The same service, the same reliability, has a different value depending on the site.

The value of information cannot be determined without considering the use of information.

Suppose that Castellana has a choice between the perfect information of Don Juan and the imperfect information of Imperfecto Inc. Which one should she buy? The expected net gains on the Tequila site are shown in Figure 8.3. The ENG when buying perfect information from Don Juan is $80 and when buying imperfect information from Imperfecto Inc. is only $78. Thus it is better to buy the perfect information from Don Juan. Compare this with the Ixtlan site. There Don Juan brings only $50, and Imperfecto Inc. brings $52. So in Ixtlan it is better to buy imperfect information from Imperfecto and in Tequila perfect information from Don Juan.

When Is Perfect Information Better?

Consider the Tequila site, where the expected net gain with perfect information is

$$\$300 - F_P$$

where F_P is the cost of perfect information. With imperfect information the expected net gain is

$$\$156 - F_I$$

where F_I is the cost of imperfect information. The perfect information is better if

$$\$300 - F_P > \$156 - F_I$$

which leads to

$$F_I > F_P - \$144$$

We must also have

$$F_P < \$280$$

$$F_I < \$136$$

because otherwise the ENG becomes negative. In Figure 8.9 we show a

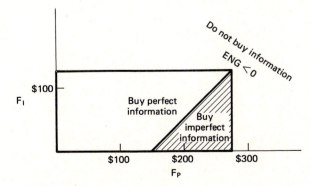

FIGURE 8.9
The choice between perfect or imperfect information depends on the price of the information.

graphical representation of our results. Take any value of the fees charged for information, and find the corresponding point on the chart. If the point is outside the quadrangle, do not buy information, and if it is in the shaded area, the imperfect information is better; otherwise, the perfect information is better.

The Site in El Dorado*

There is the possibility that the well will be a GUSHER, that is, there will be a great deal of oil. The judgmental or prior probabilities are

$$P[\text{GUSHER}] = .1$$

$$P[\text{WET}] = .2$$

$$P[\text{DRY}] = .7$$

The gain is $2000 if GUSHER and $1000 if WET, and the loss is $400 if the site is DRY. Should the owner drill? The expected monetary value is

$$(\text{EMV})_0 = .1 \times \$2000 + .2 \times \$1000 - .7 \times \$400 = \$120$$

The owner should drill. If the owner can get perfect information at no cost, the EMV is

$$(\text{EMV})_1 = .1 \times \$2000 + .2 \times \$1000 - .7 \times \$0 = \$400$$

The expected value of perfect information is

$$\text{EVPI} = (\text{EMV})_1 - (\text{EMV})_0 = \$400 - \$120 = \$280$$

which is the ceiling the owner should be willing to pay to a clairvoyant for perfect information.

Suppose imperfect information can be obtained for $118. The information received now can take three forms: SECO, MOJADO, or CHORROS.† The reliability of the imperfect information is shown in Figure 8.10 by the conditional probabilities. For example, if the site is WET, the conditional probability is .3 that the information will be SECO:

$$P[\text{SECO} \mid \text{WET}] = .3$$

---

* May be omitted without loss of continuity.
† *Chorros* means soaking in Spanish.

	SECO	MOJADO	CHORROS
Gusher	.1	.05	.85
Wet	.3	.25	.45
Dry	.7	.25	.05

FIGURE 8.10 The reliability of information is defined by the conditional probabilities.

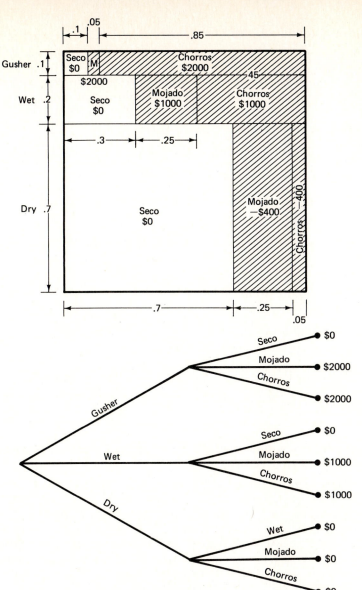

FIGURE 8.11
Thought experiment and probability tree representation of drilling
problem of the wildcatter in
Ixtlan.

The thought experiment and the corresponding probability tree are shown in Figure 8.11. Suppose the information is purchased and the decision rule is to drill when the information is MOJADO or CHOR-ROS. The gross expected monetary value is

$$(EMV)_1 = .1 \times .1 \times \$0 + .1 \times .05 \times \$2000 + .1 \times .85 \times \$2000$$

$$+ .2 \times .3 \times \$0 + .2 \times .25 \times \$1000 + .2 \times .45 \times \$1000$$

$$- .7 \times .7 \times \$0 - .7 \times .25 \times \$400 - .7 \times .05 \times \$400$$

$$= \$236$$

and the expected net gain after the fee is paid is

$$ENG = (EMV)_1 - F - (EMV)_0 = \$236 - \$118 - \$120 = -\$2$$

So you may be tempted to conclude that there is no point in purchasing the information system. Note that there is an alternate decision rule: Drill only if the information is CHORROS. With this decision rule, the gross expected monetary value is

$$(EMV)_1 = .1 \times .85 \times \$2000 + .2 \times .45 \times \$1000 - .7 \times .05 \times \$400 = \$246$$

and the expected net gain

$$ENG = (EMV)_1 - F - (EMV)_0 = \$246 - \$118 - \$120 = \$8$$

which is a positive ENG. Thus the decision is to purchase the imperfect information and to drill only if the result of the seismic test is CHOR-ROS. Bear the following in mind:

> Unless appropriate action is taken, the information may not be worth buying.

What is the expected value of the imperfect information system?

$$EVXI = (EMV)_1 - (EMV)_0 = \$246 - \$120 = \$126$$

This value holds under the assumption tht the best action is taken.

8.4 INFORMATION ANALYSIS AND DECISION MAKING: A DIALOG

Q. *Can you explain in nontechnical terms how information impacts on the state of mind of people?*

A. A story will clarify the issue.

Gambling in Las Vegas

Suppose you are in Las Vegas and consider placing a single bet on black at the roulette table. To simplify matters, ignore the 0, and assume that there are 18 black and 18 red pockets. What is the probability that the ball will stop on black?

One-half.

You are taking here the point of view of the frequency approach. But suppose that while you are watching the game, red comes up 5 times in sequence. Would you still think that the probability of black is one-half?

I certainly would. Half of the pockets are black and half red, so the probability is one-half.

Suppose red comes up 10, 20, or 50 times in sequence?

I would believe that the manager had rigged the roulette wheel.

So now you realize that your initial assessment of the probability

being one-half was a prior probability, a state of your mind, corresponding to your faith in the honesty of the manager?

Yes, I see that the subjective and frequency approaches are combined here. Can you tell me a more practical application?

Suppose that you are still in Las Vegas and want to make money by playing blackjack. The cards are on the table face down in a precise sequence. The players pick cards from this deck. There is nothing uncertain about the cards in the deck except that you are unaware of the sequence. The uncertainty is in *your mind* and not in the actual deck of cards. If you were a clairvoyant, you could read the cards, and the uncertainty in your mind would be dispelled. But you are not a clairvoyant and must be satisfied with imperfect information. The approach to winning in the long run is this. You keep a mental record of the cards dealt. For example, assume that all four aces have been dealt. You know there are no more aces in the deck and so have imperfect information about the deck. You know that the next card will not be an ace. You examine your mental record, and on the basis of decision analysis determine what action should be taken. The croupier of the casino does not keep records or use decision analysis, and so a sophisticated player has a slight advantage over the casino. This advantage may be enough so that in the long run a player has a good chance to win. This approach has been used with great success by real-life gamblers.

Q. *Why do you say that reliability is measured by conditional probabilities?*

A. A second anecdote will clarify the issue.

Murder or Suicide

One morning, upon rising and going to the bathroom, the Countess finds the Count dead in the bathtub. She suspects that the Count was unhappy and so thinks it might possibly be a suicide. But as she does not like the butler, she thinks that maybe he might have killed the Count. She does not want a scandal and so calls Sherlock Holmes to investigate the case.

Mr. Holmes arrives with Dr. Watson, and they conclude that either the Count (1) committed suicide or (2) was murdered by the butler. Also the following facts are established: (1) The Count died Saturday night, (2) he was found stabbed to death, (3) he was found in the tub, (4) he was naked, (5) he had exactly two knife wounds, (6) he was left-handed, and (7) the wound was on the left side.

Dr. Watson reasons as follows: (1) The probability that someone is murdered on a Saturday night is .1; (2) the probability that a murderer would use a knife is .1; (3) the probability that a murder is committed in a tub is .05; (4) the probability that a person found in a tub naked is .9; (5) the probability that a murderer uses exactly two stabs is .1; (6) the probability that the murdered person is left-handed is .05; (7) the probability that the wound on a murdered body is on the left side is .5. Thus the probability of murder is

$$.1 \times .1 \times .05 \times .9 \times .1 \times .5 \times .5 = .00001125$$

Dr. Watson concludes that the probability of suicide is .99998875.

However, Sherlock Holmes reasons in an entirely different manner. He says that according to his experience no one has ever committed suicide with two stabs of a knife. So this leads to the suspicion of murder. Furthermore, in his experience he has never found a left-handed man committing suicide with a knife and leaving a wound on the left side. So this again leads to the suspicion of murder. So Mr. Holmes concludes that the Count was murdered by the butler.

Note that Dr. Watson fell into the trap of working with the probabilities of what murderers do. This has no relevance to the situation where certain facts are uncovered and what happened must be derived in the light of the information provided by the facts. Specifically, the probabilities of murder and of suicide must be compared as conditioned by the information received.

Returning to our text, you will recall that Ms. Castellana was not concerned with the probability of Defectuoso Inc. finding oil. She wanted the reliability, that is, the conditional probabilities, of Defectuoso reporting MOJADO or SECO when the site is WET or DRY.

Reliability as a conditional probability is a measure of performance of Imperfecto Inc. and is independent of the geological situation at Ixtlan or Tequila.

Q. *Suppose Imperfecto Inc. charges only $50 if there is no oil but $100 if there is oil. Should they buy the information?*

A. You need to make a decision analysis. In Figure 8.5 you should delete the gate and adjust the payoffs. Let's leave this as an exercise.

Q. *How often is information analysis used?*

A. Information analysis forms the theoretical foundation of the modern approach to accounting, statistical sampling, forecasting, etc. There have also been significant advances in economic theory when the traditional assumption that information could be obtained free was abandoned.

Q. *How does information analysis fit into decision analysis?*

A. Information analysis is an essential phase of decision analysis. In the first phase of decision analysis the situation is assessed in terms of available information. However, it must also be determined whether it is worthwhile to search for more information. If so, the information must be obtained and the decision analysis repeated using the new information. Thus decision and information analysis are inseparable.

Q. *What are the advantages of information analysis?*

A. You must recognize that billions of dollars are being spent on getting information, and managers often do not get full benefit from the information obtained. Information analysis already has and will more frequently provide support to managers so they can (1) dispense with costly information which provides no benefit, (2) use the information with which they are provided to better advantage, and (3) obtain further information which increases the effectiveness of the decision-making process.

8.5 APPLICATION TO MARKET RESEARCH

The Uneeda Corporation is considering marketing a product. If sales are high, the profit will be $4 million, but if low, there will be a loss of $2,600,000. Should the corporation proceed to market the product?

Management believes that the probability of high sales is .4 and of low sales .6:

$$P[\text{HIGH}] = .4 \qquad P[\text{LOW}] = .6$$

To resolve the issue whether to market the product or not, it is proposed that a market research study be conducted. Without going into detail, we simply report that the reliability of the prediction of the market research can be stated in probabilistic terms, that is, in the language of the Mexican wildcatter:

$$P[\text{ALTO} \mid \text{HIGH}] = .8 \qquad P[\text{BAJO} \mid \text{HIGH}] = .2$$

$$P[\text{ALTO} \mid \text{LOW}] = .3 \qquad P[\text{BAJO} \mid \text{LOW}] = .7$$

The method of solution presents no difficulties and is left as an exercise. (The decision is as follows: Market if ALTO, and do not market if BAJO.)

8.6 ACCOUNTING APPLICATIONS

In Section 5.2, we discussed an auditing problem where various audits with different reliabilities were available. Considering auditing as an information system and using decision analysis, we can make a more comprehensive analysis of the situation, including the possibility of imperfect audits.

Consider the Dependable Corporation which may have a variance in the corporate accounts. If there is a variance and it is left uncorrected, a loss of $30,000 will result to the corporation. Should an audit be performed?

The management of the corporation believes that the prior probability of having a variance is 2/3, that is,

$$P[\text{VARIANCE}] = \tfrac{2}{3} \qquad P[\text{NOVARIANCE}] = \tfrac{1}{3}$$

An initial audit of the accounts can be obtained for $4000. If the accounts of the firm are rejected, the auditor will make a further investigation at a fee of $6000, which will guarantee finding and fixing the variance. The reliability of the initial audit is given by the conditional probabilities

$$P[\text{ACCEPT} \mid \text{VARIANCE}] = \tfrac{2}{5} \qquad P[\text{REJECT} \mid \text{VARIANCE}] = \tfrac{3}{5}$$

$$P[\text{ACCEPT} \mid \text{NOVARIANCE}] = \tfrac{3}{4} \qquad P[\text{REJECT} \mid \text{NOVARIANCE}] = \tfrac{1}{4}$$

To solve the problem, we develop the loss table in Figure 8.12. First assume that there is a variance. If (1) the auditor is retained but the accounts are accepted, the loss is $4000 + $30,000 = $34,000; if (2) the auditor is retained but the accounts are rejected, the loss is $4000 + $6000 = $10,000; if (3) the auditor is not retained, the loss is $30,000.

Assume that there is no variance. If (4) the auditor accepts the accounts, there is a loss of $4,000; if (5) the accounts are rejected, there is a loss of $4000 + $6000 = $10,000; if (6) the auditor is not retained the loss is $0.

The decision tree corresponding to the auditing problem is shown in Figure 8.13. Using averaging out, at fork 3 we get the expected loss of

$$\tfrac{1}{4} \times \$10,000 + \tfrac{3}{4} \times \$4000 = \$2500 + \$3000 = \$5500$$

and at fork 4,

$$\tfrac{3}{5} \times \$10,000 + \tfrac{2}{5} \times \$34,000 = \$6000 + \$13,600 = \$19,600$$

At fork 2 we get the expected loss when the auditor is retained:

$$\tfrac{1}{3} \times \$5500 + \tfrac{2}{3} \times \$19,600 = \$14,900$$

If the auditor is not retained, at fork 5 we get the expected loss of

$$\tfrac{2}{3} \times \$30,000 = \$20,000$$

Thus, Dependable Corporation is better off retaining the auditor and better off by $20,000 − $14,900 = $5100. This is the expected value of the audit.

		ACTS	
		Retain Auditor	Do Not Retain Auditor
OUTCOMES	There is a variance	(1) Account is accepted: $4000 + $30,000 = $34,000 (2) Account is rejected: $4000 + $6000 = $10,000	(3) $30,000
	There is no variance	(4) Account is accepted: $4000 (5) Account is rejected: $4000 + $6000 = $10,000	(6) $0

FIGURE 8.12 Loss table for the auditor's problem.

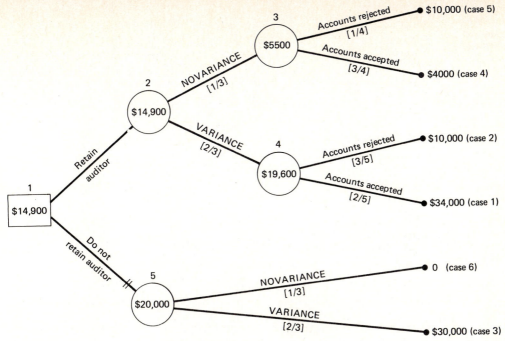

FIGURE 8.13 The decision tree for the auditor's problem. Values at the tips are from Figure 8.12.

8.7 IMPACT OF PERSONAL PREFERENCES

We have stressed already that whether or not to purchase information depends on the use of the information. Now we show how personal preferences influence this purchase decision.

Consider Don Quixote, an adventurous person, who likes danger and is a **risk seeker**. Figure 8.14 shows his utility function. The formula to convert P, pesos, into utiles U is

$$U(P) = 100 \times \left(\frac{P + \$1000}{\$2000} \right)^3$$

How would Don Quixote react to drilling in Ixtlan?

The probability is .25 of gaining $1000 and .75 of losing $400. We must convert pesos to utiles to get the expected utiles:

$$U(\$1000) = 100 \times \left(\frac{\$1000 + \$1000}{\$2000} \right)^3 = 100 \text{ utiles}$$

$$U(-\$400) = 100 \times \left(\frac{-\$400 + \$1000}{\$2000} \right)^3 = 2.7 \text{ utiles}$$

Thus the expected utiles for the venture are

$$.25U(\$1000) + .75U(-\$400) = .25 \times 100 + .75 \times 2.7 = 27.025 \text{ utiles}$$

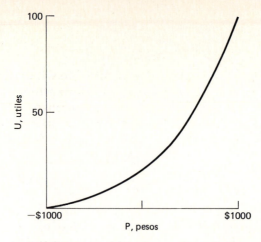

FIGURE 8.14 Utility function of Don Quixote, a risk seeker:

$$U(P) = 100 \times \left(\frac{P + \$1000}{\$2000}\right)^3$$

If Don Quixote does not drill, he gets $0, and the utiles are

$$U(\$0) = 100 \times \left(\frac{\$0 + \$1000}{\$2000}\right)^3 = 12.5 \text{ utiles}$$

which is less than the 27.025 utiles. *Don Quixote will drill.* Compare this with Ms. Castellana, a **risk avoider**, who decided not to drill. Don Quixote, being a risk seeker, prefers to take the risk of drilling to doing nothing.

Now consider whether Don Quixote should purchase perfect information from Don Juan for $200. He pays the $200, and if Don Juan says MOJADO, he drills and gets $1000. This occurs with a probability of .25, and the corresponding utiles are

$$.25U(\$1000 - \$200) = .25U(\$800)$$

If SECO, he does not drill but still pays the $200, so the corresponding utiles are

$$.75U(\$0 - \$200) = .75U(-\$200)$$

Thus the expected utiles with perfect information for $200 are

$$.25U(\$800) + .75U(-\$200)$$

But

$$U(\$800) = 100\left(\frac{\$800 + \$1000}{\$2000}\right)^3 = 72.9 \text{ utiles}$$

and

$$U(-\$200) = 100\left(\frac{-\$200 + \$1000}{\$2000}\right)^3 = 6.4 \text{ utiles}$$

and so the expected utiles are only

$$.25U(\$800) + .75U(-\$200) = .25 \times 72.9 + .75 \times 6.4 = 23.025 \text{ utiles}$$

which is less than the 27.025 utiles obtainable without information. *Don Quixote will not purchase the perfect information for $200.* Compare this with Ms. Castellana, who decided to purchase the perfect information for $200. Don Quixote prefers the risk of drilling to the certainty of paying the fee of $200.

Whether to purchase information or not depends on personal preferences.

Note that our method of information analysis can incorporate personal preferences by the simple artifice of converting monetary values to utiles. We stress, however, that the fee to be paid must be incorporated in the gains and losses and cannot be deducted after the analysis is made, as suggested in Figure 8.1. The *net* monetary values must be listed in the diagram of the dart board thought experiment. When working with decision trees, the net values must be listed at the tips of the tree.

8.8 DECISION ANALYSIS AT GULF OIL CHEMICALS: A SUCCESSFUL APPLICATION

On March 9, 1977 Mr. William C. Roher, President, Gulf Oil Chemicals Company, reported to the Commercial Development Association in New York on how the decision was made to build a new refinery for Gulf Oil Chemicals.*

Five years earlier the management of Gulf Oil Chemicals was of the opinion that a new olefin cracker plant of a certain size should be built at a certain location using a certain type of feedstock.† However, there were hundreds of millions of dollars involved, and management was searching for a more reliable method of making the decision. So Gulf Oil Chemicals undertook a decision analysis in collaboration with SRI International. According to the SRI International approach, the study was carried out in three phases: deterministic phase, probabilistic phase, and informational phase.

Deterministic Phase

First a deterministic computer-based model (like the model for La Brea Oil Company discussed in Section 1.6) was developed. The inputs to the computer included such factors as feedstock cost, product yields by the

---

* Adapted from a report of the SRI (Stanford Research Institute) International, Menlo Park, Calif., dated May 25, 1978.

† *Olefin* is an unsaturated open-chain hydrocarbon containing at least one double bond. To *crack* means to break up a chemical compound into simpler compounds by means of heat. *Feedstock* is raw material supplied to a machine or processing plant such as an olefin cracker plant.

processing plant, selling prices, plant operating cost, volume of products sold, and so on'. Initially the output of the computer was a deterministic forecast of revenues, investments, costs, and profits.

Sensitivity Phase

After the deterministic model was built and tested, a sensitivity analysis was made to determine which of the inputs were *crucial* from the viewpoint of uncertainty, that is, which of the inputs would seriously influence the future of Gulf Oil Chemicals. It was found, for example, that the forecast of price greatly influences profits and is therefore a crucial variable.

Probabilistic Phase

After the crucial variables of uncertainty were identified, it became necessary to assess the probabiity distribution for these random variables. Various experts were questioned, including Mr. Roher himself. Probability distributions for these input variables were assessed by Mr. Roher, other executives, and experts. Then the probability distributions were compared, and a consensus for each probability distribution was reached.

By using these input probability distributions, the probability distribution for the outputs were computed by risk analysis as discussed in Section 5.6.

Informational Phase

Examining the output probability distributions leads to the question of what additional information should be collected to improve the decision. To put the decision of searching for more information on a quantitative basis, the expected value of perfect information was determined by the techniques discussed in Section 5.3.

Recognizing that perfect information is impractical to obtain, the expected value of a more accurate, still imperfect engineering estimate was calculated. The calculation convinced management that it is indeed worthwhile to get a more accurate engineering estimate of the plant investment. A similar procedure was followed for other crucial variables, and it was decided which of these variables should be estimated with more accuracy.

When the better estimates for these variables were obtained, the output probability distributions were recomputed and the final results obtained. The consequence was that Gulf Oil Chemicals executives changed their minds in three ways. It was decided to

1. Build a larger plant
2. Choose a different plant site
3. Build a plant based on different feedstock

In addition, Mr. Roher stated that decision analysis made important contributions to Gulf Oil Chemicals in at least four ways:

1. It forced the management to reexamine the data carefully.
2. Management became explicit about uncertainties.
3. Managers were enabled to communicate effectively about profits in terms of risks and opportunities.
4. Executives had more confidence that a good decision was made.

Mr. Roher finished his presentation by stating that at the beginning executives had doubts but that with the help of decision analysis they ended with certainty—the certainty of having made a good decision. He concluded by stating that "Thus, if you feel as I do that the good decisions are more often than not followed by good outcomes, you should not hesitate to use decision analysis where the outcome is important."

SUMMARY

1. Managers are faced with two types of decision: (a) what information to obtain and (2) what action to take.
2. Decision analysis has four phases: (a) deterministic, (b) sensitivity, (c) probabilistic, and (d) informational.
3. The cost of information must be balanced against expected benefits before the decision to acquire the information system is made.
4. The decision maker should buy the information system if the expected net gain

$$ENG = (EMV)_1 - F - (EMV)_0 > 0$$

where (1) $(EMV)_0$ is the expected value of the venture without the information system using prior probabilities, (2) $(EMV)_1$ is the expected value of the venture with the information system using the posterior probabilities, and (3) F is the fee to be paid for the information system.

5. Information enters the theory by enabling the decision maker to update prior probabilities to posterior probabilities by the use of Bayes' theorem.
6. The expected value of an information system is

$$EVXI = (EMV)_1 - (EMV)_0$$

and so the expected net gain is

$$ENG = EVXI - F$$

When the information system is perfect, EVXI is to be replaced by EVPI, the expected value of perfect information.

7. The expected value of information can be determined by drawing the decision tree either in informational chronology or actual chronology.

8. Imperfect information may be better than perfect information if the price is right.

9. The reliability of an information system is expressed by conditional probabilities.

10. The assessment accuracy of probabilities should be tailored to the decision to be made.

11. Information can be wasted by not making proper or optimum decisions utilizing the information.

12. The expected value of perfect information EVPI is the upper bound to the value of imperfect information systems.

13. When making a decision, two judgmental factors must be considered: (1) the prior probabilities and (2) personal preferences or utilities. Both may vary from individual to individual.

SECTION EXERCISES

1. **Information Analysis and Decision Analysis**

1.1 Give examples from your own experience or knowledge for each of the following types of analysis. State the nature of the problem, the decision to be made, the decision variables, and why this problem fits this type of analysis. It is not necessary for you to formulate the problem for solution; merely define the problem itself.
   a. Deterministic analysis
   b. Sensitivity analysis
   c. Risk analysis
   d. Information analysis

1.2 Why do you think information analysis is regarded as the "most sophisticated analysis" of the four?

2. **Examples of Information Analysis**

2.1 Refer to the oil drilling problem discussed in Section 8.2. In drilling in a new region, the prior probability of oil is $P[\text{WET}] = .1$. Because of the regional situation, the profit if the site is WET is $8000, but if the site is DRY, there is a $1000 loss.
   a. Draw a decision tree representation of this situation in the absence of information similar to Figure 8.2.
   b. Calculate the expected value of the venture without information $(\text{EMV})_0$.
   c. What should Ms. Castellana decide?

2.2 Refer to the oil drilling problem discussed in Section 8.2 and Exercise 2.1. Don Genaro, the ubiquitous clairvoyant, offers his services to Ms. Castellana for $1000; he can predict with absolute certainty whether or not the site is WET.
   a. What is the expected monetary value of the venture with perfect information but before paying the fee $(\text{EMV})_1$?

b. What is the expected net gain ENG?

c. What should Ms. Castellana decide?

Don Juan now appears and offers perfect information for $500.

d. What is the expected net gain ENG?

e. What should Ms. Castellana decide?

f. What is the expected value of perfect information EVPI?

2.3 Refer to the oil drilling problem discussed in Section 8.2 and Exercises 2.1 and 2.2. The seismic sounding firm of Imperfecto Inc. is willing to provide seismic tests for $100. From the past records of Imperfecto, they show a conditional probability of .7 that a correct prediction will be made if the site is WET, $P[\text{MOJADO} \mid \text{WET}] = .7$, and when the site is dry, the relevant probability is $P[\text{MOJADO} \mid \text{DRY}] = .4$.

a. To help decide whether or not to buy the information, make a decision tree for this case similar to Figure 8.4.

b. Assign payoffs and determine probabilities for branches for this tree to produce a decision tree for this case which is ready for analysis, similar to Figure 8.5. Note that this will require you to calculate all the posterior probabilities as was done in Section 8.2.

c. Using your response to Exercise 2.2b as your guide, redraw the decision tree, and apply extensive analysis and backward induction, your result being a tree similar to Figure 8.6, with all values indicated.

d. What is the best strategy?

e. What is the expected value of imperfect information EVXI?

f. Prepare a thought experiment and probability tree in actual chronology following Figure 8.7. Define your thought experiment by making a dart board as in Figure 8.7.

g. Use your model for actual chronology of part f to show that the gross EMV, $(\text{EMV})_1$, is in agreement with the result you found in this exercise using informational chronology.

h. Defectuoso offers imperfect information for a fee of $300. Should Castellana buy the information? Support your response with the computation of ENG.

i. Suppose that Castellana has the choice of perfect information for $500 from Don Juan or imperfect information from Imperfecto Inc. for $100. What should she do?

2.4 Refer to the oil drilling problem discussed in Section 8.2. In drilling in a new region, the prior probability of oil is $P[\text{WET}] = .1$. Because of the regional situation, the profit if the site is WET is $5000, but if the site is DRY, there is a $500 loss.

a. Draw a decision tree representation of this situation in the absence of information similar to Figure 8.2.

b. Calculate the expected value of the venture without information $(\text{EMV})_0$.

c. What should Ms. Castellana decide?

2.5 Refer to the oil drilling problem discussed in Section 8.2 and Exercise 2.4. Don Genaro, the ubiquitous clairvoyant, offers his services to Ms. Castellana for $600; he can predict with absolute certainty whether or not the site is WET.

a. What is the expected monetary value of the venture with perfect information but before paying the fee $(\text{EMV})_1$?

b. What is the expected net gain ENG?

c. What should Ms. Castellana decide?

Don Juan now appears and offers perfect information for $300.

d. What is the expected net gain ENG?

e. What should Ms. Castellana decide?

f. What is the expected value of perfect information EVPI?

2.6 Refer to the oil drilling problem discussed in Section 8.2 and Exercises 2.4 and 2.5. The seismic sounding firm of Imperfecto Inc. is willing to provide seismic tests for $200. From the past records of Imperfecto, they show a conditional probability of .9 that a correct prediction will be made if the site is WET, $P[\text{MOJADO} \mid \text{WET}] = .9$, and when the site is dry, the relevant probability is $P[\text{MOJADO} \mid \text{DRY}] = .5$.

    a. To help decide whether or not to buy the information, make a decision tree for this case similar to Figure 8.4.

    b. Assign payoffs and determine probabilities for branches for this tree to produce a decision tree for this case which is ready for analysis similar to Figure 8.5. Note that this will require you to compute all the prior and posterior probabilities as was done in Section 8.2.

    c. Using your response to part b as your guide, redraw the decision tree and apply extensive analysis and backward induction, your result being a tree similar to Figure 8.6, with all values indicated.

    d. What is the best strategy?

    e. What is the expected value of imperfect information EVXI?

    f. Prepare a thought experiment and probability tree in actual chronology following Figure 8.7. Define your thought experiment by making a dart board as in Figure 8.7.

    g. Use your model for actual chronology of Exercise 2.2f to show that the gross EMV, $(\text{EMV})_1$, is in agreement with the result you found in this exercise using informational chronology.

    h. Defectuoso offers imperfect information for a fee of $500. Should Castellana buy the information? Support your response with the computation of ENG.

    i. Suppose that Castellana has the choice of perfect information for $400 from Don Juan or imperfect information from Imperfecto Inc. for $125. What should she do?

3. *The Wildcatter of Tequila*

3.1 In Section 8.3, a decision concerning the Tequila site is made to buy the imperfect information from Imperfecto and to drill only if Imperfecto predicts MOJADO (line 4, Figure 8.3, Tequila site) using actual chronology. Carry out the analysis using informational chronology, and show that the result is the same.

3.2 Refer to the Tequila site drilling example discussed in Section 8.3. In drilling here in the following year, the prior probability of oil is determined to be $P[\text{WET}] = .4$. The profit if the site is WET is $2000, but if the site is DRY, there is a $1000 loss.

    a. Draw a decision tree representation of this situation in the absence of information similar to Figure 8.2.

    b. Calculate the expected value of the venture without information $(\text{EMV})_0$.

    c. What should Ms. Castellana decide?

3.3 Refer to the Tequila site drilling example discussed in Section 8.3 and Exercise 3.2. Don Genaro, the ubiquitous clairvoyant, offers his services to Ms. Castellana for $1000; he can predict with absolute certainty whether or not the site is WET.

    a. What is the expected monetary value of the venture with perfect information but before paying the fee $(\text{EMV})_1$?

    b. What is the expected net gain ENG?

    c. What should Ms. Castellana decide?

Don Juan now appears and offers perfect information for $500.

    d. What is the expected net gain ENG?

    e. What should Ms. Castellana decide?

    f. What is the expected value of perfect information EVPI?

3.4 Refer to the Tequila site drilling example discussed in Section 8.3 and Exercises 3.2 and 3.3. Defectuoso appears on the scene and offers imperfect information for $300. The reliability of their service is as stated in Section 8.3.

    a. What is the gross EMV?

    b. What is the expected value of imperfect information EVXI?

    c. What is the expected net gain ENG?

    d. What decision should Ms. Castellana make?

3.5 Refer to the Tequila site drilling example discussed in Section 8.3 and Exercises 3.2, 3.3, and 3.4. The seismic sounding firm of Imperfecto Inc. is willing to provide seismic tests for $100. From the past records of Imperfecto, they show a conditional probability of .7 that a correct prediction will be made if the site is WET, $P[\text{MOJADO} \mid \text{WET}] = .7$, and when the site is dry, the relevant probability is $P[\text{MOJADO} \mid \text{DRY}] = .4$.

    a. To help decide whether or not to buy the information, make a decision tree for this case similar to Figure 8.4.

    b. Assign payoffs and determine probabilities for branches for this tree to produce a decision tree for this case which is ready for analysis similar to Figure 8.5. Note that this will require you to compute all the prior and posterior probabilities as was done in Section 8.3.

    c. Using your response as your guide, redraw the decision tree, and apply extensive analysis and backward induction; your result being a tree similar to Figure 8.6, with all values indicated.

    d. What is the best strategy?

    e. What is the expected value of imperfect information EVXI?

    f. Suppose that Castellana has the choice of perfect information from Don Juan or imperfect information from Imperfecto Inc. What should she do?

    g. Make a graph similar to Figure 8.9 to show graphically where imperfect information is better and worse than perfect information.

3.6 Refer to the Tequila site drilling example discussed in Section 8.3. In drilling herein by a new outfit, Mextex, the prior probability of oil is determined to be $P[\text{WET}] = .2$. The profit if the site is WET is $42,000, but if the site is DRY, there is a $10,000 loss.

    a. Draw a decision tree representation of this situation in the absence of information similar to Figure 8.2.

    b. Calculate the expected value of the venture without information $(\text{EMV})_0$.

    c. What should Mextex decide?

3.7 Refer to the Tequila site drilling example discussed in Section 8.3 and Exercise 3.6. Don Genaro, the ubiquitous clairvoyant, offers his services to Mextex for $9000; he can predict with absolute certainty whether or not the site is WET.

    a. What is the expected monetary value of the venture with perfect information but before paying the fee $(\text{EMV})_1$?

    b. What is the expected net gain ENG?

    c. What should Mextex decide?

Don Juan now appears and offers perfect information for $3000.

    d. What is the expected net gain ENG?

    e. What should Mextex decide?

    f. What is the expected value of perfect information EVPI?

3.8 Refer to the Tequila site drilling example discussed in Section 8.3 and Exercises 3.6, and 3.7. Defectuoso appears on the scene and offers imperfect information for $1500. The reliability of their service is as stated in Section 8.3.

    a. What is the gross EMV?

b. What is the expected value of imperfect information EVXI?

c. What is the expected net gain ENG?

d. What decision should Mextex make?

3.9 Refer to the Tequila site drilling example discussed in Section 8.3 and Exercises 3.6, 3.7, and 3.8. The seismic sounding firm of Imperfecto Inc. is willing to provide seismic tests for $1000. From the past records of Imperfecto, they show a conditional probability of .9 that a correct prediction will be made if the site is WET, $P[\text{MOJADO} \mid \text{WET}] = .9$, and when the site is dry, the relevant probability is $P[\text{MOJADO} \mid \text{DRY}] = .3$.

  a. To help decide whether or not to buy the information, make a decision tree for this case similar to Figure 8.4.

  b. Assign payoffs and determine probabilities for branches for this tree to produce a decision tree for this case which is ready for analysis similar to Figure 8.5. Note that this will require you to compute all the prior and posterior probabilities as was done in Section 8.3.

  c. Using your response as your guide, redraw the decision tree, and apply extensive analysis and backward induction; your result being a tree similar to Figure 8.6, with all values indicated.

  d. What is the best strategy?

  e. What is the expected value of imperfect information EVXI?

  f. Suppose that Mextex has the choice of perfect information from Don Juan or imperfect information from Imperfecto Inc. What should they do?

  g. Make a graph similar to Figure 8.9 to show graphically where imperfect information is better and worse than perfect information.

4. *Information Analysis and Decision Making: A Dialog*

4.1 In the first question-and-answer pair of Section 8.4 it is hypothesized that red comes up 10, 20, and 50 times in sequence. What other possibilities are there other than that the "manager had rigged the roulette wheel?" Note that the student should make a distinction among the possibilities of 10, 20, or 50.

4.2 Assume, as in the third question-and-answer pair of Section 8.4, that in the situation facing Ms. Castellana *as described in Section 8.2* that Imperfecto Inc. charges only $50 if there is no oil and $100 if there is oil. Modify Figure 8.5 accordingly, and decide whether or not she should buy the information.

5. *Application to Market Research*

5.1 Complete the solution of the market research problem described in Section 8.5. Using informational chronology, answer the question as to whether or not the corporation should proceed to market the product.

5.2 Refer to Exercise 5.1. Repeat the exercise using actual chronology.

6. *Accounting Applications*

6.1 Refer to the Dependable Corporation example discussed in Section 8.6. There may be a variance in the accounts which if left uncorrected will result in a loss of $100,000 to the company. The management believes that the prior probability of a variance is 8; that is;

$$P[\text{VARIANCE}] = .8$$

An internal audit can be obtained for $10,000. If the accounts of the firm are rejected, the auditor will make a further investigation for $15,000, guaranteeing finding and fixing the variance. The reliability of the initial audit is as given in Section 8.6.

  a. Make a loss table similar to Figure 8.12 for this situation.

b. Make a decision tree for this situation similar to Figure 8.13.
c. Make the decision for Dependable Corporation. Justify.

7. *Impact of Personal Preferences*

7.1 Apply the utility function of Don Quixote given below to Exercises 2.1 to 2.3.

$$U = 100 \times \left(\frac{P + 1000}{2000} \right)^3$$

    a. What is the new decision? (*Note*: It may or may not be different.)
    b. Justify your results with the utility values you obtained.

7.2 Apply the utility function of Don Quixote given in Exercise 7.1 to Exercises 2.4 to 2.6.
    a. What is the new decision? (*Note*: It may or may not be different.)
    b. Justify your results with the utility values you obtained.

7.3 Apply the utility function of Don Quixote given in Exercise 7.1 to Exercise 3.1.
    a. What is the new decision? (*Note*: It may or may not be different.)
    b. Justify your results with the utility values you obtained.

7.4 Apply the utility function of Don Quixote given in Exercise 7.1 to Exercises 3.2 to 3.5.
    a. What is the new decision? (*Note*: It may or may not be different.)
    b. Justify your results with the utility values you obtained.

CHAPTER EXERCISES AND DISCUSSION QUESTIONS

C.1 We continue to work on Ms. Castellana's drilling ventures. She is now moving operations offshore. The probability, as she sees it, of an offshore wet well is .15. Don Genaro—still following her about—offers his services for $250; he can predict with absolute certainty whether an offshore site is WET or DRY but has extra costs (boat rentals, etc.). The second clairvoyant, Don Juan, is still following Don Genaro about and undercutting his prices. He offers perfect information for $215. Underwater seismic soundings from Defectuoso cost $100. From their past records of performance offshore she finds that there is a probability of .7 that a correct prediction will be made if the site is WET. When the well is DRY, the probability of a correct prediction is .8. Defectuoso's eager competitor, Imperfecto Inc., offers the same service (and has the same record) for $60. If a well turns out to be WET, the profit is $6000; if DRY, the loss is $800.
    a. Do a complete analysis, using both forms, for this situation, and decide what she should do. For your own benefit and to justify your conclusions to Ms. Castellana, prepare a complete presentation using illustrations similar to Figures 8.2, 8.3, 8.4, 8.5, 8.6, and 8.7.
    b. How would this decision be changed if she had the same utility function as Don Quixote in Exercise 7.1?

C.2 While out in her catamaran, Ms. Castellana sees strong signs of underwater oil. Her judgmental probability of a WET well at this site is .25. The gain and all other conditions of purchase of information are as described in Discussion Exercise C.1.
    a. Do a complete analysis, using both forms, for this situation and decide what she should do. For your own benefit and to justify your

conclusions to Ms. Castellana, prepare a complete presentation using illustrations similar to Figures 8.2, 8.3, 8.4, 8.5, 8.6, and 8.7.

    b. How would this decision be changed if she had the same utility function as Don Quixote in Exercise 7.1?

C.3 The K. Niffin Company is thinking of introducing its new Niffany line of jewelry based on microprocessor-controlled luminescent gems. They think there are only two possibilities, that consumers will see their jewelry as better than or worse than their only competitor's product; and they estimate the probability of being perceived as better to be 3/4. A market survey can be made that will improve their knowledge but at a cost of $700,000. The advantage of the survey is that it would give information concerning their future position in the market, and they are fortunate in having the reliability characteristics of the survey firm based on previous experience. If the jewelry will in fact be perceived as better by the consumers, then the probability the survey will so indicate is .8. If the product will not be so perceived by the consumers, then the probability that the market survey will so determine is .4. If the new jewelry is perceived to be better by the consumers and they have marketed it, the return will be $6 million. If they do not market it, they can capitalize on the research by selling the concepts for $800,000. On the other hand, if the new jewelry is perceived as inferior and they market it, sales will be low, giving a return of $150,000. If they do not market it under these circumstances, they can yield only $250,000. What is the appropriate strategy? Fully justify using the methods of this chapter.

C.4 Marcy's Department Stores have been expanding into suburban areas. A key element in their moves is the proximity of existing or proposed parking garages. They are interested in moving into Springbrook, a town within reach of dense metropolitan centers but previously undeveloped by their type of business. Springbrook plans to build a new parking garage at either of two locations, one in the center of town and the other near the railroad station. There is land near both sites that would be suitable for Marcy's, and such land is now selling rapidly and at premium prices. Within 3 months, the City Manager will recommend one of the two sites, following which the Board of Representatives will make a choice. The board is not legally required to take the City Manager's recommendation, but it is certain that they will choose one or the other of the sites. Marcy's has had an appraisal made and has determined the following values:

	LAND VALUE		
SITE	Current	Future if Garage Built	Future if Garage Not Built
Center city	$1,000,000	$1,500,000	$1,000,000
Railroad station	2,000,000	2,250,000	1,500,000

Marcy's has the choice of purchasing any or all sites; reasoning that they can always resell the land. They have been offered 3-month options to purchase both locations at a cost of $150,000; the option purchase price being at the current values. They can make their purchase decision after the Board of Representatives has chosen a site for the garage. If Marcy's doesn't make its purchase now or purchase the options, other hungry buyers will immediately purchase the land. V. A. Shawnee, an operations researcher, has been hired to advise Marcy's. He believes that the City Manager's actions indicate a 30% chance of the center city site being chosen as the recommended site. His soundings of the body politic lead him to believe that the Board of Representatives will not totally ignore the recommendation and that the relevant probabilities are as follows:

| | CITY MANAGER RECOMMENDATION | |
BOARD CHOICE	Center City	RR Station
Center city	.8	.3
RR station	.2	.7

What should Marcy's do?

C.5 The Nowait Transportation Company has purchased franchise rights in a number of communities to provide minibus transportation services in the communities. The company has a choice of actions. They can start minibus service immediately or could first have a demographic survey (an analysis based on census data concerning the characteristics of the franchise area population with respect to their use of minibus transport) made and then decide whether to start minibus service. Or they could do a formal market survey of the region to determine whether a market exists and of what magnitude. Of course, they could first make a demographic survey and then, as a consequence of the results of the demographics, have a market survey done before making a decision. The relevant costs and benefits are as follows:

Cost of demographic survey: $10,000
Cost of market survey: $50,000
Cost of entry into the franchise market: $250,000
Value of the market exploitation: $500,000

The best current estimate of the probability of the market existing (and thereby yielding the $500,000 market exploitation value) is .2. If there is such a market existing, the probability that the market survey will show that it exists is .9, and the probability that the demographic survey will show that there is a market is .7. On the other hand, if there is no market, the probability that the market survey will show that there is a market is .2, and the probability that the demographic survey will show a market when one does not exist is .3. What strategy should the company follow?

C.6 M. A. Tour, a field salesperson, is considering an offer to become a sales manager. As Tour sees it, the immediate decision is between remaining a field salesperson or accepting the position as a sales manager. Looking to the first year after accepting or rejecting the current offer, Tour sees the following mutually exclusive complementary chance events as relevant:

  i. The sales of Tour's group grow at least 10%.
 ii. The sales of Tour's group do not grow at least 10%.

At the end of that first year, Tour sees a second decision point. At this decision point, Tour must decide whether to stay in or go to field sales, to change fields entirely, or to stay in the manager's job. Whichever decision is made at this point, Tour sees it as followed by a chance fork: Tour will either be a modest success or a great success. The annual salary 3 years after the last decision point is chosen by Tour as the decision criterion. Tour believes that the probability that the sales group's sales will increase by at least 10% is .7 and that the difference between great and moderate success in sales management is 1.5 to 1 in salary, in field sales, 2 to 1, and in another field, 1.2 to 1. Tour estimates that the probability of great success in sales management is .6, in field sales, .9, and in another field, .5. What should Tour do?

9

Inventory Management

"Not again! We are out of beer in Arizona," exclaims the president of Midwest Brewery. "Can't you rush 10,000 cases to Phoenix?" The vice-president of production responds that it would take 2 months to produce the extra cases of beer. "Is there some way to find beer in inventory?," asks the president. The marketing vice-president says, "Yes, we have beer in Alaska, but it would take at least a month to ship it to Phoenix." "We have our beer at the wrong place again," the president remarks. "It was a bad decision to cut inventory levels." But then says the vice-president of finance, "How are you going to make a profit if your money is tied up in inventory?" Then again, "If beer is kept in inventory too long, it loses its taste."

This little anecdote throws light on the problem of managing inventories. Goods must flow from the initial raw material stage through production, distribution, and transportation to customers-users. A high level of service and production cannot be provided unless there is an efficient inventory management system which coordinates workers, machines, and facilities. Inventories must serve as **buffers** between production, transportation, and consumption.

Note that there are inventories of goods everywhere, in department stores, in retail stores, in supermarkets, in factories, and at gas pumps, and the fact is that billions of dollars are tied up in inventory. Business cannot be profitable unless the right level of inventory is kept at the right place. Public utilities cannot operate efficiently without inventories. The logistics of the military depend heavily on inventories. The entire smooth operation of our economy depends on inventories.

We stress that inventory control is one of the most successful application areas of quantitative methods.

Five Reasons to Keep Inventory

Fundamentally, inventory is kept to meet demand for goods without running out of stock and at a lowest possible cost. Going into more detail, we classify the reasons for keeping inventory under five headings.

1. *To meet irregular demand.* In the introduction we stated the problem of meeting the demand for beer under varying demand conditions. This is one of the typical reasons inventories are kept.

2. *To meet the demand for perishable goods.* In Chapter 3 we discussed the problem of keeping inventories for strawberries, a highly perishable fruit. Generally fresh fruit, fresh vegetables, and fresh meat are all perishable goods. In fact, the demand for high-fashion goods is also "perishable." Thus an inventory of frozen foods is kept, because many foods in their natural state deteriorate fast.

3. *When the supply of raw materials or finished goods is irregular.* For example, we keep inventories of wheat so the product of harvest time can be used throughout the year. When you travel in some remote area, you buy gas when you see a gas station, because you are not certain when and where you can buy gas again. Large water reservoirs hold water to meet irregular demands for water.

4. *To buy and produce in quantity.* It would be impractical and too expensive to buy envelopes, paper clips, and so on daily for an office. Supermarkets and department stores buy in quantity so goods are obtained at a reduced cost.

5. *To meet material requirements.* When products are manufactured in a factory, an in-process of inventory of subassemblies and parts must be kept. For example, the manufacture of automobiles requires an inventory of motors, radios, wheels, tires, etc., so that there is a smooth flow of cars coming off the assembly line.

The Three Inventory Costs

1. **Ordering costs.** These costs include managerial and clerical costs in preparing the purchase or production order. When parts are manufactured in a machine shop in quantity, first the machine must be readied to start production; the labor cost involved in making the machines ready is called **setup cost** and should be included in the ordering cost.

2. **Carrying costs.** When inventory is kept, there are such costs as maintaining warehouse and storage facilities, insurance costs, breakage, spoilage, obsolescence, and so on. In addition there are depreciation, taxes, and the cost of capital as well as other financial costs.

3. **Stockout costs.** When demand cannot be met, a loss is incurred to the business. Profit is lost, customer goodwill impaired, and so on.

Difficulties in Obtaining Costs

While inventory theory assumes that these costs can be determined, there are often severe difficulties in getting them, and some costs are, in fact, impossible to determine. As to ordering costs, it may be difficult to determine just what costs should be associated with ordering a particular item. As to carrying costs, there is often difficulty in determining the cost of money, particularly when the enterprise has ways other than in inventory to use the money. Finally, stockout costs are extremely difficult or often impossible to determine. Such items as loss of profit may be questionable, because, for example, it may be possible to deliver goods at a later time. Loss of goodwill of customers may be even more difficult to put into dollars. Therefore, when working with inventory theory, a practical view must be kept in mind, and the issue should always be raised whether the cost can be determined, and if yes, with what accuracy. Here what-if types of dialogs and sensitivity analysis may be appropriate as they can determine what accuracy is needed for making the decision or what risks are taken if only inaccurate cost data are available.

Types of Inventory Control Systems

There are many ways to classify inventory control systems. Consider, for example, the various types of demand. If the demand is deterministic, there are no probabilistic considerations involved. For example, when products such as airplanes are delivered to meet a schedule, deterministic theories hold. In such cases there may be no need for finished goods inventory, but there may be a need to keep in-process inventories for subassemblies and parts. On the other hand, when the demand is uncertain, probabilistic models must be used, and inventories are kept to hold shortages at a low level.

We can also classify inventory systems by the method of ordering. Some systems are based on always ordering the same quantity. These are **fixed order quantity** systems. In other systems orders are placed every week, every month, or at a predetermined **fixed order period**.

We can also classify inventory control systems as single-period or multiperiod systems. For example, when dealing with perishable or fashionable goods and an order is placed and the goods sold, there may be no chance to reorder or to replenish inventory. On the other hand, in most inventory control situations, orders are placed repeatedly either in fixed quantities or at fixed times. In some situations there is a chance to order twice, three times, and so on, and then we speak of inventory systems with two, three, and so on periods. On the other hand, in many inventory control problems it is tacitly assumed that we are dealing with an ongoing problem and that orders will be placed indefinitely.

Finally, we can classify inventory control problems according to the criterion to be used to determine the optimal inventory control system. In the strawberry problem discussed in Chapter 5 (as customary in problems with perishable goods) we assumed that the objective was to maximize expected profit. But most inventory control systems are subsystems of larger systems, and the optimal inventory control system is found by minimizing cost.

Difficulties in Obtaining Information

We already stated that information about some costs is often difficult or impossible to determine. Thus there is an inherent inaccuracy in the information provided to inventory control. In addition, there are many other inaccuracies in inventory situations. When establishing **inventory control systems**, there is a need to forecast the demand and the probability of what the demand will be. Forecasts are always uncertain, and probabilities of demand are difficult to determine.

Also, there are other inaccuracies in establishing what the inventory situation really is. For example, physical inventory counts, that is, actually counting inventory, is costly and cannot be done too frequently. Consequently there may be inaccuracies in knowing what quantities of goods a firm has. For these reasons it is important to keep in mind that there is no point in determining optimal inventory control levels at a very high accuracy if the data provided are inaccurate.

> In inventory control problems the accuracy of calculations must be in balance with the accuracy of the data available.

Computers for Inventory Control

In practice most inventory control systems are computer based. Too much data must be handled, and manual processing becomes too costly, inaccurate, slow, etc. Often management information systems (MIS) contain inventory control systems as subsystems. Thus controlling inventory becomes a combined problem between computer science and quantitative methods of management. Inventory theory supports managerial decision making by taking advantage of modern computer systems.

9.2 WHEN THE DEMAND IS CERTAIN

Tyres Inc., a wholesale distributor of tires, sells 2400 tires per year and orders 200 tires every month from the manufacturer. Delivery is essentially overnight, and so ordering can be done when Tyres Inc. is out of stock. However, the clerical staff is overloaded, and so it is proposed that orders should be placed quarterly in the quantity of 600 tires. But the financial executive feels that the money tied up in inventory is already too high and would like to see semimonthly ordering of 100 tires. How much should they order? When should they order? First we need to state our assumptions.

Three Assumptions

1. Minimization of the combined inventory carrying cost and ordering cost is the criterion to be used.
2. The demand is known with certainty.
3. The daily demand rate is constant.

Economic Order Quantity

We know that demand $D = 2400$ per year but do not know what quantity Q to order each time an order is placed.* Examination of the records of the company shows that the cost of placing an order C_o is \$18.75, irrespective of the size of the order. The carrying cost, C_c per year per unit, is 40% of the cost of a tire, that is, of \$50:

$$C_c = .4 \times 50 = \$20$$

Suppose Tyres Inc. orders 600 tires four times a year, implying a cycle time of 3 months. Figure 9.1 shows the **sawtooth pattern** of the inventory level corresponding to this policy. The average inventory level is shown in Figure 9.1:

At start:	600 units
After 1st month:	400 units
After 2nd month:	200 units
After 3rd month:	0 units
	1200 units

$$\text{Average inventory:} \quad \frac{1200}{4} = 300 \text{ units}$$

If the order quantity is designated by Q, the average inventory

---

* A summary of the notation appears at the end of this chapter.

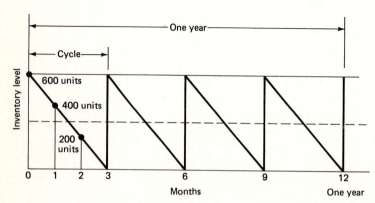

FIGURE 9.1
Saw-tooth pattern of inventory control when the demand is known.

N	Q = D/N	Z_c	Z_o	Z
1	2400	$24,000	$18.75	$24,018.75
2	1200	12,000	37.50	12,037.50
4	600	6,000	75.00	6,075.00
12	200	2,000	225.00	2,225.00
52	46	462	975.00	1,436.54

FIGURE 9.2 Inventory costs for Tyres Inc. when various ordering policies are used.

level is $Q/2$, halfway between the top Q and bottom zero. Thus the *yearly* inventory carrying cost is

$$Z_c = \tfrac{1}{2}C_c Q = \tfrac{1}{2} \times 20 \times 600 = \$6000$$

The yearly ordering cost is

$$Z_o = C_o N = 18.75 \times 4 = \$75.00$$

where N is the number of orders placed per year or frequency of ordering per year. But

$$N = \frac{D}{Q} = \frac{2400}{600} = 4$$

and so the combined yearly inventory cost is

$$Z = Z_c + Z_o = \frac{1}{2}C_c Q + \frac{C_o D}{Q} = \$6000 + \$75 = \$6075$$

In Figure 9.2 we show the various costs when $N = 1, 2, 4, 12$, or 52. Note that the lowest combined cost occurs at weekly ($N = 52$) ordering. Suppose, however, that any frequency of ordering is allowed. Would $N = 52$ still be the best ordering policy?

In Figure 9.3 we show graphically the yearly costs for various values of Q. Note that ordering costs are represented by a straight line and carrying costs by a decreasing function. The total cost is a U-shaped

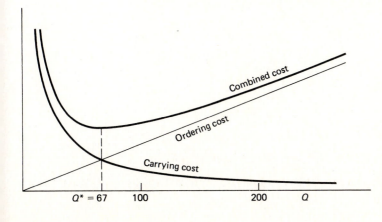

FIGURE 9.3
Inventory costs for various ordering quantities Q.

curve, and minimum cost occurs when Q has the value of about 67. In Section 9.9, the appendix to this chapter, we show that

> The minimum of such a curve occurs when the yearly inventory carrying cost Z_c equals the yearly ordering cost Z_o.

How Much to Order

From the preceding rule,

$$Z_c = Z_o$$

or by using the preceding formulas,

$$\frac{1}{2}C_cQ = \frac{C_oD}{Q}$$

Multiply both sides by

$$\frac{2Q}{C_c}$$

and get

$$Q^2 = \frac{2C_oD}{C_c}$$

or

$$Q = \sqrt{\frac{2C_oD}{C_c}}$$

It is customary to designate the best (optimum) of an unknown by a superscript asterisk. Thus the best **economic ordering quantity**, Q, is designated by $Q*$:

> The best economic ordering quantity (EOQ) is given by the square root formula
> $$Q* = \sqrt{\frac{2C_oD}{C_c}}$$

The lowest combined cost is

$$Z* = 2Z_c* = 2Z_o*$$

and

$$Z* = C_cQ* = \sqrt{2C_oC_cD}$$

For Tyres Inc. $D = 2400$ per year, $C_o = \$18.75$, and $C_c = \$20.00$ per year per unit, and so the EOQ is

$$Q^* = \sqrt{\frac{2 \times 18.75 \times 2400}{20}} = 67.082$$

$$Z_c^* = \frac{1}{2}C_c Q^* = \frac{1}{2} \times 20.00 \times 67.082 = \$670.82$$

$$Z_o^* = Z_c^* = \$670.82$$

$$Z^* = \$1341.64$$

Frequency of Ordering

The yearly demand is 2400 and the optimum order quantity is 67.082, and so Tyres Inc. should order

$$\frac{2400}{67.082} = 35.78$$

or about 36 times a year, or 3 times a month.

If the optimum order quantity is Q^*, the optimum frequency of ordering is

$$N^* = \frac{D}{Q^*} = \sqrt{\frac{C_c D}{2C_o}}$$

The optimal frequency of ordering is

$$N^* = \frac{D}{Q^*} = \sqrt{\frac{C_c D}{2C_o}}$$

We can now compare our results with the original policy of ordering 200 units every month. Using $Q = 200$, we get a yearly carrying cost of

$$Z_c = \tfrac{1}{2}C_c Q = \tfrac{1}{2} \times \$20.00 \times 200 = \$2000$$

and an ordering cost of

$$Z_o = C_o \frac{D}{Q} = \$18.75 \times \frac{2400}{200} = \$225$$

The combined yearly inventory cost is

$$Z = Z_c + Z_o = \$2000 + \$225 = \$2225.00$$

Thus the lowest cost of $Z^* = \$1341.64$ represents a yearly saving of $\$2225.00 - \$1341.64 = \$883.36$.

Sensitivity Analysis

Suppose that for some reason Tyres Inc. deviates from the EOQ. For example, they order 10% more times, say 39 times a year. Then $Q = 4500/39 = 61.5$. Using the formula for the combined inventory cost, we obtain $Z = \$1346.63$. This means that the cost is up only by .37%. Thus it is seen that a small change in the ordering quantity or in the frequency of ordering results in a small change in the inventory cost. In fact, even if $N = 52$, that is, Tyres Inc. orders weekly, the cost is only \$1437, which is only 7% above the minimum. We conclude, therefore, that in practical situations small deviations from the economic order quantity may be taken to meet convenience or other managerial factors.

It is useful to obtain an insight into the value of the EOQ as a function of the various quantities involved. Note that if the cost of ordering C_o or the demand D goes up, Q^* goes up too. But the square root formula implies that, say, a fourfold increase in D results in a doubling of Q^*. When the ordering cost C_o goes up, Q^* goes down. Of course Q^* and N^* move in opposite directions.

Applications to Production

So far we have assumed that ordering a part means to purchase it from a vendor. However, the theory developed here applies equally well to production if the production rate is high. More precisely,

> The EOQ theory as stated here can be applied to production if the rate of production is much higher than the rate of usage.

If during production a significant portion of the parts are used up, the EOQ theory developed here must be modified. However, in real life the problem would be dealt with as a problem in production scheduling, which will be discussed later in this chapter. Therefore, here we simply present the formula that can be used for gradual production without proving the formula:

> The optimum EOQ for gradual production is given by
>
> $$Q^* = \sqrt{\frac{2C_o D}{f C_c}}$$
>
> where the factor f is given by
>
> $$f = \frac{\text{rate of production} - \text{rate of usage}}{\text{rate of production}}$$

Price Breaks

Often the cost of an item varies with the order size. For example, assume the following:

> Discount category 1: Order size 0–599:
> > Unit cost = $7.50
> Discount category 2: Order size 600–999:
> > Unit cost = $6.75
> Discount category 3: Order size 1000 and up:
> > Unit cost = $5.85

What should the order quantity be? *Do not think that the lower the unit cost, the better.* We must make an economic analysis to decide.

Let us assume that the demand $D = 10,000$ per year, the ordering cost $C_o = \$30$, and the carrying cost per unit per year is 20% of the cost of the unit. Before we can apply the EOQ formula, we state the result proved with the aid of calculus in Section 9.9.

> The optimal ordering quantity must be selected from the following candidate solutions: (1) the quantities given by the EOQ formula or (2) the quantities corresponding to the price breaks.

In our problem there are three prices, so there are three quantities given by the EOQ formula. There are two price breaks and two corresponding ordering quantities, giving a total of five candidate solutions. So we solve the problem in five steps:

> *Step 1.* Find the candidate solutions from the EOQ formula.
> *Step 2.* Keep only the feasible solutions.
> *Step 3.* Find further candidate solutions by considering ordering quantities corresponding to the price breaks.
> *Step 4.* For each feasible candidate solution, calculate the total cost given by the sum of the combined inventory cost and item cost where
>
> > item cost = demand × unit cost

(Note that when price breaks are considered, the item costs must be included when calculating the total cost.)

> *Step 5.* Select as the optimal ordering quantity the candidate solution with the lowest total cost.

Calculating the EOQ

We have three costs and apply the EOQ formula three times.

Discount Category 1. $D = 10{,}000$ per year, $C_o = \$30$, and $C_c = .2 \times \$7.50 = \$1.50$*:

$$Q = \sqrt{\frac{2C_oD}{C_c}} = \sqrt{\frac{2 \times 30 \times 10{,}000}{1.5}} = 632$$

But this is *not* feasible, because the cost of \$7.50 applies to ordering quantities 0–599, and 632 is not in this range.

Discount Category 2. $D = 10{,}000$ per year, $C_o = \$30$, and $C_c = .2 \times \$6.75 = \$1.35$:

$$Q = \sqrt{\frac{2 \times 30 \times 10{,}000}{1.35}} = 667$$

This is feasible because the cost of \$6.75 applies to ordering quantities 600–999, and 667 is in this range. The combined inventory cost is

$$Z = C_cQ = 1.35 \times 667 = \$900$$

The item cost is $10{,}000 \times \$6.75 = \$67{,}500$. The total cost is $\$900 + \$67{,}500 = \$68{,}400$.

Discount Category 3. $D = 10{,}000$ per year, $C_o = \$30$, and $C_c = .2 \times \$5.85 = \$1.17$:

$$Q = \sqrt{\frac{2 \times 30 \times 10{,}000}{1.17}} = 716$$

This is *not* feasible because the cost of \$5.85 applies to ordering quantities 1000 and up, and 716 is less than 1000. Thus the EOQ gives a single candidate solution with $Q = 667$ and a total cost of \$68,400.

There are two quantities corresponding to the price breaks: 600 and 1000. The respective combined inventory costs are

$$Z = \frac{1}{2}C_cQ + \frac{C_oD}{Q} = \frac{1}{2} \times .2 \times 6.75 \times 600$$

$$+ \frac{30 \times 10{,}000}{600} = \$405 + \$500 = \$905$$

and

$$Z = \frac{1}{2}C_cQ + \frac{C_oD}{Q} = \frac{1}{2} \times .2 \times 5.85 \times 1000$$

$$+ \frac{30 \times 10{,}000}{1000} = \$585 + \$300 = \$885$$

---

* All Q values are rounded.

The corresponding total costs are

$$\$905 + 10{,}000 \times \$6.75 = \$905 + \$67{,}500 = \$68{,}405$$

and

$$\$885 + 10{,}000 \times \$5.85 = \$885 + \$58{,}500 = \$59{,}385$$

To summarize, we have three candidate solutions:

1. From the EOQ formula: $Q = 667$, and total cost = $68,400.
2. First price break: $Q = 600$, and total cost = $68,405.
3. Second price break: $Q = 1000$, and total cost = $59,385.

The optimum ordering quantity is given by the quantity corresponding to the second price break, $\sqrt{Q^*} = 1000$ and total cost = $59,385, because this quantity provides the lowest total cost.

9.4 UNCERTAIN DEMAND: SINGLE-PERIOD SYSTEM

The assumption that the demand is known may be practical in many inventory situations. However, often uncertainty about the demand dominates the problem. In Chapter 5 we discussed such situations in the example of the strawberry problem. The characteristic features of the problem were as follows: (1) Demand is a random variable with a known probability distribution; (2) once an order is placed, sales are made from the quantity ordered, and reordering is not possible; and so (3) only a single time period needs to be considered.

In Chapter 5 we discussed the strawberry problem as an illustration of decision analysis and not from the point of view of inventory management. However, the approach presented is valid, and so now that you are studying inventory control, all you need do is review the discussion in Chapter 5. Then you can proceed to work the more realistic exercises given at the end of this chapter.

9.5 UNCERTAIN DEMAND: MULTIPERIOD SYSTEM

Two-Bin Inventory Control System

To clarify the model to be used, let us go back to the old times and describe how Abraham Holton controlled the inventory of sugar in his general store. Mr. Holton used the **two-bin inventory control system**, meaning that he dispensed sugar to the customers from a large first bin, and when he ran out of sugar, he ordered sugar from the wholesaler and started to dispense sugar from a second bin. Why the second bin?

Mr. Holton knows that there will be 3 weeks **lead time** between ordering and receiving the sugar. The second bin contains sugar to cover the uncertain demand in these 3 weeks. The quantity R in the second bin equals the expected demand in the 3 weeks plus the **safety stock**. The safety stock is an extra inventory held as a hedge or protection against the possibility of stockout. The first bin contains Q units of sugar; this is the order quantity. The second bin contains R units of sugar, and this R is called the **reorder point** because when the inventory reaches R, Mr. Holton orders from the wholesaler.

Figure 9.4 shows a sample inventory record. As sugar is dispensed, inventory decreases until the first bin is depleted. At point R, the reorder point, Abraham Holton runs out of sugar in the first bin and begins to dispense sugar during the lead time from the second bin. During the first cycle the **lead-time demand** is less than R, and so Holton is not short of sugar. But during the second cycle the lead-time demand is higher than R, and so there is a stockout. Now if the second bin is too small, Holton will have stockouts frequently, provide a poor service level, and have many dissatisfied customers. If he keeps a large amount of stock in the second bin, he will rarely or perhaps never have stockout but will tie up much money in inventory. So he has the problem of how much to keep in the second bin, that is, how to set the reorder point. In addition, of course, he has the problem of how much to order to balance his cost of ordering and cost of carrying inventory. Mr. Holton knows with certainty the lead time of delivery, that is, how long it will take to receive new sugar, and has some idea about the variability in the demand for sugar. So he uses his judgment to establish the reorder point R and the ordering quantity Q so the carrying costs, ordering costs, and customer satisfaction will balance.

Using the theory developed in Chapter 5, we say that we are faced with decision making under uncertainty, where (1) the uncontrollable demand is a random variable, and (2) the controllable, decision variables are Q, the quantity ordered, and R, the reorder point. Thus *we are seeking a decision rule to determine these two variables.*

Before we proceed to derive the decision rule via an example, we remind you that

reorder point = expected lead-time demand + safety stock level

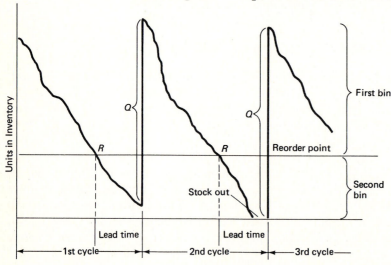

FIGURE 9.4
Two-bin inventory control system.

Fastcraft Inc.

Consider now a modern situation, Fastcraft Inc., a manufacturer of precision parts for aircraft engines. Examination of records reveals

$$\text{yearly demand} = 600 \text{ units}$$

$$\text{yearly inventory carrying cost} = C_c = \$20/\text{unit}$$

$$\text{setup cost to manufacture} = C_o = \$1500$$

$$\text{stockout cost} = \$40/\text{unit}$$

Let us assume for the moment that the demand for parts is uniform (constant demand rate) during the year. Under such an idealized condition inventory can be represented by the sawtooth diagram in Figure 9.5. So we can use the EOQ formula and calculate that the economic ordering quantity is

$$Q^* = \sqrt{\frac{2 \times 1500 \times 600}{20}} = 300 \text{ units}$$

and

$$N^* = \frac{600}{300} = 2/\text{year}$$

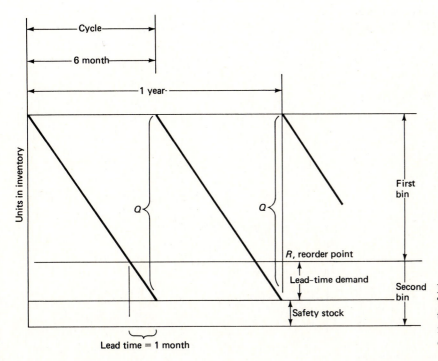

FIGURE 9.5
Two-bin inventory control system under idealized conditions for Fastcraft Inc.

Thus the cycle time is 6 months, that is, two cycles per year. We assume that this is an accurate enough approximation for the ordering quantity and proceed to determine the safety stock and reorder point.

The Safety Stock

Demand is an uncontrollable random variable, and we need probabilistic information about the demand.

Examining the records of Fastcraft, we find that the lead time is exactly 1 month and that lead-time demand can be represented by the thought experiment using the roulette wheel shown in the upper part of Figure 9.6. The lower part shows the corresponding probability mass function (PMF). The expected lead-time demand is

$$.04 \times 20 + .112 \times 30 + .2 \times 40 + .272 \times 50 + .236 \times 60 + .112 \times 70$$

$$+ .028 \times 80 = 50 \text{ units/month}$$

This of course agrees with the fact that the yearly demand is $12 \times 50 = 600$ units. Should the reorder point be 50, or should there be a safety

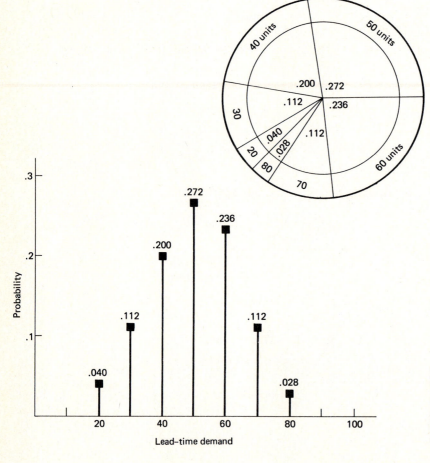

FIGURE 9.6
Thought experiment and the probability mass function of the lead-time demand for Fastcraft Inc.

stock and a higher reorder point? To answer this question, we should make an economic analysis for various safety stocks. The parts must be ordered in multiples of 10, and so we examine safety stocks of 0, 10, 20, and 30, that is, reorder points of 50, 60, 70, and 80. For each alternative we need to determine the combined expected cost of stockouts and cost of carrying safety stock. We obtain our answer by decision analysis.

Figure 9.7 shows the decision tree. At the foot of the tree are four branches corresponding to the four alternatives. For example, at chance fork 1 there are three branches corresponding to the demands of 60, 70, and 80 and stockouts of 10, 20, and 30. These values and the corresponding probabilities are listed along the four branches.

At each of the chance forks there is a gate at which a toll or fee must be paid equal to that of carrying the safety stock.*

Chance forks 2, 3, and 4 are self-explanatory.

In Figure 9.8 we show the calculations required. Let us first calculate the fees. At gate 1 there is no safety stock carrying cost and no fee to be paid. At gate 2 the carrying cost for safety stock of 10 units must be paid. The carrying cost is $20 per unit, so the fee is 10 × $20 = $200. The fees at gates 3 and 4 are 20 × $20 = $400 and 30 × $20 = $600, respectively.

Now we need to calculate the stockout costs at the tips of the tree.

---

* It may behoove you to review Figure 6.3 and the associated discussion.

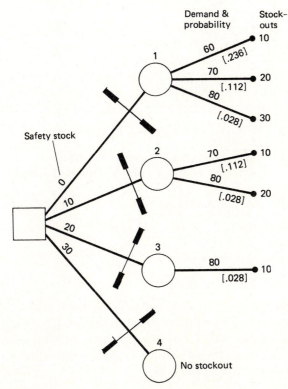

FIGURE 9.7
Decision tree to determine the best safety stock for Fastcraft Inc.

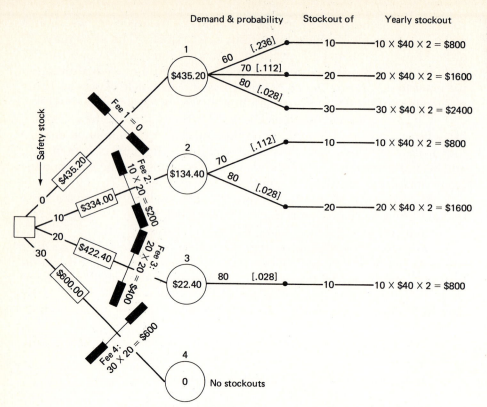

Demand & probability   Stockout of   Yearly stockout

FIGURE 9.8
The best safety stock level for Fastcraft Inc. is 10 units.

Fork 1 — $435.20

- 60   [.236] → 10 → 10 × $40 × 2 = $800
- 70 [.112] → 20 → 20 × $40 × 2 = $1600
- 80   [.028] → 30 → 30 × $40 × 2 = $2400

Fork 2 — $134.40

- 70   [.112] → 10 → 10 × $40 × 2 = $800
- 80   [.028] → 20 → 20 × $40 × 2 = $1600

Fork 3 — $22.40

- 80   [.028] → 10 → 10 × $40 × 2 = $800

Fork 4 — 0   No stockouts

Safety stock

- 0   Fee 1 = 0 $435.20
- 10   Fee 2: 10 × 20 = $200 $334.00
- 20   Fee 3: 20 × 20 = $400 $422.40
- 30   Fee 4: 30 × 20 = $600 $600.00

At the top right there is a shortage of 10 units. So in each cycle there is a cost of 10 × $40 = $400. There are two cycles per year, and so the yearly stockout cost is 10 × $40 × 2 = $800.

At the tip below, the shortage is 20 units, and so the yearly stockout cost is 20 × $40 × 2 = $1600. And so on.

Now we average out at each chance fork. For fork 1 we get

$$.236 \times \$800 + .112 \times \$1600 + .028 \times \$2400 = \$435.20$$

We mark this at fork 1. The corresponding values at forks 2, 3, and 4 are $134.40, $22.40, and $0, respectively, because at fork 4 there never is a shortage.

Now we add the fees, that is, the carrying costs, and get

For fork 1: $435.20 + 0 = $435.20.
For fork 2: $134.40 + $200 = $334.40
For fork 3: $22.40 + $400 = $422.40
For fork 4: $0 + $600 = $600

In Figure 9.9 we display the carrying costs, the stockout costs, and the combined costs. The lowest combined cost alternative is fork 2 with a safety stock of 10 units. To get the optimum reorder point, we must add the expected lead-time demand. Thus $R = 50 + 10 = 60$ units. The lowest combined cost is $334.40.

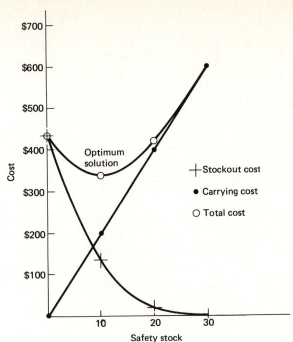

FIGURE 9.9
Carrying cost, stockout
cost, and total cost for Fastcraft Inc.

Now we summarize our approach.

Step 1. Calculate the order quantity by the economic order quantity (EOQ)
formula.
Step 2. Calculate the safety stock level and the optimum reorder quantity by
decision analysis.

Uniform Lead-Time Demand Distribution

Often there are insufficient data to determine the probability mass
function of the lead-time demand, and all one can say is the demand is
between certain limits. Suppose, for example, for Fastcraft Inc. that all
we can say is the demand is between 20 and 80 units. A practical
approach to such problems is to assume that the demand distribution is
uniform (discussed in Section 3.3). For example, for Fastcraft Inc. we can
assume that the probability mass function is shown in Figure 9.10.
Calculation of the safety stock and reorder point is similar to the one
treated before, and so the solution to the problem is left as an exercise.

Normal Lead-Time Demand Distribution

Often the lead-time distribution is specified as a normal distribution. In
such cases a simple approach is to approximate the normal distribution
by a probability mass function.
Suppose, for example, for Fastcraft Inc. it is found that the lead-

FIGURE 9.10
Uniform probability mass function of lead-time demand.

time demand distribution can be represented by a normal distribution with a mean of $\mu = 50$ and $\sigma = 15$.* We decide to approximate this distribution with a probability mass function of the demand of 20, 30, 40, 50, 60, 70, and 80 units (Figure 9.11). Designate the respective probabilities by p_2, p_3, p_4, p_5, p_6, p_7, and p_8. Then

$$p_2 = P[d \leq 25], \qquad \text{area left of 25}$$

$$p_3 = P[25 < d \leq 35], \qquad \text{area between 25 and 35}$$

$$p_4 = P[35 < d \leq 45], \qquad \text{area between 35 and 45}$$

$$p_5 = P[45 < d \leq 55], \qquad \text{area between 45 and 55}$$

$$p_6 = P[55 < d \leq 65], \qquad \text{area between 55 and 65}$$

$$p_7 = P[65 < d \leq 75], \qquad \text{area between 65 and 75}$$

$$p_8 = P[75 < d], \qquad \text{area right of 75}$$

We compute the cumulative distribution function (CDF) on the right-

_____

* The normal distribution is discussed in Section 3.5.

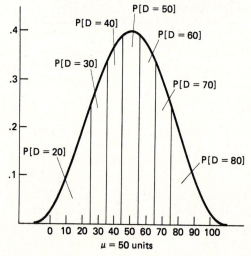

FIGURE 9.11
Normal lead-time demand probability distribution approximated by probability mass function.

hand side by the method in Chapter 3. For example, for p_2 we have

$$z = \frac{d - \mu}{\sigma} = \frac{25 - 50}{15} = -1.67$$

and the cumulative probability from Table B.1 in Appendix B is .05 (rounded). Thus,

$$p_2 = .05$$

For p_3,

$$z = \frac{35 - 50}{15} = -1.00$$

and from Table B.1 we get .16. Thus,

$$p_3 = P[25 < d \leqslant 35] = P[d \leqslant 35] - P[d \leqslant 25] = .16 - .05 = .11$$

In Figure 9.12 we tabulate our calculations and find the approximate probability mass function shown in columns 4 and 5.

Now we can proceed to determine the safety stock and reorder point. Solution of the problem is left as an exercise.

(1) d, LEAD-TIME DEMAND	(2) z, RATIO FOR NORMAL DISTRIBUTION	(3) CUMULATIVE NORMAL PROBABILITY DISTRIBUTION	(4) d, LEAD-TIME DEMAND	(5) PROBABILITY OF DEMAND
20			20	.05
25	$(25 - 50)/15 = -1.67$	.05		
30			30	.11
35	$(35 - 50)/15 = -1.00$	.16		
40			40	.21
45	$(45 - 50)/15 = -.33$	.37		
50			50	.26
55	$(55 - 50)/15 = +.33$	.63		
60			60	.21
65	$(65 - 50)/15 = +1.00$	.84		
70			70	.11
75	$(75 - 50)/15 = +1.67$	.95		
80			80	.05

FIGURE 9.12 Calculating a probability mass function to approximate a normal distribution.

Other Distributions

Occasionally neither the uniform nor the normal distributions are the most convenient distributions to use. However, our method of using an approximate probability mass distribution can be applied to any continuous probability function.

Critique of Method

In the inventory problem there are two decision variables: the quantity to be ordered and the reorder level. In the analysis we assume that first the optimum ordering quantity is determined and then the optimum reorder point. However, the performance of the system depends on both of these decision variables, and our calculation of the expected inventory level is only approximate. Namely, when a shortage occurs, there will be no units in inventory, and so an error is committed when calculating the cost of carrying the safety stock. However, more sophisticated calculations considering both decision variables simultaneously show that in practical situations our approach is accurate enough. In fact, the cost of stockout is rarely known accurately, and probability estimates are subject to errors. So now we proceed to study the problem when the stockout costs are unknown.

9.6 WHEN THE STOCKOUT COST IS NOT KNOWN

Often it is too difficult or impractical to determine stockout costs. In such cases decision making can be supported by specifying the **service level**. This means that the probability of a stockout is specified to be below a certain level, say, for example, .1. How does one determine the reorder point to meet such a specification?

Returning to Fastcraft Inc., consider the lead-time probability mass function shown in Figure 9.6. First we calculate the cumulative probability distribution shown in the upper part of Figure 9.13. We see, for example, that the probability of the lead-time demand being less than or equal to 60 units is .860. In the lower diagram we show that when the reorder point is 60 units the probability of a stockout equals $1.000 - .860 = .140$. Thus a reorder level of 60 is not enough for a service level of .1. By completing the lower diagram, we note that a reorder level of 70 units provides a stockout probability of .028, which is less than .1.

> The safety stock to provide a specified level of service can be determined with the aid of cumulative probability distribution of the lead-time demand.

The safety stock level is obtained by subtracting the expected demand: $70 - 50 = 20$ units.

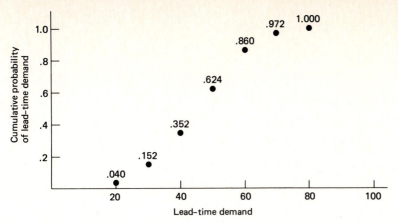

FIGURE 9.13
Establishing inventory service levels for Fastcraft Inc.

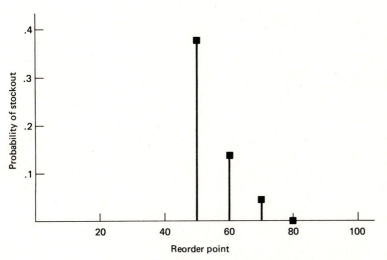

Uniform Lead-Time Demand Distribution

Suppose the lead-time demand is uniformly distributed between 20 and 80 units. What should the reorder point be for a service level of .1 of stockouts? We have to use the formulas from Section 3.3 to solve the problem. We have

$$a = 20 \text{ units}$$

$$b = 80 \text{ units}$$

$$b - a = 60 \text{ units}$$

and so the cumulative distribution for the demand d is

$$0 \qquad \text{for } d < 20$$

$$\frac{d - 20}{60} \qquad \text{for } 20 \leq d < 80$$

$$1 \qquad \text{for } d \geq 80$$

We need to find the demand d such that

$$\frac{d - 20}{60} = 1 - .1 = .9$$

or

$$d - 20 = .9 \times 60 = 54$$

$$d = 74$$

Thus the reorder point is 74 units, and the safety stock is $74 - 50 = 24$ units.

Normal Lead-Time Demand Distribution

Suppose the lead-time demand is specified by a normal distribution with a mean of $\mu = 50$ and $\sigma = 15$. What should the safety stock be to keep the stockout probability at .1? Using the notation for normal distribution, we need to find a d such that

$$z = \frac{d - 50}{15}$$

Table B.1 in Appendix B gives .900. We find that for $z = 1.28$ the value is .89973, and this is close enough for any practical purpose. So

$$\frac{d - 50}{15} = 1.28$$

and

$$d - 50 = 15 \times 1.28 = 19.2$$

Thus for any practical purpose a safety stock of 19 units will do, and the reorder point will be $50 + 19 = 69$ units.

9.7 INVENTORY SYSTEMS FOR DEPENDENT DEMAND

In Section 9.1 when we listed the reasons for keeping inventory, we stated as a fifth reason meeting material requirements. Now we develop the technique of inventory control for production which today is referred to as **material requirement planning (MRP)**, a technique which during the last few years has essentially revolutionized production control.

Suppose you are manufacturing automobiles. You know that each automobile requires four wheels and one spare wheel, five tires, one engine, one chassis, etc. Thus if a master production schedule is given for automobiles, there is no uncertainty connected with the number of wheels, tires, engines, and so on that are required. It is said that these parts must meet a *dependent demand* associated with the master production schedule. The best way to understand how schedules are prepared for such dependent demand is through an example.

Producing Skateboards

When products are manufactured, there is a need for a **bill of materials** which describes the various parts required to make the product. While a bill of materials contains a great deal of information, the fundamental logic or structure of how to put the various parts together is relatively simple. In Figure 9.14 we show the **product structure tree** of a skateboard assembly. The skateboard assembly is on *level 0*, and the two components shown are on *level 1*. The first component is the fiberglass board, and the second is the wheel assembly. Each skateboard requires one fiberglass board and two wheel subassemblies, as shown in the diagram. The subassemblies are called the *children* of the *parent* skateboard assembly. For each skateboard there is one fiberglass board and two wheel assemblies, so the *child-parent ratio* is, respectively, 1 and 2.

Note on the diagram that each wheel subassembly consists of the components on level 2. The first is the truck, and the second is the wheels. One truck and two wheels are required for each wheel subassembly, meaning that the child-parent ratio is, respectively, 1 and 2.

Suppose that it is required to make 100 skateboard assemblies in week 6, as shown in entry 1, line 1, Figure 9.15. Also suppose there is a 2-week *lead time* for manufacturing the skateboard assembly. Then the order to manufacture the skateboard assemblies should be placed in week 4, as shown in entry 1, line 2, Figure 9.15. The order placement must be *time-phased* 2 weeks ahead of the requirement date.

Entry 2, line 1, Figure 9.15 shows that 100 fiberglass boards are required in week 4 for the skateboard assembly. The lead time is 1 week, and so the order must be placed in week 3.

Entry 3, line 1, Figure 9.15 shows that 200 wheel assemblies are required in week 4 because each skateboard assembly requires two wheel assemblies; that is, the child-parent ratio is 2. The lead time for

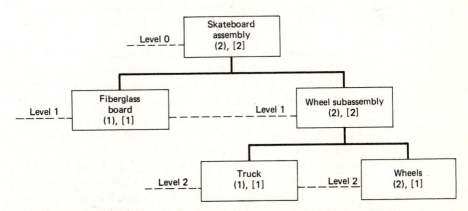

FIGURE 9.14 Product structure tree of skateboard assembly. The numbers in parentheses show the child-parent ratios. The numbers in brackets show the lead-times in weeks.

		WEEKS					
		1	2	3	4	5	6
1. *Skateboard assembly*	Requirement						100
Lead time = 2 weeks	Order placement				100		
2. *Fiberglass board*	Requirement				100		
Lead time = 1 week	Order placement			100			
3. *Wheel subassembly*	Requirement				200		
Lead time = 2 weeks	Order placement		200				
4. *Truck*	Requirement		200				
Lead time = 1 week	Order placement	200					
5. *Wheels*	Requirement		400				
Lead time = 1 week	Order placement	400					

FIGURE 9.15 Schedule for manufacturing 100 skateboard assemblies required in week 6.

wheel assemblies is 2 weeks, so orders for the wheel assemblies must be placed in week 2.

Entry 4, Figure 9.15 shows that 200 trucks are required in week 2, and the order must be placed in week 1.

Finally, entry 5, Figure 9.15 shows that 400 wheels are required in week 2 because the child-parent ratio is 2. The lead time is 1 week, and so the order must be placed in week 1.

Note then that three types of questions are answered by the schedule shown in Figure 9.15:

1. *Product structure:* What part is required?
2. *Quantity:* How many parts are required?
3. *Time phasing:* When is the part required?

So far we have assumed that 100 skateboard assemblies are required in week 6. Now we consider the problem described in Figure 9.16a when there is a gross requirement in week 6 of 150, 185, and 217 units for skateboard assemblies, fiberglass board, and wheel subassemblies and there is an inventory of *on-hand* quantities of 20, 30, and 40 units, respectively (Figure 9.16a). Also there is an inventory of on-hand quantities of 50 and 500 units for trucks and wheels, respectively. Our problem is to fill in the manufacturing schedule in Figure 9.16a.

To show how this is done, we present a copy of Figure 9.16a in Figure 9.16b, where the schedule is developed in the following manner:

Step 1. There is a given gross requirement of 150 skateboard assemblies in week 6. There are 20 units on hand, so the net requirement is $150 - 20 = 130$ units (entry 1, Figure 9.16b). There is a 2-week lead time, so we release 130 skateboard assemblies in week 4.

Step 2a. There is a gross requirement of 130 fiberglass boards for the skateboard assemblies in week 4. There are 30 on hand, so the net requirement is $130 - 30 = 100$ units. There is a lead time of 1 week, so we release 100 units in week 3 (entry 2, Figure 9.16b).

Step 2b. There is also a given gross requirement of 185 fiberglass boards in week 6. The inventory has been all used up, so the on-hand quantity is 0. The net requirement in week 6 is 185, and so these units are released in week 5 (entry 2, Figure 9.16b).

Step 3a. There is a gross requirement of 2 × 130 = 260 wheel subassemblies in week 4. There are 40 on hand, so net requirements are 260 − 40 = 220 units. The lead time is 2 weeks, so we release 220 units in week 2 (entry 3, Figure 9.16b).

Step 3b. There is also a given gross requirement of 217 units in week 6. The inventory of 40 has been used up in week 4, so the on-hand quantity is 0. Net requirements are 217 units. The lead time is 2 weeks, so 217 units are released in week 4 (entry 3, Figure 9.16b).

Step 4a. There is a gross requirement of 220 trucks in week 2. The on-hand quantity is 50, so the net requirement is 170 units. We release 170 units in week 1 (entry 4, Figure 9.16b).

Step 4b. There is also a gross requirement of 217 trucks in week 4. The on-hand quantity equals 0, so the net requirement is 217. We release 217 units in week 3.

Step 5a. There is a gross requirement of 2 × 220 = 440 wheels in week 2. There are 500 on hand, so there is a net requirement of 0 in week 2, and we release 0 in week 1.

Step 5b. There is also a gross requirement of 2 × 217 = 434 trucks in week 4. There were initially 500 units on hand, and 440 were used in week 2. So there are still 500 − 40 = 60 units on hand in week 4, and the net requirement is 434 − 60 = 374 units in week 4. So we release 374 units in week 3.

		1	2	3	4	5	6
	WEEKS						
1. *Skateboard assembly*	Gross requirement						150
	On hand: 20						
	Net requirement						
	Order release						
2. *Fiberglass board*	Gross requirement						185
	On hand: 30						
	Net requirement						
	Order release						
3. *Wheel sub- assembly*	Gross requirement						217
	On hand: 40						
	Net requirement						
	Order release						
4. *Truck*	Gross requirement						
	On hand: 50						
	Net requirement						
	Order release						
5. *Wheels*	Gross requirement						
	On hand: 500						
	Net requirement						
	Order release						

FIGURE 9.16a Gross manufacturing requirements.

ENTRY		WEEKS					
		1	2	3	4	5	6
1. *Skateboard assembly*	Gross requirement					①	150
	On hand: 20						20
	Net requirement						130
	Order release				130		
2. *Fiberglass board*	Gross requirement			②a	130	②b	185
	On hand: 30				30		0
	Net requirement				100		185
	Order release			100		185	
3. *Wheel sub-assembly*	Gross requirement			③a	260	③b	217
	On hand: 40				40		0
	Net requirement				220		217
	Order release		220		217		
4. *Truck*	Gross requirement	④a	220	④b	217		
	On hand: 50		50		0		
	Net requirement		170		217		
	Order release	170		217			
5. *Wheels*	Gross requirement	⑤a	440	⑤b	434		
	On hand: 500		500		60		
	Net requirement		0		374		
	Order release	0		374			

FIGURE 9.16b Schedule for meeting given gross manufacturing requirements.

This completes calculating the schedule for producing skateboards, and now we can discuss how this procedure is used in practice.

Computer-Based Material Requirement Planning (MRP)

Note that the fundamental logic of material requirement planning is quite simple. But when it comes to real-life applications with thousands of assemblies, subassemblies, and parts and many levels, the calculations become unmanageable by hand, and so invariably computers are used to develop the schedules for MRP. We also must remember that actual schedules are not just numbers and dates, as shown in Figure 9.16(a) and (b), but that great amounts of data must be shown to make production schedules practical. Therefore, computer-based MRPs must generate a large variety of reports.

Thus in actual practice massive files of bills of materials, inventory records, the master production schedule, orders and forecasts of requirements for products, and so on must be kept by the computer. Also these files must be frequently updated to take care of design changes for the bills of materials and to monitor inventory transactions, orders received, changes in demand forecast, and so on.

By using the basic logic of MRP that we discussed, the computer uses these files as inputs and produces a large number of outputs. For example, schedules of net requirements, orders released, inventory levels, exception reports, reports for planning for performance control, and so on are generated.

Note, therefore, that MRP requires a combination of quantitative methods of decision making and computer science and management information systems (MISs). Reports generated by MRP do not optimize production schedules; the purpose of MRP is to support managers in making production decisions.

9.8 UNITED STATES AIR FORCE SAVES WITH PROJECT EOQ*: A SUCCESSFUL APPLICATION

Nineteen cadets of the Air Force Academy were taking a course in logistic management and quantitative management techniques. They learned about the EOQ formula and wondered how the Air Force was using it. They discovered that there were 250,000 active items but that the EOQ formula was used only for 25,000 items. The reason for the limited use of the EOQ formula was that it was not known how to apply EOQ to items for which price discounts could be obtained, that is, to 90% of the items.

Note that outside of the military the EOQ formula is widely used for items with discounts. Namely, in the commercial world vendors submit prices of goods with discounts included, and buyers use the decision rules discussed earlier in this chapter on how to choose the best ordering quantities. However, the situation in the Air Force is quite different because the Armed Services Procurement Regulation (ASPR) specifies competitive (advertised) procurement in all cases. Thus suppliers must bid on quantities specified in the solicitation, and in the Air Force it was not known how to specify these alternate quantities. So the cadets concentrated on the problem of how to specify alternate quantities of goods in solicitations.

Perhaps each item should be manually reviewed and alternate quantities to be purchased specified in the solicitation? But such a procedure for the 250,000 active items would have involved a prohibitive amount of manual labor. What was needed was a *decision rule to calculate the price discount solicitation quantities*. Once such a decision rule is established, bids can be solicited by computers, and then the EOQ formula as developed in this chapter can be applied.

Decision Rule Restrictions

There are a great many restrictions involved when procuring material for the federal government and the Air Force. Without going into details of these restrictions, we simply state here three important restrictions.

1. Each item must be ordered three or less than three times a year.
2. The volume ordered must cover demand for at least 3 months.
3. Vendor solicitations must "make sense" to the vendor.

The last restriction is a particularly troublesome one because

---

* Adapted from Larry M. Austin, " 'Project EOQ': A Success Story in Implementing Academic Research," *Interfaces*, Vol. 7, No. 4, August 1977, pp. 1–14.

vendors refuse to quote on too many alternatives such as 100, 200, 300, . . . , 1000 items. Thus studies must be conducted to find out what kinds of solicitation quantities "make sense" to vendors.

We do not present details of the many decision rules examined by the cadets and show only the final decision rule.

Decision Rule to Solicit Quantity Discounts

There are two variables for each of the 250,000 active inventory items that determine the decision rule. The first of these is D_1, *the demand in dollars per year*, and the second is Q_1^*, *the dollar volume of the optimum economic order quantity* (EOQ). Thus,

$$D_1 = D \times \text{(unit cost of item)}$$

$$Q_1^* = Q^* \times \text{(unit cost of item)}$$

where D is number of units demanded per year and Q^* is optimum order quantity.

By use of these two variables, the decision rule categorizes items into five major and eight subcategories, as shown in Figure 9.17. For example, the first major category is defined by (1) the demand in dollars D_1 being equal to or more than \$10,000 per year and (2) Q_1^* being over \$2500. Note also in Figure 9.17 that there are four subcategories for this first major category. The decision rule depends on the relative magnitudes of Q_1^* and demand D_1. For example, when

$$Q_1^* < \tfrac{3}{4}D_1$$

MAJOR CATEGORY	SUBCATEGORY	PRICE DISCOUNT SOLICITATION QUANTITIES
1. $D_1 \geq \$10,000$ or $Q_1^* > \$2500$	$Q_1^* < \tfrac{3}{4}D_1$ $\tfrac{3}{4}D_1 \leq Q_1^* < D_1$ $D_1 \leq Q^* < \tfrac{3}{2}D_1$ $Q_1^* \geq \tfrac{3}{2}D_1$	$Q_1^*, 2Q_1^*, 3Q_1^*, 4Q_1^*$ $Q_1^*, 2Q_1^*, 3Q_1^*$ $Q_1^*, 2Q_1^*$ $Q_1^*, 3D_1$
2. $\$2000 \leq D_1 < \$10,000$ and $Q_1^* \leq \$2500$	Option of buyer: remain within small purchase limits Option of buyer: exceed small purchase limits	Q_1^*, any quantity up to \$2499 Same quantities as in major category 1
3. $\$833 \leq D_1 < \$2000$	$Q_1^* > \$2000$ $Q_1^* \leq \$2000$	$Q_1^*, \$2499$ $Q_1^*, (Q_1^* + \$2499)/2$ \$2499
4. $\$300 \leq D_1 < \$833$	—	$Q_1^*, 3D_1$
5. $D_1 < \$300$	—	Do not solicit price discounts

FIGURE 9.17 Solicitation inventory control decision rule for U.S. Air Force. D_1 = demand per year in dollars, and Q^* = optimum EOQ in dollars.

then price discounts are solicited on the quantities of $Q_1{}^*$, $2Q_1{}^*$, $3Q_1{}^*$, and $4Q_1{}^*$ items. When

$$\tfrac{3}{4}D_1 \leq Q_1{}^* < D$$

the quantities solicited are $Q_1{}^*$, $2Q_1{}^*$, and $3Q_1{}^*$. The rest of Figure 9.17 is self-explanatory.

A numeric example should clarify the use of the decision rule. Suppose (1) the yearly demand is 120 units, (2) the optimum economic ordering quantity is 100 units, and (3) the unit cost is \$100. First calculate the number of orders per year:

$$N = \frac{120}{100} = 1.2$$

Thus the first restriction that $N \leq 3$ is met. Second, calculate the number of months the order covers demand. The monthly demand is 100 units, and so the demand is covered for 10 months, which is more than the minimum of 3 months. So the second restriction is met.

To apply the decision rule, we need to calculate D_1 and $Q_1{}^*$:

$$D_1 = 120 \times \$100 = \$12,000$$

$$Q_1{}^* = 100 \times \$100 = \$10,000$$

Note first that (1) D_1 is over the minimum \$10,000 and (2) $Q_1{}^*$ is over the minimum \$2500, and therefore the rule for the first major category (Figure 9.17) applies.

Try first subcategory 1. Does

$$Q_1{}^* < \tfrac{3}{4}D_1$$

hold? $Q_1{}^* = \$10,000$ and

$$\tfrac{3}{4}D_1 = \tfrac{3}{4} \times 12,000 = \$9000$$

But

$$10,000 < 9000$$

is false: The first subcategory does not apply.

Try subcategory 2. Does

$$\tfrac{3}{4}D_1 \leq Q_1{}^* < D_1$$

hold? We have

$$9000 \leq 10,000 < 12,000$$

which does hold. Thus from Figure 9.14 the solicited ordering quantities in dollars are $Q_1{}^*$, $2Q_1{}^*$, and $3Q_1{}^*$ or \$10,000, \$20,000, and \$30,000. We can convert this to the solicited ordering quantities of 100, 200, and 300 units.

Finally we need to check the third restriction: Does this "make sense" to the vendor. Here we merely state that the expert opinion is affirmative.

Forecast of Benefits

Using past data for demand, exponential smoothing of forecasts (described in Section 4.4), and managerial judgment, forecasts for each item were made. But it was not possible to forecast discounts, and so they were considered as random variables. The expected value of the discounts was not known, and therefore studies were made on three levels of expected discounts, namely 3, 5, and 8%. Now how can one determine the benefits for a probabilistic problem of this type?

We are dealing here with a problem of several random variables, and the model to be used is described in Section 5.6 (Figure 5.14). The cadets used the technique of simulation (covered in Section 17.5) and computed the expected benefit. Figure 9.18 shows gross savings in annual acquisition costs and net savings in total annual costs for each expected price discount level.

These projections were so impressive that a management decision was made to proceed to implement a pilot project where a net annual saving of $600,000 was realized. After the success of the pilot project, the Air Force proceeded to a full-scale implementation of the new price discount solicitation policy.

SUMMARY

1. The scientific approach to inventory management is based on the evaluation of ordering policies in terms of economic consequences.
2. The three important costs are carrying cost, ordering cost, and stockout cost.
3. The economic ordering quantity formula provides the optimum ordering quantity for the deterministic case and minimizes the combined carrying and ordering costs.
4. Probabilistic inventory control decision rules are derived by using decision analysis.
5. The two decision variables are ordering quantity and reorder point or safety stock level.
6. Safety stocks are used to balance carrying costs and stockout costs.
7. The economic ordering quantity formula provides a good approximation to the optimum ordering quantity for the probabilistic case.

AVERAGE PRICE DISCOUNT	GROSS SAVINGS	NET SAVINGS
3%	$19.6	$10.3
5	39.9	25.9
8	67.2	50.7

FIGURE 9.18 Projected gross and net savings in millions of dollars of annual acquisition costs.

8. The optimum safety stock level and reorder point are calculated by using the probability mass function of the demand distribution and minimizing the combined carrying cost and stockout cost.

9. When the stockout cost is not known, the safety stock and reorder point can be determined by specifying a policy of maintaining a given service level for stockouts.

10. The basic model for inventory control of dependent products is simple, but implementation of material requirement planning (MRP) involves the use of computer systems.

NOTATION

A: average lead-time demand
C_c: carrying cost per unit
C_o: ordering cost per unit or setup cost per unit
D: demand per year
d: lead-time demand
f: $= (P - D)/P$
N: number of orders per year
$N*$: optimum frequency of orders per year
P: production per year
Q: quantity ordered
$Q*$: economic order quantity
R: reorder point
Z: combined yearly cost $(= Z_o + Z_c)$
Z_c: inventory carrying cost per year
Z_o: ordering cost per year
z: ratio used in normal distribution

9.9 APPENDIX: DERIVATION OF THE EOQ FORMULAS

The EOQ Formula

The combined cost is given by*

$$Z = \frac{1}{2}C_cQ + \frac{C_oD}{Q}$$

To get the minimum, we set the first derivative to zero,

$$\frac{dZ}{dQ} = \frac{1}{2}C_c - \frac{C_oD}{Q^2} = 0$$

---

* This is the bilinear function discussed in Appendix A, Section 7.

which gives the EOQ formula:

$$Q = \sqrt{\frac{2C_o D}{C_c}}$$

The carrying cost per year is

$$Z_c = \frac{1}{2}C_c Q = \frac{1}{2}C_c \sqrt{\frac{2C_o D}{C_c}} = \sqrt{\frac{1}{2}C_o C_c D}$$

The ordering cost per year is

$$Z_o = C_o \frac{D}{Q} = C_o D \frac{C_c}{2C_o D} = \sqrt{\frac{1}{2}C_o C_c D}$$

Thus for the optimal Q,

$$Z_o = Z_c$$

The Price Break Theorem

According to calculus, if the derivative of a function exists and does not equal zero at a certain point, the function *cannot* have a minimum. The total cost Z is a function of the ordering quantity Q, which has a derivative *except* at the quantities corresponding to the price breaks. Thus the minimum is either at the price breaks or at points where the derivative equals zero. These points are given by the EOQ formula. Thus the minimum point is given either by the quantities corresponding to the price breaks or by the EOQ formula.

SECTION EXERCISES

1. *The Scientific Approach to Inventory Management*

1.1 In your own words, state what is meant by the following terms used in Section 9.1, giving one practical example of each from your own experience:

    a. Ordering costs
    b. Irregular demand
    c. Perishable goods
    d. Setup cost
    e. Stockout cost

1.2 Give a real-world example from your own experience of each of the following inventory situations:

    a. Deterministic demand
    b. Uncertain demand
    c. Fixed order quantity
    d. Fixed order period
    e. Single period
    f. Multiperiod

g. Cost minimizing

h. Profit maximizing

2 *When the Demand is Certain*

2.1 In the Tyres Inc. example Section 9.2,

  a. Expand Figure 9.2, adding rows for $N = 60, 67$, and 75. Compute all values of Q, Z_c, Z_o, and Z for the new values of N.

  b. Plot Z vs. N for all values of N in your table, and connect the points using a smooth curve.

  c. What conclusion(s) do you draw?

2.2 Ogol Inc. uses 1500 correctable typewriter ribbons a year; the ribbons cost $2.50 each. There is a fixed cost of $6 associated with each order placed. Ogol management has found that the carrying cost is roughly 20% per year, based on average dollar value of the ribbons in inventory.

  a. What is the carrying cost for *one* ribbon for 1 year?

  b. Make a table similar to Figure 9.2, and get all entries for $N = 1, 10, 100, 150$, and 300.

  c. From part b, plot Z vs. N.

  d. Using your plot from part c, what value of N do you judge to give the lowest Z?

  e. Compute the optimal value of N using the EOQ formula of Section 9.2. How does this compare with your result obtained in part d?

  f. Compute the value of Z corresponding to the N you determined graphically in part d. Also compute the value of Z corresponding to the optimal value of N found by you in part e. What is the amount of difference between these two values of Z? Would you say this amount is important to Ogol?

  g. Would you change the ordering policy if the price of ribbons is increased to $3 each? Why, or why not?

2.3 Refer to the Tyres Inc. example in Section 9.2. Suppose the demand has changed to 3600 per year, the cost of placing an order has increased to $25, and the carrying cost per year per unit is down to 30% of the cost of a tire.

  a. Find the economic ordering quantity Q^*.

  b. Find the lowest combined cost Z^*.

  c. Find the optimal frequency of ordering N^*.

Assume that Tyres Inc. deviates from the EOQ and orders 10% more frequently than the optimal frequency.

  d. What is Q under these conditions?

  e. What is the corresponding Z?

  f. What is the percentage increase in combined cost?

  g. If Tyres Inc. orders every week, what is the percentage increase in the combined cost?

2.4 Refer to the Tyres Inc. example in Section 9.2. Suppose the demand has changed to 5400 per year, the cost of placing an order has decreased to $15, and the carrying cost per year per unit is down to 20% of the cost of a tire.

  a. Find the economic ordering quantity Q^*.

  b. Find the lowest combined cost Z^*.

  c. Find the optimal frequency of ordering N^*.

Assume that Tyres Inc. deviates from the EOQ and orders 20% less frequently than the optimal frequency.

  d. What is Q under these conditions?

  e. What is the corresponding Z?

  f. What is the percentage increase in combined cost?

  g. If Tyres Inc. orders every week, what is the percentage increase in the combined cost?

2.5 Omni-Cook Ltd. uses 500 foam cartons a month to pack food processors for shipment. Each pallet of 50 cartons takes up to 2.5 square meters of floor space. Shipping takes place from a high-cost port through which the units are imported; the storage area for cartons is rented as needed (unused space is not paid for) at a cost of $40 per square meter per year. Omni's products have a high rate of return; Omni figures that any cash they have on hand can be invested in increasing their other businesses for a net return of 25%. Cartons cost $.5 each.

a. Find the unit carrying cost in dollars per carton per year (C_c).

b. There is an ongoing debate in the company as to the exact cost of each order. The president says that it is $10 per order, based on costing the time spent by purchasing agents in carrying out the tasks involved in placing an order. The chief purchasing agent says that the agents are on the payroll all the time whether or not they are placing orders. She says that the only costs which should be considered are the $4 variable costs of placing an order. Find the economic order quantity using both costs.

c. For each of the two preceding cases (ordering cost $4 and $10), compute the total cost Z of maintaining the inventory. (*Hint:* The formula for Z is given at the beginning of Section 9.2.) Find the difference between these two values of Z in both dollars and percentage.

d. The warehousing manager says that the record keeping isn't too good and that there could be 10% errors in either direction for the cost of storage of cartons. What effect will this error have on total costs? (*Hint:* The error in warehouse storage costs affects only part of the cost of carrying the goods.)

2.6 Fire Flint Inc., a large manufacturer of tires, has extra warehousing capacity available and also an excellent cash position. To take advantage of this situation, Fire Flint offers to Tyres Inc. (the wholesale distributor of tires discussed in Section 9.2) the following arrangement. Fire Flint will provide warehousing in its own plant free of charge to Tyres. Fire Flint guarantees 24-hour delivery but charges a fixed amount of $50 for each order. Fire Flint hopes that this arrangement will decrease the number of orders per year placed by Tyres and will increase the order quantity. This will make it possible for Fire Flint to make longer production runs and decrease manufacturing costs. Tyres Inc. is considering accepting this offer because a cost analysis shows that carrying costs will decrease to $5.00 per year per tire. Demand is still 2400 per year, but the previous ordering cost of $18.75 is increased by the fixed charge of $50 to $68.75. Find the EOQ, N, and Z.

2.7 Refer to Exercise 2.6. Due to rapidly changing wages, Fire Flint Inc. cannot guarantee that the fixed charge for each order will be $50. They advise Tyres Inc. that this charge could vary about 14% up or down. Would this uncertainty influence the values of EOQ, N, and Z? If so, by how much?

3. *Quantity Discounts and Price Breaks*

3.1 Tyres Inc. requires 500 rims per year for special orders. The rims are purchased from S. Mir at an estimated ordering cost of $20; the carrying cost for a year is $5 per rim. The first 100 units in any order must be taken at the list price of $40 each. However, a quantity in excess of 100 units can be purchased at a 5% reduction from list; a quantity in excess of 250 can be obtained at a 10% reduction. What is the economic order quantity Z?

3.2 Ten thousand blungits a year are required by the Farr Corporation. The quoted price has been $4 per blungit, but because of a reduction in business during a recession in the blungit market, the chief supplier has offered Farr a 6% discount for quantities over 5000 (in single-lot orders). Farr has determined that their purchase cost is $4 per order and that their inventory carrying cost is 25% of the average value of the inventory of blungits.

 a. Find the EOQ, the corresponding number of times a year the order is to be placed, and the total cost Z, assuming that no discount is offered.

 b. Assuming the 6% discount is in effect, find the EOQ, the corresponding number of times a year the order is to be placed, and the total cost Z.

 c. What is your recommendation to Farr?

 d. The supplier reduced the discount to 3% when business picked up. What is your recommendation to Farr under these conditions?

 e. Can you give Farr a rule which tells them at which discount to change their ordering policies? (*Hint:* Assume a discount rate D, and carry out the analysis symbolically. Find the value of D which causes the decision to change.)

3.3 Camac Palindromes Inc. buys 20,000 pretested palindromes a year. Ordering costs are $25 per order, and the carrying costs are figured at 20% of purchase cost. The price schedule follows:

QUANTITY ORDERED	UNIT PRICE
1–1999	$7.50
2000–4999	6.75
5000–7999	6.25
8000–19,999	6.00
20,000 and up	5.75

Find the economic order quantity.

3.4 Tripartite Inc. has received a new discount schedule from their major Japanese supplier, Ichinisan, for microprocessor chips. This schedule, showing three price breaks, is as follows:

QUANTITY ORDERED	UNIT PRICE
0–49	$.50
50–99	.45
100–299	.40
300 and up	.38

If the demand is 500 units per year, the carrying costs are based on a 25% rate, and the cost of purchase is $10, what is the EOQ?

3.5 D. Y. Buck Video Enterprises requires 5000 blank video tape cassettes a year. The estimated cost of placing an order is $20, and the annual carrying cost is estimated to be $4 per average unit in inventory for a year. Their supplier has offered them the following discount schedule: First 200 units must be purchased at the list price of $40 each, the next 300 units can be obtained for 4% off the regular price, and any additional units can be obtained at a discount of 7%.

 a. What is the quantity to be ordered which will give the lowest total cost?

 b. What is the total annual cost under your recommended ordering policy?

c. What is the annual savings obtained under your policy with this discount schedule as compared to a situation where the supplier offered no discounts at all?

3.6 Tai-Tai Perfumes purchases 8000 liters of musk oil per year from Shen-Shen Enterprises, a supplier in southeast Asia. Because each order placed involves letters of credit and other special work typical of international purchases, the order cost is established as $32 per order placed. Security requirements in storage lead to an annual cost of $10 per average liter in inventory. The current discount schedule for musk oil is as follows:

QUANTITY ORDERED	UNIT PRICE	DISCOUNT ALLOWED
1–400	$20	0%
401–800	19	5
801 and up	18	10

a. What is the quantity you would recommend that Tai-Tai purchase?
b. What is the total annual cost at your recommended purchase quantity?

4. *Uncertain Demand—Single Period System*

4.1 Norman Nibble, proprietor of the Shiquor Liquor Store, was discussing the issue of how many cases he should purchase on the coming Monday of the new fast-selling pina vodkada product with Sherry Sack, his assistant.

"The problem is that this stuff is completely free of any preservatives and any pina vodkada that is not sold at the end of the week (by Saturday night, that is) will spoil over Sunday, a complete loss. Fortunately, we are the only store in the area that will carry it, so if we can't supply a customer when they come to us, all we lose is the value of that sale. They have to come back to us if they want to buy again."

"Do you have any idea of how much demand you will get in a week?," asked Sack.

"Yes. We've been selling it at $60 a case (no broken cases allowed) for the past 50 weeks, and I've got data on the number of cases sold each week [see Exhibit I]. Not bad, when you consider that we pay the distributor $42 per case."

Analyze this situation as a one-period model, and tell Norman what quantity he should purchase at the start of a week.

EXHIBIT I

DEMAND PER WEEK (CASES)	NUMBER OF WEEKS THIS DEMAND RECORDED
50	5
51	15
52	25
53	5

4.2 Dick Neer's Record Shoppe orders records for its advance-sale market each month. The purchase cost of a record is $6; they sell them at $7.30. Records not sold at the end of the month are taken back by the supplier at $5. The monthly demand has been shown to be as follows:

DEMAND (RECORDS PER MONTH)	PROBABILITY OF THIS DEMAND
0–60	.01
61–90	.04
91–120	.20
121–150	.50
151–180	.20
181–210	.04
211 and more	.01

a. How many records should they order each month?
b. If they follow your recommendation, what is the probability of a stockout?
c. If the manufacturer lowered the amount paid for records taken back to $2, what is the new order quantity which Neer's should use?

4.3 The Grim Corporation sells reapers to farmers. Reapers cost $60,000 and sell for $85,000 each. Reapers not sold at the end of the growing season usually bring $45,000. The probability distribution of demand during the season has been as follows:

NUMBER DEMANDED	PROBABILITY THIS NUMBER DEMANDED
0	.10
1	.10
2	.25
3	.25
4	.15
5	.10
6	.05

How many reapers should Grim stock at the start of each season?

5. *Uncertain Demand—Multiperiod System*

5.1 Refer to the Fastcraft Inc. example in Section 9.5. Assume that the characteristics of this inventory situation are as stated:

yearly demand = 600 units

yearly inventory carrying cost = $20/unit

setup cost = $1500

stockout cost = $40/unit

lead time = 1 month

The demand function is as given in Figure 9.10. Following the two-step procedure given in this text, calculate the reorder point and safety stock, supplying the following:
a. The decision tree for determining the best safety stock level, similar to Figure 9.8.
b. The reorder point in units
c. The optimal reorder quantity in units
d. The combined cost for your solution

5.2 Refer to the Fastcraft Inc. example in Section 9.5. Assume that the characteristics of this inventory situation are as stated:

yearly inventory carrying cost = $10/unit

setup cost = $2000

stockout cost = $20/unit

lead time = 1 month

The demand function is as given in Figure 9.6. Following the two-step procedure given in this text, calculate the reorder point and safety stock, supplying the following:
   a. The decision tree to determine the best safety stock level, similar to Figure 9.8
   b. The reorder point in units
   c. The optimal reorder quantity in units
   d. The combined cost for your solution

5.4 L&R Foot is a chain of stores selling jogging shoes. The annual demand is approximately uniform; records show that for any 6-week period demand is uniformly distributed between 3600 and 4800 pairs. The annual inventory cost to carry a pair of shoes is $1.50. The setup cost for manufacturing a lot is $2000. The production lead time is 6 weeks, and the stores are open every week of the year. The manager of the chain feels that for purposes of analysis he can reasonably think in terms of a safety stock which is integral multiples of 100 (2200, 2300, etc.) and that the same 100-unit breakdown can be used in figuring probabilities. Since joggers want to run in their shoes immediately, a stockout means a lost sale; the lost profit on each stockout is $5. Determine
   a. The reorder point in units
   b. The optimal reorder quantity in units
   c. The combined cost for your solution

5.5 In Section 9.5, the first steps are given for solving the Fastcraft Inc. inventory situation when the probability distribution of the lead-time demand is normal. Using the values assigned in the text, complete the example, finding the safety stock, the reorder point, and the combined cost for your solution.

6. *When the Stockout Cost Is Not Known*

6.1 L&R Foot wants a stockout probability less than .05 and does not want to assign a stockout cost because they feel that there is more at stake than the profit on the one sale. What safety stock should they keep?

6.2 What safety stock should be maintained for Fastcraft Inc. as modified in Exercise 5.2 for
   a. A probability of stockout less than .1?
   b. A probability of stockout less than .2?

7. *Inventory Systems for Dependent Demand*

7.1 Refer to Figure 9.14, the product structure for the skateboard assembly. Suppose that a design change has been made to have three wheels on the truck of each wheel subassembly. Redraw the product structure diagram of Figure 9.14 accordingly.

7.2 Refer to Figure 9.14, the product structure for the skateboard assembly. Suppose that a design change has been made to break the fiberglass board into two component parts called upper decorative layer and base layer. Redraw the product structure diagram of Figure 9.14 accordingly.

7.3 Make a product structure like Figure 9.14 for the following:
  a. Spiral notebook
  b. Wooden pencil
  c. Book
  d. Chair

7.4 For each of the product structures you made in Exercise 7.3 find the parent-child ratio for each component.

7.5 Refer to Figure 9.15. Suppose that the number of skateboard assemblies required in week 8 is 150. Make the revised version of Figure 9.15.

7.6 Refer to Figure 9.15. Suppose that the number of skateboard assemblies required in week 8 is 100 but that the lead time to manufacture the assembly is reduced to 1 week. Make the revised version of Figure 9.15.

7.7 Refer to Figure 9.15. Suppose that the number of skateboard assemblies required in week 8 is 150 and that the lead time for fiberglass boards is 2 weeks, the lead time for wheel assemblies is 1 week, and the lead time for wheels is 2 weeks. Make the revised version of Figure 9.15.

7.8 Refer to Figures 9.16a and b. Suppose that the on-hand rows are as shown, but that the gross requirement is changed to 50 skateboard assemblies for week 8, 100 for week 9, 50 for week 10, 0 for week 11, and 60 for week 12. Make the new version of Figure 9.16b which can be used to meet this revised master production schedule.

7.9 Refer to Figures 9.16a and b. Suppose that the on-hand rows are as shown but that the gross requirement is changed to 50 skateboard assemblies per week for weeks 8–12 inclusive. Make the new version of Figure 9.16b which can be used to meet this revised master production schedule.

7.10 Refer to Figures 9.16a and b. Suppose that the first-week on-hand row for each item is as shown below but that the gross requirement for skateboard assemblies is unchanged. Make the new version of Figure 9.16b which can be used to meet this revised master production schedule.

ROW NO.	ITEM DESCRIPTION	ON-HAND FIRST WEEK
1.	Skateboard assembly	50
2.	Fiberglass board	25
3.	Wheel subassembly	90
4.	Truck	0
5.	Wheels	100

7.11 JDS MicroComputers makes a model 432 personal computer by assembling subassemblies purchased from vendors. The model 432 personal computer includes a detachable keyboard and a video monitor. There is a separate assembly, the MQ, which houses a disk drive assembly in which there are two disk drives, purchased as subassemblies—the disk drive assembly serves as their housing and carries essential wiring. The MQ also contains the "computer," the CPU, storage, communications capabilities, etc., which come from a vendor as a unit. If all components are ready MQ can be considered ready—that is the lead time is negligible.
  a. Make the product structure for the model 432, showing quantities for the parent-child relationships.
  b. If no completed model 432s are on hand but there are 50 detachable keyboards (lead time 2 weeks), 100 video monitors (lead time 8 weeks), 400 disk drive subassemblies (lead time 6 weeks), and no disk drive assembly units (lead time 4 weeks) on hand at the start of current production, make a schedule similar to Figure 9.16 to meet

the following master production schedule:

WEEK NO.	GROSS REQUIREMENT
9	250
10	850
11	600
12	0
13	1200
14	1200

(Assembling the MQ requires negligible lead time.)

8. *United States Air Force Saves with Project EOQ: A Successful Application*

8.1 Why do you think rule 2, the volume ordered must cover demand for at least 3 months, is applied to procurements for the Air Force?

8.2 The rule of Figure 9.17 can be shown in the form of a two-dimensional plot. Make D_1 the horizontal axis and Q^* the vertical axis.
   a. Mark out the areas corresponding to categories 1–5.
   b. Do you feel that the rules could be more clearly stated to eliminate a possible source of ambiguity which your figure reveals?

CHAPTER EXERCISES AND DISCUSSION QUESTIONS

C.1 Give examples of at least five types of physical goods which you know to be inventoried in the real world. Why are they inventoried?

C.2 Give examples of at least five types of physical goods which you know not to be inventoried in the real world. Why are they not inventoried? (*Hint:* Don't limit your thinking to manufacturing situations.)

C.3 Sometimes we use the concepts of inventory analysis to deal with services. What would be "inventoried" in the following types of services:
   a. Banks
   b. Barber shops
   c. Concerts
   d. CPA firm
   e. Group of medical practitioners
   f. Taxicab company

C.4 Sometimes no one person is charged with the task of minimizing the total inventory costs. Each operating function tries to meet the goals set for it.
   a. Which inventory cost would the financial department try to minimize?
   b. Which inventory cost would the purchasing department try to minimize?
   c. Which inventory cost would the production department try to minimize?
   d. Which inventory cost would the marketing department try to minimize?
   e. Which inventory cost would the sales department try to minimize?

C.5 Make a listing of the various types of inventory control systems described in this chapter, and indicate where you would apply each based on its special characteristics.

C.6 In Section 9.2 the formula is derived for getting the EOQ when a constant production of the needed units needs to be maintained. For the case of an annual demand of 20,000 units, a daily production rate of 200 units for 250 working days per year, a production setup charge of $200, and an annual carrying cost of $1 per unit with a unit cost of $15, find the EOQ. If the lead time is 10 days, what is the reorder point? What is the frequency of ordering?

C.7 Based on studies by the industrial engineering department, a company has established that the daily need for R72 units is normally distributed with a mean of 120 and standard deviation of 14. The lead time is one day. The cost of placing an order is $20, carrying costs are $1 per unit per year, and it is desired to maintain a 95% service level (5% probability of stockout).

    a. What is the EOQ?
    b. What is the reorder point?

C.8 In several of the exercises for this chapter you were asked to perform a sensitivity analysis to determine how much the total combined costs changed when the value ordered was not the EOQ. As a consequence of your answers to these exercises, what can you say about the reasons more organizations do not use EOQ analysis in performing their purchasing?

C.9 In the first paragraph of this chapter, an example is given of an inventory problem in a brewery. The comments of the individuals in charge of production, marketing, and finance are given in this paragraph. The following is a list of situations in which inventory problems can arise. Give your version of the comments that would be given by individuals in production, marketing, and finance in the following situations:

    a. A factory making cars
    b. A distributor of video cassette recorders

In the following situations, there is no "production" as such. Instead of the comment by the "production" manager, give the comments of the "buyer" who selects and orders goods.

    c. A department store
    d. A gas station

10

Linear Programming

A central problem of quantitative managerial decision making is the optimum allocation of limited resources among various alternatives. One of the most powerful mathematical techniques of optimization is linear programming and its extensions of mathematical programming. Modern computers make it possible to solve practical problems with many thousands of constraints and unknowns. **Linear programming** has been very successful in supporting managerial decision making, both in the private and public sectors of our society, and it penetrates practically all aspects of quantitative decision making. In this and the following three chapters you will learn what linear and mathematical programming is, how it is to be used, and its scope and limitations. You will learn how to formulate models and solve them using both manual and computer-based approaches.

10.1 HOW TO BUILD A LINEAR PROGRAMMING MODEL

In Chapter 1 we presented general principles of model building and of the scientific method. These principles of course apply to building a linear programming model, and therefore it is suggested that you review Sections 1.4 and 1.5. Here we simply repeat for your guidance the sixth statement of the summary of Chapter 1: To quantitatively analyze a management decision problem, you must (1) determine the alternatives, (2) establish the consequences for each alternative, (3) define the criterion to be used, (4) evaluate the alternatives in terms of the criterion, and (5) choose an acceptable or perhaps optimum alternative in terms of the criterion.

We must stress that model building is more an art than a science and that there are no hard and fast rules which will assure success when building a model. You will learn how to master and apply the principles of model building via examples and practice. Our approach is to present model building via case studies.

Belchfire Motors is manufacturing rods, rings, and pistons for automobiles. The daily production rate is 7800 rods, 5000 rings, and 1000 pistons.

The management of Belchfire Motors wants to know whether this is the best production schedule, and if not, how the schedule can be improved. Naturally, to make a quantitative analysis of this situation, we need to have a better understanding of the problems and more data.

In Figure 10.1a some of the given constants of the production process are given. Note that only limited resources of labor, steel, and nickel are available to Belchfire. Specifically, there are 45,000 units of labor, 20,000 units of steel, and 50,000 units of nickel available. (We do not specify how the units are measured, whether labor is measured in hours or minutes, steel in tons or pounds, and so on.) Figure 10.1a shows how much resource is required to manufacture each of the rods, rings, and pistons. For example, as shown in the first row of the second column, it takes five units of labor to produce one ring.

The bottom row shows the profit contribution of each rod, ring, and piston.

We can verify that the production schedule of Belchfire satisfies the **constraints**. Namely, labor utilization is given by

$$2 \times 7800 + 5 \times 5000 + 4 \times 1100 = 45,000$$

and steel utilization by

$$7800 + 2 \times 5000 + 2 \times 1100 = 20,000$$

The nickel utilization is

$$3 \times 7800 + 3 \times 5000 + 3 \times 1100 = 41,700$$

where indeed $41,700 < 50,000$. This means that not all resources of nickel are used, and in fact there is a surplus of $50,000 - 41,700 = 8300$ units. The **payoff**, the profit contribution is

$$Z = .15 \times 7800 + .08 \times 5000 + .12 \times 1100 = \$1702$$

We know from the problem statement that the **criterion** of optimization is to maximize the profit contribution. So now we need to examine the alternatives available to Belchfire.

RESOURCES	RODS	RINGS	PISTONS	CONSTRAINTS
Labor	2	5	4	45,000
Steel	1	2	2	20,000
Nickel	3	3	3	50,000
Unit profit contribution per objective function	15¢	8¢	12¢	

FIGURE 10.1a Initial information given on Belchfire Motors.

What Are the Alternatives?

Due to the fact we allow fractional solutions to problems, there will be infinitely many alternatives available to Belchfire. Furthermore, a more detailed analysis of the production processes reveals that in addition to the processes shown in Figure 10.1a, some further possibilities are available.

As shown in Figure 10.1b, there are three different ways that rings can be manufactured. The profit contribution of the first process is the 8 cents also shown in Figure 10.1a, but there are two other possibilities, providing profit contributions of 3 and 6 cents, respectively. Note that resource requirements for these alternates are different.

Pistons can be manufactured by two different processes, each providing different profit contributions and requiring different resources.

Note now that there are six unknowns or variables in the problem: how many rods to make, how many rings to make by each of the three processes, and how many pistons to make by each of the two processes.

So now we have all the constants, all the variables, and all the constraints of the problem and can proceed to develop our mathematical model.

Developing the Model

To develop the linear programming model, we need notation for the variables. It is customary in linear programming to designate the variables by x_1, x_2, and so on. As shown in Figure 10.1b, the unknowns of our problem are therefore $x_1, x_2, \ldots, x_6$. Note that the production process Belchfire is currently using is represented by the following solution:

$$Z = \$1702$$
$$x_1 = 7800$$
$$x_2 = 5000.0$$
$$x_3 = 0$$
$$x_4 = 0$$
$$x_5 = 1100$$
$$x_6 = 0$$

So now we are ready to develop our model. The payoff function, when all six production processes are included, is given by

$$Z = .15x_1 + .08x_2 + .03x_3 + .06x_4 + .12x_5 + .15x_6$$

The labor constraint is

$$2x_1 + 5x_2 + 6x_3 + 4x_4 + 4x_5 + 5x_6 \leq 45{,}000$$

The steel constraint is

$$1x_1 + 2x_2 + 1x_3 + 3x_4 + 2x_5 + 4x_6 \leq 20{,}000$$

The nickel constraint is

$$3x_1 + 3x_2 + 2x_3 + 1x_4 + 3x_5 + 2x_6 \leq 50{,}000$$

RESOURCES	RODS		RINGS		PISTONS		CONSTRAINTS
	x_1	x_2	x_3	x_4	x_5	x_6	
Labor	2	5	6	4	4	5	$\leq 45,000$
Steel	1	2	1	3	2	4	$\leq 20,000$
Nickel	3	3	2	1	3	2	$\leq 50,000$
Unit profit contribution per objective function	15¢	8¢	3¢	6¢	12¢	15¢	Maximize

FIGURE 10.1b Complete information given for solving the resource allocation problem of Belchfire Motors.

For the sake of completeness, we should also state that all the unknowns must be positive or zero (nonnegative). However, in all linear programming problems, unless stated otherwise, the variables are automatically assumed to be nonnegative, and therefore we shall not list those inequalities.

Now we have our linear programming model with six unknowns and three constraints.

Note that in all our relationships the unknowns appear to the first power, that is, the relationships are **linear**. There are no such terms as x_1^2, x_4^3, x_2/x_5, $\sqrt{x_3}$, x_1x_6, and so on.

> In a linear programming problem all the relationships, including the **objective function**, must be linear.

Solution to the Problem

In our discussion we are now concentrating on building models and not on solving them. Therefore, we simply state that as a result of the analysis, it is found that the optimum solution to the problem, that is, the one which provides the highest profit contribution, is

$$x_1^* = 16,000$$
$$x_2^* = 0$$
$$x_3^* = 0$$
$$x_4^* = 0$$
$$x_5^* = 0$$
$$x_6^* = 1000$$

The maximum profit contribution is given by

$$Z^* = .15 \times 16,000 + .15 \times 1000 = \$2550$$

Note that this solution is $\$2550 - \$1702 = \$848$, better than the current solution Belchfire is using, and also that the solution implies making 16,000 rods and 1000 pistons by the second process. We can verify that the constraints are met:

$$\text{labor used} = 2 \times 16{,}000 + 5 \times 1000 = 37{,}000 < 45{,}000$$
$$\text{steel used} = 16{,}000 + 4 \times 1000 = 20{,}000$$
$$\text{nickel used} = 3 \times 16{,}000 + 2 \times 1000 = 50{,}000$$

Note that the optimum solution uses all the steel and nickel but *not* all the labor.

Some resources may not be utilized in the optimum solution of a problem.

You may be wondering about the surplus of $45{,}000 - 37{,}000 = 8000$ hours of labor. What does this mean in a practical situation? Note that the model assumes that (1) there is a constraint of 45,000 hours of labor, and (2) surplus labor has no value. In practice this may be true because, for instance, a worker skilled on the grinder may not be able to run another machine. However, if surplus labor does have a value, the model would have to be modified. Our solution is optimum only for the model concerned. In practice, to get an optimum solution to a situation, we may have to do more work, as shown by what follows.

Market Considerations

When the management of Belchfire is presented with the solution, they express dissatisfaction. They of course like the $848.00 improvement in profit contribution, but they don't like the fact that only rods and pistons are produced. The Vice-President of Marketing says that Belchfire must provide a more complete variety of automotive parts to satisfy customers. Therefore, after some discussion, the management specifies that a solution to the production scheduling process is acceptable only if at least 5000 rods are manufactured. Now we have a new constraint:

$$1x_1 \geq 5000$$

Management wants at least 2000 rings but does not care by which process the rings are manufactured. They just want the total to be at least 2000, and so we have the new constraint

$$1x_2 + 1x_3 + 1x_4 \geq 2000$$

Management wants at least 1600 pistons:

$$1x_5 + 1x_6 \geq 1600$$

Now we have a new model for the problem. We still have six unknowns, but we have the original three constraints and three new ones, a total of six constraints and the original objective function.

As we are not discussing here how to obtain solutions to problems, we simply state the optimum solution:

$$x_1^* = 13800$$
$$x_2^* = 200$$

$$x_3^* = 1400$$
$$x_4^* = 400$$
$$x_5^* = 1600$$
$$x_6^* = 0$$

The profit is

$$Z^* = .15 \times 13{,}800 + .08 \times 200 + .03 \times 1400$$

$$+ .06 \times 400 + .12 \times 1600 = 2344$$

This is $2550 − $2344 = $206 less than the optimum solution. However, it is better than the current solution by the amount $2344 − $1702 = $642.

We can now compute the resources utilized and the number of products made:

labor used
$$2 \times 13800 + 5 \times 200 + 6 \times 1400 + 4 \times 400 + 4 \times 1600 = 45000$$
steel used
$$13800 + 2 \times 200 + 1400 + 3 \times 400 + 2 \times 1600 = 20000$$
nickel used
$$3 \times 13800 + 3 \times 200 + 2 \times 1400 + 400 + 3 \times 1600 = 50000$$
rods made
$$13800 = 13800$$
rings made
$$200 + 1400 + 400 = 2000$$
pistons made
$$1600 = 1600$$

Note that all resources are fully utilized and also that some rings are manufactured by the second and third production processes, each with profit contributions of 3 and 6 cents, respectively, this notwithstanding the fact that the first process of manufacturing rings produces an 8-cent profit contribution.

A variable providing the highest contribution may not be utilized in the optimum solution of a problem.

Similarly, note that pistons are manufactured by the first process with the profit contribution of 12 cents, and not by the second process, which has the higher profit contribution of 15 cents.

The Four Conditions of a Linear Programming Problem

1. *All relationships must be linear.* Thus, terms such as x_2^2, $\sqrt[3]{x_5}$, x_3^5, x_3/x_2, $\log x_5$, and so on cannot occur. Linearity also implies proportionality, as, for example, if it takes three men to produce one unit, it is assumed that six men can produce two units or that one man can produce one-third of a unit.

2. *Fractional solutions are allowed.* So far all our answers are whole numbers, but it can easily happen, for instance, that the answer is 14,252.356271 pistons are to be made. Naturally in practice you will round off and make 14,252 pistons.

However, if the problem is, for example, whether to manufacture one, two, or three ships, linear programming may not give the answer because it makes no sense to manufacture 2.501 ships. Linear programming applies only when the variables are allowed to be **continuous**.

3. *The constants are known in a deterministic manner.* For example, if the probability is 1/2 that the profit contribution is 15 cents and 1/2 that it is 20 cents, linear programming cannot give an answer. To put it another way, the value of each of the constants is assigned with certainty, that is, with the probability of 1, and no uncertainty is allowed.

4. *A single payoff is maximized or minimized.* It is not possible to maximize profits, sales, and consumer satisfaction and so on at the same time. When management specifies several goals or conflicting goals, techniques of linear programming can be applied only if priorities or compromises among payoffs are developed. (Discussion of this approach is postponed to Chapter 14.)

In a resource allocation problem, when some of these conditions do not hold, we speak of extensions of linear programming, that is, nonlinear programming. The term **mathematical programming** includes all programming problems, linear or nonlinear.

10.2 ILLUSTRATIONS OF LINEAR PROGRAMMING PROBLEMS

In this section we present a series of unrelated illustrations of linear programming, so you can get an impression of the all-encompassing scope of this technique of resource allocation. In each illustration we describe the problem and develop the model. Solutions to the problems are postponed for later discussion.

The Nutrition Problem

The Abbey Chemical Corporation makes four kinds of vitamin pills. The first type of pill contains five units of vitamin C (ascorbic acid), three units of B_{12}, and one unit of B_1 (thiamine). To maintain generality, we shall simply refer to these vitamins as V_1, V_2, and V_3. In Figure 10.2 we also show the vitamin content of the second, third, and fourth kinds of pills. Suppose that Abbey Chemical makes pills for a hospital where a minimum requirement for each type of vitamin is specified: at least 100 units of V_1, 80 units of V_2, and 120 units of V_3. How many pills of each type should be made to minimize the total cost?

Designate by x_1, x_2, x_3, and x_4, respectively, the number of pills (see Figure 10.2). To meet the constraints, we must have

$$5x_1 + 2x_2 + 3x_3 + 2x_4 \geq 100$$

$$3x_1 + 5x_2 + 2x_3 + 1x_4 \geq 80$$

$$1x_1 + 3x_2 + 2x_3 + 6x_4 \geq 120$$

		VITAMIN PILLS				Requirements (Units)
		Quantity Produced				
		x_1	x_2	x_3	x_4	
Types of Vitamins	V_1	5	2	3	2	≥ 100
	V_2	3	5	2	1	≥ 80
	V_3	1	3	2	6	≥ 120
	Unit cost	40¢	50¢	35¢	40¢	Minimize

FIGURE 10.2 Information given for solving the resource allocation problem of the Abbey Chemical Corporation.

For example, producing 120 of pill 1 and no other pill,

$$x_1 = 120 \qquad x_2 = x_3 = x_4 = 0$$

is a production schedule meeting the constraints, that is, a **feasible solution** to the problem. Is this the lowest cost schedule? On the bottom line of Figure 10.2 unit costs in cents are shown for each type of pill. We must minimize the objective function Z, representing the combined cost:

$$Z = .40x_1 + .50x_2 + .35x_3 + .40x_4$$

But producing 120 of pill 1 at a cost of $48.00 is not the best. For example, you can easily verify that making 30 of pill 1 and 30 of pill 2 meets the constraints at a cost of $27.00.

This is a linear programming problem; all the relationships are linear, and fractional solutions are allowed. The optimum solution can be obtained by linear programming, and it is

$$Z^* = \$13.67$$
$$x_1^* = 11.56$$
$$x_2^* = 6.06$$
$$x_3^* = 0$$
$$x_4^* = 15.05$$

Blending of Gasolines

The La Brea Oil Company obtains two types of blending stock from an oil refinery and blends these into aviation gasoline and motor gasoline. Type 1 crude oil has a high octane rating of 104 and is available to the extent of 45,000 barrels. Type 2 crude oil has a lower octane rating of 94 and is available to the extent of 100,000 barrels. There is a demand for up to 35,000 barrels of aviation gasoline with an octane rating of at least 102. Motor gasoline can be sold in any amount, and the octane rating must be at least 96. The profit contribution is $8.50 on each barrel of aviation gasoline and $6.50 on each barrel of motor gasoline. The problem is to compute how much crude oil should be allocated to each of the products.

Note that type 1 crude can be sold either as aviation or motor gasoline, but type 2 crude cannot even be sold as motor gasoline because the octane rating is too low. So the company sells 35,000 barrels of crude 1 as aviation gasoline, blends the rest of the 10,000 barrels with 40,000 barrels of crude 2, and realizes a profit contribution of

$$8.50 \times 35,000 + 6.50 \times 50,000 = \$622,500$$

Does this allocation provide adequate octane ratings and the best profit?

Before we can proceed with the problem, we must know how to compute the octane rating when stocks are blended. For example, take 10,000 barrels of the 104 octane crude and 40,000 barrels of the 94 octane crude. The octane rating of the resulting blend is computed by the *weighted mean* of the two blends:

$$\frac{104 \times 10,000 + 94 \times 40,000}{10,000 + 40,000} = 96$$

Thus the blend meets the octane rating for motor gasoline, and of course crude 1 not only meets the aviation gasoline rating but exceeds it. This raises the question of whether a different allocation scheme may meet the requirements and provide a higher profit contribution. So let us proceed to formulate a linear programming model for the problem.

Designate the respective allocations as shown in Figure 10.3 by x_1, x_2, x_3, and x_4. Then

$$x_1 + x_3 \leq 45,000$$
$$x_2 + x_4 \leq 100,000$$
$$x_1 + x_2 \leq 35,000$$

To satisfy the octane rating, we must have

$$\frac{104x_1 + 94x_2}{x_1 + x_2} \geq 102$$

$$\frac{104x_3 + 94x_4}{x_3 + x_4} \geq 96$$

Multiply both sides of the inequalities by $x_1 + x_2$ and $x_3 + x_4$, respectively:

$$104x_1 + 94x_2 \geq 102(x_1 + x_2)$$
$$104x_3 + 94x_4 \geq 96(x_3 + x_4)$$

Carry out the multiplications, and move all terms to the left side:

$$(104 - 102)x_1 + (94 - 102)x_2 \geq 0$$
$$(104 - 96)x_3 + (94 - 96)x_4 \geq 0$$

	CRUDE GASOLINES	
	1 **High-Octane** **Rating** **104**	**2** **Low-Octane** **Rating** **94**
Aviation fuel: octane rating 102	x_1	x_2	$\leq 35,000$
Motor fuel: octane rating 96	x_3	x_4	No constraint
	$\leq 45,000$	$\leq 100,000$

FIGURE 10.3 Information given for solving the resource allocation problem of the La Brea Oil Company.

Carry out the subtractions:

$$2x_1 - 8x_2 \geq 0$$

$$8x_3 - 2x_4 \geq 0$$

In summary the constraints are

$$
\begin{aligned}
x_1 \quad\quad\ +x_3 \quad\quad &\leq 45,000 \\
x_2 \quad\quad\ + x_4 &\leq 100,000 \\
x_1 \ + \ x_2 \quad\quad\ &\leq 35,000 \\
2x_1 \ -8x_2 \quad\quad\ &\geq 0 \\
8x_3 \ -2x_4 &\geq 0
\end{aligned}
$$

The profit contribution is

$$Z = 8.5x_1 + 8.5x_2 + 6.5x_3 + 6.5x_4$$

Thus this is a linear programming problem; all the relationships are linear, and fractional solutions are admitted. The optimum solution is

$$
\begin{aligned}
Z^* &= \$995,833.33 \\
x_1^* &= 21,333.33 \\
x_2^* &= 5333.33 \\
x_3^* &= 23,666.67 \\
x_4^* &= 94,666.67
\end{aligned}
$$

A Transportation Problem

Transamerican Manufacturing, a firm which has factories in Denver, Houston, and Miami, ships goods to Seattle, Los Angeles, Dallas, Chicago, and New York. Figure 10.4(a) shows the geography of the problem and Figure 10.4(b) provides a **network** representation, because shipments must follow the lines shown. Figure 10.5 shows next month's shipping plan. Is this the lowest-cost plan?

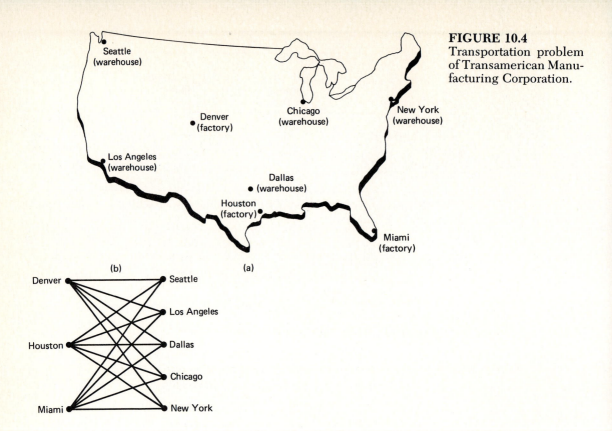

FIGURE 10.4 Transportation problem of Transamerican Manufacturing Corporation.

Note in Figure 10.5 that production capacities in Denver, Houston, and Miami are, respectively, 800, 500, and 1100 units, and demand at Seattle, Los Angeles, Dallas, Chicago, and New York is 120, 350, 590, 410, and 930 units. Unit transportation costs are also shown in Figure 10.6. The problem is to determine quantities to be shipped so that requirements are met and total transportation cost is lowest.

To formulate this linear programming problem, designate the

FROM FACTORIES	TO WAREHOUSES					PRODUCTION CAPACITIES
	Seattle	Los Angeles	Dallas	Chicago	New York	
Denver	120	350	330			800
Houston			260	240		500
Miami				170	930	1100
Demand	120	350	590	410	930	2400

FIGURE 10.5 Shipping plan for the Transamerican Manufacturing Corporation. The quantities listed show the number of units to be shipped. For example, 350 units will be shipped from Denver to Los Angeles.

FROM FACTORIES	Seattle	Los Angeles	Dallas	Chicago	New York	PRODUCTION CAPACITIES
			TO WAREHOUSES			
Denver	$150	$115	$ 80	$100	$185	800
Houston	230	155	105	110	165	500
Miami	340	270	130	135	135	1100
Demand	120	350	590	410	930	2400

FIGURE 10.6 Unit transportation costs, demand, and production capacities for the Transamerican Manufacturing Corporation.

quantities shipped by the notation listed in Figure 10.7a. For example, x_9 designates the quantity to be shipped from Houston (factory 2) to Chicago (warehouse 4). Note that there are in total 15 variables in the problem. Production capacity in each of the three cities is given, so we have the three constraints

$$
\begin{aligned}
x_1 + x_2 + x_3 + x_4 + x_5 &= 800 \\
x_6 + x_7 + x_8 + x_9 + x_{10} &= 500 \\
x_{11} + x_{12} + x_{13} + x_{14} + x_{15} &= 1100
\end{aligned}
$$

implying a total production capacity of 2400 units. Demand in each of the five warehouses provides five more constraints:

$$
\begin{aligned}
x_1 + x_6 + x_{11} &= 120 \\
x_2 + x_7 + x_{12} &= 350 \\
x_3 + x_8 + x_{13} &= 590 \\
x_4 + x_9 + x_{14} &= 410 \\
x_5 + x_{10} + x_{15} &= 930
\end{aligned}
$$

implying a total of 2400 units. The problem is to minimize total transportation costs,

$$
\begin{aligned}
Z = {}& 150x_1 + 115x_2 + 80x_3 + 100x_4 + 185x_5 \\
& + 230x_6 + 155x_7 + 105x_8 + 110x_9 + 165x_{10} \\
& + 340x_{11} + 270x_{12} + 130x_{13} + 135x_{14} + 135x_{15}
\end{aligned}
$$

under the given eight constraints.

	FROM FACTORIES	1 Seattle	2 Los Angeles	3 Dallas	4 Chicago	5 New York	PRODUCTION CAPACITIES
				TO WAREHOUSES			
1.	Denver	x_1	x_2	x_3	x_4	x_5	= 800
2.	Houston	x_6	x_7	x_8	x_9	x_{10}	= 500
3.	Miami	x_{11}	x_{12}	x_{13}	x_{14}	x_{15}	= 1100
	Demand	120	350	590	410	930	2400

FIGURE 10.7a Notation introduced to establish a mathematical model for the Transamerican Manufacturing Corporation.

The optimum solution to the problem is shown in Figure 10.7b.

The transportation problem and its generalizations are one of the most successful areas of linear programming, and all of Chapter 12 is devoted to this subject.

A Problem in Production and Inventory Control

Concrete Construction Corp. is making plans for the production of bricks for the coming fiscal year. Quarterly requirements are 50, 50, 150, and 150 million bricks, a total of 400 million. The production plan is to make 100 million bricks in each quarter, starting with no initial inventory of bricks. The corporation wishes to end up with no final inventory. Is this the best production schedule?

To simplify, from now on we shall drop the word million and simply talk about the requirement of 50, 50, 150, and 150 bricks. Production costs do not change within the year, and the total production cost is fixed. Thus inventory carrying costs will decide how to choose the best production schedule.

Why not eliminate inventory costs by making 50, 50, 150, and 150 bricks? It turns out that there is a limit to how many bricks Concrete Construction can manufacture in a quarter; this constraint is 125 bricks per quarter.

Figure 10.8 gives a graphic representation of the cumulative production schedule and requirements. In the first quarter 100 bricks are made, 50 are used, and there is an inventory of 50 bricks. In the second quarter another 100 are made, 50 are used, and there is an inventory of 100 bricks. In the third quarter another 100 are made, 150 are used, and there is an inventory of 50. Finally, in the fourth quarter 100 are made, 150 are used, and no inventory is left. Inventory carrying costs are $60 per brick per year, or $15 per brick per quarter. So the inventory carrying cost is

$$15 \times (50 + 100 + 50 + 0) = \$3000$$

Now introduce notation to establish the linear programming model.

		TO WAREHOUSES					
		1	2	3	4	5	
FROM FACTORIES		Seattle	Los Angeles	Dallas	Chicago	New York	PRODUCTION CAPACITIES
1.	Denver	120	350	330	0	0	= 800
2.	Houston	0	0	260	240	0	= 500
3.	Miami	0	0	0	170	930	= 1100
	Demand	120	350	590	410	930	2400

FIGURE 10.7b Optimum solution to the transportation problem of the Transamerican Manufacturing Corporation. The lowest transportation cost is $286,850.

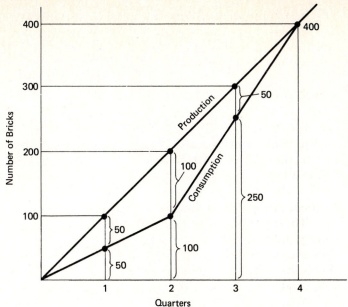

FIGURE 10.8
Graphic repre-
sentation of the
cumulative pro-
duction schedule
and require-
ments for Con-
crete Construc-
tion Corporation.
The difference
between the two
equals the inven-
tory.

Designate by x_1, x_2, x_3, and x_4 the quantity produced in each quarter. We must have

$$x_1 \leq 125$$
$$x_2 \leq 125$$
$$x_3 \leq 125$$
$$x_4 \leq 125$$

Designate the cumulative production by y_1, y_2, y_3, and y_4*:

$$y_1 = x_1$$
$$y_2 = x_1 + x_2$$
$$y_3 = x_1 + x_2 + x_3$$
$$y_4 = x_1 + x_2 + x_3 + x_4$$

The production requirements must be met:

$$y_1 \geq 50$$
$$y_2 \geq 100$$
$$y_3 \geq 250$$
$$y_4 = 400$$

Thus the following additional four constraints hold:

$$x_1 \geq 50$$
$$x_1 + x_2 \geq 100$$
$$x_1 + x_2 + x_3 \geq 250$$
$$x_1 + x_2 + x_3 + x_4 = 400$$

---

* We depart from our convention of designating all the unknowns by xs.

The problem is to minimize the total inventory cost:

$$Z = 15[(y_1 - 50) + (y_2 - 100) + (y_3 - 250)]$$
$$= 15(y_1 + y_2 + y_3) - 6000$$
$$= 15[x_1 + (x_1 + x_2) + (x_1 + x_2 + x_3)] - 6000$$

or

$$Z = 45x_1 + 30x_2 + 15x_3 - 6000$$

The constant 6000 has no influence on the optimum values of x_1, x_2, and x_3, and therefore the problem reduces to minimization of

$$45x_1 + 30x_2 + 15x_3$$

Note that y_1, y_2, y_3, y_4 and x_4 do not enter into the objective function. The optimum solution to the problem is

$$Z^* = \$1125$$
$$x_1^* = 50$$
$$x_2^* = 100$$
$$x_3^* = 125$$
$$x_4^* = 125$$

This is $\$3000 - \$1125 = \$1875$ less than the production schedule of making 100 bricks each quarter.

When Overtime Production Is Possible

To make the problem more realistic, assume that unlimited overtime production is possible. Designate by x_5, x_6, x_7, and x_8, respectively, the quantity of bricks produced on overtime. Now the cumulative production is

$$y_1 = x_1 + x_5$$
$$y_2 = x_1 + x_2 + x_5 + x_6$$
$$y_3 = x_1 + x_2 + x_3 + x_5 + x_6 + x_7$$
$$y_4 = x_1 + x_2 + x_3 + x_4 + x_5 + x_6 + x_7 + x_8$$

The constraints are

$$
\begin{array}{llll}
x_1 & & & \leq 125 \\
x_2 & & & \leq 125 \\
x_3 & & & \leq 125 \\
x_4 & & & \leq 125 \\
x_1 & + x_5 & & \geq 50 \\
x_1 + x_2 & + x_5 + x_6 & & \geq 100 \\
x_1 + x_2 + x_3 & + x_5 + x_6 + x_7 & & \geq 250 \\
x_1 + x_2 + x_3 + x_4 + x_5 + x_6 + x_7 + x_8 & = 400
\end{array}
$$

The inventory cost is

$$15[(y_1 - 50) + (y_2 - 100) + (y_3 - 250)] = 15(y_1 + y_2 + y_3) - 6000$$

$$= 45x_1 + 30x_2 + 15x_3 + 45x_5 + 30x_6 + 15x_7 - 6000$$

The production cost is no longer fixed and must be included in the total cost. Assume that the straight time production cost per brick is $50 and that overtime production is $20 more per brick, or $70 per brick. Then the combined production cost is

$$50x_1 + 50x_2 + 50x_3 + 50x_4 + 70x_5 + 70x_6 + 70x_7 + 70x_8$$

Adding inventory and production costs, we get the total cost:

$$Z = 95x_1 + 80x_2 + 65x_3 + 50x_4 + 115x_5 + 100x_6 + 85x_7 + 70x_8 - 6000$$

This is the objective function to be minimized under the constraints.
The optimum solution is

$$Z^* = \$20{,}875$$
$$x_1^* = 50$$
$$x_2^* = 75$$
$$x_3^* = 125$$
$$x_4^* = 125$$
$$x_5^* = 0$$
$$x_6^* = 0$$
$$x_7^* = 0$$
$$x_8^* = 25$$

Note that the total minimum cost is $20,875. To compare this with the straight-time solution, we need to calculate first the straight-time production cost. This is $400 \times \$50 = \$20{,}000$. Then we add the inventory cost of $1125 and get $20,000 + \$1125 = \$21{,}125$. Thus overtime saves $21,125 - \$20{,}875 = \$250$.

A Personnel Assignment Problem

The Hy-Pressure Realty Co. of Santa Monica, California operates in three sales territories: north, east, and south. The three agents of the firm, John, Ann, and George, are to be assigned to north, east, and south, respectively. Is this the best assignment of agents?

This problem is called an **assignment problem** because the issue is how to assign people (or activities, machines, facilities, etc.) to specific tasks (or places, locations, etc.).

The manager of Hy-Pressure assigns an effectiveness index to each agent when operating in each of the territories. For example, John's index is 15 in north, 17 in east, and 22 in south. In Figure 10.9 the various performance indices are shown. The management of Hy-Pres-

	NORTH	EAST	SOUTH
John	15	17	22
Ann	18	28	31
George	23	12	27

FIGURE 10.9 Effectiveness indices for Hy-Pressure Realty Company.

sure wants to assign the salespersons in such a way that the sum of the indices is maximum.

To formulate the problem mathematically, we introduce the notation shown in Figure 10.10. When an agent is assigned to a territory, the unknown is 1; otherwise it is 0. For example, when John is assigned to north, we have x_{11} equal to 1, and x_{12} and x_{13} equal to 0, and so on. An agent can be assigned to only a single territory, and so

$$x_1 + x_2 + x_3 = 1$$
$$x_4 + x_5 + x_6 = 1$$
$$x_7 + x_8 + x_9 = 1$$

Furthermore, each sales territory has only one agent, and so

$$x_1 + x_4 + x_7 = 1$$
$$x_2 + x_5 + x_8 = 1$$
$$x_3 + x_6 + x_9 = 1$$

The problem is to maximize the objective function:

$$Z = 15x_1 + 17x_2 + 22x_3$$
$$+ 18x_4 + 28x_5 + 31x_6$$
$$+ 23x_7 + 12x_8 + 27x_9$$

where the coefficients are the effectiveness indices. Is this a linear programming problem? Is this a transportation problem?

The relationships are linear, but fractional solutions are not permitted. So at first blush it appears that this is not a linear programming problem. However, an important theorem in linear programming states the following:

If in the transportation problem all the constraints are integers,* then the solution too is integer. The assignment problem is a transportation problem.

Thus if the linear programming problem is solved, the optimum solution will be automatically integer. The optimum allocation of agents is (1) John to south, (2) Ann to east, and (3) George to north.

10.3 GRAPHIC SOLUTION OF LINEAR PROGRAMMING PROBLEMS

The Indian Jewelry Problem: How to Maximize

Minnehaha, modern-day entrepreneur and namesake of the beautiful maiden in Longfellow's poem "The Song of Hiawatha", is in the business of manufacturing rings and bracelets of silver and gold. Each ring takes 3 ounces of silver and 1 ounce of gold (these are large rings); each bracelet takes 1 ounce of silver and 2 ounces of gold. It so happens

---

* The transportation costs may be fractions.

	NORTH	EAST	SOUTH	CAPACITIES
John	x_1	x_2	x_3	1
Ann	x_4	x_5	x_6	1
George	x_7	x_8	x_9	1
Demand	1	1	1	3

FIGURE 10.10 Notation introduced to establish the mathematical model for the Hy-Pressure Realty Company. For example, if $x_6 = 1$, Ann is assigned to the south; if $x_6 = 0$, she is *not* assigned to the south.

that Minnehaha has only 9 ounces of silver and 8 ounces of gold. Thus, if she makes x_1 rings and x_2 bracelets, any production schedule must satisfy the two inequalities

$$3x_1 + x_2 \leq 9 \qquad \text{silver constraint}$$
$$x_1 + 2x_2 \leq 8 \qquad \text{gold constraint}$$

Each ring brings \$4.00 profit and each bracelet \$5.00 profit. Thus the problem is to maximize the objective function, giving the combined profit

$$Z = 4x_1 + 5x_2$$

This is a linear programming problem, and it can be solved by a graphic procedure.* As a first step, convert the silver constraint into an equation:

$$3x_1 + x_2 = 9$$

How can we represent graphically combinations of rings and bracelets which exactly meet this constraint?

If we make no bracelets, $x_2 = 0$, and so the number of rings can be computed by solving the silver constraint for x_1:

$$3x_1 = 9 - x_2$$

or

$$x_1 = \frac{9 - x_2}{3} = \frac{9 - 0}{3} = 3$$

So in Figure 10.11, (a), we get point A.

Now if we make no rings, $x_1 = 0$, and we solve the silver constraint for x_2:

$$x_2 = 9 - 3x_1 = 9 - 3 \times 0 = 9$$

This gives point B in Figure 10.11. The straight line from A to B gives the combination of rings and bracelets which exactly meet the silver constraint. Combinations to the left of AB meet the silver constraint with a surplus of silver.

---

* The theory of straight lines is reviewed in Appendix A, Section 3.

FIGURE 10.11
Graphic representation of the constraint
of Minnehaha's problem.

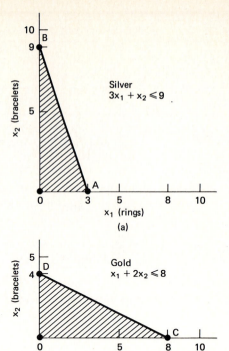

Silver
$3x_1 + x_2 \leqslant 9$

(a)

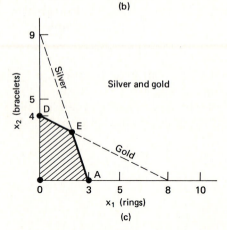

Gold
$x_1 + 2x_2 \leqslant 8$

(b)

Silver and gold

Silver

Gold

(c)

Note that both x_1 and x_2 must be nonnegative, and so solutions must lie above or on line $0A$ and to the right or on line $0B$. *Thus solutions must be within or on the border line of triangle $0AB$* [Figure 10.11, (a)].

A similar argument shows that due to the gold constraint *solutions must lie within or on the border line of triangle $0CD$* [Figure 10.11, (b)]. Finally in Figure 10.11(c) we combine Figures 10.11(a) and (b) and find that the solution must lie within or on the border of the $DEA0$ quadrangle. Now we claim that *the optimum solution cannot lie inside the quadrangle but must lie on the border of the quadrangle.*

To clarify the validity of this statement, assume that we have the *goal* of realizing a profit of $50. Then we must have

$$4x_1 + 5x_2 = 50$$

In Figure 10.12 we reproduce the quadrangle from Figure 10.11(c) and also draw the $50 **isoprofit** line. Observe that every point on this line lies outside of the quadrangle, and so it is impossible to meet the goal of a $50 profit with the available gold and silver. So instead of considering a $50 isoprofit line, consider a constant isoprofit line:

$$Z = 4x_1 + 5x_2 = \text{constant}$$

Observe that for any value of the constant we get a straight line. How do these lines compare?

To answer the question, let us calculate the slope of these isoprofit lines. We write

$$5x_2 = -4x_1 + \text{constant}$$

and

$$x_2 = -\frac{4}{5}x_1 + \frac{\text{constant}}{5}$$

Thus the slope is $-4/5$ and is independent of the value of the profit. This means that *all the constant isoprofit lines are represented by parallel straight lines*. To illustrate, we also draw the $40 isoprofit line in Figure 10.12.

So now we introduce a *roll-down* procedure to show how to solve the linear programming problem; namely, we roll down the paper, as shown in Figure 10.13, starting from the $50 isoprofit line until we reach the quadrangle. You can observe in Figure 10.13 that as we roll down the paper, we "bump" into corner E of the quadrangle. Observe also that as we roll down the paper, we steadily decrease the profit. So once we bump into corner E, there is no reason to roll down the paper further; it would only decrease the profit. Thus you can see that the maximum profit is obtained when we bump into corner E. Here

$$3x_1 + x_2 = 9$$
$$x_1 + 2x_2 = 8$$

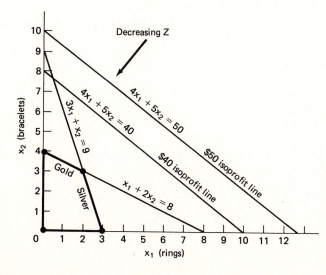

FIGURE 10.12
Feasible solutions to Minnehaha's problem must lie within or on the border of the quadrangle. Also shown is the $50 isoprofit line.

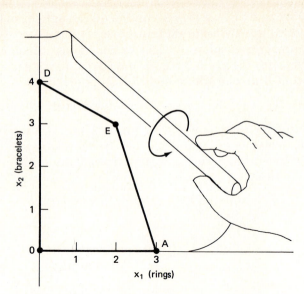

and by solving the two equations, we find the optimum solution:

$$x_1^* = 2 \qquad x_2^* = 3$$

Evaluating the objective function at this point yields a maximum profit:

$$Z^* = 4x_1^* + 5x_2^* = 8 + 15 = \$23$$

Summary of Graphic Procedure

Step 1. Convert inequalities into equations.

Step 2. Plot each equation.

Step 3. Choose an unattainable high goal for the profit (that is, for the objective function).

Step 4. Plot the corresponding isoprofit line.

Step 5. Apply the roll-down procedure, and mark the "bumped" corner.

Step 6. Calculate x_1, x_2, and Z for the bumped corner.

What If the Profit Contributions Change: Sensitivity Analysis

Suppose the profit contribution on rings increases to \$5.00. The objective function now is

$$Z = 5x_1 + 5x_2$$

and so the isoprofit line in Figure 10.13 changes a little; the slope becomes -1 (the line is a $-45°$ line). However, when the paper is rolled down, it will still bump into corner *E*. The optimum solution is still making two rings and three bracelets.

Changing the constants does not necessarily imply a change in decisions.

However, the value of the combined profit does change. Namely, the optimum combined profit is

$$Z^* = 5x_1^* + 5x_2^* = 5 \times 2 + 5 \times 3 = \$25$$

Now suppose that the profit contribution on each ring is still \$4.00 but that the profit contribution on each bracelet increases to \$12. Now the objective function is

$$Z = 4x_1 + 12x_2$$

Observe that the slope of this isoprofit line is $-4/12 = -1/3$. As an illustration of such an isoprofit line, consider the straight line for which the profit goal is \$60,

$$4x_1 + 12x_2 = 60$$

as shown in Figure 10.14. It is easy to see that if the paper rolls down parallel to this new straight line, we bump into corner *D*, and therefore the optimum solution, giving the maximum combined profit for this situation, is

$$x_1^* = 0 \qquad x_2^* = 4$$

This means that only bracelets will be manufactured, and the combined profit will be \$48. Another interesting observation about this solution is that only four units of silver will be used from the available nine units. All of the eight units of gold will be used, because gold is a scarce resource, meaning that a small decrease in the quantity of gold will

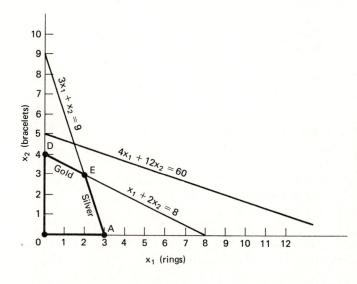

FIGURE 10.14
Feasible solution to Minnehaha's problem must lie within or on the border of the quadrangle. Profit contributions are \$4.00 and \$12.00 respectively. Also the \$60.00 profit line is shown.

decrease profits. A small decrease in the quantity of silver, however, will *not* decrease combined profits. Note, as stated earlier, that optimum allocation of resources does not necessarily mean using all resources.

Suppose that profit contribution on rings is $25 and on bracelets only $5. Now we must maximize the objective function:

$$Z = 25x_1 + 5x_2$$

Observe that the isoprofit lines are represented by straight lines with the slope of -5. For example, if we arbitrarily pick $250 as a goal, the $250 isoprofit line is given by

$$25x_1 + 5x_2 = 250$$

as shown in Figure 10.15. When we roll down this line (roll to the left), we bump into corner A of the quadrangle. Thus the optimum solution is given by

$$x_1^* = 3 \qquad x_2^* = 0$$

which yields a combined profit of $75. Observe that now only rings are made and that only three units of gold from the available eight are used. All nine units of silver are used for production, because now silver is a scarce resource.

In summary, one of the corners of the quadrilateral is the optimum solution to the problem.

1. If the profit contributions are $4 and $5, the solution is corner E, both silver and gold are scarce, and both constraints are binding.
2. If the profit contributions are $4 and $12, the solution is corner D, silver is in surplus, gold is scarce, and only the gold constraint is binding.
3. If the profit contributions are $25 and $5, the solution is corner A, silver is scarce, gold is in surplus, and only the silver constraint is binding.

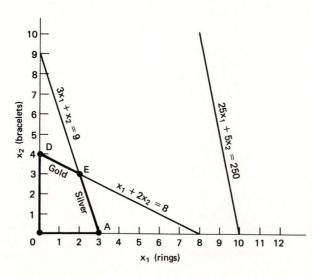

FIGURE 10.15 Feasible solutions to Minnehaha's problem must lie within or on the border of the quadrangle. Profit contributions are $25.00 and $5.00, respectively. Also shown is the $250.00 profit line. Silver is scarce; gold is in surplus.

So far we have made sensitivity analyses if the profit contributions change. In Chapter 11 we shall make sensitivity analyses on the constraints. But now we must consider also the problem of minimization.

The Feed Mix Problem: How to Minimize

The Texas Cattle Feed Corp. purchases two types of grain, each containing different amounts of four kinds of nutritional elements. To have a satisfactory feed for cattle, the grain must be mixed so that minimum requirements for each kind of nutritional element are met. This problem is similar in form to the nutrition problem already discussed and therefore requires only a quick discussion. Figure 10.16 provides the required information and is to be compared with Figure 10.2 for the Abbey Chemical Corporation.

Assume that the corporation will buy type 1 grain in quantity x_1, and type 2 grain in quantity x_2. The four constraints to meet the four types of nutrition requirements are

$$\text{type 1:} \quad 2x_1 + 3x_2 \geq 30$$
$$\text{type 2:} \quad x_1 + 4x_2 \geq 20$$
$$\text{type 3:} \quad 3x_1 + x_2 \geq 15$$
$$\text{type 4:} \quad 7x_1 + 4x_2 \geq 28$$

The problem is to minimize the cost of feed,

$$Z = 14x_1 + 14x_2$$

where the $14 is the unit cost of each type of grain.

In Figure 10.17 we show the four straight lines representing the constraints. Observe that feasible solutions will lie above and on the polygon *ABCD*. (Type 4 does not affect the solution and is called a redundant constraint.) Note also that the coefficients of x_1 and x_2 in the objective function are both 14, and so the constant cost lines will be 45° lines. We must minimize cost instead of maximizing profit and so must roll the paper up from the bottom. Suppose we start with a −45° line, going through the origin as shown by the rolled-up paper in Figure 10.17. We want to move this line up until we bump one of the corners of

| | | TYPES OF GRAIN | | |
| | | Quantity Purchased | | |
		x_1	x_2	REQUIREMENTS
Types of Grain	Type 1	2	3	≥ 30
	Type 2	1	4	≥ 20
	Type 3	3	1	≥ 15
	Type 4	7	4	≥ 28
	Unit cost	14	14	Minimize

FIGURE 10.16 Information given for solving the feed mix problem for the Texas Cattle Feed Corp.

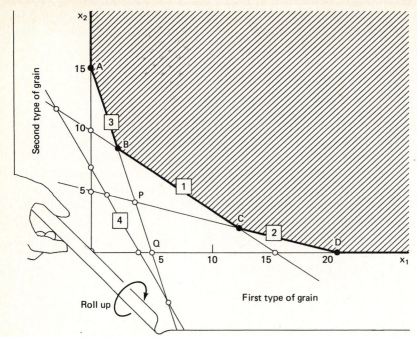

FIGURE 10.17
Feasible solutions to the Texas Cattle Feed Corporation's problem must lie within or on the border of the shaded area. The problem is solved by the "roll-up" process.

the polygon. You can easily verify that the first corner we bump will be corner B. Thus, for the objective function considered, corner B represents the optimum solution. By solving the equations

$$2x_1 + 3x_2 = 30$$
$$3x_1 + \; x_2 = 15$$

we get

$$x_1^* = \tfrac{15}{7} = 2.14$$
$$x_2^* = \tfrac{60}{7} = 8.57$$

and the lowest cost is

$$Z^* = 14x_1^* + 14x_2^* = 30 + 120 = \$150$$

Note that only constraints 1 and 3 are binding. What-if the profits change? Depending on the specific values, corners A, B, C, or D may become optimal. Study of this problem is left as an exercise.

10.4 FURTHER ILLUSTRATIONS OF LINEAR PROGRAMMING AND ITS EXTENSIONS

To clarify certain concepts of linear programming, we discuss in this section two modifications of the Indian jewelry problem.

When Resources Can Be Bought and Sold

So far we assumed that due to some unstated rules (perhaps tribal custom) Minnehaha cannot *sell* her silver and gold to be used in making rings and bracelets. Assume that she can sell one ounce of silver or gold for $.50 and $2.00, respectively. How many rings and bracelets should she make, and how many ounces of silver and gold should she sell?

This problem is quite different from the original but can be easily stated as a linear programming problem. Designate by x_3 the number of ounces of silver sold and by x_4 the number of ounces of gold sold. The silver constraint is

$$3x_1 + x_2 \leq 9 - x_3$$

or

$$3x_1 + x_2 + x_3 \leq 9$$

The gold constraint is:

$$x_1 + 2x_2 \leq 8 - x_4$$

or

$$x_1 + 2x_2 + x_4 \leq 8$$

The profit to be maximized is

$$Z = 4x_1 + 5x_2 + .5x_3 + 2x_4$$

We still have two constraints, but now we have four unknowns as well.

If you solve this new problem, you will find that the optimum solution is still making two rings and three bracelets, and Minnehaha should not sell any of her silver or gold.

But suppose the profit on each bracelet increases to $12, as discussed when we made our sensitivity analysis of the original problem, (Figure 10.14). Then the optimum solution led to a surplus of 4 ounces of silver because Minnehaha was forbidden to sell. Now she can sell her silver. In the original problem the profit was $48. Now the optimum solution is still just making four bracelets, but she can get an additional 4 × $.50 = $2.00 for her silver, and the optimum profit is $48 + $2 = $50.

Note that the purchase price of silver and gold does not enter into the calculations. These are called *sunk* costs.

Note, however, that

> Modifying a problem may or may not require a change in decisions.

A Fixed Charge Problem

A certain entrepreneur is considering the manufacture of rings and bracelets. He owns 9 ounces of silver and 8 ounces of gold. The profit contribution for rings is $4.00 and for bracelets, $5.00. All the other coefficients are the same as in the problem with Minnehaha. So you solve the problem with linear programming and find that the optimum solution is to make two rings and three bracelets and that the profit contribution is $23. Suppose, however, that there is a **fixed cost** or **charge** of $7.00 to get into the business. Thus the net profit for the entrepreneur is $23 − $7 = $16.

This is one of the alternatives the entrepreneur can consider. He can also consider the possibility of making only rings or only bracelets. Consider each of these alternatives.

Suppose he makes only rings. He can make three rings and get a profit contribution of $3 \times 4 = \$12$. Suppose the fixed charge is $5.00 for making only rings. The net profit will be $\$12 - \$5 = \$7$.

Now consider making only bracelets. He can make four bracelets and get a profit contribution of $4 \times 5 = \$20$. Suppose the fixed charge to make only bracelets is $2.00, and so there is a net profit of $\$20 - \$2 = \$18$.

We conclude, therefore, that the best plan for the entrepreneur is to make only bracelets.

Note that this is *not* a linear programming problem because the profit is not a linear function of the unknowns. Namely, the profits are not proportional to the number of rings and bracelets made.

In a fixed charge problem the cost is composed of two parts: (1) a constant cost which may or may not be zero and (2) a linear cost function.

For example, making 2 rings and 3 bracelets gives a profit of $17, but making 1 ring and 1.5 bracelets gives only a profit of

$$4 \times 1 + 5 \times 1.5 - 6 = \$5.5$$

which is not one-half of $17.

The only way we could solve this problem was to divide the problem into three alternatives and solve each alternative. As long as there are only a few alternatives, the fixed charge problem can be solved by solving a series of linear programming problems. However, if there are many or myriad alternatives, linear programming cannot deal with the problem, and more advanced techniques are needed, as described in Chapter 13.

10.5 COMPUTER-BASED SOLUTIONS AND ALGORITHMS

While graphic solutions of linear programming problems provide important insight, practical problems have too many variables and constraints to be solved by such a simple method. Manual methods are inadequate in practice, and computer-based solutions must be used. There are many computer programs available for solving linear programming problems, and here, merely for illustrative purposes, we show how to use such a program by solving the problem of Belchfire Motors. The first three constraints are

$$2x_1 + 5x_2 + 6x_3 + 4x_4 + 4x_5 + 5x_6 \leq 45,000$$
$$x_1 + 2x_2 + x_3 + 3x_4 + 2x_5 + 4x_6 \leq 20,000$$
$$3x_1 + 3x_2 + 2x_3 + x_4 + 3x_5 + 2x_6 \leq 50,000$$

The second three constraints are

$$x_1 \qquad\qquad\qquad\qquad \geq 5000$$
$$x_2 + x_3 + x_4 \qquad\qquad \geq 2000$$
$$x_5 + x_6 \geq 1600$$

and the problem is to minimize the objective function:

$$Z = .15x_1 + .08x_2 + .03x_3 + .06x_4 + .12x_5 + .15x_6$$

How do we tell the computer what the relationships are? This depends on the computer you use, and here we illustrate one particular system. In the upper part of Figure 10.18, in lines numbered 2000 to 2060, we input after the word DATA the constants of the problem in a BASIC computer language program. In line 2060 we input the constants of the objective function. Note that the unknowns are not listed, only the constants used in the relationships. (Zeros must be listed.)

Then you tell the computer to RUN the program. The computer asks whether you want to maximize or minimize and what the number of variables and constraints are. When you provide the answers, the computer proceeds to solve the problem and gives the answers, as shown in the lower part of Figure 10.18.

We stress again that this is only an illustration, and to solve a linear

---

```
2000   DATA 2, 5, 6, 4, 4, 5, '≤', 45000
2010   DATA 1, 2, 1, 3, 2, 4, '≤', 20000
2020   DATA 3, 3, 2, 1, 3, 2, '≤', 50000
2030   DATA 1, 0, 0, 0, 0, 0, '≥', 5000
2040   DATA 0, 1, 1, 1, 0, 0, '≥', 2000
2050   DATA 0, 0, 0, 0, 1, 1, '≥', 1600
2060   DATA .15, .08, .03, .06, .12, .15


RUN


DO YOU WANT TO MAXIMIZE OR MINIMIZE?MIN
NUMBER OF VARIABLES?6
NUMBER OF CONSTRAINTS?6


SOLUTION

VALUE OF THE OBJECTIVE FUNCTION IS 2344
VALUES OF THE VARIABLES ARE
     X(1) = 13800
     X(2) = 200
     X(3) = 1400
     X(4) = 400
     X(5) = 1600
     X(6) = 0
```

FIGURE 10.18 Computer-generated solution to the problem of Belchfire Motors.

programming problem in your facility, you must find out how a linear programming problem can be solved on your computer.

When There Is a Constant In the Objective Function

In the problem for the Concrete Construction Corporation we had to minimize:

$$Z = 45x_1 + 30x_2 + 15x_3 - 6000$$

But the computer does not allow you to input the constant 6000. What do you do?

You minimize,

$$45x_1 + 30x_2 + 15x_3$$

because the optimum values of x_1, x_2, and x_3 are the same for the two problems. But for minimum cost you must take the answer from the computer and subtract the 6000.

Why Study Algorithms?

While you will use computer programs, you will hardly be involved in writing or changing programs. Still, to get an insight into mathematical programming, you need some familiarity with the algorithms involved. For this reason in subsequent chapters we shall introduce you to some of the most important algorithms.

> The prime purpose of learning algorithms of mathematical programming is to obtain insight into the theory so the algorithms can be effectively applied to solving problems.

10.6 CHECKLIST FOR BUILDING A MATHEMATICAL PROGRAMMING MODEL

As stated before, building a mathematical model is more of an art than a science. The most important thing, of course, is that you understand the problem. However, even artists follow certain rules, and so the following checklist of 10 items will be useful when building the model:

1. Establish the criterion.
2. Determine the alternatives.
3. List the constraints.
4. List the unknowns.
5. List the constants.
6. Develop notation for the unknowns.
7. Develop the payoff function.

8. Establish the relationships between the unknowns and the constraints.
9. Review, summarize, and explain the model.
10. Expand and modify the model if necessary.

When you build a mathematical programming model, it is unlikely that you will be able to take these steps in the sequence listed. More likely, you will go back and forth between the steps until you cover all the necessary points.

10.7 BETTER DISTRIBUTION PLANNING BY MATHEMATICAL PROGRAMMING: A SUCCESSFUL APPLICATION

We present an application of mathematical programming to provide insight into the broad scope and wide possibilities offered. The application* describes a large problem where linear programming is not adequate, where advanced techniques of nonlinear programming must be used, and where, with relatively small effort, substantial benefits have been obtained. The application also clearly shows how computers are used in mathematical programming.

Background

Hunt-Wesson Foods Inc. produces tomato products, cooking oil, matches, pudding, shortening, and hundreds of other products at 14 locations (Wesson Refineries, Hunt Canneries and Copackers). At the time of this study, Hunt-Wesson distributed nationally through 12 distribution centers. Annual sales were in the vicinity of $400 million and growing fairly steadily. Transportation was by common rail and by both common and contract truck carriers. The company's policy was to service each of the many thousands of customers from a single distribution center for all products.

Hunt-Wesson Foods undertook a planning study because it faced pressing distribution center expansion and relocation issues. Management recognized that the solution of these problems will involve changes in the design of the company's entire national distribution system. To resolve the problem, the company decided to employ a computer-based approach. Management desired not only to resolve the immediate questions but also wanted to make a comprehensive plan to improve the distribution center locations, assignment of customers in distribution centers, and annual aggregate product flows through the system.

Some of the basic questions management sought answers for were

---

* Adapted from Arthur M. Geoffrion, "Better Distribution Planning with Computer Models," *Harvard Business Review*, Vol. 54, No. 4, July–Aug. 1976, pp. 92–99.

the following:

1. How many distribution centers should there be?
2. In which cities should they be located?
3. What size should each distribution center be, and which products should it carry?
4. Which distribution center(s) or plant(s) should service each customer?
5. How should each plant's output of each product be allocated among distribution centers or customers?
6. What should the annual transportation flows be throughout the system?
7. For a given level of customer service, how do the costs of the best distribution system compare with the projections of the current system?

(This list of unknowns is item 4 in the checklist for building a mathematical model in Section 10.6.)

The Mathematical Programming Model

We present here only an overview and omit mathematical details such as notation, system of relationships, and so on.

The many hundreds of various Hunt-Wesson Foods products were aggregated into 17 product groups. It was assumed that the 14 plants of Hunt-Wesson Foods could deliver products to 45 possible distribution center sites and serve the many thousands of customers through 121 customer zones.

The fundamental alternatives of the problem are (item 2 in the checklist) as follows: What amount of 1 of the 17 product groups should be shipped from 1 of the 14 factories via 1 of the 45 distribution center sites to 1 of the 121 customer zones? Therefore, it appears that the number of variables is

$$17 \times 14 \times 45 \times 121 = 1{,}295{,}910$$

However, not all the 17×14 combinations of product groups and factories are possible, because not every product group is made in each factory. In fact, there are only 50 of these possibilities, and so the number of variables of the problem is

$$50 \times 45 \times 121 = 272{,}250$$

The quantities to be shipped can of course be fractional values, and so these variables are continuous. However, there are also variables of the problem which can assume only the values 0 and 1. Namely, there are 45 variables which state whether a possible distribution center site is to be used or not. There are also the 0, 1 variables that state which distribution center should serve which customer zone. As there are 45 possible distribution center sites and 121 customer zones, there is a total of $45 \times 121 = 5445$ variables of this type.

Now we continue to the constraints of the problem (item 3 in the checklist). The production capacity in each plant of each product group is given by 50 constraints. The demand of each product group at each customer zone is given, providing $17 \times 121 = 2057$ constraints. The total quantity shipped through each distribution center site cannot be above a certain limit or below a certain other limit. This, then, provides $45 + 45 = 90$ constraints.

The payoff function of the problem is given by the cost function to be minimized (items 1 and 7 in the checklist). Here a distinction must be made between fixed and variable cost. Thus, the fixed cost (fixed charge) for each of the distribution center sites is given by 45 constants. The variable cost is provided by the average unit cost of producing and shipping from each factory each product group via each distribution center site to each customer zone. Thus, there are 272,250 variable cost contributions.

Note, then, that this is not a linear programming problem, but it is a fixed charge problem like the one discussed previously in this chapter. The problem we discussed, of course, had only three alternatives and so could be solved by linear programming. The real-life Hunt-Wesson Foods problem has myriad alternatives and so advanced techniques of solution and computerization were required to obtain solutions to the problem.

Role of the Computer

It is important to distinguish among the basic roles which the computer plays in supporting a mathematical programming project:

1. Prepare data and systematic, summarized forecasts based on alternate assumptions on the future.
2. Evaluate answers to the basic questions listed previously by calculating costs and other quantitative factors important to decision makers.
3. Provide answers to what-if types of questions.
4. Find the "best" solution in terms of a criterion acceptable to decision makers.

Benefits of Mathematical Programming

The study team found that the "best" solution to the problem required that six locations for distribution center sites be changed. Two of the six changes were so important that Hunt-Wesson Foods proceeded to immediate implementation. As a result of the distribution center site changes, improvements in assigning customers to distribution centers were also implemented.

A third change was not considered so important but was also

adopted because it gave additional warehouse space in a region where more space was particularly needed. Two other changes were postponed for future consideration. Finally, the sixth change was so marginal that it was dropped.

The realizable annual cost savings were estimated to be in the millions of dollars.

10.8 HOW MATHEMATICAL PROGRAMMING SUPPORTS DECISION MAKING: A DIALOG

Q. *Does mathematical programming provide the optimum decision?*

A. Be more specific.

Q. *Let's go back to Belchfire Motors. Is the solution really the best?*

A. The answers provided are best, conditioned on the assumption that the model precisely describes the situation. If the model is complete and absolutely accurate, the answer is yes.

Q. *Do models usually describe the situation completely?*

A. No, but they may come close. Remember that the first model for Belchfire was not accepted by management but that the second was.

Q. *Why not a third model?*

A. It could happen that a third and fourth, etc., model must be developed until finally management agrees that the model adequately describes the situation. Don't forget that management must make decisions within certain time frames and cannot postpone decisions indefinitely.

Q. *I wonder whether mathematical programming makes decisions at all.*

A. No, mathematical programming and computers provide information and support decision making. Only people make decisions.

Q. *Then how do you know that the model is adequate and stop making changes and computer runs?*

A. The model must be validated in two different senses. *Technical* validation means to verify that the computer gives correct answers to the model as stated, that is, that the answers satisfy the constraints and provide the optimum. *Managerial*, the more difficult type of validation, means that the decision makers agree that the model describes the situation in accordance with management's perception of the situation.

Q. *Does this mean that you have to make many computer runs?*

A. Yes indeed! This is the reason why it is so important to have mathematical programming techniques which can provide answers in relatively few steps and to have computers that can carry out the computations fast and inexpensively.

Q. *So mathematical programming does not even give answers?*

A. Yes, it does. It provides answers to specific questions. These are often the what-if type. For example, if the question is how does the answer change if the constraints are changed or the contributions are changed, then sensitivity analysis can provide specific answers. However, final decisions must be made by people.

Q. *You said that mathematical programming works only if all the constants are known with certainty. Is this often the case?*

A. Not really. Usually there is uncertainty. In fact, as the future is never known, there must always be uncertainty.

Q. *Then how can mathematical programming be useful?*

A. Go back to the jewelry problem of Minnehaha. Recall that when we solved the problem we found that two rings and three bracelets should be manufactured. When we changed the profit contribution of rings from $4 to $5, we still found that two rings and three bracelets should be manufactured. Note, then, that the solution to the problem was actually independent of whether the profit was $4 or $5. So if there is uncertainty about the profit of rings but it is known that the profit is between $4 and $5, there is certainty about the decision that the best solution is to make two rings and three bracelets.

Q. *Is, then, mathematical programming a form of decision support systems?*

A. This is a question of how words are used. The fact is that some decision support systems contain linear programming as a subsystem, and the designer of DSS should not bar the possibility of using mathematical programming.

Q. *You said your purpose for covering algorithms is to provide insight only. What algorithms will you cover, and what not?*

A. We shall cover only the algorithms which are used most frequently. In Chapter 11 we cover the simplex method, the foundation of most linear programming algorithms; in Chapter 12, the transportation algorithm; and in Chapter 13, some mathematical programming algorithms. We shall not cover algorithms for network problems and the assignment problem and other special-purpose algorithms which do not substantially increase your insight.

Q. *How do you put probability in the model?*

A. Linear programming cannot explicitly do that. However, there are advanced techniques of mathematical programming which can provide guidance under such conditions.

Q. *Are such techniques often used?*

A. Not much as yet, and that is why they are not covered in this textbook. However, in the future they will probably be used more.

Q. *So what will the future bring in your view?*

A. Techniques of mathematical programming are ever improving and applications are increasing. Computers are becoming faster and cheaper. Therefore, the prognosis is that mathematical programming will be used more and more as time goes by.

SUMMARY

1. Linear programming and its extensions are most important quantitative techniques of managerial decision making.

2. Two primary limitations of linear programming are the following: (a) All variables must appear in all relationships to the first power, and (b) fractional solutions are possible.

3. The primary purpose of linear programming—as in all quantitative analysis—is to provide information to support decision makers.

4. To build a linear programming model, you must establish (a) the alternatives, (b) the consequences of alternatives expressed by the objective function, and (c) the feasible alternatives subject to the constraints.

5. The graphic approach to linear programming is important for providing insight into the problem and its solution.

6. Exploration of the situation, model building, and interpretation are invariably performed by people, but the actual calculations required to solve a linear programming problem are usually carried out by the computer.

SECTION EXERCISES

1. *How to build a Linear Programming Model*

1.1 In the first paragraph of Section 10.1, a procedure for analyzing a management decision problem is given. From your own daily experience, find a situation in which you had to make a decision, and answer the following questions, which are similar to those given in the procedure for analyzing a management decision problem:
   a. What are the alternatives?
   b. What are the consequences of each alternative?
   c. What criterion will be used to choose among alternatives?
   d. Evaluate the alternatives using the criterion.
   d. What is the best choice? (Justify in terms of part d.)

1.2 Refer to the Belchfire Motors example of Section 10.1. Suppose that the resource constraints have been changed as follows: 50,000 hours of labor are available, but only 15,000 pounds of steel can be had, and supplies of nickel have been increased by special allocation to 40,000 pounds. Make a new version of Figure 10.1a to account for these changes.

1.3 Belchfire rings, rods, and pistons have been redesigned to fit the new, smaller engines. As a consequence, the labor input to each of the three items has been reduced by 1 unit and the amont of nickel increased by .5 unit. The amount of steel per unit has been increased in the case of the rods by .25 unit, decreased for rings by 10%, and increased for pistons by 5%. Make the new version of Figure 10.1a to account for these changes (with the original resource constraints).

1.4 Assume that all rings are produced by process x_4, all pistons by process x_6, and the production schedule is as given at the start of Section 10.1.

    a. What is the profit contribution?

    b. Is this a feasible solution?

1.5 If 5,000 rings are manufactured in equal quantities in each of the three processes and 1,100 pistons equally in each of the two piston processes,

    a. What is the profit contribution?

    b. Is this a feasible solution?

1.6 In the subsection entitled "Developing the Model" of Section 10.1, the table of Figure 10.1b is reduced to a set of equations and inequalities. Reduce the solution of Exercise 1.2 to a similar set of linear equations and inequalities.

1.7 In the subsection entitled "Developing the Model" of Section 10.1, the table of Figure 10.1b is reduced to a set of equations and inequalities. Reduce the solution of Exercise 1.3 to a similar set of linear equations and inequalities.

1.8 For each of the following conditions of a linear programming problem, give a practical example in which the condition is violated and therefore mathematical programming must be used:

    a. All relationships must be linear.

    b. Fractional solutions are allowed.

    c. Constants are known deterministically.

    d. A single payoff is maximized or minimized.

2. *Illustrations of Linear Programming Problems*

2.1 For the nutrition problem described in Section 10.2, assume that requirements have been changed as follows: a minimum of 150 units of V_1, a minimum of 100 units of V_2, and a minimum of 100 units of V_3. Make a new version of Figure 10.2.

2.2 For the nutrition problem described in Section 10.2, the compositions of the pills have been changed. Pill x_1 provides 4, 2, and 1 units of V_1, V_2, and V_3; pill x_2, 1, 6, and 3 units; pill x_3, 3 units of each; and all vitamin contents of pill x_4 have been reduced by 20%. Make a new version of Figure 10.2.

2.3 For the nutrition problem described in Section 10.2 a possible production schedule ($x_1 = 120$, all others zero) was proposed and the value of the objective function found. Find a better production (it does not have to be optimal).

2.4 In the nutrition example of Section 10.2, Figure 10.2 is reduced to a set of equations and/or inequalities. Reduce the table of Exercise 2.1 to a similar set of equations.

2.5 In the nutrition example of Section 10.2, Figure 10.2 is reduced to a set of equations and/or inequalities. Reduce the table of Exercise 2.2 to a similar set of equations.

2.6 Mr. Grumble is on doctor's orders to take at least 4 grams of iron and at least 5 grams of zinc in tablets each day. "Zincon" tablets each contain 3 grams of iron and 1 gram of zinc, and each costs $1.00. "Irozon" tablets each contain 1 gram of iron and 4 grams of zinc, and each costs $.50. How many of each type of tablet should Mr. Grumble buy to meet the doctor's order and minimize cost?

2.7 Refer to the La Brea Oil Company example of Section 10.2. Assume that the minimum octane requirement for motor oil decreases from 96 to 95. Create a new table similar to Figure 10.3 and show which of the inequalities developed in this example are changed and to what. The gasoline blending problem has become more difficult in that constraints must be placed on maximum allowable vapor pressure for the products. Assume that crude type 1 has a vapor pressure of 4 and crude type 2 a vapor pressure of 10. When you blend the crudes, a product is obtained with a vapor pressure that is the weighted average of the pressures of the crudes. The vapor pressure for aviation fuel must be less than or equal to 4.9 and for motor fuel, not greater than 8.1. Make a new table similar to Figure 10.3 for this situation, and show all equations that are associated with this model.

2.8 Refer to the transportation problem example in Section 10.2. A new warehouse is established in Philadelphia; thus, a new column must be added to Figure 10.6. The Philadelphia cost column is 130, 170, and 140. The requirements are 180 units, which increased amount is to be met by adding an additional 60 units to the capacity of each of the factories.

    a. Revise Figure 10.6 accordingly.
    b. Revise the network of shipment shown in Figure 10.4(b).
    c. Revise Figures 10.7a and b to add the additional warehouse in symbolic notation.
    d. Show the revised equations and inequalities of the form given in Section 10.2 for the original problem.
    e. Work out a new possible shipping schedule in the format of Figure 10.5.

2.9 A cereal manufacturer finds himself overstocked with "cold cereals" in the west (10,000 cases), in the east (30,000 cases), and in the south (30,000 cases). He learns that orders for cold cereals are increasing in the north and has orders from Fargo (30,000 cases), Madison (20,000 cases), and Ann Arbor (20,000 cases).

Shipping costs per case are (in cents) as follows:

	FARGO	MADISON	ANN ARBOR
West	5	2	3
East	8	4	3
South	9	7	5

Find the optimal routing for transporting the cereals north.

2.10 Refer to the production and inventory control example of Section 10.2. Change the production schedule to 75, 75, 100, and 150 bricks.

    a. Illustrate this schedule and the consumption graphically (as in Figure 10.8).
    b. Determine the inventory cost.
    c. Is this a better solution than a schedule of 100, 100, 100, and 100?
    d. How does this problem change if the maximum number of bricks that can be made in a quarter is 150?

2.11 Refer to the production and inventory control example of Section 10.2. The production requirements have been changed to a minimum of 60, 80, 100, and 160. Create a new version of Figure 10.8, and write the full set of equations and inequalities that define the problem (as is done in the text in Section 10.2).

2.12 Refer to Exercise 2.11. Make two possible production schedules for the situation of Exercise 2.11 and find the inventory carrying cost for each. Draw a graph similar to Figure 10.8 to illustrate your two solutions.

2.13 Refer to the inventory and production control example of Section 10.2 where overtime production is possible; assume that overtime is allowed under the terms and conditions discussed in Section 10.2. Choose a production schedule to provide for production requirements of 200, 150, 110, and 90 bricks; illustrate in a graph similar to Figure 10.8, and find the cost of your solution.

2.14 Refer to the personnel assignment problem discussed in Section 10.2. The effectiveness indices for John have been changed to 20, 4.5, and 15; for Ann, to 25, 16, and 25; and George's remain the same. Rewrite the objective function.

2.15 Refer to the personnel assignment problem discussed in Section 10.2. George is not to be assigned to the east under any circumstances. How might his effectiveness indices be changed to achieve this result without otherwise changing the model?

3. *Graphic Solution of Linear Programming Problems*

3.1 Minnehaha has redesigned the rings discussed in the Indian jewelry problem. Each ring now takes 20 grams of silver and 5 grams of gold; each bracelet takes only 5 grams of silver and 15 grams of gold. Because of the higher cost, she now stocks only 200 grams of silver and 150 grams of gold. Express these new constraints in the form of inequalities as done in Section 10.3, and draw new versions of Figures 10.11 (a), (b), and (c). Show the feasible solution set.

3.2 Refer to Exercise 3.1. In addition to these changes in the constraints, each ring now brings only $3 in profit and each bracelet only $4. Write the new objective function, and show it in a revised version of Figure 10.12.

3.3 Refer to Exercises 3.1 and 3.2. Use the roll-down approach to determine the optimal solution to the revised Indian jewelry problem.

3.4 Refer to Exercises 3.1, 3.2, and 3.3. Suppose that the profit on each bracelet increases to $8. What is the new objective function, and what is the new optimal solution and maximum profit?

3.5 Refer to Exercises 3.1, 3.2 and 3.3. Suppose that the profit on rings increases to $10 but that the profit on bracelets is unchanged. What is the new objective function, and what is the new optimal solution and maximum profit?

3.6 Refer to Exercises 3.1, 3.2 and 3.3. Suppose that the profit on bracelets increases to $20 and that the profit on rings increases to $10? What is the new objective function, and what is the new optimal solution and maximum profit?

3.7 Refer to the feed mix problem of Section 10.3. New discoveries at St. Ignaz University's School of Animal Nutrition have indicated that the requirements for nutrition must change to 25 of type 1, 15 of type 2, 10 of type 3, and 40 of type 4. Express these new constraints in the form of inequalities as done in Section 10.3, and show these new constraints graphically. Show the feasible solution set.

3.8 Refer to Exercise 3.7. In addition to the changed nutritional requirements, it has been discovered that the first and second types of grain contain residual insecticides. The first type of grain contains 5 milligrams of residual insecticide per unit and the second type, 2 milligrams. The limitation on the maximum amount of residual insecticide is 45 milligrams total. Express these new constraints in the form of inequalities as done in Section 10.3, and show the new constraints graphically. Show the feasible solution set.

3.9 Refer to Exercises 3.7 and 3.8. Assume that the objective function is unchanged but that the constraint changes of Exercises 3.7 and 3.8 hold. Use the roll-up method to determine the optimal solution to the feed mix problem. What is the cost of the optimal solution?

3.10 This exercise pertains to the feed mix problem as defined in Section 10.3 (without the changes in constraints of Exercises 3.7 and 3.8). Use graphical methods to determine under which conditions the corners A, B, C, and D (see Figure 10.17) successively become the optimal solutions.

4. *Further Illustrations of Linear Programming*

4.1 If Minnehaha has the option of selling gold and silver in addition to selling rings and bracelets made of those precious metals, how does the analytical formulation of the problem change? That is, how many variables does the new problem have, and how is the objective function to be altered?

4.2 Under which conditions (as defined by relative values of profit contributions in the objective function) would you expect a solution that leads to only selling gold and/or silver and not calling for any fabrication of rings and bracelets?

4.3 Suppose that Minnehaha is offered silver and gold at a price different from the silver and gold that she now has. Her current supply will soon be used up, and she has to use this new gold and silver in her future work and, consequently, in her future planning using linear programming. The new gold and silver will cost more than what she had on hand initially. In what way will the coefficients in the statement of the problem change?

4.4 Are profit functions limited to linear and quadratic forms, which are the only types you have seen illustrated in this text?

4.5 In Section 10.4 we discussed one type of situation where an entrepreneur would like to do linear programming to solve his problem but the concept of a fixed charge must be taken into account. Give two examples of other, realistic, situations where a fixed charge would be large enough to warrant consideration in the model formulation.

4.6 Give two examples of linear programming problems in which the variables can take on only integer values.

5. *Computer-based Solutions*

5.1 What do you see as being the advantages of using a computer to solve linear programming problems?

5.2 If you have a computer program readily available, run the Texas Cattle Feed Corporation problem (as modified in Section 10.5), and compare the results to those given in Figure 10.17.

6. *Checklist for Building a Mathematical Programming Model*

6.1 Use the principles of Section 10.6 to solve the chapter exercises. Keep a list of how you are using the principles.

7. *Better Distribution Planning by Mathematical Programming: A Successful Application*

7.1 Arthur M. Geoffrion, author of the article described in Section 10.7, stresses that "The purpose of computing is insight, not numbers."
   a. What might that mean in the context of this application?
   b. Can you think of an insightful question that might be asked by management and answered by the computer model?

7.2 The author of the article from which this application is taken places great importance on the ability to answer what-if types of questions. Give an example of such a question that might be answered by this model.

8. *How Mathematical Programming Supports Decision Making: A Dialog*

8.1 In the article quoted in Section 10.7, the author states that it is important to avoid claims of excessive realism for the model. Does the fact that Belchfire management accepted the second model mean that it was, in fact, completely "real?"

8.2 In the article quoted in Section 10.7, it is stated that "The purpose of computing is insight." In Section 10.8, it is stated that the purpose of mathematical programming and computers is to provide guidance and information. Provide two examples of how these statements support each other.

8.3 In Section 10.8 we discussed *managerial* validation in which the decision makers agree that the model describes the situation in accordance with management's perception of the situation. What if "management's perception of the situation" is grossly in error?

8.4 In Section 10.8 it is stated that constants are not usually known with certainty. How can sensitivity analysis help the decision maker to deal with this uncertainty? Give an example.

CHAPTER EXERCISES AND DISCUSSION QUESTIONS

Chapter Exercises C.1–C.11 are realistic business situations involving problems which can be expressed as linear programming problems. Make tables similar to Figures 10.1-3 and 10.5-10, whichever are appropriate, and express the constraints and objective function as inequalities and equations as done in the text. Thus, your solution to each of these problems should, as a minimum, include one or more tables expressing the model and the set of linear relationships that are implied by the table. In addition, you may be asked for additional information in the exercise.

C.1 Business has dropped considerably at B. N. Krupt & Co. They have 8 hours a week available on the coil winder and 25 hours a week available on their potting machine. They have a maximum of 4 hours of labor available each week; this labor force has been trained to operate any and all of the equipment in the company. Two subcontracts have been obtained. The customer's needs far exceed Krupt's ability to produce, and the customers will accept as many units as Krupt will supply each week until further notice. Krupt makes a $3 contribution to profit from each unit of product I and $6 from each unit of product II. Product I requires .2 hour of coil winder, 1 hour of the potting machine and .1 hour of labor; product II requires .4 hour of coil winder, .8 hour of the potting machine, and .25 hour of labor.

C.2 The Biker's Fruit Bar label and advertising assures a net weight of 100 grams. No more than 80 grams of cornstarch can be used in the bar, and at least 40 grams of strawberry lekvar must be used. Cornstarch of adequate quality costs 3 cents per gram, and strawberry lekvar is available from their own patch at 8 cents per gram.

C.3 Good News Advertising Corp. has found that it can predict quite accurately the response to advertisements appearing on TV. They have three different types of advertisements they use: *A*, *B*, and *C*. The effectiveness of the advertisements varies by the product being advertised. In the case of their most important client, who has three products (I, II, and III), they have found that the sales volumes (in thousands of units) are as follows: Advertisement *A* brings in 2 units of I, 2 units of II, and 20 units of III; advertisement *B* brings in 200 units of I, 20 units of II, and 20 units of III; and *C* brings in 20, 200, and 20. Advertisements are purchased in continuous units of time, and the units brought in by the advertisements given are per minute of advertising time. The customer is faced with overcapacity and has asked Good News to find the least cost advertising mix to provide the following minimum number of units of each product: I,

2; II, 50; and III, 20. The cost per minute in thousands of dollars for each type of advertisement is A, \$10; B, \$12, and C, \$.90.

C.4 The Clear Oil corporation makes a foot shampoo that is comprised of four ingredients: A, B, C, and D. They have three types of the foot shampoo specified as follows: Type I has not more than 40% of A and not less than 50% of B and must not have more than 50% of C; it sells for \$1.10 per bottle. Type II has not more than 40% of A and not less than 15% of B; it sells for \$1 a bottle. Type III has not more than 80% of A and sells for \$.75 per bottle. The ingredients A, B, C, and D are in high demand, and Clear Oil can only get guarantees of annual deliveries per week as follows: A, 6000 liters; B, 4000 liters; C, 6500 liters; and D, 3000 liters. Each bottle of finished foot shampoo contains 1 liter of the mixture. The cost per liter of the ingredients is A, \$.60; B, \$1.20; C, \$1; and D, \$.80. The company wants to maximize its profits in this product line.

C.5 Baskin, Peet and Moss, CPAs, generates an equal amount of profit for each audit produced. Sy Ferth, the chief auditor, has done a study and found that the average number of audits produced per year varies among the four auditors but that it also depends on the firm being audited. Auditor A produces 20 audits a year when working on firm I, 18 on firm II, 21 on firm III, and 19 on firm IV. Auditor B has a different pattern of performance: 25, 20, 23, and 22. Auditor C can do 18, 16, 17, and 19; auditor D, 22, 15, 19, and 21. The CPA firm wants to assign auditors so as to maximize profits for the year. (*Hint:* This is an assignment problem. Assume an auditor cannot work on more than one firm at a time.)

C.6 S. R. Pankh just graduated from Stamford University with an MBA. He has been employed by the Berea Synthetic Cotton Mills and is working directly with the president. Currently he is trying to convince the president that linear programming could be used to determine the production schedule for different styles on the different operations of carding, drawing, spinning, and weaving. Kent Du, the president, argues, "Our situation is too complex. We have only 8000 hours of spinning available but only 30 hours of carding." But, replies Pankh, "The requirements for time on the machines are different. For our seven styles we require 2, 3, 2, 2, 4, 3, and 3 hours per unit made of carding and for spinning, 650, 600, 710, 550, 580, 700, and 810 hours for each unit of each style." "Aha!," says Du. "But you don't know how much time is required for each style for drawing and weaving; we've never been able to get the foremen to keep adequate records. That's why I would rather leave machine assignment up to the people who know best how to get it done." "Yes, but you do know how much time we have available for drawing and weaving," said Pankh. "My records show that we have 260 hours of drawing time available and 280 hours of weaving. Give me the time, and I'll find out the requirements." The company controller supported Pankh and offered to supply the profit figures by unit and style, which he did: \$5, \$3, \$2.50, \$2, \$4.50, \$3.80, and \$4.10. Pankh hid himself in a rolled-up Egyptian carpet for 6 weeks and was able to observe the factory operations through a mothhole in the carpet. At the end of that time he was able to report that the time taken in drawing (per style) was 40, 20, 30, 15, 29, 35, and 25 hours; in weaving, 25, 35, 30, 40, 24, 32, and 25. Pankh and Du agreed on the corporation's goal: to maximize profit.

C.7 Tri Cot competes with Berea in styles 1 and 2. Thus, they have sufficient carding and spinning capacity to regard these limitations as nonexistent. Their constraints on weaving and drawing are the same as Berea, as are their profits. They want to maximize profit and have essentially the same machine time requirements as Berea.

C.8 The I. O. Way Animal Supply Cooperative buys corn and sorghum to feed muskrats. Three nutritional factors, *A*, *B*, and *Z*, are needed to meet the muskrats' daily minimum requirements; they require 48, 165, and 150 units. Corn supplies 8, 11, and 25 units of the nutritional factors per gram; sorghum supplies 3, 15, and 6 units. Corn is now being charged to the cooperative at $1.20 per kilogram and sorghum at $1 per kilogram. The cooperative wants to minimize the cost of supporting the muskrats.

C.9 W. R. House & Daughters has two factories and two warehouses. The factories are in Chicago and Rock Island; the warehouses are in Peoria and Morrison. There is a surplus capacity in both factories, but the requirements in both warehouses must be met exactly. Peoria requires 6 units of goods and Morrison requires 7 units. The total capacity of the Chicago factory is 10 units, and the total capacity of the Rock Island factory is 8 units. Shipping costs are as follows: Chicago to Peoria, $9 per unit; Chicago to Morrison, $8; Rock Island to Peoria, $5; and Rock Island to Morrison, $3.

C.10 Ten thousand units are to be delivered by the Standard Unit Company according to this schedule: July, 1000; August, 2000; September, 4000; and October, 3000. It costs Standard $50 to store 1 unit for 1 month, and the capacity of the company warehouse is 1500 units. The production capacity is 29,000 units per month.

C.11 Solve Exercise C.1 graphically.

C.12 Solve Exercise C.2 graphically.

C.13 Solve Exercise C.8 graphically.

C.14 Solve Exercise C.9 graphically.

C.15 Make a graphical representation of a possible solution to Exercise C.10; model your representation after Figure 10.8.

C.16 Find a feasible (not necessarily optimal) solution to Exercise C.3. What is the cost of this solution?

C.17 Find a feasible solution (not necessarily optimal) to Exercise C.4. What is the profit that will be made with your solution?

C.18 Find a feasible solution (not necessarily optimal) to Exercise C.5. What is the profit that will be made with your solution?

C.19 Find a feasible solution (not necessarily optimal) to Exercise C.6. What is the profit that will be made with your solution?

C.20 Find a feasible shipping schedule for Exercise C.9. What are the costs with your solution?

C.21 Refer to Exercise C.15. What is the cost of your solution to Exercise C.10? The following exercises may be solved graphically.

C.22 Refer to Exercise C.1. What-if the profit contribution from product I rises to $7.20 per unit? What is the optimal solution and the optimal profit?

C.23 Refer to Exercise C.1. What-if the profit contribution from product II rises to $15? What is the optimal solution and the optimal profit?

C.24 Refer to Exercise C.1. What-if the amount of labor available rises to 40 hours per week? What is the optimal solution, and what is the optimal profit?

C.25 Refer to Exercise C.7. Aggressive marketing has enabled Tri Cot to increase its profit on style 1 to $7 per unit. What is the optimal solution, and what is the optimal profit.

C.26 Refer to Exercise C.8. The cooperative is now able to get sorghum products that are equivalent to plain sorghum as by-products of another process; for cooperative purposes there is no charge for this sorghum material. What is the optimal solution, and what is the optimal cost?

C.27 An agricultural mill manufactures feed for cattle, sheep, and chickens. This is done by mixing the following main ingredients: Corn, limestone, soybeans, and fish meal. These ingredients contain the following nutrients: vitamins, proteins, calcium, and crude fat. The contents of nutrients in each kilogram of the ingredients is as follows:

INGREDIENT	NUTRIENT VITAMINS	PROTEIN	CALCIUM	CRUDE FAT
Corn	8	10	6	8
Limestone	6	5	10	6
Soybeans	10	12	6	6
Fish meal	4	8	6	9

The mill contracted to produce 10, 6, and 8 (metric) tons of cattle feed, sheep feed, and chicken feed. Because of the shortages, a limited amount of the ingredients is available, namely, 6 tons of corn, 10 tons of limestone, 4 tons of soybeans, and 5 tons of fish meal. The price per kilogram of these ingredients is, respectively, $.20, $.12, $.24, and $.12. The minimal and the maximal units of the various nutrients for a kilogram of the cattle feed, the sheep feed, and the chicken feed are as follows:

PRODUCT	NUTRIENT Vitamins Min.	Max.	Protein Min.	Max.	Calcium Min.	Max.	Crude Fat Min.	Max.
Cattle feed	6	8	6	8	7	8	4	8
Sheep feed	6	8	6	8	6	8	4	8
Chicken feed	4	6	6	8	6	8	4	8

Formulate this problem so that the total cost is minimized.

C.28 A company manufactures an assembly consisting of a frame, a shaft, and a ball bearing. The company manufactures the shaft and the frames but purchases the ball bearings from a ball bearing manufacturer. Each shaft must be processed on a forging machine, a lathe, and a grinder. These operations require .5 hour, .2 hour, and .3 hour per shaft, respectively. Each frame requires .8 hour on a forging machine, .1 hour on a drilling machine, .3 hour on a milling machine, and .5 hour on a grinder. The company has 5 lathes, 10 grinders, 20 forging machines, 3 drillers, and 6 milling machines. Assume that each machine operates a maximum of 2400 hours per year. Formulate the problem of finding the maximum number of assembled components that can be produced as a linear program.

C.29 A company wishes to decide how many large, medium, and small computers to buy. Their costs are $100, $75, and $50, respectively. Large computers have a capacity for 10 million bytes, while medium computers have a 6-million-byte capacity, and small computers have a 4-million-byte capacity. Large computers consume 200 watts; medium, 120 watts; and small, 80 watts of power. The company requires a capability of at least 80 million bytes, while it can supply only up to 10 kilowatts of power to the computers. How many of each type of computer should the company buy to minimize the cost?

C.30 Dan has $2200 to invest over the next 5 years. At the beginning of each year he can invest money in 1- or 2-year time deposits. The bank pays 8% interest on 1-year time deposits and 17% (total) on 2-year time deposits. In addition XYZ bank will offer 3-year certificates at the beginning of the second year. These certificates will return 27% (total) if Dan reinvests his money available every year. Formulate a linear programming problem to show him how to maximize his total cash on hand at the end of the fifth year.

C.31 A corporation has $30 million available for the coming year to allocate to its three subsidiaries. Because of the commitments to stability of personnel employment and for other reasons the corporation has established a minimal level of funding for each subsidiary. These funding levels are $3 million, $5 million, and $8 million, respectively. Owing to the nature of its operation, subsidiary 2 cannot utilize more than $17 million without major new capital expansion. The corporation is unwilling to undertake such expansion at this time. Each subsidiary has the opportunity to conduct various projects with the funds it receives. A rate of return (as a percent of investment) has been established for each project. In addition, certain of the projects permit only limited investment. The data for each project are as follows:

SUBSIDIARY	PROJECT	RATE OF RETURN (%)	UPPER LIMIT ON INVESTMENT
1	1	8	$6 million
	2	6	$5 million
	3	7	$9 million
2	4	5	$7 million
	5	8	$10 million
	6	9	$4 million
3	7	10	$6 million
	8	6	$3 million

Formulate this problem as a linear programming problem.

C.32 A furniture manufacturer has three plants which need 500, 700, and 600 tons of lumber weekly. The manufacturer may purchase the lumber from three lumber companies. The first two lumber manufacturers virtually have unlimited supply, and because of other commitments, the third manufacturer cannot ship more than 500 tons weekly. The first lumber manufacturer uses rail for transportation, and there is no limit on the tonnage that can be shipped to the furniture facilities. On the other hand, the last two lumber companies use trucks that limit the tonnage that can be shipped to any of the furniture companies to 200 tons. The following table gives the transportation cost from the lumber companies to the furniture manufacturers (dollars per ton):

LUMBER COMPANY	FURNITURE FACILITY		
	1	2	3
1	2	3	5
2	2.5	4	4.8
3	3	3.6	3.2

Formulate this problem as a linear programming problem.

The Simplex Algorithm, the Dual Problem, and Sensitivity Analysis

While in practice linear programming problems are solved by computers, there is a need to understand the computational method, that is, the algorithm used by computers. Therefore, in this chapter the mathematical technique of the **simplex algorithm** is presented via simple illustrations and manual calculations. Also discussed will be the important concept of the dual formulation of linear programming problems and sensitivity analysis.

11.1 INTRODUCTION TO THE SIMPLEX ALGORITHM

Solving Linear Equations

The simplex algorithm is closely related to the solution of a system of linear equations. So before we present the simplex algorithm, a few words about solving linear equations by the Gauss-Jordan elimination method will be helpful.

Suppose you need to solve

$$3x_1 + 2x_2 - x_3 = 12$$
$$5x_1 - 3x_2 + 7x_3 = 23$$
$$1x_1 + 4x_2 - 2x_3 = 12$$

You can get the answer by various computational methods* and find that

$$x_1 = 2, \qquad x_2 = 5, \qquad x_3 = 4$$

Suppose you need to solve a second set of equations:†

$$1x_1 + 0x_2 + 0x_3 = 2$$

---

* A review of solving linear equations is included in Appendix A, Sections 5 and 6.
† For the sake of clarity we shall show the coefficients 0 and 1 in our equations.

$$0x_1 + 1x_2 + 0x_3 = 5$$

$$0x_1 + 0x_2 + 1x_3 = 4$$

You know immediately that

$$x_1 = 2, \qquad x_2 = 5, \qquad x_3 = 4$$

In fact the two systems of equations are **equivalent**, because they have the same solution. The Gauss-Jordan method is a computational technique through which a sequence of steps, iterations, transforms a system of linear equations into an equivalent system such that the solution can be directly observed, as in our second set of equations. The key to the method is to make (1) the first **coefficient** in the first equation equal to 1, (2) the second coefficient in the second equation equal to 1, (3) the third coefficient in the third equation equal to 1, and so on, and to have zeros everywhere else as coefficients.

To illustrate the method, consider a simple problem:

$$(1) \quad 3x_1 + 1x_2 = 9$$

$$(2) \quad 1x_1 + 2x_2 = 8$$

The solution method is the following:

Step 1. We want to have a 1 as the coefficient of x_1 in the first equation. So we divide each coefficient by 3:

$$1x_1 + \tfrac{1}{3}x_2 = 3$$

The result is

NEW FIRST EQUATION = $\tfrac{1}{3}$ × OLD FIRST EQUATION

Our system of equations is now

$$(1) \quad 1x_1 + \tfrac{1}{3}x_2 = 3$$

$$(2) \quad 1x_1 + 2x_2 = 8$$

Step 2. We want the coefficient of x_1 in the second equation to become 0. So we subtract 1 times the first equation from the second equation:

$$0x_1 + (2 - \tfrac{1}{3})x_2 = 8 - 3$$

or

$$0x_1 + \tfrac{5}{3}x_2 = 5$$

The rule is

NEW SECOND EQUATION = OLD SECOND EQUATION − 1 ×
NEW FIRST EQUATION

Note that *OLD* refers to the system obtained in the previous step. Our system of equations now is

$$(1) \quad 1x_1 + \tfrac{1}{3}x_2 = 3$$

$$(2) \quad 0x_1 + \tfrac{5}{3}x_2 = 5$$

Step 3. We want the coefficient of x_2 in the second equation to become 1. So we divide by $\frac{5}{3}$, that is, multiply by $\frac{3}{5}$, and get

$$0x_1 + 1x_2 = 5 \times \frac{3}{5}$$

The rule is

NEW SECOND EQUATION $= \frac{3}{5} \times$ OLD SECOND EQUATION

Our system of equations is now

$$(1) \quad 1x_1 + \tfrac{1}{3}x_2 = 3$$

$$(2) \quad 0x_1 + 1x_2 = 3$$

Step 4. We want the coefficient of x_2 in the first equation to become 0. So we subtract $\frac{1}{3}$ times the second equation from the first equation:

$$1x_1 + 0x_2 = 3 - \tfrac{1}{3} \times 3 = 2$$

The rule is

NEW FIRST EQUATION = OLD FIRST EQUATION $- \frac{1}{3} \times$ NEW
SECOND EQUATION

Thus our final system of equations is

$$(1) \quad 1x_1 + 0x_2 = 2$$

$$(2) \quad 0x_1 + 1x_2 = 3$$

And the solution is

$$x_1 = 2, \qquad x_2 = 3$$

Method of Detached Coefficients

In the simplex method a great deal of writing is saved by using the method of detached coefficients. Instead of writing equations, you just write the coefficients in tableau (table) form. As shown in part (a) of Figure 11.1, start with the given coefficients in the first tableau and follow the four steps:

Step 1

NEW FIRST ROW $= \frac{1}{3} \times$ OLD FIRST ROW $= \frac{1}{3} \times [3, 1, 9]$

So write the new first row in part (b) of Figure 11.1.

Step 2

NEW SECOND ROW = OLD SECOND ROW $- 1 \times$ NEW FIRST
ROW $= [1, 2, 8] - 1 \times [1, \tfrac{1}{3}, 3]$

So complete the second tableau in part (c) of Figure 11.1.

Now we copy the second tableau in part (d) of Figure 11.1 but replace NEW by OLD.

(a)

	1	2	3	
1	3	1	9	OLD FIRST ROW
2	1	2	8	OLD SECOND ROW

First Tableau

(d)

	1	2	3	
1	1	$\frac{1}{3}$	3	OLD FIRST ROW
2	0	$\frac{5}{3}$	5	OLD SECOND ROW

Second Tableau Copied

(b)

	1	2	3	
1	1	$\frac{1}{3}$	3	NEW FIRST ROW
2				

Second Tableau Started

(e)

	1	2	3	
1				
2	0	1	3	NEW SECOND ROW

Third Tableau Started

(c)

	1	2	3	
1	1	$\frac{1}{3}$	3	
2	0	$\frac{5}{3}$	5	NEW SECOND ROW

Second Tableau Completed

(f)

	1	2	3	
1	1	0	2	NEW FIRST ROW
2	0	1	3	

Third Tableau Completed

FIGURE 11.1 Solving a system of linear equations with the method of detached coefficients.

Step 3

NEW SECOND ROW $= \frac{3}{5} \times$ OLD SECOND ROW $= \frac{3}{5} \times [0, \frac{5}{3}, 5]$

So write the new second row in part (e) of Figure 11.1.

Step 4

NEW FIRST ROW = OLD FIRST ROW $- \frac{1}{3} \times$ NEW SECOND ROW
$$= [1, \tfrac{1}{3}, 3] - \tfrac{1}{3} \times [0, 1, 3]$$

So complete the third tableau in part (f) of Figure 11.1.

Now you can reconstruct the equivalent system of equations by using the coefficients from part (f),

$$1x_1 + 0x_2 = 2$$
$$0x_1 + 1x_2 = 3$$

and conclude immediately that

$$x_1 = 2, \qquad x_2 = 3$$

Now we apply a similar technique to linear programming.

The Standard Form of Linear Programming

Let us return to the Indian jewelry problem of Minnehaha discussed in Chapter 10. Recall that she has 9 ounces of silver and 8 ounces of gold and that she manufactures rings and bracelets. Designate by x_1 the number of rings and by x_2 the number of bracelets manufactured. The silver constraint is met if

$$3x_1 + 1x_2 \leq 9 \quad \text{(silver)}$$

and the gold constraint if

$$1x_1 + 2x_2 \leq 8 \quad \text{(gold)}$$

The problem is to maximize the profit:

$$Z = 4x_1 + 5x_2$$

Before the simplex method can be applied, the relations in the linear programming problem must be brought to a **standard** form, which means that the inequalities are turned into equations.

Designate by S_1 the quantity of surplus silver and by S_2 the quantity of surplus gold. If a constraint is **binding**, there is no leftover resource, and the surplus is zero. The new variables S_1 and S_2 are called **slack variables** and produce no profit. Therefore we can now state our linear programming problem in the standard form,

$$3x_1 + 1x_2 + 1S_1 + 0S_2 = 9 \quad \text{(silver)}$$

$$1x_1 + 2x_2 + 0S_1 + 1S_2 = 8 \quad \text{(gold)}$$

and the problem is to maximize the profit,

$$Z = 4x_1 + 5x_2 + 0S_1 + 0S_2$$

because the slack variables do not contribute to the profit. The solution to the standard linear programming problem will be the same as for the original problem. However, as you will see in what follows, there is a mathematical advantage when introducing the standard form.

Namely, the simplex algorithm starts with an **initial solution** and then improves the solution through a system of equivalent equations. Now for the standard formulation of the problem it is easy to get a solution:

$$x_1 = 0, \qquad x_2 = 0, \qquad S_1 = 9, \qquad S_2 = 8$$

This is not a practical solution because the profit is zero. However, at this stage of the algorithm we do not care; all we want is an initial solution which can be improved. First we get organized to show how the calculations are carried out.

The Simplex Tableau

Instead of writing the equations of the linear programming problem, we use the method of detached coefficients, discussed earlier. Note that there are five variables in the problem, x_1, x_2, S_1, S_2, and Z, and that we

The Simplex
Algorithm, the Dual
Problem, and
Sensitivity Analysis

want each variable to appear in each equation. So first we rewrite the
equations of the problem:

$$9.0 = 3.0x_1 + 1.0x_2 + 1S_1 + 0S_2 + 0Z \quad \text{(silver)}$$
$$8.0 = 1.0x_1 + 2.0x_2 + 0S_1 + 1S_2 + 0Z \quad \text{(gold)}$$
$$0 = 4.0x_1 - 5.0x_2 + 0S_1 + 0S_2 + 12 \quad \text{(profit)}$$

Why the decimal points? For expository reasons we shall make a
distinction when a coefficient *happens* to be a whole number or when it
is so by *design*. For example, the constraint on silver being 9, the
number happens to be a whole number. So we write 9.0. But the
coefficient on the slack is precisely 1 by design, so we just write 1. This
will help to describe the calculations of the simplex method.

Figure 11.2 shows the initial (first) simplex tableau, displaying the
detached coefficients and the variables. Recall that in our initial solution

$$x_1 = 0, \qquad x_2 = 0, \qquad S_1 = 9.0, \qquad S_2 = 8.0$$

In the first column we list SILVER, GOLD, and INDEX. In the column
marked "variables" we list the variables S_1, S_2, and Z, and in the column
"values" we list the initial solutions 9.0, 8.0, and $0. Because the values
of x_1 and x_2 are zeros, we say that x_1 and x_2 are OUT of the solution and S_1
and S_2 are IN because the values are not zero.

> OUT variables must be equal to zero; IN variables may or may not be equal to
> zero.

To help find the values of S_1, S_2, and Z, we put circles around the
three 1s in the tableau.

> We find the values of the IN variables by entering the simplex tableau from
> the top, dropping to the circled 1, and moving to the left to the "variables" and
> "values" columns.

There is of course no problem in finding the values for the OUT
variables; they are equal to zero.

		VALUES	RINGS	BRACELETS	SILVER SLACK ●	GOLD SLACK ●	Z	Shuffleboard
VARIABLES			x_1	x_2	S_1	S_2	Z	
SILVER	$S_1 =$	9.0	3.0	1.0	①	0	0	
GOLD	$S_2 =$	8.0	1.0	2.0	0	①	0	
INDEX	$Z =$	$0	−$4.00	−$5.00	$0	$0	①	

FIGURE 11.2
First, initial simplex tableau. The stones are at S_1 and S_2.

To clarify which variables are IN, we display at the top of the tableau a *shuffleboard* and place the *stones* where the IN variables (S_1 and S_2 in our discussion) are located.

If we only knew the location of the stones and the associated tableau, then we would have the solution to our problem.

> The simplex algorithm consists of shuffling the stones one by one, calculating the associated tableau until the values of the IN variables provide the optimum solution to the problem.

Thus we need three rules to answer the three questions: (1) Which stone should be shuffled? (2) Where should the stone be shuffled? (3) When should shuffling be stopped?

However, before we discuss these rules, we digress a moment and provide an insight into the nature of the simplex method.

Understanding the Simplex Method

We must stress again that the crux of the matter is to find the location of the stones for the optimum solution. Suppose we know that the stones are at x_1 and x_2 and that x_1 and x_2 are IN and S_1 and S_2 are OUT. Then

$$3x_1 + 1x_2 = 9 \quad \text{(silver)}$$

$$1x_1 + 2x_2 = 8 \quad \text{(gold)}$$

We can solve two equations with two unknowns and find the solution. If we had 5, 10, or even 50 equations, we could solve 5, 10, or 50 equations with 5, 10, or 50 unknowns and find the solution. But in a new problem we do not know where the stones are.

Even in the jewelry problem discussed here we do not know where the stones are. Going back to our graphic solution in Chapter 10, recall that if

$$Z = 4x_1 + 5x_2$$

the stones are at x_1 and x_2. But if

$$Z = 4x_1 + 12x_2$$

then $x_1 = 0$, there is a silver surplus of 5 units, and so $S_1 = 5$. Thus x_2 and S_1 are IN and x_1 and S_2 are OUT. The stones are at x_2 and S_1.

We could try every possible location for the two stones, solve two equations for two unknowns in each case, and find the best solution. How many cases would we have to try?

The first stone can be put at four places and the second at the remaining three places. This gives a total of $4 \times 3 = 12$ alternatives, but we counted each twice, and so there are only 6 alternatives. It is easy to solve six times two equations with two unknowns, and therefore it is easy to solve the problem by this **brute-force method** or **exhaustive enumeration**.

But suppose you have a problem with 30 stones and 100 places. It can be shown that there are 100!/(30!70!) solutions, where "!" stands for factorial (see Section 3.6 for the meaning of factorial). This number can be calculated as approximately 294×10^{23}, meaning the number 294 followed by 23 zeros. You would have to solve 30 equations with 30 unknowns this many times. And this is a *small* linear programming problem. No computer ever could do such large jobs, not even in a million years. The simplex method gets around the problem by using an **iterative** method.

The power of the simplex algorithm is that it provides an initial solution, and then by moving one stone at a time, the solution is improved by iterations until the optimum solution is obtained. Compared with the brute-force method, the iterative method is an enormous shortcut.

We are now ready to return to our main topic, the simplex algorithm.

11.2 THE SIMPLEX ALGORITHM

Three Rules of the Simplex Algorithm

First we address ourselves to the question of where to shuffle the stones (Figure 11.2). Suppose we move one of the stones to the x_1 column, which means that we bring rings into the solution. What will happen to the profit?

First we must recognize that bringing in a ring to the solution requires 3 ounces of silver and 1 ounce of gold. Thus, if a ring is brought into the solution, S_1, the value of the first slack, must be decreased by 3 and S_2, the value of the second slack, decreased by 1. Each ring brings a profit of $4.00, and changing the slack makes no difference in the profit, because slacks are valued as zero. Therefore, bringing in a ring will produce a gain in profit of $4.00. But the simplex method works with losses, not profits, and so in the **simplex tableau** we show a negative loss, that is, a gain of −$4.00.

What about bringing in a bracelet, that is, moving a stone to the bracelet column? Each bracelet requires 1 ounce of silver and 2 ounces of gold. So the first slack must be decreased by 1 and the second slack by 2. However, the slacks are valued at zero, and so bringing in a bracelet results in a loss of −$5.00. To sum up, it looks more promising to bring bracelets into the solution than rings. So we decide to *enter x_2* in the solution. Our reasoning leads to the first rule of the simplex algorithm:

> The **ENTERING rule** of the simplex algorithm: Examine the bottom row of the simplex tableau, and move the stone to the most negative column.

In the case of a tie, move the stone to one of the most negative columns.

Now we know that the stone will be moved to the bracelet column.

FIGURE 11.3
Complete version of the first, initial simplex tableau. The stones are at S_1 and S_2. S_1 and S_2 are IN the solution, and x_1 and x_2 are OUT.

	ROW NUMBERS	VARIABLES	VALUES	RINGS x_1	BRACELETS x_2	SILVER SLACK S_1	GOLD SLACK S_2	Z	HOW MUCH?
					Enter	Leave •	•		Shuffleboard
SILVER	(1)	$S_1 =$	9.0	3.0	1.0	(1)	0	0	9.0/1.0 = 9.0
GOLD	(2)	$S_2 =$	8.0	1.0	2.0	0	(1)	0	8.0/2.0 = 4.0 *
INDEX	(3)	$Z =$	$0	−$4.00	−$5.00	$0	$0	(1)	—

To stress the point, we put a frame around the coefficients in the bracelet column (Figure 11.3) and call this the **pivot column** of the tableau. We also label the column at the top as ENTER. Now we address ourselves to the question of which stone to move to the pivot column.

Each bracelet improves the profit by $5.00 and so causes a loss of −$5.00. We call the −$5.00 the **improvement index**, or just the index associated with x_1, and call the bottom row of the simplex tableau the **index row**. Note the following:

> The indexes associated with the stones are equal to zero.

Now it makes good sense to bring in bracelets to improve the profit, and we should try to bring in as many bracelets as possible. However, bracelets require silver and gold, so there is an upper limit to the quantity we can bring in. This leads to our second rule:

> The **HOW-MUCH rule** of the simplex algorithm: Bring to the solution as many units as possible without violating the constraints.

Each bracelet requires 1 ounce of silver, and we have 9 ounces of silver. Thus, no more than nine bracelets can be introduced insofar as silver is concerned. But each bracelet requires 2 ounces of gold, and we have only 8 ounces of gold, so only four bracelets can be introduced insofar as gold is concerned. Thus the binding constraint is that the maximum number of bracelets which can be brought to the solution is four.

A more formal calculation for determining the number of bracelets to be brought in is in the last column of the tableau. Namely, we divide the numbers in the "values" column by the corresponding numbers in the pivot column. We get $9.0/1.0 = 9.0$, and $8.0/2.0 = 4.0$. The smaller of these two numbers is 4.0, which tells us that four bracelets are to be brought into the solution. We also know that no gold will be left in the solution, that is, S_2 will be 0, meaning that the second slack will disappear from the solution. So now we label the S_2 column at the top of the tableau as LEAVE. This is our third rule:

> The **LEAVING rule** of the simplex algorithm: Remove the stone as indicated by the binding constraint.

In the case of a tie, remove the stone corresponding to one of the binding constraints.

Gold disappears from the solution, as we put a frame around the second row of the tableau and call this row the **pivot row**. The intersection of the pivot row and the pivot column contains the **pivot coefficient**, the number 2.0.

In summary, we can say that we have a new solution to the problem:

$$x_1 = 0 \quad \text{(no bracelets)}$$

$$x_2 = 4.0 \quad \text{(four rings)}$$

$$S_1 = 9.0 - 3.0x_1 - 1.0x_2 = 9.0 - 0 - 4.0 = 5.0$$

$$S_2 = 0$$

The stone has been moved from S_2 to x_2; x_2 and S_1 are IN the solution; x_1 and S_2 are OUT. The profit for the second solution is

$$Z = 4.0x_1 + 5.0x_2 = 4.0 \times 0 + 5.0 \times 4.0 = 0 + 20 = \$20.00$$

which is indeed better than the profit for the first solution.

Second Simplex Tableau

Our goal now is to construct a second simplex tableau corresponding to our new solution which has x_2 and S_1 IN. This will allow us to go from the second to the third tableau, and so on, until we find the best solution to the problem.

In Figure 11.4 we start construction of the new tableau. In the first column we list SILVER, BRACELETS, and INDEX. In the "variables" column we write S_1, x_2, and Z. Our problem is to construct the second tableau so that its properties match those of the first tableau. What do we need?

In the first tableau we have S_1 and S_2 in the solution. S_1 is still IN the solution, so we list 1, 0, 0 in the S_1 column. But how do we indicate that x_2 is IN the solution? Note that in the first tableau in the S_2 column (Figure 11.3) we have the numbers 0, 1, 0, so now in the second tableau we must have 0, 1, 0 in the x_2 column. We write these three numbers in

ROW NUMBERS	VARIABLES	VALUES	RINGS x_1	BRACELETS x_2	SILVER SLACK S_1	GOLD SLACK S_2	Z	HOW MUCH?
SILVER (1)	$S_1 =$			0	1			
BRACELETS (2)	$x_2 =$			(1)	(0)			
INDEX (3)	$Z =$			$0	$0			

Shuffleboard

FIGURE 11.4
Starting the second simplex tableau.

the x_2 column in Figure 11.4. How do we fill out the rest of the tableau to get these desired numbers?

The gold (pivot) row in Figure 11.3 corresponds to the equation

$$8.0 = 1.0x_1 + 2.0x_2 + 0S_1 + 1S_2 + 0Z$$

As you know, if in a system of equations all the coefficients are divided by the same number, an equivalent system of equations results. Thus the equation for the gold constraint can be turned into a new equation by dividing the pivot coefficient (Figure 11.3) by 2.0:

$$4.0 = .5x_1 + 1x_2 + 0S_1 + .5S_2 + 0Z$$

Or the same can be written with the method of detached coefficients:

$$\frac{[8.0, 1.0, 2.0, 0, 1]}{2.0} = [4, .5, 1, 0, .5]$$

We can say the same thing in words:

$$\text{NEW SECOND ROW} = \frac{\text{OLD PIVOT ROW}}{\text{PIVOT COEFFICIENT}}$$

Note that when we refer to a ROW we consider the x_1, x_2, S_1, and S_2 columns and ignore the Z column because this column will never change.

So now you can write the new second row of the second simplex tableau as shown in Figure 11.5.

How do we get the new silver first row in the second tableau? We must have a 0 in the x_2 column. Note that an equivalent system of equations results if from one of the equations another equation is subtracted or if a multiple of another equation is subtracted. So you can say that

NEW SILVER ROW = OLD SILVER ROW − 1.0 × NEW SECOND ROW

Or in equation form we can say that

$$9.0 = 3.0x_1 + 1.0x_2 + 1S_1 + 0S_2 + 0Z \quad \text{(old silver)}$$

$$4.0 = .5x_1 + 1x_2 + 0S_1 + .5S_2 + 0Z \quad \text{(new second row)}$$

$$5.0 = 2.5x_1 + 0x_2 + 1S_1 - .5S_2 + 0Z \quad \text{(new silver)}$$

or simply

$$[9.0, 3.0, 1.0, 1, 0] - 1 \times [4.0, .5, 1, 0, .5] = [5.0, 2.5, 0, 1, -.5]$$

So write these coefficients in the second tableau in Figure 11.5. Observe that the coefficient of x_2 is indeed 0 in the silver row.

By a similar method you can find the new bottom (index) row:

NEW INDEX ROW − OLD INDEX ROW − (−5.0) × NEW SECOND ROW

Reminder: The decimal point indicates that the number happens to be a whole number. Why −5.0? This is the coefficient in the first tableau in the x_2 column, bottom row. Alternatively, you can write the equation corresponding to the bottom row:

$$20.0 = -1.5x_1 + 0x_2 + 0S_1 + 2.5S_2 + Z$$

We can verify directly the row solution from the second tableau in Figure 11.5. Namely, x_1 and S_2 are OUT, so

$$x_1 = 0, \qquad S_2 = 0$$

However, x_2 is IN, so we enter the x_2 column from the top, drop to the circled 1, move to the left, and read in the "values" column:

$$x_2 = 4.0$$

				RINGS	BRACELETS	SILVER SLACK	GOLD SLACK		Shuffleboard
ROW NUMBERS	VARIABLES	VALUES		x_1	x_2	S_1	S_2	Z	HOW MUCH?
SILVER (1)	$S_1 =$	5.0		2.5	0	①(1)	−.5	0	
BRACELETS (2)	$x_2 =$	4.0		.5	(1)	0	.5	0	
INDEX (3)	$Z =$	$20.00		−$1.50	$0	$0	$2.50	(1)	

FIGURE 11.5.
Completing the second simplex tableau. The stones are at x_2 and S_1. Thus x_2 and S_1 are IN the solution, and x_1 and S_2 are OUT.

Similarly, we enter the S_1 column from the top, drop to the circled 1, move to the left, and read in the "values" column:

$$S_1 = 5.0, \qquad Z = \$20.00$$

Note that in the x_2 column we have indeed, as desired, the numbers 0, 1, 0. S_1 is still in the solution, and correspondingly in the S_1 column we still have the numbers 1, 0, 0.

In summary, we have accomplished changing our problem from the first initial tableau (Figure 11.3) to a second tableau (Figure 11.5). The stones are not in columns S_1 and S_2 but in columns x_2 and S_1, as indicated by the stones and circles around the 1s. In these columns in the bottom row we have 0s, just as we had 0s in columns S_1 and S_2 in the first tableau. We see that the second tableau has properties similar to the first tableau.

As for the first tableau, we can ask the same question for the second tableau: Can this solution be improved?

If a ring is brought into the solution, there will be a loss of $-\$1.50$, as indicated by the index in the bottom row of Figure 11.5. This means an improvement of $1.50. If one unit of S_2 is brought into the solution, there will be a loss of $2.50, as again indicated by the index in the bottom row. Thus we conclude that we can improve the solution by bringing rings into the solution. However, before we continue to the third tableau, let us summarize the steps in our algorithm.

Recap of Algorithm

Step 1. Apply the ENTERING rule. Find the most negative index in the bottom row of the tableau. (This is -5.00 in Figure 11.2.) Write at the top ENTER, as this is the variable coming into the solution. Frame the pivot column.

Step 2. Apply the HOW-MUCH rule. Divide the "values" column by the pivot column, and star the smallest nonnegative ratio. (In Figure 11.2 this is

$$[9.0/1.0, 8.0/2.0] = [9.0, 4.0]$$

and the smallest positive value is 4.0.) Apply the LEAVING rule, identify the variable to be removed, and frame the corresponding row as the pivot row. The number at the intersection of the pivot row and pivot column is the pivot coefficient. (This is 2.0 in Figure 11.2.)

Step 3. Start the new simplex tableau. Write in the coefficients of 0s and 1s in the pivot column. Fill in the "variables" column.

Step 4. Replacing the old pivot row is

$$\text{NEW ROW} = \frac{\text{OLD PIVOT ROW}}{\text{PIVOT COEFFICIENT}}$$

Step 5. For all other rows,

$$\text{NEW ROW} = \text{OLD ROW} - \text{COEFFICIENT IN PIVOT} \\ \text{COLUMN} \times \text{NEW ROW from step 4}$$

In the example we had

$$\text{NEW ROW} = \frac{\text{OLD PIVOT ROW}}{2.0}$$

NEW SILVER ROW = OLD SILVER ROW − 1.0 × NEW ROW

and

NEW INDEX ROW = OLD INDEX ROW − (−5.0) × NEW ROW

Third Simplex Tableau

We apply the five steps of the simplex algorithm to the second simplex tableau, which is copied in Figure 11.6.

Step 1. Apply the ENTERING rule. The most negative index is −$1.50 in the x_1 column, showing that rings are to enter into the solution. Write ENTER at the top of the rings column. Frame the column as the new pivot column.

Step 2. Apply the HOW-MUCH rule. Divide the "values" column

	ROW NUMBERS	VARIABLES	VALUES	RINGS x_1	BRACELETS x_2	SILVER SLACK S_1	GOLD SLACK S_2	Z	HOW MUCH?
SILVER	(1)	$S_1 =$	5.0	2.5	0	①	−.5	0	5.0/2.5 = 2.0 ✳
BRACELETS	(2)	$x_2 =$	4.0	.5	①	0	.5	0	4.0/.5 = 8.0
INDEX	(3)	$Z =$	$20.00	−$1.50	$0	$0	$2.50	①	—

FIGURE 11.6 The solution represented by the second simplex tableau is evaluated.

by the pivot column, and star the smallest ratio, 2.0, in the first (silver) row. Frame the first row as the new pivot row. The new pivot coefficient is 2.5.

Step 3. Start the new simplex tableau in Figure 11.7. Write in the rings column the numbers 1, 0, 0. Write the new variables x_1 coming into the solution in the first row of the "variables" column and copy x_2 and Z. Write RINGS, BRACELETS, and INDEX in the first column.

Step 4. The pivot row is the silver row and therefore

$$\text{NEW FIRST ROW} = \frac{\text{OLD PIVOT ROW}}{2.5}$$

Step 5.

$$\text{NEW BRACELETS ROW} = \text{OLD BRACELETS ROW} - .5 \times \text{NEW FIRST ROW}$$

$$\text{NEW INDEX ROW} = \text{OLD INDEX ROW} - (-1.5) \times \text{NEW FIRST ROW}$$

So now in Figure 11.7 we have the third simplex tableau. The variables x_1 and x_2 are IN, and the new solution is

$$x_1 = 2, \qquad x_3 = 3.0, \qquad Z = \$23.00$$

This means that two rings and three bracelets are manufactured, there is no slack (surplus of gold or silver), and the profit is \$23.

								Shuffleboard
ROW NUMBERS	VARIABLES	VALUES	RINGS x_1	BRACELETS x_2	SILVER SLACK S_1	GOLD SLACK S_2	Z	
RINGS (1)	$x_1 =$	2.0	1	0	.4	−.2	0	
BRACELETS (2)	$x_2 =$	3.0	0	1	−.2	.6	0	
INDEX (3)	$Z =$	\$23.00	\$0	\$0	\$.60	\$2.20	1	

FIGURE 11.7 The third, final simplex tableau. The stones are at x_1 and x_2. Thus x_1 and x_2 are IN the solution, S_1 and S_2 are OUT.

There is no negative index in the bottom row, so we apply the third rule:

> **STOPPING rule:** When there are no negative indexes in the bottom row, the optimum solution has been obtained.

Thus the third tableau is the final tableau, and the third solution is the optimal one.

To appreciate the validity of the rule, let us write out explicitly the system of equations corresponding to the tableau in Figure 11.7. We have

$$2 = 1x_1 + 0x_2 + .4S_1 - .2S_2 + 0Z$$

$$3 = 0x_2 + 1x_2 = .2S_1 + .6S_2 + 0Z$$

$$23 = 0x_1 + 0x_2 + .6S_1 + 2.2S_2 + 1Z$$

where the last equation can be written as

$$Z = 0x_1 + 0x_2 - .6S_1 - 2.2S_2 + 23$$

Recall that our objective is to maximize Z. But bear in mind that all the variables must be 0s or positive numbers, and so the value of Z is less than \$23 unless S_1 and S_2 are both 0s. Then and only then can we get the profit of \$23. Therefore, it is seen that any other solution to the problem will generate less than \$23 profit.

This concludes our discussion of the simplex algorithm under the assumptions that (1) all the constraints use the $\leq$ sign, (2) the right-hand-side coefficients are nonnegative, and (3) we maximize. Now we proceed to the general case where these assumptions might not hold.

11.3 THE FEED MIX PROBLEM: HOW TO MINIMIZE

We now show how the simplex algorithm is to be modified when there are $\leq$, $=$, and $\geq$ signs and when the problem is to minimize the objective function. For illustrative purposes, we use in slightly modified form the Texas Cattle Feed Corp. problem discussed in Chapter 7. The constraints to meet the four types of nutrition requirements are

$$2x_1 + 3x_2 = 30, \quad \text{type 1}$$

$$1x_1 + 4x_2 \geq 20, \quad \text{type 2}$$

$$3x_1 + 1x_2 \geq 15, \quad \text{type 3}$$

$$1x_1 + 0x_2 \leq 10, \quad \text{type 4}$$

The problem is to minimize the objective function:

$$Z = 14x_1 + 15x_2$$

This problem can be solved by a graphic method, and we leave it as an exercise for you to show that corner B in Figure 10.17 still provides the optimal solution.

Standard Form

First we need to convert the stytem of relationships into a standard form; that is, we want to introduce additional variables to change the unequal signs to equal signs. We already know that by introducing slack variables we can change $\leq$ signs to $=$ signs. But what do we do about $\geq$ signs?

Instead of *adding*, we must be *subtracting* new variables, because the new variables must be nonnegative. So we get

$$2x_1 + 3x_2 + 0S_1 + 0S_2 + 0S_3 = 30$$

$$1x_1 - 4x_2 - 1S_1 + 0S_2 + 0S_3 = 20$$

$$3x_1 + 1x_2 + 0S_1 - 1S_2 + 0S_3 = 15$$

$$1x_1 + 0x_1 + 0S_1 + 0S_2 + 1S_3 = 10$$

where S_1 and S_2 are negative, slack, or **surplus** variables. The word surplus is due to the fact that if, for example, $S_1 = 5$, then there is a surplus of 5 units in the second constraint.

But now our problem is to find an initial solution. Examining the preceding equations, we conclude that we have no direct way to do so, because the solution cannot have negative values. Therefore we introduce the **artificial variable** A_1 in the first equation,

$$2x_1 + 3x_2 + 0S_1 + 0S_2 + 0S_3 + 1A_1 = 30$$

and for the initial solution we use $A_1 = 30$. Now inspect the second equation. We cannot use $S_1 = -20$ for the initial solution because we do not allow negative values. So we introduce a second artificial variable A_2,

$$1x_1 + 4x_2 - 1S_1 + 0S_2 + 0S_3 + 0A_1 + 1A_2 = 20$$

and use $A_2 = 20$ for our initial solution. For the third relationship we write

$$3x_1 + 1x_2 + 0S_1 - 1S_2 + 0S_3 + 0A_1 + 0A_2 + 1A_3 = 15$$

and use $A_3 = 15$ for the initial solution. In the fourth relationship we have a slack variable, and so we can use $S_3 = 10$ for the initial solution.

The preceding equations form the new standard set with the initial solution:

$$x_1 = 0, \qquad x_2 = 0$$

$$S_1 = 0, \qquad S_2 = 0, \qquad S_3 = 10$$

$$A_1 = 20, \qquad A_2 = 20, \qquad A_3 = 15$$

We now summarize our approach:

1. For each $=$ sign, introduce an artificial variable.

2. For each $\geq$ sign, introduce a surplus and an artificial variable.
3. For each $\leq$ sign, introduce a slack variable.

Objective Function

Now we have converted the relationships into equations and developed an initial solution. What do we do about the objective function?

As for the slack variables S_1, S_2, and S_3, we price them at 0 as in our earlier discussions. However, the artificial variables A_1, A_2, and A_3 require special consideration. Namely, to obtain the optimal solution, we must be certain that these variables are OUT of the solution, because otherwise our original relationships may not hold. For example, if A_1 is not zero, the first equation will not hold. Therefore, these variables must be priced at a very high value, so that when the optimum is obtained, they will automatically be driven out of the solution. Let us designate this large value by M, and then the objective function to be minimized is

$$Z = 14x_1 + 15x_2 + MA_1 + MA_2 + MA_3$$

Now we have formulated the standard form of the problem with the aid of the "big M method." How large should M be? It should be "very" large, so the artificial variables disappear. Considering that x_1 and x_2 are priced at 14 and 15, we guess that the price of 100 would be large enough. As you will see, the artificial variables will disappear in three steps. However, if they do not ultimately disappear, it means that you have not chosen M large enough, and you should take an even larger value, say 1000.

To set up the first simplex tableau, we rewrite our relationships:

$$30 = 2x_1 + 3x_2 + 1A_1 + 0S_1 + 0A_2 + 0S_2 + 0A_3 + 0S_3 + 0Z$$
$$20 = 1x_1 + 4x_2 + 0A_1 - 1S_1 + 1A_2 + 0S_2 + 0A_3 + 0S_3 + 0Z$$
$$15 = 3x_1 + 1x_2 + 0A_1 + 0S_1 + 0A_2 - 1S_2 + 1A_3 + 0S_3 + 0Z$$
$$10 = 1x_1 + 0x_2 + 0A_1 + 0S_1 + 0A_2 + 0S_2 + 0A_3 + 1S_3 + 0Z$$
$$0 = -14x_1 - 15x_2 - 100A_1 + 0S_1 - 100A_2 + 0S_2 - 100A_3 + 0S_3 = 1Z$$

For the initial solution we use

$$A_1 = 30, \quad A_2 = 20, \quad A_3 = 15, \quad S_3 = 10$$

We are in a position now to construct the first simplex tableau as shown in Figure 11.8. (Disregard for the moment row 5′ at the bottom.) Is this a valid simplex tableau?

Not so! We stated when introducing the concepts of the shuffle-board and stones that in the bottom row of the simplex tableau the indexes under the stones must be zero. (You can verify this by looking at Figures 11.2, 11.5, and 11.7.) But in Figure 11.8, row (5), we have −\$100 under A_1, A_2, and A_3. We must take steps so we have zeros under A_1, A_2, and A_3.

Row Numbers	Variables	Values	x_1	x_2	A_1	S_1	A_2	S_2	A_3	S_3	Z	Shuffleboard How Much?
(1)	$A_1 =$	30.0	2.0	3.0	1	0	0	0	0	0	0	30.0/3.0 = 10
(2)	$A_2 =$	20.0	1.0	4.0	0	−1	1	0	0	0	0	20.0/4.0 = 5 *
(3)	$A_3 =$	15.0	3.0	1.0	0	0	0	−1	1	0	0	15.0/1.0 = 15
(4)	$S_3 =$	10.0	1.0	0	0	0	0	0	0	1	0	
(5)	$Z =$	0	−$14	−$15	−$100	0	−$100	0	−$100	0	1	
(5′)	$Z =$	+$6500	+$586	+$785	0	−$100	0	−$100	0	0	1	

The top of the table shows "Enter" (over the x_2 column) and "Leave" (over the A_2 column), with stones placed on the shuffleboard bar.

FIGURE 11.8 First, initial simplex tableau for the modified Texas Cattle Feed Corp. problem.

The Initial Simplex Tableau

We fall back on our previous approach; we know how to change a system of equations into an equivalent system. We can subtract from one equation multiples of other equations. So we add to row (5) in Figure 11.8, 100 times row (1), 100 times row (2), and 100 times row (3). By this method we get a new bottom row, (5′):

$$
\begin{array}{r}
[0,\ -14,\ -15,\ -100,\ \ \ 0,\ -100,\ \ \ 0,\ -100,\ 0] \\
+\ 100\ \times\quad [30,\quad 2,\quad 3,\quad 1,\quad 0,\quad 0,\quad 0,\quad 0,\ 0] \\
+\ 100\ \times\quad [20,\quad 1,\quad 4,\quad 0,\ -1,\quad 1,\quad 0,\quad 0,\ 0] \\
+\ 100\ \times\quad [15,\quad 3,\quad 1,\quad 0,\quad 0,\quad 0,\ -1,\quad 1,\ 0] \\
=\ [+6500,\ +586,\ +785,\quad 0,\ -100,\quad 0,\ -100,\quad 0,\ 0]
\end{array}
$$

This new bottom row will do as an index row, because in columns $A_1, A_2,$ and A_3 we have 0s. So we write the valid bottom row (5′) in Figure 11.8, and by disregarding row (5), we have indeed constructed a valid initial index tableau.

Modified Simplex Rules

Now all we need to do is apply the five steps previously described. First, however, we must modify the ENTERING and STOPPING rules of the simplex algorithm:

> The ENTERING rule: Examine the bottom row of the simplex tableau. Move the stone to the most negative column if maximizing and to the most positive column if minimizing.

> The STOPPING rule: The optimal solution has been obtained (1) when maximizing and there are no negative indexes in the bottom row and (2) when minimizing and there are no positive indexes in the bottom row..

In Figure 11.8 the entering and leaving variables are x_2 and A_2, respectively. Figures 11.9, 11.10, and 11.11 show the second, third, and fourth and final simplex tableaus.

11.4 SENSITIVITY ANALYSIS

What-if some of the coefficients slightly change in a linear programming problem? As you will see, the simplex algorithm automatically provides a great deal of information on sensitivity analysis. To simplify our discussion, we assume that a change by 1 unit in a coefficient is sufficiently "small," and again we examine the Indian jewelry problem.

What-If the Constraints Change?

What-if Minnehaha happens to have 1 ounce less silver, that is, if the silver constraint is reduced by 1 unit? Write the equation in standard form:

$$3x_1 + 1x_2 + 1S_1 + 0S_2 = 9 - 1 = 8$$

$$1x_1 + 2x_2 + 0S_1 + 1S_2 = 8$$

You could solve this new linear programming problem and find that profit would decrease by $.60. However, it turns out that you can get the answer directly from the simplex tableau without any additional work. Inspect again the third, final tableau in Figure 11.7. What happens

Row Numbers	Variables	Values	x_1	x_2	A_1	S_1	A_2	S_2	A_3	S_3	Z	How Much?
(1)	$A_1 =$	15	1.25	0	1	.75	−.75	0	0	0	0	15.0/1.25 = 12
(2)	$x_2 =$	5	.25	1	0	−.25	.25	0	0	0	0	5.0/.25 = 20
(3)	$A_3 =$	10	2.75	0	0	.25	−.25	−1	1	0	0	10.0/2.75 = 3.64 ✳
(4)	$S_3 =$	10	1.0	0	0	0	0	0	0	1	0	10.0/1.0 = 10
(5)	$Z =$	$2575	$389.75	0	0	$96.25	−$196.25	−$100	0	0	1	−

Enter (above x_1/x_2 columns), *Leave* (above A_3/S_3 columns), Shuffleboard

FIGURE 11.9 Second simplex tableau for the modified Texas Cattle Feed Corp. problem.

FIGURE 11.10 Third simplex tableau for the modified Texas Cattle Feed Corp. problem.

Row Numbers	Variables	Values	x_1	x_2	A_1	S_1	A_2	S_2	A_3	S_3	Z	How Much?
(1)	$A_1 =$	10.5	0	0	①	.636	−.636	.455	−.455	0	0	10.5/.636 = 16.51 ＊
(2)	$x_2 =$	4.11	0	①	0	−.273	.273	.091	−.091	0	0	—
(3)	$x_1 =$	3.64	①	0	0	.091	−.091	−.364	.364	0	0	3.64/.091 = 40
(4)	$S_3 =$	6.36	0	0	0	−.091	.091		−.364	①	0	—
(5)	$Z =$	$1156.31	0	0	0	$60.78	−$160.78	$41.87	−$141.87	0	①	—

if we bring back 1 unit of the slack variable S_1? In the bottom row we still have (after x_1 and x_2 are properly recomputed) the profit index of $.60. But if you look at the preceding equations, you notice that setting S_1 to 1 is the same as decreasing the silver constraint by 1 unit, that is, from 9 to 8 ounces. So a *decrease in the silver constraint of 1 ounce means a loss in profit of $.60.*

Similar reasoning shows that an increase in the silver constraint by 1 unit, that is, from 9 to 10 ounces, causes an increase in profit of $.60.

What-if the gold constraint is increased by 1 unit from 8 to 9 ounces? You can read in the index row and x_2 column of Figure 11.7 that profit increases by $2.20.

You see then that increasing the constraint will increase the profit,

Row Numbers	Variables	Values	x_1	x_2	A_1	S_1	A_2	S_2	A_3	S_3	Z
(1)	$S_1 =$	16.43	0	0	1.57	①	−1	.715	−.715	0	0
(2)	$x_2 =$	8.58	0	①	−.429	0	0	.286	−.286	0	0
(3)	$x_1 =$	2.14	①	0	−.143	0	0	−.429	.429	0	0
(4)	$S_3 =$	7.86	0	0	.143	0	0	.429	−.429	①	0
(5)	$Z =$	157.7	0	0	−$95.42	0	−$100	−$1.56	−$98.44	0	①

FIGURE 11.11
Fourth and final simplex tableau for the modified Texas Cattle Feed Corp. problem.

and for each unit of increase in the constraint there is an increase in profit called the **shadow price** associated with the constraint. The shadow price of silver is $.60 and of gold, $2.20.

What-if there is a surplus in one of the constraints, that is, the constraint is not binding? Then there is no change in profit when increasing or decreasing the constraint, and the shadow price is zero. Note then that the simplex tableau not only gives answers to the allocation problem but provides shadow prices.

> The shadow prices corresponding to binding constraints can be read directly in the index row of the final simplex tableau. Shadow prices corresponding to nonbinding constraints are zero.

What-If the Contributions Change?

Suppose the contribution for rings increases by $1.00 from $4.00 to $5.00. A small change in a coefficient in the objective function does not change the signs in the bottom row of the simplex tableau, so the solution is still optimum and remains the same. The optimum solution still requires manufacturing two rings and three bracelets, and so the profit increases for each ring by $1.00, a total of $2 \times \$1.00 = \$2.00$.

Similar reasoning shows that if the profit contribution for bracelets increases by $1.00, the profit will increase by $3 \times \$1.00 = \$3.00$.

We found these results because both rings and bracelets are in the optimum solution. However, if, for example, rings are not in the optimum solution, the profit contribution of rings does not enter into the calculations, and a small change in the contribution for rings will not change the solution and the value of the optimum profit.

11.5 THE DUAL LINEAR PROGRAMMING PROBLEM

Consider the linear programming problem with the unknowns y_1, y_2, y_3, y_4 and the constraints

$$2y_1 + 1y_2 + 3y_3 + 7y_2 \leq 14$$
$$3y_1 + 4y_2 + 1y_3 + 4y_4 \leq 14$$

where the objective function

$$Y = 30y_1 + 20y_2 + 15y_3 + 28y_4$$

is to be maximized. Compare this problem with the Texas Cattle Feed problem discussed in Chapter 10, where the constraints are

$$2x_1 + 3x_2 \geq 30$$
$$1x_1 + 4x_2 \geq 20$$
$$3x_1 + 1x_2 \geq 15$$
$$7x_1 + 4x_2 \geq 28$$

and the objective function to be minimized is

$$Z = 14x_1 + 14x_2$$

Can you see the relationships between the two problems? The right-hand coefficients of the first problem and the coefficients of the objective function of the second problem are the same, namely 14 and 14. The coefficients of the objective function of the first problem and the right-hand coefficients of the second problem are the same, namely 30, 20, 15, and 28. *If you turn one problem on its "side," you obtain the other.* Also the inequality signs are reversed, and in one problem we maximize and in the other, minimize. One of the problems is called the **primal** and the other is the **dual**.

> The relationship between the primal and the dual is symmetric, meaning that the dual of the dual is the primal.

Now we state without proof an important theorem from the theory of linear programming:

> The optimal values of the objective function of the primal and the dual are the same.

For example, we know that the minimum value of the objective function for Texas Cattle Feed is $150.00. So we know right away that the maximum value of the objective function for the dual is also $150.00.

Here is another important theorem:

> The simplex tableau solution to the dual provides the shadow prices of the primal.

For example, consider Minnehaha's problem:

$$3x_1 + 1x_2 \leq 9$$
$$1x_1 + 2x_2 \leq 8$$

Maximize:

$$Z = 4x_1 + 5x_2$$

For the dual,

$$3y_1 + 1y_2 \geq 4$$
$$1y_1 + 2y_2 \geq 5$$

Minimize:

$$Y = 9y_1 + 8y_2$$

The common optimal value of the objective functions is $23.00.

We know from the final simplex tableau (Figure 11.7) that the shadow price for silver is $.60 and for gold, $2.20. So according to our theorem, this should be the value of y_1 and y_2 for the optimal solution to the dual. Indeed,

$$Y_1 = .60, \qquad Y_2 = 2.20$$

is a solution because

$$3 \times .60 + 1 \times 2.20 = 4.00$$

$$1 \times .60 + 2 \times 2.20 = 5.00$$

$$Y = 9 \times .60 + 8 \times 2.20 = \$23.00$$

and it can be shown that this is the optimal solution.

11.6 MISCELLANEOUS COMMENTS ABOUT LINEAR PROGRAMMING

The General Simplex Method

So far we have not discussed the problem of maximization when there are $\le$, $=$, and $\ge$ signs. Suppose we want to maximize the objective function under such conditions:

$$2x_1 + 10x_2 + 3x_3$$

All we have to do is change the signs in the objective function and minimize:

$$-2x_1 - 10x_2 - 3x_3$$

We can now proceed with our minimization algorithm with one modification: *The artificial variables must be assigned large negative values when using the big M method.*

So far we assumed that the right-hand sides are nonnegative. Suppose we have the constraint

$$-3x_1 + 4x_2 \le -15$$

All we need do is to multiply each term by -1 and change the sign to $\ge$:

$$3x_1 - 4x_2 \ge 15$$

Thus we can apply the simplex method directly to such problems.

Degeneracy

The LEAVING rule of the simplex method specifies that the variable which corresponds to the binding constraint is the one to be removed from the solution. In the case of a tie, the variable corresponding to one of the binding constraints is to be removed. However, under certain conditions called **degeneracy**, it may happen that the wrong variable is removed and at a later step in the simplex method the same variable reenters. Then the algorithm goes around the same loop forever, and the optimum is never reached. Fortunately, in practice this situation does not occur, and therefore this theoretically possible situation is ignored.

Multiple Solutions

Suppose in the final simplex tableau we find that one or several of the improvement indexes are 0. This means that such a variable can be brought into the solution without changing the value of the objective function.

Suppose we can bring in U units of such a variable before some other variable leaves. Then we can bring in $.1U$ or $.7U$ or FU of this variable without changing the objective function, where F may be any fraction between 0 and 1.

There may be infinitely many solutions to a linear programming problem.

Under such conditions it may become possible to maximize or minimize a second objective function, a third one, and so on.

Negative Variables

Suppose we have the constraints

$$1x_1 + 1x_2 \leq 1$$
$$-1x_1 + 1x_2 \leq 1$$
$$0x_1 + 1x_2 \geq 0$$

where it is specifically stated that x_1 may be positive, negative, or zero (x_2 cannot be negative). The problem is to maximize the objective function:

$$Z = -10x_1 + 1x_2$$

We have not yet considered problems of this nature, but such problems can easily be transformed into linear programming problems with nonnegative variables. Namely, introduce two nonnegative auxiliary variables x_3 and x_4 such that

$$x_3 - x_4 = x_1$$

Now the constraints are

$$1x_2 + 1x_3 - 1x_4 \leq 1$$
$$1x_2 - 1x_3 + 1x_4 \leq 1$$

where x_2, x_3, and x_4 are nonnegative.

The problem is to maximize

$$-10(x_3 - x_4) + 1x_2 = 1x_2 - 10x_3 - 10x_4$$

It can be shown (but the proof is omitted) that the new problem always solves the original problem. And we already know how to solve this new problem because all the variables are nonnegative.

No Feasible Solution

When using the big M method, it may happen that there is no way to get rid of an artificial variable. This indicates that there is no feasible solution to the problem and probably the model does not fit reality and the error in the model formulation must be corrected.

Unbounded Solutions

It can happen in a maximization problem that the value of an entering variable can increase indefinitely without any variable leaving. This means that the value of the objective function can increase indefinitely too. This of course cannot occur in a real-life problem, and so the conclusion is again that the model does not fit reality and the error in model formulation must be corrected.

The Dual Theorem

When discussing the dual theorem, we assumed that either (1) all the constraints use the $\leq$ sign and we maximize or (2) all the constraints use the $\geq$ sign and we minimize. Now we show that if there are mixed $\leq$, $\geq$, and $=$ signs, then the problem can be reduced to the preceding case 1 (or case 2). We need the following procedure to reduce the problem to case 1:

1. If there is a $\geq$ sign, multiply both sides of the relationship by -1. As an example,

$$2x_1 - 3x_2 \geq 5$$

is converted to

$$-2x_1 + 3x_2 \leq -5$$

2. If there is an $=$ sign, first replace the equation by two new relationships using $\leq$ and $\geq$ signs, respectively. For example,

$$3x_1 - 2x_2 = 3$$

is replaced by

$$3x_1 - 2x_2 \leq 3$$
$$3x_1 - 2x_2 \geq 3$$

The solution then must provide exactly 3 units of the resource. The second equation is changed to

$$-3x_1 + 2x_2 \leq -3$$

3. If the problem is a minimization, maximize the negative of the objective function. For example,

$$Z = 7x_1 - 5x_2, \quad \text{minimize}$$

is replaced by

$$Z = -7x_1 + 5x_2, \qquad \text{maximize}$$

A similar procedure can be used to reduce the problem to the preceding case 2. Note that the linear programming problem can be reduced to two distinct cases and that therefore there are two possible duals.

This, then, concludes our discussion of the simplex algorithm and associated methods. In Chapter 12 we discuss a special type of linear programming problem of great practical importance.

11.7 WHY STUDY THE SIMPLEX METHOD? A DIALOG

Q. *Throughout this book you stressed the need to study algorithms solely for the purpose of obtaining insight and understanding. You said that in practical problems I would use the computer anyway. So what is the point of going through the simplex method?*

A. The concept and nature of algorithms is very basic to quantitative methods. The logical discipline of developing a rigorous, step-by-step solution to a problem is essential to understanding the scientific method. You need to learn a few of the most popular algorithms to obtain this kind of understanding.

Q. *Do all concerned agree on this point?*

A. No, and some skip the specifics of algorithm. Some even think there is no need to learn multiplication tables and multiplication by hand, because you would use a calculator anyway.

Q. *Isn't this a strange point of view?*

A. Yes indeed! And some take the opposite point of view and will not allow students to use calculators but insist that all calculations be done by hand. As in all matters, moderation is best, and so I subscribe to the view that you should learn a few basic algorithms when studying quantitative methods.

SUMMARY

1. The simplex algorithm is one of the most important quantitative methods used in managerial decision making.
2. The simplex method works with detached coefficients.
3. The first step in the simplex algorithm is to bring the problem into the standard form with the aid of slack, surplus, and artificial variables.
4. The second step is to find an initial (first) feasible solution and simplex tableau.
5. The simplex method improves solutions by an iterative process.

6. Each iteration is carried out by applying the three rules of the simplex method: the ENTERING, HOW-MUCH, and LEAVING rules.

7. The STOPPING rule indicates the last iteration and optimal solution.

8. There may be infinitely many optimal solutions to a problem.

9. The bottom (index) row of the final simplex tableau provides the shadow prices for each constraint.

10. With each linear programming primal problem one can associate a dual problem. One of the problems is of maximization and the other of minimization. The value of the objective function is the same for both problems.

11. The general linear programming problem may involve (a) a mixture of $\geq$, $=$, and $\leq$ signs; (b) positive, zero, or negative right-hand sides; (c) negative variables; and (d) maximization or minimization. But all such problems can be solved by the simplex method presented in this chapter.

12. A linear programming problem may have (a) no solution, (b) a single solution, or (c) multiple, that is, infinitely many, solutions.

13. Under special conditions the problem of degeneracy and/or unbounded solutions may have to be considered.

SECTION EXERCISES

1. **Introduction to the Simplex Algorithm**

1.1 Refer to the set of simultaneous equations given at the beginning of Section 11.1 (and for which the solution is $x_1 = 2$, $x_2 = 5$, and $x_3 = 4$). Determine, by using elementary methods for calculation, whether or not each of the following sets of equations is equivalent to the original set:

a. $6x_1 + 4x_2 - 2x_3 = 24$
   $5x_1 - 3x_2 + 7x_3 = 23$
   $1x_1 + 4x_2 - 2x_3 = 14$
b. $1x_1 + 0x_2 + 0x_3 = 2$
   $2x_1 + 1x_2 + 0x_3 = 5$
   $0x_1 + 0x_2 + 1x_3 = 4$

1.2 Use the Gauss-Jordan method to find the solutions to the following sets of simultaneous equations; check your results by substitution into the original set. You should use the method of detached coefficients.

a. $2x_1 + 3x_2 = 30$
   $3x_1 + 1x_2 = 15$
b. $2x_a + 3x_b = 5$
   $-10x_a - 4x_b = 8$
c. $100x_1 + 100x_2 = 700$
   $-1x_1 + 1x_2 = -1$
d. $.5x_1 - 1x_2 = 1$
   $1.2x_1 + 1.6x_2 = 1$

1.3 In the discussion of the standard form of linear programming in Section

11.1, slack variables are introduced into the equations for the Indian jewelry problem of Minnehaha, and an initial solution is found. Minnehaha has redesigned the rings discussed in the Indian jewelry problem. Each ring now takes 20 grams of silver and 5 grams of gold; each bracelet takes only 5 grams of silver and 15 grams of gold. She now stocks only 200 grams of silver and 150 grams of gold. Find an initial solution to this new set of equations.

1.4 Refer to Figure 11.2. Write your solution to Exercise 1.3 in the same form as a simplex tableau.

2. The Simplex Algorithm

2.1 In Section 11.2, the algorithm for the simplex method is recapitulated into five steps. Use this algorithm in recapitulated form to solve your revised Indian jewelry problem (as designed in Exercises 1.3 and 1.4). Note that the objective function must be stated. It can be obtained from Exercise 3.2 of Chapter 10.

2.2 A television set manufacturing firm has to decide on the mix of color and black-and-white TVs to be produced. Market research indicates that at most 500 units and 2000 units of color and black-and-white TVs can be sold per month. The maximum number of man-hours available is 25,000 per month. A color TV requires 10 man-hours, and a black-and-white TV requires 7.5 man-hours. The unit profits of the color and black-and-white TVs are $30 and $15, respectively. Use the algorithm described in Section 11.2 to solve for the number of units of each TV type that the firm must produce in order to maximize its profit.

2.3 The supply analyst of a car rental company must decide on the amount of unleaded gas to buy from three possible vendors. The company refuels its cars regularly at the four airports it serves. The oil companies have said that they can furnish up to the following amounts of gas during the coming month: 275,000 gallons for oil company 1. 550,000 gallons for oil company 2, and 660,000 gallons for oil company 3. The required amount of unleaded gas is 110,000 gallons at airport 1. 220,000 gallons at airport 2. 330,000 gallons at airport 3, and 440,000 gallons at airport 4. When transportation costs are added to the bid price per gallon for gas from each vendor the cost of furnishing gas at a specific airport is as follows:

	COMPANY 1	COMPANY 2	COMPANY 3
Airport 1	10	7	8
Airport 2	10	11	14
Airport 3	9	12	4
Airport 4	11	13	9

    a. Formulate the decision problem as a linear programming model.
    b. Solve for the optimal buying amounts from each vendor.

2.4 A retired lady has sought help from her relative, an MBA, to advise her on maximizing the total cash on hand at the end of the fifth year. She has $2200 to invest over the next 5 years. At the beginning of each year she can invest money in 1- or 2-year time deposits. The bank pays 8% interest on 1-year time deposits and 17% (total) on 2-year time deposits. In addition, Republic National Bank will offer 3-year certificates at the beginning of the second year. These certificates will return 27% (total). If the retired lady reinvests her money available every year, how would one, as an MBA, formulate the linear program? Solve for the optimal investment amount in each year by the simplex algorithm.

2.5 Apply the simplex method to solve

$$\text{max. } 30x_1 + 23x_2 + 29x_3$$

subject to

$$6x_1 + 5x_2 + 3x_3 \leq 62$$

$$4x_1 + 2x_2 + 5x_2 \leq 40$$

$$x_1 \geq 0, \qquad x_2 \geq 0, \qquad x_3 \geq 0$$

2.6 A company manufactures refrigerators and air conditioners. The company has three warehouses and two retail stores. Sixty, 80, and 50 refrigerators and 90, 50, and 50 air conditioners are available at the three warehouses, respectively. One hundred and 90 refrigerators are required at the retail stores, respectively. The unit shipping costs which apply to both the refrigerators and air conditioners from the warehouses to the retail stores are as follows:

| | STORE | |
WAREHOUSE	1	2
1	30	50
2	20	30
3	60	30

Find the shipping pattern that minimizes the total cost by the simplex method.

2.7 A company produces dishwashers, stoves, and ovens. During the coming year, sales are expected to be the following:

| | QUARTER | | | |
PRODUCT	1	2	3	4
Dishwashers	1500	1000	2000	1200
Stoves	1500	1500	1200	1500
Ovens	1000	2000	1500	2500

The company wants a production schedule that meets the demand requirements. Management also has decided that the inventory level for each product must be at least 150 units at the end of each quarter. There is no inventory of any product at the start of the first quarter. During a quarter, only 18,000 hours of production time are available. A dishwasher requires 2 hours, a stove 4 hours, and an oven 3 hours of production time. Dishwashers cannot be manufactured in the fourth quarter because the company plans to modify tooling for an improved product line. Assume that each item left in inventory at the end of a quarter incurs a holding cost of $5. The company wants to plan its production schedule over the year in a way that meets the quarterly demands and minimizes the total inventory cost. Formulate the problem, and then solve it by the simplex method.

2.8 Consider the problem

$$\text{max. } Z = 2x_1 + 7x_2 - 3x_3$$

subject to

$$x_1 + 3x_2 + 4x_3 \leq 30$$

$$x_1 + 4x_2 - x_3 \geq 10$$

and

$$x_1 \geq 0, \qquad x_2 \geq 0, \qquad x_3 \geq 0$$

Solve for the optimal solution by the simplex method.

3. *The Feed-Mix Problem: How to Minimize*

3.1 Show that corner B in Figure 10.17 still provides an optimal solution to the revised feed mix problem described at the start of Section 11.3.

3.2 Make a table listing the slack, surplus, and artificial variables introduced in order to obtain a solution to the feed mix problem of Section 11.3. For each variable, give the reason for its introduction into the solution.

3.3 Introduce slack or surplus variables into the relationship given below for a linear programming problem as required to initiate the simplex method, and tell whether the variables you introduce are surplus or slack variables:

$$1x_1 + 2x_2 \leq 4$$

$$1x_1 + 4x_2 \leq 5$$

$$2x_1 + 3x_2 \leq 10$$

3.4 An oil refinery can buy two types of oil: light crude oil and heavy crude oil. The cost per barrel of these types is, respectively, \$11 and \$9. The following quantities of gasoline, kerosene, and jet fuel are produced per barrel of each type of oil:

	GASOLINE	KEROSENE	JET FUEL
Light crude oil	.40	.20	.35
Heavy crude oil	.32	.40	.20

The refinery has contracted to deliver 1 million barrels of gasoline, 400,000 barrels of kerosene, and 250,000 barrels of jet fuel. Find the number of barrels of each crude oil that satisfy the demand and minimize the total cost.

3.5 Solve Exercise 2.7 where you minimize $-30x_1 - 23x_2 - 29x_3$.

3.6 A baby food producer produces cereals for babies. The cereals consist of three main ingredients: raw materials A, F, and G. These ingredients contain three characteristics: sweetness, nutrition, and crunchiness. The following table gives the characteristics per pound of each ingredient. The sweetness, nutrition, and crunchiness must be in the following intervals, respectively: (18, 22), (20, 25), and (6, 12).

CHARACTERISTICS	RAW MATERIAL		
	A	*F*	*G*
Sweetness	25	15	25
Crunchiness	15	30	20
Nutrition	5	12	8

If the selling prices per pound of raw materials A, F, and G are, respectively, \$.10, \$.08, and \$.12, find the least expensive mix.

4. *Sensitivity Analysis*

4.1 Refer to Figure 11.7. Consider a new problem situation slightly different from the Indian jewelry problem stated here; the different problem resulted in a third-row solution in the final simplex tableau as follows:

ROW NO.	VAR.	VAL.	x_1	x_2	S_1	S_2	Z
(3)	Z	$25	0	0	$.50	$2.00	1

    a. What is the shadow price of silver?
    b. What is the shadow price of gold?

4.2 A farmer has 500 acres of land and wishes to determine the acreage allocated to the following three crops: wheat, corn, and soybean. The man-days, preparation cost, and profit per acre of the three crops are as follows:

CROP	MAN-DAYS	PREPARATION COST ($)	PROFIT ($)
Wheat	6	100	60
Corn	8	150	100
Soybeans	10	120	80

Suppose that the maximum number of man-days available are 5000 and that the farmer has $60,000 for preparation.

    a. Find the optimal solution.
    b. Assuming an 8-hour work day, would it be profitable to the farmer to acquire additional help at $3 per hour? Why, or why not?
    c. Suppose that the farmer has contracted to deliver at least the equivalent of 100 acres of wheat. Use sensitivity analysis to find the new optimal solution.

4.3 A product is assembled from three parts that can be manufactured on two machines, A and B. Neither machine can process different parts at the same time. The number of parts processed by each machine per hour are as follows:

	MACHINE A	MACHINE B
Part 1	12	6
Part 2	15	12
Part 3	—	25

Management seeks a daily schedule of the machines so that the number of assemblies is maximized. Currently, the company has three machines of type A and four machines of type B.

    a. Solve the problem.
    b. If only one machine can be acquired, which type would you recommend and why?
    c. Management is contemplating the purchase of a type A machine at a cost of $100,000.00. Suppose that the life of the machine is 10 years and that each year is equivalent to 2000 working hours. Would you recommend the purchase if the unit profit from each assembly is $1? Why, or why not?

5. The Dual Linear Programming Problem

5.1 Refer to the two-constraint, four-variable linear programming problem described at the beginning of Section 11.5:

$$2y_1 + 1y_2 + 3y_3 + 7y_4 \leq 14$$

$$3y_1 + 4y_2 + 1y_3 + 4y_4 \leq 14$$

max. $\quad 30y_1 + 20y_2 + 15y_3 + 28y_4$

Suppose that further investigation showed that the coefficients were not all up to date and that the new set of coefficients were as follows:

$$2.4 \quad 1.2 \quad 3.0 \quad 7.5$$

$$3.0 \quad 5.3 \quad 1.1 \quad 3.4$$

    a. Write the dual for this revised linear programming problem.
    b. Solve the dual graphically, and obtain solutions to the primal problem thereby.
    c. Find the shadow prices.
    d. Interpret the shadow prices.

5.2 Maximize $- x_1 + 7x_2 - 5x_3 + 14x_4$
subject to

$$3x_1 + 4x_2 + 5x_3 + 5x_4 \le 60$$

$$-1x_1 + 1x_2 - 2x_3 + 2x_4 \le 10$$

every $x_j \ge 0$.

    a. Write the dual problem and verify that a feasible solution is $y_1 = 1$ and $y_2 = 1$.
    b. Use the information in part a to derive an optimal solution to both the primal and dual problems.

5.3 Consider the problem

$$\text{max. } Z = 4x_1 + 3x_2 + 6x_3$$

subject to

$$3x_1 + x_2 + 3x_3 \le 30$$

$$2x_1 + 2x_2 + 3x_3 \le 40$$

and every $x_j \ge 0$. Write the dual problem and

    a. Solve the primal problem, obtain the values of the dual variables, and verify that they are optimal (without solving the dual).
    b. Solve the dual problem (graphically, if you wish) and obtain the values of the primal variables. Verify that they are optimal (without solving the primal).

6. *Miscellaneous Comments About Linear Programming*

6.1 Suppose we have the following objective functions which we wish to maximize. Show how to modify them to be used with the minimization algorithm.

    a. $6x_1 - 4x_2 + 3x_3$
    b. $-22x_1 + 0x_2 + 6x_3 - 7x_4 - 22x_5$
    c. $79x_1 - 65x_2 + 56x_3$

6.2 Suppose we have the following objective functions which we wish to maximize; they include artificial variables A_i. Show how to modify the objective functions and the values of the artificial variables to be suitable for use with the minimization algorithm:

    a. $5x_1 - 4A_1$
    b. $22x_1 - 18x_2 + x_3 - A_1 + 4A_2$
    c. $3x_1 - 0x_2 + .5x_3 - 4x_4 - 5A_1 + 6A_2 + 4A_3$

6.3 Suppose one of the constraints in a linear programming problem is

$$-4x_1 + 5x_2 - 6x_3 + 16x_4 \le -22$$

Rewrite this constraint so that the simplex method as discussed in this textbook may be used to find a solution.

6.4 Transform the following into linear programming problems with nonnegative variables where the original problem allows x_1 to be positive, negative, or zero:

a.
$$-4x_1 + 6x_2 + 5x_3 \geq 20$$
$$3x_1 - 2x_2 + 4x_3 \geq 10$$
$$8x_1 - 3x_2 + 3x_3 \geq 20$$
max. $Z = x_1 + 4x_2 - 5x_3$

b.
$$2x_1 + 3x_2 \geq 78$$
$$3x_1 + 1x_2 \leq 50$$
$$6x_1 - 5x_2 = 80$$
min. $Z = x_1 + x_2$

6.5 Introduce slack, surplus, or artificial variables into the following sets of inequalities and equations as discussed in this textbook. This is necessary to initiate the simplex method of solving the associated linear programming problems. Also indicate which variables are of the several types:

a.
$$6x_1 + 0x_2 + 0x_3 + 2x_4 \geq 50$$
$$1x_1 + 1x_2 + 1x_3 + 1x_4 = 20$$
$$0x_1 + 1x_2 + 2x_3 + 1x_4 \leq 30$$

b.
$$1x_1 + 3x_2 + 2x_3 \geq 8$$
$$10x_1 - 9x_2 + 1x_3 \geq 10$$
$$1x_1 + 2x_2 + 1x_3 \leq 4$$

c.
$$3x_1 + 1x_2 + 2x_3 \geq 14$$
$$3x_1 + 4x_2 + 4x_3 \geq 20$$
$$1x_1 + 1x_2 + 1x_3 = 12$$

CHAPTER EXERCISES AND DISCUSSION QUESTIONS

C.1 Use the Gauss-Jordan method to find the solution to the following sets of simultaneous equations:

a.
$$4x_1 - 3x_2 + 0x_3 = 8$$
$$-2x_1 + 1x_2 - 1x_3 = 0$$
$$3x_1 - 2x_2 + 0x_3 = 4$$

b.
$$2x_1 + 1x_2 = 10$$
$$3x_1 + 4x_2 = 20$$

C.2 Consider the following set of three equations in four variables:

$$1x_1 + 1x_2 + 1x_3 + 1x_4 = 8$$

$$1x_1 + 4x_2 + 0x_3 + 2x_4 = 4$$

$$1x_1 + 1x_2 + 3x_3 - 1x_4 = 10$$

The complete solution to this set of equations is one which expresses three of the unknowns in terms of the other, which can take on arbitrary values. Find this complete solution using the Gauss-Jordan method, where x_4 is the variable which can take arbitrary values.

C.3 A particular solution to the set of equations in Exercise C.2 is obtained by setting the variable x_4 to some arbitrary value. Set x_4 to zero, and find the solution.

C.4 It takes 20 tons of aggregate and 12 tons of cement to make a base for landing a new vertical takeoff domestic rocket ship. One truck from supplier A contains 3 tons of aggregate and 1 ton of cement. A truck from supplier *B* contains 2 tons of cement and 5 tons of aggregate; a truck from supplier *C* contains 3 tons of each ingredient. The new base is to be constructed under a contract from the federal government. The three suppliers all operate in areas that have been designated as distressed, and the terms of the contract require that something be purchased from each area. Also, waste from excess truckloads has been criticized in similar projects in the past, so that fractional truckloads are allowed. Find the exact amount to be ordered from each supplier to exactly provide the ingredients required for the platform.

C.5 Refer to Exercise C.1 in Chapter 10, B. N. Krupt & Company. Solve this exercise using the simplex method. If you have also solved this exercise using the graphical approach, verify your result, and identify tableaus in your simplex solution with corners of the feasible region in your graphical solution.

C.6 Refer to Chapter 10, Exercise C.2, the Biker's Fruit Bar case. Solve this exercise using the simplex method. If you have also solved this exercise using the graphical approach, verify your result, and identify the tableaus in your simplex solution with the corners of the feasible region in your graphical solution. Show by use of arrows how the simplex method moves from corner to corner.

C.7 Refer to Chapter 10, Exercise C.3, the Good News Advertising Corp. Solve this minimization problem in linear programming by using the simplex method.

C.8 Refer to Chapter 10, Exercise C.4. Solve this linear programming problem using the simplex method.

C.9 Refer to Chapter 10, Exercise C.6, concerning S. R. Pankh, recent MBA graduate. Use linear programming by the simplex method to solve this problem.

C.10 Refer to Chapter 10, Exercise C.7, the Tri Cot case. Use the simplex method to solve this linear programming problem. If your have already solved this problem using the graphical method, verify your solution.

C.11 Refer to Chapter 10, Exercise C.8 the I.O. Way Animal Supply Cooperative. Solve this problem by the simplex method. If you have already solved this problem using the graphical method, verify your solution.

C.12 From your solution to the following chapter exercises (the final simplex tableau must be available), determine the shadow prices, and explain their meaning in terms of practical what-if questions they answer:
   a. Exercise C.6
   b. Exercise C.7
   c. Exercise C.8
   d. Exercise C.9
   e. Exercise C.10
   f. Exercise C.11

C.13 In Section 11.4, the statement is made that "A small change in a coefficient does not change the signs in the bottom row (of the final simplex tableau), so the solution is still optimal and the same."
   a. In the context of asking what-if questions about the contributions, why is it necessary that the solution still be optimal and the same?
   b. How might you use the final simplex tableau to determine how large a change in a coefficient is still "small?"

C.14 Write the dual programming problems for those Exercises C.1 through C.8 in Chapter 10 which your instructor assigns. Does the dual in any case represent an easier problem to solve than the original? Why?

C.15 Refer to Exercises C.6 through C.11. For any and all of the exercises C.6

through C.11 for which you have obtained a solution and which your instructor assigns, give the following:

    a. The optimal value for the objective function of the dual problem

    b. The values of the variables for the optimal solution to the dual problem

C.16 Vladimir S. has a linear programming problem which involves maximizing the objective function that he has developed. Unfortunately, the personal computer that he just purchased to carry out linear programming tasks for him does not maximize objective functions; it only minimizes them. How can Vladimir use the dual problem to get his original problem solved?

C.17 Refer to Exercise C.16. After solving his problem as described there (using the dual), his close friend, Rodney Kvetchkoff, said that use of the dual was unnecessary. According to Rodney, Vladimir could have converted his maximization problem to a minimization problem with a simple arithmetic operation. What is he talking about?

C.18 Consider the feed mix problem discussed in Chapter 10 and described in Figure 10.16. Write the dual problem. What are the units in which the dual variable is expressed, and what is the economic interpretation of the dual variable? What is the relationship between the value of the nutrients and the cost? What is the economic interpretation of the constraints of the dual problem?

C.19 A linear programming problem has been stated as the following set of constraints and objective function, but the variables may be unrestricted in sign. Convert to a form that can be solved using the simplex method, and solve.

$$4x_1 + 5x_2 + 2x_3 = 20$$
$$6x_1 + 4x_2 + 0x_3 = 16$$
$$\text{max.} \quad Z = 4x_1 + 3x_2 + 1x_3$$

12

The Transportation Problem and Applications*

In Section 10.2 when discussing the problem of the Transamerican Manufacturing firm, we presented an illustration of a simple transportation problem. In fact, the transportation problem and similar situations represent some of the most successful applications of linear programming. These problems could be solved by the simplex algorithm, but special, extremely efficient algorithms have been developed for solving the transportation problem. With the aid of modern computers, problems with thousands of equations and unknowns can be solved quickly and at relatively low cost. In this chapter we present the basic method of solution for the transportation problem and some applications. The method is based on the simplex algorithm but takes advantage of the special structure of the transportation problem to reduce the effort required to find a solution. As in the simplex algorithm, there are three steps to solving the problem: (1) get started, (2) evaluate how good the solution is, and (3) improve the solution. A special stopping rule is given so you can determine that the optimum solution has been found.

The purpose of our presentation is again to provide insight into the algorithm, but very likely in practice you will use the computer.

12.1 THE FUNDAMENTAL ALGORITHM

Consider the problem of the Fanta-Seas Shipping firm which has three production facilities at Gondor, Mordor, and Harlindon with respective *capacities* of 51, 85, and 76 units. This means that production, that is, *supply*, cannot exceed 51, 85, and 76 units, respectively.

Fanta-Seas Shipping must deliver goods during this period to meet demand at three warehouses in different locations in quantities 71, 97, and 44 units. In Figure 12.1 we show the problem in schematic form. In

---

* This chapter can be studied without a knowledge of the simplex algorithm.

422

FROM	TO			CAPACITIES-SUPPLIES	
	W1	W2	W3		
Gondor	$2 $x_1 = ?$	$4 $x_2 = ?$	$5 $x_3 = ?$	51	
Mordor	$8 $x_4 = ?$	$12 $x_5 = ?$	$9 $x_6 = ?$	85	EAST RIM
Harlindon	$3 $x_7 = ?$	$7 $x_8 = ?$	$13 $x_9 = ?$	76	
Demand	71	97	44	212	
	SOUTH RIM				

FIGURE 12.1 Transportation problem of Fanta-Seas Shipping Corp.

each cell we list in the upper right-hand corner the transportation cost from a supplier to a warehouse and the unknown quantity to be shipped. In the **east rim** we show capacity-supply requirements and in the **south rim** demand requirements. Note that supplies and demands balance to 212 units.

The capacity-supply constraints mean that

$$x_1 + x_2 + x_3 = 51$$
$$x_4 + x_5 + x_6 = 85$$
$$x_7 + x_8 + x_9 = 76$$

The demand constraints mean that

$$x_1 + x_4 + x_7 = 71$$
$$x_2 + x_5 + x_8 = 97$$
$$x_3 + x_6 + x_9 = 44$$

The payoff function to be minimized is the total cost:

$$Z = 2x_1 + 4x_2 + 5x_3$$
$$+ 8x_4 + 12x_5 + 9x_6$$
$$+ 3x_7 + 7x_8 + 13x_9$$

This is, then, a linear programming problem with nine unknowns, and we present a computational technique to find the optimum solution.

Northwest Corner Rule

The northwest corner rule tells you how to get started in solving the problem. As shown in Figure 12.2 on the flowchart, we start by placing an answer in the northwest corner, that is, shipping from Gondor to W1, the first warehouse. As box 2 in the flowchart indicates, you should place

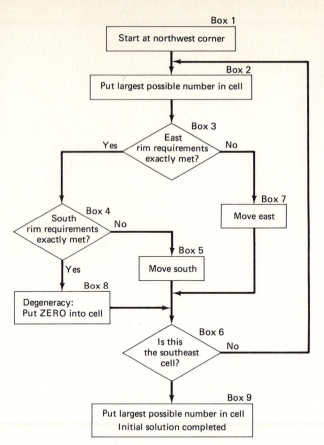

FIGURE 12.2
Flowchart describing
the northwest corner
rule.

Box 1
Start at northwest corner

Box 2
Put largest possible number in cell

Box 3
East rim requirements exactly met?

Yes   No

Box 7
Move east

Box 4
South rim requirements exactly met?   No

Box 5
Move south

Yes

Box 8
Degeneracy: Put ZERO into cell

Box 6
Is this the southeast cell?   No

Box 9
Put largest possible number in cell
Initial solution completed

the largest possible number in this **cell**. The capacity at Gondor is 51, and so

$$x_1 \leq 51$$

The demand at W1 is 71, and so

$$x_2 \leq 71$$

Thus the largest possible value of x_1 is 51, and by putting 51 units into the northwest corner, you start to build the initial solution (Figure 12.3).

Now, as shown in box 3 in the flowchart, you must decide into which cell you want to move. Are the east requirements exactly met? Yes, because we are shipping 51 units from Gondor to W1, and capacity at Gondor is 51. According to the flowchart, we move to box 4 and ask whether the south rim requirements are met. No, because demand at W1 is 71, and we shipped only 51 to W1. So box 5 in the flowchart tells us to move south. That is, we want to ship from Mordor to W1. On the flowchart we go to box 6, which asks whether we reached the southeast cell in Figure 12.3. The answer is no, so we go back to box 2 and put the largest possible number into this cell. What is this number? Capacity at Mordor is 85, and demand at W1 is 71. We already shipped 51 units to W1, and therefore the largest possible number that can be shipped is 71 − 51 = 20 units, so we put 20 in the Mordor-W1 cell (Figure 12.3). Now that we are finished with box 2 in the flowchart, we move to box 3 and again ask whether each of the rim requirements is met. It is not, so we move east to the cell for shipping from Mordor to W2. We have not reached the southeast corner, so we go back to box 2 and put the largest possible number, that is, 65, into the cell from Mordor to W2 (Figure 12.3). Then again we move south, put in the largest possible number, 32, and move east. Now we are in the southeast cell, so move from box 6 to box 9, put in the largest possible number, 44, and complete the initial solution to the problem. Note that we have not reached box 8 where the problem of degeneracy is raised. We shall postpone for now discussing the meaning of this box.

Does this solution make sense? Certainly the rim requirements are met, but we have not even considered the transportation cost. Thus this solution may be very bad and result in the high cost of

$$2 \times 51 + 8 \times 20 + 12 \times 65 + 7 \times 32 + 13 \times 44 = \$1838$$

Now the fact is there are clever ways to get a good initial solution, and then you can save time when solving the problem manually. However, we are interested here in providing you with an insight into the algorithm and not with efficiency of solution. Therefore we are satisfied with the solution obtained by the northwest corner rule and raise the question whether this solution is the best and if not, how it can be improved.

The Shuffleboard Model of the Transportation Problem*

Observe in Figure 12.3 that we have numbers in five of the cells and no numbers in the rest of the cells, meaning that zero unit is shipped through these cells. Let us put stones into the cells where we have

---

* This model is based on the so-called *stepping stone* method.

		TO		CAPACITIES-	
	W1	**W2**	**W3**	**SUPPLIES**	
Gondor	$2 (51)	$4	$5	51	
Mordor	$8 (20) →	$12 (65)	$9	85	EAST RIM
Harlindon	$3	$7 (32) →	$13 (44)	76	
Demand	71	97	44	212	
		SOUTH RIM			

FIGURE 12.3 Initial solution to the transportation problem of Fanta-Seas Shipping Corp. The total cost is $1838.

FIGURE 12.4
Transportation problem compared with
shuffling stones on a shuffleboard.

numbers and imagine the problem of finding the best solution as shuffling the stones until the best location is obtained. Considering the problem as a shuffleboard problem (see Figure 12.4), we state that our problem involves three different questions:

1. Where to put the stone initially
2. How to evaluate the solution
3. If the solution is not the best, which stone to shuffle where to get a better solution

We already know how to get started, and if we can answer the second and third questions, we have a way to solve the transportation problem. Let us proceed now to our technique of evaluating solutions.

Improvement Indices

We shall develop now the technique of establishing an improvement index for each empty cell which tells us whether or not a stone should be moved there. The method will be such that if all the improvement indices are positive or zero (that is, nonnegative), then the solution is optimal. With the concept of the improvement index, we can describe our strategy of solving the transportation problem with the aid of the flowchart in Figure 12.5.

In box 1 we state that first we need to establish a shuffleboard **transportation matrix** model of the problem. In box 2 we state that the initial solution is obtained by placing the stones according to the **northwest corner rule**. In box 3 we compute the improvement indices and in box 4 we make a decision. If all the improvement indices are positive or zero, we have obtained the optimal solution. Otherwise, we generate an improved solution by moving the stone with the most negative improvement index. Let us now develop the approach in detail.

For the moment, freeze all shipments from Gondor to the warehouses and also all shipments arriving at W1. In other words, allow only changes in shipments from Mordor to W2 and W3 and from Harlindon to W2 and W3. As shown in Figure 12.6, Part (a), we have a reduced transportation problem, shipping from two **sources** to two **destinations**. We do not allow change of shipment from Mordor to W1, so the 20 units are frozen, and we can say that the available capacity is only 65 at Mordor. There are 76 units available from Harlindon. As to demand at

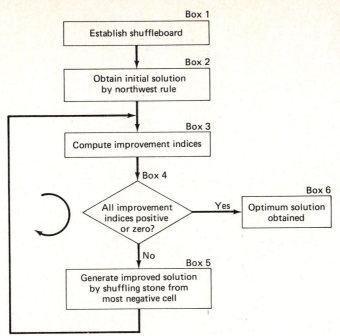

the warehouses, we observe that because we have not shipped anything from Gondor to $W2$ and $W3$, we still need 97 units at $W2$ and 44 units at $W3$. Now we wish to examine whether we can find a better solution to this two-by-two reduced transportation problem.

Suppose we ship 1 unit from Mordor to $W3$. Simultaneously, we must balance rim requirements, and so we must reduce shipments from Mordor to $W2$ and from Harlindon to $W3$ by 1 unit. Finally, we must ship 1 more unit from Harlindon to $W2$. These changes are shown in Figure 12.6, part (b). Is this new solution better or worse?

Observe that the shipping cost from Mordor to $W3$ is \$9.00. Thus, by shipping 1 unit we are increasing the shipping cost by \$9.00. Now look at the Mordor to $W2$ cell. Here we are decreasing shipments by 1 unit and the shipping cost is \$12.00, so we decrease the cost by \$12.00 or increase the cost by $-\$12.00$.* In the Harlindon to $W2$ cell the shipping cost is \$7.00, so here we increase the cost by \$7.00, and finally in the Harlindon to $W3$ cell we have an increase of $-\$13.00$. To summarize, by the proposed change in the solution we increase cost by

$$+9 - 12 + 7 - 13$$

as shown in Figure 12.7(a). This amounts to $-\$9.00$, and we call this the *improvement* index because a $-\$9.00$ increase implies a $+\$9.00$ decrease in cost, and we want to minimize cost. So we see that we have a

---

* This is strange language, but this is the convention used in the transportation algorithm.

Part (a)

		TO		CAPACITIES- SUPPLIES	
		W1	W2	W3	
FROM	Gondor	$2 ⑤①	$4	$5	51
	Mordor	$8 ㉑	$12 ㉕	$9	85
	Harlindon	$3	$7 ㉜	$13 ㊹	76
	Demand	71	97	44	212

SOUTH RIM — EAST RIM

Part (b)

		TO		CAPACITIES- SUPPLIES
		W2	W3	
FROM	Mordor	$12 ⊖① ←	$9 ⊕①	65
	Harlindon	$7 ⊕① →	$13 ⊖①	76
	Demand	97	44	

FIGURE 12.6 Reducing the transportation problem to shipping from two sources to two destinations.

cost saving of $9.00 for each unit shipped from Mordor to W3, provided the corresponding changes are made in the other cells.

> The improvement index of an empty cell equals the cost of one unit shipped through the empty cell.

This proposed change makes sense, and you might ask why not follow up and ship the maximum number of units from Mordor to W3. We are not doing so because there may be a better improvement.

After all, we have no reason to believe that the best place to ship is to the Mordor-W3 cell. What we want to do is to evaluate each of the empty cells and find the most promising one, that is, the one with the smallest, that is, most negative, improvement index. The evaluation is done by the following rules:

1. Start drawing a path at the empty cell to be evaluated. You may go clockwise or counterclockwise. (We draw all our paths counterclockwise.)

2. Move straight until you hit a stone.

3. Turn 90°, and proceed until you hit a second stone.

4. Continue until you return to the empty cell or reach a dead end.

5. If you are at a dead end, backtrack and try an alternate path until you find a **closed path**.

6. List the transportation costs at each corner of the path.

7. Sum the transportation costs at the corners of the path with alternating signs to obtain the improvement index.

The approach to be followed is illustrated in detail in Figure 12.7 where all four empty cells are evaluated. We already have the −9 improvement index in the Mordor-W3 cell, and we list this improvement index in the lower left-hand corner of the cell in Figure 12.8. Suppose you want to evaluate the Gondor-W2 cell. As shown in Figure 12.7, we must follow a path starting at the Gondor-W2 cell, going through Gondor-W1, Mordor-W1, and Mordor-W2. By introducing 1 unit in the upper right- and lower left-hand corners of the pattern and reducing shipment by 1 in the upper left- and lower right-hand corners, we can change our solution and still not violate the rim requirements. The corresponding improvement index is

$$4 - 2 + 8 - 12 = -\$2$$

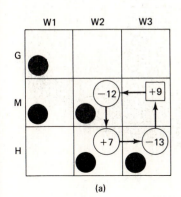

(a)

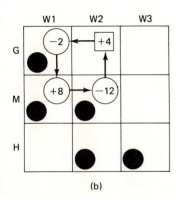

(b)

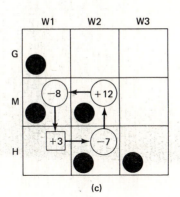

(c)

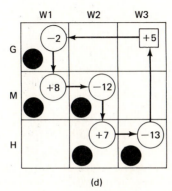

(d)

FIGURE 12.7
Closed paths used to evaluate the initial solution to the transportation problem. Transportation costs with alternating signs are in circles at each stone and in squares at cells being evaluated.

FROM	TO: W1	TO: W2	TO: W3	CAPACITIES-SUPPLIES
Gondor	\$2 (51)	\$4 −2	\$5 −7	51
Mordor	\$8 (20)	\$12 (65)	\$9 −9	85
Harlindon	\$3 0	\$7 (32)	\$13 (44)	76
Demand	71	97	44	212
	SOUTH RIM			EAST RIM

FIGURE 12.8 Evaluation of the initial solution to the transportation problem.

and we list this in the lower left-hand corner of the Gondor-*W*2 cell in Figure 12.8.

Note that when we were at the stone at the Mordor-*W*2 cell, we did not move down to the Harlindon-*W*2 cell because that would have led to the Harlindon-*W*3 stone—a dead end.

The Harlindon-*W*1 cell can be evaluated by the closed path in Figure 12.7(c). The improvement index is

$$3 - 7 + 12 - 8 = \$0$$

and we list this in Figure 12.8.

Finally, the Gondor-*W*3 cell is evaluated by the path in Figure 12.7(d). For this path the improvement index is

$$5 - 2 + 8 - 12 + 7 - 13 = -\$7$$

We put this index into the Gondor-*W*3 cell of Figure 12.8.

This then concludes the evaluation of each of the empty cells. We know we have not yet reached the optimum solution because there are negative indices, indicating potential cost saving. Now we proceed to improve the solution.

How to Improve the Solution

We shall shuffle one of the stones to a new place. Which one?

Move the stone with the most negative improvement index.

(In the case of a tie, use one of the most negative indices.) In Figure 12.8 the most negative improvement index is −9, which indicates shipments from Mordor to *W*3. How much can we ship from Mordor to *W*3?

As we increase shipment from Mordor to *W*3, shown by the path in Figure 12.7(a), we must decrease shipments from Mordor to *W*2 and

Harlindon to W3 to keep rim requirements in balance. The corresponding shipments are 65 and 44 units, and we conclude that we cannot ship more than 44 units from Mordor to W3 without specifying negative shipments from Harlindon to W3. So we decide to ship 44 units and put this number into the cell in Figure 12.9 where the second solution is being constructed. We know now that we shall move a stone in the Mordor-W3 cell. Which of the stones should be moved there? Observe that when shipping 44 units from Mordor to W3 we must decrease simultaneously by 44 units shipments from Harlindon to W3. Thus, in this cell we shall have 0 shipment, that is, no stone.

To sum up, what we have decided is to move the stone from the Harlindon-W3 cell to the Mordor-W3 cell. Now we can fill in the rest of the values for the second solution in Figure 12.9. Shipments from Mordor to W2 will be 65 − 44 = 21 and from Harlindon to W2, 32 + 44 = 76. Shipments to W1 remain unchanged. This then concludes shuffling the stones and construction of the second solution to the transportation problem.

By shipping 44 units to W3 and making the corresponding adjustments, we increase transportation costs by -$9 × 44 = −$396, where the −$9 is the improvement index. Thus the new cost for the second solution is $1838 − $396 = $1442. We have clearly improved our solution, but is this solution the best?

Evaluating and Improving the Second Solution

Now we must repeat our algorithm as specified by the loop in the flowchart in Figure 12.5 and compute the improvement indices. The paths to be used to evaluate the second solution are shown in Figure 12.10. (Note that when evaluating the Gondor-W3 cell we go to Gondor-W1, Mordor-W1, and Mordor-W3 and skip Mordor-W2, because if we go to Mordor-W2 and turn to Harlindon-W2, we reach a dead end.) The

		TO			CAPACITIES-SUPPLIES	
		W1	**W2**	**W3**		
	Gondor	⑤① $2	$4	$5	51	
FROM	Mordor	②⓪ $8	㉑ $12	㊹ $9	85	**EAST RIM**
	Harlindon	$3	⑦⑥ $7	$13	76	
	Demand	71	97	44	212	
		SOUTH RIM				

FIGURE 12.9 Second solution to the transportation problem. The total cost is $1442.

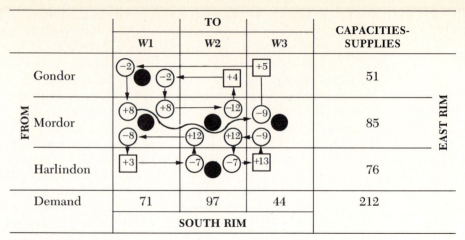

FIGURE 12.10 Closed paths used to evaluate the second solution to the transportation problem.

evaluation of the second solution, that is, the improvement indices, is shown in Figure 12.11. There is a negative index in the Gondor-W2 cell, and so our second solution is not the best. The (only and most negative) index equals −2, and so there is a third solution with an increase of transportation cost of −$2 × 21 = −$42. Thus the cost for the third solution is $1442 − $42 = $1400. Again we must test this solution for optimality.

The Third Solution

The third solution is shown in Figure 12.12, the closed paths to be used for evaluation in Figure 12.13, and the improvement indices of the third solution in Figure 12.14. The most negative index is −2 in the Harlin-

	TO			CAPACITIES-SUPPLIES	
	W1	**W2**	**W3**		
Gondor	$2 51	$4 −2	$5 +2	51	
Mordor	$8 20	$12 21	$9 44	85	
Harlindon	$3 0	$7 76	$13 +9	76	
Demand	71	97	44	212	
	SOUTH RIM				

FIGURE 12.11 Evaluation of the second solution to the transportation problem.

FROM	TO			CAPACITIES-SUPPLIES	EAST RIM
	W1	W2	W3		
Gondor	30 $2	21 $4	$5	51	
Mordor	41 $8	$12	44 $9	85	
Harlindon	$3	76 $7	$13	76	
Demand	71	97	44	212	
	SOUTH RIM				

FIGURE 12.12 Third solution to the transportation problem. The total cost is $1400.

don-W1 cell. The increase in costs is $-2 \times 30 = -\$60$, and so the cost for the fourth solution is $\$1,400 - \$60 = \$1340$.

The Fourth and Final Solution

Finally, we show the fourth solution in Figure 12.15 and observe that all the indices are either 0 or positive and so no further improvement is possible. Thus the lowest possible cost is $1340. A direct calculation verifies the result:

$$4 \times 51 + 8 \times 41 + 9 \times 44 + 3 \times 30 + 7 \times 46 = \$1340$$

We can summarize our approach with the flowchart in Figure 12.5. We obtained an initial solution (box 2) with the northwest corner rule for

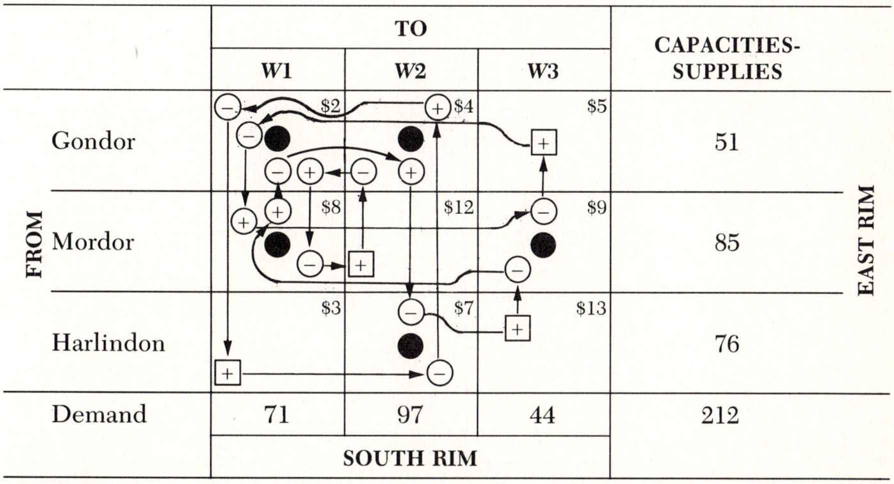

FIGURE 12.13 Closed paths used to evaluate the third solution to the transportation problem.

FROM	TO			CAPACITIES-SUPPLIES	
	W1	W2	W3		
Gondor	$2 30	$4 21	$5 +2	51	EAST RIM
Mordor	$8 41	$12 +2	$9 44	85	
Harlindon	$3 -2	$7 76	$13 +7	76	
Demand	71	97	44	212	
	SOUTH RIM				

FIGURE 12.14 Evaluation of third solution to the transportation problem.

a total cost of $1838. Then we computed the improvement indices (box 3), found the most negative one, and generated the second solution (box 5) for a total cost of $1442. We went around the loop (boxes 3, 4, and 5) twice more and ended with the fourth solution, which had only positive or 0 indices. Thus we reached the optimum solution (box 6) with a total cost of $1340.

12.2 ALTERNATE OPTIMUM SOLUTIONS

Observe in Figure 12.15 that the improvement index in the Mordor-W2 cell is 0. This means that if shipments are introduced from Mordor to W2 there will be no change in the total transportation cost. Of course you must realize if 1 unit is shipped from Mordor to W2, shipments from Harlindon to W1 must be increased by 1 and shipments from Mordor to W1 and from Harlindon to W2 decreased by 1. Note then that there are alternate optimum solutions to the problem, all having the same total transportation cost of $1340.

FROM	TO			CAPACITIES-SUPPLIES	
	W1	W2	W3		
Gondor	$2 +2	$4 51	$5 +4	51	EAST RIM
Mordor	$8 41	$12 0	$9 44	85	
Harlindon	$3 30	$7 46	$13 +9	76	
Demand	71	97	44	212	
	SOUTH RIM				

FIGURE 12.15 Fourth solution to the transportation problem. The evaluation shows that this is the final, optimum solution. The total (lowest) cost is $1340.

		W1	W2	W3	CAPACITIES-SUPPLIES	
			TO			
	Gondor	$2	$4 51	$5	51	
FROM	Mordor	$8	$12 41	$9 44	85	EAST RIM
	Harlindon	$3 71	$7 5	$13	76	
	Demand	71	97	44	212	
		SOUTH RIM				

FIGURE 12.16 Alternate optimum solution to the transportation problem.

The maximum quantity that can be shipped from Mordor to W2 is 41 units, because if we ship more than 41, negative shipments would be required from Mordor to W1 to satisfy the rim conditions. If 41 units are shipped from Mordor to W2, nothing will be shipped from Mordor to W1, $30 + 41 = 71$ units from Harlindon to W1, and $46 - 41 = 5$ units from Harlindon to W2. This alternate optimum solution is shown in Figure 12.16. Of course, any shipment between 0 and 41 units, even fractional shipments, will provide alternate optimum solutions to the problem. As an example, in Figure 12.17 we show an alternate solution when 10.5 units are shipped from Mordor to W2.

12.3 DEGENERACY

Suppose that in the problem of Fanta-Seas Shipping requirements at W2 drop by 32 to 65 and at W3 increase by 32 to 76, as shown in Figure 12.18. When you apply the northwest corner rule, you get stuck in the Mordor-W2 cell, as there is no stone either to the south or to the east. As pointed out in Figure 12.2, box 8, this is the case of *degeneracy*.

A simple way to get around degeneracy is to move south and use a ZERO stone. To make certain you know in the course of the solution that this is not an empty cell but that there is a stone in the cell, we put a ZERO stone in the transportation tableau. Now you can continue with the northwest corner rule as shown in Figure 12.2, box 6. If you reach box 2, the largest possible number in the cell is 0, that is, ZERO. Thus you can complete the initial solution to the problem. Now you can calculate the improvement indices (Figure 12.5) and use the transportation algorithm, always remembering that a ZERO stone represents the 0 value.

Note in Figure 12.3 that

Number of stones = number of rows + number of columns − 1.

FROM	TO			CAPACITIES-SUPPLIES	
	W1	W2	W3		
Gondor	$2	$4 51.0	$5	51	EAST RIM
Mordor	$8 30.5	$12 10.5	$9 44.0	85	
Harlindon	$3 40.5	$7 35.5	$13	76	
Demand	71	97	44	212	
		SOUTH RIM			

FIGURE 12.17 Second alternate optimum solution to the transportation problem.

Bear in mind that in the case of degeneracy the ZERO stones must be counted too.

The Assignment Problem

In Section 10.2 we discussed the Hy-Pressure Realty Co. to illustrate the assignment problem. If you try to solve the problem by starting with the northwest corner rule, you get a 1 in the northwest corner cell and discover you are faced with degeneracy. You insert a ZERO stone but again face degeneracy. You end up with 1s in the diagonal cells and ZERO stones. The assignment problem is a highly degenerate problem, and you can solve it by our algorithm, but in fact there are special, highly efficient algorithms for solving the assignment problem. However, learning the special algorithm would not add substantially to your insight and so is not included here.

FROM	TO			CAPACITIES-SUPPLIES	
	W1	W2	W3		
Gondor	$2 51	$4	$5	51	EAST RIM
Mordor	$8 20	$12 65	$9	85	
Harlindon	$3	$7 ZERO	$13 76	76	
Demand	71	65	76	212	
		SOUTH RIM			

FIGURE 12.18 Example of the case of degeneracy in the transportation problem.

Drawing paths, as in Figure 12.13, can become too time-consuming, so to overcome this difficulty, we introduce the modified distribution (MODI) method as a shortcut. Here we describe the method without mathematical proof. The MODI method consists of assigning values of n to the **north rim** and of w to the **west rim** of the transportation tableau as shown in Figure 12.19. The value of w_1, in the top of the west rim, is always 0. The rest of the values satisfy the first MODI rule:

First MODI rule: The sum of a w and n must equal the transportation cost at the crossroad stone.

(The rule does not hold for empty cells.) For example, we must have

$$w_2 + n_3 = 9$$

because the transportation cost in Figure 12.19 in the second row, third column, is \$9.00.

What is the point in finding the north and west rim values? Suppose for the moment that we have the values. Then we could compute the improvement indices by the second rule of the MODI method.

Second MODI rule: The improvement index in each empty cell can be obtained by subtracting from the transportation cost the sum of corresponding values of w and n.

Let us then proceed to determine the w and n values. We know that w_1 is 0, so we have five remaining unknowns w_2, w_3, n_1, n_2, and n_3. According to the first MODI rule, we have five equations, as shown schematically in Figure 12.20. This system of linear equations is easy to

		NORTH RIM		
		$n_1 = ?$	$n_2 = ?$	$n_3 = ?$
WEST RIM	$w_1 = 0$	● \$2	● \$4	
	$w_2 = ?$	● \$8		● \$9
	$w_3 = ?$		● \$7	

FIGURE 12.19 MODI method for evaluating the third solution (Figure 9.12) to the transportation problem. Note that w_1 is always 0.

EQUATION	WEST RIM			NORTH RIM			COST
1	w_1			$+n_1$			$= 2$
2	w_1				$+n_2$		$= 4$
3		w_2		$+n_1$			$= 8$
4		w_2				$+n_3$	$= 9$
5			w_3		$+n_2$		$= 7$

FIGURE 12.20 Stating the first MODI rule as a system of linear equations.

solve. We know that w_1 is 0, so from equation 1 we get

$$n_1 = 2 - w_1 = 2 - 0 = 2$$

From equation 2 we get

$$n_2 = 4 - w_1 = 4 - 0 = 4$$

We know that $n_1 = 2$, so from equation 3 we get

$$w_2 = 8 - n_1 = 8 - 2 = 6$$

From equation 4 we get

$$n_3 = 9 - w_2 = 9 - 6 = 3$$

and finally from equation 5 we get

$$w_3 = 7 - n_2 = 7 - 4 = 3$$

In Figure 12.21 we show these values. Now the improvement index for the empty cells can be simply computed by using the second MODI rule.

With a little practice you can learn to determine the values of w and n without writing the equations, just working with the transportation tableau. When you find the most negative improvement index, you know where to move a stone. Now you draw the closed path required to evaluate this cell. You ship the largest possible amount through this cell and modify the solution along the path accordingly.

Thus the MODI method by a simple calculation allows you to compute all the improvement indices. Otherwise, the solution method is precisely the same as before.

	$n_1 = 2$	$n_2 = 4$	$n_3 = 3$
$w_1 = 0$	●	●	\$5 $5 - 0 - 3 = +2$
$w_2 = 6$	●	\$12 $12 - 6 - 4 = +2$	●
$w_3 = 3$	\$3 $3 - 3 - 2 = -2$	●	\$13 $13 - 3 - 3 = +7$

FIGURE 12.21 Calculating the improvement indices with the MODI method.

Consider the transportation problem shown in Figure 12.22. The total capacity in the plants is 221 units, while demand at the warehouses is only 208. This means that there is a surplus capacity. Which plant should ship to which warehouse and in what quantity?

This problem can be solved with the transportation algorithm by modifying the transportation problem. Namely, we introduce a fourth dummy warehouse with 0 transportation cost for the surplus capacity, as shown in Figure 12.23. Now we have a transportation problem we know how to deal with, and by applying our algorithm, we can solve the problem.

Now suppose that the demand in warehouse W1 increases to 75 units. So the total demand is 258, which is more than the capacity of 221; there is insufficient capacity. However, if management allows partial fulfillment of demand, then the problem can again be solved by the transportation algorithm by simply introducing in the bottom row a dummy plant for unfilled demand at 0 transportation cost.

> **Unbalanced transportation problems** can be solved by introducing dummy variables.

You can see that the transportation algorithm has a broader scope than would appear at first glance. Now we show another important application of the transportation algorithm.

12.6 SHIPPING THROUGH TIME

Consider again the production and inventory control problem of the Concrete Construction Corp. discussed in Section 10.2. We show now (Figure 12.24) that problems of this type can be formulated as transportation problems.

Recall that capacities are 125 bricks in each quarter and demands are 50, 50, 150, and 150 bricks, respectively (see the east and south rims in Figure 12.24).

	WAREHOUSES			
	W1	W2	W3	CAPACITIES-SUPPLIES
Plant A	?	?	?	55
Plant B	?	?	?	68
Plant C	?	?	?	98
Demand	25	72	111	208 221

FIGURE 12.22 Transportation problem where there is surplus capacity to meet requirements.

439

	WAREHOUSES				
	W1	W2	W3	Dummy	CAPACITIES
Plant A				$0	55
Plant B				$0	68
Plant C				$0	98
Demand	25	72	111	13	221

FIGURE 12.23 Solving an unbalanced transportation problem by the introduction of a dummy variable.

Concrete Construction proposed to make 100 bricks in each quarter. In Figure 12.24 we show how the bricks are made and used. In each row we show the bricks made in the respective quarter and in each column the bricks used in the respective quarter.

In quarter 1, 100 bricks are made − 50 used in quarter 1, 50 earmarked for quarter 2. There is a surplus capacity of 25 bricks in quarter 1, as in all the other quarters.

In quarter 2, 100 bricks are made, all earmarked for quarter 3. In quarter 3, 100 bricks are made − 50 used in quarter 3, 50 earmarked for quarter 4. Finally, in quarter 4, 100 bricks are made, all used in quarter 4.

The shaded portion of the tableau indicates cells where no numbers must be put. For example, it is impossible to make bricks in the second quarter to be earmarked for use in the first quarter, etc.

Observe that this problem is a transportation problem because the 20 cells of the tableau must be filled so that rim requirements are met and the total inventory cost is to be minimized. Let us find these costs.

Consider, for example, the cell in the first row, second column. This represents 50 bricks manufactured in the first quarter, earmarked to be used in the second quarter. Inventory carrying costs are $15.00 per quarter per brick. Thus, carrying these 50 bricks in inventory costs 50 ×

SUPPLY-PRODUCTION	DEMAND-USAGE				SURPLUS	CAPACITIES-SUPPLIES
	Quarter 1	Quarter 2	Quarter 3	Quarter 4	Dummy	
Quarter 1	$0 50	$15 50	$30	$45	$0 25	125
Quarter 2		$0 0	$15 100	$30	$0 25	125
Quarter 3			$0 50	$15 50	$0 25	125
Quarter 4				$0 100	$0 25	125
Demand	50	50	150	150	100	

EAST RIM

SOUTH RIM

FIGURE 12.24. Formulating the production and inventory control problem of the Concrete Construction Corp. as a shipping problem through time.

$15 = \$750$. Now consider the cell in the first row, third column. These bricks must be carried for two quarters, and so the costs will be $30 per brick. Thus the $15 and $30 correspond to transportation costs in the transportation problem, and we can list these costs in the upper right-hand corner of each cell. What about the shaded cells?

You do not need costs here because as you develop the solution with the aid of the transportation algorithm, you block these cells from the solution and apply the algorithm only to the unshaded cells.

You can see, therefore, that this and similar problems can be solved by the transportation method. Solution of this problem and other related problems are left as exercises.

12.7 SENSITIVITY ANALYSIS

What-if some of the numerical values slightly change in the transportation problem? As you will see, the transportation algorithm automatically provides a great deal of information on sensitivity analysis. To simplify our discussion, we assume that a change by one unit in any of the numerical values is sufficiently "small," and we present our discussion by examining again the problem of the Fanta-Seas Shipping Corp.

What-If the Rim Values Change?

Suppose in Figure 12.15 the capacity at Gondor is increased by 1 unit to 52 units and the demand in W2 is increased by 1 unit to 98. What is the solution to this transportation problem?

None of the transportation costs have changed; none of the improvement indices will change, and therefore the stones are located optimally. So we simply increase by 1 unit (to 52) the quantity shipped from Gondor to W2. The total transportation cost will increase by $4.00.

What-if the capacity at Gondor is decreased by 1 unit and the demand at W2 is similarly decreased by 1 unit. Again the stones are optimally located, and we drop shipments from Gondor to W2 by 1 unit, that is, from 51 to 50. The total transportation cost is decreased by $4.00.

Suppose now that the capacity at Harlindon is increased by 1 unit and the demand at W3 is increased by 1 unit. Note that the Harlindon-W3 cell is empty because the shipping cost of $13 is too high. But suppose we ship 1 unit from Harlindon to W3. The total transportation cost will go up by $13.00. Is this an optimum solution to the problem? No, because we have now six stones, and the optimum solution has only five.

Bear in mind that we have evaluated the empty Harlindon-W3 cell with the improvement index of $9.00. This means that by introducing a unit shipment from Harlindon to W3 and making the appropriate adjustments (Figure 12.25) along the path of evaluation (to maintain rim conditions) we increase the cost by $13.00 - \$9.00 + \$8.00 - \$3.00 = \$9.00$. So if we *reduce* by 1 unit shipments from Harlindon to W3, we *reduce* the cost by $9.00. To summarize: (1) Introduce 1 unit, and

		TO			CAPACITIES-SUPPLIES	
		W1	W2	W3		
FROM	Gondor	$2	$4 51	$5	51	EAST RIM
	Mordor	($8) 41 − 1	$12	($9) 44 + 1	85	
	Harlindon	($3) 30 + 1	$7 46	[$13] +9	76 + 1	
	Demand	71	97	44 + 1	212 + 1	
			SOUTH RIM			

FIGURE 12.25 Sensitivity analysis for Fanta-Seas Shipping Corp. when two rim values are changed.

increase cost by $13.00; (2) reduce by 1 unit, and decrease cost by $9.00. Thus the net effect is that the optimal solution shown in Figure 12.25 increases the total cost by $13.00 − $9.00 = $4.00. Of course you can directly verify from Figure 9.25 that the increase in cost is $9.00 − $8.00 + $3.00 = $4.00.

In summary, we see that when the two rim requirements are changed, two different situations must be considered.

Condition 1. The cell involved contains a stone. Under this condition the shipments in this cell are to be changed, and the change in total transportation cost is given by the cost in the cell.

Condition 2. If the cell is empty, it will remain empty, because shipping through the empty cell is too expensive:

change in transportation cost = improvement index − transportation cost

The solution is obtained by carrying out the required modification along the evaluation path of the cell.

What-If the Transportation Costs Change?

Suppose in Figure 12.25 the transportation cost from Gondor to W1 is increased by $1.00. This route, even at $2.00, is too expensive, and an increase in cost to $3.00 will make the route even more expensive, so the route will not be used. There will be no change in the total transportation cost.

In fact, a small change in transportation cost will cause only a small change in improvement indices, and so positive improvement indices will remain positive, and the stones will remain placed optimally.

As an example, assume that the transportation cost from Gondor to W2 is increased by $1.00. None of the improvement indices will become negative, so the stones are still placed optimally. Consequently the solution is unchanged, but the total cost of shipping 51 units from

Gondor to *W2* will increase by $51.00. If the cost of shipping from Gondor to *W2* is decreased by $1.00, the total cost will drop by $51.00.

How to Increase Capacity

Suppose demand in Figure 12.25 increases at *W3* to 44 + 1 = 45 units. Which of the capacities should be increased?

Suppose we increase the capacity at Gondor to 51 + 1 = 52. This implies a change at an empty cell, so the increase in cost is the difference between the transportation cost of $5.00 and the improvement index of $4.00. So the increase is $5.00 − $4.00 = $1.00.

If we increase the capacity at Mordor, the increase is given by the transportation cost of $9.00.

If we increase the capacity at Harlindon, the increase is given by the difference of $13.00 − $9.00 = $4.00.

Thus it is clear that the optimum solution is to increase capacity at Gondor. The optimum solution is given in Figure 12.26, and direct calculation shows that the increase in cost is indeed $4.00 − $7.00 + $3.00 − $8.00 + $9.00 = $1.00.

12.8 EXTENSIONS OF THE TRANSPORTATION PROBLEM: NETWORK ANALYSIS

If you go back to the transportation problem of Transamerica Manufacturing Corporation in Section 10.2, you notice in Figure 10.4 a *network* representation of the problem. We can of course represent the problems in our current chapter by networks also. In fact, there is a broad class of linear programming problems which can be represented by various networks. This topic is very important because of the many successful applications, but discussion is postponed to Chapter 18, as you need knowledge of other areas of quantitative analysis before the topic of networks can be covered.

	W1	W2	W3	CAPACITIES-SUPPLIES
Gondor	$2	($4) 51 + 1	$5 4	51 + 1
Mordor	($8) 41 − 1	$12	($9) 44 + 1	85
Harlindon	($3) 30 + 1	($7) 46 − 1	$13 +9	76
Demand	71	97	44 + 1	212 + 1

TO (over W1 W2 W3), FROM (left), EAST RIM (right), SOUTH RIM (bottom)

FIGURE 12.26 Finding the optimum solution to the problem of increasing capacity.

Q. *How large are the transportation problems that have been solved?*

A. Hundreds of sources and hundreds of destinations.

Q. *How can you determine the equations and the coefficients in the equations for such large problems? How do you input the coefficients when there are hundreds of thousands of them?*

A. You use the computer to calculate the coefficients and to set up the equations.

Q. *How?*

A. Let me illustrate. Suppose you want to send a package from city *A* to city *B*. There are millions of combinations. But the clerk who takes the package uses a manual to calculate the charge. The manual provides charges for a limited number of combinations of cities and also provides rules on how to calculate the charge from one city to another. Thus the clerk only "inputs" the data from the customer, from where to where to send the package, weighs the package, and then calculates the charge. The computer works in a similar manner; the rate structure and rules for calculating the coefficients of the equations are stored. Then there are special computer programs which take the input provided by humans, calculate the coefficients for the linear programming problem, and set up the equations. After all this work is completed, the optimization program proper is called in to find the solution to the problem.

SUMMARY

1. The transportation model and its extensions are some of the most important models of quantitative methods.

2. The transportation algorithm consists of the following rules: (a) Develop the initial solution by the northwest rule; (b) calculate the improvement indices; (c) if there is a negative improvement index, put a stone at the cell with the most negative improvement index and remove a stone at the appropriate cell; (d) if there is no negative index, you have the optimum solution.

3. A transportation problem may have infinitely many optimum solutions.

4. The MODI method is a convenient shortcut for calculating improvement indices.

5. The transportation algorithm directly provides a great deal of information for sensitivity analysis.

SECTION EXERCISES

1. **The Fundamental Algorithm**

1.1 Refer to Figure 12.1. Suppose that the requirements to warehouse 1 (W1) are changed to 84 and the capacities of Gondor and Mordor increased by 25 and reduced by 12, respectively. Draw the revised schematic chart (similar to Figure 12.1) to account for the situation after these changes.

1.2 Refer to Figure 12.1. Suppose that the costs of shipping from Gondor to all warehouses are increased by 25% and the costs of shipping from Harlindon to warehouses 2 and 3 are increased by $1 to account for high losses en route. Draw the revised schematic chart (similar to Figure 12.1) for this revised situation.

1.3 Refer to Figure 12.2. The choice of the northwest corner is arbitrary. The starting place could be chosen to be the southwest corner. Redraw the flowchart of Figure 12.2 to start from the southwest corner; be sure to make all appropriate changes in rules and decisions.

1.4 Refer to Exercise 1.1. Start at the southwest corner, and find an initial solution for the Fanta-Seas case as described in Figure 12.1. What is the cost of this solution? Is it less or greater than the cost of the initial solution obtained by the northwest corner starting rule? Why?

1.5 Refer to the initial solution shown in Figure 12.3. This solution represents action to be taken; write out the instructions given by this table.

1.6 Figures 12.6, 12.7, and 12.8 show the formation of paths originating in empty cells and having corners corresponding to cells with stones as the basis for obtaining the improvement indices. Use the same method to determine the improvement indices using the initial solution that you found in Exercise 1.4.

1.7 Refer to Figures 12.7 and 12.8. Suppose that the shipping cost from Mordor to warehouse 2 were decreased to $3. Calculate the improvement indices that now hold.

2. **Alternate Optimal Solutions**

2.1 The following is a table showing the optimal solution to a transportation problem involving three factories shipping and five warehouses receiving goods. Show whether or not this is the only optimal solution; if not, find another optimal solution.

FROM	W1	W2	W3	W4	W5	Total
F1	3 40	2 40	3 20	4 0	4 0	100
F2	3 0	3 0	3 20	2 0	0 80	100
F3	4 0	4 0	3 40	2 80	3 0	120
Total	40	40	80	80	80	320

2.2 Refer to Exercises 1.1, 1.4, and 1.6. Complete the use of the stepping stone algorithm to obtain the optimal solution for this transportation problem.

2.3 The following table gives the costs and rim values for a transportation problem to be solved at minimum cost.

    a. Find an initial feasible solution by use of the northwest corner rule.

    b. Starting from that solution, find the optimal solution.

    c. Are there alternate optimal solutions? If so, find them.

	W1	W2	W3	W4	W5	Total
F1	55	39	40	50	40	40
F2	35	30	100	45	60	20
F3	40	60	95	35	30	40
Total	25	10	20	30	15	100

2.4 Refer to Exercise 2.1. In this exercise, one optimal solution to a transportation problem is given and you are requested to find a second. In fact, there is an infinity of optimal solutions to this problem. Find the linear expression for this infinite set of solutions.

3. Degeneracy

3.1 The following is a transportation problem with a solution indicated. What is the next step? What is the term applied to situations like this?

	W1	W2	W3	W4	W5	TOTAL
F1	140					140
F2	40	220				260
F3			150	200	10	360
F4					120	120
Total	180	220	150	200	130	880

4. The MODI Method

4.1 Work through from initial solution (by the northwest corner method) to the optimal solution the Fanta-Seas Shipping firm transportation problem of Section 12.1 using the MODI method of solution.

4.2 Work through from the initial solution obtained in Exercises 1.1 and 1.4 to the optimal solution using the MODI method of solution.

5. When Supply and Demand Do Not Balance

5.1 The following is a transportation problem with surplus capacity. Introduce a dummy variable, and create the new problem which can be solved by the methods of this chapter.

	W1	W2	W3	W4	TOTAL
F1					600
F2					200
F3					100
					900
Total	110	220	90	80	510

5.2 The following is a transportation problem with insufficient capacity.

Introduce a dummy variable, and create a new problem which can be solved by the methods of this chapter.

	W1	W2	W3	TOTAL
F1				500
F2				2,800
F3				6,200
F4				900
				10,400
Total	5000	4500	1200	10,700

5.3 Consider the transportation problem defined in the following table.
   a. Redraw the table so that the transportation method as described in this chapter may be used.
   b. Find an initial feasible solution.
   c. Find the optimal solution.
   d. Is the optimal solution you have found unique? If not, what are the alternate optimal solutions?
   (*Hint*: Think about linear combinations.)

	W1	W2	W3	W4	TOTAL
F1	28	40	36	38	140
F2	18	28	24	30	260
F3	42	54	52	54	360
F4	36	48	40	46	220
					980
Total	180	280	150	20	630

5.4 Refer to Exercise 5.3. In this statement of the problem, only transportation costs have been considered. This would be a valid practical solution if production costs are the same at all locations. As it turns out, an analysis by the industrial engineering department of this organization shows that the following production costs hold at the various factories:

FACTORY	UNIT COST OF PRODUCTION
F1	$60
F2	72
F3	48
F4	60

Taking these production costs into account to obtain total costs for each cell in the statement of the problem (Exercise 5.3),
   a. Redraw the table so that the transportation method may be used.
   b. Find an initial feasible solution.
   c. Find the optimal solution for the problem including these production costs.
   d. Is the optimal solution you have found unique? If not, find all alternate optimal solutions.

6. *Shipping Through Time*
6.1 In Section 12.6, a time-dependent shipping problem is described and illustrated in Figure 12.24. Solve this problem.

7. *Sensitivity Analysis*

7.1 Refer to the solution to the Fanta-Seas problem as shown in Figure 12.15. What if the capacity at Gondor is increased by 1 and the requirement at warehouse 2 increased by 1?

7.2 Refer to the alternate solution to the Fanta-Seas problem as shown in Figure 12.16
   a. What if the capacity at Harlindon is increased by 1 and the requirement at warehouse 3 also is increased by 1?
   b. What if the capacity at Gondor is decreased by 1 and the requirement at warehouse 2 is decreased by 1?

7.3 Refer to the solution to the Fanta-Seas problem as shown in Figure 12.15. What if the capacity at Mordor is increased by 1 and the requirement at warehouse 2 is increased by 1?

7.4 Refer to the alternate solution to the Fanta-Seas problem as shown in Figure 12.16. What if the capacity at Mordor is increased by 1 and the requirement at warehouse 1 is also increased by 1?

7.5 Refer to the transportation problem of Exercise 2.3.
   a. What if the capacity of F2 drops to 70 and simultaneously the requirements at W3 drop to 50?
   b. What if the capacity of F2 drops to 90 units and at the same time requirements at W3 drop to 70?
   c. What if the capacity at F3 increase to 130 and requirements at W3 increase to 90?
   d. What if the cost of shipping from F3 to W2 increases from $3 to $5?

7.6 Refer to the transportation problem of Exercise 2.1. What if the shipping route from F2 to W5 experiences a growth of profitable activity, and it is decided that a subsidy no longer applies. Shipping costs of $3 per unit are now assigned to this route. What is the optimal solution under these circumstances? Is the resulting change in total costs what you would have expected?

7.7 What if the capacity at Harlindon is decreased by 1 and the requirement at warehouse 2 is decreased by 1 for
   a. The optimal solution of Figure 12.15.
   b. The alternate solution of Figure 12.16.

7.8 What is the effect of increasing the shipping cost from Mordor to warehouse 3 for
   a. The optimal solution of Figure 12.15.
   b. The alternate solution of Figure 12.16

7.9 At which location is it optimal to increase capacity if
   a. In Figure 12.15 requirements at warehouse 2 increase by 1?
   b. In Figure 12.16 requirements at warehouse 2 increase by 1?

CHAPTER EXERCISES AND DISCUSSION QUESTIONS

C.1 Extel Inc. can produce microprocessor CPU chips at two locations: Westbury and Southbury. Westbury can produce 300,000 a month and Southbury, 450,000. Three companies, MEP, KCN, and LDO, require 100,000, 200,000, and 150,000 units per month, respectively. Since the three companies require different characteristics and the two producing plants have different capabilities, the cost of producing chips for the various customers at the two plants differ. The production costs can be summarized as follows:

PRODUCING PLANT	CUSTOMER		
	MEP	KCN	LDO
Westbury	$.50	$.90	$.20
Southbury	.60	.50	.50

Determine how many units should be produced at each plant to minimize production costs.

C.2 X. Sess Corporation is introducing three products into the market. They have five plants in which these products could be manufactured. The distriburors have offered to take 600, 400, and 700 of these products which cost different amounts to produce in the different plants. Also the fourth and fifth plants cannot produce the third product. All plants can manufacture the second product which costs $50, $60, $55, $65, and $52 per unit to manufacture in all the five plants, respectively. The costs of manufacturing the first product in all plants are $60, $65, $55, $65, and $60 in the five plants, respectively. The costs of manufacturing the third product in the three plants which can manufacture it are $80, $85, and $75, respectively. The plants do not all have equal capacity. For purposes of capacity planning, the products can be considered to require the same capacity. The total numbers of units that can be produced in the five plants (no matter what kind of unit) are 400, 800, 400, 1000, and 700. All capacities and demands are in units per month. What is the optimum assignment of manufacturing for the five plants?

C.3 In the introductory part of this chapter, it is stated that the type of problem which is called a transportation problem can be solved using the simplex method. Why, then, is there a special method for solving this type of problem?

C.4 Yivas and Son manufactures four products: *A*, *B*, *C*, and *D*. Each of these products can be made from three different materials: I, II, and III. The amount of each material that goes into each product is the same: Three units of *A* require one unit each of materials I, II, and III. Similarly, six units of *B* require two units each of I, II, and III. In this case, we wish to maximize profits where the profit contribution of each material when used in each product is given in the following table. There is a limited amount of each material and upper limits to the market demand potential for each product.

   a. Formulate as a transportation problem what can be done by the methods of this chapter.

   b. Find the optimal solution(s).

MATERIALS	PRODUCTS				MATERIALS AVAILABLE
	1	2	3	4	
1	78	120	78	117	200
2	66	90	72	90	300
3	54	81	69	45	500
Potential market	200	100	160	50	

Note: The "cost" figures in small type are not costs; they are profit contributions.

13

Mathematical Programming: A Survey

So far we have assumed that we are dealing with resource allocation problems where all the relationships are linear or that a linear approximation is an accurate enough model for the problem. While linear programming has a very wide range of applications, there still are many resource allocation problems where the assumptions of linear programming do not hold. In this chapter we survey the generalization of linear programming. Specifically, we study

1. Resource allocation problems where all the variables must be whole numbers or integers
2. Mixed integer linear programming problems, where some of the variables are integers, while others are continuous
3. Nonlinear programming problems where either the constraints and/or the payoff function are no longer linear
4. Dynamic programming, a technique capable of dealing with a wide variety of resource allocation problems, linear or nonlinear

In this chapter we stress problem formulation and present algorithms for solving simple problems only through illustrative examples. Bear in mind that algorithms for solving mathematical programming problems may be unlike the simplex or transportation algorithms. Namely, there may be no absolute guarantee that these more complex algorithms lead rapidly or at all to optimum solutions. There is still much research needed in this field to obtain definitive answers. In practical situations dealing with mathematical programming problems, it is common practice to combine judgment, the algorithm, and the computer to support decision making.

One of the most important limitations of linear programming is that the variables are assumed to be continuous. Often by rounding off the answers, a valid solution or at least a good approximation to a solution requiring integer values can be obtained. In this section we study problems where every one of the values of the variables must be integers, that is, **pure integer linear programming problems**. Here are some examples where solutions must be all integers:

Selection of projects to achieve goals

Routing of police cars, street sweeping equipment, locating fire stations, and other location problems

Capital budgeting

Assignment of personnel to projects

Planning menus for hospitals, schools, penitentiaries, etc.

It may happen that by **complete enumeration**, that is, by brute force, it is possible to examine all possible integer solutions to a problem and select the best. Such an approach may be possible because of the extreme speed of modern computers, which can examine millions of alternatives. However, when the number of alternatives is very large, as is often the case, even the largest of computers is inadequate for obtaining solutions. This, then, is where special integer programming algorithms are needed. The illustrations we give in this textbook have relatively few alternatives and can be solved by brute force. However, the problems presented apply to real-life problems with a large number of variables, in which case special algorithms are required to solve the problems.

Now we proceed to present some typical pure integer programming problems.

Project Selection for a Government Agency

A government agency is planning to sponsor two types of projects. Each type 1 project requires $1,721,000 and each type 2, $1,356,000. Total available funds are $20,500,000. Designate by x_1 the number of type 1 projects sponsored and by x_2 the number of type 2 projects sponsored. Here x_1 and x_2 are integers, because fractional projects cannot be sponsored. Thus,

$$1.721x_1 + 1.356x_2 \leq 20.50$$

where amounts are in millions of dollars.

Projects of type 2 are more risky than projects of type 1, and to work with risk in a quantitative manner, the agency applied the concept of the **linear risk factor**. For example, the risk factor of .122 was assigned to type 1 projects and .450 to type 2 projects. Suppose, for example, that $2 million are assigned to type 1 projects and $5 million to type 2 projects.

Then the agency assigns a risk factor to this resource allocation of

$$2 \times .122 + 5 \times .450 = .244 + 2.250 = 2.494$$

Namely, the combined risk factor is calculated by multiplying for each project the dollar amount by the respective risk factor and adding the products.

The policy of the agency required that the combined risk factor be less than .207. This then leads to the constraint

$$.122(1.721)x_1 + .450(1.356)x_2 \leq .207(20.50)$$

or

$$.21x_1 + .61x_2 \leq 4.25$$

The agency made a **cost benefit analysis** and found that projects of type 1 bring benefits with the monetary equivalent of 7% of the costs; that is, for project type 1 the benefit is $.07 \times 1.721 = \$.120$ in millions. The benefit from x_1 projects of type 1 is therefore $.120x_1$. For type 2 the benefit is 18%, and these projects are more risky. Thus the combined benefit from x_1 projects of type 1 and x_2 of type 2 is

$$Z = .120x_1 + .244x_2$$

The problem is to maximize Z, subject to the two inequalities

$$1.721x_1 + 1.356x_2 \leq 20.50$$

$$.21x_1 + .61x_2 \leq 4.25$$

under the assumption that x_1 and x_2 must be integers.

Routing of Police Cars

A certain city is divided into a number of equal zones to be patrolled by police cars (Figure 13.1). Each rectangle is x_1 units long and x_2 units wide, where distances are measured in units of thousands of feet, and so x_1 and x_2 must be integers.

The minimum driving distance from the southwest corner to the northeast corner of each zone is

$$x_1 + x_2$$

and experience shows that patrolling is inefficient if this driving distance is less than 19,500 feet. So the following constraint results:

$$x_1 + x_2 \geq 19.5$$

Inefficiencies occur also if x_2 is less than 75% of x_1, leading to the second constraint:

$$x_2 \geq .75x_1$$

A third potential inefficiency leads to the constraint

$$x_2 \leq 18.5$$

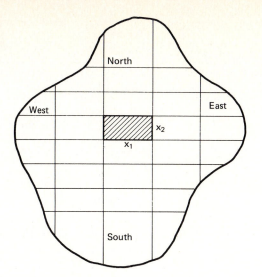

FIGURE 13.1
A city is divided into a number of equal zones to be patrolled by police cars.

and a fourth to

$$x_1 \geq 2.5$$

The objective is to minimize *expected* travel time within each zone. How does one calculate this value?

We can fall back to our dart board model in Chapter 2. Namely, we represent each city zone by a rectangular dart board. We throw a dart: This is the location of the police car. We throw a second dart: This is where the car must go. What is the expected distance between the darts? How long does it take to cover the distance?

With the aid of probability theory it can be shown that the expected distance covered in the west-east (or east-west) direction is $x_1/3$ and in the north-south (or south-north) direction, $x_2/3$. Respective average cruising speeds are 30 miles per hour = 158,400 feet per hour and 15 miles per hour = 79,200 feet per hour. The problem is to minimize the expected travel time:

$$Z = \frac{x_1}{3 \times 158.4} + \frac{x_2}{3 \times 79.2}$$

or

$$Z = .0021x_1 + .0042x_2$$

subject to the previously stated four inequalities.

A Capital Budgeting Problem

A corporation considers establishing five capital investment projects with the expected cash flows shown in Figure 13.2. For example, project 1 requires an outflow (from the corporation) of $150,000 and $50,000 in the first and second years, respectively, and inflow (to the corporation) of $90,000 and $400,000 in the fourth and fifth years.

PROJECTS	YEARS						TOTAL
	1	2	3	4	5	6	
1	−$150	−$50	$0	$90	$550	$0	$440
2	−$80	−$180	−$200	$120	$210	$520	$390
3	−$220	−$300	−$120	$150	$290	$550	$350
4	−$110	−$60	$70	$130	$0	$0	$30
5	$0	−$100	$10	$90	$220	$630	$850

FIGURE 13.2 Five capital investment projects and their associated 6-year cash flows.

Let x_1, x_2, x_3, x_4, and x_5 be 1 or 0, depending on whether the respective capital investment is undertaken or not. The total outflow in the first year is subject to the budgetary constraint of $500,000:

$$150x_1 + 80x_2 + 220x_3 + 110x_4 \leq 500$$

The budgetary constraint for the second year is $650,000:

$$50x_1 + 180x_2 + 300x_3 + 60x_4 + 100x_5 \leq 650$$

The corporation wants to maximize the combined cash flow of the projects. The total cash flow for each project is shown in the right-most column of Figure 13.2, and so the problem is to maximize

$$Z = 440x_1 + 390x_2 + 350x_3 + 30x_4 + 850x_5$$

To complete formulation of the problem, various interrelationships among the projects must be considered.

Project 5 is a follow-up to project 4 and cannot be undertaken unless 4 is undertaken:

$$x_5 \leq x_4$$

Thus if x_4 is zero, x_5 will also be zero. Projects 1 and 2 cannot both be undertaken:

$$x_1 + x_2 \leq 1$$

Thus, if either x_1 or x_2 is 1, the other x will be zero. *Either* projects 3 *or* 4 *must* be undertaken:

$$x_3 + x_4 = 1$$

Thus, either x_3 or x_4 must be 1, but the other x is 0. At least two projects *must* be undertaken:

$$x_1 + x_2 + x_3 + x_4 + x_5 \geq 2$$

Thus at least two xs will be 1. It is not allowed to undertake more than three projects:

$$x_1 + x_2 + x_3 + x_4 + x_5 \leq 3$$

Thus only three xs can be 1.

This is a 0-1 programming problem with five unknowns and seven constraints.

Project Supervision for a Federal Agency

A federal agency assigns six civil servants to supervise three projects. Figure 13.3 shows the effectiveness factor of each civil servant with each of the projects. The figure size shows the variables to be used in solving this assignment problem. For example, if person 3 is assigned to project 2, we have

$$x_8 = 1$$

and

$$x_7 = 0$$

and

$$x_9 = 0$$

because

1. The value 1 refers to an assignment.
2. The value 0 refers to a nonassignment.

Note that the xs are 0s or 1s. Note also that each person must be assigned to exactly one project. So, for example, for the first person we must have

$$x_1 + x_2 + x_3 = 1$$

		PROJECTS			
		1	**2**	**3**	
	1	35 x_1	28 x_2	28 x_3	= 1
	2	26 x_4	21 x_5	18 x_6	= 1
CIVIL SERVANTS	**3**	17 x_7	15 x_8	12 x_9	= 1
	4	24 x_{10}	21 x_{11}	15 x_{12}	= 1
	5	32 x_{13}	29 x_{14}	17 x_{15}	= 1
	6	47 x_{16}	39 x_{17}	31 x_{18}	= 1
		≥ 1	≥ 2	≤ 2	

FIGURE 13.3 Assignment of six civil servants to three federal projects.

Because one of these xs must be 1, the other two xs must be 0s. Similarly, for the other persons,

$$x_4 + x_5 + x_6 = 1$$

$$x_7 + x_8 + x_9 = 1$$

$$x_{10} + x_{11} + x_{12} = 1$$

$$x_{13} + x_{14} + x_{15} = 1$$

$$x_{16} + x_{17} + x_{18} = 1$$

Further assignment policies are as follows:

1. Each project must have at least one person assigned to it:

$$x_1 + x_4 + x_7 + x_{10} + x_{13} + x_{16} \geq 1$$

$$x_2 + x_5 + x_8 + x_{11} + x_{14} + x_{17} \geq 1$$

$$x_3 + x_6 + x_9 + x_{12} + x_{15} + x_{18} \geq 1$$

2. At least two persons must be assigned to project 2:

$$x_2 + x_5 + x_8 + x_{11} + x_{14} + x_{17} \geq 2$$

3. Not more than two persons can be assigned to project 3:

$$x_3 + x_6 + x_9 + x_{12} + x_{15} + x_{18} \leq 2$$

4. Persons 4 and 5 are married and work together:

$$x_{10} = x_{13}$$

$$x_{11} = x_{14}$$

$$x_{12} = x_{15}$$

The objective function to be maximized is obtained by adding the products of the xs and the respective effectiveness indices:

$$Z = 35x_1 + 28x_2 + 28x_3 + 26x_4 + 21x_5 + 18x_6 + \cdots$$

Locating Fire Stations

A certain city has four fire stations and seven fire districts, as shown in Figure 13.4a. (Circles represent stations and squares, districts.) Each district can be serviced by several stations (as shown by the broken lines), and the question is whether some of the stations could be closed down.

In a simple problem a solution can be found by trial and error. For example, it is clear that station 1 could be shut down, as districts 1, 3, and 6 are serviced by station 1, but districts 3 and 6 could be serviced by station 3 and district 1 by station 2 or station 4. However, for a large problem it is more efficient to solve the problem by integer programming.

Introduce the variables x_1, x_2, x_3, and x_4 which assume values of 0 or

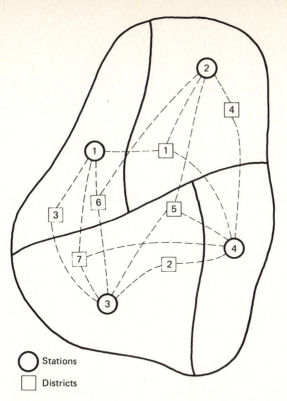

FIGURE 13.4a
A certain city has four fire
stations and seven fire districts.

Stations

Districts

1 depending on whether the respective station is to be shut down or not. We must minimize the number of stations kept open, given by the objective function

$$Z = x_1 + x_2 + x_3 + x_4$$

District 1 must be serviced at least from one station. As shown in Figure 13.4a, district 1 can be serviced from station 1, 2, or 4. Thus,

$$x_1 + x_2 + x_4 \geq 1$$

meaning that one cannot shut down stations 1, 2, and 4 simultaneously. District 2 can be serviced from stations 3 and 4:

$$x_3 + x_4 \geq 1$$

Similar reasoning provides the constraints for district 3,

$$x_1 + x_3 \geq 1$$

district 4,

$$x_2 + x_4 \geq 1$$

district 5,

$$x_2 + x_3 + x_4 \geq 1$$

district 6,

$$x_1 + x_2 + x_3 \geq 1$$

and district 7,

$$x_1 + x_3 + x_4 \geq 1$$

The problem discussed here is a special type of **location problem**. Other important applications of location theory are positioning of ambulances, street cleaning units, police centers, etc.

Assigning Crews to Aircraft

In Section 10.2 we discussed the personnel assignment problem for the Hy-Pressure Realty Co. The problem was to assign people to jobs. Now we consider an extension, the *covering* problem, where, for example, crews are scheduled or assigned to tasks. Consider, for instance, the problem of the Blasting Jets Corporation.

Blasting Jets flies only four different *trips*, where a trip means flying an airplane from one city to another, either nonstop or with intermediary stops. Of course crews must be assigned to each trip. However, the crews are based in San Antonio and may have to be flown back to the base by commercial flight or flown between other cities. This is an expensive operation, so a good plan will minimize the number of these *deadhead* trips.

A naive and inefficient plan would be to assign a crew to trip 1 which originates in San Antonio and terminates in Los Angeles and then fly the crew back to San Antonio by commercial aircraft. Trip 2 starts at Los Angeles and terminates in San Francisco. A second crew would be flown to Los Angeles, assigned to trip 2, and then flown back from San Francisco to San Antonio. And so on.

To minimize these deadhead trips, it is proposed that trips 1, 2, and 3 be combined into a single *pairing* unit, as these three trips can be flown by a crew without a rest break. Trip 4 is not included because all four trips cannot be flown without a rest period. Thus trip 4 stays by itself as a single crew aircraft pairing. Estimating the cost of this new crew plan reveals considerable savings to Blasting Jets. But is it the most efficient plan?

Figure 13.4b shows the data for the problem. There are 11 possible pairings as shown by the 11 columns. The 1s indicate the pairings. For example, pairing 10 shows the possibility of flying trips 1, 2, and 3 in

TRIPS	PAIRINGS										
	1	2	3	4	5	6	7	8	9	10	11
1	1				1	1	1			1	1
2		1			1			1	1	1	1
3			1			1		1		1	
4				1			1		1		1
	12	9	10	11	18	15	16	14	20	23	25

FIGURE 13.4b Four trips and 11 possible pairings for Blasting Jets.

sequence as a unit, without a rest break for the crew. Note, however, this *cannot* be done for all trips, not for trips 2, 3, and 4 or for some other combinations. The problem is to decide which pairing should be included in the best plan. Now we can formulate the mathematical model of the problem.

Introduce the 0, 1 variables $x_1, x_2, \ldots, x_{11}$. If pairing 1 is included, then set x_1 to 1 and otherwise to 0. If pairing 2 is included, then set x_2 to 1 and otherwise to 0. And so on for the rest of the variables.

Note that if pairing 1 is included, trip 1 is taken care of, is *covered*, and so pairings 5, 6, 7, 10, and 11 must be excluded. Thus we must have

$$x_1 + x_5 + x_6 + x_7 + x_{10} + x_{11} = 1$$

because only one of the variables $x_1, x_5, x_6, x_7, x_{10}$, or x_{11} can be 1; the others must be zero. Similarly,

$$x_2 + x_5 + x_8 + x_9 + x_{10} + x_{11} = 1$$

$$x_3 + x_6 + x_8 + x_{10} = 1$$

and

$$x_4 + x_7 + x_9 + x_{11} = 1$$

Thus these four constraints for the 11 variables must be satisfied.

Assume that the cost associated with each pairing is determined and that the cost coefficients of the objective function are listed in the bottom row of Figure 13.4b. Then the problem is to minimize

$$Z = 12x_1 + 9x_2 + 10x_3 + 11x_4 + 18x_5 + 15x_6 + 16x_7$$
$$+ 14x_8 + 20x_9 + 23x_{10} + 25x_{11}$$

under the given constraints.

This is a 0-1 programming problem with 11 unknowns and four constraints. The problem can be solved by direct enumeration, as it has only 12 possible solutions. The actual solution is left as an exercise. The answer is

$$x_7 = 1, \quad x_8 = 1, \quad \text{all other } xs \text{ are zero}$$

$$Z = 30$$

13.2 MIXED INTEGER LINEAR PROGRAMMING PROBLEMS

In many real life situations some variables may be integers while others are continuous. In this section we examine such mixed integer linear programming problems.

Examples of such problems can be found by reformulating many of the problems treated in this textbook under linear programming or in the previous section, under pure integer programming. For example, in production problems some of the items may be of high value, like ships, airplanes and buildings and a solution of say 2.73 buildings makes no sense. On the other hand small value items like screws, bolts or envelopes can be considered continuous, as manufacturing say 12,513.68 parts is essentially the same as 12,514 parts. Therefore such problems are formulated as mixed integer programming problems.

In a similar way capital budgeting problems may include the possibility of investing in real estate and in stocks and bonds, or other items which can be obtained in essentially continuous quantities. There again we are dealing with mixed programming problems.

Another illustration is problems in inventory control where large value items must be represented by integer variables, but small value items as continuous.

Now we proceed to present some typical examples of mixed integer linear programming problems.

When Alternate Production Facilities Are Available

In Section 10.4 we considered Minnehaha's problem subject to the fixed charge condition that it was possible to

1. Manufacture only rings with a fixed cost of $5.00
2. Manufacture only bracelets with a fixed cost of $2.00
3. Manufacture both bracelets and rings with a fixed cost of $7.00

We solved this fixed charge problem by brute force, solving for each of the three alternatives and finding the best alternative. We now formulate the problem as a mixed linear programming problem and allow the manufacture of fractional rings and bracelets.

The original problem was to maximize

$$Z = 4x_1 + 5x_2$$

subject to

$$3x_1 + x_2 \le 9$$

$$x_1 + 2x_2 \le 8$$

We introduce two 0-1 variables y_1 and y_2 such that

If $y_1 = 0$, no rings are made.
If $y_1 = 1$, rings are made.
If $y_2 = 0$, no bracelets are made.
If $y_2 = 1$, bracelets are made.

(0-1 variables are often denoted by ys.)

The silver and gold constraints remain the same, but how do we introduce the fixed cost?

If only rings are manufactured, the profit is $4x_1 - 5$, and if only bracelets, $5x_2 - 2$, and if both, $4x_1 + 5x_2 - 7$. So we can try

$$Z = 4x_1 + 5x_2 - 5y_1 - 2y_2$$

But the trouble is that if we maximize this we get zeros for y_1 and y_2, meaning that nothing is manufactured, which makes no sense. Somehow we must make certain that this cannot happen. So the procedure is as follows: Select a large number, say 100, and write

$$x_1 \leq 100y_1$$

Now if $y_1 = 0$, that is, no rings are made, x_1 will also be zero, as it should. If $y_1 = 1$, rings are made, and so

$$x_1 \leq 100$$

which is an unnecessary constraint, because the silver constraint

$$3x_1 + x_2 \leq 9$$

implies that $x_1 \leq 3$ anyway. Similarly for bracelets we introduce the constraint

$$x_2 \leq 100y_2$$

which makes $x_2 = 0$ when $y_2 = 0$. When $y_2 = 1$, we get

$$x_2 \leq 100$$

which is an unnecessary constraint, because the gold constraint

$$x_1 + 2x_2 \leq 8$$

implies that $x_2 \leq 8/2 = 4$ anyway. So if we maximize

$$Z = 4x_1 + 5x_2 - 5y_1 - 2y_2$$

we can be certain that both y_1 and y_2 cannot be zero, because then both x_1 and x_2 are zero and so is Z, which is certainly not the optimum solution. If the solution yields $y_1 = 0$, then x_1 will be automatically 0; if $y_2 = 0$, then x_2 will be automatically 0, as it should be.

Thus our problem is to maximize

$$Z = 4x_1 + 5x_2 - 5y_1 - 2y_2$$

subject to

$$3x_1 + x_2 \leq 9$$

$$x_1 + 2x_2 \leq 8$$

$$x_1 \leq 100y_1$$

$$x_2 \leq 100y_2$$

where y_1 and y_2 are 0-1 variables.

How did we select the number 100? We know that $x_1 \leq 3$ and $x_2 \leq 4$, so in fact any number greater than 4 would have been sufficiently large.

Expanding Production Capacity

In Section 12.7 (Figure 12.26) we studied a combined production and transportation problem. Suppose that in Figure 12.26 requirements are increased at W3 by 50 units and the problem is to determine which of the plant capacities should be increased. Here we asume again that only a single plant expansion is possible.

Requirements must be met:

$$x_1 + x_4 + x_6 = 71$$
$$x_2 + x_5 + x_8 = 97$$
$$x_3 + x_6 + x_9 = 94$$

Introduce the 0-1 variables y_1, y_2, and y_3, designating the production facility to be expanded:

$$y_1 + y_2 + y_3 = 1$$

Then

$$x_1 + x_2 + x_3 = 51 + 50y_1$$
$$x_4 + x_5 + x_6 = 85 + 50y_2$$
$$x_7 + x_8 + x_9 = 76 + 50y_3$$

The problem is to minimize the total transportation cost as given in the original problem.

13.3 BRANCH-AND-BOUND ALGORITHM

We illustrate the effective and often used branch-and-bound algorithm to solve integer and mixed linear programming problems with the aid of the project selection problem from Section 13.1.

We want to maximize

$$Z = .120x_1 + .244x_2$$

subject to the constraints

$$1.721x_1 + 1.356x_2 \leq 20.50$$

$$.21x_1 + .61 x_2 \leq 4.25$$

where x_1 and x_2 are integers.

The Associated Continuous Problem

First we relax the constraints of x_1 and x_2 being integers. This leads to a linear programming problem. In a practical situation we would solve the problem with the simplex algorithm, but in our illustrative problem we can use the graphical approach from Chapter 10. In Figure 13.5 we first plot the constraints. Then as a first step we arbitrarily assume a profit goal of $3.00 and plot the corresponding isoprofit line. Then we roll down this line and bump into corner C. Thus for the optimum solution,

$$1.721x_1 + 1.356x_2 = 20.50$$

$$.21x_1 + .61x_2 = 4.25$$

Solving for x_1 and x_2, we get

$$x_1 = 8.812, \quad x_2 = 3.933$$

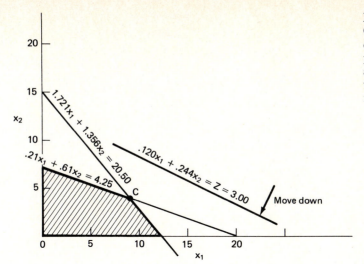

and

$$Z = .120 \times 8.812 + .244 \times 3.933 = 2.017$$

This is not an integer solution, and when the constraint of an integer solution is reestablished, the solution will move away from corner C and will stay inside or on the boundary of the shaded quadrangle.

> The optimum solution to the integer programming problem can never be better than the solution to the associated continuous linear programming problem.

This must be true because the continuous problem considers all possible solutions, including integer solutions.

Branching the Solution

We now choose arbitrarily to examine one of the unknowns, say x_1. The solution to the integer programming problem will not be 8.812, but it will be such that either $x_1 \leq 8.00$ or $x_1 \geq 9.00$. So we split the original problem into two new problems with new constraints, that is, we **branch** to two new problems (Figure 13.6).

Problem A

$$\left.\begin{array}{r} 1.721x_1 + 1.356x_2 \leq 20.50 \\ .21x_1 + .61x_2 \leq 4.25 \end{array}\right\} \text{old constraints}$$
$$x_1 \qquad\qquad \leq 8 \qquad \text{new constraint}$$

Problem B

$$\left.\begin{array}{r} 1.721x_1 + 1.356x_2 \leq 20.50 \\ .21x_1 + .61x_2 \leq 4.25 \end{array}\right\} \text{old constraints}$$
$$x_1 \qquad\qquad \geq 9 \qquad \text{new constraint}$$

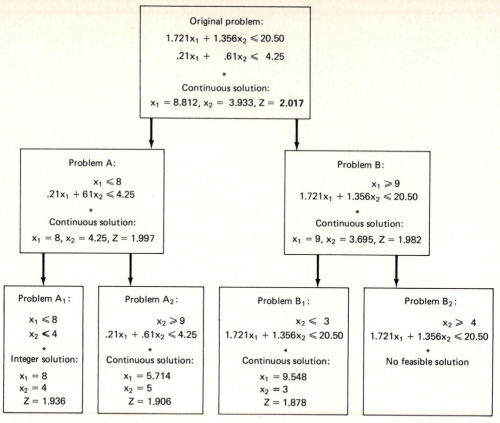

FIGURE 13.6 Example of the branch-and-bound algorithm.

We do not change the objective function:

$$Z = .120x_1 + .244x_2$$

Suppose that we now solve both problems without constraining x_1 and x_2 to integers and that the optimum solutions happen to be integers. *The better of the two solutions is then the optimum solution to the original problem.* But suppose A or B or both yield fractional values. Then we split the problems again and continue this *branching* until finally the linear programming solutions yield integer values. Then we have the solution to the original integer programming problem. Now we illustrate our approach by solving problems A and B.

In real life we would solve problems A and B with the simplex algorithm. Here we use the graphical approach shown in Figure 13.7. The optimum solution to problem A is

$$x_1 = 8$$

$$x_2 = \frac{1}{.61}(4.25 - .21x_1) = 4.213$$

and to problem B is

$$x_1 = 9$$

$$x_2 = \frac{1}{1.356} (20.50 - 1.721x_1) = 3.695$$

Branching Again

Neither of these solutions are integers. So now we split A into A_1 and A_2 (Figure 13.6).

    Problem A_1: Add the constraint

$$x_2 \leq 4$$

    Problem A_2: Add the constraint

$$x_2 \geq 5$$

and split B into B_1 and B_2 (Figure 13.6).

    Problem B_1: Add the constraint

$$x_2 \leq 3$$

    Problem B_2: Add the constraint

$$x_2 \geq 4$$

    We solve these problems by our graphical method (Figure 13.8).

Problem A_1

$$x_1 = 8, \qquad x_2 = 4$$

$$Z = .120 \times 8 + .244 \times 4 = 1.936$$

Problem A_2

$$x_2 = 5, \qquad x_1 = \frac{1}{.21} (4.25 - .61x_2) = 5.714$$

$$Z = .120 \times 5.714 + .244 \times 5 = 1.906$$

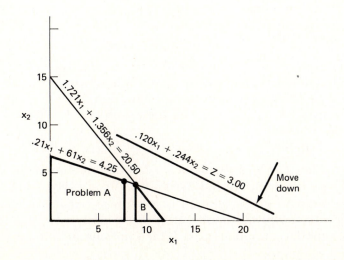

FIGURE 13.7
The original integer programming problem is replaced by problems A and B.

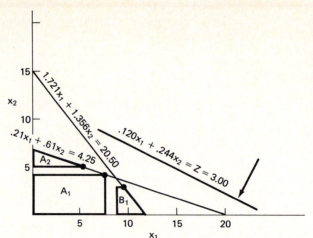

FIGURE 13.8
Problems *A* and *B* in
Figure 13.7 are replaced
by problems A_1, A_2 and
B_1, and B_2, respectively.
Problem B_2 is not shown
because it has no feasi-
ble solution.

Problem B_1

$$x_2 = 3, \qquad x_1 = \frac{1}{1.721}(20.50 - 1.356x_2) = 9.548$$

$$Z = .120 \times 9.548 + .244 \times 3 = 1.878$$

Problem B_2

There is no feasible solution.

Now we have an integer solution with $x_1 = 8$, $x_2 = 4$, and $Z = \$1.936$. Problem B_2 is infeasible. Should we split A_2? Here $Z = \$1.906$, which is less than $\$1.936$. Splitting A_2 cannot improve the solution because the introduction of new constraints cannot improve the solution. *The bound of $\$1.906$ tells us that A_2 is a dead-end problem.* Similarly, there is no point in splitting B_1, which is bound by $Z = \$1.878$, a value less than $\$1.936$. So the only candidate problem is A_1, which already has an integer solution. Thus the optimum solution is $x_1 = 8$, $x_2 = 4$, and $Z = \$1.936$.

Recapitulation

The **branch-and-bound algorithm** is an effective search for finding the optimum solution to integer programming problems. It also works for mixed integer programming problems. For example, if in our problem x_2 is allowed to take any value, then problem *B* (Figure 13.6) yields the optimum solution.

Thus the method consists of the following steps:

Step 1. Solve the associated continuous problem. If the solution yields integer values, you have already solved the problem.

Step 2. If the solution is not integer, select one of the variables arbitrarily and branch to two new problems. Solve both problems for the continuous case. If the solutions are integer, choose the best.

Step 3. If the solutions are not integer, throw away the *bound* problems. Split the other problems, and continue the algorithm until you find the optimum solution.

13.4 THE CUTTING PLANE ALGORITHM

Another often used algorithm for solving pure or mixed integer programming problems is the **cutting plane algorithm**. This algorithm starts by solving the associated continuous linear programming program and if the solution is not integer, continues step by step, introducing new contraints which "cut away" noninteger solutions. We provide an insight into how the algorithm works by an illustration.

Routing of Police Cars

The illustrative problem is (Section 13.1) to minimize

$$Z = .00607x_1 + .0133x_2$$

subject to

$$x_1 + x_2 \geq 19.5$$

$$.75x_1 - x_2 \leq 0$$

$$x_2 \leq 18.5$$

$$x_1 \qquad \geq 2.5$$

Figure 13.9 shows a graphical representation of the problem. The quadrangle $A_1A_2A_3A_4$ shows the feasible area for the corresponding continuous problem. This area includes fractional solutions which are infeasible for the integer programming problem.

Consider the integer feasible solutions inside or on the edge of $A_1A_2A_3A_4$. The smallest polygon, the hexagon $B_1B_2B_3B_4B_5B_6$, contains all the feasible integer solutions, where the coordinates of the corners are

$$B_1: 11, \ 9; \qquad B_2: 12, \ 9; \qquad B_3: 20, \ 15;$$
$$B_4: 23, \ 18; \qquad B_5: \ 3, \ 18; \qquad B_6: \ 3, \ 17$$

This polygon is called the *convex hull* of the feasible integer solutions. If we know the convex hull, we can search the corners and find the optimum solution to the integer programming problem. Thus the crux of the matter is to find the convex hull, or at least a part which contains the optimum solution. This can be accomplished by the cutting plane algorithm.

Step by step we cut away the noninteger solutions until the optimum integer solution is found. Usually it is not necessary to find the entire convex hull, because the optimum solution is found by an earlier cut.

The cutting plane algorithm uses the simplex method and finds appropriate new constraints to cut away noninteger solutions. To illus-

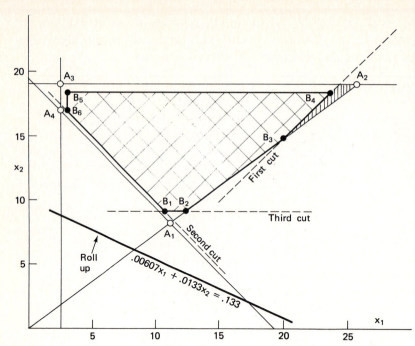

FIGURE 13.9
Illustration of the cutting plane algorithm. The quadrangle $A_1A_2A_3A_4$ represents the feasible area for the associated continuous problem. The hexagon $B_1B_2B_3B_4B_5B_6$ represents the convex hull of the integer programming problem.

trate, consider as the first new constraint

$$x_1 - x_2 \leq 5$$

This is the relationship defining the straight line through points B_3 and B_4. Thus the shaded area in Figure 13.9 is cut away. As a second constraint, consider the line B_1B_6:

$$x_1 + x_2 \geq 20$$

This cuts away a thin long region, on the lower left, from the feasible area. If the constraint

$$x_2 \geq 9$$

is applied (line B_1B_2), only the lower portion of the convex hull remains (crosshatched), and the corner B_1 is found as the solution by the *roll-up* procedure. For B_1, $x_1 = 11$, $x_2 = 9$, and this is the integer solution to the problem.

In summary, the cutting plane method uses constraints to remove noninteger solutions. Compared with the branch-and-bound method, note that only constraints *perpendicular* to the axes are used and that the problem is replaced at each step with several new problems. Details of the theory of the cutting plane algorithm are not included here because in this chapter we stress problem formulation.

13.5 NONLINEAR PROGRAMMING

In many of the resource allocation problems treated in this book it may happen that a linear approximation to the constraints and/or to the objective function may not be valid. Often quadratic functions such as

$$x_1^2 + 3x_1x_2 + x_2^2 + x_3^2$$

are to be maximized or minimized, or functions involving higher powers of variables or other more complicated functions occur in the constraints and/or in the payoff function. So let us discuss some of the typical areas where nonlinear functions may be required.

Earlier we dealt with the problem of *blending materials*, including blending of crude oils to produce fuel to meet minimum standards. In real life, the constraints of octane rating, vapor pressure, etc., are often nonlinear functions.

In many *production problems* the quantities produced are nonlinear functions of dollars expended. The cost of purchasing parts and/or labor costs may also be nonlinear functions. Often there is cost associated with changing levels of production or changing capacities, and they may require nonlinear relationships.

In many *marketing problems*, sales generated by promotion or advertising are nonlinear functions of dollars expended, because of the effect of diminishing returns. Also frequently there is an interaction among sales territories. For example, if sales go up in one territory, they may go up in another territory as well. Moreover, there is an interaction between monthly or yearly sales, and so the allocation of funds to territories or different time periods may require nonlinear functions.

Inventory control problems often lead to nonlinear relationships. The combined cost of activities in several locations and/or in a sequence of time periods may not be the sum of the individual costs. Frequently goods must be ordered in batches, which leads to nonlinear relationships. When the safety level of stocks in inventory control is determined and such costs as unfilled demand and capacity are included, nonlinear relationships are often called for.

Capital budgeting problems and *portfolio selection problems* may require nonlinear payoff functions.

In Chapter 7 we stated that utility theory allows the conversion of *multiobjective problems* to standard maximization problems. When there are myriad or infinitely many alternatives, there is a need for mathematical solution techniques to find the optimum solution. Nonlinear programming provides such a technique.

When all the variables of the problem are integers, we may have an integer, nonlinear programming problem. When some variables are and some not, we may have a mixed integer, nonlinear programming problem.

So far, in all our mathematical programming problems we assumed that a deterministic approach is valid. However, when some of the quantitites in a mathematical programming problem are uncertain, probabilities must be considered, and so the resource allocation models become more involved and nonlinear. In relatively simple cases, the payoff functions can be replaced by using expected values. However, it can be shown that just using expected values may lead to erroneous answers. When probabilistic considerations must be included, often complex and nonlinear problems must be solved.

We now present a set of typical nonlinear programming problems.

Optimum Allocation of Advertising Budget

A corporation wants to allocate $5 million between advertising in the north and the south. In the north x_1 million of advertising generates

$$S_1 = -20x_1^2 + 105x_1$$

millions of dollars in sales. In the south x_2 million of advertising generates

$$S_2 = -5x_2^2 + 55x_2$$

millions of dollars in sales. The profit margin is 20% of sales. So total profit is 20% of total sales, less the amount spent on advertising, or

$$Z = .2(S_1 + S_2) - (x_1 + x_2)$$
$$Z = .2(-20x_1^2 + 105x_1) + .2(-5x_2^2 + 55x_2) - (x_1 + x_2)$$

or

$$Z = -4x_1^2 + 20x_1 - x_2^2 + 10x_2$$

The problem is to maximize this profit subject to

$$x_1 + x_2 = 5$$

First we ignore the constraints and solve the unconstrained problem. The maximum of the quadratic

$$-4x_1^2 + 20x_1$$

can be obtained with the formula in Appendix A, Section 7.5,

$$a = -4$$
$$b = 20$$

and so

$$x_1 = -\frac{b}{2a} = -\frac{20}{2(-4)} = 2.5$$

The second quadratic is

$$-x_2^2 + 10x_2$$

and so

$$a = -1$$
$$b = 10$$

and

$$x_2 = -\frac{10}{2(-1)} = 5$$

However,

$$x_1 + x_2 = 7.5 \geq 5$$

Thus this solution is not feasible. So we proceed to solve the constrained problem.

We solve the constraint for x_1:

$$x_1 = 5 - x_2$$

Now we substitute in the profit function:

$$Z = -4(5 - x_2)^2 + 20(5 - x_2) - x_2^2 + 10x_2 = -5x_2^2 + 30x_2$$

This is a quadratic function, and we can use the formula from Appendix A again:

$$a = -5$$
$$b = 30$$
$$c = 0$$

The optimum value of x_2 is

$$x_2{}^* = -\frac{b}{2a} = -\frac{30}{2(-5)} = 3$$

Also

$$x_1{}^* = 5 - x_2 = 2$$

and the profit is

$$Z = -4 \times 2^2 + 20 \times 2 - 3^2 + 10 \times 3 = \$45 \text{ million}$$

The Portfolio Selection Problem

A certain investor considers investing $100,000 in three different stocks. The objective of the investor is to obtain a return of 16% under a condition of minimum risk.

Designate by x_1, x_2, and x_3 the amounts invested in thousands of dollars in stocks 1, 2, and 3, respectively. We have

$$x_1 + x_2 + x_3 = 100$$

Stock 1 has an expected return of 8%; stock 2, 12%; and stock 3, 20%. The combined expected return is

$$.08x_1 + .12x_2 + .20x_3 = .16 \times 100 = 16$$

In modern portfolio theory the risk of a stock is measured by the variance of the return and the risk of a portfolio by the variance of the combined return of investments.* Assume that the standard deviation of the return of the stocks is .0200, .0245, and .0283, respectively, and that

---

* This is a different approach from the one discussed earlier in connection with a project selection for a government agency.

the returns of stocks are statistically independent. The variance of the return of the portfolio is obtained by adding the variances of each of the investments:

$$Z = (.020x_1)^2 + (.0245x_2)^2 + (.0283x_3)^2$$

or

$$Z = .0004x_1{}^2 + .0006x_2{}^2 + .0008x_3{}^2$$

Thus the problem is to minimize the risk Z under the two constraints stated.

First we eliminate x_1 and x_2 from the objective function. From the first constraint we get

$$x_1 = 100 - x_2 - x_3$$

Substituting into the second constraint, we get

$$.08(100 - x_2 - x_3) + .12x_2 + .20x_3 = 16$$

By simplifying, we get

$$x_2 = 200 - 3x_3$$

Also

$$x_1 = 100 - x_2 - x_3 = 2x_3 - 100$$

Substituting into the equation for Z, we get

$$Z = .0004(2x_3 - 100)^2 + .0006(200 - 3x_3)^2 + .0008x_3{}^2$$

By simplifying, we get

$$Z = .0078x_3{}^2 - .88x_3 + 28$$

This is a quadratic, and we can use the formula in the Appendix A again:

$$a = .0078$$

$$b = -.88x_3$$

$$x_3{}^* = \$56.43 \qquad \text{(all in thousands)}$$

$$x_2{}^* = 200 - 3x_3{}^* = 200 - 3x(56.43) = \$30.77$$

$$x_1{}^* = 100 - x_2{}^* - x_3{}^* = 100 - 56.43 - 30.77 = \$12.82$$

Thus the investor should invest $12,820, $30,770, and $56,430 into stocks 1, 2, and 3, respectively.

13.6 DYNAMIC PROGRAMMING PROBLEMS

Dynamic programming is not so much a specific technique as an approach or a point of view to optimization. Dynamic programming is applicable whether the problem is linear or not, but the problem must have a special structure; it must be *sequential*, involving an interrelated series of subproblems. Typical examples will illustrate the scope and nature of dynamic programming.

Construction of Oil Pipelines*

Figure 13.10 describes the problem of building a pipeline from point A to point B. The grid shows that the pipes must be laid along the rectangular set of branches shown in the diagram. The cost of each branch of pipe from node to node changes depending on many different factors. For example, the cost of construction depends on the price of obtaining the right-of-way (through farmland, towns, cities, industrial sites, possibility of sharing with a railroad or a highway, etc.). The cost also depends on the nature of the terrain (level land, rolling hills, rough territory, etc.) and the nature of the soil (sandy, rocky, depending on the percentage of rocks, etc.).

To illustrate the approach to solving the problem, we mark along each branch the cost of the pipeline. For example, the route shown in Figure 13.10 has a combined cost of

$$
\begin{aligned}
&1 + 2 + 1 + 5 + 3 + 4 + 1 + 2 + 2 + 1 + 2 + 1 + 2 + 2 \\
&+ 2 + 1 + 2 + 3 + 2 = 39
\end{aligned}
$$

This problem could be formulated as an integer programming problem and solved as such. However, the problem can be formulated as a dynamic programming problem, and the solution can be obtained in a much shorter time and at less expense.

The Stagecoach Problem

The oil pipeline problem in Figure 13.10 can be formulated as routing a stagecoach in the shortest time from point A to point B under the assumption that travel time is not related to distance but is measured in dollars as specified by the cost of the pipeline. The fact is that many dynamic programming problems can be formulated as routing a stagecoach.

---

* R. P. Jefferis and K. A. Fegley, "Application of Dynamic Programming to Routing Problems," *IEEE Transactions on Systems Science and Cybernetics*, Vol. SSC-1, No. 1, Nov. 1965, pp. 21–26.

Top branch costs (left to right): 1 2 3 4 1 2 1 8

	Col 1	Col 2	Col 3	Col 4	Col 5	Col 6	Col 7	Col 8	right
Row 1	1 / 2	2 / 3	2 / 5	2 / 1	4 / 6	5 / 2	2 / 1	2 / 3	2
Row 2	3 / 3	4 / 5	2 / 4	5 / 3	8 / 1	4 / 2	2 / 6	3 / 2	3
Row 3	1 / 3	2 / 5	3 / 1	1 / 7	5 / 5	1 / 3	3 / 2	1 / 1	5
Row 4	2 / 2	1 / 1	3 / 4	2 / 2	3 / 1	2 / 3	5 / 4	4 / 5	1
Row 5 (A)	1 / 10	2 / 3	2 / 4	3 / 2	2 / 4	3 / 5	2 / 3	2 / 1	2

FIGURE 13.10
Problem of building a pipeline from point A to point B.

In Figure 13.11 we show a simple stagecoach problem. There are 10 nodes, and the problem is to travel from node 1 to node 10 in the shortest possible time. Travel time between the nodes is marked along the branches and is in no way related to the actual distance between the nodes. Solution to this problem will be given in Section 13.7.

As to the oil pipeline problem, nodes *A* and *B* in Figure 13.10 correspond to nodes 1 and 2 in Figure 13.11; and the other nodes of the grid to nodes 2–9.

Production and Inventory Control

A corporation is developing a 12-month production and inventory plan to meet the monthly demand for goods. Initial and final inventories are specified. Production and inventory costs vary from month to month and are given. Various pricing strategies are available, and corresponding demand functions are known. Monthly production rates can be changed, and the cost of increasing or decreasing production rates is known. Thus smooth production is associated with low cost.

The problem is to maximize profit under the condition that demand must be met.

A more general formulation of the problem allows back orders and loss of sales. Solution of the more general problem requires knowledge of the cost of back ordering and the penalty cost of not meeting demand.

Distribution of Advertising Effort

A corporation is developing a plan to advertise in various media in several sales territories. The productivity of advertising, that is, sales generated, is known for each medium in each territory and is a nonlinear function of dollars expended. The problem is how to distribute a given budget, that is, a given level of dollars, among the various sales territories and media so profit will be maximized.

The problem of distributing a given amount of effort between

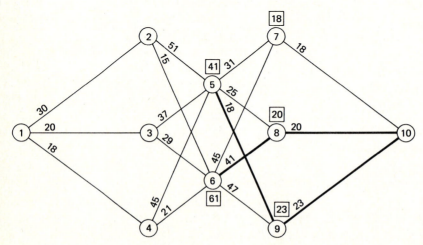

FIGURE 13.11 Stagecoach problem: how to travel in the shortest time from node 1 to node 10.

various possibilities is called the **distribution of effort problem** and is applicable to many resource allocation problems. For example, the problem of allocating a certain amount of money among various types of investments is a distribution of effort problem. Note that the variables may be continuous or constrained to integer values.

Equipment Replacement

A car rental agency maintains a fleet of cars for hire. Should these cars be replaced each 12 months, 18 months, 24 months? To maximize profit, the cost of maintenance, the cost of buying new cars, and the loss of business due to shortages must be balanced. Such problems are complicated by the fact that as cars age, maintenance costs increase and, also due to inflation, the cost of new cars increases.

Similar problems exist for other kinds of equipment which wear out and need to be replaced. In addition to replacement of entire units, the possibility of replacing only parts of the equipment must also be allowed. This leads to the problem of maintaining an inventory of spare parts. A typical example is the maintenance of a fleet of airplanes where engines and other equipment must be periodically overhauled and spare parts for engines and other types of equipment must be held.

Timber Harvesting

A firm in the Pacific Northwest is planning to plant trees in a new area. As the trees grow, they are cut down, and sales and profits depend on the quantity of timber sold.

To compute profit, the cost of planting, maintaining the forest, harvesting, and transporting the timber must be considered. There is an optimum time to cut and replant trees, and dynamic programming helps in determining the optimum plan.

Should the firm consider a plan of 50, 100, or 200 years? Problems of this sort are best handled by assuming an **unbound time horizon**. In this framework it is assumed that the trees will be planted and harvested forever, and then the problem is to maximize yearly profit or the discounted value of the infinite stream of future profits.

There are many practical problems where the unbounded horizon approach is preferred. For example, consider installing a new production tool which eventually must be replaced, or the daily control of inventory, or a plan for yearly capital investments. In each of these problems it is difficult or impossible to specify the time horizon. Thus the assumption of an infinite or unbounded horizon provides the most realistic answer.

Probabilistic Problems

Almost any of the variables discussed in the previous problems may be uncertain and require probabilistic treatment. For example, in the oil pipeline problem costs may be uncertain, and only the probability distribution of costs may be available. In a production and inventory control problem the monthly demand and carrying costs may be uncertain. In the advertising allocation problem the generation of sales may be subject to uncertainty. In equipment failure and maintenance problems it may not be known precisely how long equipment may be operational, and only the probability distribution of failures may be available. Such problems are common, and the payoffs frequently become nonlinear functions. Such sequential resource allocation problems can be dealt with best by dynamic programming.

Now that we have surveyed a number of typical dynamic programming problems, we proceed to illustrate the algorithms to be used to solve such problems.

13.7 DYNAMIC PROGRAMMING ALGORITHM

The Stagecoach Problem

We need to find the shortest route from node 1 to node 10 (Figure 13.11). This may look difficult, so first let us solve some simple problems.

Suppose the coach is at node 7. It will take 18 hours to get to node 10. We mark this 18 hours above node 7 in a small square. Similarly, it takes 20 hours from node 8 and 23 hours from node 9 to get to node 10.

Suppose the coach is at node 5. There are three ways to get to node 10:

Via node 7: Travel time = 31 + $\boxed{18}$ = 49 hours.

Via node 8: Travel time = 25 + $\boxed{20}$ = 45 hours.

Via node 9: Travel time = 18 + $\boxed{23}$ = $\boxed{41}$ hours.

The shortest route is via node 9, and travel time is 41 hours. We mark this 9 above node 5 in a small square box and mark the 5–9–10 route with a heavy line.

Suppose the coach is at node 6. There are three ways to get to node 10:

Via node 7: Travel time = 45 + $\boxed{18}$ = 63 hours.

Via node 8: Travel time = 41 + $\boxed{20}$ = $\boxed{61}$ hours.

Via node 9: Travel time = 47 + $\boxed{23}$ = 70 hours.

The shortest route is via node 8, and the shortest travel time is 61 hours. We mark this 61 in a small square above node 6 and mark the route 6–8–10 with the heavy line.

Now comes the surprise. We redraw Figure 13.11 in Figure 13.12, but ignore nodes 7, 8, 9, and 10. *We do not need these nodes.* The problem is to travel from node 1 to either node 5 or node 6 in the shortest possible time, where travel time includes the 41 and 61 hours in the small squares. Namely, if we solve this new, smaller problem, we shall know what to do when we reach either node 5 or 6. So let us solve this new problem.

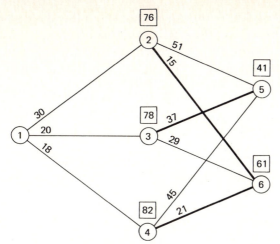

FIGURE 13.12
Illustration of dynamic programming algorithm by the stagecoach problem. The original problem is reduced to the problem of traveling in the shortest possible time from node 1 to node 5 or node 6.

There are two ways to go from node 2. Travel times are as follows:

Via node 5: Travel time = 51 + $\boxed{41}$ = 92 hours.

Via node 6: Travel time = 15 + $\boxed{61}$ = $\boxed{76}$ hours.

There are two ways to go from node 3. Travel times are as follows:

Via node 5: Travel time = 37 + $\boxed{41}$ = $\boxed{78}$ hours.

Via node 6: Travel time = 29 + $\boxed{61}$ = 90 hours.

There are two ways to go from node 4. Travel times are as follows:

Via node 5: Travel time = 45 + $\boxed{41}$ = 86 hours.

Via node 6: Travel time = 21 + $\boxed{61}$ = $\boxed{82}$ hours.

We mark these travel times above nodes 2, 3, and 4. Now we redraw Figure 13.12 as shown in Figure 13.13, displaying only nodes 1, 2, 3, and 4. Our problem is to travel in the shortest time from node 1 to node 2 or 3 or 4. There are three ways to go from node 1. Travel times are as follows:

Via node 2: Travel time = 30 + $\boxed{76}$ = 106 hours.

Via node 3: Travel time = 20 + $\boxed{78}$ = $\boxed{98}$ hours.

Via node 4: Travel time = 18 + $\boxed{82}$ = 100 hours.

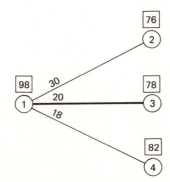

FIGURE 13.13
The stagecoach problem is reduced to the problem of traveling in the shortest possible time from node 1 to node 2 or 3 or 4.

Thus the best route is through node 3, and the shortest travel time is 98 hours. Figure 13.14 shows the optimum solution.

Now we know that the coach must first go to node 3. Figure 13.12 shows that from node 3 it must go to node 5 and Figure 13.11 that from node 5 it must go to node 9 and then to node 10. Thus we have solved the problem.

A Pricing Problem

A corporation is pricing a product for five future periods. Alternate prices are $3.00, $4.00, $5.00, and $6.00, with profits varying from period to period, as shown in Figure 13.15. For example, a price of $5.00 brings $35.00 in period 1, $20 in period 2, etc. The corporation wants to develop an optimum schedule of prices to maximize total profit. However, due to marketing policy, the price cannot be changed by more than $1.00 from period to period. For example, if the price in the first period is $5.00, the price in the second period can be only $4.00, $5.00, or $6.00.

This problem can be formulated as an integer programming problem, but the solution is much easier by using dynamic programming.

Figure 13.16 shows the problem in the form of the stagecoach problem. There are 21 nodes, and we must determine the longest route from node 1 to either node 18, 19, 20, or 21 to obtain the maximum profit. The branches indicate that the price cannot be changed by more than $1.00 from period to period. Profits corresponding to prices are shown along the branches. For example, node 11 indicates a price of $4.00 in period 3, and the branches terminating in node 11 are marked by the profit of $45.00

Solution of the problem is left as an exercise.

A Production Smoothing Problem

A firm is preparing a four-period production schedule to deliver two units of a product in each period, a total of eight units. There is a setup cost of $350 in each period, but the firm can also keep an inventory at a

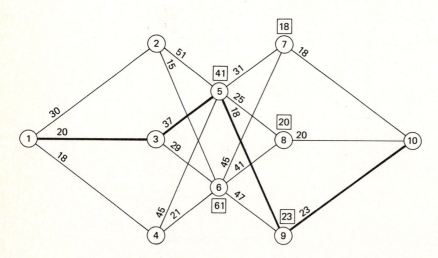

FIGURE 13.14
Optimum solution to the stagecoach problem

PRICES	PERIODS				
	1	2	3	4	5
$3.00	$40	$35	$35	$35	$15
$4.00	$30	$25	$45	$30	$20
$5.00	$35	$20	$40	$10	$10
$6.00	$45	$10	$20	$25	$40

FIGURE 13.15 Profits generated by four prices in five different time periods.

cost of $80 per unit per period. Furthermore, it is impractical to produce more than four units in any period. Unit production costs are $1000 and are independent of when the units are manufactured. Thus the problem is to develop a schedule such that combined setup and inventory costs are at a minimum.

Figure 13.17 describes the problem as a stagecoach routing problem. There are 13 nodes, and the branches correspond to feasible production schedules. The horizontal scale represents the production periods and the vertical scale, the cumulative production. For example, node 6 corresponds to the end of period 2 and a cumulative production of 5 units. Cumulative requirements are 2 + 2 = 4 units, and so node 6 corresponds to an inventory of 5 − 4 = 1 unit and an inventory carrying cost of $80. The three branches starting at node 6 represent the production of 1, 2, or 3 units in period 3. The numbers along the

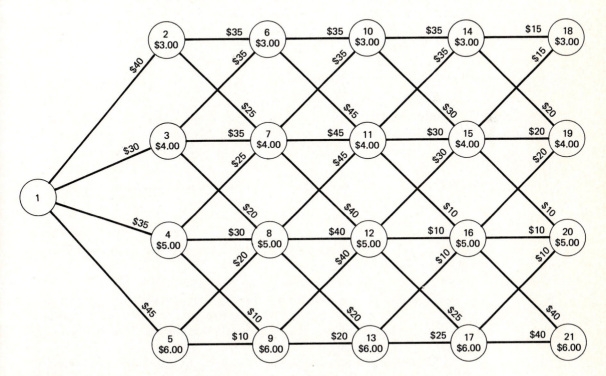

FIGURE 13.16 Pricing problem formulated as a stagecoach routing problem.

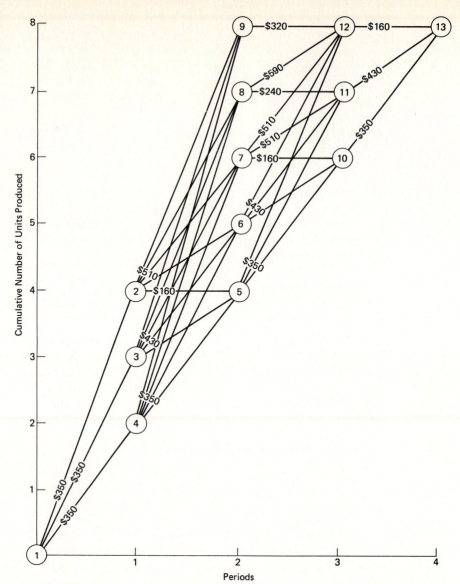

FIGURE 13.17 Production smoothing problem formulated as a stagecoach routing problem.

branches represent combined setup and inventory costs or $350 + $80 = $430 for these branches.

As a further illustration, consider the branch from node 7 to node 11, corresponding to a cumulative production level of 6 units and the production of 1 unit in period 3. The setup cost is $350, the inventory cost is 2 × $80 = $160, and the combined cost, shown along the branch, is $350 + $160 = $510.

The problem is to find the lowest cost route from node 1 to node 13. Solution of the problem is left as an exercise.

Basic Concepts of Dynamic Programming

We are now ready to describe the salient features of dynamic programming. First, the problem must be a multistage problem which can be subdivided into a sequence of subproblems. Production and inventory control provide excellent illustrations, as in these problems a sequence of subproblems must be solved.

The basic computational approach we described is a **recursion** procedure, or **backward recursion**, which starts solving the problem in the last stage and then proceeds backward to the preceding stage, etc.

After each subproblem at each stage is solved, the results are recorded, and from then on only stages of the problem must be considered which precede the one just solved.

The principle behind the dynamic programming algorithm is the **principle of optimality**.

> An optimal policy has the property that whatever the initial state and initial decision are, the remaining decisions must constitute an optimal policy with regard to the state resulting from the initial decision.

As an example, consider the stagecoach problem shown in Figure 13.11. Assume that the coach is in state 5, that is, at node 5. We determined that the best route from node 5 is to node 9 and then to node 10. This policy of using route 5–9–10 is independent of decisions made prior to reaching node 5. In whatever manner the coach reaches node 5, from then on the best route is 5–9–10.

Advantages of Dynamic Programming

The dynamic programming algorithm represents an immense reduction in the number of computations that need to be performed. To illustrate, consider a 20-stage problem where at each stage 10 alternatives are available. In the first two stages there will be $10 \times 10 = 100$ alternatives which can be represented by a tree with 100 tips. By the third stage there will be $10 \times 10 \times 10 = 1000$ alternatives or 1000 tips on the tree, and then 10,000 alternatives or 10,000 tips, etc. As the number of stages increases, the number of alternatives increases unthinkably. This is what Richard Bellman, the discoverer of dynamic programming, calls the **curse of dimensionality**. For example, by the twentieth stage there are 10^{20} possibilities, requiring this many tips on the tree. This is the number 1 followed by 20 zeros.

To appreciate how large this number is, it can be shown that if you had 1000 computers each examining 1 million possibilities every second, it would still take more than 3000 years to examine the 10^{20} alternatives.

Consider now the dynamic programming algorithm. In the last subproblem there are $10 \times 10 = 100$ alternatives. The calculations preceding the last one will require examining another 100 alternatives and so on. Thus there will be $19 \times 100 = 1900$ alternatives to examine. This is, of course, a very modest load for a modern computer.

In section 13.1 a simplified model of the crew scheduling problem was presented. Now we show how Flying Tiger, the world's largest air cargo carrier, uses this approach.

Flying Tiger has two fleets, one consisting of 18 DC-8s and the other of 6 Boeing 747s. Crews must be scheduled to fly the planes, and the DC-8 and 747 crews are scheduled separately, each crew consisting of three pilots. Crew costs account for approximately 10–15% of the company's total expenses.

The Crew Planning Process

In preparing a typical plan for the 747 aircraft, there were 156 *basic legs*, meaning that there were 156 flight segments specified. Each basic leg consists of a single takeoff and a single landing. These basic legs were linked together to form 107 *resolved legs* where a resolved leg means a sequence of basic legs that must be flown as a unit; that is, the crew cannot change planes. Of the 107 legs, 29 were *deadheads*, meaning that for these flight units the crew must be flown back on a commercial flight as passengers. Deadheads are necessary because crews live at a base city, and it is not possible to construct round trips for the crew just by flying the Flying Tiger planes.

The 107 resolved legs are linked together to form 114 *trips*, where a trip means a sequence of resolved legs that can be flown in one *duty period*. A duty period is the period of time during which a crew may operate a plane without a rest break. Then the 114 trips were combined into 18,799 possible *pairings*, where a pairing is a sequence of trips which together make up a round trip beginning and ending at a crew base.

The first problem then is to develop an optimal list of pairings that covers every resolved leg during the planning horizon of 1 week. The second problem is to extend the schedule for a month, called the *bid lines*, which is then the schedule for the entire month.

Before an optimal solution to the problem can be found, the objective function must be defined. The management of Flying Tiger decided that the problem was to minimize the total cost of operation. This cost consists primarily of payments to the crew, which depends on the length of time the crew spends away from its base and not just on the time spent flying. This is the incentive for trying to find a "tight" crew schedule, that is, one for which the ratio

$$\text{RATIO} = \frac{\text{FLYING TIME}}{\text{TIME AWAY FROM BASE}}$$

* Adapted from R. E. Marsten, M. R. Muller, and C. L. Killiom, "Crew Planning at Flying Tiger: A Successful Application of Integer Programming," *Management Science*, Vol. 25, No. 12, Dec. 1979, pp. 1175–1183.

is high. In addition, other costs such as the cost of deadhead flights, hotels, meals, taxis, and so on are included in the objective function.

Mathematical Model and Computer Programs

Note that this model is similar to the one already discussed in Section 13.1 except that here the basic legs are combined into resolved legs, trips, and pairings. In a typical problem there were 79 constraints and 14,328 0-1 variables. The optimization is performed by an integer programming computer package, and the inputs to the program are specifications such as the following:

> Admissible starting and ending cities for trips
> Minimum and maximum number of flying hours in duty periods
> Crew bases admissible starting and ending cities for pairings
> Admissible layover cities

The computer program carries out the optimization for a 1-week schedule, and then another computer program prepares the bid lines for the entire month.

Benefits

Direct benefits include savings of approximately $300,000 per year on crew costs for the 747 aircraft. Precise statements of savings on the DC-8 crews were not given because here the objective function for the bid-line selection problem was not directly expressible in dollars. As a further benefit it was also noted that while the number of pilots increased from 400 to 520 during the year the system was installed, the number of crew planning personnel was unchanged.

In addition to these quantifiable benefits, intangible benefits were also obtained, such as the greater ease of producing crew schedules, which was particularly significant because Flying Tiger experienced a rapid expansion in operations during this period.

13.9 ABOUT LARGE MATHEMATICAL PROGRAMMING PROBLEMS: A DIALOG

> **Q.** *When describing crew planning at Flying Tiger you mentioned that there were 14,328 0-1 variables and 79 constraints. If I multiply this out, it seems to me that there must be at least 1,131,912 coefficients in the equations. How is it possible to work with such a large number of data?*
>
> **A.** We already discussed this problem in Section 12.9 in connection with the transportation problem. The coefficients are not provided manually, and if you review our discussion, you find that the inputs to the problem are specifications like the following: "admissible

starting and ending cities for trips" and so on. At Flying Tiger a special computer programming package was developed which takes these types of inputs that characterize the problem. Then the program proceeds to compute the coefficients of the mathematical programming equations and sets up the equations themselves. Thus the coefficients for the equations are not input data but are derived by the computer from the input.

Q. *Our computing center has several efficient programs to solve linear programming problems but not for integer or mixed integer or nonlinear programs. Why?*

A. The states of the art of computer programs for linear programming problems and mathematical programming problems are quite different. Very large linear programming problems can be solved with relative ease. But when the assumption of linearity is dropped, things get much more difficult, and the programs become much more complex. In fact, for some nonlinear programming problems or large integer and mixed integer programming problems there may not be adequate computer programs available at all.

Q. *How then do we know what to do in such situations?*

A. You must consult an expert who specializes in solving such problems.

SUMMARY

1. Many practical resource allocation problems cannot be modeled by linear programming.

2. In pure integer programming all the unknowns must be integers.

3. In mixed integer programming some unknowns must be integers; the others may take on any values.

4. The branch-and-bound algorithm systematically replaces integer and mixed integer linear programming problems with new linear programming problems. These in turn are solved by the simplex method.

5. The cutting plane algorithm systematically cuts away noninteger solutions from an integer or mixed linear program and solves each new problem with the simplex algorithm.

6. In nonlinear programming the constraints and/or the objective function are nonlinear.

7. There is no universal algorithm to solve nonlinear programming problems. Each problem must be examined and a suitable algorithm applied.

8. Dynamic programming problems are sequential and involve an interrelated series of subproblems.

9. Dynamic programming problems can be solved by the backward recursion computational process.

10. Very sophisticated algorithm and computer programs are available for solving complex mathematical programming problems with many thousands of unknowns and constraints.

11. Mathematical programming has been successfully applied to a large variety of practical problems.

SECTION EXERCISES

1. *Pure Integer Programming Problems*

1.1 In Section 13.1 a government agency project selection problem is discussed. The following changes have been announced:

Each type 1 project requires $2 million.
Each type 2 project requires 8% less.
The total available funds have been reduced to $19 million.

Assuming that none of the other inputs has changed,
    a. Write the linear constraint equation for total funds.
    b. Write the linear equation for the constraint of risk factor.
    c. Write the linear equation for the constraint of maximizing cost benefit.

1.2 In Section 13.1 a government agency project selection problem is discussed. The following changes have been announced:

The risk factor for type 1 projects is increased to .15.
The risk factor for type 2 projects is increased to .6.
The combined risk factor should be less than .2.
The cost benefit factor of type 2 projects is increased to 1.3.
The cost benefit factor of type 1 projects is reduced to 1.05.
    a. Write the linear constraint equation for total funds.
    b. Write the linear equation for the constraint of risk factor.
    c. Write the linear equation for the constraint of maximizing cost benefit.

1.3 In Section 13.1 a government agency project selection problem is discussed. The agency has been given additional funds for a total of $30 million, but they are now required to also support type 3 projects, each of which requires $2.5 million. The risk factor assigned to type 3 projects is .2; the agency is now required to keep the combined risk factor below 5.5. A cost benefit factor of 1.08 has been assigned to type 3 projects.
    a. Write the linear constraint equation for total funds.
    b. Write the linear equation for the constraint of risk factor.
    c. Write the linear equation for constraint of maximizing cost benefit.
    d. Why is this an integer programming problem?

1.4 In Section 13.1 a police car routing problem is discussed. Assume the following changes in policy: The minimum driving distance from the southwest corner to the northeast corner of each rectangle is increased to 20,000 feet, x_2 must be more than 80% of x_1, and x_2 must be less than 16, while x_1 must exceed 3.0. Cruising speeds have been reduced to 25,000 and 20,000, respectively, to conserve energy.

  a. State in a linear form the relationship for the minimum driving distance from the southwest corner to the northeast corner of each square.
  b. Write the linear expression for the constraint relating x_2 to a fraction of x_1.
  c. Write the linear constraint equation for the maximum value of x_2.
  d. Write the linear constraint equation for the minimum value of x_1.
  e. Use the information given in Section 13.1 concerning the expected distance covered in either direction to write the objective function.
  f. Why is this an integer programming problem?

1.5 A capital budgeting problem is discussed in Section 13.1. Assume that the expected cash flows have changed; they are given by the accompanying figure which replaces Figure 13.2.

Cash flows (thousands of dollars)

PROJECT	YEAR					
	1	2	3	4	5	6
1	−200	+25	0	200	300	50
2	−100	−200	−300	0	500	800
3	−500	0	200	200	−500	800
4	−100	0	80	100	0	0
5	0	−300	−50	0	500	600

  a. Assuming that all other conditions of the problem as stated in the text are the same, write the objective function for this problem.
  b. Assuming that the other conditions are the same as in the text, write the set of constraint equations for this problem.
  c. Assume that the budget constraints have been relaxed. The total sum available for all projects is $750,000 for the first year and $1 million for the second year. New relationships among the jobs have been recognized. Job 5 must come ahead of 4, and 4 cannot be undertaken unless 5 is undertaken. Projects 2 and 3 cannot both be undertaken, but either project 1 or 2 must be undertaken, and at least three must be undertaken. However, not all five can be undertaken. All other relationships expressed in the text are no longer in effect. Write the objective functions and all constraints.

1.6 In Section 13.1 a project supervision problem for a federal agency is discussed showing that it can be expressed as an assignment problem. The efficiency coefficients for this situation are shown in Figure 13.3.
  a. Write the objective function for the problem.
  b. Persons 4 and 5 got divorced, and 5 married 6. Also, it now appears that three persons must be assigned to project 2 and not more than two persons can be assigned to either 1 or 3. Rewrite the constraints to account for this new set of conditions.

2. Mixed integer linear programming problems

2.1 In Section 13.2, Minnehaha's problem is discussed and a mixed integer expression of the problem is outlined. Assume that the conditions and technological coefficients have been changed as follows:
  1. Minnehaha can manufacture only rings at a setup cost of $6.
  2. Minnehaha can manufacture only bracelets with a setup cost of $3.
  3. Minnehaha can manufacture both bracelets and rings with a setup cost of $9.
  4. The objective function for the original problem is changed to $Z = 5x_1 + 7x_2$.

a. Introducing three 0-1 variables, write the objective function in mixed integer form.
b. Write the constraint equations in mixed integer form.
c. Following the text, examine the solutions under the same three mutually exclusive conditions.

3. Branch-and-bound algorithm

3.1 Following the text of Section 13.3, solve the following integer programming problem by the branch-and-bound algorithm:

$$x_1 + 2x_2 \leq 3$$

$$x_2 \leq .8$$

$$x_1, x_2 = 0, 1, 2, \ldots$$

$$\max Z = 1x_1 + 4x_2$$

(*Hint*: This is a two-variable problem as is the one carried through in the text. Follow the presentation of the text in working through your solution; make a two-dimensional plot so that you can find a graphical solution to the linear problem and move from there, branching into new problems and drawing graphs similar to Figures 13.7 and 13.8 to follow your progress.)

3.2 Following the text of Section 13.3, solve the following integer programming problem by the branch-and-bound algorithm:

$$3x_1 + 2x_2 \leq 42$$

$$x_2 \leq 14$$

$$x_1 \leq 8$$

$$x_1 + 2x_2 \leq 30$$

$$x_1, x_2 = 0, 1, 2, \ldots$$

$$\max Z = x_1 + x_2$$

(*Hint*: See the hint for Exercise 3.1.)

4. Cutting plane algorithm

4.1 Refer to Section 13.4, where the cutting plane algorithm is discussed. Consider the following integer programming problem in two variables:

$$x_1 \leq 4.5$$

$$8x_1 + x_2 \leq 30.5$$

$$x_1, x_2 = 0, 1, 2, \ldots$$

$$\max Z = x_1 + x_2$$

a. Plot the constraints on x_1-x_2 axes, and show the feasible integer solutions with large dots on the intersections of the corresponding integer values on the ordinate and abscissa.
b. On your plot, draw the outlines of the polygon which corresponds to the convex hull of feasible integer solutions.
c. Write the new constraints which define the convex hull. Eliminate any redundant original constraints, and fully specify the new linear programming problem.
d. On your plot, show the regions (by shading) that are eliminated by the new constraints.

e. Find the optimal solution to the original integer programming problem (which you do by reference to your revised problem, of course).

4.2 Consider the following integer programming problem in two variables:

$$-3x_1 + 5x_2 \geq 0$$

$$x_1 \geq 1$$

$$2x_1 + 2x_2 \geq 7$$

$$x_1, x_2 = 0, 1, 2, \ldots$$

$$\min Z = 3x_1 + 4x_2$$

a. Plot the constraints on x_1-x_2 axes, and show the feasible integer solutions as large dots on the intersections of the integer values on the ordinate and abscissa. (*Hint*: It is impossible to show the full set of feasible integer solutions, and there are infinitely many of them.)

b. On your plot, draw the outlines of the portion of a polygon which corresponds to the convex hull of feasible integer solutions.

c. Write the new constraints which define the convex hull. Eliminate any original constraints which are redundant, and fully specify the new linear programming problem.

d. On your plot, show the regions (by shading) which are eliminated by the new constraints.

e. Find the optimal solution to the original integer programming problem (which you do by reference to your revised problem, of course).

5. *Non-Linear Programming*

5.1 The Engels Toy Company is making a decision on its magazine advertising campaign. There are two media available; each generates sales in accordance with the formula $S = 20 \times A - 4 \times A^2$, where S is sales generated and A is the amount spent advertising in the medium. Advertising expenditures can be any value up to $2 million. Follow the reasoning of Section 13.5 to obtain the following:

a. The optimal values of funds to be allocated to each medium

b. The total net gain at optimum

5.2 Refer to the advertising budget allocation example of Section 13.5. During the subsequent planning period, the corporation decides to allocate $7 million between advertising in the midwest and southwest. In the midwest, x_1 million of advertising expenditure generates

$$-6x_1^2 + 50x_1$$

million dollars in sales. In the southwest, x_2 million of advertising expenditure generates

$$-15x_2^2 + 100x_2$$

million dollars in sales. The profit margin is 25% of sales.

a. Express the total profit in terms of x_1 and x_2.

b. Write the constraint equation(s) that apply in this case.

c. Solve the unconstrained problem. Is the unconstrained solution feasible?

d. Express the total profit in terms of x_2 only.

e. Find the optimal values for x_1 and x_2.

f. What is the total profit at the optimal values for the allocations?

5.3 Refer to the portfolio selection example in Section 13.5. The investor feels that under present conditions 16% is too low even under minimum risk; the investor now seeks 17%. Under these conditions the investor has been able to form a syndicate and now has a total of $1 million to invest. Available stocks are as before; their ratings remain unchanged.

    a. State the constraints for the investor.

    b. State the objective function in terms of the total variance of the investments.

    c. Eliminate two of the three portfolio variables from the objective function, and state the objective function in terms of only one such variable.

    d. Find the optimal values of the variables in terms of the investments to be made. What is the risk (as expressed in variance) of this portfolio?

6. Dynamic Programming Problems

No exercises are supplied for this section.

7. Dynamic Programming Algorithm

7.1 Refer to the stagecoach problem as discussed in Section 13.7 and illustrated in Figure 13.12–13.14. While the connections between stops (nodes) remain the same, the times to traverse them have been changed to the values defined in the following matrix:

Travel time in days.

FROM NODE NUMBER	TO NODE NUMBER									
	1	2	3	4	5	6	7	8	9	10
1		10	14	18						
2					30	25				
3					26	29				
4					20	22				
5							31	25	18	
6							25	41	17	
7										30
8										20
9										10

    a. Find the shortest route from node 1 to node 10. (*Hint*: Follow the process shown in Section 13.7; draw a sequence of charts as in Figures 13.2 - 13.14)

    b. What is the time along the shortest route?

7.2 Find the shortest route from node 0 to node 10 in the accompanying stagecoach problem.

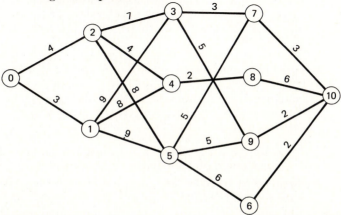

7.3 Refer to the pricing problem given as an example in Section 13.7. Figure 13.16 states the problem as a network which can be solved in the same manner as the stagecoach example of the first part of this section. Find the optimal pricing policy.

7.4 Refer to the production smoothing problem given as an example in Section 13.7. Figure 13.17 states the problem as a network which can be solved in the same manner as the stagecoach example of the first part of this section. Find the optimal production policy.

7.5 You should have no difficulty now in finding the *longest* routes through a network of the stagecoach type. (*Hint*: Follow the procedure of Section 13.7, but enter the time for the longest route at each stage in the square box above the node.) Find the longest routes

    a. Through the stagecoach problem at the beginning of this section.

    b. To traverse the stagecoach problem with the revised times as given in Exercise 7.1.

    c. To get from node 0 to node 10 in the stagecoach problem of Exercise 7.2.

    d. In the pricing problem of Section 13.7, interpret the "profits" as "costs," and find the policy which minimizes total cost.

7.7 A company has four plants of equal size and capacity in different locations. The owner is over 90 years old and wants to capitalize these plants by selling them at the maximum total return. Having great faith in his good health, the owner will sell these plants over a 4-year period if he can maximize his total selling price by so doing. Each plant yields a profit of $1 million per year. A large company has offered him the following deal. They will purchase at the beginning of any of the years 0, 1, 2, 3, or 4 plants. The amount they will pay at any one time depends on the number of plants offered for sale as given by the following table:

PLANTS SOLD AT START OF YEAR	AMOUNT BUYER WILL PAY (PER PLANT)
0	$0
1	4,000,000
2	3,400,000
3	3,000,000
4	2,225,000

Find the optimal sequence of sales and what the total income of the aged owner will be during that period of selling off. (*Hint*: This can be solved as a dynamic programming problem. Don't overlook the loss of revenue in selling a plant.)

8. *Crew planning at Flying Tiger: A Successful Application*

8.1 The management of Flying Tiger is reported in Section 13.8 as having concluded that the "problem was to minimize the total cost of operation." The examples of cost given are all expressible in "immediate" dollar expenditures (taxis, deadhead flights, etc.).

    a. Are there any nondollar costs you can think of?

    b. Are there any dollar costs which are not immediate but which you feel might be included in such a model?

8.2 Why do you think the crew planning model made it possible to increase the number of pilots from 400 to 520 without increasing the planning staff?

9. *About Large Mathematical Programming Problems: A Dialog*
No exercises are provided for this section.

CHAPTER EXERCISES AND DISCUSSION QUESTIONS

C.1 Give three examples of situations which would fit the linear programming model except that the variables are not linearly related. (*Hint*: Pick a realistic situation, and express as a linear programming problem. Then examine in turn constraints and the objective function to see if a more realistic expression would be nonlinear.)

C.2 Give three examples of situations which would fit the linear programming model except that the variables are not continuous. (*Hint*: Pick a realistic situation, and express as a linear programming problem. Then examine in turn constraints and the objective function to see if a more realistic expression would be nonlinear.)

C.3 The Vulture Tower Convalescent Home has two sections, one for ambulatory geriatric patients and the other for those who are confined to bed. The capacity of the ambulatory section is 180 and of the bed section, 120. As the home uses a common kitchen, they cannot handle more than a total of 250 patients of both kinds. The profit on an ambulatory patient is $600 per month; the profit on a bed-confined patient is $800 per month. Patients cannot be divided into fractional parts, so that a solution for this programming problem must be restricted to integer numbers of patients. Find the solution.

14

Goal Programming and Multiobjectives

In Chapter 10 when we stated the four conditions of linear programming, the fourth condition was the following: A single payoff is maximized or minimized. This condition holds so far also for integer, mixed, nonlinear, dynamic, etc., programming. We now show how this limitation of mathematical programming can be relaxed. But first we must review why there is a need to relax it.

Many practical problems have **multiobjectives**. In fact, we discussed this matter in detail in Chapter 7 for decision making under uncertainty, and our rationale holds as well for deterministic problems. You should, therefore, review the introduction to Chapter 7.

The central concept of **goal programming** is to determine the individual preferences of decision makers in terms of goals and to establish either (1) a single, overall function which is to be minimized under the given constraints or (2) a series of goal functions which are to be minimized in the sequence of their relative importance. While the purpose of goal programming is to deal with **multigoal** problems, a good start is to deal with a problem with a single goal.

14.1 WHEN PROFIT IS THE SINGLE GOAL

Consider again the Indian jewelry problem in Section 10.3. Designate by x_1 the number of rings made and by x_2 the number of bracelets, where x_1 and x_2 may be fractions. Each ring requires 3 units of silver and 1 unit of gold. Each bracelet requires 1 and 2 units, respectively. There are 9 units of silver and 8 units of gold available and so the **resource constraints** are

$$3x_1 + x_2 \leq 9 \qquad \text{silver constraint}$$
$$x_1 + 2x_2 \leq 8 \qquad \text{gold constraint}$$

The profit is

$$4x_1 + 5x_2$$

Suppose the goal of the decision maker is to achieve a profit of at least $50. If you return now to Figure 10.12 you note that the profit represented by the $50 isoprofit line cannot be realized. (The highest profit is $23.) *The problem as stated is infeasible.* But goal programming and decision makers realize the following:

Goals may be **underachieved**, met exactly, or overachieved.

There is no standard mathematical notation to express the desire of the decision maker to achieve a goal. So as a mathematical abbreviation we state that

$$4x_1 + 5x_2 \geq 50 \qquad \text{(as a goal)}$$

meaning that the goal is to achieve the inequality

$$4x_1 + 5x_2 \geq 50$$

Goal constraints are **flexible**; resource constraints are **absolute-rigid**.

Now our problem is to put the goal constraint into standard mathematical notation. We (the analysts) know that in this problem the goal constraint will be underachieved. Designate the **deviational variable** of underachievement by D^-. Then we can say that

$$4x_1 + 5x_2 + D^- = 50$$

But in a new problem no one knows whether the goal will be underachieved, exactly met, or overachieved. Designate the deviational variable of overachievement by D^+. Then always

$$4x_1 + 5x_2 + D^- - D^+ = 50$$

where (1) the deviational variables D^- and D^+ are either positive or zero, and (2) either D^- or D^+ is zero or (3) both D^- and D^+ are zero. Note that the preceding relationship can always be met. For instance, in the problem considered,

$$x_1 = 0, \qquad x_2 = 0, \qquad D^- = 50, \qquad D^+ = 0$$

is a solution.

Flexible goal constraints can always be converted into rigid-absolute constraints by the introduction of deviational variables.

Now we have two resource constraints and one converted goal constraint, and the problem is to find the best solution. How can we do this?

We must convert the problem to a standard minimization or maximization problem. The conversion is effected by the concept of the **goal function**. We say we want to get as close as possible to the profit of $50; that is, we want to minimize D^-, the underachievement.

To summarize, our problem is to find the values of the nonnegative variables x_1, x_2, and D^+, and D^- which minimize the goal function

$$Z = D^-$$

What kind of problem is this? For the moment designate D^+ by x_3 and D^- by x_4. Then the three constraints are

$$3x_1 + x_2 \qquad \le 9$$

$$x_1 + 3x_2 \qquad \le 8$$

$$4x_1 + 5x_2 - x_3 + x_4 = 50$$

and the objective function is

$$\text{minimize } Z = x_4$$

We have converted our goal programming problem into a linear programming program.

Later we shall show that the solution to this problem is

$$x_1 = 2, \qquad x_2 = 3, \qquad D^- = 27, \qquad D^+ = 0, \qquad \text{profit} = \$23$$

meaning that the profit goal is underachieved by $27 and that the best profit is $23. The problem has the same solution as the original jewelry problem discussed in Chapter 10.

We now proceed to study a more relevant situation with two or more goals.

14.2 SEVERAL GOALS

Consider the manufacture of two products, where each of the first product takes 3 hours to manufacture and each of the second, 2 hours. The total time available is 60 hours, and so the resource constraint

$$3x_1 + 2x_2 \le 60$$

must be satisfied. The profits are $2.00 and $5.00, respectively, and the firm has a goal of having a profit of at least $100.

$$2x_1 + 5x_2 \ge 100 \qquad \text{(as a goal)}$$

The firm also wants a balanced sale between the two products, which is expressed by the desire to produce at least 30 units of the first product:

$$x_1 \ge 30 \qquad \text{(as a goal)}$$

We need to replace the flexible goal constraints with rigid constraints. Designate by D_P^- the profit underachievement and by D_P^+ the profit overachievement. Then

$$2x_1 + 5x_2 + D_P^- - D_P^+ = 100$$

Designate under- and overachievement in producing the first product by D_1^- and D_1^+, respectively. Then

$$x_1 + D_1^- - D_1^+ = 30$$

What should the overall objective function, the goal function, be? This must of course be specified by the decision maker. Assume that the decision maker has a strong desire not to underachieve the profit of \$100 but attaches no significance to overachieving. Similarly, the decision maker does not wish to underachieve the production of the first product. Thus a goal function of

$$Z = D_P^- + D_1^-$$

is suggested. Note that we converted the goal programming problem into a linear programming problem.

Note also that we assigned equal importance to the two deviational variables D_P^- and D_1^-. Now the decision maker may feel that under-achievement in profit is more serious than underachievement in producing the first product. In fact, he may feel that it is three times more important. This can be translated into mathematics by using the **weighted goal function**:

$$Z = 3D_P^- + D_1^-$$

Now supose the decision maker in addition does not want to have a profit of over \$100. The firm may not want to have an adverse public image or may have some other rationale for this policy. So now the goal function should have a term containing D_P^+. For example, the decision maker may specify a goal function of

$$Z = 3D_P^- + D_P^+ + D_1^-$$

Or suppose the decision maker also wants x_1 to be between 25 and 35 units or strives for the goals

$$x_1 \geq 25 \quad \text{(as a goal)}$$

$$x_1 \leq 35 \quad \text{(as a goal)}$$

Such a problem is called **interval goal programming** problem, and the goal constraints can be converted into absolute constraints:

$$x_1 + D_{25}^- - D_{25}^+ = 25$$

$$x_1 + D_{35}^- - D_{35}^+ = 35$$

where D_{25}^-, D_{25}^+, D_{35}^-, and D_{35}^+ are under- and overachivement in producing product 1 in quantities of 25 or 35, respectively. The goal function now could possibly be

$$Z = 5D_P^- + 2D_P^+ + D_{25}^- + D_{35}^+ + D_1^-$$

because the decision maker does not want product 1 to be under 25 or over 35 units.

Finally, let us return to our original problem and reconsider the rigid time constraint of

$$3x_1 + 2x_2 \leq 60$$

Suppose there is a possibility for overtime and/or subcontracting at a higher cost. So the rigid time constraint is converted into a goal constraint,

$$3x_1 + 2x_2 \leq 60 \qquad \text{(as a goal)}$$

which can be written as

$$3x_1 + 2x_2 - D_T^+ + D_T^- = 60$$

where D_T^+ and D_T^- are over- and underachievement in time, measured in hours of labor. Now the goal function may be written as

$$Z = D_P^- + D_1^- + D_T^+$$

which shows that a penalty is attached in overachieving the time constraint of 60 hours, in addition to underachieving the profit and underachieving the number of units of the first product (as specified in the original problem). Now we summarize our approach to goal functions:

---

1. The goal function is specified by a weighted mean of the deviational variables.
2. The goal function is always minimized.

Of course some of the weights may be 0s, and some or all may be 1s.

Note that so far all our goal programming problems have been converted into linear programming problems, or we might say we have dealt only with **linear goal programming**, that is, with goal programming problems where all the constraints are linear. When the constraints are nonlinear and the variables are integer or mixed integer, etc., we deal with **mathematical goal programming**.

Now we turn our attention to another type of goal programming.

14.3 THE MEDIA ALLOCATION PROBLEM: PREEMPTIVE PRIORITIES

A certain firm wants to allocate its advertising budget of x_1, x_2, and x_3 dollars among television, national magazines, and local newspapers. Each media exposes 15,000, 10,000, and 8000 people, respectively, per $1000 of expenditure. The firm pursues three goals:

1. Keep total expenditures under $250,000.
2. Expose at least 600,000 people.
3. Keep television expenditures between $100,000 and $150,000.

Thus the goal constraints are

$$x_1 + x_2 + x_3 \leq 250{,}000 \quad \text{(as goal 1)}$$

$$15x_1 + 10x_2 + 8x_3 \geq 600{,}000 \quad \text{(as goal 2)}$$

$$\left. \begin{array}{l} x_1 \geq 100{,}000 \\ x_1 \leq 150{,}000 \end{array} \right\} \quad \text{(as goal 3)}$$

These goal constraints can be converted into absolute constraints:

$$x_1 + x_2 + x_3 + D_T^- - D_T^+ = 250{,}000$$

$$15x_1 + 10x_2 + 8x_3 + D_E^- - D_E^+ = 600{,}000$$

$$x_1 + D_{100}^- - D_{100}^+ = 100{,}000$$

$$x_1 + D_{150}^- + D_{150}^+ = 150{,}000$$

where the subscripts T, E, 100, and 150 stand for total expenditure, exposure, \$100,000, and \$150,000. Now we turn our attention to the goal function.

Management attaches extreme importance to the first goal, namely to keep total expenditure under \$250,000. In fact management desires to ignore goals 2 and 3 until the best is done for goal 1. We say that management assigns preemptive priority to minimize overachievement of total expenditure, that is, the value of D_T^+.

After the best is done for goal 1, the highest-**ranking** goal, management wants to pay attention to the second goal of exposing at least 600,000 people. The desire is then to do the best for goal 2 *without any detrimental effect on goal 1.* This means minimizing D_T^+ without changing D_T^+.

Similarly, goal 3 is considered only after the best is done for goals 1 and 2, and improving performance toward goal 3 is allowed only without jeopardy to goals 1 and 2.

Recall now that television expenditures are to be kept to not lower than 100,000 and not higher than 150,000, meaning that $D_{100}^- + D_{150}^+$ is to be minimized without changing the values of D_T^+ and D_E^- established earlier.

It is customary to designate the goal function by

$$Z \sim P_1 D_T^+ + P_2 D_E^- + P_3(D_{100}^- + D_{150}^+)$$

where P_1, P_2, and P_3 serve to identify the priority level or rank of the respective goals. Thus the right-hand side is not an ordinary mathematical expression but a reminder of priorities. However, if P_1, P_2, and P_3 are interpreted as weights and it is assumed that P_1 is much greater than P_2 and P_2 is much greater than P_3, then the right-hand side becomes an ordinary mathematical expression, and, in fact, we have a weighted goal function.

> A goal programming problem with preemptive priorities can be interpreted as a goal programming problem with a weighted goal function, provided the use of very large weights is allowed.

Real-life programs are solved on the computer, but graphic methods still
provide important insight into goal programming. As an illustration,
consider again the Indian jewelry problem with the goal of realizing a
profit of at least $50.

The solid lines in Figure 14.1 show the rigid resource constraints
and the dashed line, the flexible goal constraint. Points to the right
(above) the dashed line are points with overachievement of profit where
$D^+ > 0$; points below are underachievement, where $D^- > 0$. The shaded
feasible area is below the goal line, and so clearly there would be no
feasible solution if the goal line were rigid. But it is not. So we must find
the point in (or on the border of) the shaded quadrangle which minimizes underachievement or D^-.

We can use the principle of *roll-down* (see Chapter 10, Figure
10.13) and find that corner B is the point with the minimum D^-. Thus
point B is the solution to the problem, just as in the original Indian
jewelry problem.

To make the problem more representative, assume that the decision maker has three preemptive goals:

1. Realize a profit of at least $15.00.
2. Make at least 1.8 bracelets.*
3. Make at least 3.2 rings.

---

* Recall that fractional quantities are permitted.

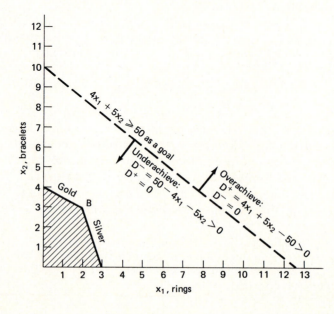

FIGURE 14.1
Indian jewelry prob-
lem with the single
goal of achieving a
profit of $50.

Thus, in addition to the resource constraints,

$$3x_1 + x_2 \leq 9 \quad \text{(silver)}$$

$$x_1 + 2x_2 \leq 8 \quad \text{(gold)}$$

we have three goal constraints:

$$4x_1 + 5x_2 \geq 15 \quad \text{(as goal 1: profit)}$$

$$x_2 \geq 1.8 \quad \text{(as goal 2: bracelets)}$$

$$x_1 \qquad \geq 3.2 \quad \text{(as goal 3: rings)}$$

The last three goal constraints can be converted to

$$4x_1 + 5x_2 + D_P^- - D_P^+ = 15$$

$$x_2 + D_B^- - D_B^+ = 1.8$$

$$x_1 \qquad + D_R^- - D_R^+ = 3.2$$

where the subscripts P, B, and R stand for profit, bracelets, and rings, respectively. We solve the problem in three steps.

In the first step we concentrate on the first priority: Minimize D_P^-. So in Figure 14.2 we show the resource and the goal constraints. All points above (or on) the (dashed) goal line meet the first goal, because the profit of $15 is overachieved. Thus we can replace the flexible goal constraint with the rigid constraint:

$$4x_1 + 5x_2 \geq 15$$

We see, therefore, that our problem is to solve the goal programming problem with three rigid constraints,

$$3x_1 + x_2 \leq 9$$

$$x_1 + 2x_2 \leq 8$$

$$4x_1 + 5x_2 \geq 15$$

and with goals 2 and 3. (We have taken care of goal 1.)

In the second step of our approach we concentrate on the second goal: Minimize D_B^-. In Figure 14.3 we reproduce Figure 14.2, but now goal 2 is represented by the dashed line $x_2 = 1.8$.

Note that all points above the dashed line overachieve goal 2, and therefore all points within the border of the shaded pentagon achieve both goals 1 and 2. So our problem is to find in (or on the border of) the shaded area the point to meet goal 3 in the best manner.

Thus in the third step of our approach we must solve the problem with the four constraints

$$3x_1 + x_2 \leq 9$$

$$x_1 + 2x_2 \leq 8$$

$$4x_1 + 5x_2 \geq 15$$

$$x_2 \geq 1.8$$

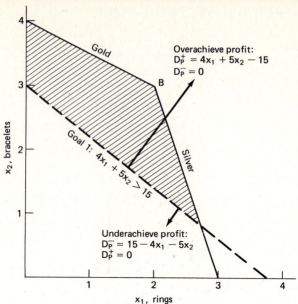

FIGURE 14.2
First preemptive priority:
Realize a profit of at least
$15.00.

and must minimize underachievement for the third goal. The third goal is represented by the dashed line in Figure 14.4. Points to the right overachieve and to the left, underachieve. Note that goal 3 will have to be underachieved.

So now we have a linear programming problem: Find the point closest to the dashed goal 3 line in (or on the border of) the shaded pentagon.

We use again the principle of roll-down, though now the goal line is

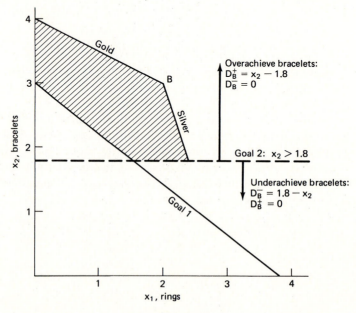

FIGURE 14.3
Second preemptive priority: Make at least 1.8 bracelets.

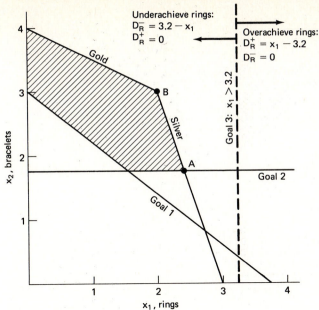

Underachieve rings:
$$D_R^- = 3.2 - x_1$$
$$D_R^+ = 0$$

Overachieve rings:
$$D_R^+ = x_1 - 3.2$$
$$D_R^- = 0$$

FIGURE 14.4
Third preemptive priority: Make at least 3.2 rings.

really to be rolled to the left. We bump into corner A, and so the solution to the problem is

$$x_2 = 1.8$$

To get the value of x_1, we must compute the intersection of the dashed line and the silver constraint in Figure 14.3:

$$3x_1 + x_2 = 9$$

We get

$$3x_1 = 9 - x_2$$

$$x_1 = \tfrac{1}{3}(9 - x_2) = \tfrac{1}{3}(9 - 1.8) = 2.4$$

So the solution to the problem is to make 2.4 rings and 1.8 bracelets. The profit is

$$4x_1 + 5x_1 = 4 \times 2.4 + 5 \times 1.8 = \$18.60$$

Thus goal 1 is overachieved by $\$18.60 - \$15.00 = \$3.60$, goal 2 is met exactly by making 1.8 bracelets, and the third goal is underachieved by making $3.2 - 2.4 = .8$ rings less than the goal of 3.2.

In Figure 14.5 we show our approach in flowchart form. First we draw the resource constraints (box 1) and then the goal constraint(s) for the first-priority goal (box 2). Then we make a test (diamond-shaped box 3) as to whether the goal can be met. If yes, we replace the flexible goal constraint(s) by rigid constraint(s) (box 4). If not, find the optimum solution(s) by roll down (box 7). Then test if there are more (lower-ranking) goals (box 5). If there are none, we have the solution; otherwise, we must repeat the process for the next (lower-ranking) goal (box 6).

FIGURE 14.5
Flowchart for solving a
problem with preemptive
priorities.

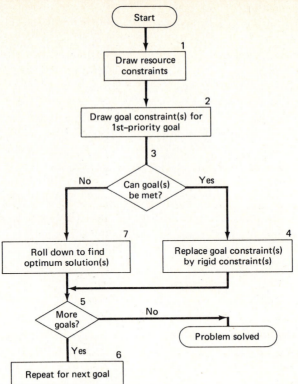

14.5 COMPUTER-BASED SOLUTIONS

A linear goal programming problem for which the goal function is a weighted mean of the deviation variables presents no particular difficulty because the simplex method of linear programming can be directly applied. For problems with preemptive priorities, the situation is somewhat different.

The problem can be solved by using large weights, but it is not immediately clear what weights should be used. Fortunately, by appropriate modification of the simplex method, direct and efficient algorithms can be developed. Solution techniques fall into two types.

The first type of approach, **sequential linear goal programming**, first solves the problem by the simplex method, considering only the top-ranking goal. Suppose the goal is to minimize the deviational variable D_1^-; designate the minimum value by D_1^*. (D_1^* could of course be zero.) Now the first goal is replaced by the rigid constraint

$$D_1^- = D_1^*$$

and the computer proceeds to the second step, which is to solve the linear programming problem with the preceding added constraint and considering only the second-ranking goal. (The first goal will be automatically taken care of.)

After this second linear programming problem is solved by the simplex method, a new second constraint is added, and the computer proceeds to solve this new third linear programming problem. And so on.

The second type of approach, the **multiphase simplex method**, is a simple extension of the classical simplex method we discussed in Chapter 11. Instead of a single bottom row (the index row in Figure 11.4), a separate index row is added for each preemptive goal. The initial solution to the problem is obtained exactly the same as described in Chapter 11. Without going into detail, you should know that the computer proceeds to successive solutions of the simplex method, first considering the top-ranking goal, then the second-ranking, and so on. Thus,

> Efficient computer programs based on the simplex method are available for solving linear goal programming problems.

Finally we wish to say a few words about mathematical goal programming. In these situations the traditional algorithm for mathematical programming must be modified, or new algorithms must be developed, and consequently the computer programs become more complex and less efficient. However,

> Computer programs for mathematical goal programming are available and are continuously being improved.

14.6 SCOPE AND ADVANTAGES OF GOAL PROGRAMMING

As stated before, many practical situations involve multiple, competitive, and often conflicting goals, and therefore in such situations considering a single objective is inadequate, and so there is the potential of applying goal programming. Thus the scope of goal programming is essentially unlimited and applies to all manner of resource allocation problems. There are, however, certain special features of goal programming which have been used in practical problems, and we review some of these now.

Goal programming permits experimentation in a simple and flexible manner with various constraints, goal levels, trade-offs, priorities, policies, and levels of goal attainment.

Goal programming has been used for justification of budgets in organizations where multiple goals must be considered. Budget requests can be justified in terms of viable goals, alternatives, and expected results.

Many organizations have unique institutional factors and constraints which can be dealt with by goal programming. Decisions made by administrative policy-making groups can be associated with goals, and decisions can be supported in organizations with many stakeholders.

In many organizations often bitter and emotional arguments arise, and true individual preferences are unknown and remain hidden. Goal programming makes it possible to fit individual objective functions to existing data, thereby revealing hidden individual preferences. Explicit recognition of these preferences leads to better decisions.

Furthermore, the explicit identification of the source of different opinions can clarify situations, and this in turn can lead to resolution of otherwise unresolvable conflicts.

Development of objective functions and evaluation of goals in terms of results are often performed on a computer in an interactive mode. This provides immediate feedback to decision makers and allows them to change and adapt their goals to accommodate other stakeholders. Thus computer-supported goal programming can lead to better decisions which could not be reached without either the computer or goal programming.

14.7 ACADEMIC PLANNING BY GOAL PROGRAMMING: SUCCESSFUL APPLICATIONS

Background

There is perhaps no managerial field where decision making must be made in a more confusing environment than in academic planning. There are always many objectives, goals, and constraints which are often conflicting, and in fact academic planning and management are full of fuzzy situations. There are always many stakeholders involved, such as students, faculty, university administration, board of trustees, legislators, general public, prospective employees, and so on.

Specifically at least the following factors must be considered*:

1. Demand of accountability by funding sources and by the general public
2. Demographic changes which may result in an overall decline in college-age youth
3. Significant shifts into certain academic areas such as business schools
4. Faculty turnover as a result of these shifts, such as a greater opportunity at nonacademic organizations
5. Inflationary pressures

The traditional approach to academic planning is the use of qualitative methods, bargaining, negotiating, yielding to various pressures, and arbitrary and ad hoc decisions. However, recently quantitative methods have been successfully applied to these problems. There are two approaches to support decision making in such situations: (1) the

---

* See Carl Joiner, "Academic Planning Through the Goal Programming Model," *Interfaces*, Vol. 10, No. 4, Aug. 1980, pp. 86–91.

use of preference theory (utility theory), covered in Chapter 7, and (2) goal programming to be covered now.

We start by presenting a model and then shall describe a specific successful application.

Model*

The general model uses 15 variables. One of them is the total payroll increase from prior years, while the others are the number of faculty members, such as

1. Number of research assistants
2. Number of instructors
3. Number of full professors
4. Number of nonacademic staff members

and so on.

The model uses 71 constants, such as

1. Percentage of staff classified as full-time faculty
2. Estimated number of undergraduate student credit hours required per session
3. Desired graduate faculty to student ratio
4. Desired percentage increase in salary for faculty

In addition, there are constants specifying teaching load, desired proportion of each faculty type, average annual salaries, etc.

The model includes seven goal constraints:

1. Accreditation
2. Total number of academic staff
3. Distribution of academic staff
4. Number of nonacademic staff
5. Number of graduate research assistants
6. Salary increase
7. Total payroll budget

Now we move on to the objective function to be minimized. The model uses a preemptive priority list established by the university administration in accordance with policies, existing conditions, and judgment. Thus the objective function is to minimize deviations either negative or positive, that is, under- and overachievement in accordance with the established priority list.

Application at the University of Nebraska at Omaha

Professor Carl Joiner in the previously cited article reported on how goal programming is used at the College of Business Administration at the University of Nebraska at Omaha.

---

* S. M. Lee and E. R. Clayton, "A Goal Programming Model for Academic Resource Allocation," *Management Science*, Vol. 18, No. 8, April 1972, pp. B395–B408.

The first model was constructed to describe the existing goal and resource processes of the college. Nine goals were established with decreasing priority. We list here only the first four goals and the ninth goal, namely,

1. Generate staff needs.
2. Maintain 75% full-time faculty.
3. Maintain 40% undergraduate faculty with a terminal degree.
4. Generate department heads.
9. Minimize budget.

The model was programmed on a computer, and as a first run a solution was obtained which met all the goals at the lowest possible cost. The cost of achieving all goals was $2,318,224. These dollar values are hypothetical and do not correspond to the salaries paid at the University of Nebraska at Omaha.

Now of course there was not enough money to reach all the goals of the college, and so there was a need to apply goal programming to determine the cost of allowing underachievement of certain goals. One approach would be to set a realistic budget and by goal programming determine which of the goals will be underachieved and to what extent. A more sophisticated approach is to consider a set of alternate priority lists, determine by goal programming the optimum solution for each of them, and then compare them. To follow the latter approach, six *goal packages* were established. The first of these is a "bare bones" goal, defined as generating staff, department heads, student credit hours, and dean's office requirements. The cost of achieving this minimum goal package was found to be $1,298,724.

Now we state the second and third goal packages. We omit the fourth to ninth packages, as they would not add to understanding the approach.

2. "Bare bones" plus 45% graduate faculty at a cost of $1,319,635
3. Bare bones plus 40% of undergraduate faculty with a terminal degree at a cost of $1,553,749

By using the nine goals and six goal packages, a systematic sensitivity analysis was performed to support the decision-making activities of the dean. Thus by making repeated computer runs and solving a series of goal programming problems, a comprehensive panorama of the alternatives and costs was presented to the dean.

Benefits at the University of Nebraska

The Dean of the College of Business Administration stated that the advantage of the goal programming is not so much in cost savings as in exploring various policy and procedural alternatives. He found that the results provided by goal programming had been quite meaningful in developing and reformulating the priorities of the college. The methodology was appropriate for examining the various trade-offs in resource planning and testing the sensitivity of various allocation possibilities.

The goal programming approach was also found particularly useful when a budgetary cutback occurred and the plans of the college had to be changed.

14.8 A DIALOG

Q. *What are the most successful applications of goal programming?*

A. Here are some:

Design and development of antenna systems for space vehicles
Managing university admissions
Training of troops to support military exercises
Pollution control
Marine environmental control
Planning naval officer accessions (promotions)
Emergency medical services planning
Managing medical libraries
Antenna and radar systems design

Q. *Are most applications in the public domain?*

A. Yes, so far, but business applications are increasing.

Q. *Why is this so?*

A. Quantitative techniques have been quite successful in business for many years, because it was possible to formulate goals with single objective functions. But in the public domain goals are very difficult to establish, and so quantitative techniques were lagging. Now goal programming has become successful in the public domain and is leading in the number of successful applications. But this is only a temporary situation.

Q. *How do you determine the goals anyway?*

A. Organizations often have explicit policies which can be formulated as goals. In fact, the analyst often finds that goals have already been stated, and so formulating the problem as a goal programming problem may not be so prohibitively difficult.

Q. *How do you get the weights when dealing with a weighted goal function?*

A. You try a set of weights, and if the preferences resulting from the goal function do not meet the approval of the decision makers, you change the weights. You may do this by trial and error, but there are also systematic procedures available to determine the weights most acceptable to the decision maker. Often the answers are relatively independent from the particular weights, and in practice the problem is not as serious as it appears in theory. Furthermore, if the answers depend a great deal on the exact value of the weights, probably the problem has not been formulated quite right.

Q. *Don't managers want the best? Can they be satisfied with statements such as the profit should be at least $200,000?*

A. They are often satisfied with a "good" solution. As already discussed in the dialog in Chapter 1, managers often *satisfice*, using the term of Professor Herbert A. Simon.

Q. *I am dubious about your discussion of profit in the Indian jewelry problem. You give no credit for overachievement. Isn't it always the more, the better?*

A. Consider, for example, when you buy gas with a certain octane rating. You do not want your car to knock, and if there is an adequate octane rating, your car will perform properly. So there is no advantage to having a higher octane rating or aviation fuel for your automobile. In fact it could be a disadvantage if your engine cannot cope with a high octane rating. Or when you pick up your phone, you want to get a fast dial tone so you can dial. But it wouldn't really help to get an immediate response because it would not make any difference to you. The target for delivering a daily report may be 8:00 o'clock in the morning when the executive arrives at the office, and there is no advantage to delivering the report before he gets there. And so on.

Q. *I am confused about the stakeholders and the decision makers. Who is the decision maker?*

A. There is a real problem, particularly in the public domain. Who decides about the level of allowable air pollution? The executive branch? Congress? The mayor of the city? In such situations the analyst must be very careful in developing the goals, constraints, and objective function. A great deal of verification with several people must be carried out.

Q. *In Chapter 7 you discussed multiobjectives under uncertainty, and your approach was totally different from the one discussed now. Why?*

A. There seem to be two schools of thought when approaching multiobjective problems. The analysts, following the approach in Chapter 7, are primarily concerned with problems of uncertainty and use utility theory. The goal programming people manage to use a deterministic approach and follow the mathematical programming approach. There have been proposals to integrate the two theories, but so far there is no general acceptance of a unified approach.

Q. *I don't remember you talking about constraints in Chapter 7.*

A. The utility theory people, that is, the decision analysts, seem to be working with problems where the alternatives can be explicitly listed and where the number of alternatives is small or large but not myriad or infinite. The goal programming people work with alternatives subject to constraints, and the number of alternatives may be infinite. But of course there is an overlap of situations which can be dealt with by either of the approaches.

Q. *So which approach should I use?*

A. You should search the literature, consult experts, and use the most suitable approach.

Q. *What is your prognosis for goal programming?*

A. Successful applications of multiobjective or multigoal approaches will increase in the future.

SUMMARY

1. Goal programming supports decision making with multiple goals and thereby allows the modeling of human judgment in a flexible way.

2. Goal programming allows the simultaneous support of several stakeholders and decision makers.

3. In goal programming (a) the decision variables are augmented by deviational variables, (b) resource constraints are augmented by goal constraints, and (c) the function to be minimized is the goal function.

4. Linear goal programming problems, whether the goal function is a weighted mean of the deviational variables or preemptive priorities are used, can be solved by modifications of the simplex method.

SECTION EXERCISES

1. **When profit is the single goal.**

1.1 Assume that the goal for the Indian jewelry problem discussed in Section 14.1 and illustrated in Figure 14.1 is to make a profit of at least $30.

   a. Redraw Figure 14.1 showing the new isoprofit line.

   b. Formulate the underachievement and overachievement expressions (as is done on either side of the isoprofit line in Figure 14.1) using the deviational variables D^+ and D^-.

   c. Convert the objective function to a rigid (absolute) constraint equation incorporating the two deviational variables.

   d. Using the rigid constraint equation obtained in part c, follow the discussion in the text to convert the goal programming problem to a linear programming problem with three constraints and an objective function which is expressed in terms of the deviational variable. Follow the notation of Section 14.1 in which the deviational variables become x_3 and x_4.

1.2 Assume that the goal for the Indian jewelry problem discussed in Section 14.1 and illustrated in Figure 14.1 is to make a profit of at least $70.

   a. Redraw Figure 14.1 showing the new isoprofit line.

   b. Formulate the underachievement and overachievement expressions (as is done on either side of the isoprofit line in Figure 14.1) using the deviational variables D^+ and D^-.

c. Convert the objective function to a rigid constraint equation incorporating the two deviational variables.

d. Using the rigid constraint equation obtained in part c, follow the discussion in the text to convert the goal programming problem to a linear programming problem with three constraints and an objective function which is expressed in terms of the deviational variable. Follow the notation of Section 14.1 in which the deviational variables become x_3 and x_4.

2. **Two Goals: Profit and Diversification**

2.1 Refer to the example concerning the manufacture of two products in Section 14.2. Assume that the resource constraint is unchanged. The firm's goal is a profit of at least $200. The firm wants to produce at least 50 units of the first product.

   a. Designating profit underachievement and overachievement by D_p^- and D_p^+, replace the flexible goal constraints with rigid constraints for this goal.

   b. Designating underachievement and overachievement in producing the first product by D_1^- and D_1^+, replace the flexible goal constraints with rigid constraints for this goal.

   c. Write the goal function which assumes that both profit and production goals are equally important.

   d. Write the goal function which assumes that profit is twice as important as production.

   e. Assume the decision maker wishes x_1 to be between 45 and 55. Following the approach in the text, write the two absolute interval goal programming constraint equations.

   f. Following your work in part e, write the rigid goal function incorporating the interval goal into the goal function, assuming all goals are equally important.

   g. Following your work in part f, write the rigid goal function for this situation assuming that the decision maker gives the profit goal twice the importance of the product diversity goal and the interval goal one-half the importance of the product diversity goal.

2.2 Refer to the example concerning the manufacture of two products in Section 14.2. Assume that the resource constraint is unchanged. The firm's goal is a profit of at least $80. The firm wants to produce at least 20 units of the first product.

   a. Designating profit underachievement and overachievement by D_p^- and D_p^+, replace the flexible goal constraints with rigid constraints for this goal.

   b. Designating underachievement and overachievement in producing the first product by D_1^- and D_1^+, replace the flexible goal constraints with rigid constraints for this goal.

   c. Write the goal function which assumes that both profit and production goals are equally important.

   d. Write the goal function which assumes that profit is half as important as production.

   e. Assume the decision maker wishes x_1 to be between 10 and 30. Following the approach in the text, write the two absolute interval goal programming constraint equations.

   f. Following your work in part e, write the rigid goal function incorporating the interval goal into the goal function, assuming all goals are equally important.

   g. Following your work in part f, write the rigid goal function for this situation assuming that the decision maker gives the profit goal four times the importance of the product diversity goal and the interval goal twice the importance of the product diversity goal.

2.3 Refer to the example concerning the manufacture of two products in Section 14.2. Assume that the resource constraint is unchanged. The firm's goal is a profit of at least $250. The firm wants to produce at least 35 units of the first product.

a. Designating profit underachievement and overachievement by D_p^- and D_p^+, replace the flexible goal constraints with rigid constraints for this goal.

b. Designating underachievement and overachievement in producing the first product by D_1^- and D_1^+, replace the flexible goal constraints with rigid constraints for this goal.

c. Write the goal function which assumes that both profit and production goals are equally important.

d. Write the goal function which assumes that profit is six times as important as production.

e. Assume the decision maker wishes x_1 to be between 25 and 55. Following the approach in the text, write the two absolute interval goal programming constraint equations.

f. Following your work in part e, write the rigid goal function incorporating the interval goal into the goal function, assuming all goals are equally important.

g. Following your work in part f, write the rigid goal function for this situation assuming that the decision maker gives the profit goal one-quarter the importance of the product diversity goal and the interval goal one-half the importance of the product diversity goal.

3. *The Media Allocation Problem: Preemptive Priorities*

3.1 Refer to the firm which wants to allocate its advertising budget, discussed in Section 14.3. Assume that the media TV, national magazines, and local newspapers expose 20,000, 8000, and 10,000 people, respectively, per $1000 of advertising expenditure. The firm pursues the following three goals:

1. Keep total expenditures under $200,000.

2. Expose at least 1 million people.

3. Keep TV expenditures between $200,000 and $300,000.

a. Using the notation in the text, write the equations of the goal constraints.

b. Convert the goal constraints into absolute constraints.

c. Assume that management attaches most importance to the second goal, exposure to a given audience. *Preemptive* priority is assigned to minimizing overachievement of total expenditure. Using the notation $P_1, P_2, \ldots$, write the goal function in symbolic terms as is done in the text.

3.2 Refer to the firm which wants to allocate its advertising budget, discussed in Section 14.3. Assume that the media TV, national magazines, and local newspapers expose 10,000, 18,000, and 12,000 people, respectively, per $1000 of advertising expenditure. The firm pursues the following three goals:

1. Keep total expenditures under $500,000.

2. Expose at least 2 million people.

3. Keep TV expenditures between $100,000 and $200,000.

a. Using the notation in the text, write the equations of the goal constraints.

b. Convert the goal constraints into absolute constraints.

c. Assume that management attaches most importance to the second goal, exposure to a given audience. *Preemptive* priority is assigned to minimizing overachievement of total expenditure. Using the notation

$P_1, P_2, \ldots$, write the goal function in symbolic terms as is done in the text.

3.3 Refer to the firm which wants to allocate its advertising budget, discussed in Section 14.3. Assume that the media TV, national magazines, and local newspapers expose 5000, 10,000 and 15,000 people, respectively, per $1000 of advertising expenditure. The firm pursues the following three goals:

1. Keep total expenditures under $600,000.
2. Expose at least 2 million people.
3. Keep TV expenditures between $400,000 and $600,000.

    a. Using the notation in the text, write the equations of the goal constraints.
    b. Convert the goal constraints into absolute constraints.
    c. Assume that management attaches most importance to the second goal, exposure to a given audience. *Preemptive* priority is assigned to minimizing overachievement of total expenditure. Using the notation $P_1, P_2, \ldots$, write the goal function in symbolic terms as is done in the text.

4. Graphic Solution of Goal Programming Problems

4.1 Refer to the Indian jewelry example as discussed in Section 14.4. Assume that the decision maker has three preemptive goals:

1. Realize a profit of at least $10.00.
2. Make at least 1.6 bracelets.
3. Make at least 3 rings.

    a. Write the three goal constraints (profit, bracelets, rings).
    b. Convert the three goal constraints to three rigid constraints using deviational variables, following the text in Section 14.4.
    c. Concentrate on the first priority; make a new version of Figure 14.2, replacing the flexible goal constraint for profit with a rigid constraint; write the new constraint. Show the feasible region in your new figure as a shaded region.
    d. Summarize the problem as it now stands, giving the three rigid constraints and following the approach in Section 14.4.
    e. Draw a new version of Figure 14.3 corresponding to the new values and conditions and showing the problem at this stage.
    f. Summarize the problem as it now stands, giving the four rigid constraints.
    g. Draw a new version of Figure 14.4 corresponding to the new values and conditions and showing the problem at this stage.
    h. Find the solution, and give the solution values for all deviational variables.

4.2 Refer to the Indian jewelry example as discussed in Section 14.4. Assume that the decision maker has three preemptive goals:

1. Realize a profit of at least $20.00.
2. Make at least 1.2 bracelets.
3. Make at least 1.4 rings.

    a. Write the three goal constraints (profit, bracelets, rings).
    b. Convert the three goal constraints to three rigid constraints using deviational variables, following the text in Section 14.4.
    c. Concentrate on the first priority; make a new version of Figure 14.2, replacing the flexible goal constraint for profit with a rigid constraint; write the new constraint. Show the feasible region in your new figure as a shaded region.

d. Summarize the problem as it now stands, giving the three rigid constraints and following the approach in Section 14.4.

e. Draw a new version of Figure 14.3 corresponding to the new values and conditions and showing the problem at this stage.

f. Summarize the problem as it now stands, giving the four rigid constraints.

g. Draw a new version of Figure 14.4 corresponding to the new values and conditions and showing the problem at this stage.

h. Find the solution, and give the solution values for all deviational variables.

4.3 Refer to the Indian jewelry example as discussed in Section 14.4. Assume that the decision maker has three preemptive goals:

1. Realize a profit of at least $8.00.
2. Make at least 2.5 bracelets.
3. Make at least 4 rings.

a. Write the three goal constraints (profit, bracelets, rings).

b. Convert the three goal constraints to three rigid constraints using deviational variables, following the text in Section 14.4.

c. Concentrate on the first priority; make a new version of Figure 14.2, replacing the flexible goal constraint for profit with a rigid constraint; write the new constraint. Show the feasible region in your new figure as a shaded region.

d. Summarize the problem as it now stands, giving the three rigid constraints and following the approach in Section 14.4.

e. Draw a new version of Figure 14.3 corresponding to the new values and conditions; showing the problem at this stage.

f. Summarize the problem as it now stands, giving the four rigid constraints.

g. Draw a new version of Figure 14.4 corresponding to the new values and conditions and showing the problem at this stage.

h. Find the solution, and give the solution values for all deviational variables.

5. Computer-Based Solutions

5.1 In Section 14.5, the sequential linear goal programming approach to solving goal programming problems involving preemptive priorities is described. Make a flowchart to show the process as it is described in Section 14.5.

5.2 What is the importance to the managerial decision maker of the following statement appearing in Section 14.5: Efficient computer programs based on the simplex method are available for solving linear goal programming problems.

6. Scope and Advantages of Goal Programming

6.1 In what sense does goal programming support the asking of what-if questions?

6.2 Do you think that the business enterprises you are familiar with would use the results of goal programming analyses to make their decisions? Why, or why not?

7. Academic Planning by Goal Programming: Successful Applications

7.1 Give an example of a situation other than academic planning where "there are many objectives, goals, and constraints which are often conflicting . . .full of fuzzy situations" and where "there are always many stakeholders involved."

7.2 In Section 14.7 it is stated that the general model uses 15 variables, and 5 variables are given. Give as many more as you can think of.

7.3 In Section 14.7 it is stated that the general model uses 71 constants, and 4 constants are given. Give as many more as you can think of.

7.4 In Section 14.7 it is stated that the model uses a preemptive priority list established by the university administration. Give your version of the priorities which you feel would be set by

    a. The board of trustees, assuming this is a public institution

    b. The faculty

    c. The students

    d. Any other stakeholder you choose

7.5 The cost of three of the six goal packages are presented along with their conditions. Make a table showing the conditions for the package (that is, its description), the cost achieved, the difference between this goal package cost and the minimal, and the percentage difference between this goal package cost and that of the minimal cost package.

7.6 It is stated in Section 14.7 that the "goal programming approach was also found particularly useful when a budgetary cutback occurred and the plans of the college had to be changed." Why do you think this would be so?

8. *Goal Programming and Multiobjectives: A Dialog*

8.1 Can you think of or find a way to systematize assigning weights when working with a group of decision makers?

8.2 What is the process by which goals might be specified suitably for goal programming if they do not already exist in the form of policies?

8.3 In Section 14.8 the statement is made "if the answers depend a great deal on the exact value of the weights, probably the problem has not been formulated quite right." Why do you think this is so?

CHAPTER EXERCISES AND DISCUSSION QUESTIONS

C.1 G. N. Sberg produces Danish and Swedish pancakes as a precooked, frozen shelf item. Each Danish pancake requires 20 grams of baking soda and 60 grams of flour. Each Swedish pancake requires 30 grams of baking soda and 40 grams of flour. The total amount of flour and baking soda per day is limited by boat transportation to the factory to 6 and 3 kilograms, respectively. The following is the prioritized statement of the goals set by Sberg:

1. Get as close as possible to producing 100 pancakes a day.

2. Get out at least 65 Swedish pancakes a day.

3. Produce at least 50 Danish pancakes per day.

    a. Solve this goal programming problem graphically.

    b. Assume that goals 1 and 3 are interchanged in priority. Solve the resulting goal programming problem graphically.

C.2 GP University is a private institution which believes in the profit motive. GP has a faculty consisting of a dean and 20 instructors who have been rated as satisfactory for use by the school. Some of the instructional staff is adjunct, working only part time. The dean is on a regular salary, but to encourage the instructors, they receive $50 per student per course if they are part-time instructors and $100 per student per course if they are full-time (which group is required to carry out tasks beyond instruction which are believed to increase with student numbers, such as registration, etc.).

Full-time faculty can teach a maximum of 200 students per term and part-time faculty, a maximum of 100. To maintain the school's accreditation, instruction by the part-time staff is supposed to be kept to less than 30% of the total instruction. The revenue per student is $300 per student. The dean is allowed to teach up to 30 students. When the dean teaches, she receives $25 per student in addition to the fixed payment of $4000 per term.

    a. Solve this as a linear programming problem to maximize revenue. (*Hint:* The variables can be number of students contacted in a course by the dean and full-time or part-time faculty.)

    b. It is recognized that the long-term future of the institution depends on more than profit maximization. The following is a prioritized listing of goals; find the goal programming solution assuming that all goals are given equal importance.

    1. Achieve a minimum profit of 10% of revenue.

    2. Achieve a minimum profit of $40,000.

    3. Keep the part- to full-time faculty teaching ratio to less than 40%.

    4. Reduce the dean's teaching to zero.

    Formulate this as a goal programming problem.

    c. Find a solution for the problem as defined in parts a and b.

C.3 Mommy Warbucks has $400,000 available for investment. She sees her choices as being to put her money into any of the following: stocks, bonds, money funds, gold, and bank money market certificates. Because this money is part of her personal pension fund, she is limited as to when she can make investments. She can invest in stocks on January 1 and antici-pates a 50% return after 2 years. At the same time, she could also purchase corporate bonds through her broker which at the present time she feels can yield a 25% gain in 3 years. On the following December 31, she can buy shares in a money fund from which she expects 100% gain in 5 years. Unfortunately, she was detected by the Swiss government in a minor bank fraud and cannot invest again in a gold account in Switzerland (which she prefers since she has a retirement estate there) until the beginning of the fifth year. However, she believes that at that time the gold will grow by 100% in 2 years. Any funds which she does not invest in any of the preceding she will put into bank money market certificates which pay 14% per year. She has been struggling with how to invest while supporting the following goals:

1. Put no more than $125,000 in any one type of investment for diversity.

2. Put at least $100,000 into bank money market certificates to provide safety.

3. Put at least $50,000 into stocks because she believes the greatest chance for high growth is there.

4. Withdraw at least $100,000 for spending at the beginning of the fourth year.

5. Maximize total return at the end of 6 years.

    a. Assuming all investments come to an end on her ninety-fourth birthday (end of the sixth year), formulate this as a goal programming solution based on this prioritization.

    b. Solve this goal programming problem.

Markov Processes

While there is uncertainty in all managerial decision-making situations, often a deterministic approach can provide adequate solutions. Therefore, in Chapters 10–14 we concentrated on mathematical programming, a deterministic approach for solving resource allocation problems. In Chapters 4–9 we already considered managerial situations under uncertainty, and now we resume the study of probabilistic managerial problems where it is impossible to predict with accuracy what will happen, yet one can make useful forecasts in a probabilistic sense by employing the laws of chance.

If you consider a sequence of random experiments, such as a series of thought experiments, you are dealing with an ongoing process, a **stochastic process**. You are already familiar with a simple example from Section 3.6, where you studied the Bernoulli trial process. A more complex example is in Chapter 9 where we studied inventory control under uncertainty. Due to the uncertainty of demand, the decisions made and inventory levels realized are controlled by a stochastic process. There are many important managerial applications of such processes, and in this chapter we treat a particular class of such stochastic processes called Markov processes.

The best way to introduce **Markov processes** is through an actual business situation.

15.1 HOW TO INFLUENCE CONSUMER BEHAVIOR

Americans drink something like 400 million cups of coffee a day, and no one would venture to predict what brand of coffee a particular consumer would buy. Aromatic Coffee Bean Corp. (ACB) sells in a region of the United States where $100 million worth of coffee is bought each month. ACB has 20% of the market, that is, $20 million sales per month. The competitors have 80% or $80 million. We can also say that the probability that a coffee buyer buys from ACB or a competitor is, respectively, .2

or .8. ACB is unhappy about its **market share**, and the problem is how to raise the market share.

Consumer Behavior

Management feels that customers switch *away* from ACB too often but do not switch often enough *to* ACB. Customers should be influenced in such a way that a higher market share for ACB results. Figure 15.1 shows a sample record of individual purchases. To simplify, it is assumed that each consumer buys once a month. As you can see, consumer 1 bought coffee from ACB in January and then again in February but in March switched to a competitor. Observe from the Table how consumers switch between ACB and the competitors.

Now suppose records for thousands of consumers over many years are available. We could examine the record of a single customer and find that the consumer bought about 20% of the time from ACB. Or we could examine the January record and find that about 20% of the consumers bought from ACB, meaning that the ACB share of the market is 20%.

There are two ways to look at the problem:

1. Study the behavior of a single customer.
2. Study the variations of the market share in time.

Both approaches are valid, and we shall use the one which is more convenient and provides more insight to the managerial situation.

ACB wants to influence the consumer's behavior, and in Figure 15.2 we present a summary record of brand switching from the month of January to the month of February. The right-hand column shows that in January out of 100 consumers 20 purchase coffee from ACB and 80 from competitors. In the upper left-hand corner we show that 12 of the ACB customers will purchase again in February. This means that 60% of ACB customers are loyal to their brand. The other 8 ACB customers are lost to the competitors and purchase a competitive brand. This means that 60% are loyal, while 40% switch to competitors.

The second row of Figure 15.2 shows the behavior of the consumers of the competitors. Out of the 80 consumers, 8, that is, 10%, switch to ACB; 72, that is 90%, repeat buying from the competitors. Note then that ACB loses 8 customers but also gains 8 customers, and so in February

	CONSUMERS							
MONTH	**1**	**2**	**3**	**4**	**5**	**6**	**7**	**8**
January	Yes	No	No	No	No	No	Yes	No
February	Yes	No	Yes	No	No	No	No	No
March	No	No	Yes	No	No	No	No	Yes
April	No	No	No	No	Yes	Yes	No	No
—								
—								

FIGURE 15.1 Sample record of individual purchases for ACB Corp.

FROM	TO		
	ACB	**Competitors**	
ACB	12 customers of ACB (60% of 20) stay with ACB	8 customers of ACB (40% of 20) switch to competitors	There are 20 customers of ACB in January
Competitors	8 customers of competitors (10% of 80) switch to ACB	72 customers of competitors (90% of 80) stay with competitors	There are 80 customers of competitors in January
	There will be 20 customers of ACB in February	There will be 80 customers of competitors in February	100 consumers are considered

FIGURE 15.2 Summary record of brand switching between ACB Corp. and competitors.

the market share stays at 20%. Similarly, the competitors lose 8 consumers to ACB but gain 8 from ACB, so their market share stays at the 80% level; it is in **equilibrium.**

> Equilibrium market share means that the loss of consumers is exactly balanced by the gain of others.

We summarize Figure 15.2 by saying that the table describes how consumers switch FROM ACB and competitors TO ACB and competitors. Note that FROM ACB to ACB means staying with ACB and FROM competitors TO competitors means staying with competitors.

The scientific approach deals with uncertainty in terms of probability. Therefore, the switching behavior of customers is expressed in terms of probabilities. In Figure 15.3 we show the **transition probability matrix** of the FROM-TO switching behavior. The upper left-hand corner shows the probability of .6 that a customer remains loyal to ACB. The probability that a customer switches to a competitor (is lost to a competitor) is .4.

The lower left-hand corner shows the probability of .1 that a competitor loses a consumer to ACB, and the lower right-hand corner shows a probability of .9 that competitors retain a customer.

This process of brand switching is a typical Markov process, and the switching behavior described by the Markov process is specified by the transition probabilities.

> A Markov process is characterized by the *transition* probability matrix.

Note that the sum of the probabilities in each row of the transition probability matrix must add to 1 because a consumer either stays with ACB or switches to a competitor. (Column numbers may or may not add to 1.)

FROM	TO	
	ACB	Comps
ACB	.6	.4
Comps	.1	.9

FIGURE 15.3 Transition probability table for brand switching between ACB Corp. and competitors.

Decision Alternatives

ACB wants to increase its market share by influencing customers. Management is considering two different advertising strategies to increase market share. The first of these consists of a series of advertisements aimed at convincing customers of ACB to continue purchasing from ACB. Such a strategy could be called **defensive**, since it aims to increase the loyalty of customers.

An alternate advertising campaign under consideration is an **aggressive** campaign, aimed at convincing users of competitive brands to swtich to ACB. The cost of each of these advertising campaigns is $500,000 a month. Which campaign should ACB choose?

In terms of quantitative analysis, the problem reduces to prediction of the market shares resulting from each of the campaigns. If ACB can predict the market shares for each of the campaigns, then dollar sales and profits can be predicted. What we need is a method for predicting market shares. So we proceed to establish a mathematical model for consumer behavior and the computation of market shares.

15.2 MARKOV MODEL OF CONSUMER BEHAVIOR

Earlier in this book we found it useful to use thought experiments when modeling managerial situations under uncertainty. We shall discuss Markov models in terms of a sequence of chance experiments with random devices. But first we present Markov models in terms of a metaphor.

The Frogs of Monte Carlo

Assume that the world of our mathematical investigation consists of a lily pond covered with many pads, occupied by a large population of leaping, intelligent amphibians designated in everyday language as *frogs*[*] (Figure 15.4). There is also a giant clock loudly ticking time. At each tick each frog jumps and lands either on the same pad or onto another one but never into the pond. A pad may hold any number of frogs.

---

[*] See Ronald A. Howard, *Dynamic Probabilistic Systems*, 2 vols., Wiley, New York 1971.

The probability of a frog landing on any pad depends only on the pad he presently occupies and not on how the frog reached the pad.

More precisely, we say that the transition probability matrix describes the probabilities of a frog jumping from any pad to any pad.

We stress that it is impossible to tell *where* the frog will land, but we know exactly the *probabilities* of where it will land.

Observe that each consumer is modeled by a frog and each brand by a lily pad. Suppose pad 1 represents ACB and pad 2 all the competitors. Frogs on pad 1 are customers of ACB. ACB has 20% of the market, so about 20% of the frogs are on pad 1. We can also say that the probability of a frog being on pads 1 and 2 is .2 and .8, respectively. In the terminology of Markov models we say that the process had two **states,** 1 and 2, and that the **state probabilities** are .2 and .8, respectively.

Thought Experiment

As shown in Figure 15.5 we attach a roulette wheel to each of the two lily pads. The wheel attached to pad 1 has a larger sector, representing the probability .6, and a smaller one the probability .4. The second wheel is attached to lily pad 2, and the sectors are now in the ratio of .9 and .1. Suppose a frog sits on pad 1. He spins the wheel and observes where the ball stops. If it stops in the sector marked 1, he will jump and fall back on pad 1. But if the ball stops in sector 2, he will jump over to pad 2. Similarly, if a frog is on pad 2, he will stay on the same pad with a probability of .9 and jump to pad 1 with a probability of .1. Thus, this experiment corresponds precisely to the behavior of consumers when considering ACB's problem.

In the lower part of Figure 15.5 we show a **transition diagram** describing graphically the same thought experiment. The circles represent states and the arcs and arrows, transitions.

Do not confuse the state probabilities with the transition probabilities. The state probabilities are *unconditional*: The probability is .2 and .8 that the frog is in state 1 or state 2, respectively. The transition

FIGURE 15.4
Frogs of Monte Carlo.

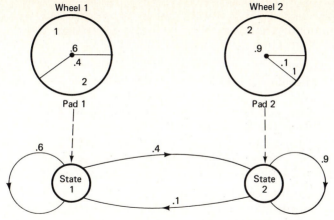

FIGURE 15.5
Thought experiment
of brand switching.

probabilities are *conditional*. For example, the probability that the frog will be next in state 2 if it is now in state 1 equals .4.

In Figure 15.6 we show a graphic representation of the Markov model with the aid of a tree diagram. At the foot of the tree there are two branches describing whether a consumer buys or does not buy coffee from ACB. The respective probabilities are .2 and .8. At branch *A* we are dealing with a customer of ACB, and so the probability of a repeat buy is .6 and of switching to the competitor is .4.

At branch *B* we are dealing with a consumer buying from competitors. Thus the probability that the consumer switches to ACB is .1, and the probability that the consumer will again buy from a competitor is .9. The tree diagram describes how consumers switch from one month to the next. You would have to continue attaching branches to the tree to

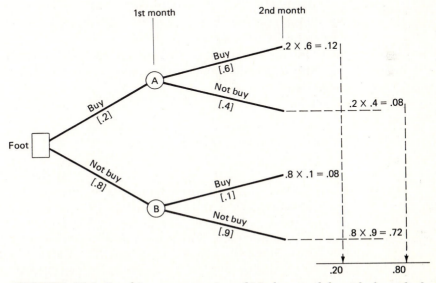

FIGURE 15.6 Graphic representation of Markov models with the aid of a tree diagram.

describe the third, fourth, and so on months. Let us compute the market shares for a given month, provided the market shares for the preceding month are given.

At the foot of the tree the probability that a consumer buys from ACB is indicated as .2 and so the market share is 20%, as it should be. The probability, as shown at the branch emanating from point A, is .6 that this customer will stay loyal to ACB. Thus, the probability of a repeat purchase is $.2 \times .6 = .12$.

At the foot of the tree the probability is .8 that the consumer does not buy from ACB. The probability, as shown at the branch emanating from point B, is .1 that this consumer switches to ACB. Thus the probability that a nonbuyer turns into a buyer is $.8 \times .1 = .08$. The probability that a consumer buys in the second month is $.12 + .08 = .20$. Thus it is seen that the market share stays at the 20% level. A similar computation, shown in Figure 15.6 shows that the competitors' share stays at the 80% level.

Dependent Versus Independent Experiments

Note that the experiment to be performed, that is, which roulette wheel to use, depends on whether the frog is on pad 1 or pad 2. We are dealing with a sequence of dependent experiments; the experiment to be performed depends on the outcome of the previous experiment. Contrast this to the Bernoulli process (Chapter 3, Section 6), which can be looked upon as a sequence of coin tossings. The probability of tossing heads or tails never changes; the experiments are *independent* of each other. Outcomes do not influence the experiments.

Note that in a Markov process the experiment depends on the *last* outcome, but on on earlier outcomes. The probability of landing on a particular pad does not depend on where the frog came from, but only on where the frog is.

> In a Markov process each experiment depends only on the outcome of the last experiment.

Equilibrium Market Shares

So far we assumed that ACB takes no advertising action and that the shares of the market stay the same; that is, they are in equilibrium. But suppose ACB starts a purely defensive advertising campaign which tries to convince customers to stay loyal but has no influence whatever on consumers using competitive products. Assume that the first line of the transition probability matrix in Figure 15.3 suddenly changes to the first line shown in Figure 15.7. Note that the probability of a repeat purchase is increased from .6 to .7 and that the probability of losing a customer is decreased from .4 to .3. The second line of the matrix remains un-

	TO	
FROM	**ACB**	**Comps**
ACB	.7	.3
Comps	.1	.9

FIGURE 15.7 Transition probability matrix for defensive advertising campaign.

changed, as consumers not using ACB coffee are not influenced by a purely defensive campaign. Thus ACB still gains consumers from the competitors at a probability of .1, and consumers still stay with the competitors at a probability of .9. What happens to the market shares?

Compare the situation with the one on a winter morning when on awakening you turn up the thermostat. The house will not suddenly get warm, but the temperature will begin to increase. Increasing the temperature is designated as **transient** temperature. Eventually your house reaches a **steady-state** temperature corresponding to the thermostat setting.

The same happens when ACB begins to advertise. As the months go by, the market share increases until a new equilibrium, steady-state market share is reached. Assuming that you have adequate furnace capacity, your house will heat up rapidly, and you are primarily interested in the equilibrium temperature. You will see later that the equilibrium market share is reached fairly rapidly, and so usually management is primarily interested in the equilibrium market share. Therefore, we postpone discussing the transient behavior of market share and proceed directly to compute the equilibrium share.

Calculating Equilibrium Market Shares

To solve our problem, we redraw in Figure 15.8 the tree first drawn in Figure 15.6. This time, however, we do not know the market share and so replace the probability .2 by the unknown probability S_1 and the probability .8 by an unknown probability S_2. Thus S_1 and S_2 are the unknown **equilibrium probabilities** that a consumer buys from ACB when the defensive advertising campaign is in effect. You can also look upon S_1 and S_2 as the fractional expressions of the market share. Designate by S_1' the probability that a consumer will buy from ACB in the second month. Following the same argument as in Figure 15.6, we must have

$$S_1' = .7S_1 + .1S_2$$

We are interested in the equilibrium market share, meaning that probabilities stay the same. Thus we must have

$$S_1' = S_1$$

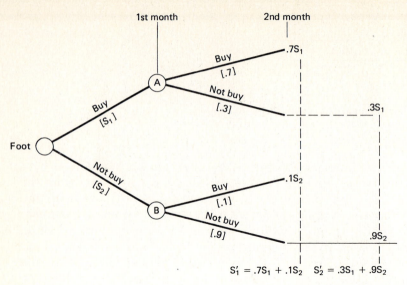

FIGURE 15.8
Determining equilibrium market shares with the aid of a tree diagram.

$$S'_1 = .7S_1 + .1S_2 \qquad S'_2 = .3S_1 + .9S_2$$

Consequently,

$$S_1 = .7S_1 + .1S_2 = .7S_1 + .1(1 - S_1)$$

Solving for S_1, we obtain

$$S_1 = .25$$

Naturally,

$$S_2 = 1 - S_1 = .75$$

We could also compute S_2 using the relationship

$$S_2 = S_2' = .3S_1 + .9S_2$$

from Figure 15.8. We of course would get the same answer.

After the campaign is in effect for a sufficiently long time, ACB will have 25% of the market. Sales will be $25 million; profit before considering the cost of advertising is 20% of this, or $5 million. Subtracting the $500,000 cost of advertising, we find that ACB will net $4.5 million. Thus the long-run effect of the defensive advertising campaign is beneficial, because profits increase by $.5 million dollars. What about the aggressive advertising campaign?

Management has information to indicate that the aggressive campaign will increase the probability of gaining a customer from the competitor from the previous .1 to .15, as shown by the transition probability matrix in Figure 15.9 (lower left corner). Now only 85% of the buyers of competitors will continue buying from them. The first line in the matrix remains unchanged, because the aggressive advertising campaign is not addressed to customers of ACB.

The calculations to be performed are precisely the same, and so we leave this computation as an exercise. We state only that the aggressive campaign leads to a market share of 27.3% and to a gross profit of

FROM	TO	
	ACB	Comps
ACB	.6	.4
Comps	.15	.85

FIGURE 15.9 Transition probability matrix for aggressive advertising campaign.

$5,454,000. The net profit, after paying for the advertising campaign, is $4,954,000. Thus it is seen that of the three alternatives—doing nothing, advertising defensively, or advertising aggressively—the best choice of action lies in aggressive advertising.

When There Are More Than Two States

In our problem we had two states and determined the equilibrium probabilities by solving two linear equations with two unknowns. When there are three states, we need to solve three linear equations with three unknowns, and so on. When there are many states, special computer-based solution techniques provide quick and accurate answers.

15.3 MARKOV MODEL OF BLOOD BANKS

In Section 5.1 we studied the problem of selling strawberries, a highly perishable commodity. In Chapter 9 we studied inventory control and included the situation when the demand is uncertain. Now we are ready to study an important inventory control problem: the control of blood banks to provide blood for transfusions to patients. In Section 15.7 we shall describe an application dealing with this problem; now we present a simplified Markov model for dealing with the problem.

   The demand for blood in a hospital is a perishable commodity because blood has a limited lifetime during which it can be transfused to patients. After this time span it becomes *outdated* and must be discarded. The problem is how to balance most efficiently availability and the outdating of blood. So the problem we consider now is how to determine the number of units of blood to be shipped to a hospital to replenish inventory in the blood bank. While in Section 15.7 we shall consider the problem under realistic conditions, here, as an introduction, we shall make some simplifying assumptions.

The Thought Experiment

Consider a perishable commodity with a lifetime of only 2 days and with a demand probability mass function of

Number of units demanded	0	1	2	3
Probability of demand	.11	.22	.29	.38

We also need to specify the inventory policy to be used. We assume that the inventory control policy is first-in-first-out (FIFO), meaning that the oldest commodity is always used first. Each morning a fixed number of fresh commodity arrives, and the problem is to determine the best quantity of fresh commodity to be delivered then.

Note that the expected demand per day is

$$.11 \times 0 + .22 \times 1 + .29 \times 2 + .38 \times 3 = 1.94$$

Consider now a thought experiment where two units of commodity are delivered every morning. Replacing the demand probability mass function with an appropriate roulette wheel, you can generate daily demand and calculate inventory levels. Figure 15.10 shows the result of such a thought experiment.

In line 1 we assume that we start with an inventory of 6 units in the morning. The asterisks show that there are 2 fresh units, 2 one-day-old and 2 two-day-old units. The demand in line 1 happens to be 3 units. So 3 units are used up. According to FIFO policy, the oldest commodity is used first. Thus the 2 two-day-old and 1 of the one-day-old units will be used. As shown in line 1, in the evening there will still be 2 fresh units but only 1 one-day-old unit and no two-day-old units.* There is no shortage, and no commodity is discarded.

Now we are ready to consider the next day in line 2. There will be 3 units from the day before and 2 more delivered, a total inventory of 5 units in the morning. There will be 2 fresh units, as shown by the two asterisks, 2 one-day-old units, and 1 two-day-old unit. Assume again that the demand is 3, and so 3 units are used. In the evening there will be only 2 fresh units left, as the 2 one-day-old and 1 two-day-old units will be used up. There is still no shortage and no commodity discarded. And so, line by line, you can verify the inventory records in Figure 15.10.

---

* We assume that the commodity does not age during the day, only at night.

| | | MORNING | | | | | EVENING | | | | |
	INVENTORY	Fresh	One-Day-Old	Two-Day-Old	DEMAND	USAGE	Fresh	One-Day-Old	Two-Day-Old	SHORT	DISCARDED
1	6	**	**	**	3	3	**	*	—	0	0
2	5	**	**	*	3	3	**	—	—	0	0
3	4	**	**	—	3	3	*	—	—	0	0
4	3	**	*	—	3	3	—	—	—	0	0
5	2	**	—	—	3	2	—	—	—	1	0
6	2	**	—	—	0	0	**	—	—	0	0
7	4	**	**	—	0	0	**	*	*	0	0
8	6	**	**	**	0	0	**	**	**	0	2

FIGURE 15.10 Inventory record for the control of a perishable commodity. The asterisks represent units of commodity.

	MORNING		DEMAND	USAGE	DISCARDED	SHORTAGE	EVENING INVENTORY	NEXT MORNING		PROBABILITY OF DEMAND	TRANSITION PROBABILITY
	State	Inventory						Inventory	State		
1	1	2	0	0	0	0	2	4	3	.11	.11
2	1	2	1	1	0	0	1	3	2	.22	.22
3	1	2	2	2	0	0	0	2	1	.29 ⎫	.67
4	1	2	3	2	0	1	0	2	1	.38 ⎭	
5	2	3	0	0	0	0	3	5	4	.11	.11
6	2	3	1	1	0	0	2	4	3	.22	.22
7	2	3	2	2	0	0	1	3	2	.29	.29
8	2	3	3	3	0	0	0	2	1	.38	.38
9	3	4	0	0	0	0	4	6	5	.11	.11
10	3	4	1	1	0	0	3	5	4	.22	.22
11	3	4	2	2	0	0	2	4	3	.29	.29
12	3	4	3	3	0	0	1	3	2	.38	.38
13	4	5	0	0	1	0	5	6	5	.11 ⎫	.33
14	4	5	1	1	0	0	4	6	5	.22 ⎭	
15	4	5	2	2	0	0	3	5	4	.29	.29
16	4	5	3	3	0	0	2	4	3	.38	.38
17	5	6	0	0	2	0	6	6	5	.11 ⎫	.62
18	5	6	1	1	1	0	4	6	5	.22 ⎬	
19	5	6	2	2	0	0	3	6	5	.29 ⎭	
20	5	6	3	3	0	0	2	5	4	.38	.38

FIGURE 15.11 Calculation of transition probabilities.

Our problem is to determine the expected number of units (1) short, (2) outdated-discarded, and (3) used.

The Markov Model

We define the state of the system as the number of units of commodity in inventory in the morning. Note that there are at least 2 units in inventory every morning because 2 fresh units are delivered. Note also that there cannot be more than 6 units in inventory because after 2 days units are outdated and discarded. Thus states 1, 2, 3, 4, and 5 correspond to morning inventories of 2, 3, 4, 5, and 6 units. Changes in states of the system are governed by a Markov process, and in Figure 15.11 we show how to determine the transition probabilities.

In the first four lines it is assumed that the system is in state 1, meaning that the morning inventory is 2. The demand can be 0, 1, 2, and 3. So as the figure shows, the number of units used will be 0, 1, 2, and 2. No units will be discarded. The first three lines show that there will be no shortage, but the fourth line shows that when the demand is 3, there will be a shortage of 1. Now we can compute the evening inventory as 2,

1, 0, and 0, respectively. So the next morning the inventory will be, after the 2 fresh units are added, 4, 3, 2, and 2, respectively. And the following morning the states will be 3, 2, 1, and 1.

Now we need to compute the transition probability. Line 1 shows that the probability of moving from state 1 to state 3 is the same as the probability of 0 demand, which is .11. Line 2 shows that the probability of moving from state 1 to state 2 equals the probability of the demand being 1, which .22. However, to compute the probability of moving from state 1 to state 1 (meaning no change in state), we must be a little more careful. Namely, this can happen in two different ways: The demand may be 2 or 3 with the respective probabilities of .29 and .38. Thus the probability of the system moving from state 1 to state 1 equals .29 + .38 = .67.

The system cannot go from state 1 to either state 4 or state 5, and so these transition probabilities are zero. In Figure 15.12 we now begin to build up the transition probability matrix. In row 1 we show the transition probabilities from state 1 to states 1, 2, 3, 4, and 5. The probabilities are in reverse order to our computations in Figure 15.11 and equal .67, .22, .11, 0, and 0 respectively.

The other rows of the transition probability matrix in Figure 15.12 are computed in a similar manner by using the probabilities from Figure 15.11 This then completes the calculations involved in determining the transition probability matrix.

Using a computer, we have calculated the equilibrium probabilities for each state, and here we merely report the results:

$$P[\text{state} = 1] = S_1 = .187$$

$$P[\text{state} = 2] = S_2 = .162$$

$$P[\text{state} = 3] = S_3 = .194$$

$$P[\text{state} = 4] = S_4 = .215$$

$$P[\text{state} = 5] = S_5 = .242$$

The Answers

What is the expected number of shortages per day?

The only way a shortage can occur, as you can verify in line 4 of Figure 15.11 is if (1) the morning inventory is 2, that is, the system is in

FROM STATE 1	TO STATE 2				
	1	2	3	4	5
1	.67	.22	.11	0	0
2	.38	.29	.22	.11	0
3	0	.38	.29	.22	.11
4	0	0	.38	.29	.33
5	0	0	0	.38	.62

FIGURE 15.12 Transition probability matrix.

state 1, or (2) the demand is 3. In all other cases there will be no shortage because the demand cannot exceed 3 units. So

expected number of shortages = (equilibrium probability of state 1)

$$\times \text{ probability of [demand} = 3]$$

$$= .187 \times .38 = .071 \text{ units}$$

What is the expected number of units outdated per day? This can happen in three different ways.

1. Line 13 in Figure 15.11 Morning inventory is 5, meaning that the system is in state 4 and the demand 0. There is 1 unit outdated. The conditional expected value is

$$P[\text{state} = 4] \times P[\text{demand} = 0] = .215 \times .11 = .0237 \text{ unit}$$

2. Line 17 in Figure 15.11 The conditional expected value is

$$P[\text{state} = 5] \times P[\text{demand} = 0] \times 2 = .242 \times .11 \times 2 = .0532 \text{ unit}$$

because 2 units are outdated.

3. Line 18 in Figure 15.12 The conditional expected value is

$$P[\text{state} = 5] \times P[\text{demand} = 1] = .242 \times .22 = .0532 \text{ unit}$$

Thus the expected number of units outdated = .0237 + .0532 + .0532 = .1301 unit. Also,

expected number of units used =

expected demand − expected number outdated = 1.94 − .1301
$$= 1.8099 \text{ units}$$

Note then that the Markov model allows computation of performance of the inventory control system. To make a decision as to how many units should be delivered each morning, the following three steps must be undertaken:

Step 1. Calculate the performance for various inventory control policies.

Step 2. Establish a preference criterion in terms of an objective function.

Step 3. Choose the solution which maximizes (or minimizes, as the case may be) the objective function.

15.4 MARKET SHARE DYNAMICS

So far we have studied only the equilibrium or steady-state values of the market share. When you buy a furnace, you want to know how fast it will heat your house. In the same way management of the ACB Corp. wants to know how long it will take for the advertising campaign to take hold. Let us calculate now how long it will take with the defensive advertising campaign for the market share to rise from 20 to 25%.

In Figure 15.13 we show brand switching from one month to another. In January ACB has 20 customers out of 100, 70% of whom will stay loyal. So, as the upper left-hand corner shows, there will be 14 consumers buying again; 30% or 6 of the customers are lost to competitors.

The lower left-hand corner shows that out of 80 consumers who bought in January from competitors, 10% or 8 will switch to ACB. Thus in February there will be 14 + 8 = 22 customers of ACB. The competitors will have 6 + 72 = 78. Note that the market share does not jump suddenly to 25% but only to 22%.

We now have the February market share. In the same way we can compute the March market share for ACB:

$$.7 \times .22 + .1 \times .78 = .232$$

The competitors' share is .768 in March.

In Figure 15.14 we show the graph of how the market share increases, that is, the dynamics of market share. Strictly speaking, the market share *never* reaches the 25%, but from the practical point of view, very rapidly the difference between the actual market share and the equilibrium share of 25% becomes negligible. For example, you can verify that in April the market share will be 23.92%.

The growth in market share for the aggressive advertising campaign can be computed in exactly the same manner and is left as an exercise.

15.5 TWO-STATE MARKOV MODELS

In Section 15.2 we calculated the equilibrium market share for Aromatic Coffee Bean Corp. (ACB) but omitted calculating the time it takes to get to equilibrium. Now we present a formula for determining both the

	TO		
FROM	**ACB**	**Competitors**	
ACB	14 customers of ACB (70% of 20) stay with ACB	6 customers of ACB (30% of 20) switch to competitors	There are 20 customers of ACB in January
Competitors	8 customers of competitors (10% of 80) switch to ACB	72 customers of competitors (90% of 80) stay with competitors	There are 80 customers of competitors in January.
	There will be 22 customers of ACB in February	There will be 78 customers of competitors in February	100 consumers are considered

FIGURE 15.13 Summary of brand switching for defensive advertising campaign.

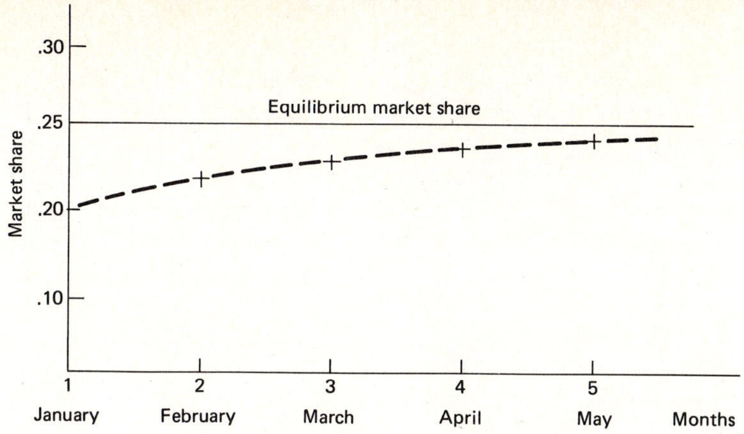

FIGURE 15.14
Growth of Market share for defensive advertising campaign.

equilibrium probabilities and the transient performance of two-state Markov processes.

First introduce the notation shown in Figure 15.15 where p_1 designates the probability that consumers stay in state 1 and p_2 the corresponding probability for state 2. Using this notation, we can redraw the tree from Figure 15.8 as shown in Figure 15.16 and establish the relationships among market shares:

$$S_1' = p_1 S_1 + (1 - p_2)S_2$$

But

$$S_2 = 1 - S_1$$

and for equilibrium there is no change in market share:

$$S_1' = S_1$$

Thus,

$$S_1 = p_1 S_1 + (1 - p_2)(1 - S_1)$$

Solve for S_1:

$$S_1 = \frac{1 - p_2}{2 - p_1 - p_2}$$

Also,

$$S_2 = 1 - S_1 = \frac{1 - p_1}{2 - p_1 - p_2}$$

	TO	
FROM	**ACB**	**Comps**
ACB	p_1	$1 - p_1$
Comps	$1 - p_2$	p_2

FIGURE 15.15 Transition probability matrix for two-state Markov process.

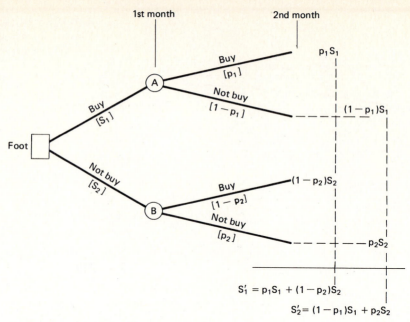

1st month   2nd month

Foot

Buy [S₁]

Not buy [S₂]

A

B

Buy [p₁]

Not buy [1−p₁]

Buy [1−p₂]

Not buy [p₂]

$p_1 S_1$

$(1-p_1)S_1$

$(1-p_2)S_2$

$p_2 S_2$

$$S_1' = p_1 S_1 + (1 - p_2)S_2$$
$$S_2' = (1 - p_1)S_1 + p_2 S_2$$

FIGURE 15.16 Representation of two-state Markov process with tree diagram.

Growth Rate of Market Share

In Figure 15.14 we show graphically the way the market share approaches the equilibrium share. Now we present a formula to compute the growth of market share.

Designate by D the difference between the actual and equilibrium shares in month 1 and by D', in month 2. Then, as we show at the end of this Section,

$$\frac{D'}{D} = F \qquad \text{or} \qquad D' = FD$$

where

$$F = p_1 + p_2 - 1$$

Application to Aromatic Coffee Bean Corporation

We have

$$p_1 = .7, \qquad p_2 = .9$$

and so

$$S_1 = \frac{1 - .9}{2 - .7 - .9} = .25$$

$$S_2 = 1 - S_1 = .75$$

$$F = .7 + .9 - 1 = .6$$

The initial market share is .2, and so the January difference D is

$$D = .25 - .20 = .05$$

The February difference is

$$FD = .6 \times .0500 = .03$$

and the February share is

$$.25 - .03 = .22$$

The March difference is

$$FD = .6 \times .03 = .6^2 \times .05 = .018$$

and the March share is

$$.25 - .018 = .232$$

The April difference is

$$FD = .6 \times .018 = .6^3 \times .05 = .0108$$

and the April share is

$$.25 - .0108 = .2392$$

After 6 months the difference is

$$.6^6 \times .05 = .0466 \times .05 = .00233$$

Note then that the actual market does indeed get rapidly close to the equilibrium share. Namely, we started with an initial difference of .05, that is, 20% of .25, and in the sixth month we have a difference of .000233, that is, only about .1%.

Derivation Formula*

$$D = S_1 - \frac{1 - p_2}{2 - p_1 - p_2}$$

$$D' = S_1' - \frac{1 - p_2}{2 - p_1 - p_2}$$

But

$$S_1' = p_1 S_1 + (1 - p_2)(1 - S_1)$$

and so

$$D' = [p_1 S_1 + (1 - p_2)(1 - S_1)] - \frac{1 - p_2}{2 - p_1 - p_2}$$

---

* Study of the derivation may be omitted.

Thus,

$$F = \frac{D'}{D} = \frac{[p_1 S_1 + (1 - p_2)(1 - S_1)] - (1 - p_2)/(2 - p_1 - p_2)}{S_1 - (1 - p_2)/(2 - p_1 - p_2)}$$

Multiply the numerator and denominator by $2 - p_1 - p_2$

$$F = \frac{[p_1 S_1 + (1 - p_2)(1 - S_1)](2 - p_1 - p_2) - (1 - p_2)}{S_1(2 - p_1 - p_2) - (1 - p_2)}$$

After extensive manipulation, you get

$$F = p_1 + p_2 - 1$$

15.6 HOW TO CONTROL ACCOUNTS RECEIVABLE

The You-May-Charge-All (YMCA) Credit Corp. is alarmed by the increase in costs associated with accounts receivable. Various proposals are being considered to decrease costs. For example, it is proposed that a more strict scoring system for accepting accounts should be introduced to eliminate high-risk accounts. Another possibility is to introduce penalties for late payments, or again YMCA is considering changing their method of collecting doubtful accounts. For example, campaigns of phoning delinquent customers or following up by strongly worded warnings are being considered. To determine what action should be taken, a quantitative analysis of the accounts receivable problem is initiated.

To simplify, assume that YMCA classifies accounts into three classes: good, delinquent, and doubtful. We shall not discuss the specifics of how the account classification is performed, since this is a matter of business policy and varies from firm to firm.

Figure 15.17 shows how the accounts switch from month to month. The right-hand column shows, for example, that out of 100 accounts 60 are good in the month of May. The upper left-hand corner shows that 42, that is, 70% stay good in June. Out of the 60 good accounts, 30% or 18 become delinquent in June, and none of the good accounts become doubtful in June.

You can give a similar interpretation to the other numbers in Figure 15.17. Also, by adding columns you observe that there will be 45 good, 38 delinquent, and 17 doubtful accounts in June.

Note then that the switching of accounts can be described by a Markov model, and the transition probability matrix is given in Figure 15.18.

In Figure 15.19 we now compute the distribution of accounts in July. For example, you can see in the upper left-hand corner that 70% of the 45 good accounts, that is, $.7 \times 45 = 31.5$ accounts, will stay good; $.3 \times 45 = 13.5$ good accounts will become delinquent; etc. By adding the columns, you observe that in July there will be only 35.3 good, 39.7

FROM	TO			MAY
	Good	Delinquent	Doubtful	
Good	42	18	0	60
	70%	30%	0%	
Delinquent	3	18	9	30
	10%	60%	30%	
Doubtful	0	2	8	10
	0%	20%	80%	
June	45	38	17	100

FIGURE 15.17 Summary record of account switching.

delinquent, and 25.0 doubtful accounts. What will be the equilibrium distribution of the accounts?

We can repeat the same calculations as in Figure 15.19, but now in the right-hand column we should write the unknown probabilities of "good," "delinquent," and "doubtful," that is S_1, S_2, and S_3 (Figure 15.20). The bottom row probabilities are obtained by adding the columns.

$$S_1' = .7S_1 + .1S_2$$

$$S_2' = .3S_1 + .6S_2 + .2S_3$$

$$S_3' = \qquad .3S_2 + .8S_3$$

We want to compute the equilibrium probabilities, so must have

$$S_1' = S_1, \qquad S_2' = S_2, \qquad S_3' = S_3$$

Thus we get

$$\text{Eq. (1):} \quad S_1 = .7S_1 + .1S_2$$

$$\text{Eq. (2):} \quad S_2 = .3S_1 + .6S_2 + .2S_3$$

$$\text{Eq. (3):} \quad S_3 = \qquad .3S_2 + .8S_3$$

From Eq. (1),

$$S_2 = 2S_1$$

From Eq. (3),

$$S_3 = \tfrac{3}{2}S_2$$

FROM	TO		
	Good	Delinquent	Doubtful
Good	.7	.3	0
Delinquent	.1	.6	.3
Doubtful	0	.2	.8

FIGURE 15.18 Transition probability matrix for account switching.

FROM	TO			JUNE
	Good	Delinquent	Doubtful	
Good	.7 × 45 = 31.5	.3 × 45 = 13.5	0	45
Delinquent	.1 × 38 = 3.8	.6 × 38 = 22.8	.3 × 38 = 11.4	38
Doubtful	0	.2 × 17 = 3.4	.8 × 17 = 13.6	17
July	35.3	39.7	25.0	100

FIGURE 15.19 Distribution of accounts in the month of July.

Therefore,

$$S_3 = \tfrac{9}{2} S_1$$

But,

$$S_1 + S_2 + S_3 = 1$$

or

$$S_1 + 3S_1 + \tfrac{9}{2} S_1 = 1$$

Therefore,

$$S_1 = \tfrac{2}{17} = .1176$$

$$S_2 = \tfrac{6}{17} = .3529$$

$$S_3 = \tfrac{9}{17} = .5294$$

Thus in equilibrium there will be only 11.76 good accounts, an alarming decrease from the initial 60 good accounts. The number of delinquent accounts does not change much; it increases from 30 to 35.29. But the number of doubtful accounts increases from 10 to 52.94.

You can see then that YMCA is properly concerned about the degradation of the quality of their accounts receivable. We shall not continue the analysis to its economic completion because our prime purpose here is to demonstrate how Markov models are to be used in such an accounts receivable problem. It suffices to say that YMCA must

FROM	TO			MONTH 1
	Good	Delinquent	Doubtful	
Good	$.7S_1$	$.3S_1$	0	S_1
Delinquent	$.1S_2$	$.6S_2$	$.3S_2$	S_2
Doubtful	0	$.2S_3$	$.8S_3$	S_3
Month 2	S_1'	S_2'	S_3'	

FIGURE 15.20 Change in distribution of accounts from one month to another.

determine the various alternative actions and the transition probability matrices associated with each action. Then, by determining the equilibrium distribution of the accounts and the associated cost and profit, a decision can be made as to the optimum action to be taken.

15.7 BLOOD DISTRIBUTION SYSTEMS: A SUCCESSFUL APPLICATION

In Section 15.3 we presented a Markov model for controlling the inventory of blood banks. Now we present a successful application using this type of model.

The Blood Bank Problem*

Each year over 2 million Americans need the right type of blood from 6000 hospital blood banks in the United States. If the right blood is not available, medical complications and/or postponement of surgery can result, which leads to unnecessary human suffering, extra days of hospitalization, emergency shipments of blood, and other additional costs.

The traditional approach to resolving this problem consists in the establishment of regional blood centers which then supply blood to hospital blood banks. Each hospital orders blood from the center as the demand for blood is estimated, and the regional blood center decides, based on availability, what quantity of blood to ship. This approach leads not only to delivery uncertainties and delays, much waste of blood, and extra cost of transportation but also to an adversary relationship between management of the regional center and the hospitals. The efficient management of blood banks is a complex and difficult task, and executives of the Greater New York Blood Program decided to turn to quantitative methods of management and computer-based systems to resolve the situation. With the aid of quantitative techniques it was possible to examine alternative policies for controlling blood banks and to develop a satisfactory and efficient policy. First we describe the model used in this work.

The Markov Model

In Section 15.3 we already discussed a simplified Markov model for controlling the blood bank in a single hospital. We assumed a life span of 2 days, though the actual life span is 21 days. We assumed a single

---

* Adapted from Erich Brodheim and G. P. Prastacos, "The Long Island Blood Distribution System as a Prototype for Regional Blood Management," *Interfaces*, Vol. 9, No. 5, Nov. 1979, pp. 3–20. Also see the following by the same authors: "PBDS: A Decision Support System for Regional Blood Management," *Management Science*, Vol. 26, No. 5, May 1980, pp. 451–463. This work received the Management Science Achievement Award of the Institute of Management Science in 1979.

random variable in the model, namely the demand for blood transfusion. We also assumed a single system parameter, a decision variable which specifies the quantity of blood to be delivered each morning to each hospital. This implies that once blood is delivered to a hospital it stays there. The study of regional blood centers distributing blood to many hospitals shows that such a system leads to waste of blood. A more efficient system can be obtained if some method is employed to enable hospitals to return some blood. Specifically, it was found that when fresh blood is received at a hospital and not used soon, it is more efficient to return the blood to the regional blood center for transshipment to other hospitals. This then led to the concept that hospitals be provided with (1) *rotational* blood to be returned to the regional blood center if not used soon and (2) *retention* units to be kept until either transfused or discarded after 21 days.

Thus there is a need for a model which determines how many rotational and how many retention units should be sent to each hospital. Consequently a new system parameter, the desired inventory level of rotational units in hospitals, was introduced. In Section 15.3 we did not consider this system parameter, but it must be included in the more comprehensive model.

Finally the question is raised as to whether it is efficient to ship to every hospital every day. In fact it is not, and so the concept of periodic delivery was developed, meaning that blood is delivered to some hospitals every day, to others every second or third day, and so on. Thus the four system parameters to be determined for each hospital are the following:

1. Length of period between blood deliveries to each hospital
2. Number of rotational units shipped at each delivery at each hospital
3. Number of retention units shipped at each delivery at each hospital
4. Desired inventory of rotational units to be kept at each hospital

Setting these four system parameters is called the establishment of an inventory distribution policy.

Now we must consider the random variables of the problem. In Section 15.3 we assumed a single random variable—the demand for blood transfusion. However, closer examination of the operation of hospitals reveals that a single variable is not adequate, namely when surgery is scheduled for the day blood is earmarked for transfusion as specified by the demand. However, as surgery is undertaken, some of the blood is not used and is returned to the hospital blood bank. Thus a second random variable, the *usage* of blood, is significant when designing the system. To summarize, there is a need to specify two statistically dependent random variables:

1. The *demand* for units of blood
2. The actual *usage* of units of blood

To develop an efficient inventory distribution policy, it is necessary to compare and evaluate various policies. The first important measure of the performance of a system is the expected number of units of blood short per day, or *shortage rate*, at each hospital.

The second important performance measure is the expected number of units of blood outdated (discarded) per day, or the *outdate rate*. This leads to the cost of wasted blood—a commodity that is difficult to obtain.

Could both of these performance measures be minimized simultaneously? As you know, in many or most problems it is not possible to minimize two objective functions simultaneously. However, in this problem it is possible, and the following mathematical theorem can be proved (derivation not included here).

> Policy Theorem 1. Optimal policy minimizes both shortage rate and outdate rate.

As a consequence of this theorem there is no need to determine the cost of shortages and outdates, because both of these costs will be minimized simultaneously, independent of the respective costs. Now the question arises of how to distribute blood among the various hospitals. Here again we state an important theorem derived by mathematical analysis:

> Policy Theorem 2. Optimal inventory distribution policy equalizes outdate and shortage rates among hospitals.

In addition to these two *objective* measures of performance, there is also a third important *subjective* measure that must be considered. Namely, when not enough blood is in the blood bank, management of a hospital feels "uncomfortable" and expresses concern over the inadequacy of the blood supply. To meet this judgmental consideration, the concept of the *replacement factor* is introduced, which makes hospitals "feel safe." Specifically, a safety policy is established, meaning that at each period a minimum shipment, which is above the mean usage rate, is delivered. For example, a policy based on judgment may be established which specifies a shipment of 110% of the expected usage at each delivery to each hospital. This policy is designated as using a safety factor of 110% or 1.10.

Optimization

Development of the best inventory distribution policy begins by establishing performance *targets* for the following three system parameters:

1. Shortage rate

2. Outdate rate
3. Minimum acceptable safety factor

Note that because of the policy theorem already stated these parameters are the same for every hospital.

By using these parameters as input, it is possible to develop a mathematical programming model which when solved calculates the following two-system parameters:

1. Minimum quantity of fresh blood to be collected by the regional blood bank
2. Optimal inventory distribution policy for each hospital consisting of the following four system parameters: (a) length of period between deliveries, (b) number of rotational units shipped, (c) number of retention units shipped, and (d) desired inventory level of rotational units.

System Operation

The system was developed and installed first at the Long Island Blood Services Division of the Greater New York Program. To implement such a system, the following four important activities must be performed:

1. Collect demand and usage data from hospitals.
2. Set performance targets, and policies.
3. Calculate optimal inventory distribution policy.
4. Monitor demand and usage levels, and adjust the system to changes if necessary.

Efficient operation of the system could not be performed without the use of computers. With the aid of minicomputers each hospital monitors demand, usage, and inventory. Information is transmitted to regional blood centers where all activities of the system are monitored and adjustments are made as time goes on. Note that the computer is used not only for processing the data involved in the system but also for making decisions as required on shipments to various hospitals.

A Decision Support System

In developing the blood control system, the principal investigators called the system a decision support system for the following reasons.

Note first that performance targets are set by judgment and are not derived from an optimization model, because at the regional blood center decision makers are faced with several objectives, some of which are conflicting and so are resolved by subjective judgments and performance trade-offs. Furthermore, quantitative cost measurement of system performance is well nigh impossible due to the many judgmental and human factors involved. Also, a blood distribution policy must conform to local laws and medical and management policies. Note also that it is necessary to install not merely an efficient allocation of a scarce resource but also a "fair" one. A final reason that this system is described as a decision support system stems from the fact that the computer forms an absolutely essential basis for the system. Not only are data collected on the system so that an up-to-the-minute picture of the situation is provided to decision makers, but also finding the best inventory distribution policy requires solution of nonlinear programming problems on the computer.

Advantages and Benefits

Introduction of the system based on quantitative methods led to dramatic improvements. Prior to installing the system, the outdate rate was 20%, which was reduced to 4%. This converts to a $500,000 savings per year in avoiding waste of blood. In addition, prior to installing the system there were 7.8 deliveries on the average per week, which was reduced to 4.2 deliveries per week. This translates to a savings of $100,000 per year in transportation cost, thus resulting in a total direct cost saving of $600,000 per year.

However, the intangible benefits, which would be very difficult to translate into dollars, are at least equally significant. First, the availability of blood to patients is improved. Second, the relationship between managers of regional blood centers and hospitals is improved, and earlier "adversary" relationships are replaced by a cooperative arrangement between regional and hospital management.

In the words of Johannah Pindyck, Vice President and Director of the Greater New York Blood Program, "This system has given us a mechanism to do exactly what we urgently needed—*Take the Crisis Out of Blood Banking.* We have offered to our hospitals a rational, effective functioning system—which will soon be extended both throughout our service area and elsewhere in the United States and abroad. It is not unfair to state that this program *can* and *will* contribute to improvement in health care throughout our nation and therefore touch each and every one of us at some time in our life."

15.8 NON-MARKOVIAN PROCESSES: A DIALOG

Q. *You mentioned stochastic processes but discussed only Markov processes. Can you give an example of a non-Markovian process?*

A. Consider an urn containing 10 black and 10 red balls. You draw 1 ball and replace it. What kind of process is this?

Q. *This is a Bernoulli process, and the probability is one-half of drawing either a black or red ball. What's new here?*

A. Nothing yet. But now consider the process invented by George Polya, a mathematician of Hungarian origin. After you draw a ball, replace it but add a ball of the same color. Suppose you draw a black ball. You put back *two* black balls. If you draw a red ball, you put back *two* red balls. Now this is not a Bernoulli or, in fact, a Markovian process. Namely, the probability of drawing a black or red ball changes as time goes on, and the particular value of the probability depends on how many red or black balls happen to be in the urn at a particular instant. This depends on the history of the color of balls already drawn.

Q. *Can you give a practical example?*

A. Consider again the coffee problem described in Section 15.1. If a customer buys coffee many times in succession from ACB, it is more likely that he will continue buying coffee from ACB than another customer who just happened to switch over from a competitor for the first time. Brand loyalty strengthens as a customer keeps buying the same brand. Thus, a more accurate analysis of the problem should factor in these changes in probabilities. These are non-Markovian processes and have been studied extensively to describe consumer behavior.

Q. *Here is another matter. You studied the situation when ACB starts to advertise. But you assumed that the competitors sit still and do nothing in response to the advertising campaign. What if the competitors respond with a counterstrategy?*

A. Now you have a more complex situation. You would have to draw a decision tree, consider the various possibilities, and apply techniques of decision analysis in combination with the theory of Markov processes. The problem gets more complex, but the techniques of solution presented in this textbook apply equally well.

SUMMARY

1. There is a variety of managerial situations where uncertainty dominates, but the situation can be modeled by Markov processes.

2. Markov processes consist of a sequence of random experiments where the experiment itself depends only on the outcome of the last experiment.

3. While it is impossible to predict *which* state will be next in a Markov process, the probability of *what* the next state will be is known with certainty and is given by the transition probability matrix.

4. To apply Markov models, a careful distinction must be made between (1) the equilibrium and transient solution of the system and (2) the transition probabilities and state probabilities.

5. Stochastic processes are more general than Markov processes, and the probability laws governing their behavior are more complex.

6. When the probability matrix suddenly changes in a Markov proc-

ess, a new Markov process starts, governed by the new transition probability matrix. Thus managerial decision making does not result in controlling the outcomes; it results in changes in transition probabilities.

7. In a two-state Markov process the equilibrium market shares are given by

$$S_1 = \frac{1 - p_2}{2 - p_1 - p_2}$$

$$S_2 = \frac{1 - p_1}{2 - p_1 - p_2}$$

and the market share growth is given by

$$\frac{D'}{D} = p_1 + p_2 - 1$$

where

P_1 = probability that the process stays in state 1

P_2 = probability that the process stays in state 2

SECTION EXERCISES

1. *How to Influence Consumer Behavior*

1.1 Refer to Figure 15.2. Suppose that ACB had considered 200 customers rather than 100. Prepare the new version of Figure 15.2 which reflects this change.

1.2 Suppose that ACB has a subsidiary which sells tea. A study of 1000 tea consumers for the years 1981 and 1982 showed that from the first year to the second the number of consumers

1. Staying with ACB was 420
2. Switching to ACB from competitors was 150

ACB's market share in 1981 was .60. With this information,
   a. Make a table similar to Figure 15.2.
   b. Make a transition probability matrix similar to Figure 15.3.
   c. Determine ACB's market share in 1982.

1.3 Suppose that ACB has a subsidiary which sells frozen peas. A study of 500 pea consumers for the months of June and July showed that from the first year to the second the number of consumers

1. Staying with ACB was 120
2. Switching to ACB from competitors was 150

ACB's market share in June was .30. With this information,
   a. Make a table similar to Figure 15.2.
   b. Make a transition probability matrix similar to Figure 15.3.

c. Using Figure 15.3 and the transition probability matrix you made in part b, evaluate the relative differences in market position and status of ACB for these two products.

d. Define an aggressive strategy for ACB.

1.4 Suppose that ACB has a subsidiary which sells macaroons. A study of 5000 macaroon consumers for the years of 1979 and 1980 showed that from the first year to the second the number of consumers

1. Staying with ACB was 3000
2. Switching to ACB from competitors was 500

ACB's market share in 1979 was .80. With this information,

a. Make a table similar to Figure 15.2.

b. Make a transition probability matrix similar to Figure 15.3.

c. Using Figure 15.3 and the transition probability matrix you made in part b, evaluate the relative differences in market position and status of ACB for these two products.

d. Define a defensive strategy for ACB.

2. *Markov Model of Consumer Behavior*

2.1 In Section 15.2, the calculations for equilibrium market share are shown for the ACB coffee example when a defensive strategy is in place. After that calculation, an aggressive strategy is defined. Find the equilibrium shares under the aggressive strategy.

2.2 Refer to Exercise 1.2 For this situation,

a. Prepare a new version of the thought experiment for both parts of Figure 15.5 where pad 1 represents ACB and pad 2 represents all the competitors.

b. Prepare a new version of Figure 15.6 to show this situation as a tree diagram.

c. Following the discussion in Section 15.2, find the market shares for 1982.

A defensive market strategy is introduced under which consumer behavior from 1981 to 1982 is to be predicted. Under this new strategy, marketing expects to increase the probability of holding consumers with ACB by 25%.

d. Prepare a new version of Figure 15.7 to show this situation as a transition probability matrix.

e. Prepare a new version of Figure 15.6 to show this situation as a tree diagram.

f. Determine the equilibrium market shares and illustrate your computation with a new version of Figure 15.8.

2.3 Refer to Exercise 1.3. For this situation,

a. Prepare a new version of the thought experiment for both parts of Figure 15.5 where pad 1 represents ACB and pad 2 represents all the competitors.

b. Prepare a new version of Figure 15.6 to show this situation as a tree diagram.

c. Following the discussion in Section 15.2, find the market shares for July.

An aggressive market strategy is introduced under which consumer behavior from June to July is to be predicted. Under this new strategy, marketing expects to decrease the probability of the competitor holding onto consumers by 20%.

d. Prepare a new version of Figure 15.7 to show this situation as a transition probability matrix.

e. Prepare a new version of Figure 15.6 to show this situation as a tree diagram.

f. Determine the equilibrium market shares and illustrate your computation with a new version of Figure 15.8.

2.4 Refer to Exercise 1.4. For this situation,

a. Prepare a new version of the thought experiment for both parts of Figure 15.5 where pad 1 represents ACB and pad 2 represents all the competitors.

b. Prepare a new version of Figure 15.6 to show this situation as a tree diagram.

c. Following the discussion in Section 15.2, find the market shares for 1977.

A defensive market strategy is introduced under which consumer behavior is to be predicted. Under this new strategy, marketing expects to increase the probability of holding consumers with ACB to .8.

d. Prepare a new version of Figure 15.7 to show this situation as a transition probability matrix.

e. Prepare a new version of Figure 15.6 to show this situation as a tree diagram.

f. Determine the equilibrium market shares and illustrate your computation with a new version of Figure 15.8.

3. *Markov Model of Blood Banks*

3.1 Consider a perishable commodity with a lifetime of 2 days and a demand probability mass function of

Units demanded	0	1	2	3
Prob. demand	.4	.3	.2	.1

A FIFO inventory policy is used.

a. Find the expected demand per day.

Assume that 2 units of the commodity are delivered every morning.

b. Make an appropriate thought experiment (you can make a wheel with a spinner, use a random number table, use a random number generator in a calculator or computer, or use a lottery-type drawing). Simulate the situation for 8 days, presenting your results in your own inventory summary similarly to Figure 15.10.

c. Determine the transition probabilities. To do this, create your own version of Figure 15.11.

d. Summarize your transition probabilities in your own version of Figure 15.12.

e. What is the expected number of shortages per day?

f. What is the expected number of units outdated per day?

g. What is the expected number of units used?

3.2 Consider a perishable commodity with a lifetime of 2 days and a demand probability mass function of

Units demanded	0	1	2	3
Prob. demand	.2	.5	.2	.1

A FIFO inventory policy is used.

a. Find the expected demand per day.

Assume that 2 units of the commodity are delivered every morning.

b. Make an appropriate thought experiment (you can make a wheel with a spinner, use a random number table, use a random number generator in a calculator or computer, or use a lottery-type drawing).

Simulate the situation for 8 days, presenting your results in your own inventory summary similarly to Figure 15.10.

c. Determine the transition probabilities. To do this, create your version of Figure 15.11.

d. Summarize your transition probabilities in your own version of Figure 15.12.

e. What is the expected number of shortages per day?

f. What is the expected number of units outdated per day?

g. What is the expected number of units used?

3.3 Consider a perishable commodity with a lifetime of 2 days and a demand probability mass function of

Units demanded	0	1	2	3
Prob. demand	.1	.4	.4	.1

A FIFO inventory policy is used.

a. Find the expected demand per day.

Assume that 2 units of the commodity are delivered every morning.

b. Make an appropriate thought experiment (you can make a wheel with a spinner, use a random number table, use a random number generator in a calculator or computer, or use a lottery-type drawing). Simulate the situation for 8 days, presenting your results in your own inventory summary similarly to Figure 15.10.

c. Determine the transition probabilities. To do this, create your own version of Figure 15.11.

d. Summarize your transition probabilities in your own version of Figure 15.12.

e. What is the expected number of shortages per day?

f. What is the expected number of units outdated per day?

g. What is the expected number of units used?

4. *Market Share Dynamics*

4.1 Make a summary table similar to Figure 5.13 for the aggressive coffee advertising campaign of ACB. From that table, make a probability transition matrix, and then

a. Use an analysis similar to that in the text of Section 15.4 to determine the market share under the aggressive campaign for February.

b. Use an analysis similar to that in the text of Section 15.4 to determine the market share under the aggressive campaign for March, April, May, June, July, and August.

c. Plot the market share vs. month in a plot similar to Figure 15.14.

d. Show with a horizontal line the equilibrium market share under this campaign.

4.2 Refer to Exercises 1.2 and 2.2. From the probability transition matrix you made there for behavior under the defensive market strategy,

a. Use an analysis similar to that in the text of Section 15.4 to determine the market share under the defensive campaign for 1982.

b. Use an analysis similar to that in the text of Section 15.4 to determine the market share under the defensive campaign for 1983, 1984, 1985, and 1986.

c. Plot the market share vs. year in a plot similar to Figure 15.14.

d. Show with a horizontal line the equilibrium market share under this campaign.

4.3 Refer to Exercises 1.3 and 2.3. From the probability transition matrix you made there for behavior under the aggressive market strategy,

a. Use an analysis similar to that in the text of Section 15.4 to determine the market share under the aggressive campaign for July.

b. Use an analysis similar to that in the text of Section 15.4 to determine the market share under the aggressive campaign for August, September, October, November, and December.

c. Plot the market share vs. month in a plot similar to Figure 15.14.

d. Show with a horizontal line the equilibrium market share under this campaign.

4.4 Refer to Exercises 1.4 and 2.4. From the probability transition matrix you made there for behavior under the defensive market strategy,

a. Use an analysis similar to that in the text of Section 15.4 to determine the market share under the defensive campaign for 1977.

b. Use an analysis similar to that in the text of Section 15.4 to determine the market share under the defensive campaign for the next 6 years.

c. Plot the market share vs. month in a plot similar to Figure 15.14.

d. Show with a horizontal line the equilibrium market share under this campaign.

5. Two-State Markov Models

5.1 In Section 15.2 an aggressive campaign for ACB's coffee sales is defined; the corresponding transition probability matrix is shown in Figure 15.9.

a. Get the values for P_1 and P_2 using the transition probability matrix which is defined in the description of the campaign in Section 15.2.

b. Draw a tree for this situation, following the discussion in this text and the tree shown in Figure 15.16.

c. Following the discussion in this text, establish the relationships between market shares, finding the values of S_1', S_1, S_2, and F.

d. Find the market share for the following 6 months.

e. Compute the *percentage* difference between the market share at the end of this period and the equilibrium value you calculated for it in Exercise 2.1.

5.2 In Exercise 2.2 a defensive campaign for ACB's tea sales is defined; the corresponding transition probability matrix was to be found by you in part d of Exercise 2.2.

a. Get the values for P_1 and P_2 using the transition probability matrix which you found in part d of Exercise 2.2.

b. Draw a tree for this situation, following the discussion in this text and the tree shown in Figure 15.16.

c. Following the discussion in this text, establish the relationships between market shares, finding the values of S_1', S_1, S_2, and F.

d. Find the market shares for the following 10 years.

e. Compute the *percentage* difference between the market share at the end of this period and the equilibrium value you calculated for it in part f of Exercise 2.2.

5.3 In Exercise 2.3 an aggressive campaign for ACB's frozen pea sales is defined; the corresponding transition probability matrix was found by you in part d of that exercise.

a. Get the values for P_1 and P_2 using the transition probability matrix which you found in part d of that exercise.

b. Draw a tree for this situation, following the discussion in this text and the tree shown in Figure 15.16.

c. Following the discussion in this text, establish the relationships between market shares, finding the values of S_1', S_1, S_2, and F.

d. Find the market shares for the following 6 months.

e. Compute the *percentage* difference between the market share at the end of this period and the equilibrium value you calculated for it in part f of Exercise 2.3.

5.4 In Exercise 2.4 a defensive campaign for ACB's macaroon sales is defined; the corresponding transition probability matrix was found by you in part d of Exercise 2.4.

    a. Get the values for P_1 and P_2 using the transition probability matrix which you found in part d of that exercise.

    b. Draw a tree for this situation, following the discussion in this text and the tree shown in Figure 15.16.

    c. Following the discussion in this text, establish the relationships between market shares, finding the values of S_1', S_1, and S_2, and F.

    d. Find the market shares for the following 5 years.

    e. Compute the *percentage* difference between the market share at the end of this period and the equilibrium value you calculated for it in part f of Exercise 2.4.

6. How to Control Accounts Receivable

6.1 The following is a version of Figure 15.18 obtained by a study of the records of the D. Ed Beet Company:

FROM-TO	GOOD	DELINQ.	DOUBTF.	AUGUST
Good	30	60	0	90
Delinquent	1	40	59	100
Doubtful	0	5	5	10
July	31	105	64	200

    a. Enter percentages in this table so that it corresponds to the information presented in Figure 15.17.

    b. Prepare the transition probability matrix for this situation similar to Figure 15.18.

    c. Prepare a table similar to Figure 15.19, showing the distribution of accounts in the month of August.

    d. Prepare a table similar to Figure 15.20, showing the initial distribution (S_1, S_2, S_3) and the next-period distribution (S_1', S_2', S_3').

    e. Compute the equilibrium probabilities.

    f. Discuss the resulting equilibrium probabilities from the standpoint of managerial action. What conclusions do you draw?

6.2 The following is a version of Figure 15.18 obtained by a study of the loan repayment records of the credit union at the Bowes Chutney Corporation:

FROM-TO	GOOD	DELINQ.	DOUBTF.	FIRST QUARTER
Good	250	50	0	300
Delinquent	100	40	50	190
Doubtful	0	90	20	110
Second quarter	350	180	70	600

    a. Enter percentages in this table so that it corresponds to the information presented in Figure 15.17.

    b. Prepare the transition probability matrix for this situation similar to Figure 15.18.

    c. Prepare a table similar to Figure 15.19, showing the distribution of accounts in the second quarter.

    d. Prepare a table similar to Figure 15.20, showing the initial distribution (S_1, S_2, S_3) and the next-period distribution (S_1', S_2', S_3').

    e. Compute the equilibrium probabilities.

f. Discuss the resulting equilibrium probabilities from the standpoint of managerial action. What conclusions do you draw?

6.3 The following is a version of Figure 15.18 obtained by a study of the records of the Passport Credit Plan. Customers who never allow charges for interest to accumulate are called "convenience" users of the Passport Credit Card and are not desirable. Convenience users receive heavy mailings to move them into the other categories, which are "excellent" for people whose charges in a month are over $200 and "good" for those whose charges are between $10 and $199.99.

FROM-TO	EXCEL.	GOOD	CONVEN.	JAN.
Excellent	80	10	0	90
Good	20	60	20	100
Convenience	10	20	80	110
Feb.	110	90	100	300

a. Enter percentages in this table so that it corresponds to the information presented in Figure 15.17.
b. Prepare the transition probability matrix for the situation similar to Figure 15.18.
c. Prepare a table similar to Figure 15.19, showing the distribution of accounts in the month of February.
d. Prepare a table similar to Figure 15.20, showing the initial distribution (S_1, S_2, S_3) and the next-period distribution (S_1', S_2', S_3').
e. Compute the equilibrium probabilities.
f. Discuss the resulting equilibrium probabilities from the standpoint of managerial action. What conclusions do you draw?

6.4 The following is a version of Figure 15.18 obtained by a study of the records of the D. Ed Beet Company:

FROM-TO	GOOD	DELINQ.	DOUBTF.	AUGUST
Good	30	60	0	90
Delinquent	1	40	59	100
Doubtful	0	5	5	10
July	31	105	64	200

a. Enter percentages in this table so that it corresponds to the information presented in Figure 15.17.
b. Prepare the transition probability matrix for this situation similar to Figure 15.18.
c. Prepare a table similar to Figure 15.19, showing the distribution of accounts in the month of August.
d. Prepare a table similar to Figure 15.20, showing the initial distribution (S_1, S_2, S_3) and the next-period distribution (S_1', S_2', S_3').
e. Compute the equilibrium probabilities.
f. Discuss the resulting equilibrium probabilities from the standpoint of mangerial action. What conclusions do you draw?

7. *Blood Distribution Systems: A Successfu' Application*

7.1 Can you think of other situations in which "efficient management. . .is a complex and difficult task" in which executives and managers would be well advised to "turn to quantitative methods of management. . .to resolve the system?"

7.2 Do you think the "replacement factor" is set to the same value for all hospitals. Why, or why not?

7.3 Based on the savings reported for the system, estimate the following:
   a. The dollars per year cost of 1% outdate, averaged over the range 4–20%
   b. The dollar cost per delivery, averaged over the range 4.2–7.8 deliveries per week

8. *Non-Markovian Processes: A Dialog*

8.1 Assume there is an urn containing four red and four black balls. Assume that you are drawing balls under the process invented by George Polya described in Section 15.8.
   a. What is the probability of drawing a red ball on the first draw?
   b. If the first draw yields a red ball, what is the probability of getting a red ball on the second draw?
   c. If the first draw yields a black ball, what is the probability of getting a red ball on the second draw?
   d. If the first draw and second draw yield red balls on both draws, what is the probability of getting a red ball on the third draw?

8.2 In Section 15.8, an example of a non-Markovian process involving a coffee customer is given. Give a different example, and explain why it is a non-Markovian process.

CHAPTER EXERCISES AND DISCUSSION QUESTIONS

C.1 Which of the following situations in business and administration are deterministic and which are probabilistic:
   a. Designing gears for a new automobile transmission
   b. Determining tax liability for a state tax
   c. Deciding on the number of clerks to have on duty at the town clerk's office
   d. Finding the cost of making a part using workers' time sheets
   e. Predicting the cost of a nuclear power plant before all regulatory approvals are received

C.2 Why have each of the following been called stochastic processes:
   a. The time it takes to service an applicant for unemployment compensation
   b. The time to obtain a spare part
   c. The number of vacancies per decade on the Supreme Court
   d. The number of customers arriving at the door of a retail store at 10:00–10:30 a.m. each morning.

C.3 The Upper Venus Development Commission and Board of Representatives are having a dispute over the level of taxation. Upper Venus is next to Lower Venus. Both communities are on the shore of the only lake in the center of an otherwise desert-like region; the nearest other communities are hundreds of kilometers away. For this reason, any movement of industries takes place between those two communities only. The development commission says that Upper Venus is in trouble because 30 of the 60 businesses that were in Upper Venus have moved to Lower Venus in the past year. The board of representatives says that there is no real problem since 30 of the 100 businesses which were in Lower Venus have moved to

Upper Venus in the same period. Settle this discussion, and show what the long-term future of the two communities is with respect to business development. Fully justify every statement you make with appropriate quantitative support.

C.4 Refer to Exercise C.3.
   a. Define an aggressive strategy for the community (Upper or Lower Venus) which is most likely to lose out in the long run.
   b. Define a defensive strategy for the community (Upper or Lower Venus) which is most likely to lose out in the long run.

C.5 Refer to Figure 15.9, the transition probability matrix for the aggressive advertising campaign for ACB. A special promotion costing $100,000 additional has been proposed which it is believed will increase the switching to ACB from the competitors. Unfortunately, this campaign will cause some switching away from ACB: the new transition probability matrix has the following first column:

.55

.25

Is it worth paying the extra $100,000? Justify your decision. (*Note*: You start by assuming that the market is in equilibrium.)

C.6 The Public Health Department of Upper Venus is concerned with the failure of businesses to respond to citations for excessive emission of pollutants. They have established three categories of offenders, A, B, and C. An A offender is one who was cited but has corrected the problem; a B offender is one who was cited and is taking action; a C offender is one who was cited but is taking no action. Offenders are reviewed each month because it has been observed that transitions among types of offenders are frequent, being the following:

1. An A offender may allow the problem to recur, as a consequence of lax control or an increase in activity beyond the ability of corrective measures to offset, and thus switch to B.
2. A B offender may succeed in correcting the problem and thus switch to A.
3. A B offender may cease its activities to correct the problem and become a C.
4. A C offender may institute corrective action and become a B.
5. No other switches occur.
6. It is not uncommon for an offender to stay in the same category from month to month.

A summary record of switching for several months has led to the following transition matrix:

FROM-TO	A	B	C
A	.8	.2	0
B	.4	.4	.2
C	0	.2	.8

   a. Assuming that equilibrium has been reached, what proportion of the Upper Venus businesses that have been cited are category A, B, or C? A two-part regulatory scheme has been proposed to improve pollution control. Any firm which appears on the C list for two successive months will be fined; any firm which moves from B to A will be given a tax rebate. The new city manager estimates the new transition probability matrix to be as follows:

FROM-TO	A	B	C
A	.8	.2	0
B	.8	.15	.05
C	0	.5	.5

b. What is the equilibrium distribution of the various categories if the scheme works according to this matrix?
c. What is the growth of the proportion of cited businesses in the A category?
d. What projections can you make for the future?

16

Waiting Lines: Queuing Theory

Most of us spend part of our waking hours waiting for something—to pay at the checkout counter at a market, get a ticket at a theatre, pay a toll at a bridge or tunnel, land at an airport, mail a letter in the post office, get food in a cafeteria, borrow a book from the library, deposit a check in a bank, register for courses in a college, cross a street, etc. Frustrated, we ask why can't enough checkout clerks be provided, enough toll booths, landing strips, etc.? Why is there always insufficient capacity? Why isn't something done about it?

16.1 THE SCIENTIFIC APPROACH TO WAITING LINES

Is time really wasted when waiting? Suppose there were twice as many clerks at the post office, so you would very rarely have to **queue**. The increase in wages to clerks would result in an increase in postal rates. Suppose there were more landing strips at the airport. In busy hours there would be less waiting and circling, but we would have to pay for the extra capacity. Look at it this way: (1) At busy times you wait, lose time, and the servers are busy; (2) when no one is queuing, servers and facilities are idle, wasting time, waiting for customers.

> The scientific approach to problems of waiting lines (queuing) is to balance the cost of waiting against the cost of service.

As the level of service increases (more clerks, landing strips, etc.), the cost of waiting decreases, and the cost of service increases. The optimum service level is obtained by minimizing combined costs (see Figure 16.1) or maximizing combined benefits.

To make optimum decisions, it becomes necessary to predict the **operating characteristics** of waiting-line systems, such as the average number of people waiting, people being served, and attendants idling

FIGURE 16.1
The central issue is to balance the cost of waiting against the cost of idle servers.

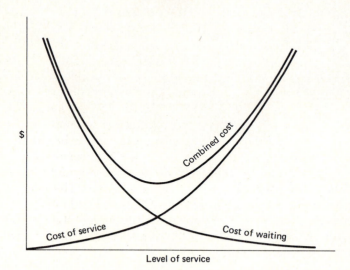

and the average time spent waiting, being served, idling, etc. Once these operating characteristics are known, one can proceed to an economic analysis and optimize.

Note that waiting-time problems are dominated by uncertainty; the variables of the problem are usually random. For example, (1) the number of customers arriving in an hour, (2) the time to service a customer, (3) the number of customers in the queue, (4) the number of customers being served, etc., are all random variables. Thus we are dealing here with stochastic processes and need stochastic models.

When a **waiting-line system** is designed, management is usually interested in overall performance and economic consequences as time goes by, or on the average. Thus decisions are based on performance characteristics such as (1) the average (expected) number of customers arriving per hour, (2) the average time to service a customer, (3) the average number of customers in the queue, etc.

Before we proceed to present a business application of waiting lines, we stress that the models we discuss in this chapter have broad applicability. Just to mention a few, note the following:

1. Cars waiting for service at a gas station
2. Checkout stands in supermarkets
3. Machines waiting for repairs
4. Waiting at telephones due to busy signals

5. Waiting in a doctor's office
6. Ships waiting for docks in a harbor
7. Drivers waiting to enter a bridge or tunnel
8. Students waiting to register

How to Staff a Tool Crib

Chubby Cherubs Corp. (CCC) is a manufacturer of children's furniture. The tools to manufacture the furniture are kept in a tool crib, and workers, before starting to work on a job, go to the tool crib and request the tools necessary. CCC has a single attendant at the tool crib to give out the tools. The workers arrive with the list of tools they need; the attendant provides the tools. Management observes that long queues form to get the tools and that much skilled labor time is lost. The supervisor of production recommends that a second attendant be provided. However, the second attendant will have to be paid, and so operating the tool crib will be more costly. The Vice President of Finance of CCC objects, because he feels that the second attendant will often be idle and so CCC will be worse off with two attendants. The assistant supervisor of production, however, thinks that three attendants would be better, so there would be no loss of skilled labor time. To perform an economic analysis of the situation, we need to establish the operating characteristics of this waiting-line system.

Basic Concepts of Waiting-Line Systems

Figure 16.2 shows schematically the basic aspects of a typical waiting-line system with three **channels**. Customers arrive from a **source** (or **calling population**) and proceed for service to an idle channel. If all channels are busy, customers form a single queue. When a customer arrives, the customer joins the queue at the tail. When a channel becomes idle, the customer at the head of the queue proceeds to the idle channel. It is said that the **queuing discipline** is first-come, first-served or **first-in-first-out (FIFO)**. After a customer is served, the customer departs.

Do not be confused between the number of channels and number of attendants. Suppose trucks are unloaded in a factory at two docks, but unloading at each dock is done by four attendants, a total of eight attendants. If there is only one truckload being unloaded, four attendants will be idle, and so this is a **two-channel system**. Ships arriving at a single dock may be unloaded by a team of 50; still this is a single-channel system. In a supermarket there may be five checkout counters, each attended by two clerks. This is still a five-channel system. But a barbershop with two chairs and two barbers is a two-channel system.

The source of the calling population may be large (*infinite*), and then the probability of an arrival does not depend on the length of the queue. On the other hand, the calling population may be finite, as when

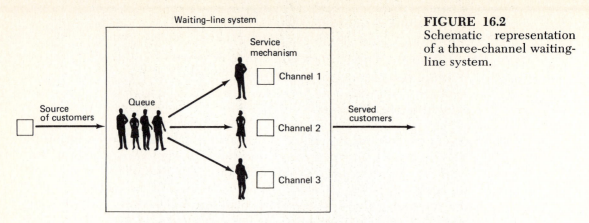

FIGURE 16.2
Schematic representation of a three-channel waiting-line system.

the problem is to maintain a fleet of three airplanes. If all airplanes are grounded and are in the queue for repairs, the probability of a new arrival is zero.

Now we describe a mathematical model of a simple waiting-line system.

Birth and Death Processes

Many biological situations as well as business situations can be modeled by so-called **birth and death processes**.

> Birth and death processes are characterized by the assumption that the probability of birth (or death) is the same in any fixed time period, regardless of the time of day, month, year, etc.

Birth corresponds to arrivals in a waiting-line system and death to the termination of a service.

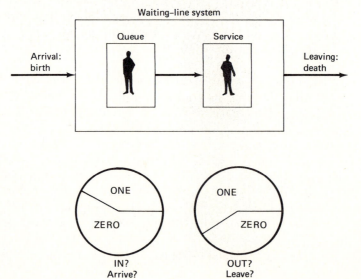

FIGURE 16.3
Thought experiment for single-channel waiting-line system.

The thought experiment (Figure 16.3) should help in understanding the process we are considering. Assume that there is a *single channel* and that there are two customers in the system, one in queue waiting and one being served. Now we spin the OUT wheel, shown in the lower right-hand part of the Figure 16.3. Suppose the ball stops at ZERO, so no one leaves. Then we spin the IN wheel and observe that there is ONE arrival. As shown in the first row of Figure 16.4a, this implies a change of +1 in the system, and so there will be two customers waiting at the end of the first step of the thought experiment, and the total number of customers in the system will be 3. Note that the thought experiment does not allow the arrival or leaving of two or more customers. Figure 16.4b presents graphically the outcomes of the thought experiment.

The second row in Figure 16.4a shows that there are three customers in the system and that two are waiting. There is no leaving, no arrival, and no change in the system. Thus we proceed line by line and simulate the waiting-line system characterized by the birth-death process. Observe that at the end of the fifth period there is no one in the system. Thus, at the beginning of the sixth period the OUT wheel need not be spun, because if no one is in the system, no one can leave. As shown in the sixth line, there is an arrival, so at the end of the sixth period one customer is being served, and the total number of customers in the system is 1.

Note that arrival is generated by the IN wheel and is independent of the length of the queue. This then tacitly assumes an infinite calling population. If the calling population is finite, say, for example, eight, and if there are eight customers in the queue, the IN wheel should not be spun.

16.2 ARRIVAL AND SERVICE TIME DISTRIBUTIONS

The thought experiment in Figure 16.3 is not adequate to describe real-life waiting-line situations. A more realistic situation requires specification of the probability mass functions of arrivals as illustrated in Figure 16.5.

Poisson Arrival

Experience has shown that many arrival patterns can be described by the Poisson distribution:

Poisson distribution:

$$P(x) = \frac{A^x e^{-A}}{x!}$$

where

A = average (mean) number of arrivals

STEP NUMBER	NUMBER IN SYSTEM AT START	NUMBER IN QUEUE (QUEUE LENGTH) AT START	NUMBER LEAVING	NUMBER ARRIVING	CHANGE IN NUMBER IN SYSTEM	NUMBER IN SYSTEM AT END	NUMBER IN QUEUE (QUEUE LENGTH) AT END
1	2	1	ZERO	ONE	+1	3	2
2	3	2	ZERO	ZERO	0	3	2
3	3	2	ONE	ZERO	−1	2	1
4	2	1	ONE	ZERO	−1	1	0
5	1	0	ONE	ZERO	−1	0	0
6	0	0	ZERO[a]	ONE	+1	1	0
7	1	0	ONE	ONE	0	1	0
8	1	0	ZERO	ONE	+1	2	1
9	2	1	ZERO	ONE	+1	3	2
10	3	2	ZERO	ONE	+1	4	3

[a] *Do not spin "leaving" wheel.*

FIGURE 16.4a Results of thought experiment for single-channel waiting-line system.

x = specific value of the number of arrivals

$x!$ = x **factorial**, for example, $3! = 3 \times 2 \times 1,\quad 5! = 5 \times 4 \times 3 \times 2 \times 1$

e = 2.718, the base of natural logarithms

For example, assume that on the average 4 patients arrive per hour

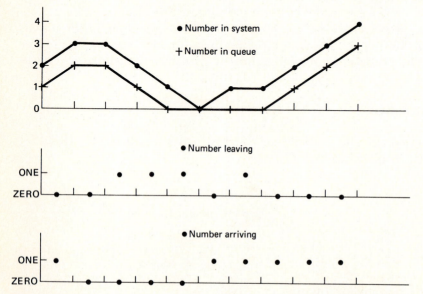

FIGURE 16.4b
Graphical representation of thought experiment for single-channel waiting-line system.

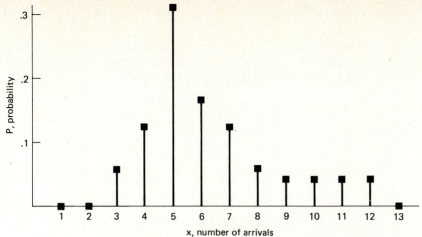

FIGURE 16.5
Example of a given arrival probability mass function.

in the emergency room of St. Mary's Hospital. What is the probability that 3 patients will arrive between 2:00 p.m. and 3:00 p.m.? We have

$$A = 4$$

$$x = 3$$

and so

$$P(3) = \frac{A^x e^{-A}}{x!} = \frac{4^3 e^{-4}}{3!} = \frac{64 e^{-4}}{3 \times 2} = .195367$$

As a further illustration, Figure 16.6 shows the probability mass function for the Poisson arrival with an average arrival rate of $A = 3$.

If the **arrival distribution** rate can be described by the Poisson distribution, the mathematical theory of waiting lines can be greatly simplified. Thus when the data for the situation are analyzed, it is important to determine whether the Poisson distribution applies.

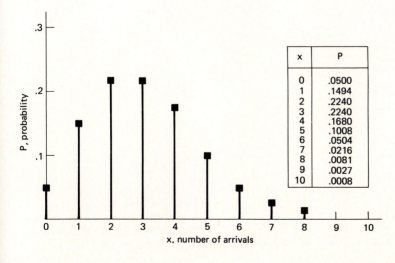

x	P
0	.0500
1	.1494
2	.2240
3	.2240
4	.1680
5	.1008
6	.0504
7	.0216
8	.0081
9	.0027
10	.0008

FIGURE 16.6
Poisson probability distribution of arrivals when A, the average arrival rate, is 3 per hour.

Exponential Service Times

Typically, service time is also a random variable and is characterized by the cumulative probability distribution. As an illustration, in Figure 16.7 you can read that for patients in St. Mary's Hospital

$$\text{probability}[t \le .25 \text{ hour}] = 0$$

$$\text{probability}[t \le .50 \text{ hour}] = .16$$

$$\text{probability}[t \le .75 \text{ hour}] = .57$$

$$\text{probability}[t \le 1.00 \text{ hour}] = .80$$

$$\text{probability}[t \le 1.25 \text{ hours}] = .87$$

$$\text{probability}[t \le 1.50 \text{ hours}] = 1.0$$

where t is the service time in hours. Note then that **service time distribution** is characterized by specifying

$$\text{probability } [t \le C]$$

for all values of the constant C.

Experience has shown that many·service time patterns can be described by the exponential distribution:

Exponential distribution:

$$\text{probability } [t \le C] = 1 - e^{-SC}$$

---

where

t = service time
S = expected number of units the service facility
      can handle in a specified period of time
C = any constant

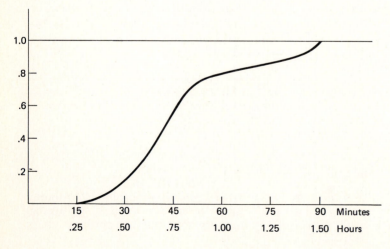

FIGURE 16.7
An example of a given cumulative probability distribution of service time.

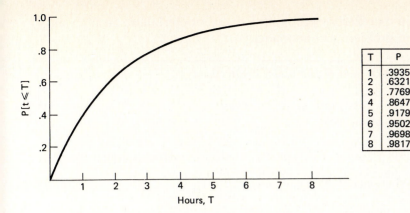

FIGURE 16.8
Exponential service time
distribution with an average
service rate of .5 per hour:
$P[t \leq T] = 1 - C^{-.5T}$.

T	P
1	.3935
2	.6321
3	.7769
4	.8647
5	.9179
6	.9502
7	.9698
8	.9817

As an illustration, assume that a maintenance crew of two can take care of four computers per day (an 8-hour day) and that the service time distribution is exponential. Then (Figure 16.8)

$$S = .5/\text{hour}$$

$$P[t \leq C] = 1 - e^{-SC} = 1 - e^{-.5C}$$

For example, the probability that service is completed in $C = 4$ hours is

$$P[t \leq 4] = 1 - e^{-.5 \times 4} = 1 - e^{-2} = 1 - .1353 = .8647$$

When service time data are analyzed, it is important to determine whether the distribution is exponential before the theory can be applied.

Interarrival Distribution

So far we have characterized arrivals by giving the probability distribution of the number of arrivals. There is, however, another way to characterize arrivals. Namely, we can consider the time elapsed *between* successive arrivals and state the probability distribution of the **interarrival times**.

A simple example is the following. Interarrival times can be either 5 or 10 minutes. The probability is .5 for each of these possibilities. You can visualize this arrival process by tossing a coin: If heads, the interarrival time is 5 minutes; if tails, it is 10 minutes.

Now the following important theorem holds:

> The interarrival time distribution for the Poisson distribution is exponential—and vice versa: If the interarrival time distribution is exponential, the number of arrivals per unit of time is Poisson.

Random Variables

This is just a reminder that the number of arrivals per unit of time, the service time, the interarrival time, the number of customers waiting in line, and the number of people being served are all random variables

561

and must be specified by probability distributions before an analysis of a waiting-line problem can be made.

16.3 BASIC WAITING-LINE THEORY FOR A SINGLE CHANNEL

We cover first the mathematical theory of waiting lines under the following assumptions:

---

1. Poisson distribution of arrivals (this implies an infinite calling population)
2. Exponential distribution of service times
3. First-in-first-out (FIFO) queue discipline

We refer to such systems as the **Poisson exponential system**. We shall not describe the theory but only results of the theory. Here we consider the single-channel case and later, in Section 16.5, the multichannel case.

Operating Characteristics

We introduce the following notation to define the waiting-line system:

A = average number of arrivals per unit of time = arrival rate (birth rate)

T = average (mean) service time

S = average number served per unit of time = service rate

ρ = utilization factor = fraction of time the service facility is busy

W_q = average waiting time

L_q = average number of customers in queue

W_S = average transit time from entering to leaving the system = time from birth to death (includes waiting time W)

L_S = average number of customers in the system (customers in the queue plus those being served)

We shall always assume that $A < S$, because otherwise the system cannot handle the arrivals, and the waiting line will get longer and longer.

Discussion of Operating Characteristics

Suppose A = 4 customers per hour. Then, on the average, there is an arrival each

$$\frac{1}{A} = \frac{1}{4} \text{ hour} = .25 \text{ hour} = 15 \text{ minutes}$$

The average time between arrivals is 15 minutes.

Suppose now the average service time is T = .2 hour. If there is a long queue, the servers will be busy, and there will be no idle time until everyone is served. The system can service 5 customers per hour, so the service rate is $S = 5$ customers per hour. In general,

$$S = \frac{1}{T}$$

We can also say that the system is capable of servicing 5 customers per hour or that the capacity of the system is 5 per hour:

$$\text{capacity} = \text{service rate} = S$$

You must be careful when using the $S = 1/T$ formula, because you must measure time in the same units for S and T. For example, we could have said that $T = 12$ minutes. Now the capacity or service rate is

$$S = \frac{1}{T} = \frac{1}{12} = .083333/\text{minute}$$

It is good practice to choose the unit of time so that the numbers involved are easy to handle.

An important performance characteristic of waiting-line systems is ρ, the utilization factor, that is, that fraction of time the service facility is busy. For single-channel Poisson exponential systems it can be shown that

$$\rho = \frac{A}{S}$$

For example, if $A = 4$ per hour and $S = 5$ per hour, the utilization is

$$\rho = \frac{A}{S} = \frac{4}{5} = .8$$

meaning that the system is busy 80% of the time.

Suppose first that $\rho > 1$, that is, $A > S$. This means that the arrival rate is greater than the capacity. For example, 10 customers per hour arrive, but the capacity is only 5 per hour. More and more customers will wait, and the queue will grow indefinitely. In fact even when $\rho = 1$, that is $A = S$, it can be shown that the queue will increase indefinitely.

We always assume that the utilization is less than 100%; that is,

$$\rho < 1$$

and

$$A < S$$

To obtain an insight into the meaning of ρ, the **utilization factor**, and the formula

$$\rho = \frac{A}{S}$$

consider an unusual waiting-line system where both arrival and service rates are constant. Suppose that customers can be scheduled to arrive exactly 15 minutes apart, meaning that the interval time is exactly 15 minutes. Suppose also that each service time is exactly 12 minutes. The system will be busy 12 minutes in each 15-minute period. So the system will be busy or utilized $12/15 = .8$ fraction of the time. But we have

$$A = 4/\text{hour}$$

$$S = 5/\text{hour}$$

and

$$\frac{A}{S} = \frac{4}{5} = .8$$

Thus the utilization for this system is the same as the corresponding Poisson exponential system.

Note, however, that in the latter system the probability of waiting is .8, while in the constant arrival and service time case the customer *never* has to wait. The two systems have the same utilization but otherwise very different characteristics.

The Average Number of Customers in the System*

This all-important quantity is given for single-channel Poisson exponential systems by (see Eq. 2, Figure 16.14)

$$L_S = \frac{A}{S - A}$$

or

$$L_S = \frac{\rho}{1 - \rho}$$

Note that if the utilization ρ is low, the average number of customers in the system is small, as on the average there will be few customers waiting. As ρ increases (Figure 16.9), L_S increases too, and as ρ nears 1, L_S grows indefinitely. This makes sense, because as the utilization factor

---

* At the end of the chapter in Figure 16.14 a summary of the most important waiting-line formulas is given. Each time we use one of these equations, we refer to Figure 16.14 in parentheses.

FIGURE 16.9
Average number of customers
L_S in a single-channel, Poisson exponential system.

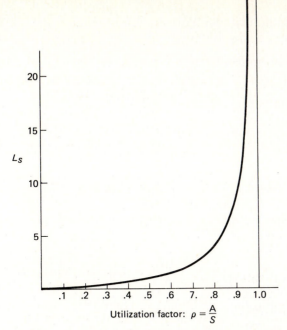

nears 1, the number of customers waiting should grow beyond bounds.

To better understand this important phenomenon, consider that exactly 100 customers are served per hour. This means that the service time is one-hundredth of an hour, or 36 seconds. Suppose that exactly 101 customers arrive per hour. This means that more arrive than can be served, and so as time goes on, the queue grows indefinitely. On the other hand, suppose that exactly 100 customers arrive per hour. If there is the slightest delay in service, the queue gets longer and will not get shorter, since there is no way for the service to catch up. Small disturbances add up, and so the line grows indefinitely.

Consider now an arrival rate of 99 customers per hour, providing an excess capacity of only 1 customer per hour. Observe in Figure 16.9 that the number of customers in the system is extremely sensitive to ρ, the value of the utilization factor, when ρ is close to 1. A utilization factor of ρ = .99 means that the average number of customers is 99. From the formula given in the next section, you can compute that the waiting time is .99 hour, that is, almost an entire hour. Suppose that for some reason service shuts down for one-tenth of an hour, that is, for 6 minutes. The arrival rate is 99 per hour, so in 6 minutes there will be approximately 10 arrivals, and the population will be 99 + 10 = 109. How long will it take to reduce the number of customers in the system to 99? There is only 1 customer per hour of excess capacity. So it will take approximately 10 hours to absorb the additional 10 customers. A 6-minute shutdown causes a 10-hour upset.

Five Basic Formulas

For the single-channel Poisson exponential system with given A, $S = 1/T$, and $A < S$, the following formulas hold:

1. Utilization factor*:

$$\rho = \frac{A}{S} < 1$$

2. Average number of customers in the system (including queue and service)*:

$$L_S = \frac{A}{S - A} = \frac{\rho}{1 - \rho} \qquad \text{(Eq. 2, Figure 16.14)}$$

3. Average time a customer spends in the system (includes waiting and service):

$$W_S = \frac{1}{S - A} = \frac{L_S}{A} \qquad \text{(Eq. 1a, Figure 16.14)}$$

4. Average time a customer spends in the queue waiting for service:

$$W_q = \frac{A}{S(S - A)} = W_S - T \qquad \text{(Eq. 1c, Figure 16.14)}$$

5. Average number of customers in the queue (waiting for service):

$$L_q = \frac{A^2}{S(S - A)} = \frac{\rho^2}{1 - \rho}$$

and

$$L_q = AW_q \qquad \text{(Eq. 1b, Figure 16.14)}$$

An Application: The-Rocks Copying Machine

Assume that jobs arrive 4 per hour to this machine and that it takes, on the average, $T = 12$ minutes $= .2$ hour to complete a job. We have $A = 4$ per hour and $S = 1/T = 5$ per hour. The utilization factor is

$$\rho = \frac{A}{S} = \frac{4}{5} = .8$$

The number of customers in the system (Eq. 2, Figure 16.14) is

$$L_S = \frac{\rho}{1 - \rho} = \frac{.8}{1 - .8} = \frac{.8}{.2} = 4 \text{ customers}$$

---

* We stated this formula earlier.

The average time the customers spend in the system (Eq. 1a, Figure 16.14) is

$$W_S = \frac{L_S}{A} = \frac{4}{4} = 1 \text{ hour} = 60 \text{ minutes}$$

The average time a customer spends in the queue (Eq. lc, Figure 16.14) is

$$W_q = W_S - T = 1.0 - .2 = .8 \text{ hour} = 48 \text{ minutes}$$

The average number of customers in the queue (Eq. 1b, Figure 16.14) is

$$L_q = AW_q = 4 \times .8 = 3.2 \text{ customers}$$

16.4 SOLVING THE TOOL-CRIB PROBLEM

Chubby Cherubs Corp. operates 24 hours per day. Assume that there are on the average 648 arrivals per day at the tool crib. This means 27 arrivals per hour, and so $A = 27$ per hour. Assume that a Poisson exponential system describes the situation.

Single Attendant

Assume that the average service time is

$$T = 2 \text{ minutes} = 0.333 \text{ hour}$$

The service rate is

$$S = \frac{1}{T} = \frac{1}{2} \bigg/ \text{minute} = 30/\text{hour}$$

The total number of workers in the system on the average is (Eq. 2, Figure 16.14)

$$L_S = \frac{A}{S - A} = \frac{27}{30 - 27} = \frac{27}{3} = 9 \text{ workers}$$

Workers will wait in line to get service and continue waiting while being serviced. Thus, if we assume an hourly wage of $15, the cost of servicing (including waiting time and service time) is

$$C_S = 9 \times 24 \times 15 = \$3240$$

The attendant's hourly wage is $12, so the daily cost for the attendant is

$$C_A = 24 \times 12 = \$288$$

and the total daily cost is

$$C_T = C_S + C_A = \$3240 + \$288 = \$3528$$

To gain insight into the operating characteristics of the system, we compute the following quantities:

Utilization factor:

$$\rho = \frac{27}{30} = .9$$

Average time spent in the system (Eq. 1a, Figure 16.14)

$$W_S = \frac{L_S}{A} = \frac{9}{27} = \frac{1}{3} \text{ hour} = 20 \text{ minutes}$$

Average time spent waiting in the queue (Eq. 1c, Figure 16.14)

$$W_q = W_S - T = 20 - 2 = 18 \text{ minutes} = .3 \text{ hour}$$

Average number of workers in the queue (Eq. 1b, Figure 16.14)

$$L_q = AW_q = 27 \times .3 = 8.1 \text{ workers}$$

Two Attendants

Assume that two attendants share the job of providing tools. When a worker arrives, the list of tools is examined jointly by the two attendants, and the job of getting the tools is split. Note that this is a single-channel system because the two attendants take care of customers jointly. Assume that two attendants work faster than one but not twice as fast. Namely, assume that the service time is 1.2 minutes to get the tools when there are two attendants. This, then, means that the capacity S is $60/1.2 = 50$ per hour. So we have

$$A = 27/\text{hour}, \quad S = 50/\text{hour}, \quad T = 1.2 \text{ minutes} = .02 \text{ hour}$$

The total number in the system on the average is (Eq. 2, Figure 16.14)

$$L_S = \frac{A}{S - A} = \frac{27}{50 - 27} = \frac{27}{23} = 1.1739 \text{ workers}$$

The costs are

$$C_S = \frac{27}{23} \times 24 \times 15 = \$422.61$$

$$C_A = 2 \times 24 \times 12 = \$576.00$$

$$C_T = \$998.61$$

Note that using two attendants is less costly than using one. To gain insight into the operating characteristics of the system, we compute the following:

Utilization factor:

$$\rho = \frac{A}{S} = \frac{27}{50} = .54$$

Average time spent in the system (Eq. 1a, Figure 16.14)

$$W_S = \frac{L_S}{A} = \frac{27}{23 \times 27} = .0435 \text{ hour} = 2.609 \text{ minutes}$$

Average time spent waiting in the queue (Eq. 1c, Figure 16.14):

$$W_q = W_S - T = .0435 - .0200 = .0235 \text{ hour} = 1.409 \text{ minutes}$$

Average number of workers in the queue (Eq. 1b, Figure 16.14):

$$L_q = AW_q = 27 \times .0235 = .6345 \text{ worker}$$

Three Attendants

Assume that three attendants working jointly in the tool crib can take care of 70 workers per hour, meaning that the service rate is $S = 70$ per hour and that the service time is

$$T = \frac{60}{70} = .857 \text{ minute} = .0143 \text{ hour}$$

(This is still a single-channel system.) The arrival rate is still $A = 27$ per hour, and so the total number in the system on the average is (Eq. 2, Figure 16.14)

$$L_S = \frac{A}{S - A} = \frac{27}{70 - 27} = \frac{27}{43} = .6279 \text{ worker}$$

The costs are

$$C_S = \frac{27}{43} \times 24 \times 15 = \$226.05$$

$$C_A = 3 \times 24 \times 12 = \underline{\$864.00}$$

$$C_T = \$1090.05$$

Note that three attendants are more costly than two. Thus it is best to have two attendants. To gain insight into the operating characteristics of the system, we compute the following quantities:

Utilization factor:

$$\rho = \frac{A}{S} = \frac{27}{70} = .386$$

Average time spent in the system (Eq. 1a, Figure 16.14)

$$W_S = \frac{L_S}{A} = \frac{27}{43 \times 27} = .0233 \text{ hour} = 1.395 \text{ minutes}$$

Average time spent waiting in the queue (Eq. 1c, Figure 16.14):

$$W_q = W_S - T = .0233 - .0143 = .009 \text{ hour} = .54 \text{ minute}$$

Average number of workers in the queue (Eq. 1b, Figure 16.14):

$$L_q = AW_q = 27 \times .009 = .243 \text{ worker}$$

In Figure 16.10 we summarize the performance of the three systems considered.

16.5 PROBABILISTIC PERFORMANCE MEASURES

In real-life situations it is often difficult or impractical to estimate accurately the cost incurred by customers waiting. Therefore, management may specify the performance of the system in terms of probabilities.

Let us recall that if the jobs scheduled to arrive at The-Rocks copy machine were exactly 15 minutes apart and if each job took exactly 12 minutes, the machine would be busy exactly

$$\rho = \frac{A}{S} = .8$$

fraction of the time, where ρ is the utilization factor. For a Poisson exponential system, the following theorem can be proved:

1. The probability P_W that a single-channel Poisson exponential system is busy is

$$P_W = \rho = \frac{A}{S}$$

2. The probability P_0 that the system is idle, that is, the number of customers in the system is 0, is

$$P_0 = 1 - P_W = 1 - \rho = 1 - \frac{A}{S}$$

3. The probability P_n that there are n or more customers in the system is

$$P_n = \rho^n$$

	SINGLE ATTENDANT	TWO ATTENDANTS	THREE ATTENDANTS
T	2 min	1.2 min	.857 min
S	30/hr	50/hr	70/hr
ρ	.9	.54	.386
L_S	9 workers	1.1739 workers	.6279 worker
W_S	20 min	2.609 min	1.395 min
W_q	18 min	1.409 min	.540 min
L_q	8.1 workers	.6345 worker	.243 worker
C_T	$3528.00	$998.61	$1090.05

FIGURE 16.10 Performance of a single-channel waiting-line system for Chubby Cherubs Corp. when A, the average arrival rate, is 27 workers per hour and one, two, or three attendants work in the tool crib.

The-Rocks Copying Machine Again

The probability of a machine being busy is

$$P_W = \rho = .8$$

The probability of the system being idle is

$$1 - P_W = 1 - \rho = .2$$

The probability of having (1) 1 or more than 1, (2) 2 or more than 2, and (3) 3 or more than 3 customers in the system is given by

(1) $P_1 = \rho = .8$ (meaning that the system is busy)

(2) $P_2 = \rho^2 = .8^2 = .64$

(3) $P_3 = \rho^3 = .8^3 = .512$

Performance Specifications

Suppose management knows from experience at other facilities that a utilization over 60% is unsatisfactory and specifies that utilization be not more than 60%. This means that

$$\rho \le .6$$

or

$$\frac{A}{S} \le .6$$

or

$$S \ge \frac{A}{.6}$$

But $A = 4$ per hour, and so

$$S \ge \frac{4}{.6} = 6.67$$

This means that the machine should be able to complete at least 6.67 jobs per hour or on the average a job should take not more than

$$T = \frac{1}{S} = \frac{1}{6.67} = 0.15 \text{ hour} = 9 \text{ minutes}$$

But the copying machine can complete a job on the average only each 12 minutes. *Thus management desires a faster copying machine.*

Suppose as an alternative management specifies that the probability of 3 or more customers in the system be less than .1. Then

$$P_3 < .1$$

or

$$\rho^3 < .1$$

Thus*

$$\rho < .1^{1/3} = .464$$

or

$$\frac{A}{S} < .464$$

Repeating the method just used, we find that on the average each job must be completed in less than

$$T = \frac{1}{S} = \frac{.464}{A} = \frac{.464}{4} = .116 \text{ hour} = 6.96 \text{ minutes}$$

Thus this specification requires an even faster machine.

Suppose now management specifies that there *never* should be more than 5 customers in the system. But *never* is a big word, and after some discussion, management agrees that the probability of 5 or more customers in the system should be .01. So

$$P_5 = \rho^5 = .01$$

and

$$\rho = .01^{1/5} = .398$$

or

$$\frac{A}{S} = .398$$

This leads to

$$T = \frac{.4}{A} = \frac{.4}{4} = .0995 \text{ hour} = 6 \text{ minutes}$$

Thus *this specification requires the fastest machine of all.*

16.6 MULTICHANNEL SYSTEMS

So far we have considered only single-channel systems even if we allowed several attendants working jointly. Now we consider the Poisson exponential system with several channels. Characterization of these systems is precisely the same as the single system.

We extend the definition of the utilization factor to

$$\rho = \frac{A}{CS}$$

---

* These calculations were done on an electronic calculator.

where C is the number of channels. For the single-channel system $C = 1$, $\rho = A/S$, which agrees with our old definition.

Seven Basic Formulas for Multichannel Systems

For Poisson exponential systems with C channels and given A and $S = 1/T$ the following formulas hold:

1. The utilization factor is

$$\rho = \frac{A}{CS}$$

2. The probability P_0 of zero customers in the system is

$$P_0 = \frac{1}{[R^C/C!(1 - \rho)] + 1 + (R/1!) + (R^2/2!) + \cdots + [R^{C-1}/(C - 1)!]}$$

where

$$R = \frac{A}{S}$$

and ! means factorial ($2! = 2 \times 1$, $3! = 3 \times 2 \times 1$, $4! = 4 \times 3 \times 2 \times 1$, $5! = 5 \times 4 \times 3 \times 2 \times 1$, etc.).

For example, for two channels $C = 2$, and

$$P_0 = \frac{1}{[R^2/2(1 - \rho)] + 1 + (R/1)}$$

For $C = 3$,

$$P_0 = \frac{1}{[R^3/3 \times 2 \times 1 \times (1 - \rho)] + 1 + (R/1) + (R^2/2)}$$

and so on.

3. The important factor F shown in Figure 16.11* and tabulated in Appendix B in Table B.3 is

$$F = \frac{W_q}{T} = \frac{SR^{C+1}P_0}{AC \times C! \times (1 - \rho)^2}$$

For example, for $C = 2$,

$$F = \frac{W_q}{T} = \frac{SR^3 P_0}{A \times 2 \times 2 \times 1 \times (1 - \rho)^2}$$

Note that F measures the ratio of average waiting time in the queue and the average service time.[†]

---

* The vertical scale is logarithmic.

[†] For the single-channel system, $C = 1$, and $F = A(S - A) = L_S$. Note that Figure 16.9 shows L_S or F for $C = 1$.

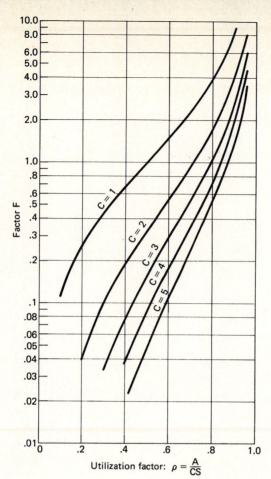

FIGURE 16.11

Factor $F = W_q/T$ for multichannel Poisson exponential systems.

4. The average waiting in the queue (Eq. 3, Figure 16.14) is

$$W_q = FT = \frac{F}{S}$$

5. The average number of customers in the queue waiting for service (Eq. 1b, Figure 16.14)

$$L_q = AW_q$$

6. The average time a customer spends in the system (includes waiting and service) (Eq. 1c, Figure 16.14) is

$$W_S = W_q + T = W_q + \frac{1}{S}$$

7. The average number of customers in the system (includes queue and service) (Eq. 1a, Figure 16.14) is

$$L_S = AW_S$$

The Burger Queen Restaurant

Assume an arrival rate of $A = 27$ per hour; two channels, $C = 2$; and a service time of $T = 2$ minutes. The service rate is

$$S = \frac{1}{T} = \frac{1}{2} = .5/\text{minute} = 30/\text{hour}$$

The utilization factor is

$$\rho = \frac{A}{CS} = \frac{27}{2 \times 30} = .45$$

To calculate P_0, we need R,

$$R = \frac{A}{S} = \frac{27}{30} = .9$$

so

$$P_0 = \frac{1}{[R^2/2(1 - \rho)] + 1 + (R/1)} = \frac{1}{[.9^2/(2 \times .55)] + 1 + .9} = .3793$$

$$F = \frac{SR^3P_0}{A \times 2 \times 2 \times 1 \times (1 - \rho)^2} = \frac{30 \times .9^3 \times .3793}{27 \times 2 \times 2 \times .55^2} = .2539$$

Note we could have read F from Figure 16.11 or determined F from Table B.3 in Appendix B. Namely, for $\rho = .44$ and $C = 2$, we get $F = .24008$. For $\rho = .46$ and $C = 2$, $F = .26839$. For $\rho = .45$, we go halfway and get

$$F = \frac{.24008 + .26839}{2} = .2542$$

which is also good enough for all practical purposes.

The rest of the calculations are straightforward (Eq. 3, Figure 16.14):

$$W_q = \frac{F}{S} = \frac{.2539}{30} = .008463 \text{ hour} = .5078 \text{ minutes}$$

and (Eq. 1b)

$$L_q = AW_q = 27 \times .008463 = .228501 \text{ customer}$$

and (Eq. 1c)

$$W_S = W_q + T = W_q + \frac{1}{S} = .008463 + \frac{1}{30} = .04180 \text{ hour}$$

$$= 2.508 \text{ minutes}$$

and (Eq. 1a)

$$L_S = AW_S = 27 \times .04180 = 1.1286 \text{ customers}$$

Three Channels for Burger Queen

Assume now that $C = 3$. Then

$$\rho = \frac{A}{CS} = \frac{27}{3 \times 30} = .3$$

From Figure 16.11 and Table B.3 in Appendix B, $F = .03335$. Thus,

$$W_q = \frac{F}{S} = \frac{.0333}{30} = .00111 \text{ hour} = .0666 \text{ minute}$$

(Eq. 3, Figure 16.14)

$$L_q = AW_q = 27 \times .00111 = .02997 \text{ customer}$$

$$W_S = W_q + T = .00111 + \tfrac{1}{30} = .03444 \text{ hour} = 2.0664 \text{ minutes}$$

$$L_S = AW_S = 27 \times .03444 = .9300 \text{ customer}$$

(Eqs. 1a, 1b, and 1c).

Summarizing the Results for Burger Queen

Before we review our results, consider the single-channel situation. The utilization factor is

$$\rho = \frac{A}{S} = \frac{27}{30} = .9$$

and so (Eqs. 2 and 1a, 1b, and 1c)

$$L_S = \frac{\rho}{1 - \rho} = \frac{.9}{1 - .9} = \frac{.9}{.1} = 9 \text{ customers}$$

$$W_S = \frac{L_S}{A} = \frac{9}{27} = \frac{1}{3} \text{ hour} = 20 \text{ minutes}$$

$$W_q = W_S - T = 20 - 2 = 18 \text{ minutes} = .3 \text{ hour}$$

$$L_q = AW_q = 27 \times .3 = 8.1 \text{ customers}$$

In Figure 16.12 we summarize our results. The single-channel system involves the average waiting time of 18 minutes. Service takes only 2 minutes on the average, and customers will probably get very unhappy under this arrangement. Two channels reduce the average waiting time to .51 minute or 30.1 seconds, a very satisfactory arrangement. Three channels further reduce average waiting time to .07 minute or 4.2 seconds, meaning essentially instantaneous service.

	C, NUMBER OF CHANNELS		
	1	**2**	**3**
ρ	.90	.45	.30
W_q	18 min	.5078 min	.0666 min
L_q	8.1 customers	.2285 customer	.0297 customer
W_S	20 min	2.508 min	2.0664 min
L_S	9 customers	1.1286 customers	.9230 customer

FIGURE 16.12 Performance of three waiting-line systems for Burger Queen Restaurant, where $A = 27$ per hour, $T = 2$ minutes, and $S = 30$ customers per hour.

The Tool-Crib Problem Again

We found (Figure 16.10) that the best thing for CCC is to employ two attendants in the tool crib. However, two objections were raised against the proposed system. First, management thought that too much time was wasted by two attendants discussing how to split the job. It would be better if each attendant took on one entire job. Also, the union objected to the technique of splitting jobs. Therefore, it was proposed that each attendant should work independently. To deal with this situation, we need to consider a two-channel system. Thus,

$$A = 27/\text{hour}, \quad S = 30/\text{hour}, \quad C = 2$$

This happens to be the Burger Queen problem we just studied, and so the number of customers in the system is 1.130. Thus the costs are

$$C_S = 1.13 \times 24 \times 15 = \$406.80$$
$$C_A = 2 \quad \times 24 \times 12 = \underline{\$576.00}$$
$$C_T = \$982.80$$

Observe that the two-channel approach is better than the sharing approach, which had a cost of $998.60. So management complies with the union's wishes not to force the attendants to split their jobs.

Three Channels for the Tool-Crib

How about using three attendants and three channels? Suppose for the moment that waiting time becomes negligible or $W_q = 0$. Then

$$W_S = W_q + T = 0 + \tfrac{1}{30} = .0333 \text{ hour} \quad \text{(Eq. lc, Figure 16.14)}$$

and (Eq. 1a)

$$L_S = AW_S = \tfrac{27}{30} = .9 \text{ customer}$$

Thus the service cost is

$$C_S = .9 \times 24 \times 15 = \$324$$

The cost of three attendants is

$$C_A = \$864$$

The total cost is

$$C_T = \$1188$$

So even if there is no waiting at all, the three-channel system is worse than the two-channel system. Thus the best thing for CCC is to use two attendants working in two channels.

Medical Test Laboratory Associates

This laboratory is considering automating certain tests on medical specimens. Each testing instrument can handle on the average $S = 25$ specimens per hour, and on the average $A = 80$ specimens arrive per hour. How many instruments should the laboratory purchase?

For one instrument, $C = 1$, and

$$\rho = \frac{A}{CS} = \frac{80}{25} = 3.2$$

For $C = 2$,

$$\rho = \frac{A}{2S} = \frac{80}{50} = 1.6$$

for $C = 3$,

$$\rho = \frac{A}{3S} = \frac{80}{75} = 1.0667$$

and for $C = 4$,

$$\rho = \frac{A}{4S} = \frac{80}{100} = .8$$

Thus unless at least four instruments are used, the lines will grow infinitely long.

> By introducing a sufficient number of channels, the queue can always be reduced to a satisfactory level.

The performance characteristics for $C = 4$ channels can be determined by reading the factor from Figure 16.11 or more accurately from Table B.3 in Appendix B. We find that

$$F = .7455$$

Thus (Eqs. 3, 1b, 1c, and 1a, Figure 16.14)

$$W_q = \frac{F}{S} = \frac{.7455}{25} = .02982 \text{ hour} = 1.7892 \text{ minutes}$$

$L_q = AW_q = 80 \times .0298 = 2.3856$ specimens

$$W_S = W_q + T = W_q + \frac{1}{S} = .0298 + \frac{1}{25} = .0298 + .04 = .0698 \text{ hour}$$

$$= 4.189 \text{ minutes}$$

and

$$L_S = AW_S = 80 \times .0698 = 5.586 \text{ specimens}$$

Is this the best number of instruments? The answer can only be obtained by an economic analysis. Here we concentrate only on determining the operating characteristics.

16.7 SINGLE-CHANNEL POISSON ARRIVAL SYSTEMS

So far we have considered only the Poisson exponential system. However, the mathematical theory of queues provides formulas to solve the single-channel case when arrival is Poisson and distribution of the service time is a given general probability distribution. For the single-channel **Poisson general system** the following assumptions are made:

1. Poisson distribution of arrivals (this implies an infinite calling population)
2. An arbitrary distribution of service time for which T is the average service time and σ is the standard deviation of the service time distribution
3. First-in-first-out (FIFO) queue discipline

Note that for the probability distribution of the service only the values of T, the average service time, and σ, the standard deviation, are required. If two service time distributions have the same T and σ, the performance formulas will be identical. Namely, it can be proved that for the single-channel Poisson general system with given A, $S = 1/T$, and $A < S$, the following formulas hold:

1. utilization factor:

$$\rho = \frac{A}{S}$$

where A is the average arrival rate. Assume that $A < S$ and $\rho < 1$.

2. Average number of customers in the queue (includes waiting and service) (see Eq. 4, Figure 16.14)*:

$$L_q = \frac{\rho^2}{1 - \rho} \times \frac{1 + f^2}{2}$$

---

* This is the Khintchine-Pollaczek formula. An alternate equivalent form of the formula is

$$L_S = \rho + \frac{A^2\sigma^2 + \rho^2}{2(1 - \rho)}$$

where the factor f is the standard deviation σ divided by the average service time T:

$$f = \frac{\sigma}{T}$$

3. Average time a customer spends in the queue waiting (Eq. 1b, Figure 16.14):

$$W_q = \frac{L_q}{A}$$

4. Average time a customer spends in the system (includes waiting and service) (Eq. 1c, Fig. 16.4):

$$W_S = W_q + T$$

5. Average number of customers in the system (includes waiting and service) (Eq. 1a, Figure 16.14)

$$L_S = AW_S$$

Applications should clarify the use of these formulas.

The Debug Computer Softwarehouse

The Debug Computer Softwarehouse, DCS (a one-programmer organization), provides service to computer users when they have trouble with computer programs or computer software.

Fixing (debugging) software falls into two classes. Minor problems, when the user is just stuck, takes only 10 minutes or .16667 hour to straighten out, but serious problems, requiring expert programming guidance, take 2 hours. What are the operating characteristics of this waiting-line problem?

Records show that arrival is Poisson, with five arrivals for each 8-hour workday or

$$A = \tfrac{5}{8} = .625/\text{hour}$$

The probability of a job being either minor or major is .5 as shown graphically by the probability distribution of the service time (Figure 16.13). The mean service time is

$$T = .5 \times .1667 + .5 \times 2 = .0833 + 1 = 1.08335 \text{ hours}$$

The service rate is

$$S = \frac{1}{T} = .9231 \text{ computer user/hour}$$

and the utilization factor is

$$\rho = \frac{A}{S} = \frac{.625}{.9231} = .6771$$

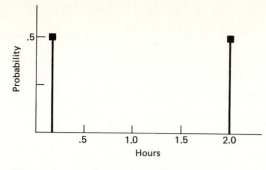

FIGURE 16.13
Probability distribution of service time for Debug Computer Softwarehouse.

Next we need to calculate the variance of the service time. In Section 3.1 we showed how this is done:

Step 1. The mean is $\mu = T = 1.0833$.

Step 2. The deviations are

$$x_1 - \mu = .1667 - 1.0833 = -.9166$$

$$x_2 - \mu = 2.000 - 1.0833 = .9167$$

Step 3. The squares of the deviations are

$$(x_1 - \mu)^2 = (-.9167)^2 = .8403$$

$$(x_2 - \mu)^2 = .9167^2 = .8403$$

Step 4. Multiply each probability by the corresponding deviation:

$$p_1(x_1 - \mu)^2 = .5 \times .8402 = .4201$$

$$p_2(x_2 - \mu)^2 = .5 \times .8402 = .4201$$

Step 5. Add the terms in step 4:

$$\sigma^2 = .4201 + .4201 = .8402$$

The square of the factor f is

$$f^2 = \frac{\sigma^2}{T^2} = \frac{.8402}{1.0833^2} = \frac{.8402}{1.1735} = .7160$$

and

$$\frac{1 + f^2}{2} = \frac{1 + .7160}{2} = .858$$

Therefore the average number of computer users in queue is

$$L_q = \frac{\rho^2}{1 - \rho} \times \frac{1 + f^2}{2} = \frac{.6771^2}{1 - .6771} \times .858 = \frac{.4585}{.3229} \times .858$$

$$= 1.42 \times .858 = 1.2184 \text{ computer users}$$

Thus (Eqs. 1b, 1c, and 1a, Figure 16.14)

$$W_q = \frac{L_q}{A} = \frac{1.2184}{.625} = 1.9494 \text{ hours}$$

$$W_S = W_q + T = 1.9494 + 1.0833 = 3.0327 \text{ hours}$$

$$L_S = AW_S = .625 \times 3.0327 = 1.8954 \text{ computer users}$$

How does this compare with the system with exponential distribution of service time? Assuming again an average service time of $T = 1.0833$ hours, we again have

$$S = \frac{1}{T} = .9231/\text{hour}$$

and

$$\rho = .6771$$

But what about the standard deviation of the exponential service time distribution? It can be shown that

> For the exponential service time distribution,
>
> standard deviation = average service time
>
> $$\sigma = T$$

Thus the factor f is

$$f = \frac{\sigma}{T} = 1$$

and

$$\frac{1 + f^2}{2} = 1$$

So for the exponential service time distribution system (Eq. 4, Figure 16.14)

$$L_q = \frac{\rho^2}{1 - \rho} \times \frac{1 + f^2}{2} = \frac{\rho^2}{1 - \rho}$$

But

$$\frac{\rho^2}{1 - \rho} = \frac{(A/S)^2}{1 - (A/S)} = \frac{A^2}{S - A}$$

which agrees with the fifth formula given for the single-channel Poisson exponential system. Thus,*

$$L_q = \frac{\rho^2}{1 - \rho} = \frac{.6771^2}{1 - .6771} = 1.42$$

---

* As an alternate we could of course use the sequence of calculations used earlier for the Poisson exponential system. (See Eqs. 2 and then 1a, 1c, and 1b, Figure 16.14.)

and (Eqs. 1b, 1c, and 1a)

$$W_q = \frac{L_q}{A} = \frac{1.42}{.625} = 2.272 \text{ hours}$$

$$W_S = W_q + T = 2.272 + 1.0833 = 3.3553 \text{ hours}$$

$$L_S = AW_S = .625 \times 3.3553 = 2.0971 \text{ computer users}$$

This shows that the exponential service system (with the same average service time) implies a somewhat slower system.

The Quickfix Softwarehouse

This softwarehouse specializes in minor problems, and the probability of occurrence of a minor problem is .9, requiring a fixing time of .1667 hour. The probability of occurrence of a serious problem is only .1, requiring a fixing time of 2 hours. So the mean service time is

$$T = .9 \times .1667 + .1 \times 2 = .1500 + .2 = .35 \text{ hour}$$

and the service rate is

$$S = \frac{1}{T} = \frac{1}{.35} = 2.857 \text{ computer users/hour}$$

As expected, Quickfix can take care of more customers than Debug Computer Softwarehouse. In fact, the average arrival rate is

$$A = 2.5 \text{ customers/hour}$$

or 20 customers per 8-hour workday. The utilization factor is

$$\rho = \frac{A}{S} = \frac{2.5}{2.857} = .8750$$

The variance of the probability distribution of the service time is

$$\sigma^2 = .9(.1667 - T)^2 + .1(2 - T)^2 = .9(.1667 - .35)^2 + .1(2 - .35)^2$$

$$= .9 \times .1833^2 + .1 \times 1.65^2 = .9 \times .0340 + .1 \times 2.7225 = .3025$$

$$f^2 = \frac{\sigma^2}{T^2} = \frac{.3025}{.35^2} = \frac{.3025}{.1225} = 2.4694$$

and

$$\frac{1 + f^2}{2} = \frac{1 + 2.4694}{2} = 1.7347$$

$$L_q = \frac{\rho^2}{1 - \rho} \times \frac{1 + f^2}{2} = \frac{.8750^2}{1 - .8750} \times 1.7346$$

(Eq. 4, Figure 16.14)

For a broad class of waiting-line problems:

$$\text{Eq. 1a:} \quad L_S = AW_S$$

$$\text{Eq. 1b:} \quad L_q = AW_q$$

$$\text{Eq. 1c:} \quad W_S = W_q + T = W_q + \frac{1}{S}$$

For the single-channel Poisson exponential system:

$$\text{Eq. 2:} \quad L_S = \frac{A}{S - A} = \frac{\rho}{1 - \rho}$$

For the multichannel Poisson exponential system:

$$\text{Eq. 3:} \quad W_q = FT = \frac{F}{S}$$

where F is obtained from Figure 15.11 or from table B.3 in Appendix B.
For the Poisson general system:

$$\text{Eq. 4:} \quad L_q = \frac{\rho^2}{1 - \rho} \times \frac{1 + f^2}{2} = \frac{\rho^2}{1 - \rho} \times \frac{1 + (\sigma/T)^2}{2}$$

where σ is the standard deviation of the service time distribution.
For the Poisson constant service time system:

$$\text{Eq. 5:} \quad L_q = \frac{\rho^2}{2(1 - \rho)}$$

FIGURE 16.14 Summary of equations for solving waiting-line problems.

$$= \frac{.7656}{.125} \times 1.7346 = 6.1248 \times 1.7346 = 10.6355 \text{ computer users}$$

$$W_q = \frac{L_q}{A} = \frac{10.624}{2.5} = 4.2496 \qquad \text{(Eq. 1b, Figure 16.14)}$$

$$W_S = W_q + T = 4.2540 + .35 = 4.600 \quad \text{(Eq. 1c, Figure 16.14)}$$

$$L_S = AW_S = 2.5 \times 4.604 = 11.50 \text{ customers}$$

(Eq. 1a, Figure 16.14)

Note then that while Quickfix can take care of more computer users, more time is spent in the system. There are many more users in queue and more waiting time by customers.

Let us compare the system with the corresponding exponential service time system. We have $f = 1$ and so (Eq. 4, Fig. 16.14)

$$L_q = \frac{\rho^2}{1 - \rho} \times \frac{1 + f^2}{2} = 6.1248 \text{ computer users}$$

$$W_q = \frac{L_q}{A} = \frac{6.1248}{2.5} = 2.4499 \text{ hours} \qquad \text{(Eq. 1b, Figure 16.14)}$$

$$W_S = W_q + T = 2.4499 + .35 = 2.8000 \text{ hours} \qquad \text{(Eq. 1c, Figure 16.14)}$$

and

$$L_S = 2.5 \times 2.8 = 7 \text{ computer users} \qquad \text{(Eq. 1a, Figure 16.14)}$$

Note that the exponential service time system implies a significantly faster system.

Constant Service Time: The Sparkle Plenty Car Wash

This single-line car wash is fully automatic, and it takes exactly $T = 10$ minutes $= .1667$ hour for a car to go through the system. Thus this is a problem with a **constant service time**. Arrival is Poisson, so this system is covered by our theory. We have $\sigma = 0$, and so

$$f = \frac{\sigma}{T} = \frac{0}{.1667} = 0$$

$$\frac{1 + f^2}{2} = .5$$

For the single-channel Poisson arrival constant service time system the average number of customers in the system (including queuing and service) is

$$L_q = \frac{\rho^2}{2(1 - \rho)} \qquad \text{(see Eq. 5, Figure 16.14)}$$

Note that for the corresponding exponential system (the fifth basic formula in Section 16.3)

$$L_q = \frac{\rho^2}{1 - \rho}$$

The constant service time system has on the average half as many customers in queue as the corresponding exponential system.

The arrival rate for Sparkle Plenty is

$$A = 5 \text{ cars/hour}$$

The service rate is

$$S = \frac{1}{T} = \frac{60}{10} = 6 \text{ cars/hour}$$

The utilization factor is

$$\rho = \frac{A}{S} = \frac{5}{6} = .8333$$

Thus (see Eq. 4),

$$L_q = \frac{\rho^2}{2(1 - \rho)} = \frac{1}{2} \times \frac{.8333^2}{1 - .8333} = \frac{1}{2} \times \frac{.6944}{.1667} = \frac{1}{2} \times 4.1656 = 2.0833$$

Also,

$$W_q = \frac{L_q}{A} = \frac{2.0828}{5} = .4166 \text{ hour} \qquad \text{(Eq. 1b, Figure 16.14)}$$

$$W_S = W_q + T = .4166 + .1667 = .5833 \text{ hour} \qquad \text{(Eq. 1c, Figure 16.14)}$$

$$L_S = AW_S = 5 \times .5833 = 2.9165 \text{ cars} \qquad \text{(Eq. 1a, Figure 16.14)}$$

Let us compare this system with the corresponding system with exponential service time. We have on the average twice as many cars waiting:

$$L_q = \frac{\rho^2}{1 - \rho} \times \frac{1 + f^2}{2} = \frac{\rho^2}{1 - \rho} \times \frac{1 + 1}{2} = \frac{\rho^2}{1 - \rho} = 4.1666 \text{ cars}$$

$$\text{(Eq. 4, Figure 16.14)}$$

$$W_q = \frac{L_q}{A} = \frac{4.1656}{5} = .8331 \text{ hour} \qquad \text{(Eq. 1b, Figure 16.14)}$$

$$W_S = W_q + T = .8331 + .1667 = 1.00 \text{ hour} \qquad \text{(Eq. 1c, Figure 16.14)}$$

$$L_S = AW_S = 5 \times 1 = 5 \text{ cars} \qquad \text{(Eq. 1a, Figure 16.14)}$$

Note then that the exponential time system implies a significantly slower system.

Another Attendant for Sparkle Plenty

Records show that two attendants wash a car more than twice as fast as a single attendant. In fact now $T = 4$ minutes $= .0667$ hour. Now

$$S = \frac{1}{T} = \frac{60}{4} = 15 \text{ cars/hour}$$

$$\rho = \frac{A}{S} = \frac{5}{15} = .3333$$

and (Eq. 4, Figure 16.14)

$$L_q = \frac{\rho^2}{2(1 - \rho)} = \frac{.3333^2}{2(1 - .3333)} = \frac{1}{2} \times \frac{.3333^2}{.6667} = \frac{1}{2} \times .1666 = .0833 \text{ car}$$

Thus,

$$W_q = \frac{L_q}{A} = \frac{.0833}{5} = .0167 \text{ hour} \qquad \text{(Eq. 1b, Figure 16.14)}$$

$$W_S = W_q + T = .0167 + .0667 = .0834 \text{ hour} \qquad \text{(Eq. 1c, Figure 16.14)}$$

and

$$L_S = AW_S = 5 \times .0834 = .417 \text{ car} \qquad \text{(Eq. 1a, Figure 16.14)}$$

Comparison with the corresponding exponential system is left as an exercise.

Impact of the Standard Deviation of Service Time Distribution

One would expect that when the standard deviation goes up, the system becomes slower, because there is more uncertainty (and variability) in service time. The formula for L_q does indeed bear out this expectation because the factor

$$1 + f^2 = 1 + \frac{\sigma^2}{T^2}$$

increases as σ increases. The fastest system with the smallest f is when $\sigma = 0$, meaning that the service time is fixed. For the exponential service time system, as already stated,

$$\sigma = T$$

and

$$f = \frac{\sigma}{T} = 1$$

We can now summarize our results:

1. If σ is significantly smaller than T, the system is significantly faster than the corresponding exponential system.
2. If σ is close to T, the system performs approximately the same as the corresponding exponential system.
3. If σ is significantly larger than T, the system performs significantly slower than the corresponding exponential system.

16.8 OTHER WAITING-LINE SYSTEMS

Queuing theory has been applied to many managerial situations not discussed in this textbook. Here we simply make a brief review of some of these other situations.

We always assumed that arrival is governed by the Poisson distribution. In real life this often is not the case, and so problems have been studied with other types of arrival distribution. For example, the problem when the time between arrivals is a constant has been studied extensively. Some of these studies assume exponential service time, while others assume more general types of distribution.

However, waiting-line theory has been applied to much more difficult situations. Let us illustrate some by example.

Transient Phenomena

Suppose in a waiting-line system some disturbance occurs such as the breakdown of service, a traffic jam, or a sudden increase in traffic. In such situations one wants to know how long it will take for the system to return to normal operating conditions, that is, to **steady-state conditions**. When the impact of disturbances or other unusual occurrences is studied, it is said that **transient phenomena** are under investigation. For example, if at a post office or at a bank a line of customers is waiting at opening time, one wants to know how long it will take for the situation to return to normal or to **equilibrium**. When studying such situations, various emergencies and solutions to these emergencies are considered. For example, the operating characteristics of systems where in the case of emergency there is a redirection of traffic or rerouting of customers through facilities have been studied.

Time-Dependent Systems

Traffic coming to a bridge or a tunnel may be light during the night but may peak during the rush hours and in the morning and afternoon. Such arrivals are clearly not Poisson, as the rate of arrival depends on the time of day or perhaps on the day of the week. Here one is interested in the operating characteristics of such systems and how they can be improved.

For example, the level of service may be changed as time goes on. In a supermarket, for instance, more checkout counters may be opened during peak loads.

Another solution to such problems is to increase the service level when the lines are too long and decrease the service level when the load is light.

Finite Queues

Consider the problem of servicing a fixed number of airplanes or machines in a shop. If there are only four machines, there will never be more than four in queue waiting for service. It is said, then, that the source of customers is *finite*.

Another type of finite line is where there are only a certain number of places in queue, and while the source is infinite, when there is no room in queue, customers will not join the queue. For example, in a gas station there may be only a limited space available for cars if cars are not allowed to queue on the street. Or the number of chairs in the waiting room of a medical office is limited, and if patients refuse to stand, their number in queue also becomes limited or finite.

Queuing Disciplines

So far we have considered only the first-in-first-out (FIFO) queuing discipline. But there are other possible queuing disciplines. For example, one could have a last-in-first-out system.

It is also possible that customers *balk*. This means that when the waiting time is too long, customers refuse to join the line and leave. Another possibility is to have *impatient* customers, meaning that after waiting a certain length of time, customers leave.

It is possible to have multichannel systems, where customers can *switch* from one line to another. For example, in a bank, as people wait for service and one of the lines gets shorter, a customer may switch to join a shorter line.

A common system of improving service to waiting lines is to specify *priorities*. A high-priority message goes through a communication network first, and so important messages have to wait less. In some systems, as in the emergency ward of a hospital, when a very high-priority patient arrives, treatment of a patient may be interrupted to give immediate attention to the higher-priority patient. After the priority case is completed, treatment is resumed on the interrupted patient. Another priority system is to provide a special line for special customers. For example, in supermarkets, customers with a limited number of purchases may be routed to the fast line. However, if the queue in the fast line becomes too long, customers may choose to join another line.

There are many situations where customers must go through facilities in sequence. For example, in a hospital where a battery of tests are given, the patient must go through various stations. In a production shop parts may have to go through various assembly lines and production facilities. Such systems are referred to as *waiting-line networks*.

While there is a large body of theory available on waiting lines, the fact is that real-life waiting-line situations can become exceedingly complex, and often there is no theory available to resolve the issues. In such cases the technique of simulation (discussed in Chapter 17) is a most popular methodology employed.

16.9 HYPING UP PRODUCTION BY QUEUING THEORY: A SUCCESSFUL APPLICATION*

Background

The Becton Dickinson Division of Becton Dickinson Company, Rutherford, New Jersey, manufactures hypodermic needles and syringes for health care. The company foresaw an increase in demand for their

---

* Adapted from Myles A. Vogel, "Queuing Theory Applied to Machine Manning," *Interfaces*, Vol. 9, No. 4, Aug. 1979, pp. 1–7.

product and desired to increase production capacity without lowering the quality of products. Attempts to improve the situation by traditional industrial engineering approaches, such as improved layout time and ratio delay studies, all failed.

A simple walk through the facility by management made it clear that there was a problem in operating the production machines. The major function of attendants was "clearing jams" in the production machines to avoid downtime of production machines when they were "jammed." But attendants were ineffective, products did not flow properly, and machine speeds were not set at optimum level. The introduction of higher-speed equipment to expand capacity only increased the frequency of jams and downtime. Attempts to make the machines more reliable and thereby reduce jams and downtimes failed, and so it became apparent that the problem was to improve attendant effectiveness.

Introduction of a Queuing Model

The analysts at Becton Dickinson realized that machine jams occurred in a random manner and so could be modeled by the arrival of customers at a waiting-line system. While ordinarily customers arriving at a waiting-line system are visualized as people, there is no reason why machine jams could not be considered as *customers*. Similarly, the channels can be represented by the attendant assigned to clearing the jams. Each attendant is assigned to a number of machines, and so each attendant is a single-channel waiting-line system where the customers are the machine jams.

To apply the formulas of waiting-line theory, it was necessary to determine whether the arrival followed the Poisson distribution and whether the service time for clearing jams followed the exponential distribution. That the system was indeed a Poisson exponential system was established in five steps:

1. Statistical data regarding time of arrivals and services were collected.
2. Frequency histograms for both arrivals and service time distributions were established, checking that mean arrival rate and service time did not change while the data were collected.
3. By using statistical theory, appropriate probability distributions were fitted to the pattern of arrivals and service times.
4. The hypothesis was postulated that the system is a Poisson exponential type.
5. Use of the chi-square goodness-of-fit test established that the hypothesis of dealing with a Poisson exponential system was valid.

Applying the Model and Economic Analysis

The management of Becton Dickinson was now in a position to predict the operating characteristics of the production system under alternate assignments of machines to attendants. However, it was noted that attendants performed not only the clearing of jams but also "other tasks." Recognizing the major significance of clearing jams, the decision was made to assign attendants exclusively to the task of clearing jams and to assign the other tasks to lower-paid personnel who routinely serviced machines relative to material handling and quality control. Then the cost of waiting and the cost of providing service were established, and so any proposed redistribution of assignment of machines to attendants could be examined and economically evaluated. By considering various alternatives, it became possible to determine the optimum allocation of attendants to machines.

Results and Analysis

On the basis of the study management decided to reduce step by step the machine attendant force to 115. This resulted in savings in labor of $575,000 during the first year of operation. At the same time there was a sudden increase in demand for syringes in the health care field, and an 80% increase in production level was made possible by the increased productivity and reduced labor costs resulting from the study.

The same analysis was implemented at two other Becton Dickinson plants in Nebraska, and the technology was transferred to manufacturing in Ireland with similar results.

16.10 THE USEFULNESS OF QUEUING THEORY: A DIALOG

Q. *Do most real-life waiting-line systems satisfy the probability distributions required by the Poisson exponential model?*

A. There are many situations which are at least approximately of the Poisson exponential type but many more where these assumptions do not hold.

Q. *Then what is the good of your theory?*

A. You have seen only an introduction to the theory, as there are many other waiting-line situations covered by mathematical theory.

Q. *Is there theory available for most waiting-line situations?*

A. I must admit that, on the contrary, many waiting-line situations are not covered by the theory, and answers can be obtained only by using simulation techniques on the computer.

Q. *Then I am back to my original question. What is the point to your theory?*

A. You must understand the meaning of the word *theory*. Theory is not the same as a set of formulas. Theory provides a useful guide and a systematic view to dealing with problems. You can organize your thoughts in a rational and efficient manner. Consider, for example, the concept of utilization. You know that when utilization is near 1, there will be trouble and small upsets will make the waiting lines very long. The Poisson exponential system tells you precisely how long the lines will become. However, in real-life situations you want to avoid having utilization near 1, and you are more interested in designing a system which will not run into trouble. Thus, even if your system is not of the Poisson exponential type, your knowledge of the theory will help you in resolving difficulties. Thus, while most real-life situations are solved by simulation, theory provides you with guidance and possible checking of the validity of your simulation techniques.

Q. *Queuing theory is then more of a body of knowledge to provide general guidance and to organize and structure your thoughts, to discipline your thought processes, than a set of specific formulas.*

A. That is right. But you must not forget that there are many real-life situations where queuing theory is directly applicable. To sum up, queuing-line theory is an important discipline for supporting managerial decision making.

SUMMARY

1. Waiting lines are one of the successful application areas of operations research and management science.

2. The scientific approach to solving waiting-line problems is to balance the cost of waiting and the cost of service.

3. The economic analysis of waiting lines is based on the operating characteristics of waiting-line systems.

4. Many practical waiting-line problems can be solved under the assumption of the Poisson exponential system.

5. Figure 16.14 summarizes the formulas used in this textbook for waiting-line problems.

6. In real-life problems data must be obtained and analyzed to determine the arrival and service time characteristics of waiting lines.

7. There are special formulas, charts, and computer programs available for solving many types of waiting-line problems.

8. Many real-life waiting-line problems can be resolved only by simulation.

SECTION EXERCISES

1. *The Scientific Approach to Waiting Lines*

1.1 Section 16.1 opens with the quotation, "Is time really wasted when waiting?" In the examples given for clerks and for landing planes, it should be clear that the real issue is, *whose* time is spent in waiting? If you don't wait, someone else does. For example, in a hairdressing shop, if you don't wait, then the hairdressers will wait when there are no customers. In the following table for showing this relationship, add three examples from your own experience:

IF I DON'T WAIT AT THE:	THEN THESE PERSONS OR MACHINES WILL BE WAITING:
1. Barber shop	Barbers
2.	
3.	
4.	

1.2 As discussed in Section 16.1, the scientific approach balances the costs of waiting against the costs of service. In some cases (for example, where the person waiting for service is an engineer at a copy machine) we can accurately estimate the cost of the waiting time. But in other cases we have no direct monetary cost. For example, if you wait at an airline ticket counter for an undue length of time, you may not use that airline in the future. In such cases we can make a list of intangible (but real) costs due to waiting. In the following list we show some of the intangible costs in the example of the undue wait at the airline ticket counter. Add three examples to this list from your own experience. Try to list as many possible intangible costs as you can think of.

1. Airline ticket counter: Lost business if customer never uses airline again
Empty seat on plane if delay causes customer to miss plane
Lost business due to customer telling friends to avoid the airline
Cost of responding to complaint letter
Cost of responding to regulatory agency if complaint made
Low productivity of clerks due to tension and pressure
High turnover of clerks
2.
3.
4.

1.3 In Section 16.1, it is pointed out that waiting-line problems are dominated by uncertainty and that the variables are *usually* random. However, sometimes the variables mentioned here are not random but *deterministic*. There are many real-world situations in which deterministic variables arise. For example, the arrivals of ships at a port may be predictable according to a schedule. Given the date, you can tell how many will arrive on that date. Give three examples of situations in which either or both of the following are deterministic:
a. The number of "customers" arriving in a given time.
b. The time to service a customer is deterministic.

1.4 For the CCC tool-crib example in Section 16.1, identify those costs which go with the rising curve of the graph of the lower part of Figure 16.1 and which costs go with the declining curve.

1.5 Figure 16.2 shows a queue with a first-in-first-out discipline. What other disciplines are possible? Give at least three.

1.6 Give three examples from your own experience of a calling population which is

  a. Infinite

  b. Finite

1.7 Give three examples of processes in the real world in which it is reasonable to assume that the probability of birth or death is the same in any fixed time period.

1.8 Give three examples of processes in the real world in which it is *not* reasonable to assume that the probability of birth or death is the same in any fixed time period.

1.9 You can easily "run" the thought experiment of Figure 16.3. Assign the IN wheel a YES sector of 30° and the OUT wheel a sector of 60°. Cut a wheel from an index card or cardboard, and use a pin through the center (or use a pencil as a spinner). It is not necessary that your wheel be a precision instrument. Make a chart similar to the table of Figure 16.4, and spin the wheels 15 steps worth. Use your data to answer the following questions:

  a. What is the average number in the queue at the end?

  b. What is the average number in the system (at the end)?

  c. What is the average number of arrivals per period?

  d. What is the average number of departures per period?

2. *Arrival and Service Time Distributions*

2.1 The number of patients per hour arriving at the Pest Medical Clinic has been shown to conform to a Poisson distribution with an average of two patients per hour. What is the probablity that

  a. Exactly four arrive in an hour?

  b. There are anywhere from two to five arrivals in an hour?

  c. More than one patient arrives in an hour?

2.2 The arrival of boats carrying marlin catches at the docks of Brando, Inc. occurs at an average rate of five per day. Assuming that the Poisson probability distribution applies, what is the probability that

  a. Exactly five arrive in one day?

  b. There are anywhere from two to three arrivals in a day?

  c. More than five arrive in a day?

2.3 The service time for patients at the Buda Medical Center is known to be exponentially distributed with an expected capacity of five patients per hour ($S = 5$). What is the probability that the service of a patient can be completed in

  a. Exactly 10 minutes?

  b. Less than half an hour?

  c. More than 1 hour?

2.4 The servicing of ships carrying marlin catches at the docks of Brando, Inc. is carried out by 10 dockworkers. They can service one ship an hour on the average. What is the probability that a ship will be serviced in

  a. Less than 1 hour?

  b. Between 2 and 3 hours?

  c. More than 5 hours?

2.5 Management has found that records for the past several years show that the arrivals at the drawing copy center of the engineering department are Poisson distributed with a mean number of arrivals of two per minute.

  a. What is the interarrival time distribution of arrivals at the engineering reproduction center?

  b. What is the probability that the time between arrivals exceeds 1.5 minutes?

  c. What is the probability that the time between arrivals is between .5 and 1 minute?

d. What is the probability that the time between arrivals is less than .8 minute?

2.6 The mean time breakdowns (also called the MTBF, the mean time between failure) for a computer is known to be 360 minutes and is well modeled by the exponential distribution.

 a. What is the distribution of the number of breakdowns per 24-hour day?
 b. What is the mean of the distribution of the number of breakdowns per 24-hour day?
 c. What is the probability that the time between breakdowns exceeds 108 minutes?
 d. What is the probability that the number of breakdowns in a 24-hour day is zero?
 e. What is the probability that the number of breakdowns in a 24-hour day is greater than 3?
 f. What is the probability that the number of breakdowns in a 24-hour day is less than 2?

3. Basic Waiting Line Theory for Single Channel

3.1 The average number of arrivals at the dockside complaint counter of Vigorish Enterprises is 15 per week. Service is at the average rate of 28 per week.

 a. What is the utilization factor?
 b. What is the average number of customers in the system?
 c. What is the average amount of time a customer spends in the system?
 d. What is the average time a customer spends in the queue waiting for service?
 e. What is the average number of customers in the queue?

3.2 The average time between arrivals of phone calls at Litvak's Drug Store is 2 minutes, and the average number of phone calls that can be serviced in an hour is 90.

 a. What is the utilization factor?
 b. What is the average number of customers in the system?
 c. What is the average amount of time a customer spends in the system?
 d. What is the average time a customer spends in the queue waiting for service?
 e. What is the average number of customers in the queue?

3.3 The average number of arrivals at the The-Rocks copying machine example of Section 16.3 drops to two per hour as a consequence of competition. All other characteristics of the system are unchanged.

 a. What is the utilization factor?
 b. What is the average number of customers in the system?
 c. What is the average amount of time a customer spends in the system?
 d. What is the average time a customer spends in the queue waiting for service?
 e. What is the average number of customers in the queue?

3.4 The office manager in the The-Rocks copying machine example of Section 16.3 prefers not to see more than three customers in the system—both in the queue and copying—on the average.

 a. What is the utilization factor which must be obtained to meet this requirement?
 b. What is the average amount of time a customer spends in the system?
 c. What is the average time a customer spends in the queue waiting for service?
 d. What is the average number of customers in the queue?

3.5 The line at the machine in the The-Rocks copying machine example of

Section 16.3 has been interfering with traffic in the corridor, and it is necessary to reduce the average queue length to .7. Assume that we have no way to change the rate of arrival.

    a. What is the average waiting time?

    b. Find an expression for the utilization factor as a function of the average queue length.

Hints:

    1. Express L_q as a function of W_q and A.

    2. Substitute the expression for W_q as a function of W_s and T and express in terms of L_s, A, and S only.

    3. Express L_s in terms of the utilization factor, and reduce the whole expression to L_q as a function of the utilization factor.

    4. Solve for the utilization factor using the formula for the roots of a quadratic equation in Appendix A.

    c. With the result of part b, find the value of the utilization factor needed to achieve the desired value of L_q.

    d. Find the value of S needed to achieve the desired value for L_q.

3.6 The average number of inquiries at the motor vehicle bureau of Westucket is three per hour. The average service time is 4 minutes.

    a. What is the utilization factor?

    b. What is the average number of customers in the system?

    c. What is the average amount of time a customer spends in the system?

    d. What is the average time a customer spends in the queue waiting for service?

    e. What is the average number of customers in the queue?

4. Solving the Tool Crib Problem

4.1 Refer to the tool-crib problem of Section 16.4. Assume that the average service time is reduced to .7 minute using four attendants. Compute all system performance characteristics found in Figure 16.10 (T, S, etc.), and enter them into a fourth column entitled "Four Attendants."

4.2 Refer to the tool-crib problem of Section 16.4. Assume that the average service time is reduced to .7 minute using four attendants and that all other characteristics of the system are the same as in the text. However, the wages of the attendants have been raised to $25 per hour. Find C_T, the total cost, for one, two, three, and four attendants, and enter the costs into a table similar to Figure 16.10. Find the optimal number of attendants.

4.3 A hospital emergency room has observed that the attendants share work. Studies under experimental conditions show that the average time for service of an emergency patient is as follows:

NUMBER OF ATTENDANTS	MEAN SERVICE TIME (MIN)
1	30
2	20
3	13
4	9
5	6

Patients arrive at an average rate of one per hour.

    a. Make a table similar to Figure 16.10, replacing C_T with C_S, the cost of the service. Compute values for the variables T through L_q, and enter them into the table.

    b. Assume that the emergency room runs on a 24-hour-per-day basis and that each attendant earns $10 an hour. Complete the entries for C_S.

c. Plot the average waiting time vs. the cost of service.

d. What is the cost of reducing the average waiting time to 10 minutes?

5. *Probabilistic Performance Measures*

5.1 Refer to the copying machine example of Section 16.3. Assume that jobs arrive at the rate of $A = 2$ per hour. All other characteristics of the system remain unchanged. What is the probability of
    a. The machine being idle?
    b. Having exactly 2 or 3 customers in the system?
    c. Having 10 customers in the system?

5.2 Refer to Exercise 3.4 in which the copying machine situation of Section 16.3 is revised to limit the average number in the queue to 3. Under these conditions, what is the probability that the number of customers in the queue
    a. Is 0, 1, 2, 3?
    b. Is less than 1, less than 2, less than 3, less than 4?

5.3 Refer to Exercise 3.5 in which the average queue length is limited to .7. Under these conditions,
    a. What is the probability of the terminal being idle?

(*Hint*: See Section 16.4.)
    b. What is the probability of having exactly 1, 2, 3, or 4 customers in the system?

(*Hint*: See Section 16.4.)
    c. What is the probability of having fewer than 3 customers in the system?
    d. What is the probability of having 2 or more customers in the system?

5.4 Refer to Exercise 4.2. For each of the four different numbers of attendants given there, find the probability for 0–13 workers in line. (*Hint*: You can make it easier to check your results by adding columns to your table for these probabilities.)

5.5 Refer to Exercise 3.6. A person who applied at the office complained that the wait was excessive. This person claimed to have counted 10 people in line. When a query was made of the personnel working at the terminal, they said that the complainer was continually dropping out of the line. To decide if the person's complaint was likely to be correct, the director of motor vehicle registrations asked for a computation that there will be 10 or more people in the system at any one time. If this probability is extremely low, then he will reject the complaint. To help make this decision, compute the probability. What do you think the director did?

6. *Multi-Channel Systems*

6.1 In the Burger Queen Restaurant example of Section 16.6, assume that the arrival rate drops to 20 per hour and as a consequence of Parkinson's law[*] the average service time increases to 2.2 minutes. Make a new version of Figure 16.12 and enter the values found by you for one, two, and three channels.

6.2 In the Burger Queen Restaurant example of Section 16.6 a fourth channel is opened. All other characteristics of the system remain as described in the section discussion.
    a. Make a fourth column for Figure 16.12 and enter the values you get.
    b. Based on the reduction in L_q and W_S that the fourth channel gives, do you think the customers will notice the difference?

6.3 The Loxtown Parking Commission is planning new parking areas to be set

---

[*] The work tends to expand to fit the time available.

aside for short-term parking. The problem they had in the past was that shoppers wanting to use the short-term parking will queue up to get into the lot because of the frequent comings and goings (the average time a space is occupied is 20 minutes). Whenever the queue exceeds three cars, traffic in an adjoining driveway is blocked. Cars arrive at an average rate of one every 6 minutes.

    a. Make a table similar to Figure 16.12 for $C = 1$ to $C = 10$ slots in the parking area.

    b. Choose a value for C to recommend to the commission. Justify your choice.

    c. One of the city planners points out that the existence of more parking spaces always brings in more cars. He estimates that the existence of another lot of any size will reduce the time between arrivals to 4 minutes on the average. Choose a new value for C, and justify it.

6.4 In the multichannel tool-crib situation described in Section 16.6, assume that the hourly wage of workers is increased to $25.

    a. For the case of two channels, make a table similar to Figure 16.12, including a row for C_T.

    b. Repeat part a for three channels.

    c. Has the optimal number of channels been changed as a consequence of this revised hourly wage? Explain.

6.5 It has been suggested that having attendants share the work in a hospital emergency room (a multiserver situation with one channel) is not the best way to handle patients. In this situation, patients can see the treatments given to others while they wait, patients criticize the services, and a survey showed that the patients feel the personal element is lost when several attendants work on one patient. It has been proposed that a one-on-one arrangement be set up (a multichannel operation with one server per channel). At the hospital in question patients arrive at the emergency room at an average rate of one per hour. Each attendant can service an average of two patients per hour. Attendants are paid $10 per hour. A 24-hour day with a constant average rate of arrival and service may be assumed.

    a. Make a table similar to Figure 16.12 including a row for C_S.

    b. Plot the average waiting time vs. the cost of service.

    c. What conclusions do you draw about the cost of service, and what is a reasonable number of channels?

7. Single Channel Poisson Arrival System

7.1 Refer to the Debug Computer Softwarehouse example of Section 16.7. Assume that the probability of a job being major or minor has been revised to be .7 for major and .3 for minor. All other characteristics of the situation remain the same. Find the values of T, S, utilization factor, L_q, W_q, W_S, and L_S.

7.2 Refer to the Debug Computer Softwarehouse example of Section 16.7. The exponentially distributed service with the same average service time gives a larger value of L_S. To what value must the average service time be reduced to give a system that has the same L_S?

7.3 Refer to the Quickfix Softwarehouse example of Section 16.7. Records show that the probability of occurrence of a minor problem has declined to .85 but that the fixing time has increased to .2 hour. The probability of occurrence of a major problem remains the same.

    a. Find the mean service time.

    b. Find the average service rate.

    c. Find the average arrival rate.

    d. What is the utilization factor?

    e. What is the variance of the probability distribution of service time?

    f. What is the average number of customers in the queue?

    g. What is the average waiting time?

    h. What is the average transit time, including waiting time?

    i. What is the average number of customers in the system?

    j. Compare this system to the corresponding exponential service time system.

7.4 Refer to the Quickfix Softwarehouse example of Section 16.7. Records show that the probability of occurrence of a major problem has increased to .2 but that the fixing time has decreased to 1.5 hours. The probability of occurrence of a minor problem remains the same.

    a. Find the mean service time.

    b. Find the average service rate.

    c. Find the average arrival rate.

    d. What is the utilization factor?

    e. What is the variance of the probability distribution of service time?

    f. What is the average number of customers in the queue?

    g. What is the average waiting time?

    h. What is the average transit time, including waiting time?

    i. What is the average number of customers in the system?

    j. Compare this system to the corresponding exponential service time system.

7.5 Refer to the Quickfix Softwarehouse example of Section 16.7. Records show that the probability of occurrence of a minor problem has declined to .8 but that the fixing time has increased to .2 hour. The probability of occurrence of a major problem has increased to .2, and the fixing time has decreased to 1 hour.

    a. Find the mean service time.

    b. Find the average service rate.

    c. Find the average arrival rate.

    d. What is the utilization factor?

    e. What is the variance of the probability distribution of service time?

    f. What is the average number of customers in the queue?

    g. What is the average waiting time?

    h. What is the average transit time, including waiting time?

    i. What is the average number of customers in the system?

    j. Compare this system to the corresponding exponential service time system.

7.6 Pop Eye's Optometrists fit contact lenses with one attendant. Their walk-in trade arrives at the rate of three per hour average; the arrival distribution has been found to be Poisson. A fitting can be accomplished in a fixed time of 10 minutes (note that this is a constant service time situation).

    a. Find values for S, L_q, W_S, L_S, and utilization factor.

    b. Add another channel, and find values for the performance characteristics of part a.

7.7 A mass transit system has converted to automatic ticket dispensers. Observation shows that the time for service is a constant, being determined by a fixed mechanical operation of dispensing. The city management wants to make decisions concerning the installation of these dispensers in a new station. The service time is a constant 6 seconds; the flow of customers into the stations is estimated at one every 2 seconds on the average, conforming to a Poisson distribution (for the rush-hour period of 2 hours, which is the period which is used to determine service characteristics). Make a table similar to Figure 16.12 showing the performance characteristics for 1, 2, 3, 5, 7, 10, and 20 dispensers.

7.8 Refer to the Sparkle Plenty Car Wash example of Section 16.7. Attendants cost $4 an hour; the car wash is open 1500 hours a year. A channel costs

$10,000, which reduces to an annual equivalent cost of $2500 per year. The amount that can be charged for a car is dependent on the transit time T according to the following relationship:

$$\text{revenue/car} = .5 - 3.24 \times (\log T)$$

a. Consider the situation with constant service time described in the text and one attendant. Make a table similar to Figure 16.12, adding rows for revenue R and cost of service C_S and the gross profit $R - C_S$.

b. Consider the situation with constant service time described in the text and two attendants. Make a table as in part a, and compute all performance characteristics and the annualized costs.

c. Consider the situation with a Poisson exponential process with one attendant. Make a table as described in part a, and compute all performance characteristics and the annualized costs.

d. Repeat part c for the case of a Poisson exponential process with two attendants.

e. Consider the situation with constant service time and one attendant per channel; perform the analysis described in part a for two channels with one attendant per channel.

(*Hint*: Remember to include the annualized channel cost.)

f. Consider the situation with constant service time and two attendants per channel; perform the analysis described in part a for two channels with two attendants per channel.

g. If you have done parts a–g of this exercise, which situation and combination of channels and attendants is optimal?

8. *Other Waiting-Line Systems*

8.1 In real life how would you go about determining whether or not the arrival distribution was governed by the Poisson distribution?

8.2 Consider the problem of performing an analysis of time-dependent systems. Suppose you had no more knowledge of the analysis of queuing systems than you have gotten from this chapter. How would you go about getting some solutions which you could use for staffing policy, etc., using the tools you have?

8.3 Give your own examples of the following:
a. A situation where we are concerned with transient phenomena
b. A time-dependent system
c. A finite queue
d. Customer balking
e. Customer switching
f. Waiting-line network

9. *Hyping up Production by Queuing Theory: A Successful Application*

9.1 Give another example where you can consider some mechanical or device failure as an "arrival."

9.2 Give an example of a situation you can think of where queuing theory might be applied to improve service or reduce costs or improve quality.

10. *The Usefulness of Queuing Theory: A Dialog*

10.1 If you have no data concerning the nature of the arrival time-service time distribution, what will you use in your analysis?

10.2 How would you know when you have a situation where the queuing theory described in this chapter is directly applicable?

CHAPTER EXERCISES AND DISCUSSION QUESTIONS

C.1 In the dialogs in this text we frequently find discussions of the usefulness and relevance of theory, because we so often find theory being questioned. What is good about the frequent questioning of theory, and what is bad?

C.2 It is possible to rent communications facilities which for a set fee of $5000 per line allow unlimited long-distance calls to be made. Assume that the demand for calls is Poisson distributed with a mean of 100 per 8-hour workday and that the average length of a call is 10 minutes. If the toll charges for an organization considering use of the special service are averaging $20,000 per month and the executive time involved is valued at $25 per hour, how many—if any—special lines should be installed? Support your recommendation.

C.3 Video Vision Centers is a chain of stores providing contact lenses. Their unique characteristic is small staffs located in convenient places (shopping centers, parking lots, railroad stations, etc.). The average arrival rate is nine customers per hour, each attendant can service an average of three customers per hour, and it is the company's policy to have only four attendants in each store. Using the Poisson exponential model,
   a. What is the utilization factor?
   b. What is the average number of customers in the queue?
   c. What is the average waiting time?
   d. What is the average transit time, including waiting time?

C.4 A handling crew unloads and loads (as required) forklift trucks moving to and from the loading platform of Southern Naptucket Engineering Truckers. Forklift truck arrivals have been found to conform to the Poisson distribution as has the rate of serviced departures of forklift trucks. The distribution of the number of completed services per unit time is unaffected by the size of the crew, but the average time required by a crew decreases proportionally to its size (a 2-person crew takes half the time of a 1-person crew, etc.). A 10-person crew unloads a forklift truck in an average time of .1 hour. Crew salaries are $10 per hour. An idling truck costs $30 per hour. Working hours are 40 hours per week.
   a. What should the size of the crew be?
   b. What is the total annual cost at the optimal value of crew size?
   c. Perform a sensitivity analysis of your solution, considering the possibility of plus or minus 10% variations in the dollar values given. How important is high precision in these values to the optimal size of the crew?

C.5 Long waiting lines were experienced for a certain production machine. Examples of past records show an average arrival rate of $A = 24$ parts per hour. On the average it takes about 2 minutes to manufacture a part, and thus $S = 30$ per hour. Assuming Poisson arrival and exponential service time, we get

$$\text{utilization factor} = \frac{A}{S} = \frac{24}{30} = .8$$

and so the expected number of parts in the queue waiting for service becomes

$$L_q = \frac{\rho^2}{2(1 - \rho)} = \frac{.64}{2(1 - .8)} = 1.6 \text{ parts}$$

This value is contrary to experience. A more careful study of the system is made, and it is found that arrival is Poisson distributed but that service time is not. Ninety-nine percent of the parts take exactly 1 minute to produce, but 1% of the time a particular complex part arrives. This complex part takes exactly 100 minutes to produce. Calculate

a. The average time required to make a part
b. The value of S
c. The value of ρ, the utilization factor
d. The value L_q.

Explain and discuss your results.

17

Simulation

While there is a large variety of mathematical models for managerial situations, for many real-life situations support for decisions cannot be obtained by purely mathematical techniques. In such situations computer-based simulation becomes a most popular computational technique. The word simulation may be applied to deterministic models, such as the financial planning models and decision support systems discussed in Section 1.6, or more often to probabilistic models. In this chapter we cover probabilistic simulation, also called Monte Carlo simulation.

Throughout this book we modeled decision making under uncertainty with the aid of thought experiments. Why can't we turn thought experiments into actual experiments to solve decision problems? The difficulty is that the use of chance devices is time-consuming, and so turning thought experiments into manual experiments is impractical. However, due to the phenomenal speed of computers, you can make a computer "spin wheels" thousands of times per second and consequently turn thought experiments into computer experiments. Thus simulation allows us to determine the consequences of trial decisions, and thereby it becomes possible to support the decision maker, even if a purely mathematical solution to the problem is not available.

You need not become an expert in computers to learn and apply simulation. The principles of simulation can be learned by doing the calculations with paper and pencil and a calculator. Therefore, in this textbook we shall avoid using computer concepts and shall rely solely on the principles of simulation.

17.1 TABLE OF RANDOM NUMBERS

In many of our thought experiments we used a roulette wheel as a chance device (see, for example, Figure 5.14). Note now that a roulette wheel can be replaced by a dart board with a vertical rectangular shape, as shown in Figure 17.1. For example, a spin ending with the ball stopping in sector 3 is equivalent to throwing a dart at the rectangular dart board and observing that the dart lands in sector 3. Each landing of a dart on the vertical, rectangular dart board corresponds to a fractional number between 0 and 1.0. So if someone were to throw a dart at the board thousands of times and record the corresponding fractional numbers in a table, we would not need to throw darts again but could use the **table of random numbers.** The authors have performed such an experiment with the aid of a computer. Table B.4 in Appendix B shows a table of random numbers uniformly distributed between 0 and 1. (The decimal points are omitted.)

The first number in Table B.4 is .48836, which corresponds to point *A* in Figure 17.1. The second number, .63729, corresponds to point *B*; the third number, .57895, corresponds to point *C*; and so on. Note, then, that by reading the numbers from the table of random numbers you can perform the thought experiment of spinning a wheel or throwing a dart.

> Any thought experiment can be turned into a sequence of calculations by using the table of random numbers.

Suppose you want to simulate the toss of an unbiased coin. Using computer notation, designate by RND the random number (between 0 and 1) read from the table. You can generate the sequence of heads or tails by using the following rule:

1. If RND $\leq$ .5, then the toss is heads.
2. If RND $>$ .5, then the toss is tails.

(In accordance with our discussion in Section 3.3, the probability of RND = .5 is zero.)

In Figure 17.2 in the first column, we show our random numbers, and in the second column we generate the toss of heads or tails. (Ignore for the moment columns 3 and 4.)

Suppose you want to generate heads or tails for a bent coin such

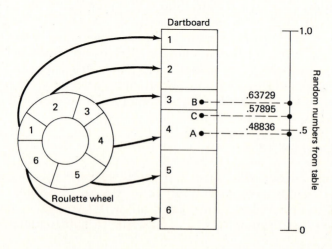

FIGURE 17.1
Replacing a roulette wheel with a dart board.

RANDOM NUMBERS	UNBIASED COIN	BENT COIN	NUMBER OF ARRIVALS
.48836	Head	Head	1
.63729	Tail	Tail	2
.57895	Tail	Head	2
.44468	Head	Head	1
.73332	Tail	Tail	2
⋮			

FIGURE 17.2 Simulation of coin tossing (the far right-hand column will be discussed later).

that the probability of tossing heads is .6 and of tails is .4. The rule is then the following:

1. If RND $\leq$ .6, the toss is heads.
2. If RND $>$ .6, the toss is tails.

In the third column of Figure 17.2 we show the generation of heads or tails for this bent coin.

Suppose now you need to know the probability of obtaining exactly three heads out of 5 tosses. You could estimate this probability in the following way. Repeat the tosses in Figure 17.2 for the bent coin a total of 500 times. Are there three heads in the first 5 tosses? Suppose *yes*. The second 5 tosses? Suppose *no*. And so on. Count the number of yeses for 100 sets of tosses. Divide by 100. This is the estimate in question.

The authors simulated this problem on a minicomputer. Five tosses were generated 50, 100, 200, and 500 times. The respective probability estimates are .4, .27, .34, and .35. We know from Chapter 3 that the exact value is given by the binomial distribution:

$$\frac{5!}{2!3!} \times .6^3 \times .4^2 = .3456$$

Thus a trial of 200 cases gives an accurate enough answer from the practical point of view.

Random Numbers of Given Probability Distribution

Now we show how to generate a random variable corresponding to any given probability distribution. As an example, consider the discrete random variable with the values 0, 1, 2, and 3 and with the probability distribution shown in Part (a) of Figure 17.3. Let us draw the cumulative distribution function shown in Part (b) of Figure 17.3. Let RND be a random number from our table of random numbers. We can generate the values of the desired random variable by the following rule:

1. If RND ≤ .15, the value is 0.
2. If .15 < RND ≤ .52, the value is 1.
3. If .52 < RND ≤ .79, the value is 2.
4. If .79 < RND, the value is 3.

The rationale of this rule is that the probability of the dart landing (1) in area 0 is .15, (2) in area 1 is .37, (3) in area 2 is .27, and (4) in area 3 is .21. This is as specified by the given probability distribution.

This technique of generating random values corresponding to a given probability distribution can be summarized by the following rule (see Figure 17.4):

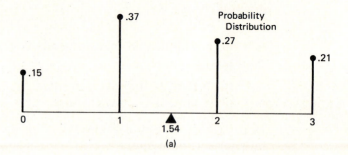

(a)

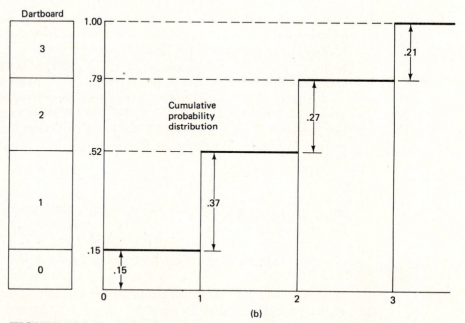

(b)

FIGURE 17.3 Generating random numbers corresponding to a given probability distribution.

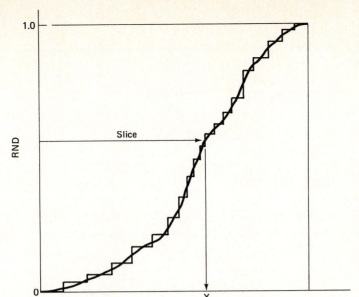

FIGURE 17.4
Generating ran-
dom numbers
with the slicing
rule.

Slicing Rule*

Step 1. Calculate the cumulative probability distribution.
Step 2. Read a random number RND from the table of random numbers.
Step 3. Slice the cumulative distribution function horizontally at point RND.
Step 4. Drop vertically to obtain the value of the random variable X.

If the probability distribution is continuous, you may have to approximate it by a step-by-step function first (Figure 17.4).

We can perform any random experiment by the use of our slicing rule and our table of random numbers. In practice it is the computer that generates the random numbers and carries out the calculations.

Linear Slicing Formula

Suppose we need to generate a random number X with a uniform distribution between A and B. The cumulative distribution is a straight line, as shown in Figure 17.5. From the slicing rule it follows that

$$\text{RND} = \frac{X - A}{B - A}$$

---

*A more scholarly term is the rule of the cumulative probability distribution function.

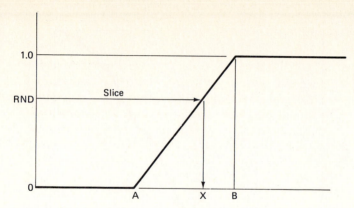

FIGURE 17.5
Generating a random number X of uniform distribution with the linear slicing formula.

Thus we have the following simple formula:

> *Linear slicing formula.* If
> $$X = (B - A)\text{RND} + A$$
> then X is uniformly distributed between A and B.

You can verify the formula by observing that (1) if RND is very small, X is just greater than A; (2) if RND is just less than 1, X is just less than $B - A + A = B$; and (3) the cumulative distribution is a straight line.

Getting and Using Answers

In practice a computer program is written to implement the simulation. The program includes counting the outcomes of the simulation and estimating the probabilities and expected values by computing averages.

Thus the approach to supporting the decision maker with simulation consists of repetition of the following two steps:

> *Step 1.* A tentative decision is made.
> *Step 2.* Consequences of the decision are determined by simulation.

Then a new decision is made, and the new consequences are determined. Actually, in practice a number of tentative decisions may be made, and the computer can provide the outcomes for each.

By trial and error, or systematic search, an acceptable solution for the decision maker is found.

We now illustrate with some typical examples how simulation is used.

As a first illustration we show how to simulate a single-channel waiting-line system. The thought experiment is shown in Figure 16.3, and we now show how to turn the thought experiment into a simulation calculation. First we must specify the probabilities.

Characteristics of the system are as follows: (1) the probability (ONE leaving on the OUT wheel) of service terminating within a 10-minute interval is .58; (2) the probability (ONE arriving on the IN wheel) of a customer arriving within 10 minutes is .45; (3) the probability of no customer arriving is .55. (The probability of more than one customer arriving is zero.) The rules for simulating this waiting-line problem are simple. If a customer is being served and the first random number is RND ≤ .58, the customer leaves, and if the second random number is RND ≤ .45, a customer arrives.

Figure 17.6 shows the first 10 steps of calculations. Assume that there are two customers in the system at the beginning, one in queue and one being served. The first random number is .48836, and so a customer leaves. The second random number is .63729, which means that no customer arrives. The change in the number of customers in the system is −1, and so at the end of the 10-minute period we have one customer in the system and no customer waiting.

The line-by-line simulation in Figure 17.6 is self-explanatory. Note, however, that in the tenth step there is no customer in the system, so no one can possibly leave, and there is no need to read from the table

STEP NUMBER	NUMBER IN SYSTEM AT BEGINNING	NUMBER IN QUEUE AT BEGINNING	1ST RANDOM NUMBER, RND	LEAVE?	2ND RANDOM NUMBER, RND	ARRIVE?	CHANGE IN NUMBER IN SYSTEM	NUMBER IN SYSTEM AT END	NUMBER IN QUEUE AT END
1	2	1	.48836	Yes	.63729	No	−1	1	0
2	1	0	.57895	Yes	.44468	Yes	0	1	0
3	1	0	.73332	No	.76234	No	0	1	0
4	1	0	.60967	No	.69193	No	0	1	0
5	1	0	.98368	No	.62535	No	0	1	0
6	1	0	.67712	No	.05503	Yes	+1	2	1
7	2	1	.34235	Yes	.68746	No	−1	1	0
8	1	0	.67049	No	.53034	No	0	1	0
9	1	0	.30004	Yes	.62626	No	−1	0	0
10	0	0	—	—	.26928	Yes	+1	1	0

FIGURE 17.6 Simulating a waiting-line system.

the random number corresponding to leaving. To estimate the average number of customers waiting, the average number in the system, etc., requires that many steps be calculated and the averages computed.

We simulated this problem on a computer for 100, 1000, 5000, and 100,000 cases and estimated the number of people in the system to be .97, 1.676, 1.7352, and 1.82741, respectively. The average number in queue were .47, .904, .9634, and 1.05516, respectively.*

Note that simulation provides the type of performance characteristics we calculated by formulas for waiting lines in Chapter 16. To make a decision, we would have to simulate the system for one, two, or possibly three channels and so on. Then we must perform economic calculations similar to those discussed in Chapter 16.

17.3 SCHEDULING UNDER UNCERTAINTY

In Section 5.5 we studied the 8-track cartridge problem of the Bop & Rock Studio (Figure 5.12). Due to uncertainties in the time spans of production, there was a question as to whether the market could be "met." With the aid of the probability tree in Figure 5.13 we showed that the market could not be met.

But suppose that there are not 3 but 10 activities and that each has an alternative of 10 time spans. The probability tree corresponding to Figure 5.13 would have $10^{10} = 10$ billion tips, and so the decision tree

---

* With the aid of Markov chain theory it can be shown that the average number of people in the system is precisely $.45 \times .55/.13$ (= 1.9038).

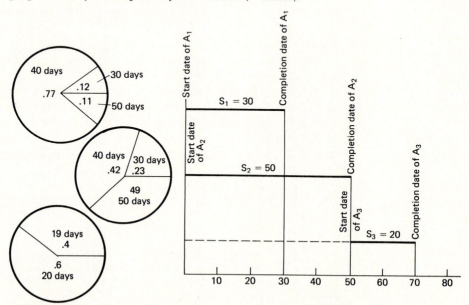

FIGURE 17.7 Scheduling problem for Bop & Rock Studio when the random variables S_1, S_2, and S_3 are, respectively, 30, 50, and 20 days.

DURATION	PROBABILITY	CUMULATIVE PROBABILITY	CONDITION FOR RND
$S_1 = 30$	.12	.12	RND $\leq$ .12
$S_1 = 40$	.77	.89	.12 < RND $\leq$ .89
$S_1 = 50$	.11	1.00	.89 < RND $\leq$ 1.0
$S_2 = 30$	.23	.23	RND $\leq$ .23
$S_2 = 40$	.42	.65	.23 < RND $\leq$ .65
$S_2 = 50$	.49	1.00	.65 < RND $\leq$ 1.0
$S_3 = 19$	.60	.60	RND $\leq$ .60
$S_3 = 20$	.40	1.00	.60 < RND $\leq$ 1.0

FIGURE 17.8 Rules for generating random numbers for Bop & Rock Studio.

approach becomes impractical. Simulation, however, provides the answer.

To simplify our presentation, we assume that the thought experiment for the system can be described by Figure 17.7. There are three activities involved: A_1, A_2, and A_3 with respective duration-time spans of S_1, S_2, and S_3. Activity A_3 cannot be started before both activities A_1 and A_2 are completed. Duration of the activities are uncertain, and the probability mass function of durations is given in the second column of Figure 17.8.

To use our slicing rule, we compute the cumulative probability distributions and then state the rule on how we compute the duration from the random number RND. For example, for activity A_1 we have the following: (1) If the random number is RND $\leq$ .12, the duration is 30 days; (2) if .12 < RND $\leq$ .89, it is 40 days; (3) otherwise it is 50 days.

In Figure 17.9 we show a few steps of the simulation. The first random number is .48836, and so the duration of the first activity is 40 days. The second random number is .63729, and so the duration of the second activity is 40 days. Thus we can start the third activity at day 40.

	RND	S_1	RND	S_2	START DATE OF A_3	RND	S_3	PRODUCTION SPAN S	PROFIT P
Step 1	.48836	40	.63729	40	40	.57895	19	59	$170
Step 2	.44468	40	.73332	50	50	.76234	20	70	−$19
Step 3	.60967	40	.69193	50	50	.98368	20	70	−$19
⋮									

FIGURE 17.9 Simulating the scheduling problem for Bop & Rock Studio.

The third random number is .57895, and so the duration of the third activity is 19 days. The production span is $S = 59$ days.

In the last column we show the profit, which is computed from the formula from Section 5.5:

$$P = \$4300 - \$70S = 4300 - 70 \times 59 = \$170$$

Computation of the other rows in Figure 17.9 is self-explanatory.

We ran this simulation on a computer 100 and 500 times and found profit estimates of $-\$136.60$ and $-\$154.10$. So the decision is not to market the cartridge.

17.4 DOCKING SHIPS IN HARBOR

Consider ships arriving to unload at pier 17, New York City. Ships arrive in the morning, and it takes exactly half a day to unload a ship. The rest of the ships form a waiting line in the harbor. The probability distribution and the cumulative probability distribution of arrivals are shown in Figure 17.3. The expected number of ships arriving daily is

$$0 \times .15 + 1 \times .37 + 2 \times .27 + 3 \times .21 = 1.54 \text{ ships/day}$$

Capacity is two ships per day, so this is a waiting-line problem where there is adequate capacity to unload the ships but a queue will form. Let us simulate the behavior of this waiting-line system.

We have already determined the rules for generating arrivals, and in fact in the fourth column of Figure 17.2 we have generated a sequence of arrivals. Thus we can directly proceed to the simulation shown in Figure 17.10. Assume that there is one ship waiting the first morning. There is one arrival, so there are two ships in the system. Both ships will be unloaded, and none is left waiting.

On the second day no ship is in queue, there are two arrivals, and there are two ships in the system; both will be unloaded. The same thing

	NUMBER IN QUEUE AT BEGINNING	RANDOM NUMBER, RND	NUMBER ARRIVING	NUMBER IN SYSTEM	NUMBER UNLOADED	NUMBER IN QUEUE, AT END
Step 1	1	.48836	1	2	2	0
2	0	.63729	2	2	2	0
3	0	.57895	2	2	2	0
4	0	.44468	1	1	1	0
5	0	.73332	2	2	2	0
6	0	.76234	2	2	2	0

FIGURE 17.10 Simulating the arrival and unloading of ships.

happens on the third day. The fourth day no ship is in queue, there is only one arrival, and so one ship will be unloaded and no ship is left waiting. On the fifth day there are two arrivals and two ships in the system, and both will be unloaded.

Thus step by step we can simulate the behavior of the system and by counting outcomes estimate the various probabilities involved. So simulation provides the performance characteristics of a system. Suppose, for example, the question arises as to whether the facility should be expanded. Then both the existing and proposed system would have to be simulated and an economic analysis made before a rational decision could be made.

17.5 RISK ANALYSIS FOR DECISION SUPPORT SYSTEMS

In Section 5.6, we discussed risk analysis (Figure 5.14), an important computer-based technique for supporting decision making under uncertainty. Now with the aid of simulation we show how complex risk analysis problems can be solved. We describe the approach with an example.

The Panacea Pharmaceutical Firm (PPF) is planning to market a new kind of cough drop. Here are next year's forecasts for the important factors of the problem and the notation to be used:

T: Total industry sales will be 15 million ounces of cough drops.

F: PPF will have a .35 fraction of the market; that is, the market share will be 35%.

Q: Forecast of quantity of cough drops sold by PPF: $Q = FT = .35 \times 15,000,000 = 5,250,000$ ounces.

P: Price per ounce: 15 cents.

R: Estimated revenue: $R = PQ = .15 \times 5,250,000 = \$787,500$.

a: Fixed cost: \$200,000.

b: Cost per ounce: 7.5 cents.

V: Variable cost: $V = bQ = .075 \times 5,250,000 = \$393,750$.

C: Total cost: $C = a + V = \$593,750$.

$Z = R - C$, profit: \$193,750.

Note that the profit of \$193,750, which is 24.6% of revenue, is computed by deterministic analysis. However, there is uncertainty in these numbers, and management wants to make a risk analysis to know the probability distribution of profit. We assume that the values are uniformly distributed within the following limits:

T: 10 to 20 million ounces

F: .2 to .5, that is, between 20 and 50%

P: 10 to 20 cents

a: \$100,000 to \$300,000

b: 5 to 10 cents

To gain an insight into the problem, we make a sensitivity analysis by computing the best and worst possible profit. The best possible profit is

$$T = 20,000,000 \text{ ounces}, \quad F = .5, \quad Q = 10,000,000 \text{ ounces}, \quad P = 20 \text{ cents}$$

$$R = PQ = \$2,000,000, \quad a = \$100,000, \quad b = 5 \text{ cents}, \quad V = 500,000$$

$$C = \$600,000, \quad Z = \$1,400,000$$

The worst possible profit, that is, the greatest possible loss, is

$$T = 10,000,000 \text{ ounces}, \quad F = .2, \quad Q = 2,000,000 \text{ ounces}, \quad P = 10 \text{ cents}$$

$$R = PQ = \$200,000, \quad a = \$300,000, \quad b = 10 \text{ cents}, \quad V = \$200,000$$

$$C = \$500,000, \quad Z = -\$300,000$$

Any other profit will be between these two extremes.

Risk Analysis by Simulation

Step 1. Generate the total industry sales T. We need a uniform distribution between $A = 10$ million and $B = 20$ million. From the linear slicing formula,

$$T = 10,000,000 \times \text{RND} + 10,000,000$$

Our first random number is RND = .48836, and so

$$T = 4,833,600 + 10,000,000 = 14,883,600 \text{ ounces}$$

Step 2. Generate the market share F. With the aid of the linear slicing formula for $A = .2$ and $B = .5$, we get

$$F = .3\text{RND} + .2$$

Our second random number is RND = .63729. Thus,

$$F = .3 \times .63729 + .2 = .191187 + .2 = .391187$$

Step 3. Generate the price P. From the linear slicing formula for $A = .1$ and $B = .2$,

$$P = .1\text{RND} + .1$$

The third random number is RND = .57895. Thus,

$$P = .1 \times .57895 + .1 = .157895 \text{ cents}$$

Step 4. Generate the fixed cost a. Now $A = 100,000$ and $B = 300,000$, and so

$$a = 200,000\text{RND} + 100,000$$

The fourth random number is RND = .44468, and so

$$a = 200,000 \times .44468 + 100,000 = \$188,936$$

Step 5. Generate the cost per ounce b. Now $A = .05$ and $B = .10$, and so

$$b = .05\text{RND} + .05$$

The fifth random number is RND = .73332, and so

$$b = .05 \times .73332 + .05 = .03666 + .05 = .086666$$

Now we have T, F, P, a, and b and can complete our calculations. The quantity sold is

$$Q = FT = .391187 \times 14{,}883{,}600 = 5{,}822{,}271 \text{ ounces}$$

The revenue is

$$R = PQ = .157895 \times 5{,}822{,}271 = \$919{,}307$$

The total cost is

$$C = a + V = a + bQ = 188{,}936 + .086666 \times 5{,}822{,}271 = \$693{,}529$$

and the profit is

$$Z = R - C = \$225{,}778$$

This then completes the first line in the simulation. Calculation of the second line is left as an exercise.

We carried out this simulation on a computer. To determine the probability distribution, we split the profit range, (−\$300,000 to \$1,400,000), into 17 segments, each \$100,000, and then made the program count when the profit was between −\$300,000 and −\$200,000, −\$200,000 and −\$100,000, and so on. Figure 17.11 shows the probability distribution obtained by running the computer for 5000 cases. The expected profit is \$191,740. How does this compare with our earlier results based on deterministic analysis?

We then had a profit of \$193,750. We can calculate the percent error we would make by using deterministic calculation. Namely,

$$\frac{193{,}750 - 191{,}740}{193{,}750} = \frac{2010}{193{,}750} = .0104$$

which shows that we would have overestimated the profit only by a fraction of .0104, that is, 1.04%.

In other problems, of course, the difference could be much larger. However, the importance of risk analysis does not lie so much in the accuracy of the estimate but in the attitude of the decision maker in examining the probability distribution. As explained in Chapter 5, the preferred alternative is chosen by applying judgment to the probability distribution and not by maximizing expected payoff.

17.6 TWO-BIN INVENTORY CONTROL SYSTEM

In Section 9.5, we already studied a two-bin inventory control system. Now we want to show how such problems can be solved by simulation.

Consider the problem of the North Pole Corp., which is wholesaling refrigerators. The following conditions hold for the system:

1. Monthly demand is uniform between 40 and 160 units (where 40 is included but 160 is not).
2. The probability of delivery in 2 months is .7 and in 3 months is .3.

Management wishes to simulate the system under the following inventory control policy: (1) If there are less than or exactly 150 refrigerators in inventory, refrigerators are ordered in such quantity that an immediate delivery would bring inventory up to 300 units; (2) there is no possibility for back ordering; that is, if there is a pending order, no second order can be placed.

Our first problem is to generate a random demand between 40 and 160 units. We use our linear slicing formula,

$$RND = (D - 40)/120$$

and try the corresponding formula

$$D = 120 \times RND + 40$$

However, this will not do, because we may get a demand for a fractional number of refrigerators, and we need whole numbers. So we drop the digits after the decimal point—we **truncate**. We write that the demand is

$$D = INT(120 \times RND) + 40$$

where the symbol INT, borrowed from computer work, designates truncation. We can verify the truncated linear slicing formula by noting the following: (1) If RND is very small, $120 \times RND$ is also very small, $INT(120 \times RND) = 0$, and $D = 40$; (2) if RND is just below 1, $120 \times RND$ is just below 120, and so $INT(120 \times RND) = 119$, and $D = 159$ (the probability of RND $= 1$ is zero); (3) the cumulative distribution is a straight line.

Assume that in the first month nothing is received and that there are 160 refrigerators in inventory (Figure 17.12). The first random number is RND = .48836. Thus we have

$$120 \times RND = 58.6032$$

$$INT(120 \times RND) = 58$$

Therefore D, the demand, is $40 + 58 = 98$ units. There is an inventory of 160 units, so 98 units are sold, and 62 units are left in inventory. There are less than 150 refrigerators in inventory, so there will be a reorder placed, and the quantity of the order will be $300 - 62 = 238$ units to bring it up to a total of 300.

Now we need to generate the lead time for the shipment to arrive. We use the rule that if the random number RND is less than or equal to .7, the lead time is 2 months and otherwise 3 months. Our second random number is RND = .63729, and so the lead time is 2 months. We also note in Figure 17.12 that there have been no lost sales.

In the second month nothing is received, so there are only 62 units in inventory, the value of RND is .57895, the demand is 109 units, only 62 are sold, and so there is a lost sale of 47 units. The inventory is down to 0, but there is no reorder because there is a pending order.

In the third month the 238 units which were ordered in the first month arrive, and so there are 238 units in inventory. The value of RND is .44468, the demand is 93, and so 93 units are sold, and 145 units are left in inventory. There is a reorder of $300 - 145 = 155$ units. The value

STEP NUMBER	NUMBER RECEIVED	NUMBER IN INVENTORY AT BEGINNING	1ST RANDOM NUMBER, RND	DEMAND, D	NUMBER SOLD	NUMBER IN INVENTORY AT END	ORDER?	ORDER QUANTITY	2ND RANDOM NUMBER, RND	LEAD TIME	LOST SALES
1	0	160	.48836	98	98	62	Yes	238	.63729	2	0
2	0	62	.57895	109	62	0	No	—	—	—	47
3	238	238	.44468	93	93	145	Yes	155	.73332	3	0
4	0	145	.76234	131	131	14	No	—	—	—	0
5	0	14	.60967	113	14	0	No	—	—	—	99
6	155	155	.69193	123	123	32	Yes	268	.98386	3	0
7	0	32	.62535	115	32	0	No	—	—	—	83
8	0	0	.67712	121	0	0	No	—	—	—	121
9	268	268	.05503	47	47	221	No	—	—	—	0
10 (:)	0	221	.34235	81	81	140	Yes	160	.68746	2	0

FIGURE 17.12 Simulating the inventory control system of the North Pole Corp.

of RND is .73332, and the lead time is now 3 months. There are no lost sales.

Calculating the next three lines in the simulation is left as an exercise.

In practice, in addition to the quantities we calculated, cost and/or other measures of performance must be calculated. Then the system should be simulated for various inventory control policies (such as varying the reorder quantity of 150 units and the replenishment quantity of 300 units) until support to decision makers can be given.

17.7 ADVANTAGES AND DISADVANTAGES OF SIMULATION

The great success and popularity of simulation lies in the fact that extremely complex situations can be dealt with in a realistic manner. The list of applications of simulation is practically unlimited.

The disadvantage of simulation is that specific numbers must be used when a simulation is performed, and no general formulas can be obtained. As a comparison, note that in some situations we can solve Markov processes and waiting-line problems with the aid of formulas. Generally speaking, the mathematical approach is preferable when available. Sensitivity analysis and optimization can be performed with the aid of simulation only at considerable time and expense. Thus, simulation is used as a last recourse when other mathematical approaches fail.

Finally, it is to be mentioned that it is a very difficult theoretical problem to determine how many trials to make and how to validate results of simulation. Details of sophisticated statistical procedures for answering such questions are beyond the scope of this textbook. However, in many practical situations a surprisingly small number of cases such as 50 to 100 appear to give answers of adequate accuracy to support decision making.

17.8 REDUCING AIRPORT DELAYS: A SUCCESSFUL APPLICATION

Many of us have had the frustrating experience when traveling by air of our airplane taxiing to a queue of planes, waiting for takeoff. Again when we arrive at our destination the plane may have to circle before it can land and await taxiing to the terminal. Clearly there is wasted time for passengers as well as a waste of scarce aircraft fuel. In fact congestion at airports in the United States results in over 25,000 hours of delay per month and in an increase of more than $10 million in direct operating cost per month for the airline industry. Also 15 million gallons of high-quality aircraft fuel is wasted per month. Delays are bad business for the airlines.

To reduce serious congestion delays the Federal Aviation Administration (FAA) and the airlines jointly have undertaken a program to determine the causes of delays and to make recommendations for their reduction.

The first study covered O'Hare International Airport at Chicago because this is the busiest airport in the country with approximately 2000 operations (arrivals and departures) per day. Our presentation is based on a report of United Airlines, a major participant in the study.*

Airport Congestion as a Waiting-Line Problem

Airplane operations at an airport can be modeled as a waiting-line system. The movement of airplanes consists of three major phases: (1) taxi out and hold for takeoff; (2) cruising, hold for landing, and landing; and (3) taxi in to the terminal. You already know from your study of waiting-line systems that the most economical operation of any waiting-line system requires a balancing of cost of waiting against the cost of capital investment, operating expenses, and other costs. The same is true for congestion at airports, and so one should not expect to eliminate all waiting but should strive to establish an optimal level of delay. It is also clear that by building additional runways or building new airports congestion could be reduced, but the purpose of the study discussed is whether congestion could be reduced without the expansion of airports by better control equipment, information systems, and operating procedures.

To reduce the congestion, it was necessary to find first the most critical component of the system. A detailed study of delays showed that the delay in holding inbound traffic is most critical, and in fact at O'Hare there was an average of 15 minutes of delay per operation. The cost of delays is between $10 to $25 per minute, which then leads to a cost per operation of about $150 to $375. If you multiply this by 2000, the number of operations per day at O'Hare, you get a daily cost of $300,000 to $750,000.

To tackle the problem of reducing delays, first there is a need to understand the performance characteristics of the system. What is needed is a relationship (curve) like the one we developed for the single-channel Poisson arrival and exponential waiting-time system displayed in Figure 16.9. Unfortunately, mathematical theory is inadequate for providing such a relationship basically for two reasons: (1) The airport waiting-line problem is such that the rate of arrival varies from a very low rate during the night to a very high rate in the afternoon (not a Poisson arrival); (2) the service time depends on which type of airplane is landing (not exponential service time), and so the sequence of arrivals is of significance. For these and other complicating reasons, instead of developing a mathematical model, a simulation model on a computer was developed, and performance characteristics were obtained by computer runs.

The left-hand scale of Figure 17.13 shows the relationship between average delay per operation in minutes and average demand for number

---

* Herbert B. Hubbard, "Terminal Airspace/Airport Congestion Delays," *Interfaces*, Vol. 8, No. 2, Feb. 1978, pp. 1–14.

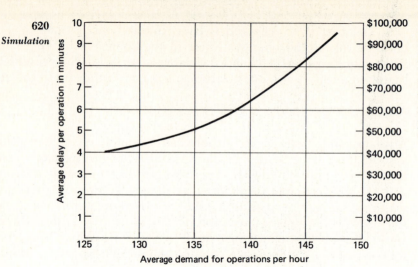

FIGURE 17.13 Average delay per operation vs. average demand for operations per hour for O'Hare airport during peak 5 hours.

of operations per hour during the peak 5 hours of operation. The right-hand scale shows the average delay cost per day. For example, when there are 136 operations per hour, it can be determined with the aid of a more accurate chart that there is an average delay per operation of about 5.2 minutes at a cost of about $52,000 per day. It can also be determined by calculating the slope of the curve that a single additional operation at an average of 137 operations will incur an additional cost of about $300. (At an average of 127 and 147 operations, the respective additional costs are $100 and $600.)

By using this simulation model, methods to reduce delays were considered that we shall now discuss.

Three Ways to Reduce Delays

The first approach to reducing delays is to change the method of using runways. O'Hare has six runways, and they can be combined into various configurations, depending on wind and weather conditions. The simulation model allowed the study of various configurations, and it was found that by introducing new policies for establishing runway configurations, significant increases in the effective capacity of the airport could be brought about.

The second approach to decreasing inbound delays is to allow airplanes to land closer to one another. However, the in-trail separation between airplanes is controlled by the turbulence of air created by the airplane. The seriousness of the turbulence depends on weather conditions, and so if better turbulence detection systems were available and the information were given to air controllers, the in-trail separation between airplanes could be decreased.

The third approach entails the limitation of arrivals-departures during peak hours and tighter control of the system flow at the airport.

To summarize, the following policies can reduce congestion at airports (without building additional runways):

1. Selecting the best runway configuration for existing wind and weather conditions
2. Installing operational turbulence detection and information systems
3. Improving the system for controlling the traffic demand during the peak period of the day

Four Benefits

1. The average inbound holding delay at O'Hare has been reduced by 2–3 minutes per arrival as the result of increased use of low delay runway configurations for existing wind and weather conditions.
2. The FAA conducted a series of tests for several turbulence detection systems which resulted in further reduction of airport congestion.
3. The FAA acquired a computer simulation model of airport operation for a joint program with the airlines and airport operators which resulted in further reduction of airport congestion.
4. The FAA developed an airport delay report and sponsored a standardized airline delay reporting system which further aided air controllers in reducing airport congestion.

17.9 MARKOV PROCESSES AND WAITING LINES: A DIALOG

Q. *When you discussed your example about a waiting line in Section 17.2, you stated in a footnote that you could get the exact answer without simulation. How do you do this?*

A. I will spare you the details, though I can explain the approach. First you must realize that a waiting-line process is a Markov process. Consider the single-channel waiting-line problem under discussion, and define the state of the process by the number of people in the system. Then there are three possible changes in state:

1. An increase by 1: This occurs when there is one arrival, but no one leaves.
2. No change: This occurs when there is neither an arrival nor leaving or there is one arrival and one leaving.
3. A decrease by 1: This occurs when no one arrives, and one person leaves.

Q. *I see that the problem can be described as a Markov process. But what do you do next?*

A. The problem can be solved by the method described in Section 15.2. Note, however, that there are infinitely many states, at least in theory, because the line can grow infinitely long. Thus there will be infinitely many unknowns and an infinite system of linear equations relating the unknowns. But due to the very special structure that the state can either increase, not change, or decrease by 1, this infinite system of linear equations can be solved, and the equilibrium probabilities can be determined.

Q. *I see your approach and am glad you spared me the details.*

SUMMARY

1. Simulation is one of the most powerful and popular techniques for supporting decision making under uncertainty.
2. To simulate means to actually carry out the calculations implied by a thought experiment.
3. The methodology of simulation with paper and pencil is based on the use of a table of random numbers. Real-life problems are invariably simulated by computer, and the random numbers are calculated by the computer.
4. The slicing rule serves to generate random numbers of a given probability distribution.
5. Random numbers of uniform distribution can be generated by the linear slicing formula.
6. Random whole numbers of uniform probability distribution can be generated by the truncated linear slicing formula.
7. Simulation is the principal computer-based technique for risk analysis.
8. The consequences of each tentative decision must be determined by an individual simulation.
9. Optimization and sensitivity analysis by simulation may be a time-consuming and expensive proposition.

SECTION EXERCISES

1. **Table of Random Numbers**
1.1 Refer to the rule given in Section 17.1 for simulating the tosses of an unbiased coin.
    a. List 10 numbers chosen in sequence from the random number table.
    b. Determine the number of heads in simulation.
1.2 Refer to the rule giving in Section 17.1 for simulating the tosses of an unbiased coin. A coin is bent so that the probability of tossing heads is .3.
    a. Describe a random number rule for the experiment.
    b. Using the random number table, generate 10 tosses of this coin.
1.3 Let X be the number of days needed to receive an order. The following probability distribution is based on those records:

X (DAYS)	PROB.
1	.3
2	.5
3	.2

a. Calculate the cumulative probability distribution.
b. Determine the random number rule for simulating this activity.
c. Read 15 numbers in sequence from the random number table. For each number, record the corresponding number of days needed to receive an order.

1.4 Let X be the time in minutes to repair a word processor. The following probability distribution is based on those records:

X (MIN)	PROB.
30	.13
40	.26
50	.44
60	.17

a. Calculate the cumulative probability distribution.
b. Determine the random number rule for simulating this activity.
c. Read 15 numbers in sequence from the random number table. For each number, record the corresponding number of minutes needed to repair the word processor.

1.5 The daily sales of a computer software package follows the binomial distribution with $n = 5$, $p = 4$.
a. Calculate the cumulative probability distribution.
b. Determine the random number rule for simulating this activity.
c. Read 15 numbers in sequence from the random number table. For each number, record the corresponding number of daily sales.

(*Hint:* You may want to review the discussion of the binomial distribution in Chapter 3.)

1.6 Refer to the linear slicing formula of Section 17.1 for obtaining random numbers with a random distribution. Different uniform distributions are specified in I–V:

	A	*B*
I	0	75
II	20	80
III	.01	.05
IV	−1	1
V	−6	−3

Carry out instructions a and b for each.
a. Obtain 25 values of X.
b. Plot the cumulative distribution for the 25 values of X you obtained.
c. Compare the cumulative distribution to a straight line and the desired range. Comment on your comparison.

2. *A Waiting-Line Problem*

2.1 Refer to the waiting-line problem of Section 17.2 and the table of Figure 17.6 for simulating that problem.
a. Carry through the simulation for steps 11–25 inclusive.
b. Based on your simulation, what is the mean number of customers in the system?
c. Based on your simulation, what is the mean length of the queue?

2.2 Refer to the waiting-line problem of Section 17.2 and the table of Figure 17.6 for simulating that problem. Assume that the probability of a service terminating is changed to .8, the probability of a customer arriving is .6, and the probability of no customer arriving is .4.
a. Carry through the simulation for steps 11–25 inclusive.

b. Based on your simulation, what is the mean number of customers in the system?

c. Based on your simulation, what is the mean length of the queue?

2.3 Refer to the waiting-line problem of Section 17.2 and the table of Figure 17.6 for simulating that problem; apply the same principles to solving the problem facing a branch office with a single clerk taking orders. Experience shows that the probability of an arrival in a 5-minute interval is .42. There is never more than one arrival in any 5-minute period. The probability that service will be completed in a 5-minute interval is .67. There are three people waiting at the door when the clerk arrives in the morning. Follow the procedure of Section 17.2 to create a table similar to Figure 17.6 for 20 5-minute intervals.

    a. Carry through the simulation for steps 1–20 inclusive.

    b. From your simulation, what do you estimate as the mean number of customers in the system?

    c. From your simulation, what do you estimate as the mean length of the queue?

2.4 Refer to the waiting-line problem of Section 17.2 and the table of Figure 17.6 for simulating that problem; apply the same principles to solving the problem facing a branch office with a single clerk taking orders. Experience shows that the probability of an arrival in a 6-minute interval is .24. There is never more than one arrival in any 6-minute period. The probability that service will be completed in a 6-minute interval is .5. There are no people waiting at the door when the clerk arrives in the morning. Follow the procedure of Section 17.2 to create a table similar to Figure 17.6 for 20 5-minute intervals.

    a. Carry through the simulation for steps 1–20 inclusive.

    b. From your simulation, what do you estimate as the mean number of customers in the system?

    c. From your simulation, what do you estimate as the mean length of the queue?

3. Scheduling Under Uncertainty

3.1 Refer to the Bop & Rock scheduling problem discussed in Section 17.3 and illustrated in Figures 17.7–17.9.

    a. Complete the table of Figure 17.9 for a total of 15 steps.

    b. Draw the probability mass function for the completion date as determined by your simulation in part a.

    c. Compute the probability mass function by direct calculation as outlined in Section 17.3.

    d. Compare the results of parts b and c.

3.2 The management of Bop & Rock revised the probabilities for the scheduling problem to the following:

ACTIVITY S_1		ACTIVITY S_2	
S_1	$p[S_1]$	S_2	$p[S_2]$
30	.2	30	.2
40	.2	40	.1
50	.6	50	.7

Activity A_3 has a time duration of exactly 20 days.

    a. Refer to Figure 17.8. Make a similar table showing the rules you will use to obtain random values for the activity times.

    b. Refer to Figure 17.9. Make a similar table showing the steps in the simulation of the project. Carry out the simulation manually for 15 steps.

c. Draw the PMF for the time to complete as determined by you.

4. Docking Ships in Harbor

4.1 Refer to the ship docking example of Section 17.4 for which Figure 17.10 is the simulation.

   a. Carry out this simulation for a total of 25 steps.
   b. Based on your simulation, what is the mean number of ships in the system?
   c. Based on the simulation, what is the mean length of the queue?
   d. Plot the mean length of the queue vs. step number for your simulation. To do this, calculate the running mean of queue length vs. step number; find the mean length of the queue at each step using the added value of that step.
   e. Plot the mean number of ships in the system vs. step number.
   f. What use could you make of the knowledge gained from parts d and e of this exercise?

4.2 Refer to the ship docking example of Section 17.4 for which Figure 17.10 is the simulation. Assume that arrival probabilities have changed as follows:

SHIPS	PROB.
0	.01
1	.09
2	.30
3	.45
4	.15

   a. Carry out this simulation for a total of 25 steps.
   b. Based on your simulation, what is the mean number of ships in the system?
   c. Based on your simulation, what is the mean length of the queue?
   d. Plot the mean length of the queue vs. step number for your simulation. To do this, calculate the running mean of queue length vs. step number; find the mean length of the queue at each step using the added value of that step.
   e. Plot the mean number of ships in the system vs. step number.
   f. What use could you make of the knowledge gained from parts d and e of this exercise?

5. Probabilistic Breakeven Analysis and Risk Analysis

5.1 Refer to the Panacea Pharmaceutical Firm example of Section 17.5. Assume that as a consequence of new information from market surveys and management conferences, the input information is as follows:

T (000,000 oz)	F (%)	P ($)	a ($000)	b ($)
20	50	.10	300	.08

   a. Find forecasted market share in ounces for PPF.
   b. Find the total forecasted revenue.
   c. Find the variable cost.
   d. Find the total cost.
   e. Find the forecasted profit.

Information concerning the uniform probability distributions for the relevant variables is as follows:

VARIABLE	LOWER LIMIT	UPPER LIMIT
T	10,000,000 oz	30,000,000 oz
F	30%	70%
P	$.08	$.12
a	$200,000	$400,000
b	$.06	$.10

f. Compute the best possible profit.
g. Compute the worst possible profit.
h. Simulate this situation following the steps in the text. If you do this by hand, carry out the simulation for 4 random values. If you use a calculator or computer, do it for at least 10.
i. Illustrate the results of your simulation in Probability Mass Function for the profit, similar to Figure 17.11.
j. Find the expected value of profit from your simulation, and compare (percentage difference) with the estimated value obtained before the simulation.

5.2 Refer to the Panacea Pharmaceutical Firm example of Section 17.5. Assume that as a consequence of new information from market surveys and management conferences, the input information is as follows:

T (000,000 oz)	F (%)	P ($)	a ($000)	b ($)
5	15	.05	100	.04

a. Find forecasted market share in ounces for PPF.
b. Find the total forecasted revenue.
c. Find the variable cost.
d. Find the total cost.
e. Find the forecasted profit.

Information concerning the uniform probability distributions for the relevant variables is as follows:

VARIABLE	LOWER LIMIT	UPPER LIMIT
T	0 oz	10,000,000 oz
F	5%	25%
P	$.025	$.075
a	$50,000	$150,000
b	$.02	$.06

f. Compute the best possible profit.
g. Compute the worst possible profit.
h. Simulate this situation following the steps in the text. If you do this by hand, carry out the simulation for 4 random values. If you use a calculator or computer, do it for at least 10.
i. Illustrate the results of your simulation in a Probability Mass Function for the profit, similar to Figure 17.11.
j. Find the expected value of profit from your simulation, and compare (percentage difference) with the estimated value obtained before the simulation.

5.3 Refer to the Panacea Pharmaceutical Firm example of Section 17.5. Assume that as a consequence of new information from market surveys and management conferences, the input information is as follows:

T (000,000 oz)	F (%)	P ($)	a ($000)	b ($)
20	30	.10	200	.05

a. Find forecasted market share in ounces for PPF.
b. Find the total forecasted revenue.
c. Find the variable cost.
d. Find the total cost.
e. Find the forecasted profit.

Information concerning the uniform probability distributions for the relevant variables is as follows:

VARIABLE	LOWER LIMIT	UPPER LIMIT
T	10,000,000 oz	30,000,000 oz
F	25%	35%
P	$.08	$.12
a	$50,000	$350,000
b	$.04	$.06

f. Compute the best possible profit.
g. Compute the worst possible profit.
h. Simulate this situation following the steps in the text. If you do this by hand, carry out the simulation for 4 random values. If you use a calculator or computer, do it for at least 25.
i. Illustrate the results of your simulation in a Probability Mass Function for the profit, similar to Figure 17.11.
j. Find the expected value of profit from your simulation, and compare (percentage difference) with the estimated value obtained before the simulation.

5.4 Refer to the Panacea Pharmaceutical Firm example of Section 17.5 for the definition of symbols used in this exercise. The National Illumen Corporation is considering introducing an energy-saving light bulb. Forecasts for the coming year's sales are as follows:

T (000,000 boxes)	F (%)	P ($)	a ($000)	b ($)
.85	20	4.65	320	1.25

a. Find forecasted market share in ounces for NIC.
b. Find the total forecasted revenue.
c. Fine the variable cost.
d. Find the total cost.
e. Find the forecasted profit.

Information concerning the uniform probability distributions for the relevant variables is as follows:

VARIABLE	LOWER LIMIT	UPPER LIMIT
T	.7	.9
F	5%	35%
P	$4.15	$5.15
a	$220,000	$420,000
b	$1.00	$1.50

f. Compute the best possible profit.

g. Compute the worst possible profit.

h. Simulate this situation following the steps in the text. If you do this by hand, carry out the simulation for 4 random values. If you use a calculator or computer, do it for at least 10.

i. Illustrate the results of your simulation in a Probability Mass Function for the profit, similar to Figure 17.11.

j. Find the expected value of profit from your simulation, and compare (percentage difference) with the estimated value obtained before the simulation.

5.5 Refer to the National Illumen Corporation in Exercise 5.4. Assume that as a consequence of new information from market surveys and management conferences, the input information is as follows:

T (000,000 boxes)	F (%)	P ($)	a ($000)	b ($)
1	40	4	200	1

a. Find forecasted market share in ounces for NIC.

b. Find the total forecasted revenue.

c. Find the variable cost.

d. Find the total cost.

e. Find the forecasted profit.

Information concerning the uniform probability distributions for the relevant variables is as follows:

VARIABLE	LOWER LIMIT	UPPER LIMIT
T	.5	1.5
F	5%	75%
P	$3.90	$4.10
a	$180,000	$220,000
b	$.90	$1.10

f. Compute the best possible profit.

g. Compute the worst possible profit.

h. Simulate this situation following the steps in the text. If you do this by hand, carry out the simulation for 4 random values. If you use a calculator or computer, do it for at least 10.

i. Illustrate the results of your simulation in a Probability Mass Function for the profit, similar to Figure 17.11.

j. Find the expected value of profit from your simulation, and compare (percentage difference) with the estimated value obtained before the simulation.

6. **Two-Bin Inventory Control System**

6.1 In Section 17.6, a simulation for the North Pole Corp.'s two-bin inventory problem is started, and the first three steps are illustrated in Figure 17.12. Carry out the simulation for 12 more steps, and complete Figure 17.12 for those steps. Based on your simulation, answer the following questions:

a. What is the average number of units in inventory at the end of the period?

b. What is the average number of lost sales?

c. What is the average order quantity?

d. What is the average number of orders?

6.2 In Section 17.6, a simulation for the North Pole Corp.'s two-bin inventory problem is started, and the first three steps are illustrated in Figure 17.12. Assume that North Pole management wants to reduce the average number of units in inventory and sets the reorder quantity at 100 and the order quantity is set to bring the inventory up to 200 units. Carry out the simulation for 15 steps, and make an illustration of your results similar to Figure 17.12. Based on your simulation, answer the following questions:

a. What is the average number of units in inventory at the end of the period?

b. What is the average number of lost sales?

c. What is the average order quantity?

d. What is the average number of orders?

e. If you have done Exercise 6.1, then compare results. Do you feel that management has achieved its goal?

8. *Reducing Airport Delays: A Successful Application*

8.1 Explain what is meant by the statement "airplane operations at an airport can be modeled as a waiting-line system."

8.2 Why would the first study be applied to the "busiest airport in the country?"

8.3 In the airport case discussed in Section 17.8, assume that there are 142 operations per hour. Use Figure 17.13 to answer the following:

a. What is the average delay per operation?

b. What is the daily cost?

c. What is the additional cost for one more operation per hour?

CHAPTER EXERCISES AND DISCUSSION QUESTIONS

C.1 Refer to the pier 17 ship docking problem of Section 17.4. At pier *18*, the following conditions hold for the probability of arrivals:

NUMBER OF SHIPS	PROB.
0	.23
1	.35
2	.22
3	.12
4	.05
5	.03

All ships arrive in the morning and take half a day to unload. It is possible to unload at most two ships per day. There is no ship at pier 18 to start.

a. Simulate 10 days of operation.

b. More dockworkers are hired to unload faster so that the upper limit of unloading is increased to three per day. Simulate 10 days of operation.

C.2 Refer to Figure 17.2 and the discussion of the use of random number tables in Section 17.1. Make a table similar to Figure 17.2 with 25 rows.

a. Select 25 random numbers, and enter them in the table appropriately.

b. Use the rule of Section 17.1 for an unbiased coin to determine the entry to be made in the appropriate column.

c. Find the proportion of heads you obtained.

d. Compare the value you obtained with .5, and explain any differences.

e. Within what range should the proportion of heads fall?. (*Hint:* You know the population proportion, so probability theory will tell you the probability distribution for the number of heads in samples of size $n = 25$.)

C.3 Refer to Figure 17.2 and the discussion of the use of random number tables in Section 17.1. Make a table similar to Figure 17.2 with 25 rows.

a. Select 25 random numbers in sequence, and enter them in the table appropriately.

b. Use the rule of Section 17.1 for a biased coin with a .6 probability of heads to determine the entry to be made in the appropriate column.

c. Find the proportion of heads you obtained.

d. Compare the value you obtained with .6, and explain any differences.

e. Within what range would you expect the proportion of heads to fall. (*Hint:* You know the population proportion, so probability theory will tell you the probability distribution for the number of heads in samples of size $n = 25$.)

C.4 "The most popular dice game in the United States is called craps. It is played with two dice; the underlying principle of the game is the fact that the most probable throw is a 7. On the first throw, if a player shoots 7 or 11 (called a natural) he wins and throws again, but if he shoots a 2, 3 or 12 (called craps) he loses. If he shoots 4, 5, 6, 8, 9, or 10 that number becomes his point, and he continues to shoot until he makes his point, in which case he wins and retains the dice, or until he shoots a 7, in which case he loses and relinquishes the dice to the next player."[*]

a. Using either a random number table or generator, simulate this game 30 times, and find the probability of winning.

b. From the same simulation, draw a conclusion about the statement that 7 is the most likely throw.

C.5 The following are the characteristics of a waiting line similar to that of Section 17.2 but where arrival probabilities depend on the length of the queue:

1. The probability of a service terminating within a 10-minute interval is .60.

2. The probability of no customer arriving is .50 if there are no customers in the system, and the probability of more than one customer arriving is 0.

3. If there is a customer in the system, the probability of a customer arriving drops to .20.

a. Using either a random number table or generator, simulate this waiting-line system 30 times. (*Hint:* You should make a table similar to Figure 17.6)

b. From your simulation, what is the mean number of customers in the system?

c. From your simulation, what is the mean length of the queue?

C.6 S. Presso sells custom-made cookies at premium prices and is noted for the long lines that occur during certain rush periods. Presso set up the operation by testing the cookie-making machine on individual runs and

---

[*] "Dice," W. H. Harris and J. S. Levey, eds., *The New Columbia Encyclopedia*, Columbia University Press, New York, 1975, p. 759.

found that the time to produce a cookie was 50 seconds plus or minus 10 seconds; the distribution of time is uniform. Unfortunately, what they failed to do in the test was to check the time it takes after one cookie has been run through. If there is only 10 seconds between cookies, then it takes a constant 100 seconds for the next cookie. If there is no gap before others after the second, the same constant 100-second time holds. Worse yet, they have found that if there are two 100-second cookie waiting times in a row, the last customer in the queue will depart. Knowing that customers would arrive during the rush periods according to the exponential distribution of interarrival times, with a mean of 120 seconds, Presso had estimated that they would sell an average of 30 cookies per hour. Use a simulation of 30 arrivals to determine an average value for the number of cookies per hour which Presso can sell.

18

Project Management by Network Models

"Both plasterers and plumbers arrived this morning," reports the foreman to the manager of the Hidden Valley Home Construction (HVHC) project. "But we cannot plaster before rough plumbing is in. How can things like that happen?" exclaims the manager.

It turns out that the plumbing was not finished on time, and the plasterers were not notified about the delay. The plumbers will finish the job in 3 days and then the plasterers can start, except that their schedule commits them to another project then, so they cannot come back until the following week. Thus there is loss of wages, and the completion date of the project will slip.

This anecdote throws light on problems involving managing projects. Before the 1950s such difficulties were considered unavoidable or were blamed on human incompetence. In the 1950s organizations were faced with very large and complex projects, and major difficulties in managing such projects occurred. Therefore, scientifically oriented efforts were initiated to provide assistance to managers of projects.

Under the pressure of real-life problems and emerging management science-operations research techniques, new concepts and formal approaches were developed. Initially, these techniques went under the labels PERT (program evaluation and review technique) and CPM (critical path method). Today the distinction between these techniques is blurred, and the name activity **network** models or just network models describes more appropriately the fundamental techniques involved.

Projects in all walks of life, particularly large complex projects, may have thousands of interdependent activities which must be scheduled, coordinated, and dovetailed during periods of many months or even years. The decision of what to do at what time, how to avoid delays and waste of funds, can be supported by the use of network models. Management science-operations research, relying on computers, has been particularly successful in supporting project management in such areas as the maintenance of plants, engineering and construction projects (highways, bridges, buildings, etc.), and research and development of complex technological systems (missiles, space vehicles, airplanes, weapons systems, computer-based information systems). We introduce techniques of planning and controlling projects by network models through an illustrative example.

18.1 HIDDEN VALLEY HOME CONSTRUCTION PROJECT

In Hidden Valley Home Construction Project (HVHC) hundreds of homes will be built on a large suburban tract. Due to the complexity of the project, management desires to use network models. The first task is to break the project into component parts called **activities**. An activity is the smallest unit of work considered in project planning and is characterized by the fact that (unless it is a *dummy*, defined later) it takes time, consumes resources, and will be started and finished at a well-defined point in time. Figure 18.1 shows the activity list for an HVHC home.

The second task is to establish the **precedence** *relationships* and required **duration** for each activity. Look, for example, at activity *K* in the HV home construction project (Figure 18.2). The duration of this activity (fasten plasterboard and plaster) will be 10 days, meaning that 10 days

---

A   Start
B   Excavate and pour footings
C   Pour concrete foundation
D   Erect wooden frame
E   Lay brickwork
F   Install basement drains and plumbing
G   Pour basement floor
H   Rough plumbing
I   Rough wiring
J   Heating and ventilating
K   Fasten plasterboard and plaster
L   Lay finishing flooring
M   Kitchen fixtures
N   Finish plumbing
O   Finish carpentry
P   Finish roofing and flashing
Q   Fasten gutters and downspouts
R   Lay storm drains for rainwater
S   Sand and varnish flooring
T   Paint
U   Finish electrical work
V   Finish grading
W   Pour walks and complete landscaping
X   Finish

FIGURE 18.1 Activity list for the Hidden Valley Home Construction (HVHC) project.
Adapted from F. K. Levy, G. L. Thompson, and J. D. Weist, "The ABC's of the Critical Path Method," Harvard Business Review, *Sept.–Oct. 1963, pp. 98–108.*

ACTIVITIES	IMMEDIATE PREDECESSORS	DURATION (DAYS)
A: Start		0
B: Excavate and pour footings	A	4
C: Pour concrete foundation	B	2
D: Erect wooden frame	C	4
E: Lay brickwork	D	6
F: Install basement drains and plumbing	C	1
G: Pour basement floor	F	2
H: Rough plumbing	F	3
I: Rough wiring	D	2
J: Heating and ventilating	D, G	4
K: Fasten plasterboard and plaster	I, J, H	10
L: Lay finishing flooring	K	3
M: Kitchen fixtures	L	1
N: Finish plumbing	L	2
O: Finish carpentry	L	3
P: Finish roofing and flashing	E	2
Q: Fasten gutters and downspouts	P	1
R: Lay storm drains for rainwater	C	1
S: Sand and varnish flooring	O, T	2
T: Paint	M, N	3
U: Finish electrical work	T	1
V: Finish grading	Q, R	2
W: Pour walks and complete landscaping	V	5
X: Finish	S, U, W	0

FIGURE 18.2 Precedence relations and durations for the activities of the Hidden Valley Home Construction project.

will elapse between the start and finish dates of plastering. The figure also shows that the **immediate predecessors** of plastering are activities *I*, *J*, and *H*, that is, rough wiring, heating and ventilating, and rough plumbing. We also say that activities *I*, *J*, and *H* *terminate* in activity *K*.

However, from Figure 18.2 we cannot directly tell how long it will take to do a group of activities, or the entire project, or what the appropriate sequence of activities will be. For example, is it necessary to complete activity *I* (rough wiring) before activity *N* (finish plumbing) can be started? These and other questions can only be answered after the network model is constructed.

18.2 NETWORK MODELS: SCIENTIFIC APPROACH TO PROJECT MANAGEMENT

Figure 18.3 shows a partial network for constructing an HV home. The network is a graph or diagram representing the structure of the activities to be performed. Each activity is represented by an arrow. Note that the arrows start and terminate in **nodes** of the diagram, representing **events**.

> An event occurs (materializes) when all activities terminating in the node have been finished and when all activities emanating from the node can be started.

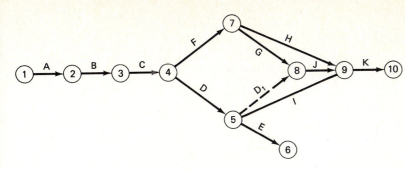

FIGURE 18.3
Partial network for Hidden Valley Home Construction project.

For example, event 9 occurs after activities H, J, and I are finished and activity K can be started. Events are characterized by the fact that they occur instantaneously in time, have no duration, and consume no resources.

The network diagram provides information on the sequence of activities. For example, you can see directly that activity C must be completed much before activity K can be started. Why is there a dashed line from event 5 to event 8?

Observe in Figure 18.2 that the immediate predecessors of J are D and G. The immediate predecessor of I is D. Suppose you draw the diagram as shown in Figure 18.4. You are facing two difficulties in this incorrect network. First, G is not a predecessor of I, as you can verify in Figure 18.2. Furthermore, there is the difficulty that activities I and J both emanate from event 5 and terminate in event 9. But it is a rule of network planning that it must be possible to identify an activity by a pair of events, and so the diagram in Figure 18.4 violates this rule. The correct network in Figure 18.3 contains a **dummy activity** D_1 between events 5 and 8. The time duration of a dummy activity is 0, and there is no resource required to complete it. The diagram as drawn in Figure 18.3 makes it clear that G is an immediate predecessor of J and that D is an immediate predecessor of I and E. Also we can identify activity J by events 8 and 9 and activity I by events 5 and 9. In summary, you need to obey the following two rules:

> Each activity is represented by one arrow and one pair of events.
> No two activities can start and end in the same pair of events.

Figure 18.5 shows the complete network for HV homes. Note that we can designate each activity in two different ways: (1) by name, such as B, E, and Q; (2) by the corresponding pair of events, such as 2–3, 5–6, and 15–16.

18.3 HOW TO DRAW A NETWORK

Drawing a network is a step-by-step method and can be learned best by an example. Consider the precedence relationships for building a swimming pool in Figure 18.6. We start drawing the network by activity

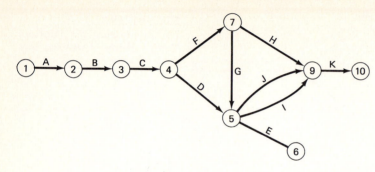

FIGURE 18.4
Example of an incorrectly drawn network.

a, which has no predecessor (Figure 18.7, part a). Then we scan the second column for activities for which *a* is a predecessor. We find activity *ċ*. So now we have path *a*, *c* (Figure 18.7, part a). Next we look for an activity for which *c* is a predecessor. We find *f*. So we have path *a*, *c*, *f*, and so on until we find path *a*, *c*, *f*, *g*, *j*.

Then we start again with *b* and construct path *b*, *e*, *d*, *f*, *g*, *j*, (Figure 18.7, part a). But now we realize that *f*, *g*, *j* appear twice, and so we redraw the diagram (Figure 18.7, part b).

We return to Figure 18.6 and realize that activities *h* and *i* are missing and draw them in Figure 18.7, part c. We also draw the paths *h*, *g*, *j* and *i*, *j* by following the precedence relationships in Figure 18.6. So now we redraw the diagram in Figure 18.7, part d.

Checking the precedence relationships in Figure 18.6, we realize that *e* has two immediate predecessors, *a* and *b*. So we insert a dummy activity (Figure 18.7, part d). Now we have the correct network.

Of course as you practice drawing networks, you will develop shortcuts and will be able to skip some of the steps described here. Also, computer programs are available which draw networks; then all you need to be able to do is read and interpret the computer output.

18.4 TIME PHASING

So far we have considered only precedence relationships and the interrelationship of activities and events. In fact, we drew the diagram and the arrows, ignoring all time considerations. Managers of projects, of

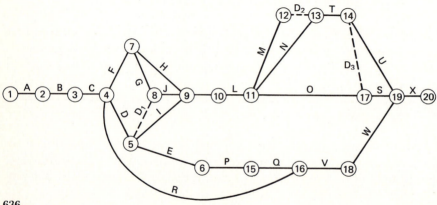

FIGURE 18.5
Network for Hidden Valley Home Construction project

ACTIVITY	IMMEDIATE PREDECESSOR
a	None
b	None
c	*a*
d	*e*
e	*a, b*
f	*c, d*
g	*h, f*
h	*a*
i	*e*
j	*g, i*

FIGURE 18.6 Precedence relationships for building a swimming pool.

course, need to know when to do the various jobs, and network models provide information on time phasing.

We find it useful to think about timing in two different ways. Each activity can be started at the *earliest possible* date, and then each event will occur at the *earliest possible* date. Or if management desires to complete the project at a certain time, each activity may be started at the *latest allowable* date, and then each event will occur at the *latest allowable* date. We shall represent both of these views of network models.

Earliest Possible Occurrence

The **earliest possible occurrence** (EPO) date of each event is calculated by a **forward pass** of the network. The best way to learn this procedure is by an example. So let us apply the procedure to the Fail Safe Mainte-

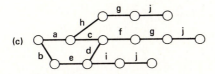

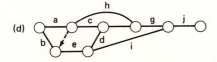

FIGURE 18.7
Steps in drawing a network for building a swimming pool.

ACTIVITY		IMMEDIATE PREDECESSOR	DURATION
Name	Pair of Events		
A	1–3	None	1
B	1–4	None	2
C	1–2	None	5
D	3–4	A	3
E	2–4	C	0
F	3–5	A	4
G	4–5	BCD	6
H	2–5	C	3

FIGURE 18.8 Precedence relations and durations for the Fail Safe Maintenance (FSM) project.

nance (FSM) project for which the precedence and duration information is given in Figure 18.8 and the network in Figure 18.9.

First we set the EPO of event 1 to zero:

$$EPO(1) = 0$$

Then we observe that the duration of activity A is 1 day. If we start working on A on day 0, it will be finished by day 1. The *earliest possible finish* (EPF) date of A is 1:

$$EPF(A) = 1$$

Similarly,

$$EPF(B) = 2$$

and

$$EPF(C) = 5$$

(We summarize our results in lines 1–4, Figure 18.10.) Note that we used

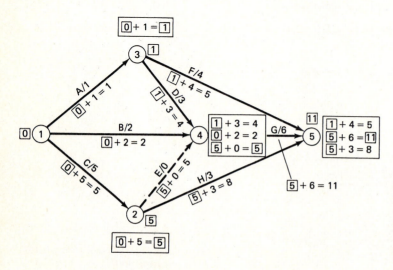

FIGURE 18.9
Earliest possible occurrence (EPO) dates (shown in squares). The number after the / shows the duration of the activity in days.

the following rule:

Rule of earliest possible finish (EPF):

EPF of an activity = EPO of event which starts activity

+ duration of activity

or

EPF = EPO + duration

The EPO of event 3 equals EPF of activity A, and so .

$$EPO(3) = EPF(A) = 1$$

Similarly,

$$EPO(2) = EPF(C) = 5$$

(See lines 5 and 6 in Figure 18.10). We display the EPOs in Figure 18.9 in small squares. Now we can proceed to calculate EPO(4). We can reach event 4 in three ways:

1. *Via activity D.* We can start D at EPO(3) = 1. Add the duration of D of 3 days:

$$EPF(D) = EPO(3) + \text{duration of } D$$

$$= 1 + 3 = 4$$

(line 7 in Figure 18.10)

2. *Via activity B.* We already have

$$EPF(B) = 2$$

(line 3 in Figure 18.10)

1.	Start:	EPO(1) = 0
2.	Rule of EPF:	EPF(A) = 0 + 1 = 1
3.	Rule of EPF:	EPF(B) = 0 + 2 = 2
4.	Rule of EPF:	EPF(C) = 0 + 5 = 5
5.	Rule of EPO:	EPO(3) = EPF(A) = 1
6.	Rule of EPO:	EPO(2) = EPF(C) = 5
7.	Rule of EPF:	EPF(D) = 1 + 3 = 4
8.	Rule of EPF:	EPF(E) = 5 + 0 = 5
9.	Rule of EPO:	EPO(4) = EPF(E) = 5
10.	Rule of EPF:	EPF(F) = 1 + 4 = 5
11.	Rule of EPF:	EPF(G) = 5 + 6 = 11
12.	Rule of EPF:	EPF(H) = 5 + 3 = 8
13.	Rule of EPO:	EPO(5) = EPF(G) = 11

FIGURE 18.10 Computation of EPO dates in days for Fail Safe Maintenance project.

3. *Via activity E.*

$$EPF(E) = EPO(2) + \text{duration of } E$$

$$= 5 + 0 = 5$$

(line 8 in Figure 18.10)

But event 4 cannot occur unless D, B, and E are finished; that is, we must select the latest date of the EPFs. The latest of 4, 2, and 5 days is 5 days. Thus,

$$EPO(4) = EPF(E) = 5$$

(line 9 in Figure 18.10)
Note that we used the following rule:

> *Rule of earliest possible occurrence (EPO):* The EPO of an event equals the latest EPF of the activities which end in the event. When only a single activity ends in the event, then the EPO of the event equals the EPF of the activity.

We calculate the EPF of F, G, and H:

$$EPF(F) = EPO(3) + \text{duration of } F$$

$$= 1 + 4 = 5$$

$$EPF(G) = EPO(4) + \text{duration of } G$$

$$= 5 + 6 = 11$$

$$EPF(H) = EPO(2) + \text{duration of } H$$

$$= 5 + 3 = 8$$

(lines 10–12 in Figure 18.10)

Now we can calculate the EPO of event 5, which is the EPO of the project. Namely, we have to take the latest of the EPFs of activities F, G, and H. The latest of 4, 11, and 8 days is 11 days, and so

$$EPO(5) = EPF(H) = 11$$

(See line 13 in Figure 18.10.)
Thus the project can be completed in 11 days or in more than 11 days. This then completes the calculation of the earliest possible occurrence dates.

Before we proceed to our next topic, it is to be pointed out that this formal mathematical approach serves primarily to acquaint you with the theory of network analysis. Once you understand the concepts clearly and have some practice, you can carry out the calculations directly with graphical representation of the network, as shown in Figure 18.9.

Suppose management insists on completing the project discussed on day 11 but wants to know the **latest allowable occurrence** (LAO) for each event that will still allow the project to be completed on time. These dates can be computed by modifying the two rules presented earlier and carrying out a **backward pass** of the network. We discuss the procedure again by the example of the Fail Safe Maintenance project. (See Figures 18.11 and 18.12).

First we set the latest allowable occurrence (LAO) of event 5 to 11 days,

$$LAO(5) = 11$$

to assure that the project will be finished on schedule (line 1, Figure 18.12). We show the LAOs in circles.

Next we calculate the latest allowable start (LAS) date of activity F. Note that F must be finished when event 5 occurs and that it takes 4 days to finish F. Thus the latest allowable start date of F is

$$LAS(F) = LAO(5) - \text{duration of } F$$
$$= 11 - 4 = 7$$

(See line 2, Figure 18.12.)
Similarly,

$$LAS(G) = LAO(5) - \text{duration of } G$$
$$= 11 - 6 = 5$$

and

$$LAS(H) = LAO(5) - \text{duration of } H$$
$$= 11 - 3 = 8$$

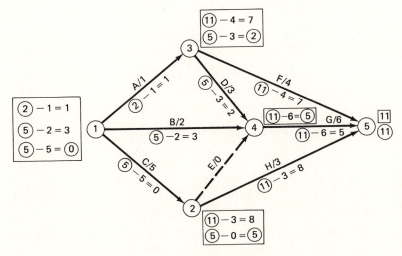

FIGURE 18.11
Latest allowable occurrence (LAO) dates (shown in circles) are determined by backward pass for the Fail Safe Maintenance project.

1. Start: $\qquad$ LAO(5) = 11
2. Rule of LAS: $\quad$ LAS(F) = LAO(5) − 4 = 11 − 4 = 7
3. Rule of LAS: $\quad$ LAS(G) = LAO(5) − 6 = 11 − 6 = 5
4. Rule of LAS: $\quad$ LAS(H) = LAO(5) − 3 = 11 − 3 = 8

5. Rule of LAO: $\quad$ LAO(4) = LAS(G) = 5

6. Rule of LAS: $\quad$ LAS(D) = LAO(4) − 3 = 5 − 3 = 2
7. Rule of LAS: $\quad$ LAS(E) = LAO(4) − 0 = 5 − 0 = 5

8. Rule of LAO: $\quad$ LAO(3) = LAS(D) = 2
9. Rule of LAO: $\quad$ LAO(2) = LAS(E) = 5

10. Rule of LAS: $\quad$ LAS(A) = LAO(3) − 1 = 2 − 1 = 1
11. Rule of LAS: $\quad$ LAS(B) = LAO(4) − 2 = 5 − 2 = 3
12. Rule of LAS: $\quad$ LAS(C) = LAO(2) − 5 = 5 − 5 = 0

13. Rule of LAO: $\quad$ LAO(1) = LAS(C) = 0

FIGURE 18.12 Computation of latest allowable occurrence (LAO) dates for the Fail Safe Maintenance project.

(See lines 3 and 4, Figure 18.12.)
Note that we used the following rule:

> *Rule of latest allowable finish (LAF):*
>
> LAF of an activity = LAO of event which ends the activity
>
> − duration of activity
>
> or
>
> LAF = LAO − duration

Now we can calculate the LAO of event 4. Namely, 4 must not occur later than the LAS of activity G. But as shown in line 3, Figure 18.12, LAS(G) = 5, and so

$$LAO(4) = LAS(G) = 5$$

(line 5, Figure 18.12)
Now we can calculate

$$LAS(D) = LAO(4) − 3$$
$$= 5 − 3 = 2$$

and

$$LAF(E) = LAO(4) − 0$$
$$= 5 − 0 = 5$$

(See lines 6 and 7 in Figure 18.12.)
We proceed now to determine the LAO of event 3. Moving backward from event 5, we can reach 3 in two ways:

1. *Via activity F.* We know that the LAS of F is 7 days (line 2 of Figure 18.12). So the LAO of event 3 cannot be later than 7 days.

2. *Via activity D.* We know that the LAS of *D* is 2 days (line 6 of Figure 18.12). So the LAO of event 3 cannot be later than 2 days.

We note therefore that the LAO of event 3 cannot be later than 7 or 2 days, and so we must choose the earlier of these dates:

$$LAO(3) = LAS(D) = 2$$

(line 8, Figure 18.12)

Note that we used the following rule:

> *Rule of latest allowable occurrence (LAO):* The LAO of an event equals the earliest LAS of the activities which leave the event. When only a single activity leaves the event, then the LAO equals the LAS of the activity.

We can calculate the LAO of event 2. Namely, the LAS of *E* is 5 days (line 7, Figure 18.12); and the LAS of *H* is 8 days (line 4, Figure 18.12). The earlier date of 5 and 8 days is 5 days, and so

$$LAO(2) = LAS(E) = 5$$

Now we can calculate the LASs of the three activities leaving event 1:

$$LAS(A) = LAO(3) - 1$$
$$= 2 - 1 = 1$$
$$LAS(B) = LAO(4) - 2$$
$$= 5 - 2 = 3$$

and

$$LAS(C) = LAO(2) - 5$$
$$= 5 - 5 = 0$$

(See lines 10, 11, and 12 in Figure 18.12.) Of these three dates of 1, 3, and 0 days, the earliest is day 0; the latest allowable occurrence of event 1, that is, the start date of the project, is day 0:

$$LAO(1) = 0$$

(See line 13, Figure 18.12.)

This then completes calculation of the latest allowable occurrence dates. Before proceeding we repeat that the primary purpose of the mathematical approach (Figure 18.12) is to acquaint you with the underlying concepts. Actual calculations, with some practice, can be carried out directly, as shown in Figure 18.11.

Slack and Critical Path

In Figures 18.13 and 18.14 we summarize our results on earliest possible occurrence and latest allowable occurrence dates. Note that these dates are the same for events 1, 2, 4, and 5 but that for event 3 the EPO date is 1

EVENTS	EARLIEST POSSIBLE OCCURRENCE, EPO	LATEST ALLOWABLE OCCURRENCE, LAO	S	CRITICAL
1	0	0	0	Yes
2	5	5	0	Yes
3	1	2	1	No
4	5	5	0	Yes
5	11	11	0	Yes

FIGURE 18.13 Slack and critical path information for the Fail Safe Maintenance project.

day and the LAO date is 2 days. This means that for event 3 there is a **slack** of $2 - 1 = 1$ day, meaning that if this event occurs anywhere between 1 and 2 days, there will still be time to complete the project on schedule.

In a more realistic network there will be many events with various amounts of slack. The value of the slack is an important piece of information for the manager, because he/she knows what the leeway is in carrying out certain activities. A slack of 20 days, for example, would mean that the manager has quite a bit of flexibility as to the occurrence of the particular event.

Events 1, 2, 4, and 5 have 0 slack. If any of these events slip schedule, there is no way to catch up, and the entire project will be delayed. Events 1, 2, 4, and 5 are connected by a **path** formed by activities *C*, *E*, and *G*. *E* is a dummy activity, requiring no resources. However, activities *C* and *G* will be critical, because if either of these are late, the entire project will be late. Therefore, the path *C–E–G* or 1–2–4–5 is called the **critical path** of the project, shown by the double line in Figure 18.14.

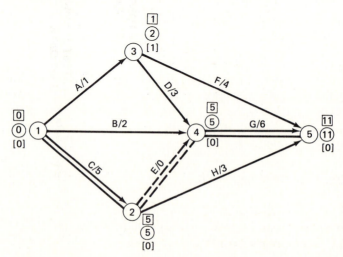

FIGURE 18.14 Network and critical path (shown by double line) for the Fail Safe Maintenance project. Earliest possible occurrence (EPO) dates are in squares, latest allowable occurrence (LAO) dates are in circles, and slacks are in brackets.

Activities on the critical path must be completed exactly on time, or else the entire project will be late.

Recognition of the critical path in a network is of great importance to the manager because the activities on the critical path are the ones that the manager must monitor and control with the greatest attention.

Note that activities A, B, D, F, and H are not on the critical path, and so the manager may take a more relaxed view in completing these activities. Let us now examine in quantitative terms how completion dates of activities influence the completion of the entire project.

18.5 SCHEDULING OF ACTIVITIES

In Figure 18.15 we present various information to support decision making for the Fail Safe Maintenance project. In the first column we show the names of activities and in the second the respective durations. Consider, for example, activity F in Figure 18.14. Activity F leaves from 3 and ends in 5 as shown in Figure 18.14. The earliest possible occurrence date of event 3 is 1, and so the earliest possible start date of activity F is 1 (column 3, Figure 18.15). Activity F takes 4 days to complete, and so the earliest possible finish date of activity F is $1 + 4 = 5$

(1)	(2)	(3)	(4)	(5)	(6)	(7)
ACTIVITY	DURATION, D	EARLIEST POSSIBLE START (EPS) DATE	EARLIEST POSSIBLE FINISH DATE, EPF = EPS + D	LATEST ALLOWABLE FINISH (LAF) DATE	LATEST ALLOWABLE START DATE, LAS = LAF − D	ACTIVITY SLACK, LAF − EPF = LAS − EPS
A	1	0	1	2	1	1
B	2	0	2	5	3	3
C	5	0	5	5	0	0
D	3	1	4	5	2	1
E	0	5	5	5	5	0
F	4	1	5	11	7	6
G	6	5	11	11	5	0
H	3	5	8	11	8	3

FIGURE 18.15 Various scheduling information for the activities of the Fail Safe Maintenance project.

days (column 4, Figure 18.15). The latest allowable occurrence date of event 5 is 11 days, and so the latest allowable finish date of activity *F* is also 11 days (column 5, Figure 18.15). Activity *F* takes 4 days to complete, and so the latest allowable start date for activity *F* is $11 - 4 = 7$ days (column 6, Figure 18.15).

The difference between the latest allowable start date of 7 days and earliest possible start date of 1 day is 6 days, and this is called the **activity slack** for *F*. (Earlier we considered the slack of an event, which can be called **event slack**.) The difference between the latest allowable finish of 11 days and earliest possible finish of 5 days is also 6 days, which again is the activity slack. Now the manager knows that there is a flexibility of 6 days in performing activity *F*. This is important information for the planning and control of activity *F*.

The other values in Figure 18.15 have been calculated in the same manner, using the information from the network in Figure 18.14.

18.6 TIME COST TRADE-OFFS

So far we assumed that the duration of each activity is fixed. However, if more resources are assigned to a job, it is ordinarily possible to shorten the duration. Typically, if more people work on an activity or more effort is expended, it will take less time to complete it. We therefore assume that there is a relationship between dollars expended on an activity and its duration.

Consider, for example, activity *C* of the Fail Safe Maintenance project. Earlier it was assumed that the duration of activity *C* is 5 days (Figure 18.8). Now we refer to this as the **normal duration** of the activity. Suppose a cost analysis reveals that it costs $800 to perform activity *C* in 5 days and that if expenditures are increased to $1000 the activity can be performed on a **crash** basis in 3 days. In fact, as shown by the time-cost trade-off curve (Figure 18.16), the activity can be performed in 4 days if $900 is expended.

In Figure 18.17 we show for each of the activities of the Fail Safe Maintenance project the duration and corresponding cost of each activity. For example, activity *A* can be performed in only a single way: in 1 day at a cost of $100.

Activity *B* can be performed in a normal way in 2 days at a cost of $300. At an additional cost (marginal cost) of $10, it can be performed in a crash manner in 1 day. Activity *C* can be performed in a normal way in 5 days at a cost of $800. A marginal increase of $100 reduces the duration to 4 days and a second $100 to 3 days. And so on for activities *D, E, F, G,* and *H*.

Now let us put all the information together. How many possible networks can we construct?

There is a single alternative for activity *A*, two for *B*, three for *C*, and so on, as shown in the far right-hand column in Figure 18.17. Thus

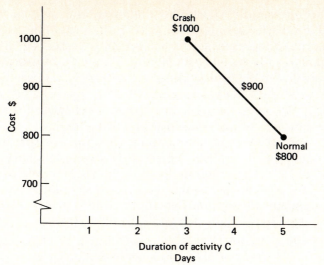

FIGURE 18.16
Time-cost trade-off for
activity *C* of the Fail
Safe Maintenance pro-
ject.

the total number of alternatives is

$$1 \times 2 \times 3 \times 2 \times 1 \times 2 \times 3 \times 3 = 216$$

But we are only interested in the lowest cost alternative for each time span, that is, in the time-cost relationship of the project. We show now how to determine this relationship.

The normal completion time for the project is 11 days (Figure 18.14) at a total cost of $3700 (Figure 18.17). Suppose management wants to complete the project earlier. Which of the activities should be selected for an increase of expenditure? To answer this, examine the marginal costs listed in the fourth column of Figure 18.17.

ACTIVITY	DURATION IN DAYS Normal	DURATION IN DAYS Crash	COST IN DOLLARS Normal	COST IN DOLLARS Crash	MARGINAL COST IN-CREASE IN DOLLARS PER DAY	NUMBER OF ALTERNATIVES
A	1	1	100	100	—	1
B	2	1	300	310	10	2
C	5	3	800	1000	100	3
D	3	2	500	550	50	2
E	0	0	0	0	—	1
F	4	3	400	430	30	2
G	6	4	1000	1400	200	3
H	3	1	600	640	20	3
		Total cost:	$3700	$4430		

FIGURE 18.17 Possible durations and corresponding costs for the activities of the Fail Safe Maintenance project.

For example, shortening the duration of activity *B* by 1 day from 2 to 1 increases cost by only $10. But shortening activity *C* by 1 day requires an increase of as much as $100 (one-half the difference between the crash and normal cost). Note in Figure 18:14 that activity *B* is *not* on the critical path, and so when activity *B* is shortened, the completion date is still 11 days, and management buys nothing for the extra $10 spent. We see, then, that a more sophisticated approach than just consideration of marginal increases is needed.

Suppose we crash all projects. The fully crashed network is shown in Figure 18.18. You can determine that completion time is reduced by 4 days to 11 − 4 = 7 days and that costs are increased as shown in Figure 18.17 from $3700 to $4430. Figure 18.18 also shows results of a complete critical path calculation. The double line shows that the project has two critical paths: (1) 1–3–4–5 and (2) 1–2–4–5.

> A project may have more than one critical path.

Observe in Figure 18.18 that each event is on a critical path but that activities *B*, *F*, and *H* are not on the critical path, and so it is pointless to fully crash these activities. In fact, as shown in Figure 18.19, these activities can be restored to normal effort without changing the critical paths and the completion date of 7 days. Note in Figure 18.17 that by restoring activities *B*, *F*, and *H* to normal effort, we save, respectively, $10, $30, and $40, a total of $80. Therefore, the *lowest-cost 7-day schedule is $80 less than the fully crashed schedule.* So this cost is $4430 − $80 = $4350.

Now we have the lowest-cost 7- and 11-day schedules. (Figure 18.19) What is the lowest-cost 10-day schedule? Examine the network in Figure 18.14 and find the activity on the critical path which can be reduced by 1 day at the lowest possible cost. Activity *E* is a dummy activity, and there are no resources involved. Figure 18.17 shows that

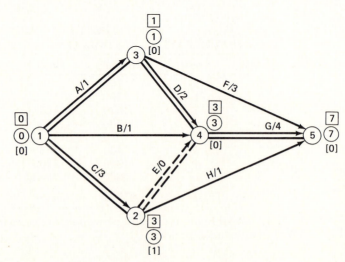

FIGURE 18.18
Fully crashed network for the Fail Safe Maintenance project. The two critical paths are shown by double lines.

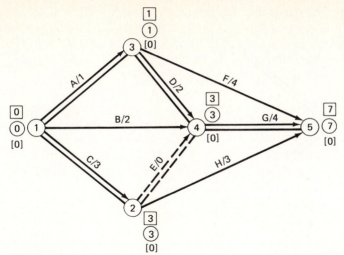

FIGURE 18.19
L o w e s t - c o s t
($4350) 7-day net-
work for the Fail
Safe Maintenance
project.

the marginal increase in cost per day is $100 for *C* and $200 for *G*. Therefore, we conclude that it is best to reduce the duration of activity *C* from 5 days to 4 days at an additional cost of $100. This will reduce the completion date from 11 days to 10 days. The total cost will increase by $100, and so we get a total cost for the project of $3700 + $100 = $3800. *Thus the lowest-cost 10-day schedule is $3800.* Figure 18.20 shows the corresponding network. Note that the project has two critical paths.

Suppose management wants to complete the project in 9 days. Which of the activities on the critical paths in Figure 18.20 do we shorten? Activity *A* cannot be crashed, and *E* is a dummy activity. We must reduce both critical paths, which can be accomplished in two ways. We can either reduce activity *G* or reduce both activities *C* and *D*. As shown in Figure 18.17, reducing *G* by 1 day costs an additional $200, while reducing both *C* and *D* costs only $150. Therefore, it is best to

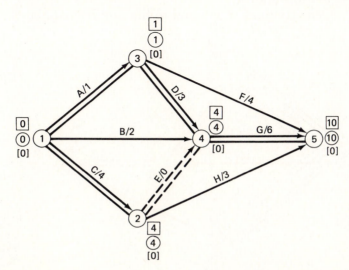

FIGURE 18.20
Lowest-cost ($3800)
10-day network for
the Fail Safe Main-
tenance project.

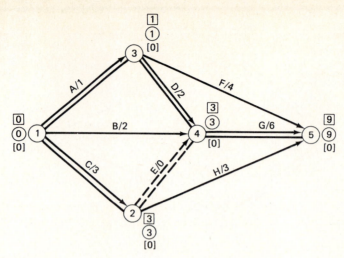

FIGURE 18.21
Lowest-cost ($3950)
9-day network for
the Fail Safe Main-
tenance project.

reduce *C* to 3 days and *D* to 2 days (Figure 18.21) and so reduce the entire project to 9 days. As compared to the 10-day schedule, there is an additional $150 incurred. *The lowest-cost 9-day schedule is $3800 + $150 = $3950.*

Let us finally compute the lowest-cost 8-day schedule. By inspecting the activities on the critical paths in Figure 18.21 we see that only *C* or *G* can be reduced. Reducing *C* will not help because *A* and *D* already take 3 days. Thus the only choice is to reduce activity *G* by 1 day at an additional cost of $200. *So the lowest-cost 8-day schedule is $3950 + $200 = $4150* (Figure 18.22).

This then concludes the time-cost trade-off calculations for the Fail Safe Maintenance project. In Figure 18.23 we summarize the lowest-cost schedules for any completion date between 7 and 11 days. In Figure 18.24 we show the time-cost trade-off curve for the lowest-cost solution. Any other solution would be represented by a point lying above the broken line shown.

Our method of solution of the problem can be characterized as a

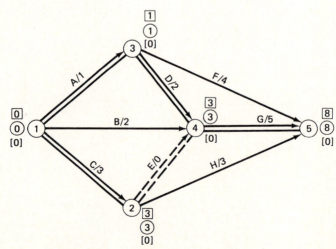

FIGURE 18.22
Lowest-cost ($4150)
8-day network for
the Fail Safe Main-
tenance project.

	7-day		8-day		9-day		10-day		11-day	
	Duration	Cost	Duration	Cost	Duration	Cost	Duration	Cost	Duration	Cost
A	1	100	1	100	1	100	1	100	1	100
B	2	300	2	300	2	300	2	300	2	300
C	3	1000	3	1000	3	1000	4	900	5	800
D	2	550	2	550	2	550	3	500	3	500
E	0	0	0	0	0	0	0	0	0	0
F	4	400	4	400	4	400	4	400	4	400
G	4	1400	5	1200	6	1000	6	1000	6	1000
H	3	600	3	600	3	600	3	600	3	600
Total cost:		$4350		$4150		$3950		$3800		$3700

FIGURE 18.23 Summary presentation of time-cost information on lowest-cost networks for the Fail Safe Maintenance project.

systematic search for the best solution. In large-scale real-life problems such an approach would be impractical, and so computer-based mathematical techniques have been developed which can provide the required answers at low cost and in a short time.

Our basic time-cost trade-off relationship (Figure 18.16) assumes that as there is more time available for an activity, the cost of completion of the activity will decrease. However, it has been found in practice that as activities unduly stretch out, indirect costs become important and costs begin to rise again, as shown in Figure 18.25. Determination of lowest-cost project networks under these conditions become more complicated, but computer programs are available, and so there are practical ways to deal with problems when crash, normal, and **slow methods** of allocating resources are possible.

18.7 PROBABILISTIC NETWORK MODELS

So far we assumed that the duration of each activity can be predicted exactly. Now we discuss the more complex problem when durations are uncertain.

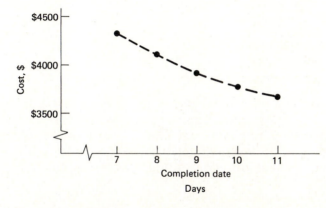

FIGURE 18.24
Time cost tradeoff curve for lowest cost networks for Fail Safe Maintenance project.

651

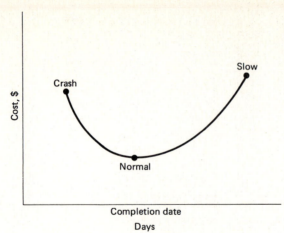

FIGURE 18.25
Time-cost trade-off for activities when indirect costs are
also included.

You must realize that in such cases two types of difficulties arise. Suppose, for example, that a new project involves 100 uncertain activities. How could management state these uncertainties? From the theoretical point of view we would require that the manager specify the probability distribution functions for each activity. However, this would be a superhuman demand on management. Thus *there is a need for a simplified approach to specifying uncertainties.*

Suppose, however, the probability function for each activity were known. How could this information be put together for scheduling purposes? How could one determine the probability distribution functions for each event and the start and completion dates? There is no mathematical technique known for calculating these functions, and so extensive simulation techniques would have to be used. Thus *there is a need to develop an approximate technique for calculating probability distribution functions for events and start and completion dates.*

Now we describe how these needs can be met.

Approximate Techniques for Probabilistic Networks

Instead of using a probability distribution for each duration, it is customary to assume that there are three estimates available for the duration of each activity:

a: most optimistic

b: most pessimistic

m: most likely

For the Fail Safe Maintenance project the three estimates are shown in the second, third, and fourth columns of Figure 18.26. The approximate method of calculation assumes that the distribution of duration for each activity follows a particular type of distribution (to be specific, **beta distribution**). Under this assumption it can be shown that

(1) ACTIVITY	(2) a	(3) b	(4) m	(5) d	(6) σ	(7) σ²
A	.5	4	1	1.42	.583	.340
B	1	4	2	2.17	.500	.250
C	4	7	5	5.17	.500	.250
D	1	6	3	3.17	.833	.694
E	0	0	0	0	0	0
F	2	8	4	4.33	1.000	1.000
G	4	9	6	6.16	.833	.694
H	1	5	3	3.00	.667	.445

FIGURE 18.26 Information on activity durations required for the approximate analysis of the probabilistic network of the Fail Safe Maintenance project.

the expected duration is approximately

$$d = \frac{a + 4m + b}{6}$$

and that the standard deviation of the duration is

$$\sigma = \frac{b - a}{6}$$

For example, for activity G in Figure 18.26 we get the expected duration of 6.16 days and for the standard deviation, .833 day (columns 5 and 6, Figure 18.26).

Using the same method of calculation, we determine the expected duration, standard deviation, and variance for each of the activities (Figure 18.26). But now how do we compute the expected completion date of the project and the standard deviation?

First we construct the network for the Fail Safe Maintenance project with the expected durations. This new network and the new earliest possible occurrence dates are shown in Figure 18.27. Note that the earliest possible occurrence date for completion is 11.33 days and that the critical path is still 1–2–4–5.

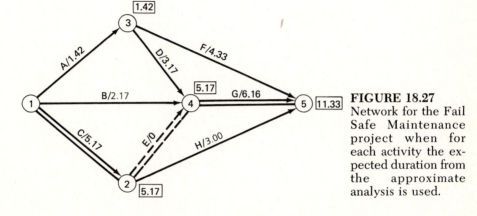

FIGURE 18.27
Network for the Fail Safe Maintenance project when for each activity the expected duration from the approximate analysis is used.

The approximate calculation assumes that (1) the sum of the expected durations on the critical path gives the expected value of the earliest possible occurrence of the completion date, (2) the variance is the sum of the variances of the activities on the critical path, and (3) the project completion date is distributed normally.

Adding the variances along the critical path in Figure 18.26, we get

$$\sigma^2 = .25 + 0 + .694 = .944$$

$$\sigma = .972 \text{ day}$$

What is the probability that the project is completed, for example, in 12 days? Using the approach for normal distribution in Chapter 3, we get

$$z = \frac{x - \mu}{\sigma} = \frac{12 - 11.34}{.972} = .679$$

and from Table B.1 in Appendix B we determine that the probability is .7517

Suppose management considers a probability of .7517 too low to complete the project in 12 days. What action can be taken to increase this probability?

Management decides to shorten the expected duration of the project to 10 days. Then $\mu = 10$, and

$$z = \frac{x - \mu}{\sigma} = \frac{12 - 10}{.972} = \frac{2}{.972} = 2.058$$

From Table B.1 we get .9803 for the probability.

As an alternate, it can be decided to control the project more carefully and decrease the standard deviation. Suppose, for example, σ becomes .5 day. Then

$$z = \frac{x - \mu}{\sigma} = \frac{12 - 11.34}{.5} = \frac{.76}{.5} = 1.53$$

and the probability becomes .9370.

Let us stress once more that in some situations the approximate technique may yield incorrect answers.* However, there are techniques available for combining accurately the random variables of the network. In simple situations, such as the one in Chapter 5 (Figure 5.12), the calculation can be carried out manually, but in many practical situations the only approach is simulation by computer.

Let us now summarize the steps required in the network procedure.

---

* See R. J. Schonberger, "Why Projects Are 'Always' Late: A Rationale Based on Manual Simulation of a PERT/CPM Network," *Interfaces*, Vol. 11, No. 5, Oct. 1981, pp. 66–70.

18.8 THE STEPS OF NETWORK PROCEDURE

Step 1. Develop a list of activities.

Step 2. List immediate predecessors.

Step 3. List activity durations.

Step 4. Draw the network.

Step 5. Determine the earliest possible occurrence (EPO) date of each event and the earliest allowable finish (EAF) date of each activity by making a forward pass.

Step 6. Determine the latest allowable occurrence (LAO) date for each event and the latest allowable start (LAS) date for each activity by a backward pass.

Step 7. Compute the slack for each activity and event.

Step 8. Construct the critical path(s) from the zero slack activities.

If a probabilistic network model is used, the following five additional steps need to be included:

Step 9. Determine the most optimistic, most pessimistic, and most likely durations for each activity.

Step 10. Calculate the expected duration of each activity, and use these values in step 3.

Step 11. Calculate the standard deviation of duration for each activity.

Step 12. Calculate the expected completion date of the project and the standard deviation.

Step 13. Calculate the probability of completion for a few sample dates.

Note that steps 5–8 are to be carried out after steps 9 and 10 are completed.

18.9 ADVANTAGES AND EXTENSIONS

Advantages

Here are some of the advantages of using network models which explain the popularity of these techniques:

1. The graphical representation provides an easily understandable visual representation.
2. Potential managerial problems can be identified and resolved early.
3. A discipline of careful planning is forced on project management personnel.
4. A better system of communication among project personnel is provided.
5. More effective allocation of resources among activities results.
6. Cost-time trade-off analysis provides better performance.

7. Uncertainty issues can be dealt with by probabilistic concepts.

Finally, it is to be pointed out that widely available computer programs make the use of network techniques practical and inexpensive.

Extensions

Due to the fact that a large number of types of organizations are involved in project management, there is a multitude of extensions of network models in use. The various issues of project management, such as organization, decentralization, communication, planning and control, and cost control, are all aided by network models. Specific techniques deal with problems such as the following:

1. Resource allocation, in particular the leveling of work loads and resources among various activities
2. Complex cost accounting and cost control issues
3. Efficient monitoring and controlling of large projects by providing status reports to management and allowing rescheduling by modifying networks

18.10 NETWORK MODELS: A DIALOG

Q. *A friend of mine took a course on quantitative methods, and in the textbook a careful distinction was made between PERT and CPM. You glossed over such differences. Why?*

A. In theoretical literature a distinction is being made. Namely, there seems to be a tendency to stress costs when dealing with CPM and uncertainty when dealing with PERT. But in practice costs must always be considered, and so in successful practical applications, the distinction between the two approaches is blurred. We have taken here a practical approach and stressed the view taken by successful analysts.

Q. *How accurate is the approximate technique you used for probabilistic networks?*

A. There is no way to tell. Let me give you an example. Suppose that an assembly consists of 100 parts and the expected duration for making each part is 1.5 months. Specifically, for each part the duration may be 1 month or 2 months, each with a probability of .5. After the 100 parts are completed, they are assembled in the final product in a matter of hours, so the duration for assembling is negligible. What is the expected value of the earliest possible occurrence of the completion date?

Q. *Isn't this a strange network? You have 100 activities, each forming its own critical path. The expected duration of each critical path is 1.5 months, and therefore, according to the approximate calculation, the expected value of the earliest possible occurrence of the completion date is 1.5 months. Am I right?*

A. Let's fall back on a thought experiment. Suppose I represent the duration for making each part by tossing a coin. If the coin shows heads, the duration is 1 month and if tails, it's 2 months. Do you accept this as a correct thought experiment for the problem?

Q. *Yes, I think you have modeled the problem correctly.*

A. The only way the project can be completed in 1 month is if all the coins show heads, indicating 1-month completion. How likely would all 100 coins show heads?

Q. *That's impossible.*

A. Well, not exactly impossible, but it certainly is extremely unlikely. So it is extremely likely that at least one of the durations will be 2 months and that the expected value of the EPO will also be almost 2 months. This shows that approximate calculation can be completely off.

Q. *Thank you. Now another question. Would you say that project management by network models is really a decision support system?*

A. This depends on how you do the work and whom you ask. If the work is done on a computer and the manager conducts a dialog with the computer, some may call this a DSS. If there is no computer involved or the manager is not directly involved in running the computer, some may not choose to call the system a DSS. But it is not really important what you call the system. The important thing is that the system makes it possible to make better decisions.

Q. *Thank you.*

SUMMARY

1. Network models are widely used in problems for the management of projects.
2. A network diagram graphically relates the activities and events of a project and directly shows precedence relationships.
3. Network models and managers decide (1) when to start, (2) when to complete, (3) when and how to speed up, and (4) when and how to slow down an activity.
4. Events are defined via start and completion dates of activities.
5. Events have no duration and consume no resources; activities require time and do consume resources.
6. Earliest possible occurrence (EPO) and latest allowable occurrence (LAO) dates provide time phasing information of events.
7. Earliest possible start (EPS), earliest possible finish (EPF), latest allowable start (LAS), and latest allowable finish (LAF) dates provide time phasing information of activities.
8. Critical path, event slack, and activity slack alert management to the relative urgency of meeting various schedules.

9. Time-cost trade-off analysis provides lowest-cost schedules which meet specified completion dates.

10. Issues of uncertainty in project management can be resolved by probabilistic network models.

11. Probabilistic networks are dealt with by approximate methods.

SECTION EXERCISES

1. *Hidden Valley Home Construction Project*

1.1 Choose some relatively simple project of interest to you (for example, a term paper, project for school, remodeling project, construction of a model). Identify the *major* activities (try to hold the number of activities below 20), and

    a. Make an activity list (similar to Figure 18.1).

    b. Make a list of the immediate predecessors (similar to Figure 18.2).

1.2 In a real-world project of some scope, such as the construction of a ship, large building, canal, dam, etc., how do you think the precedence relationships are determined?

2. *Network Models: Scientific Approach to Project Management*

2.1 Figure 18.28 is a network drawn by a newcomer to the project.

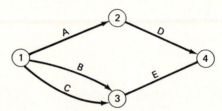

FIGURE 18.28

    a. What is wrong with this network?

    b. Correct the network. (*Hint*: Dummy activities may be necessary.)

2.2 Figure 18.29 is a network for a project. Can you reduce the number of dummy activities?

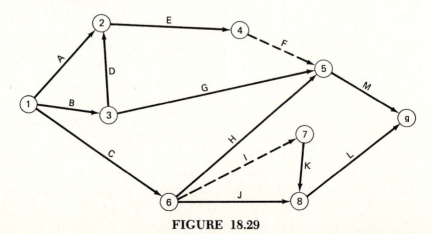

FIGURE 18.29

2.3 Figure 18.30 is a network for a project. Can you reduce the number of dummy activities?

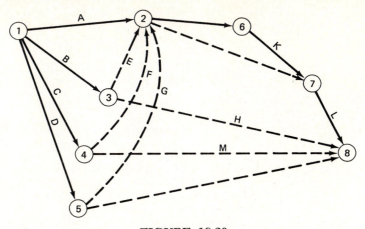

FIGURE 18.30

2.4 The section of a network shown in Figure 18.31 is not an allowable form.

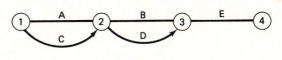

FIGURE 18.31

a. Why is this configuration not allowable?
b. Redraw this section of the network using dummy activities to make it allowable.

2.5 What is wrong with the network of Figure 18.32? (*Hint*: There are two occurrences of the same type of error.)

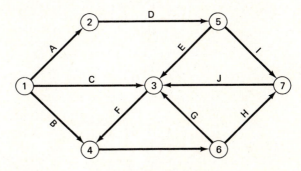

FIGURE 18.32

3. *How to Draw a Network*

3.1 The following is a table giving the precedence relations for a hospital product development project. Draw the network.

ACTIVITY	DESCRIPTION	IMMEDIATE PREDECESSOR
A	Product rationale	—
B	Develop formula	A
C	Product specification	B
D	Regulatory documents	B
E	Develop packaging concept	A
F	Design package	E
G	Develop processing system	C, D
H	Develop packaging system	F
I	Study facility requirements	G, H
J	Prepare capital equipment list	I
K	Purchase process equipment	J
L	Purchase packaging equipment	J
M	Purchase facilities	J
N	Install process equipment	K
O	Install packaging equipment	L
P	Install & construct facilities	M
Q	Prepare written procedures PH.I	G, H
Q'	Prepare written procedures PH.II	N, O, P, Q
R	Pilot test	Q'

3.2 The following is a table giving the precedence relations for a marketing engineering project. Draw the network.

ACTIVITY	DESCRIPTION	IMMEDIATE PREDECESSOR
A	Obtain approval	—
B	Prepare phase 1	A
C	Select sales personnel	A
D	Relocate salesmen to HO	C
E	Execute phase 1	B, D
F	Prepare phase 2	B, D
G	Execute phase 2	E, F, J
H	Study manuals	G, CC
I	Salesmen return home	H
J	Determine general marketing approach	A
K	Select marketing personnel	J
L	Relocate marketing personnel to HO	K
M	Consolidate marketing training plans	J
N	Design familiarization course	M
O	Train marketing personnel	L, N
P	Consolidate advertising plan	J
Q	Prepare paper	P
R	Print paper	Q
S	Prepare advertising	J
T	Approve advertising	S
U	Distribute advertising	T
V	Release & carry advertising	O, R, U
W	Draft & approve general brochure	P
X	Layout brochure	W
Y	Print brochure	X
Z	Prepare customer instruction manual	W
AA	Approve CIM	Z

ACTIVITY	DESCRIPTION	IMMEDIATE PREDECESSOR
BB	Print CIM	AA
CC	Send CIM to training center for familiarization	BB
DD	Package & deliver brochure & CIM	Y, BB
EE	End program	DD, I, V

4. *Time Phasing**

4.1 Figure 18.33 is the network for a project of the MKT Company.

  1. Questionnaires are distributed with follow-up on nonrespondents.

  2. Based on the analysis of the responses, telephone needs are determined and WATS (Wide Area Telephone Service) and FX (foreign exchanges lines in geographical regions) lines ordered and installed.

  3. All of this is accompanied by the recruiting and training of personnel to man the resulting telephone configurations.

  4. Note that the numbers in parentheses are activity durations.

    a. Refer to Figure 18.2; make a similar table from the network of Figure 18.33, showing activity letters (to identify them), description of activities, immediate predecessors, and the duration. (Include all dummy activities.)

    b. Refer to Figure 18.10; make a similar table from the network of Figure 18.33, determining the EPO for all events and EPF times for all activities.

    c. Refer to Figure 18.12; make a similar table from the network of Figure 18.33 finding the LAO for all events and LAS times for all activities.

    d. Refer to Figure 18.13; make a similar table from the network of Figure 18.33, getting the slack S for each event; indicate which events are on a critical path.

    e. Refer to Figure 18.15; make a similar table from the network of Figure 18.33, showing the duration D, EPS, EPF, LAF, LAS, and the activity slack.

---

* These exercises also include principles from Section 5.

ACTIVITY	DESCRIPTION	IMMEDIATE PREDECESSOR	DURATION IN WEEKS
AA	Start		0
A	Design minicomputer feasibility model	AA	8
B	Prepare purchase orders, obtain quotes, evaluate and place orders for units for model	A	4
C	Receive & inspect noncritical units	B	3
D	Complete specifications for critical units, prepare purchase orders for unordered unit, obtain quotes and place orders, receive, & inspect	C	10
E	Complete & distribute drawings & specifications for construction of feasibility model	A	8
F	Dummy	C	0
G	Assemble critical & noncritical units into feasibility model	D	12

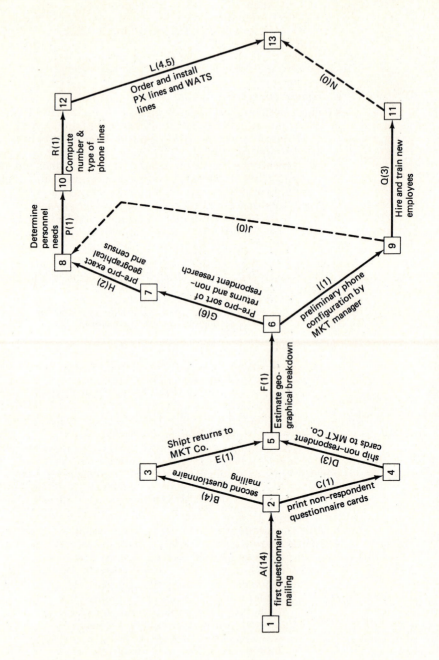

FIGURE 18.33 PERT network for the MKT Co.

ACTIVITY	DESCRIPTION	IMMEDIATE PREDECESSOR	DURATION IN WEEKS
H	Construct minicomputer feasibility model	F, E	20
I	Test minicomputer feasibility model, debug, rework, debug again, verify performance	G, H	10
J	Prepare interface for linking minicomputer & terminal	I	2
K	Dummy	J	0
L	Prepare contract, obtain quotes, & place contract for terminal	AA	9
M	Monitor vendor performance, receive terminal, verify performing to specification	L	5
N	Dummy	M	0
O	Write test specifications	AA	4
P	Write test programs	O	18
Q	Dummy	P	0
R	Verify system performance	K, N	11
S	Carry out proof tests	R, Q	7
	FINISH	S	0

Adapted from H. F. Spirer, *Engineering Manager Game Seminar* and *Project Management for Engineers*, MGI Management Institute, Inc., Larchmont, N.Y., Copyright 1974, used by permission.

FIGURE 18.34 Activity list precedence relations, and durations for bank minicomputer project.

4.2 Figure 18.34 is a listing of the activities, the precedence relations, and durations for a minicomputer development project of a bank.
    a. From Figure 18.34, draw the network corresponding to the relationships given there.
    b. Refer to Figure 18.10; make a similar table, finding the EPO for all events and the EPF times for all activities.
    c. Refer to Figure 18.12; make a similar table, finding the LAO for all events and the LAS times for all activities.
    d. Refer to Figure 18.13; make a similar table, getting the slack S for each event and indicating which events are on a critical path.
    e. Refer to Figure 18.15; make a similar table showing the duration D, EPS, EPF, LAF, LAS, and the activity slack.

4.3 Figure 18.35 is the listing of precedence relations and durations for the activities involved in creating an assembly and test operation for a new central processor unit by a computer supplier.
    a. From Figure 18.35, draw the network corresponding to the relationships given there.

ACTIVITY	DESCRIPTION	IMMEDIATE PREDECESSOR	DURATION IN DAYS
AA	Start		0
A	Select the site	I	15
B	Negotiate the lease	A	20
C	Design layout & power, AC requirements	B	10
D	Get bids from contractors	C	10
E	Select contractors	D	5

ACTIVITY	DESCRIPTION	IMMEDIATE PREDECESSOR	DURATION IN DAYS
F	Install air conditioning	E	70
G	Install electrical wiring	E	20
H	Install floors, lighting, walls	E	30
I	Brief manager of the facility	AA	2
J	Hire manager of quality control	I	20
K	Hire manager of logistics	I	30
L	Hire technicians	J	30
M	Train technicians	L, T, U	30
N	Hire test engineer	J	20
O	Design test procedures	N	30
P	Develop quality control procedures	J	30
Q	Order & deliver test equipment	O	60
R	Hire quality control inspector	J	20
S	Design inventory control system	K	60
T	Order & deliver training equipment	I	60
U	Prepare training courses	Z	60
V	Train inspector	P, R, T, U	10
W	Hire shipping & receiving clerk	I	15
X	Prepare shipping & receiving documents	W, S	60
Y	Check out test procedures	M, Q, V	10
Z	Hire training manager	I	30
	FINISH	F, G, H, X, Y	0

FIGURE 18.35

b. Refer to Figure 18.10; make a similar table, finding the EPO for all events and the EPF times for all activities.

c. Refer to Figure 18.12; make a similar table, finding the LAO for all events and the LAS times for all activities.

d. Refer to Figure 18.13; make a similar table, getting the slack S for each event and indicating which events are on a critical path.

e. Refer to Figure 18.15; make a similar table showing the duration D, EPS, EPF, LAF, LAS, and the activity slack.

4.4 Refer to the Fail Safe Maintenance project example of Section 18.4. Suppose that the marginal increase in dollars per day reduction for activity G is reduced to $100 per day and that the marginal increase for activity C is increased to $200 per day. Make a table similar to Figure 18.23 for this revised situation, and present the relationship between completion time and cost in a graph similar to Figure 18.24.

4.5 Refer to the Fail Safe Maintenance project example of Section 18.4. Suppose that the normal duration for activity D is 5 days and that the marginal cost of reduction in time is as stated. Revise Table 18.23 accordingly, and present the relationship between completion time and cost in a graph similar to Figure 18.24.

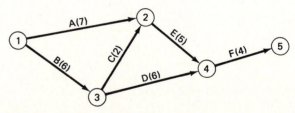

FIGURE 18.36 Network for Exercises 6.1 and 7.2.

ACTIVITY	DURATION IN DAYS		COST IN DOLLARS (000)	
	Normal	Crash	Normal	Crash
A	7	4	15	18
B	6	5	10	14
C	2	1	1	2
D	6	4	10	12
E	5	2	14	18
F	4	3	6	4

FIGURE 18.37 Possible durations and corresponding costs for the activities of the project in Exercise 6.1.

5. *Scheduling of Activities*
   Exercises for this section are integrated with those of section 4.

6. *Time Cost Benefits*
6.1 Figure 18.36 shows a network; activities are identified on the network and their durations in weeks are shown in parentheses. Figure 18.37 shows the time-cost relationships for the activities in this project.
   a. Find the critical path(s) for this project under normal scheduling.
   b. Determine the cost for this project under a normal schedule.
   c. The project manager wants to know the cost and feasibility of completing the job in any possible number of weeks from 10 to normal time. Compute the cost of completing the job in 10, 11, 12, . . . weeks, stopping at the normal time. If any time is infeasible, indicate this.

7. *Probabilistic Network Models*
7.1 Refer to the example of Section 18.7, shown in Figures 18.26 and 18.27. Assume that all activities have the same probability distribution for the duration of the activity as described:

DURATION (weeks)	PROBABILITY
2	.2
3	.5
8	.3

   a. What is the expected time for completing the project?
   b. What is the variance of the activity time duration for one activity?
   c. What is the variance of the time to complete the project? The standard deviation?
   d. What is the probability that the project will be completed in 21 weeks or less? (*Hint*: Be sure to find the probability of all possible ways of completing in a given time.)
   e. Find the same probability as requested in part d using the normal probability curve.
   f. What is the probability that the project will be completed in 18 weeks (use a normal probability curve)?

7.2 Refer to the network of Figure 18.36. The following values have been obtained for the optimistic, most likely, and pessimistic times for each activity:

ACTIVITY	a	b	m	d	σ	σ²
A	5	9	7			
B	3	10	5.75			
C	1	3	2			
D	2	6	7			
E	4	8	3			
F	3	9	3			

    a. Complete the column marked d in the table.
    b. Complete the columns marked σ and σ^2 in the table.
    c. Find the expected time for completing the project. (*Hint*: Assume that the critical path is the determining path.)
    d. Find the variance and standard deviation of the time for completing the project.

7.3 Refer to the network of Figure 18.29. The following values have been obtained for the optimistic, most likely, and pessimistic times for each activity:

ACTIVITY	a	b	m	d	σ	σ²
A	13	20	12.75			
B	1	5	4.50			
C	.5	1.5	1			
D	2	4	3			
E	.5	3	.625			
F	Dummy					
G	5	12	4.75			
H	.2	3	.7			
I	Dummy					
J	2.3	1.2	.7			
K	2	6	2.5			
L	3	10	3.5			
M	1	4	2			

    a. Complete the column marked d in the table.
    b. Complete the columns marked σ and σ^2 in the table.
    c. Find the expected time for completing the project. (*Hint*: Assume that the critical path as determined by the expected times establishes the determining path.)
    d. Find the variance and standard deviation of the time for completing the project.

CHAPTER EXERCISES AND DISCUSSION QUESTIONS

    C.1 In the example concerning the failure of the plumbing to be finished on time in the Hidden Valley Home Construction project, two examples of the "costs" of failure to coordinate project activities were given: loss of wages and the slipping of the completion date of the project. Give additional examples of costs that are a possible consequence of this failure.

    C.2 What kind of difficulties in the Hidden Valley Home Construction project can be considered to be "unavoidable?"

C.3 The statement is made in the text that "large complex projects . . . may have thousands of interdependent activities." One chart showing thousands of activities can be hard to use in the direct managerial function of any one individual. How do you think you could handle this problem? (*Hint*: Think first of how many activities any one individual could *directly* manage and then how each activity might itself become someone else's project.)

C.4 Given a set of precedence relations, there are two possible network representations. The one you have been shown in this text where activities are assigned to arrows and nodes to events is called *event on node* or *activity on arrow* or also PERT. In the other form of representation, arrows indicate only the precedence relationships, and the nodes are the activities. Hence, this is called *activity-on-node* or also PDM (for precedence diagramming method). Draw activity-on-node networks for the following:
  a. The precedence relationships shown in Figure 18.2.
  b. The precedence relationships shown in Figure 18.6.
  c. The precedence relationships shown in Figure 18.8.
  d. The precedence relationships shown in the precedence relationship table given in Exercise 3.1.
  e. The precedence relationships shown in the precedence relationship table given in Exercise 3.2.

C.5 Refer to Discussion Exercise 4. Will there be dummies in an activity-on-node diagram? If the answer is yes, what role will they play? If you answer no, why?

C.6 Suppose that management imposes a latest allowable occurrence time on a project as a whole which is less than the earliest possible occurrence of the last task on the project.
  a. What happens to the slack on the critical path?
  b. What happens to the slack on the noncritical paths?

C.7 If a project manager schedules all the tasks on a project to start at the latest allowable starting time, how many critical paths will there be in the project?

C.8 What information is required to carry out a project if an activity is missing from the network?

C.9 In the type of network illustrated here, the length of the arrow can be made proportional to the time to perform that activity. Show how this convention can be used to develop a chart which is both a schedule and a network. (Such networks are called *time-based networks* and are in widespread use.)

C.10 How might the precedence diagram (activity on node) be used in manufacturing work to describe assembly processes?

C.11 Make a network for your academic program where the activities become particular courses you take. (*Hint*: Use the prerequisite requirements of your school to determine precedence relations.)

C.12 Very few major construction projects are carried out today without using networks and the associated managerial techniques. Yet it is acknowledged that somewhere between 3 and 5% of the project costs are in such methods. Why are these methods used so widely?

19 Your Stake in Quantitative Methods

Our world is complex, uncertain, and confusing. This holds for small and big businesses and for organizations in the private and public sectors of our society. Also we have every reason to believe that the world is getting more complex. Should it also get more confusing?

Most of us feel dissatisfied with the world around us. There is nothing wrong about this, because most of us want to do better, and we believe that there is a better way. Thus there is a need, as well as an opportunity, to do better and to make better decisions.

You now know that when we discuss decision makers we do not think exclusively of managers of business or even of the public sector but of physicians, legislators, lawyers, etc., as well—all individuals who have choices of action.

We stated all this at the beginning of the textbook and developed our theme of how quantitative methods offer a better way to support decisions. Now that you have completed the course, we can review the role of decision making in our world and use the knowledge you obtained in this textbook to be more specific about the advantages and opportunities offered you by quantitative methods.

Naturally, you expect to get a good job, good pay, good working conditions, and a good living standard. But these goals are incomplete. You also want an interesting and challenging position. You want to obtain satisfaction and fulfillment. Material goods are not quite enough; psychological, societal, and other satisfactions are also important. You would like to see a better world in the future, to take part in bringing about the change for the better. We claim that better decision making can help you achieve your goals and believe that the scientific approach to decision making, when coupled with the new technology of computers and communication, can make a significant contribution to bringing about this better world.

The Scientific Method

We began this textbook by advocating the application of the scientific method to decision making. Now that you know a great deal about how the scientific method is applied to decision making, a review of the scientific method itself is appropriate.

René Descartes in 1637 published his *Essay on the Discourse of the Method.* The purpose of this essay, which caused a revolution in Western thought and philosophy, was to develop a method to think better. Descartes starts out his essay by saying that common sense alone is not enough to think straight. He says that we all feel we already have enough common sense and that no one wants to have more. But Descartes observes that some people are more effective than others in their way of thinking. Why do some people think straight and others not? Descartes says that the difference is that there is a *method* to thinking straight and that it is not common sense or judgment but the method that makes people different and better thinkers.

The quantitative method of decision making, the application of the scientific method, or the method advocated by Descartes is none other than to think in a more systematic, disciplined, and thorough way about the situation under consideration. We must list, analyze, and examine in a systematic manner our objectives, goals, judgments, opinions, facts, and potential benefits. We must strive for clarity and remove confusion from our world.

The most basic principle of Descartes is to start with skepticism and doubt—the Cartesian principle of doubt. People think in a certain way because they have been doing so for many years and have come to believe it is the only right way to think. You now have a method for examining assumptions, questions, and approaches and know how to find better solutions. You know about models, mathematical models, the salient and essential feature of the quantitative approach. You know how to build models, how to verify them, how to solve them, and how to put them to use. You know from the many successful applications how in a short period of 25 years the quantitative method of supporting decision making reached wide acceptance and scored many successes. You know how the quantitative method combines judgment and science and are aware that the acceptance and validation of models depend a great deal on judgment. You know through your work on probabilities, preference, and utility theory how judgment must be fed into models and coupled with the quantitative method. You are also aware of the limitations of the scientific approach, but a few more words are in order.

Limitations

You know now that we do not advocate the replacement of the human element, intuition, and judgment by mathematical formulas or computers. You learned from the problems and successful applications that all our work is really an extension and augmentation of human reasoning.

Behavioral aspects are not neglected but carefully scrutinized. Organizational, psychological, and societal considerations are all included when the quantitative method is applied to support decision making.

It has been claimed that the human brain consists of the right and left hemispheres. The right hemisphere deals with feeling, senses, intuition, the creative, the artistic, the romantic, and the heroic. On the other hand, the left hemisphere deals with the rational, logical, and systematic. The quantitative method stresses the left hemisphere but in no way ignores or denies the existence of the right hemisphere.

The quantitative method advocates the viewpoint and perspective of the strengthening of the left hemisphere of the brain. *Matters pertaining to the right hemisphere belong to the right hemisphere.* Basic goals and objectives, morality, ethics, quality of life, and social equity belong rightly to the right hemisphere. The scientific method is in no way in conflict with the right hemisphere and does not attempt to remove the human element.

But we advocate the scientific method of decision making as a better way to find creative alternatives and decide on actions to achieve goals and objectives. The quantitative method provides a comparative advantage to you when dealing with complex and uncertain situations. You also know, when it comes to implementing decision making, that when the quantitative approach is turned into reality, the technology of computers enters the picture as indispensable. Thus a few more words on this subject are in order.

Computers and Information Systems

We stressed throughout the textbook that it is impossible to think rationally and apply the scientific method to decision making without data and information. Staggering advances in the technology of computers have revolutionized our ability to obtain and manage data and information about our world at an ever-decreasing cost. In fact, today our ability to produce data overshadows our capability to turn the data into information so we can make better decisions and better manage our affairs. Therefore, we believe that a combination of the quantitative technique of decision making and the ever-advancing computer technology offer an unprecedented opportunity for reaching individual and societal benefits.

Where You Are

Through examples, problems, and applications you know a great deal about models and their use. You learned the importance and advantage of using the quantitative method and computers. You appreciate the difference between the formulation of models and the solution technique or algorithm required to solve models on computers.

You learned the two mainstreams of modeling: deterministic and probabilistic. After a brief introduction to the quantitative approach and mathematical models of Chapter 1, you learned the powerful deterministic method of resource allocation with the aid of linear programming and its extension (Chapters 10–14).

You were introduced to decision making under uncertainty by reviewing the concepts of probability theory in Chapters 2 and 3. Then you learned about statistical forecasting, fundamental to the quantitative analysis of business decisions. In Chapters 5 and 6 you learned decision analysis, the scientific technique of making decisions under uncertainty and how judgments about uncertainty can be made explicit by the introduction of probability. You also learned that individuals differ in their goals and preferences and learned how to apply the scientific method to such situations both under uncertainty (Chapter 7) and certainty (Chapter 14). You of course knew before starting this study that information is vital to decision making, but in Chapter 8 you learned how to put information into quantitative terms and the method for dealing with the value of information in a scientific manner.

In Chapter 9 you learned about techniques of controlling inventories and in Chapter 18 of managing projects. In Chapters 15, 16, and 17 you learned important probabilistic techniques required to solve advanced types of problems where uncertainty dominates.

You have developed and strengthened your knowledge about using quantitative methods for problem solving and have learned to appreciate the scope and applicability of these quantitative techniques by studying realistic case studies.

Throughout the text we stressed the limitations and potential errors in using quantitative methods, and now we summarize and highlight some of the more common traps and fallacies.

Five Traps in Model Building

Trap 1. Overemphasis on model. Suppose you build an elaborate financial planning system and all the inputs and outputs are related correctly. But suppose the goals of the organization are misunderstood. Suppose the model eliminates the position of the sponsor of your effort. Very likely the recommendation will be ignored.

Trap 2. Oversimplification. Someone builds a linear programming model and assumes continuous variables. However, it is impossible to have one-half of a warehouse, and so the results of the linear programming problem become useless. The model is proved simplistic and cannot deal with the realities of the situation.

Trap 3. Overcomplication. Suppose a stochastic model of a research allocation problem is built and it is found impossible to get a solution. However, a deterministic approach to the problem, using linear programming, is capable of getting good enough answers. The overcomplicated stochastic model misses the problem and is useless.

Trap 4. Assuming that data will be available. A waiting-line model is built to describe the situation, but after the model is constructed and tested, it turns out that it is impossible to obtain reliable data on arrival rates and services. The model cannot be implemented and is useless.

Trap 5. Assuming that the model will be accepted by the power of its logic. A complex PERT model is developed to control a project. However, the system is quite complex and is poorly explained to the project manager. Not only is he unable to understand how to use PERT, but he also fails to see the benefits of using the model. The model is perfectly logical but is not acceptable, because no manager will take the risk of using a technique he cannot completely understand.

Five Fallacies About Mathematics

Fallacy 1. Mathematics has magic powers. Some people erroneously think that once you have a mathematical model and put it on the computer, you will have the answer. The computer says so, it must be true! With the wrong model and the wrong data, mathematics becomes useless.

Fallacy 2. Mathematics is the most important thing in resolving the situation. Suppose a correct model for controlling inventory is established. The model assumes that the problem is to control inventory to meet a specified demand. However, the demand decreases substantially, and the problem becomes not how to control the inventory but how to regain the sales of the product.

Fallacy 3. Mathematical techniques yield complete and optimum solutions. Suppose with the aid of the transportation algorithm an optimum solution to a complex distribution problem is obtained. However, a more careful analysis shows that the constraints assumed are uncertain and unpredictable. A sensitivity analysis shows that changing the constraints has a dramatic impact on the solution. While the transportation algorithm provides important information to the decision maker, there is a serious question in what sense the solution obtained is optimum.

Fallacy 4. Mathematical techniques are always superior to verbal techniques. A mathematical model is built for a situation, and through the model a good solution is discovered. When the results are presented to the decision makers, complex mathematical notation is used and the managers fail to understand the substance of the proposition and reject the recommendation.

When solutions obtained through mathematical techniques are presented to management, verbal, graphical, and tabular discussions are more effective than the detailed mathematical representation. In fact, often the mathematics can be completely eliminated from the explanation.

Fallacy 5. Mathematical techniques can be applied to all situations. We have already stressed repeatedly that such methods as selecting overall goals and aims, life styles, social equity, an ethical framework, etc., are not subject to purely mathematical treatment.

Implementation and Theory of Change

In Chapter 1, when applying the scientific method in decision making, we distinguished five phases: (1) exploration, (2) model building, (3) model interpretation, (4) decision making, and (5) implementation. Now that you have completed your studies, we should say a few words about the last phase, implementation.

The purpose of the quantitative approach to decision making is to support decision making, and unless the effort is implemented, nothing is gained. However, as of today, there is no generally accepted theory of implementation, and so you will master implementation when taking part in real-life projects. Here we can give only general guidance to assist you when faced with issues of implementation.

Implementation is a process of innovation and organizational change. Thus implementation is dominated by behavioral aspects. Human beings, as they are, resist change because they can best satisfy their needs in a stable environment. Change is usually considered a threat to the status quo, and so when faced with implementation, you are faced with the issue of how to overcome resistance.

There has been much research in behavioral sciences on the subject of how to bring about change, and Lewin and Schein* have developed a framework for analysis. According to Lewin and Schein, there is a three-step approach required to overcome resistance to change to ensure long-term achievement.

Step 1. Unfreezing. Unfreezing is overcoming resistance to change. Encouraging dissatisfaction with current behavior leads to unlearning current behavior and creating the desire to learn new behavior. Unfreezing involves reducing defensiveness to learning, so the individual will search and explore new and improved ways of behavior.

Step 2. Changing. Changing is exposure to new information, attitude, and theory in order to achieve new perception and learn new behavior patterns. It involves gathering new information, interpreting information, and developing alternative courses of action which could lead to learning new behavior patterns. In this process a method of choosing from alternatives may need to be developed or the method modified.

Step 3. Refreezing. Refreezing is reinforcement and confirmation of support for new behavior. It requires integrating new responses in the personality of the individual and establishing meaningful relationships within the organization. Refreezing can be achieved through positive feedback and is necessary for the resulting stability of the new situation.

This framework for change has been verified and found useful by many people facing implementation. However, it is not a detailed set of specific instruction but more of a road map to guide action. Implementation is more art than science.

Prescription for Success

No one can tell you precisely how to succeed. Still it is useful to summarize the common experience of successful practitioners. So here are eight points:

1. Know your sponsor. Analysts often fail to understand clearly who

---

* Edgar H. Schein, "The Mechanism of Change," in *Interpersonal Dynamics*, W. G. Bennis, E. Schein, F. Steele, and D. Berlew, eds., Dorsey Press, Homewood, Ill., 1964, pp. 362–378.

is really in charge and pays the cost of a project, what is his/her authority, how does he/she see the problem, what are his/her motives, goals, emotions. Is he/she the decision maker? Is he/she receptive, and will he/she really support the effort? What are his/her ambitions, and what will he/she get out of the project?

2. *Understand the meaning of success.* Never fail to ask yourself, "Suppose I am successful in all. What would the consequences be?"

What is it your sponsor and other managers expect to get? Is there a real need for the project? Is there clear agreement on goals, benefits, and risks? Is it clearly understood what it will cost and how long it will take?

Choose your problem well! No matter how hard you work, if the problem is ill-chosen, you will fail. Raise this question repeatedly during the project because it is better to cancel than to fail in the end.

3. *Conceptualize the system behind the management process.* Make every effort to perceive the enterprise as a total process and keep refining your formal statement on goals, objectives, and the environment. Do not rely on formal organization charts but ferret out the informal behavioral processes of management.

Raise the issue continuously about what is important, what can be ignored, and what changes will be required in the existing situation to implement the results of your work.

4. *Insist on management participation, guidance, and commitment.* Quantitative analysis often fails because of inadequate top management approval and monitoring. You are certain to fail if resources are not committed.

Top management support is not adequate in itself because implementation will very likely involve middle management. Thus you must receive active participation from all levels of management and must insist that your effort is properly located in a formal and informal organizational structure. The best plan can fail in an unsympathetic organizational climate.

5. *Employ project planning and control techniques (see Chapter 18).* Do not believe that quantitative analysis is so totally different from other management projects that traditional project planning and control techniques do not apply. You need budgets and plans, an awareness of difficulties, and contingency plans to overcome them. You must recognize throughout that eventually you face implementation. Think in terms of the management process of innovation and not on just delivering a report which will stand on its own without further modification and updating.

6. *Use an information systems perspective.* To implement your recommendations, you need to have data and an information system to support them. Many projects have failed simply because there were no data to feed into the model. Results must be formulated as providing better quantitative information to management.

7. *Develop a good reputation.* You cannot assume that your work will speak for itself. Benefits are not self-evident from implementing quantitative analysis, and proving an expected economic advantage is often difficult. Start your project simply and keep it simple and under-

standable to management. Create credibility by scoring early benefits and by demonstrating these benefits. Express the inputs and outputs of the model in a familiar form to management and insist that your work be visible and clear to management.

8. *Be people oriented.* You must be sensitive to the needs and motives of others and strive to develop in them an understanding and desire for the changes you propose. You must be aware of your own feelings and emotions, perceive people realistically, and establish good and informal communication channels with those who will be influenced by your work.

Your Stake

Your purpose in seeking higher education is to simulate and guide your self-development. While you study today, you are concerned with your future. You aim your efforts toward a moving target. To succeed in this uncertain future environment, you must be flexible and concentrate on fundamentals. Also you must be concerned with the living world about you, not with dead knowledge. The quantitative analysis of decision making you have just learned is practical knowledge which you can soon put to direct and beneficial use. The future for people who can apply quantitative methods to support decision making is bright. Whatever change the future brings, if you know how to think straight, it will be very much to your advantage. And this is what the quantitative approach to decision making is all about.

Appendix

A

Review of Basic Mathematics

The purpose of this appendix is to provide a review of basic mathematics and numerous exercises. First, a set of initial tests on arithmetic and algebra are provided without text so you can verify your knowledge of the preliminaries. Then brief explanations and corresponding exercises follow.

A.1 ARITHMETIC AND ALGEBRA

1.1. Encircle the number on the left of the statements that are correct:

1. $48/5 + 3 = 6$

2. $9 + 5 - 2 = 5 - 2 + 9$

3. $18/5 + 1 = 3$

4. $(\frac{1}{4})^2 = \frac{1}{16}$

5. $15 \times \frac{3}{4} = 5 \times \frac{9}{4}$

6. $\frac{5}{7} \times \frac{8}{9} \times \frac{6}{11} = \frac{5}{9} \times \frac{6}{7} \times \frac{8}{11}$

7. $\frac{1}{7}(28 + 3) = 4 + 3$

8. $54/(3 \times 2) = 9$

9. $2 + 17/3 = 19/3$

10. $\dfrac{2 + 3}{2 + 5} = \dfrac{2}{3} + \dfrac{3}{5}$

11. $\dfrac{6 + 8}{2 \times 5} = \dfrac{6}{2} + \dfrac{8}{5}$

12. $\dfrac{7 \times 9}{11 \times 15} = \dfrac{7}{15} \times \dfrac{9}{11}$

13. $\dfrac{15 + 3}{5} = 3 + 3$

14. $\sqrt{49 - 25} = 7 - 5$

15. $\dfrac{15 \times 7 \times 9}{3} = 5 \times 7 \times 9$

16. $\frac{1}{9}(18 - \frac{3}{5}) = 2 - \frac{1}{15}$

17. $\dfrac{5 \times 7}{6} = \dfrac{5}{6} \times \dfrac{7}{6}$

18. $5 + \frac{2}{3} \times \frac{1}{2} = 5\frac{1}{3}$

19. $\dfrac{15 + 7}{5} = 3\frac{7}{5}$

20. $\dfrac{54 + 7}{6} = 9 + 7$

21. $\sqrt{1 - (.4)^2} = \sqrt{.6}$

22. $3 \times \sqrt{43 + 2 \times 3} = 21$

23. $\left(\frac{2}{3}\right)^2 = \frac{4}{25}$

24. $36 - 16/7 + 3 = 2$

25. $2 \times (5 \times 7) = 10 \times 14$

26. $(36 - 16)/(7 + 3) = 2$

27. $\frac{1}{5} \times (10 \times 7) = 2 \times \frac{7}{5}$

28. $1 + 2 + 3 = 1 \times 2 \times 3$

29. $2 \times 3 + 1 \times 4 = 32$

30. $2 \times 3 + 4 \times 4 = 22$

31. $2 \times 4 + 1 \times 4 = 14$

32. $2 \times 3 + 2 \times 2 = 28$

33. $5 - (-3 \times 2) = -1$

34. $2 - \dfrac{-6}{3} = 4$

1.2. Indicate on the left the letter that gives the correct answer:

		A	B	C
1.	$\frac{3}{8} \div \frac{9}{2}$	$\frac{12}{10}$	$\frac{1}{12}$	$\frac{27}{16}$
2.	$\frac{3}{4} + \frac{1}{6}$	$\frac{4}{10}$	$\frac{22}{24}$	$\frac{4}{24}$
3.	$6/6$	0	1	2
4.	$27{,}000$	2.7×10^3	2.7×10^4	2.7×10^5
5.	$9\frac{2}{3}$	6	$\frac{29}{3}$	$\frac{18}{27}$
6.	$.027$	$\frac{27}{10}$	$\frac{27}{100}$	$\frac{27}{1000}$
7.	$\dfrac{a}{b} + \dfrac{c}{d}$	$\dfrac{ac}{bd}$	$\dfrac{ad + bc}{bd}$	$\dfrac{a + c}{b + d}$
8.	$ab\left(\dfrac{a}{b}\right)$	ab	a^2	b^2
9.	$\dfrac{ab - c}{b}$	$\dfrac{a - c}{b}$	$a - \dfrac{c}{b}$	$a - c$
10.	$\dfrac{x^2}{x}$	0	x	1
11.	$\dfrac{4}{3} \dfrac{xy}{8} \dfrac{x}{4yz}$	$\dfrac{xyz}{24}$	$\dfrac{x^2}{24z}$	$\dfrac{x^2 y^2 z}{24}$
12.	$\dfrac{ab}{y} + \dfrac{y}{a}$	$\dfrac{ab + y}{ay}$	$\dfrac{a^2 b + y^2}{ay}$	$\dfrac{a^2 b + y^2}{ay}$
13.	$\frac{2}{3} + \frac{1}{5}$	$\frac{3}{8}$	$\frac{13}{15}$	$\frac{2}{15}$
14.	3.05	$\frac{305}{10}$	$\frac{305}{100}$	$\frac{305}{1000}$
15.	$\frac{3}{4} \div \frac{5}{4}$	$\frac{5}{3}$	$\frac{3}{5}$	$\frac{15}{16}$
16.	$.3$	$\frac{10}{3}$	$\frac{20}{10}$	$\frac{1}{10} + \frac{1}{10} + \frac{1}{10}$
17.	$12 \times \frac{2}{3}$	$\frac{38}{3}$	8	$\frac{24}{36}$
18.	$7 \div \frac{4}{5}$	$\frac{39}{5}$	$\frac{35}{4}$	$\frac{28}{35}$

1.3. Perform the following additions:

1. $\begin{aligned} 6a - 5b + 2c \\ -5a + 3b - 4c \\ \underline{2a - 3b - 10c} \end{aligned}$

2. $\begin{aligned} -3x + 4y - 2z \\ 4x - 2y - 3z \\ \underline{-2x - 3y + 4z} \end{aligned}$

3. $\begin{aligned} 3p - 7q - 4r \\ 5p + 9q + 7r \\ \underline{-7p - 2q - 3r} \end{aligned}$

1.4. Perform the following subtractions (subtract the second row from the first):

1. $2a - 4b + 3c$
    $-3a + 7b - 2c$

2. $8x + 9y - 7z$
    $10x - 7y + 8z$

3. $3p - 7q - 4r$
    $4p + 9q + 7r$

1.5. Simplify and check each answer by using $a = 2$, $b = 3$, $c = 5$ or $x = 2$, $y = 3$, $z = 5$:

1. $[3a - (4b - 2c)] - [4a - (b - 2c)] + [4a - (2b - 3c)]$
2. $(-3a - 5b + 2c) - (7a + 2b - 3c) + (5a + 3b - 2c)$
3. $\{[2x - 3(y + 1)] - (3y + 4z)\} - [2x - (3x - 4y - 2z)]$

1.6. Perform the following operations:

1. $(36b^2 - 5b)(-2b)$
2. $(-3n)(5n^2)$
3. $\sqrt[3]{-64y^3}$
4. $(-5x^2)(-7y^2)$
5. $r(p - 2) - 3(p + r)$
6. $5 + 2(a - 5) - 4(b + 3)$
7. $(abc - 2abd)/(-ab)$
8. $(24x^2 - 36xy + 18xz)/(-3x)$

1.7. Simplify the following expressions and check each answer with a set of numerical values of your own choice:

1. $(a - \frac{3}{2})(a - \frac{1}{2})$
2. $2xy - \{3z - [7xy - (5z - 6xyz)]\}$
3. $5a[(b - a) - 2a(1 - 3b)]$
4. $(4a - 5b)(a + b)$
5. $(1 - 3x)(x + 7) - (x + 3)(3 - 2x)$
6. $\dfrac{5a^2b^2 - 6a^3b + 8ab^3}{2a^3b}$
7. $(x^3 - 4x^2 + 7x - 12)/(x - 3)$
8. $(12a^2 + 8a - 15)/(6a - 5)$

1.8. Encircle the number on the left of the statements that are correct:

1. $(3x + 2)/(x - 4) = 3x + 2/x - 4$
2. $3a - b - c = 3(a - b - c)$
3. $\dfrac{a - b}{c - d} \cdot \dfrac{b - c}{a - c} = \dfrac{(a - b)(b - c)}{(c - d)(a - c)}$
4. $\dfrac{a - b}{c - d} \cdot \dfrac{b - c}{a - c} = \dfrac{a - b^2 - bc}{c - ad - cd}$
5. $-\dfrac{x - 2y}{2y - x} = 1$

6. $\dfrac{a - b}{a - c} \cdot \dfrac{d - b}{d - c} = \dfrac{b - a}{c - a} \cdot \dfrac{b - d}{c - d}$
7. $a(b - ac + x) = a[(b - ac) + x]$
8. $\dfrac{5x - y}{3} = \dfrac{y - 5x}{3}$
9. $-\dfrac{1}{2}(a - b) = \dfrac{b - a}{2}$

10. $\dfrac{a - b}{a - d} \cdot \dfrac{5x}{4y} = \dfrac{5}{4} \cdot \dfrac{x(b - a)}{y(d - a)}$

11. $\dfrac{6x - 8x + 2x}{x} = 0$

12. $\dfrac{2a - 5b}{2a - 5b} = 1$

13. $(u + 2)^1 = 1$

14. $\dfrac{(2u + 3v)^2}{2u + 3v} = 2u + 3v$

15. $(p - 3q)^0 = 1$

16. $(x - 7)^0 = 0$

17. $(a - b)^{-1} = b - a$

18. $\dfrac{2a - 5 - 2(a + 1)}{6a - 4 - 2(3a - 2)} = \dfrac{a}{b}$

1.9. Perform the operations, simplify, and verify by numerical values of your own choice:

1. $\dfrac{2}{x} - \dfrac{6}{y} - \dfrac{9}{z}$

2. $\dfrac{xy}{az} \cdot \dfrac{yz}{bx} \cdot \dfrac{xz}{ay}$

3. $\dfrac{a}{x} - \dfrac{b}{x^2}$

4. $\dfrac{xy}{az} \div \dfrac{bz}{ay}$

5. $\dfrac{4}{a(a + 1)} - \dfrac{3}{2a}$

6. $\dfrac{x - 3}{a} - \dfrac{x}{2a}$

7. $(a - b)\dfrac{a + 2b}{a^2 - b^2}$

8. $\dfrac{x^2 - 9}{x} \div (x + 3)^2$

9. $\dfrac{6}{a^2 - b^2} - \dfrac{9}{a - b}$

10. $\dfrac{1 + (1/y)}{1 - (1/y)}$

11. $\dfrac{9a^2 - 16}{a + 1} \div (4 - 3a)$

1.10 Show the validity of the following statements:

1. If $3(x - 2) = 0$, then $x = 2$.
2. If $5u = 0$, then $u = 0$.
3. If $xy = 0$, then either x or y is zero.
4. If $x(x - y) = 0$, then either $x = y$ or $x = 0$.
5. If $(x + y)(x - y) = 0$, then $x = \pm y$.
6. If $(x - 2)(x + 5) = 0$, then either $x = 2$ or $x = -5$.
7. If $(u - a)(u + b) = 0$, then either $u = a$ or $u = b$.
8. If $(x - 2)^2 = 0$, then $x = 2$.
9. If $a^2 - b^2 = 0$, then $a = \pm b$.
10. If $(x + a)^3 = 0$, then $a = -x$.

A.2 FUNCTIONS

2.1. Plot the points whose coordinates are $(2,7)$, $(-1,-2)$, $(-4,2)$, $(3,.5)$, $(-6,0)$, $(-3.5,-7)$, $(0,-2)$, $(2.5,6.5)$, $(-6.5,0)$, $(0,-2.5)$.

2.2. Where are the points whose abscissas (x coordinates) are 1? -2? Whose ordinates (y coordinates) are 1.5? $-.5$? Whose abscissas equal their ordinates? What is the abscissa of all points on the y axis? What is the ordinate of all points on the x axis?

2.3. The four quadrants of the plane are defined by (a) $x \geq 0$, $y \geq 0$; (b) $x \leq 0$, $y \geq 0$; (c) $x \leq 0$, $y \leq 0$; (d) $x \geq 0$, $y \leq 0$.

2.4. Plot the following functions:

a. $y = x(1 - x)$

b. $y = -(x - 2)(3 - x)$

c. $y = x + \dfrac{1}{x}$

d. $y = \dfrac{1}{x(1 - x)}$

e. $y = -\dfrac{1}{(x - 2)(3 - x)}$

2.5. Plot the following families of functions:

a. $y = ax^2$, where $a = 5, 7, 8$ for $-3 \leq x \leq 4$

b. $y = x^3 + a$, where $a = 5, 7, 8$ for $-1 \leq x$

2.6. Consider the following 11 functions:

a. $y = 3x + 5$

b. $y = 3x^2 - 3$

c. $y = -\dfrac{x}{3} + 2$

d. $y = -3x - 3$

e. $y = x^2 + 4x$

f. $y = -3x$

g. $y = .5x - 3$

h. $y = 10x^4$

i. $y = 3x - 3$

j. $y = 2x$

k. $y = 5$

2.7. Which of the following qualities do these functions possess?

1. Nonlinear function
2. Passes through the origin
3. Parallel to the line $y = 3x$
4. Passes through the point $(0, -3)$
5. Passes through the point $(0, 5)$
6. Straight line with negative slope
7. Parallel to the x axis

2.8. Consider the following function of two variables:

$$z = 2x^2 - y^2 + 2xy + y + 3$$

a. Calculate z for $x = 0$, $y = 0$; $\quad x = 1$, $y = 0$; $\quad x = 0$, $y = 1$; $\quad x = 1$, $y = -1$; $\quad x = 1$, $y = 1$

b. Plot z vs. x provided $y = 0$.

c. Plot z vs. y provided $x = .5$.

A.3. THE MATHEMATICS OF STRAIGHT LINES

A.3.1 Theory

The general equation for a straight line is

$$ax + by = c$$

If $b = 0$ but $a \neq 0$, the line is parallel to the y axis; if $b \neq 0$, we can divide by b and get

$$y = -\frac{a}{b}x + \frac{c}{b}$$

or

$$y = mx + k$$

where $m = -(a/b)$ and $k = c/b$. Here m is the *slope* of the straight line and k is the y *intercept*, meaning that if $x = 0$, then $y = k$. The x intercept is given by $l = c/a$ provided $a \neq 0$, meaning that if $y = 0$, then $x = l$. If $m = 0$, the line is parallel to the x axis.

You can plot a straight line by taking two values of x, x_1, and x_2 computing the corresponding y_1 and y_2, and connecting the points (x_1,y_1) and (x_2,y_2) by drawing a line with a straightedge. Or you can determine the intercepts and then put through a straight line.

If k and l are given, then the equation of the straight line is

$$\frac{x}{l} + \frac{y}{k} = 1$$

and so

$$a = k, \qquad b = l, \qquad c = kl$$

If two points (x_1,y_1) and (x_2,y_2) are given, then the equation of the straight line through the points is given by

$$y = \frac{y_2 - y_1}{x_2 - x_1}(x - x_1) + y_1$$

and so

$$m = \frac{y_2 - y_1}{x_2 - x_1}$$

A.3.2 Exercises

Plot the following straight lines. Determine the x and y intercepts, and the slope when applicable.

1. $y = x + 50$ for $100 \leq x \leq 200$

2. $y = 2x - 30$ for $-50 \le x \le +50$

3. $y = -x + 1$ for $-10 \le x \le +10$

4. $\dfrac{x}{2} + \dfrac{y}{3} = 1$ for $-1 \le x \le 5$

5. $-\dfrac{x}{2} + \dfrac{y}{3} = 1$ for $-5 \le x \le 5$

6. $-\dfrac{x}{2} - \dfrac{y}{3} = 1$ for $-5 \le x \le +2$

Derive the equation of the straight line going through the following pair of points. Also determine the slope and intercepts.

7. $(2,6)$, $(3,2)$

8. $(+1,-4)$, $(+2,-2)$

9. $(-2,-2)$, $(-1,-4)$

A.4 INEQUALITIES

A.4.1 Basic Rules

1. $a < b$ and $b > a$ have the same meaning.
2. $a \le b$ and $b \ge a$ have the same meaning.
3. If $a < b < c$, then $a < c$; if $a > b > c$, then $a > c$.
4. If $a < b = c$, then $a < c$; if $a > b = c$, then $a > c$.
5. If $a = b < c$, then $a < c$; if $a = b > c$, then $a > c$.
6. If $a < b$, then $a + c < b + c$ and $a - c < b - c$.
7. If $a < b$ and $c > 0$, then $ac < bc$.
8. If $a < b$ and $c < 0$, then $ac > bc$.
9. If $a + c < b$, then $a < b - c$.
10. If $a < b$ and $c < d$, then $a + c < b + d$.
11. If $a < b$ and $0 < c < d$, then $ac < bd$.

A.4.2 Solving Inequalities

1. *Solve:*

$$-3 < \frac{x - 2}{5} < 8$$

Solution: Multiply by 5: $-15 < x - 2 < 40$. Add 2: $-13 < x < 42$.

2. *Solve:* $y^2 < 9$.

Solution: $-3 < y < 3$.

3. *Solve:* $y^2 > 9$.

Solution: Either $y > 3$ or $y < -3$.

4. *Solve:*

$$4 < \frac{16}{y^2} < 9$$

Solution: Multiply by y^2: $4y^2 < 16 < 9y^2$. So

$$-2 < y < 2$$

and

$$y > \frac{4}{3} \quad \text{or} \quad y < -\frac{4}{3}$$

Thus,

$$\frac{4}{3} < y < 2 \quad \text{or} \quad -2 < y < -\frac{4}{3}$$

A.4.3 Exercises Solving Inequalities

Solve the following inequalities:

1. $3 < \dfrac{x+2}{6} < 7$

2. $2x - 4 < 6x + 12$

3. $-3 < \dfrac{30 - x}{5} < 3$

4. $\dfrac{25a^2}{y^2} < c^2$

5. $2 < \dfrac{8}{\sqrt{x}} < 4$

6. $16 < \dfrac{64}{y^2} < 64$

A.5 LINEAR EQUATIONS WITH ONE UNKNOWN

A.5.1 Theory

The standard form for a linear equation with one unknown is

$$ax + b = 0, \quad a \neq 0$$

The solution is

$$x = -\frac{b}{a}$$

Some equations with one unknown can be reduced to a standard linear equation. For example,

$$px + q = rx + s$$

is equivalent to

$$(p - r)x + (q - s) = 0$$

The equation

$$\frac{px}{x - q} = r$$

can be reduced to

$$(p - r)x + rq = 0$$

The equation

$$(x - a)^2 = (x - b)^2, \qquad a \neq b$$

means that either

$$x - a = x - b$$

or

$$x - a = -(x - b)$$

The first of these is a contradiction, but the second leads to the solution

$$x = \frac{a + b}{2}$$

A.5.2 Exercises

Solve the following equations for the indicated unknowns.

1. $5x + 12 = -4x + 22$; $x = ?$

2. $-9y + 11 = 6y - 15$; $y = ?$

3. $-9a - 11 = -6a - 15$; $a = ?$

4. $3p + 4[2p - 3(p + 2)] = 25 - 7x$; $x = ?$

5. $(y - 3)^2 = y^2 + 2$; $y = ?$

6. $(y - 2)^2 = (y - 3)^2$; $y = ?$

7. $(3z + 1)^2 + (4z - 1)^2 = (5z + 2)^2$; $z = ?$

8. $(x + 1)^2 - 1 = (2x - 1)^2 - 3x^2$; $x = ?$

9. $\dfrac{x}{y} = \dfrac{1}{z}$; $z = ?$

10. $\dfrac{1}{a} = \dfrac{1}{b} + \dfrac{1}{c}$; $b = ?$

11. $\dfrac{z}{2} + \dfrac{z}{7} = z - 6$; $z = ?$

12. $\dfrac{4}{2 - x} = \dfrac{92}{6 + 2x}$; $x = ?$

13. $ab - 2abcd + d = 7$; $d = ?$

14. $2x + 3xy + 7y = 15$; $y = ?$

15. $\dfrac{25 - 2x}{5} = 3$; $x = ?$

16. $a + \dfrac{2}{c + x} = \dfrac{3}{c + x}$; $x = ?$

17. $P = \dfrac{A}{1 + ni}$; $n = ?$

18. $\dfrac{x}{a} + \dfrac{y}{b} = 1$; $y = ?$

19. $\dfrac{1 - a}{1 - b} = \dfrac{1 - c}{1 - d}$; $c = ?$

A.6. LINEAR EQUATIONS WITH TWO UNKNOWNS

A.6.1 Theory

The general form of two linear equations with two unknowns is

$$ax + by = c, \quad \text{where } a \neq 0$$
$$dx + ey = f$$

To solve for x and y, we rearrange the first equation,

$$ax = -by + c$$

divide by a,

$$x = -\frac{b}{a}y + \frac{c}{a}$$

and substitute the value of x into the second equation,

$$d\left(-\frac{b}{a}y + \frac{c}{a}\right) + ey = f$$

Multiply by a:

$$-bdy + cd + aey = af$$

Rearrange:

$$(ae - bd)y = af - cd$$

If

$$ae - bd = 0$$

then it can be shown that either (1) there is no solution or (2) there are infinitely many solutions. Therefore assume that

$$ae - bd \neq 0$$

Then

$$y = \frac{af - cd}{ae - bd}$$

Substitute this into the first equation:

$$ax + b\frac{af - cd}{ae - bd} = c$$

Thus,

$$x = -\frac{b}{a}\frac{af - cd}{ae - bd} + \frac{c}{a}$$

Carrying out the operations on the right-hand side leads to

$$x = \frac{ce - bf}{ae - bd}$$

A.6.2 Exercises

1. Solve

$$2x + 5y = 12$$
$$4x - y = p$$

where p is a variable. Plot x and y vs. p.

2. Solve

$$x - y = 2$$
$$x - qy = 3$$

where q is a variable. Plot x and y vs. q. What happens when $q = 1$?

A.7 SQUARE ROOTS, QUADRATIC EQUATIONS, AND FUNCTIONS

A.7.1 Operations with Square Roots

If $a^2 = b \geq 0$, then a is called the square root of b. If also $a \geq 0$, then a is denoted by

$$a = \sqrt{b}$$

Here are some simple operations with square roots:

$$\sqrt{a}\,\sqrt{b} = \sqrt{ab}$$
$$\sqrt{c^2 a} = c\sqrt{a}$$
$$\frac{\sqrt{a}}{\sqrt{b}} = \sqrt{\frac{a}{b}} = \frac{\sqrt{ab}}{b}$$

if $x = \sqrt{a}$ and $y = \sqrt{b}$, then $xy = \sqrt{ab}$

A.7.2 Exercises with Square Roots

Carry out operation on the following:

$$\sqrt{16}, \quad \sqrt{256}, \quad \sqrt{\frac{36}{49}}, \quad \sqrt{16 \times 25}, \quad \sqrt{4 + \sqrt{25}}$$

$$\sqrt{\frac{1}{2} + \frac{\sqrt{25}}{10}}, \qquad \sqrt{\frac{\sqrt{25}}{2.5} + \frac{\sqrt{36}}{3}}$$

A.7.3 The Mathematics of the Quadratic Equation

The standard form for a quadratic equation is

$$ax^2 + bx + c = 0, \qquad a \neq 0$$

This can also be written as

$$\left(x + \frac{b}{2a}\right)^2 = \frac{b^2 - 4ac}{4a^2}$$

and therefore the two roots of the equation are

$$x = \frac{-b \pm \sqrt{b^2 - 4ac}}{2a}$$

There are now three possibilities: If $b^2 > 4ac$, the equation has two real roots. If $b^2 < 4ac$, the equation has two complex roots. If $b^2 = 4ac$, the equation has a double root.

The quadratic equation can be factored:

$$ax^2 + bx + c = a(x - x_1)(x - x_2)$$

where x_1 and x_2 are the two roots. Consequently,

$$x_1 + x_2 = -\frac{b}{a}$$

and

$$x_1 x_2 = \frac{c}{a}$$

A.7.4 Exercises for Solving Quadratic Equations

Solve the following seven quadratic equations:

1. $x^2 = 6 + x$
2. $x^2 - 2x = 24$
3. $6 - 5x + x^2 = 0$
4. $x^2 + 2x - 35 = 0$
5. $5x^2 - 6x + 1 = 0$
6. $1 - 4x + 3x^2 = 0$
7. $2 + 5x + 2x^2 = 0$

Factor these seven equations.

Show that for these seven equations

$$x_1 + x_2 = -\frac{b}{a}$$

$$x_1 x_2 = \frac{c}{a}$$

A.7.5 The Quadratic Function

The standard form for a quadratic function is

$$y = ax^2 + bx + c, \qquad a \neq 0$$

and the geometric representation is the parabola. If $a > 0$, the parabola has a minimum; if $a < 0$, it has a maximum. The abscissa (x value) of the extremum can be shown to be at

$$x = -\frac{b}{2a}$$

and the corresponding value (the ordinate) is

$$y = a\left(\frac{b}{2a}\right)^2 - b\frac{b}{2a} + c = c - \frac{b^2}{4a}$$

If the roots x_1 and x_2 of the equation $ax^2 + bx + c = 0$ are real, they represent the intersection of the parabola $y = ax^2 + bx + c$ with the x axis. If there is a double root ($x_1 = x_2$), the parabola is tangent to the x axis.

The parabola representing the quadratic function is a symmetric curve, the axis of symmetry being the straight line $x = -b/2a$, parallel to the y axis and going through the extremum point. The extremum point is called the *vertex* of the parabola.

A.7.6 Exercises for Quadratic Functions

Plot the following functions. Determine in each case the location of the maximum or minimum (the vertex), the axis of symmetry, and the roots (if they are real). State when the parabola goes through the origin or when it is tangent to the x axis.

1. $y = 4x - x^2$
2. $y = 9 + 4x^2$
3. $y = \frac{1}{4}(x^2 + 4x + 4)$
4. $y = 27 - 12x - 4x^2$
5. $y = x^2 - 5x + 7$
6. $y = -x^2 + 6x - 6$

A.7.7 The Bilinear Function

The bilinear function is defined by

$$y = ax + \frac{b}{x - c} + d$$

For example, if $a = 1$, $b = 1$, $c = 0$, and $d = 0$,

$$y = x + \frac{1}{x}$$

A practical example is the cost function used in deriving the economic order quantity (EOQ) in inventory control (Chapter 9).

We show now that

1. If both a and b are positive, the minimum occurs at

$$x^* = c + \sqrt{\frac{b}{a}}$$

2. If both a and b are negative, the preceding formula yields the maximum.

Proof. The first derivative of the function is

$$\frac{dy}{dx} = a - \frac{b}{(x - c)^2} = 0$$

This yields

$$(x - c)^2 = \frac{b}{a}$$

$$(x - c) = \sqrt{\frac{b}{a}}$$

and so

$$x^* = c + \sqrt{\frac{b}{a}}$$

where it is assumed that

$$\frac{b}{a} > 0$$

The second derivative is

$$\frac{dy^2}{dx^2} = -\frac{2b}{(x - c)^2}$$

Thus if $b > 0$, we have a minimum and if $b < 0$, a maximum.

A.7.8 Exercises for the Bilinear Function

1. Find the maximum of

$$y = x + \frac{1}{x}$$

2. Find the minimum of

$$y = x - \frac{x}{x + 1}$$

Hint:

$$\frac{x}{x + 1} = \frac{x + 1 - 1}{x + 1} = \frac{x + 1}{x + 1} + \frac{-1}{x + 1} = 1 + \frac{-1}{x + 1}$$

A.8 EXPONENTS AND RADICALS

A.8.1 Positive and Negative Integral Exponents

Let n, m, and k be positive integers and $a > 0$. Then

$$a^n a^m = a^{n+m}$$

$$\frac{a^n}{a^m} = \begin{cases} a^{n-m} & \text{if } n > m \\ 1 & \text{if } n = m \\ \dfrac{1}{a^{m-n}} & \text{if } n < m \end{cases}$$

$$(a^n)^k = a^{nk}$$

$$(ab)^n = a^n b^n$$

$$\left(\frac{a}{b}\right)^n = \frac{a^n}{b^n}$$

If $p = 0$, then

$$a^p = 1$$

Let p be a positive integer; then

$$a^{-p} = \frac{1}{a^p}$$

Consider the product $a^n a^m$, where m is a negative integer such that $m = -p$. Then

$$a^n a^m = a^n a^{-p} = \frac{a^n}{a^p}$$

To evaluate a^n/a^p, consider three cases:

1. $n > p$;

$$\frac{a^n}{a^p} = a^{n-p} = a^{n+m}$$

2. $n = p$;

$$\frac{a^n}{a^p} = 1 = a^0 = a^{n-p} = a^{n+m}$$

3. $n < p$;

$$\frac{a^n}{a^p} = \frac{1}{a^{p-n}} = a^{n-p} = a^{n+m}$$

Thus the same rules hold for positive and negative integer exponents. Also,

$$(a^n)^m = (a^n)^{-p} = \frac{1}{(a^n)^p} = \frac{1}{a^{np}} = a^{nm}$$

A.8.2. Fractional Exponents and Radicals

If $x^q = a > 0$, where q is a positive integer, then x is the qth root of a. If also $x \geq 0$, then x is denoted as

$$x = \sqrt[q]{a} = a^{1/q}$$

If $a > 0$ and p and q are positive integers, then

$$a^{p/q} = (a^{1/q})^p = (a^p)^{1/q}$$

A.8.3 Exercises for Exponents and Radicals

1. Write each of the following without a radical sign:

a. $\sqrt{x^3}$

b. $\sqrt[3]{(x+y)^2}$

c. $\sqrt[6]{a^5}$

d. $\sqrt{y^6}$

e. $\sqrt[3]{(a+b)^4}$

f. $\sqrt{a^r}$

g. $\sqrt[a]{b^c}$

h. $\sqrt{10}$

i. $\sqrt[3]{30}$

j. $\sqrt[4]{81}$

k. $\sqrt[9]{9}$

l. $\sqrt[3]{125}$

m. $\sqrt[5]{32}$

2. Write each of the following with a radical sign:

a. $a^{3/4}$

b. $(a+b)^{1/2}$

c. $x^{3/10}$

d. $(x+y)^{4/5}$

e. $a^{x/y}$

f. $(a+b)^{x/y}$

g. $a^{(b+c)/(d+e)}$

h. $7^{1/3}$

i. $49^{1/2}$

j. $729^{1/3}$ l. $27^{1/3}$ m. $4^{3/2}$

k. $64^{1/3}$

3. Evaluate the following:

a. $9^{-.5}$ e. $(-3)^{-2}$ i. $(10^{.2})^{-5}$

b. $4^{.5}$ f. 1^7 j. $(9^{-1.75})(9^{.75})$

c. $16^{.25}$ g. $(3^{1.5})(3^{1.5})$

d. $(-8)^0$ h. $(5^{-2.5})(5^{1.5})$

A.8.4 The Exponential Function

The function

$$y = e^x$$

is important in probability theory, utility theory, and many other fields of pure and applied mathematics. The constant e (the first letter in the last name of the Swiss mathematician Leonhard Euler, 1707–1783) has the approximate value of 2.71828. It also serves as the basis of natural logarithms.

A.8.5 Exercises

Plot the following functions (a calculator is needed for the calculations):

1. $y = e^x$ for $-1 \le x \le 1$
2. $y = e^x$ for $-3 \le x \le 5$
3. $y = e^{-x^2}$ for $-2 \le x \le 2$

A.9 MORE ABOUT FUNCTIONS

A.9.1 Functional Notation

$f(x)$ is to be read "ef of ex." Note that $f(x)$ is a number to be computed for a given x by the procedure specified by the function f.

The procedure specified by a function may be stated by a formula:

1. $f(x) = 2x^2 - 2x + 3$
2. $g(x) = -x^2 + 3x + 5$
3. $h(y) = 2^y$
4. $i(z) = 1/(z^2 + z + 1)$

The meaning of functions of several variables is similar. Following are examples of functions defined by formulas:

5. $f(x,y) = 2x + 5y$
6. $g(x,y) = -x^2 + 2xy + 5$

7. $h(x,y,z) = 3x - 2y + 5z$

8. $i(x,y) = 2^{x-y}$

9. $j(x,z) = e^{2x} - e^{-3z}$

10. $k(x,\mu) = -3e^{-.5x^2 + \mu}$

A.9.2 Exercises

Using the preceding formulas, plot the values of the following functions:

1. $f(x,2)$ vs. x

2. $g(x,2)$ vs. x

3. $h(1,y,-1)$ vs. y

4. $i(2,y)$ vs. y

5. $j(.5,z)$ vs. z

6. $k(x,5)$ vs. x

A.9.3 Functions Defined by Words and Formulas

1. *The absolute value function.* The usual symbol is $|x|$, where

$$|x| = x \quad \text{if} \quad 0 \le x$$

$$|x| = -x \quad \text{if} \quad x < 0$$

2. *The integer function.* The computer usage symbol is INT, where INT(x) is the integer obtained by dropping the digits after the decimal point. For example,

1. INT$(2.53) = 2$

2. INT$(0.73) = 0$

3. INT$(5.00) = 5$

3. *The maximum function.* The function max(x,y) is equal to the larger of the two numbers x and y. For example,

$$\max(2,5) = 5$$

$$\max(7,2) = 7$$

$$\max(-1,3) = 3$$

$$\max(-5,-2) = -2$$

4. *The minimum function.* The function min(x,y) is the smaller of the two numbers x and y. For example,

$$\min(2,5) = 2$$

$$\min(7,3) = 3$$

$$\min(-8,4) = -8$$

$$\min(-9,-3) = -9$$

A.9.4 Exercises

Plot the following functions:

1. $y = x + |x|$ for $-10 \leq x \leq 10$
2. $y = x - \text{INT}(x)$ for $0 \leq x \leq 5$
3. $y = \max(x, 5)$ for $0 \leq x \leq 10$
4. $y = \min(x, -2)$ for $-5 \leq x \leq 5$

A.10 SUBSCRIPTED NOTATION, ARRAYS, AND MATRICES

A.10.1 Single Subscripts

René Descartes (1596–1650), French philosopher and scientist, introduced the custom of calling known quantities a, b, c, etc., and unknowns x, y, z. Subscripted notation extends this notation and allows working with any number of unknowns. For example, we may designate sales in three territories by s_1, s_2, and s_3 or profits for five products by z_1, z_2, z_3, z_4, and z_5.

We designate by

$$x_1, x_2, \ldots, x_n$$

n variables, where n is a positive integer. The three dots between the commas is the traditional notation when the variables are not explicitly listed. We can also designate a subscripted sequence of variables by a single letter:

$$\{x\} = [x_1, x_2, \ldots, x_n]$$

where the braces serve to remind us that we are dealing with a sequence of variables.

A.10.2 Exercises

Consider the following three arrays:

$$\{a\} = [5, 7, -3, 6, 1, 2]$$
$$\{b\} = [12, 21, 0, 5, 31, -4]$$
$$\{c\} = [2, 1, -2, -1, 1, -4]$$

Calculate the following:

1. $a_2 b_3 - b_2 c_3 + a_2/c_2$
2. $b_1^2 - c_3^2 + a_3 b_1 c_6$
3. $(a_1 + 2a_2 + 10c_5)(b_3 - 12c_2)^2 - 5c_4^{10}$
4. $x_i = a_i + b_i, \quad i = 1, \ldots, 6$
5. $y_i = a_i + b_i + b_i/c_i, \quad i = 1, \ldots, 6$
6. $z_j = a_j c_j(a_j + b_j + b_j/c_j), \quad j = 1, \ldots, 6$

7. $e_k = a_k + b_k + 3 + a_3, \quad k = 1, \ldots, 6$

8. $f_n = (b_1 - a_2)(b_n/c_n) + 4a_1c_3(a_n + b_n + b_2/c_3) + 10, \quad n = 1, \ldots, 6$

9. $g_m = a_{7-m}, \quad m = 1, \ldots, 6$

A.10.3 Doubly Subscripted Notation

Rectangular tables or arrays of numbers are called matrices. The concise mathematical notation uses two subscripts; the first refers to the row number and the second to the column number. For example, if $\{X\}$, a two by three matrix, is defined by

$$\{X\} = \begin{vmatrix} -3 & 4 & 2 \\ 7 & -9 & 1 \end{vmatrix}$$

then

$$x_{11} = -3, \quad x_{12} = 4, \quad x_{13} = 2$$
$$x_{21} = 7, \quad x_{22} = -9, \quad x_{23} = 1$$

A.10.4 Exercises

Consider the following three matrices:

$$\{A\} = \begin{vmatrix} 1 & -2 & 2 \\ 2 & -1 & 0 \\ -1 & 5 & 1 \end{vmatrix} \quad \{B\} = \begin{vmatrix} 1 & 2 & -1 \\ -2 & 1 & 5 \\ 2 & 0 & -1 \end{vmatrix} \quad \{C\} = \begin{vmatrix} -5 & -1 & 2 \\ 1 & 5 & 2 \\ -2 & 10 & 5 \end{vmatrix}$$

Calculate the following:

1. $a_{21}b_{12} - b_{32}c_{33}$

Calculate the matrices defined by the following:

2. $x_{ij} = a_{ij} + b_{ij}$

3. $y_{ij} = a_{ij}b_{ij} + a_{12} - c_{23}$

4. $z_{ij} = a_{ij} + 3b_{ij} - 2c_{ij} + 4b_{23}/a_{23}$

5. $f_{ij} = a_{i,4-j}$

6. $g_{ij} = b_{3-i,j}$

7. $h_{ij} = c_{ji}$

Appendix B

Tables

TABLE B.1 Values of the Standard Normal Distribution Function.

z	0	1	2	3	4	5	6	7	8	9
−3.0	0.0013	0.0010	0.0007	0.0005	0.0003	0.0002	0.0002	0.0001	0.0001	0.0000
−2.9	0.0019	0.0018	0.0017	0.0016	0.0016	0.0016	0.0015	0.0015	0.0014	0.0014
−2.8	0.0026	0.0025	0.0024	0.0023	0.0023	0.0022	0.0021	0.0021	0.0020	0.0019
−2.7	0.0035	0.0034	0.0033	0.0032	0.0031	0.0030	0.0029	0.0028	0.0027	0.0026
−2.6	0.0047	0.0045	0.0044	0.0043	0.0041	0.0040	0.0039	0.0038	0.0037	0.0036
−2.5	0.0062	0.0060	0.0059	0.0057	0.0055	0.0054	0.0052	0.0051	0.0049	0.0048
−2.4	0.0082	0.0080	0.0078	0.0075	0.0073	0.0071	0.0069	0.0068	0.0066	0.0064
−2.3	0.0107	0.0104	0.0102	0.0099	0.0096	0.0094	0.0091	0.0089	0.0087	0.0084
−2.2	0.0139	0.0136	0.0132	0.0129	0.0126	0.0122	0.0119	0.0116	0.0113	0.0110
−2.1	0.0179	0.0174	0.0170	0.0166	0.0162	0.0158	0.0154	0.0150	0.0146	0.0143
−2.0	0.0228	0.0222	0.0217	0.0212	0.0207	0.0202	0.0197	0.0192	0.0188	0.0183
−1.9	0.0287	0.0281	0.0274	0.0268	0.0262	0.0256	0.0250	0.0244	0.0238	0.0233
−1.8	0.0359	0.0352	0.0344	0.0336	0.0329	0.0322	0.0314	0.0307	0.0300	0.0294
−1.7	0.0446	0.0436	0.0427	0.0418	0.0409	0.0401	0.0392	0.0384	0.0375	0.0367
−1.6	0.0548	0.0537	0.0526	0.0516	0.0505	0.0495	0.0485	0.0475	0.0465	0.0455
−1.5	0.0668	0.0655	0.0643	0.0630	0.0618	0.0606	0.0594	0.0582	0.0570	0.0559
−1.4	0.0808	0.0793	0.0778	0.0764	0.0749	0.0735	0.0722	0.0708	0.0694	0.0681
−1.3	0.0968	0.0951	0.0934	0.0918	0.0901	0.0885	0.0869	0.0853	0.0838	0.0823
−1.2	0.1151	0.1131	0.1112	0.1093	0.1075	0.1056	0.1038	0.1020	0.1003	0.0985
−1.1	0.1357	0.1335	0.1314	0.1292	0.1271	0.1251	0.1230	0.1210	0.1190	0.1170
−1.0	0.1587	0.1562	0.1539	0.1515	0.1492	0.1469	0.1446	0.1423	0.1401	0.1379
−0.9	0.1841	0.1814	0.1788	0.1762	0.1736	0.1711	0.1685	0.1660	0.1635	0.1611
−0.8	0.2119	0.2090	0.2061	0.2033	0.2005	0.1977	0.1949	0.1922	0.1894	0.1867
−0.7	0.2420	0.2389	0.2358	0.2327	0.2297	0.2266	0.2236	0.2206	0.2177	0.2148
−0.6	0.2743	0.2709	0.2676	0.2643	0.2611	0.2578	0.2546	0.2514	0.2483	0.2451
−0.5	0.3085	0.3050	0.3015	0.2981	0.2946	0.2912	0.2877	0.2843	0.2810	0.2776
−0.4	0.3446	0.3409	0.3372	0.3336	0.3300	0.3264	0.3228	0.3192	0.3156	0.3121
−0.3	0.3821	0.3783	0.3745	0.3707	0.3669	0.3632	0.3594	0.3557	0.3520	0.3483
−0.2	0.4207	0.4168	0.4129	0.4090	0.4052	0.4013	0.3974	0.3936	0.3897	0.3859
−0.1	0.4602	0.4562	0.4522	0.4483	0.4443	0.4404	0.4364	0.4325	0.4286	0.4247
−0.0	0.5000	0.4960	0.4920	0.4880	0.4840	0.4801	0.4761	0.4721	0.4681	0.4641
0.0	0.5000	0.5040	0.5080	0.5120	0.5160	0.5199	0.5239	0.5279	0.5319	0.5359
0.1	0.5398	0.5438	0.5478	0.5517	0.5557	0.5596	0.5636	0.5675	0.5714	0.5753

z	0	1	2	3	4	5	6	7	8	9
0.2	0.5793	0.5832	0.5871	0.5910	0.5948	0.5987	0.6026	0.6064	0.6103	0.6141
0.3	0.6179	0.6217	0.6255	0.6293	0.6331	0.6368	0.6406	0.6443	0.6480	0.6517
0.4	0.6554	0.6591	0.6628	0.6664	0.6700	0.6736	0.6772	0.6808	0.6844	0.6879
0.5	0.6915	0.6950	0.6985	0.7019	0.7054	0.7088	0.7123	0.7157	0.7190	0.7224
0.6	0.7257	0.7291	0.7324	0.7357	0.7389	0.7422	0.7454	0.7486	0.7517	0.7549
0.7	0.7580	0.7611	0.7642	0.7673	0.7703	0.7734	0.7764	0.7794	0.7823	0.7852
0.8	0.7881	0.7910	0.7939	0.7967	0.7995	0.8023	0.8051	0.8078	0.8106	0.8133
0.9	0.8159	0.8186	0.8212	0.8238	0.8264	0.8289	0.8315	0.8340	0.8365	0.8389
1.0	0.8413	0.8438	0.8461	0.8485	0.8508	0.8531	0.8554	0.8577	0.8599	0.8621
1.1	0.8643	0.8665	0.8686	0.8708	0.8729	0.8749	0.8770	0.8790	0.8810	0.8830
1.2	0.8849	0.8869	0.8888	0.8907	0.8925	0.8944	0.8962	0.8980	0.8997	0.9015
1.3	0.9032	0.9049	0.9066	0.9082	0.9099	0.9115	0.9131	0.9147	0.9162	0.9177
1.4	0.9192	0.9207	0.9222	0.9236	0.9251	0.9265	0.9278	0.9292	0.9306	0.9319
1.5	0.9332	0.9345	0.9357	0.9370	0.9382	0.9394	0.9406	0.9418	0.9430	0.9441
1.6	0.9452	0.9463	0.9474	0.9484	0.9495	0.9505	0.9515	0.9525	0.9535	0.9545
1.7	0.9554	0.9564	0.9573	0.9582	0.9591	0.9599	0.9608	0.9616	0.9625	0.9633
1.8	0.9641	0.9648	0.9656	0.9664	0.9671	0.9678	0.9686	0.9693	0.9700	0.9706
1.9	0.9713	0.9719	0.9726	0.9732	0.9738	0.9744	0.9750	0.9756	0.9762	0.9767
2.0	0.9772	0.9778	0.9783	0.9788	0.9793	0.9798	0.9803	0.9808	0.9812	0.9817
2.1	0.9821	0.9826	0.9830	0.9834	0.9838	0.9842	0.9846	0.9850	0.9854	0.9857
2.2	0.9861	0.9864	0.9868	0.9871	0.9874	0.9878	0.9881	0.9884	0.9887	0.9890
2.3	0.9893	0.9896	0.9898	0.9901	0.9904	0.9906	0.9909	0.9911	0.9913	0.9916
2.4	0.9918	0.9920	0.9922	0.9925	0.9927	0.9929	0.9931	0.9932	0.9934	0.9936
2.5	0.9938	0.9940	0.9941	0.9943	0.9945	0.9946	0.9948	0.9949	0.9951	0.9952
2.6	0.9953	0.9955	0.9956	0.9957	0.9959	0.9960	0.9961	0.9962	0.9963	0.9964
2.7	0.9965	0.9966	0.9967	0.9968	0.9969	0.9970	0.9971	0.9972	0.9973	0.9974
2.8	0.9974	0.9975	0.9976	0.9977	0.9977	0.9978	0.9979	0.9979	0.9980	0.9981
2.9	0.9981	0.9982	0.9982	0.9983	0.9984	0.9984	0.9985	0.9985	0.9986	0.9986
3.0	0.9987	0.9990	0.9993	0.9995	0.9997	0.9998	0.9998	0.9999	0.9999	1.0000

Extracted with permission from Ya-Lun Chou, Probability and Statistics for Decision Making, *Holt, Rinehart and Winston, New York, 1972.*

TABLE B.2 Table of the Cumulative Binomial Distribution[a]

n	x	p = 0.10	p = 0.20	p = 0.25	p = 0.30	p = 0.40	p = 0.50
5	0	0.59049	0.32768	0.23730	0.16807	0.07776	0.03125
	1	0.91854	0.73728	0.63281	0.52822	0.33696	0.18750
	2	0.99144	0.94208	0.89648	0.83692	0.68256	0.50000
	3	0.99954	0.99328	0.98437	0.96922	0.91296	0.81250
	4	0.99999	0.99968	0.99902	0.99757	0.98976	0.96875
	5	1.00000	1.00000	1.00000	1.00000	1.00000	1.00000
10	0	0.34868	0.10737	0.05631	0.02825	0.00605	0.00098
	1	0.73610	0.37581	0.24403	0.14931	0.04636	0.01074
	2	0.92981	0.67780	0.52559	0.38278	0.16729	0.05469
	3	0.98720	0.87913	0.77588	0.64961	0.38228	0.17187
	4	0.99837	0.96721	0.92187	0.84973	0.63310	0.37695
	5	0.99985	0.99363	0.98027	0.95265	0.83376	0.62305
	6	0.99999	0.99914	0.99649	0.98941	0.94524	0.82812
	7	1.00000	0.99992	0.99958	0.99841	0.98771	0.94531
	8		1.00000	0.99997	0.99986	0.99832	0.98926
	9			1.00000	0.99999	0.99990	0.99902
	10				1.00000	1.00000	1.00000
15	0	0.20589	0.03518	0.01336	0.00475	0.00047	0.00003
	1	0.54904	0.16713	0.08018	0.03527	0.00517	0.00049
	2	0.81594	0.39802	0.23609	0.12683	0.02711	0.00369
	3	0.94444	0.64816	0.46129	0.29687	0.09050	0.01758
	4	0.98728	0.83577	0.68649	0.51549	0.21728	0.05923
	5	0.99775	0.93895	0.85163	0.72162	0.40322	0.15088
	6	0.99969	0.98194	0.94338	0.86886	0.60981	0.30362
	7	0.99997	0.99576	0.98270	0.94999	0.78690	0.50000
	8	1.00000	0.99921	0.99581	0.98476	0.90495	0.69638
	9		0.99989	0.99921	0.99635	0.96617	0.84912
	10		0.99999	0.99988	0.99933	0.99065	0.94077
	11		1.00000	0.99999	0.99991	0.99807	0.98242
	12			1.00000	0.99999	0.99972	0.99631
	13				1.00000	0.99997	0.99951
	14					1.00000	0.99997
	15						1.00000
20	0	0.12158	0.01153	0.00317	0.00080	0.00004	0.00000
	1	0.39175	0.06918	0.02431	0.00764	0.00052	0.00002
	2	0.67693	0.20608	0.09126	0.03548	0.00361	0.00020
	3	0.86705	0.41145	0.22516	0.10709	0.01596	0.00129
	4	0.95683	0.62965	0.41484	0.23751	0.05095	0.00591
	5	0.98875	0.80421	0.61717	0.41637	0.12560	0.02069
	6	0.99761	0.91331	0.78578	0.60801	0.25001	0.05766
	7	0.99958	0.96786	0.89819	0.77227	0.41589	0.13159
	8	0.99994	0.99002	0.95907	0.88667	0.59560	0.25172
	9	0.99999	0.99741	0.98614	0.95204	0.75534	0.41190
	10	1.00000	0.99944	0.99606	0.98286	0.87248	0.58810
	11		0.99990	0.99906	0.99486	0.94347	0.74828
	12		0.99998	0.99982	0.99872	0.97897	0.86841
	13		1.00000	0.99997	0.99974	0.99353	0.94234

[a] *E. C. Molina,* Poisson's Binomial Exponential Limit, *D. Van Nostrand (Princeton, N.J., 1949), pp. 276–280. Extracted with permission from Ya-Lun Chou,* Probability and Statistics for Decision Making, *Holt, Rinehart, and Winston, New York, 1972.*

TABLE B.2 Cont'd

n	x	p = 0.10	p = 0.20	p = 0.25	p = 0.30	p = 0.40	p = 0.50
20	14			1.00000	0.99996	0.99839	0.97931
	15				0.99999	0.99968	0.99409
	16				1.00000	0.99995	0.99871
	17					0.99999	0.99980
	18					1.00000	0.99998
	19						1.00000
25	0	0.07179	0.00378	0.00075	0.00013	0.00000	0.00000
	1	0.27121	0.02739	0.00702	0.00157	0.00005	0.00000
	2	0.53709	0.09823	0.03211	0.00896	0.00043	0.00001
	3	0.76359	0.23399	0.09621	0.03324	0.00237	0.00008
	4	0.90201	0.42067	0.21374	0.09047	0.00947	0.00046
	5	0.96660	0.61669	0.37828	0.19349	0.02936	0.00204
	6	0.99052	0.78004	0.56110	0.34065	0.07357	0.00732
	7	0.99774	0.89088	0.72651	0.51185	0.15355	0.02164
	8	0.99954	0.95323	0.85056	0.67693	0.27353	0.05388
	9	0.99992	0.98267	0.92867	0.81056	0.42462	0.11476
	10	0.99999	0.99445	0.97033	0.90220	0.58577	0.21218
	11	1.00000	0.99846	0.98027	0.95575	0.73228	0.34502
	12		0.99963	0.99663	0.98253	0.84623	0.50000
	13		0.99992	0.99908	0.99401	0.92220	0.65498
	14		0.99999	0.99979	0.99822	0.96561	0.78782
	15		1.00000	0.99996	0.99955	0.98683	0.88524
	16			0.99999	0.99990	0.99567	0.94612
	17			1.00000	0.99998	0.99879	0.97836
	18				1.00000	0.99972	0.99268
	19					0.99995	0.99796
	20					0.99999	0.99954
	21					1.00000	0.99992
	22						0.99999
	23						1.00000
50	0	0.00515	0.00001	0.00000	0.00000		
	1	0.03379	0.00019	0.00001	0.00000		
	2	0.11173	0.00129	0.00009	0.00000		
	3	0.25029	0.00566	0.00050	0.00003		
	4	0.43120	0.01850	0.00211	0.00017		
	5	0.61612	0.04803	0.00705	0.00072	0.00000	
	6	0.77023	0.10340	0.01939	0.00249	0.00001	
	7	0.87785	0.19041	0.04526	0.00726	0.00006	
	8	0.94213	0.30733	0.09160	0.01825	0.00023	
	9	0.97546	0.44374	0.16368	0.04023	0.00076	0.00000
	10	0.99065	0.58356	0.26220	0.07885	0.00220	0.00001
	11	0.99678	0.71067	0.38162	0.13904	0.00569	0.00005
	12	0.99900	0.81394	0.51099	0.22287	0.01325	0.00015
	13	0.99971	0.88941	0.63704	0.32788	0.02799	0.00047
	14	0.99993	0.93928	0.74808	0.44683	0.05396	0.00130
	15	0.99998	0.96920	0.83692	0.56918	0.09550	0.00330
	16	1.00000	0.98556	0.90169	0.68388	0.15609	0.00767
	17		0.99374	0.94488	0.78219	0.23688	0.01642
50	18		0.99749	0.97127	0.85944	0.33561	0.03245
	19		0.99907	0.98608	0.91520	0.44648	0.05946
	20		0.99968	0.99374	0.95224	0.56103	0.10132
	21		0.99990	0.99738	0.97491	0.67014	0.16112
	22		0.99997	0.99898	0.98772	0.76602	0.23994
	23		0.99999	0.99963	0.99441	0.84383	0.33591

TABLE B.2 Cont'd

n	x	p = 0.10	p = 0.20	p = 0.25	p = 0.30	p = 0.40	p = 0.50
	24		1.00000	0.99988	0.99763	0.90219	0.44386
	25			0.99996	0.99907	0.94266	0.55614
	26			0.99999	0.99966	0.96859	0.66409
	27			1.00000	0.99988	0.98397	0.76006
	28				0.99996	0.99238	0.83888
	29				0.99999	0.99664	0.89868
	30				1.00000	0.99863	0.94054
	31					0.99948	0.96755
	32					0.99982	0.98358
	33					0.99994	0.99233
	34					0.99998	0.99670
	35					1.00000	0.99870
	36						0.99953
	37						0.99985
	38						0.99995
	39						0.99999
	40						1.00000
100	0	0.00003					
	1	0.00032					
	2	0.00194					
	3	0.00784					
	4	0.02371	0.00000				
	5	0.05758	0.00002				
	6	0.11716	0.00008				
	7	0.20605	0.00028	0.00000			
	8	0.32087	0.00086	0.00001			
	9	0.45129	0.00233	0.00004			
	10	0.58316	0.00570	0.00014	0.00000		
	11	0.70303	0.01257	0.00039	0.00001		
	12	0.80182	0.02533	0.00103	0.00002		
	13	0.87612	0.04691	0.00246	0.00006		
	14	0.92743	0.08044	0.00542	0.00016		
	15	0.96011	0.12851	0.01108	0.00040		
	16	0.97940	0.19234	0.02111	0.00097		
	17	0.98999	0.27119	0.03763	0.00216		
	18	0.99542	0.36209	0.06301	0.00452	0.00000	
	19	0.99802	0.46016	0.09953	0.00889	0.00001	
	20	0.99919	0.55946	0.14883	0.01646	0.00002	
	21	0.99969	0.65403	0.21144	0.02883	0.00004	
	22	0.99989	0.73893	0.28637	0.04787	0.00011	
	23	0.99996	0.81091	0.37018	0.07553	0.00025	
	24	0.99999	0.86865	0.46167	0.11357	0.00056	
	25	1.00000	0.91252	0.55347	0.16313	0.00119	

TABLE B.3 $F = W/T$ for Multichannel Poisson Exponential System

$\rho = A/CS$	NUMBER OF SERVICE CHANNELS, C									
	1	2	3	4	5	6	7	8	9	10
.02	.02041	.00040	.00001	.00000	.00000	.00000	.00000	.00000	.00000	.00000
.04	.04167	.00160	.00009	.00001	.00000	.00000	.00000	.00000	.00000	.00000
.06	.06383	.00361	.00031	.00003	.00000	.00000	.00000	.00000	.00000	.00000
.08	.08696	.00644	.00071	.00009	.00001	.00000	.00000	.00000	.00000	.00000
.10	.11111	.01010	.00137	.00022	.00004	.00001	.00000	.00000	.00000	.00000
.12	.13636	.01461	.00233	.00044	.00009	.00002	.00000	.00000	.00000	.00000
.14	.16279	.01999	.00366	.00079	.00019	.00005	.00001	.00000	.00000	.00000
.16	.19048	.02627	.00538	.00131	.00035	.00010	.00003	.00001	.00000	.00000
.18	.21951	.03348	.00757	.00203	.00060	.00019	.00006	.00002	.00001	.00000
.20	.25000	.04167	.01027	.00299	.00096	.00033	.00012	.00004	.00002	.00001
.22	.28205	.05086	.01354	.00426	.00147	.00054	.00021	.00008	.00003	.00001
.24	.31579	.06112	.01742	.00586	.00216	.00085	.00035	.00015	.00006	.00003
.26	.35135	.07250	.02197	.00785	.00308	.00128	.00055	.00025	.00011	.00005
.28	.38889	.08507	.02726	.01029	.00426	.00187	.00086	.00040	.00019	.00010
.30	.42857	.09890	.03335	.01323	.00575	.00265	.00128	.00063	.00032	.00017
.32	.47059	.11408	.04030	.01674	.00761	.00367	.00185	.00096	.00051	.00027
.34	.51515	.13071	.04820	.02087	.00989	.00497	.00260	.00140	.00078	.00044
.36	.56250	.14890	.05712	.02570	.01266	.00660	.00359	.00201	.00115	.00067
.38	.61290	.16877	.06716	.03131	.01597	.00862	.00485	.00281	.00167	.00101
.40	.66667	.19048	.07843	.03779	.01990	.01110	.00644	.00385	.00236	.00147
.42	.72414	.21418	.09104	.04523	.02454	.01409	.00843	.00519	.00327	.00210
.44	.78571	.24008	.10513	.05373	.02997	.01769	.01089	.00687	.00445	.00293
.46	.85185	.26839	.12084	.06343	.03631	.02198	.01384	.00898	.00595	.00402
.48	.92308	.29938	.13837	.07445	.04366	.02706	.01745	.01158	.00786	.00543
.50	1.00000	.33333	.15789	.08696	.05215	.03305	.02177	.01476	.01023	.00722
.52	1.08333	.37061	.17967	.10113	.06194	.04007	.02693	.01863	.01317	.00948
.54	1.17391	.41163	.20397	.11719	.07320	.04827	.03307	.02330	.01678	.01230
.56	1.27273	.45688	.23112	.13538	.08614	.05783	.04032	.02891	.02118	.01579
.58	1.38095	.50693	.26151	.15600	.10101	.06896	.04888	.03561	.02651	.02008

.60	1.50000	.56250	.29562	.17940	.11808	.08190	.05895	.04361	.03295	.02532
.62	1.63158	.62443	.33401	.20602	.13770	.09695	.07079	.05311	.04070	.03171
.64	1.77778	.69377	.37737	.23638	.16031	.11445	.08471	.06440	.04999	.03945
.66	1.94118	.77179	.42657	.27112	.18641	.13485	.10109	.07781	.06114	.04883
.68	2.12500	.86012	.48268	.31106	.21667	.15869	.12039	.09375	.07451	.06018
.70	2.33333	.96078	.54705	.35721	.25189	.18665	.14321	.11275	.09056	.07391
.72	2.57143	1.07641	.62144	.41089	.29314	.21963	.17031	.13547	.10990	.09057
.74	2.84615	1.21043	.70813	.47382	.34178	.25877	.20267	.16277	.13330	.11086
.76	3.16667	1.36742	.81018	.54828	.39966	.30559	.24161	.19582	.16177	.13570
.78	3.54545	1.55363	.93175	.63740	.46927	.36219	.28892	.23617	.19673	.16636
.80	4.00000	1.77778	1.07865	.74554	.55411	.43148	.34710	.28603	.24012	.20459
.82	4.55556	2.05250	1.25931	.87903	.65924	.51767	.41976	.34855	.29476	.25293
.84	5.25000	2.39674	1.48636	1.04732	.79222	.62708	.51233	.42848	.36486	.31517
.86	6.14286	2.84025	1.77962	1.26530	.96496	.76964	.63330	.53326	.45704	.39727
.88	7.33333	3.43262	2.17217	1.55778	1.19731	.96187	.79686	.67530	.58234	.50917
.90	9.00000	4.26316	2.72354	1.96938	1.52499	1.23354	1.02851	.87692	.76059	.66873
.92	11.50000	5.51042	3.55275	2.58941	2.01941	1.64418	1.37928	1.18277	1.03150	.91167
.94	15.66667	7.59107	4.93760	3.62618	2.84725	2.33268	1.96822	1.69702	1.48764	1.32132
.96	24.00000	11.75510	7.71142	5.70470	4.50850	3.71571	3.15248	2.73217	2.40682	2.14770
.98	49.00000	24.25253	16.04086	11.94997	9.50317	7.87659	6.71776	5.85074	5.17791	4.64081

TABLE B.4 Random Numbers

48836	46380	32072	58708	23625
63729	18808	10535	49737	77415
57895	29434	96847	49071	37845
44468	30305	75367	92893	16692
73332	38611	82076	31392	05413
76234	43179	42350	21959	92110
60967	06709	55232	17294	94644
69193	10591	40089	25823	69863
98386	02679	99406	70334	70079
62535	90164	52405	26865	66639
67712	42556	49950	11703	72869
05503	94380	08434	62744	84541
34235	34445	63236	51167	29876
68746	02209	07258	65404	84597
67049	53248	16454	01980	39549
53034	62394	48334	99240	24320
30004	16190	22387	04563	08602
62626	80541	74448	26024	22160
26928	19000	07763	88381	17732
86250	92190	63590	27322	25558
91981	19387	23607	23830	23272
08807	53697	29493	00313	94898
03031	06549	65421	55136	94135
75488	38574	30451	48968	90290
35003	33517	64737	53076	65163
02895	75088	90729	36472	66289
87225	04428	16951	42678	23464
33259	44090	23184	28886	96093
49514	43719	93274	51372	95483
58500	88205	03635	55087	85329
73421	28433	29708	57207	49129
68275	92184	69807	29915	29985
23145	05780	89100	42025	50288
63362	79179	72741	71776	19855
78204	84601	91784	25107	21485
64019	26034	12521	74558	70376
26180	28713	69465	27837	08735
89137	35032	25776	39730	19204
02387	05538	53654	52959	20982
28614	17974	68285	69374	42516
58892	83528	92363	26259	02412
09548	90919	14367	62920	73870
02828	82822	98057	89508	38901
64731	80681	10337	89749	15978
47764	91813	27950	82702	02373
38944	91232	97464	96833	34484
81138	45533	87946	69606	66250
45358	76951	32038	44120	71785
75472	22203	00321	47125	28960
30474	54151	55503	28093	60635
59708	61346	05757	95040	58830
31210	21528	77885	40155	92745
68428	97243	06488	73782	53092
48337	94659	27759	55744	02375
30190	89111	97293	77154	03980
64672	84713	97079	95680	19492

TABLE B.4 Cont'd

05057	31958	01029	58919	94498
70759	56913	43104	42041	51564
78282	38287	15868	55704	65657
70994	93855	26427	78450	64119
11754	55208	53411	17127	52022
30428	64933	19254	64180	97243
19003	65354	49484	08202	44942
35120	07807	61394	03257	36271
06788	99267	72057	59063	46994
44138	98853	19445	51700	41251
31477	59955	49336	59670	73151
88201	74167	25087	14803	04110
28809	54878	61220	00809	36778
29371	09133	68596	12724	17693
77682	94947	21928	76960	84767
12859	65397	18638	25701	96596
56278	55793	00071	15126	19787
37819	15799	30461	63666	05506
90780	91873	87485	70616	42047
28993	62917	67794	52216	58970
60998	71167	43166	83989	65323
06825	90851	63649	41947	60293
91895	57880	40409	75597	85579
31647	14073	61560	19661	12027
74083	96076	90543	81620	72251
29162	56050	10020	31270	86227
09175	82454	56508	89284	46267
21665	07928	10247	91037	42307
24023	24408	15335	26641	83858
52139	14024	71940	96939	96522
08551	53802	60144	98823	72297
31190	19580	55045	40019	87461
95167	40497	78864	32966	96336
00099	39952	83212	67058	94833
23217	62794	17465	99907	27996
95730	64803	74970	00171	98509
72825	92418	03483	98215	37015
58020	07294	09323	42872	83563
44315	19981	67501	95668	44569
79726	68850	34504	67293	56579
92367	19240	20615	62298	85549
03819	15959	81571	70835	02559
46521	43753	67603	67041	15603
69354	07342	84986	93304	16428

Chapter 1: Basic Texts on Quantitative Methods

Churchman, C. W., R. L. Ackoff, and E. L. Arnoff, *Introduction to Operations Research*, Wiley, New York, 1957.

Hillier, F. S., and G. J. Lieberman, *Introduction to Operations Research*, 3rd ed., Holden-Day, San Francisco, 1980.

Wagner, H. M., *Principles of Operations Research*, 2nd ed., Prentice-Hall, Englewood Cliffs, N.J., 1975.

Chapters 2–8: Decision Making Under Uncertainty

Box, G. E. P., and G. M. Jenkins, *Time Series Analysis: Forecasting and Control*, rev. ed., Holden-Day, San Francisco, 1976.

Chernoff, H., and L. E. Moses, *Elementary Decision Theory*, Wiley, New York, 1959.

DeGroot, M. H., *Probability and Statistics*, Addison-Wesley, Reading, Mass., 1975.

Feller, W., *An Introduction to Probability Theory and Its Applications*, 3rd ed., Wiley, New York, 1968.

Freund, J. E., *Introduction to Probability*, Dickenson Publishing Co., Inc., Belmont, Calif., 1973.

Hillier, F. S., and G. J. Lieberman, *Introduction to Operations Research*, 3rd ed., Holden-Day, San Francisco, 1980.

Keeney, R. L., and H. Raiffa, *Decisions with Multiple Objectives: Preferences and Value Tradeoffs*, Wiley, New York, 1976.

Raiffa, H., *Decision Analysis*, Addison-Wesley, Reading, Mass., 1968.

Schlaifer, R., *Analysis of Decisions Under Uncertainty*, McGraw-Hill, New York, 1969.

Wagner, H. M., *Principles of Operations Research*, 2nd ed., Prentice-Hall, Englewood Cliffs, N.J., 1975.

Chapter 9: Inventory Management

Buffa, E. S., and J. G. Miller, *Production, Inventory Systems, Planning and Control*, 3rd ed., Richard D. Irwin, Homewood, Ill., 1979.

Hillier, F. S., and G. J. Lieberman, *Introduction to Operations Research*, 3rd ed., Holden-Day, San Francisco, 1980.

Orlicky, J., *Materials Requirements Planning*, McGraw-Hill, New York, 1975.

Wagner, H. M., *Principles of Operations Research*, 2nd ed., Prentice-Hall, Englewood Cliffs, N.J., 1975.

Chapters 10–14: Mathematical Programming

Charnes, A., and W. W. Cooper, *Management Models and Industrial Applications of Linear Programming*, Wiley, New York, 1961.

Dantzig, G. B., *Linear Programming and Extensions*, Princeton University Press, Princeton, N.J., 1963.

Gass, Saul J., *Linear Programming*, 4th ed., McGraw-Hill, New York, 1975.

Hillier, F. S., and G. J. Lieberman, *Introduction to Operations Research*, 3rd ed., Holden-Day, San Francisco, 1980.

Ignizio, J. P., *Goal Programming and Extensions*, Heath, Lexington, Mass., 1976.

Wagner, H. M., *Principles of Operations Research*, 2nd ed., Prentice-Hall, Englewood Cliffs, N.J., 1975.

Chapter 15: Markov Processes

Derman, C., *Finite State Markovian Decision Processes*, Academic Press, New York, 1970.

Hillier, F. S., and G. J. Lieberman, *Introduction to Operations Research*, 3rd ed., Holden-Day, San Francisco, 1980.

Howard, R. A., *Dynamic Programming and Markov Processes*, M.I.T. Press, Cambridge, Mass., 1960.

Howard, R. A., *Dynamic Probabilistic Systems*, vols. 1 and 2, Wiley, New York, 1971.

Wagner, H. M., *Principles of Operations Research*, 2nd ed., Prentice-Hall, Englewood Cliffs, N.J., 1975.

Chapter 16: Waiting Lines: Queuing Theory

Conway, R. W., W. L. Maxwell, and L. W. Miller, *Theory of Scheduling*, Addison-Wesley, Reading, Mass., 1967.

Hillier, F. S., and G. J. Lieberman, *Introduction to Operations Research*, 3rd ed., Holden-Day, San Francisco, 1980.

Kleinrock, L., *Queuing Systems*, vols. I and II, Wiley, New York, 1975 and 1976.

Wagner, H. M., *Principles of Operations Research*, 2nd ed., Prentice-Hall, Englewood Cliffs, N.J., 1975.

Chapter 17: Simulation

Fishman, G. S., *Concepts and Methods in Discrete Event Digital Simulation*, 2nd ed., Wiley, New York, 1973.

Gordon, Geoffrey, *System Simulation*, 2nd ed., Prentice-Hall, Englewood Cliffs, N.J., 1978.

Hillier, F. S., and G. J. Lieberman, *Introduction to Operations Research*, 3rd ed., Holden-Day, San Francisco, 1980.

Schrieber, A. N., editor, *Corporate Simulation Models*, The University of Washington Printing Plant, Seattle, 1970.

Wagner, H. M., *Principles of Operations Research*, 2nd ed., Prentice-Hall, Englewood Cliffs, N.J., 1975.

Chapter 18: Project Management by Network Models

Hillier, F. S., and G. J. Lieberman, *Introduction to Operations Research*, 3rd ed., Holden-Day, San Francisco, 1980.

Moder, J. J., and C. R. Phillips, *Project Management with CPM and PERT*, 2nd ed., Van Nostrand, New York, 1970.

Wagner, H. M., *Principles of Operations Research*, 2nd ed., Prentice-Hall, Englewood Cliffs, N.J., 1975.

Chapter 19: Your Stake in Quantitative Methods

Churchman, C. W., *The Systems Approach*, Dell, New York, 1968.

Simon, H. A., *The Sciences of the Artificial*, M.I.T. Press, Cambridge, Mass., 1969.

Simon, H. A., *The New Science of Management Decision*, rev. ed., Prentice-Hall, Englewood Cliffs, N.J., 1977.

Appendix

D

Glossary

A

absolute constraint: a resource constraint that cannot be adapted by the decision maker.

accounting variance: a difference between the actual value and the recorded value.

act: one of the set of alternative actions available to the decision maker for which there is a set of possible outcomes.

activity: the smallest unit of work in a project plan.

activity slack: the difference between the latest start date and the earliest start date of an activity.

actual chronology: arrangement of a decision tree in the order in which physical events and decisions occur in the real world.

aggressive advertising: advertising aimed at persuading customers who buy competitive brands to switch to the company's product.

algorithm: in mathematics, any special method of solving a certain kind of problem; step-by-step rule for solving a problem.

alternative: that which may be chosen or omitted as one of two or many incompatible things, so that if one is taken, the others must be left.

arrival distribution: the probability distribution of the rate of arrivals into the waiting line.

artificial variable: a nonnegative variable used in linear programming with a positive

sign to change an inequality into an equation.

assignment problem: a special transportation problem in which the goal is to allocate optimally a set of objects (resources) to another set of objects (demands).

audit: an examination of an account or accounts by proper officers or persons appointed for that purpose.

averaging out: calculating the expected value of a set of branches emanating from a chance fork.

B

backward induction: See *extensive analysis.*

backward pass: finding the LAOs by working backward through the network.

backward recursion: using the recursion method but starting from the last stage of a sequential problem.

Bernoulli trial: a random experiment in which each trial has only two possible outcomes (usually called successes and failures) and where the successive trials are statistically independent.

beta distribution: a specific probability distribution used as a model for activity time distributions; it is used often because of its convenience.

bill of materials: a list of the quantities and types of materials and components required to make a particular product.

binding constraint: a limit on the availability of a resource such that in the optimum solution all the resource is used up.

binomial probability distribution: the discrete distribution of the number of successes in a series of Bernoulli trials.

birth and death process: a model of a real-world situation in which the arrival of the customer into the system is seen as a birth and the departure or disappearance from the system is seen as a death.

bound: an upper or lower value of the objective function against which other solutions can be compared.

branch: splitting the original problem into two or more problems with new constraints, creating two or more new problems.

branch-and-bound algorithm: a particular step-by-step procedure for solving integer and mixed integer linear programming problems by splitting the solution and branching and checking against bounds.

break-even point: the point at which the gains obtained from choosing an action equal the costs that result from choosing that action.

buffer: anything serving to lessen and absorb shock; a cushion against fluctuation.

C

calling population: See *source*.

capital budgeting problem: the problem of allocating capital (money) to different projects.

carrying cost: the cost of keeping inventory, i.e., storage, maintenance, breakage, cost of money, etc.

causal: pertaining to something which produces a result.

cell: the location of a matrix element in the table for a transportation problem in which the amount shipped from a source to a sink as well as the cost are given.

certainty: See *deterministic*.

certainty monetary equivalent (CME): the monetary value of a gamble venture.

chance fork: a fork of a decision tree which has probabilities associated with it.

channel: a facility at which a "customer" may get service.

closed path: a path through the cells of the transportation matrix that ends in the same cell from which it started.

coefficient: a given number or symbol used as a multiplier to a variable.

collectively exhaustive: all possible events as a group representing all possible outcomes.

complete enumeration: a method for solving problems by setting all variables to all possible combinations and finding the payoff for each combination.

compound event: an event made up of two or more simple events.

conditional probability: given that a particular event has occurred, the probability that another event will occur.

constant service time: the amount of time necessary to complete a service remains the same.

constraints: limits on the availability of resources.

continuous variable: a variable which takes on any real number value within a given range.

controllable factor: an element in the forecast whose value can be influenced by the decision maker.

cost benefit analysis: an analysis of both the cost of a solution and economic benefits of that particular solution.

crash duration: the estimated duration of an activity under special conditions created to reduce the duration from the normal state.

criterion: a standard of judging on which a decision may be based.

critical path: among all the paths through the network, that path (or paths) which has the least slack and, hence, along which any delay will be reflected directly in delay of the project.

cumulative distribution function: (1) a rule which assigns a probability to the event of obtaining a value of a random variable below an upper bound; (2) the probabilities assigned by this rule.

curse of dimensionality: the problem of dimensionality in that as the number of variables (dimensions) increases, there is an exponential (or greater than exponential) increase in the number of alternatives (after Richard Bellman).

cutting plane algorithm: a particular step-by-step procedure for solving integer and mixed integer programming problems.

cyclic variation: periodic patterns in the data with a time frame of more than 1 year.

D

decision analysis: the quantitative and rational approach to decision making under conditions of uncertainty.

decision fork: the node of a decision tree at which decision alternatives are available.

decision tree: a graph of the decision process indicating decision alternatives and chance events.

decision variable: an element in the forecast whose value can be selected by executive action.

defensive advertising: advertising aimed at persuading current customers to continue purchasing the company's product.

degeneracy: (1) when there is a tie in applying the entering rule of the simplex method; (2) when there is no stone either to the south or to the east, following the method of solution of Chapter 12.

dependent events: two or more events which are said to be statistically dependent if the probability of joint occurrence does not equal the product of the individual probabilities.

dependent variable: a variable whose value is determined by some independent variables.

destination: in a transportation problem the place to which the shipment goes.

deterministic: no uncertainty in the outcomes.

deviational variable: a variable that represents the quantity by which the goal is under- or overachieved.

distribution of effort problem: a problem in allocating resources seen as "efforts."

drift: lack of average or trend value in the data, showing no long-term position or pattern.

dual problem: a related linear programming problem using the same data as the primal.

dummy activity: an activity introduced to show logical constraint only, which takes no time or effort to perform; the duration of a dummy (activity) is zero.

duration: the time required to complete the activity of interest.

dynamic programming: a particular mathematical solution of technique applicable to problems where the decisions can be reduced to a sequential process involving a succession of subproblems.

dynamic rollback: See *extensive analysis*.

E

earliest possible occurrence (EPO): the earliest time at which an event can occur.

east rim: the right-hand margin of the technological table for a transportation problem, giving the capacity-supply requirements.

economic ordering quantity: the reorder quantity which if ordered at the time inventory needs replenishment minimizes the cost of ordering and carrying the inventory.

empirical: relying or based solely upon experiments or experience.

entering rule: tells which variable to enter a variable into a solution when carrying out the simplex algorithm.

equilibrium: a position that a Markov process reaches in the long run, after which the opposing factors in the process balance.

equilibrium: a return to normal, long-term operating conditions after a disturbance or transient phenomenon.

equilibrium probabilities: the probability of finding the process in one of the steady states after a large number of transitions.

equivalent systems of equations: systems of equations having the same solution.

event: one or more items from the list of all possible outcomes of a random experiment.

event: in a project, an occurrence which may be the end of an activity or several activities.

event slack: See *slack*.

exclusive events: events that cannot occur simultaneously as results of an experiment; the occurrence of one precludes the occurrence of the others.

exhaustive enumeration (brute force): solving a problem by finding the consequences of every alternative (thereby *exhausting* all alternatives).

expected monetary value (EMV): the expected monetary value of benefits (in dollars in the United States).

expected value: on the basis of a random experiment which is run for a long period of time, a weighted average of the outcomes of the experiment.

expected value of information (EVXI): the difference between the expected monetary value of the venture with the information system and that of the venture without the information system.

expected value of perfect information (EVPI): the difference between the expected value and what can be obtained, given perfect information.

experiment: any action taken to discover something not yet known or to demonstrate something known.

exponential service times: service times which conform to the exponential probability distribution.

exponential smoothing: a forecasting method in which a weighted average of past data is calculated, using decreasing weights for more remote past data.

extensive analysis: a decision tree procedure used to find the best strategy by starting with the tip of the tree moving toward the foot of the tree and by averaging out and folding back.

external audit: an examination of an account or accounts by independent auditors who are not employees of the firm being audited.

F

factorial: for a positive integer n the product of all the positive integers less than or equal to n.

feasible solution: the solution which satisfies all the constraints in a problem.

first-in-first-out (FIFO): a queuing discipline in which the items in the queue are serviced in the same order in which they arrived.

fixed charge problem: a mathematical programming problem in which cost consists of two items: (1) a fixed given amount and (2) a term which is a linear function of the unknown.

fixed order period system: an inventory system for reorder at or after a fixed period of time.

fixed order quantity system: an inventory system for reorder of the same quantity of an item(s).

flexible constraint: a goal constraint that can be changed or adapted by the decision maker.

folding back: choosing the optimum alternative from a decision fork.

forecast: to estimate or calculate in advance; to predict.

forward pass: finding the EPOs of the events in a network by working forward through the network.

function: (1) a variable quantity whose value depends on and varies with that of another quantity or quantities; (2) a rule to calculate this variable quantity.

G

goal: the end or final purpose; the end toward which a design or effort tends or a person aims to reach or accomplish.

goal function: the function to be minimized in a goal programming problem; it takes into account different goals.

goal programming: an application of linear programming which enables the decision maker to take into account different goals simultaneously.

gross profit: the difference between income and costs.

growth curve: a graphic representation illustrating a regular increase in trend values in the data.

H

hedging: trying to avoid or lessen loss (in a bet, risk, etc.) by making counterbalancing bets, investments, etc.

how-much rule: specifics how much of a variable can be introduced without violating the constraints.

hypothesis: a proposition or principle which is supposed or taken for granted in order to draw a conclusion.

I

immediate predecessor: the activity of interest which comes just before another activity.

improvement index: the amount by which the solution can be improved by entering a unit of a particular variable into the next solution of the simplex algorithm.

improvement index: the reduction in shipping cost obtained if one unit is shipped through an empty cell; when all are zero or positive, no reduction can be obtained.

independent events: two or more events are said to be statistically independent if the probability of joint occurrence equals the product of the individual probabilities.

independent variable: a variable whose values may change without respect to other variables.

index row: the improvement indexes for all variables at any step of solution of the simplex algorithm.

informational chronology: arrangement of decision tree in the time sequence information is received by the decision maker.

information system: a set or arrangement of things which uses manual, electromechanical, or electronic data processing systems to collect, process, and disseminate information.

initial solution: a (nonnegative) solution satisfying the constraints, which is chosen in order to start the simplex algorithm.

interactive: implying a conversational dialog mode of cooperation between the user and the computer system.

interarrival time: the time between arrivals.

intercept of a line (*a*): the graphic representation illustrating the value of the dependent variable when the value of the independent variable is 0.

internal audit: an examination of an account or accounts by employees of the firm being audited.

interval goal programming: a goal programming problem in which a goal is to take on a value between two constants.

inventory: the quantity of goods or materials on hand.

inventory control system: a system to ensure that inventory levels are maintained so as to operate a business in an efficient manner.

isoprofit: a graphical representation of solutions yielding a fixed profit.

iterative method: a step-by-step procedure for solving a problem in which an improved solution is substituted for the previous solution and the process is repeated until a stopping rule is satisfied.

J

joint probability: the probability that two or more events will occur simultaneously or in succession.

judgmental approach to probability: probabilities of an event occurring based on the degree of confidence or belief of the decision maker that the event will occur.

judgmental forecast: a forecasting method which is based on intuition, judgment, experience, and opinion; a method particularly suited to long-range forecasts.

L

latest allowable occurrence (LAO): the latest time at which an event can occur without delaying the completion time of a project as a whole.

lead time: the time between ordering and receiving the order.

lead-time demand: the demand for an item between reordering and receiving in inventory.

leaving rule: tells which variable to remove at a given step in the simplex algorithm.

linear: an algebraic expression whose variable quantity or quantities are in the first power only.

linear goal programming: a goal programming problem in which all the constraints and the objective function are linear.

linear programming: a particular mathematical technique for solving certain problems involving the allocation of limited resources.

linear regression: the process in forecasting which relates the future dependent variable to one or more past independent variables using linear equations.

linear relationship: a mathematical expression which describes the relationship between two or more variables in which the relationship is proportional and when the values are plotted the result is a straight line.

linear risk factor: a numerical value assigned (often subjectively by a particular method) to assess the level of risk in a specific alternative.

linear slicing formula: a linear equation to transform a uniform random number between 0 and 1 into a uniform random number between any two given limits.

location problem: an integer programming problem concerned with the location of facilities such as production, warehouses, etc.

lottery: allotment or distribution of anything by fate or chance.

M

management: the art, act, or matter of managing, or handling, controlling, directing, planning, etc., to accomplish an end.

management science: See *operations research.*

managerial decision making: choosing among alternative courses of action to obtain a defined objective.

marginal probability: in a situation where joint probabilities are considered, the probability of a particular event.

market research: collecting and analyzing all the relevant information as to consumer preferences for goods and services.

market share: the ratio of a firm's sales of a product to the total sales of that product during a specified period of time in a particular market.

Markov process: a stochastic process in which the probability of outcome of each experiment depends only on the outcome of the previous experiment.

material requirement planning (MRP): an inventory control system organized around the needs of a particular manufacturing production schedule.

mathematical expression: a symbol or set of symbols expressing a mathematical fact or statement as a quantity or operation.

mathematical formula: a set of algebraic symbols expressing a mathematical fact, principle, rule, etc.

mathematical goal programming: a goal programming problem in which, for example, (1) the constraints are not linear, or (2) the variables are integer, or (3) the variables are mixed integer and continuous.

mathematical model: See *model*.

mathematical programming: a mathematical technique for solving a broad class of problems involving the allocation of limited resources; includes linear programming.

mathematical relationship: a mathematical connection by which two things may be compared.

maximize: to increase to the highest value attainable.

mean: See *expected value*.

mixed integer linear programming problem: a linear programming problem in which both integer and continuous variables appear.

model: an abstract representation of some real-life object generally using mathematical symbols.

MODI (modified distribution) method: a simple computational method for solving the transportation problem.

moving average: an average that is revised as data become available and is based on a fixed number of past data.

multigoal: more than one goal or final purpose.

multiobjective: more than one objective (goal) for a decison-making activity.

multiphase simplex method: a way of solving the preemptive priority goal programming problem where a series of objective functions are solved in the rank sequence of the goals.

multiple solution: when two different solutions to a linear programming problem yield the same optimal value of the objective function.

net profit: gross profit less taxes and other costs as determined by the accounting system.

network: a graphic representation in which modes are connected by lines.

network: a graph that represents the interrelationships between various events and activities.

node: in a graph (of which a network is a special form) composed of lines or arrows, the point at which an arrow or line ends.

nonlinear programming problem: a programming problem which resembles a linear programming problem except that one or more of the constraints or the objective function have terms with nonlinear variables.

normal analysis: a procedure involving decision and probability trees used to find the best strategy; this analysis starts at the foot of the tree and works toward the tip of the tree.

normal distribution: a distribution of a continuous random variable where the curve has a particular bell-shaped, symmetrical distribution around a vertical line drawn at the mean and where the two ends of the curve never touch the horizontal axis; an approximation to the binomial distribution.

normal duration: the estimated duration of an activity under usual conditions.

north rim: the upper margin of the transportation matrix.

northwest corner rule: a starting rule that involves placing the largest possible value in the upper left-hand cell of the transportation matrix.

O

objective function: a mathematical expression which shows the net benefit derived from a decision alternative.

operating characteristics: the properties of the queue under analysis, including how the line is formed and how it is serviced.

operations research: scientific method applied to problem solving for executive management.

optimization: the development of a system to produce the best outcome in any circumstance.

optimum solution: the best or most favorable solution to a problem.

ordering cost: the cost, managerial and/or clerical, that is incurred in getting an item into inventory; includes cost of purchasing.

outcome: one item from the list of all possible results of a random experiment.

outlier: a data value that is unusually large or small when compared with other pertinent data.

P

path: the sequence of activities.

pattern of data: the regular structure observed in the data, such as trends (long term), seasonal (periodic—less than 1 year), cyclical (other, longer periods), etc.

payoff: the net benefit which accrues from a specific decision alternative in a given situation.

pivot coefficient: the entry in the simplex tableau in the pivot row and the pivot column.

pivot column: the most negative column used in the entering rule of the simplex algorithm.

pivot row: the row corresponding to the binding constraint as determined by the leaving rule.

Poisson arrivals: arrivals for which the number of arrivals per unit time conforms to the Poisson probability distribution.

Poisson-exponential system: a waiting-line system with Poisson arrivals, exponential service times, and a first-in-first-out (FIFO) queue discipline.

Poisson general system: a waiting-line system with Poisson arrivals, an arbitrary distribution of service times, and a first-in-first-out (FIFO) queue discipline.

posterior probability: a probability that has been recalculated after new information has been obtained.

precedence: the relationship between one activity and another, determining which activity should be done first.

preemptive priority: when a goal designated as the most important must be satisfied first, then the next goal, etc.

preference theory: See *utility theory.*

primal problem: the original statement of the linear programming problem.

principle of optimality: Given any initial state and decision, the optimal course of action is independent of the way in which a state is reached.

prior probability: the probability of the occurrence of an event before information pertinent to the event has been observed.

probability: a mathematical basis for predicting the ratio of the outcomes that would produce a given event to the total number of possible outcomes.

probability density function: the rate at which probability increases in the cumulative distribution function as the value of the random variable increases.

probability distribution function: (1) a rule which assigns a probability to the values of a random variable; (2) probabilities assigned to the values of a random variable.

probability mass function: The probability distribution function may be called by this name when the number of values of the random variable is finite.

probability tree: a graphic representation illustrating outcomes and their probabilities.

product structure tree: a graphic representation of the relationship among the components of a particular product.

pruning the tree: (1) replacing a chance fork with the expected value calculated from the branches of this fork; (2) replacing a decision fork by the optimum alternative.

pure integer linear programming problem: a linear programming problem in which the variables are all integers.

Q

quadratic function: an algebraic expression pertaining to or involving the square or second power of an unknown quantity but no higher power.

qualitative: relating to quality or qualities; distinguished from quantitative.

quantitative: capable of being measured.

quantitative analysis: See *operations research.*

queue: a line or file of people or things waiting to be served or brought into service.

queuing discipline: the order in which people in a queue receive service.

R

random variable: a variable that takes on different values as the result of a random experiment.

range: the difference between the largest and smallest value of a random variable.

ranking: ordering the goals using a criterion of importance to the organization.

recursion: a problem solving method using the result from an earlier step to get the answer to the current step.

relative frequency: the proportion of times that an event will occur in the long run if the experiment is repeated a number of times.

reorder point: the level of inventory when it is time to reorder.

resource: something that lies ready for use or can be drawn upon for aid; a supply of something to take care of a need.

resource constraint: a restriction or limitation placed on the availability of a resource.

revenue: the return from property or investment; income.

rigid constraint: See *absolute constraint*.

risk analysis: probabilistic analysis of the possibilities of gain or loss for each factor affecting an investment project.

risk avoider: a person who avoids taking chances for fear of taking a loss.

risk seeker: a person who will take chances in the hope of making a profit.

roulette wheel: a shallow revolving disk. The circumference of the disk is usually divided into 36 compartments colored red and black alternately and numbered from 1 to 36, with zero and/or double zero colored green; used in gambling game in which small ball is made to move rapidly around the wheel; in this textbook a wheel with a single zero is assumed.

S

safety stock: extra inventory held in case of stockout or delays.

sampling: the random method used to choose the sample.

sawtooth pattern: a graphic representation. for a fixed order quantity system or fixed order period system.

science: systematized knowledge derived from observation, study, and experimentation carried on in order to determine the nature or principles of what is being studied.

scientific method: general logic and procedures common to all the physical and social sciences; the free and utmost use of human intelligence.

seasonal index: a proportion which is a measure of how overall trend values are affected at a particular season.

seasonal variation: periodic variation within a time frame of 1 year or less.

sensitivity analysis: the study of the effect upon the final result of small changes in each of the variables.

sensitivity analysis: a method for answering the what-if questions under the assumption that only relatively small changes are introduced into the problem under study.

sequential linear goal programming: a method of solution to the preemptive priority goal programming problem using linear programming methods.

service level: inventory level to assure that an excessive number of stockouts will not occur.

service time distribution: the probability distribution of the amount of time needed to service a customer.

setup cost: start-up labor costs; the cost of setting up machines, etc.

shadow price: the increase in the optimal value of the objective function to be gained from adding another unit of a scarce resource.

simple event: See *outcome*.

simplex algorithm: a method of solving linear programming problems by starting from an initial solution and moving from solution to solution so as to always increase the value of the objective function until the optimum is reached.

simplex tableau: a conventional format for a table listing all relevant values for each step in carrying out the simplex algorithm.

slack: the difference between the LAO and the EPO.

slack variable: a nonnegative variable used in linear programming with a positive sign to change an inequality to an equality.

slicing rule: a technique of generating random values corresponding to any probability distribution using a table of random numbers.

slope of a straight line (designated by *b*): the change occurring in the dependent variable when there is a one-unit increase in the independent variable.

slow methods: implies special conditions created to increase the duration of an activity to save money or to improve resource utilization.

source: (1) in a transportation problem the place from which a shipment originates; (2)

the pool of customers from which entrants into a queuing system come.

south rim: the bottom margin of the table for a transportation problem, giving the demand requirements.

standard deviation: the measure of the spread of the values around the mean given by the square root of the variance.

standard form: changing the inequalities of the constraints in a linear programming problem to equalities.

standard gamble venture: two monetary values are selected to provide a standard for making comparison. Any other monetary value is measured by comparing it with the two standard values.

state: possible outcome of an experiment.

state probability: the probability of being in a particular state.

statistical forecast: a forecasting method which is based on the analysis of data; a method particularly suited for short-range forecasts.

statistical inference: quantitative statements about properties of a population as a result of a sample.

statistics: facts or data of a numerical kind assembled, classified, and tabulated so as to present significant information about a given subject.

steady state: one of the long-term, recurring states in the process.

steady-state conditions: normal, long-term operating conditions.

stochastic process: a sequence of random experiments.

stockout cost: the cost of not having sufficient inventory to satisfy demand; cost of lost profit and goodwill.

stopping rule: tells when to end an interaction solution method.

strategy: a decision rule specifying the action to take in any and all foreseeable situations.

surplus variable: a nonnegative variable used in linear programming with a negative sign to change an inequality into an equation.

symbolic representation: See *model.*

T

table of random numbers: a set of numbers corresponding to values drawn from a uniform distribution between 0 and 1.0.

thought experiment: an activity which is carried out only in the mind but which clarifies a real-world situation.

time-dependent system: a system in which the arrival rate, service time, etc., change with time.

tip of the tree: the terminal point at the end of the path through a decision tree.

transient phenomenon: a disturbance or passing occurrence.

transient state: a temporary state in the process.

transition diagram: a graph using arrows and conditional probabilities to show the possible outcomes of a move from one state in the process to the next one.

transition probability matrix: a matrix in which the rows represent origins, the columns destinations, and the cells the probability of a transition from the respective origin to the respective destination.

transportation matrix: the technological table for a transportation problem, giving the capacity, supply, and demand requirements and costs.

transportation problem: a linear programming problem concerned with finding the optimal route for a product being shipped from warehouses to customers.

trend: the general direction of movement in data, extending over a relatively long period of time, 5 to 15 years or more.

truncate: to drop the decimal part of a number.

two-bin inventory control system: a system of stock control which divides a quantity of an item into two parts: one for normal use, to be reordered when exhausted, and one for the interim, while waiting for replacements.

two-channel system: a system in which there are two facilities at which a customer may obtain service.

U

unbalanced transportation problem: condition in a transportation problem when demand and supply do not match.

unbounded time horizon: a situation in which there is no time limit to how long the process can exist and go on.

unbound solution: a situation where there is no limit to values of the objective function associated with solutions to the problem; this usually indicates that the problem was formulated incorrectly.

uncertainty: a situation where states and/or

outcomes are known only in terms of probability.

unconditional probability: the probability that an event will occur.

uncontrollable factor: an element in the forecast whose value cannot be influenced by the decision maker.

underachieve: to perform or execute less than the goal requires.

uniform probability distribution: a probability distribution where the probability of any outcome, in the allowable range of values for the random variable, is the same value.

unit cost of production: the total cost of producing a lot divided by the number of individual items in the lot.

utile: the numerical value assigned to the personal satisfaction received from a specific quantity of goods or service.

utility function: a mathematical function that assigns to each quantity of goods or service received the utile (or numerical value) of the personal satisfaction experienced.

utility theory: a technique used to analyze the personal satisfaction received from a payoff or outcome.

utilization factor: the proportion of time that the service facility is busy.

V

value (of a random variable): numeric outcome of a random experiment.

value added: the difference between gross revenue and cost of a product.

variance: the expected value of the square of the difference between the values of the random variable and the mean; the mean of the squares.

W

waiting-line: See *queue*.

waiting-line system: the operating characteristics of a particular queue.

weighted average: an average in which data used to compute the average are assigned different weights indicative of their age or relative importance.

weighted goal function: the function to be minimized in a goal programming problem; it accounts for the relative importance of different goals.

west rim: the left margin of the transportation matrix.

Index